Voices from the Margin

Voices
from the Margin

INTERPRETING THE BIBLE
IN THE THIRD WORLD

New Edition

Edited by

R. S. Sugirtharajah

ORBIS / SPCK

This new edition first published 1995
First published in Great Britain 1991
Society for Promoting Christian Knowledge
Holy Trinity Church
Marylebone Road
London NW1 4DU

New edition first published in the United States of America 1995
by Orbis Books, Maryknoll, NY 10545

Fourth Printing, December 2000

The Catholic Foreign Mission Society of America (Maryknoll) recruits and trains people for overseas missionary service. Through Orbis Books Maryknoll aims to foster the international dialogue that is essential to mission. The books published, however, reflect the opinions of their authors and are not meant to represent the official position of the Society.

British Library Cataloguing-in-Publication Data
A catalogue record for this book is available
from the British Library

SPCK/ISBN 0-281-04895-9

Library of Congress Cataloging-in-Publication Data
Voices from the margin/edited by R. S. Sugirtharajah
p.cm.
Includes bibliographical references and indexes.
ISBN 1-57075-046-7 (pbk.)
1. Bible—Hermeneutics—Comparative studies.
2. Christianity—Developing countries.
3. Christianity and culture.
4. Bible. O.T. Exodus—Hermeneutics—Comparative studies.
I. Sugirtharajah, R. S. (Rasiah S.)
BS476.V65 1995
220.6'01—dc2091-7323 CIP

Typeset by Rowland Phototypesetting Limited
Bury St Edmunds, Suffolk

Printed in Great Britain by Redwood Books,
Trowbridge, Wiltshire

Contents

Acknowledgements   viii
Introduction: The Margin as a Site of Creative Re-visioning
R. S. Sugirtharajah (Sri Lanka)   1

Part One   Using the Bible: Reading Strategies and Issues

1 Scripture and Scriptures *Stanley J. Samartha (India)*   9
2 Is There a Calypso Exegesis? *George M. Mulrain*
   (Trinidad and Tobago)   37
3 Women's Rereading of the Bible *Elsa Tamez (Costa Rica)*   48
4 Marxist Critical Tools: Are they Helpful in Breaking the
   Stranglehold of Idealist Hermeneutics? *José Miguez-Bonino*
   (Argentina)   58
5 The Case for a New Bible *Canaan S. Banana (Zimbabwe)*   69

Part Two   Re-use of the Bible: Subaltern Readings

6 Jesus and the Minjung in the Gospel of Mark *Ahn Byung-*
   Mu (South Korea)   85
7 Yahweh the Defender of the Dalits: A Reflection on
   Isaiah 3.12–15 *George Koonthanam (India)*   105
8 Anti-Greed and Anti-Pride: Mark 10.17–27 and
   10.35–45 in the Light of Tribal Values
   George M. Soares-Prabhu (India)   117
9 The Syrophoenician Woman: Mark 7.24–30 *Hisako*
   Kinukawa (Japan)   138
10 Water – God's Extravaganza: John 2.1–11
   Sr Vandana (India)   156

v

11 The Implications of the Text of Esther for African
Women's Struggle for Liberation in South Africa
Itumeleng J. Mosala (South Africa)   168
12 The Gospel of Economy from a Solomon Islands
Perspective *Leslie Boseto (Solomon Islands)*   179
13 The Equality of Women: Form or Substance
(1 Corinthians 11.2–16) *Christine Amjad-Ali (Pakistan)*   185
14 Racial Motifs in the Biblical Narratives *Cain Hope
Felder (USA)*   194

Part Three   The Exodus: One Narrative, Many Readings

15 A Latin American Perspective: The Option for the Poor
in the Old Testament *George V. Pixley (Nicaragua) and
Clodovis Boff (Brazil)*   215
16 A Korean Minjung Perspective: The Hebrews and the
Exodus *Cyris H. S. Moon (South Korea)*   228
17 A Black African Perspective: An African Reading of
Exodus *Jean-Marc Ela (Cameroon)*   244
18 An Asian Feminist Perspective: The Exodus Story
(Exodus 1.8–22; 2.1–10) *An Asian Group Work*   255
19 A Palestinian Perspective: Biblical Perspectives on the
Land *Naim S. Ateek (Israel)*   267
20 A Native American Perspective: Canaanites, Cowboys,
and Indians *Robert Allen Warrior (USA)*   277

Part Four   The Text and the Texts: Multi-faith Readings

21 Discovering the Bible in the Non-Biblical World
Kwok Pui Lan (Hong Kong)   289
22 Inter-faith Hermeneutics: An Example and Some
Implications *R. S. Sugirtharajah (Sri Lanka)*   306
23 Two Mission Commands: An Interpretation of Matthew
28.16–20 in the Light of a Buddhist Text *George M.
Soares-Prabhu (India)*   319
24 The Book of Ecclesiastes and Thai Buddhism *Seree
Lorgunpai (Thailand)*   339
25 The Rhetorical Hermeneutic of 1 Corinthians 8 and
Chinese Ancestor Worship *Khiok-Khng Yeo (Malaysia)*   349
26 The Chinese Creation Myth of Nu Kua and the Biblical
Narrative in Genesis 1–11 *Archie C. C. Lee (Hong Kong)*   368
27 The Communion of Saints: Christian and Tamil Śaiva
Perspectives *S. Gangadaran and Israel Selvanayagam (India)*   381

Contents

28 On Developing Liberation Theology in Islam *Asghar Ali Engineer (India)*   394

Part Five   People as Exegetes: Popular Readings

29 A Brazilian Example: 'Listening to What the Spirit is Saying to the Churches'. Popular Interpretation of the Bible in Brazil *Carlos Mesters (Brazil)*   407

30 A Malawian Example: The Bible and Non-literate Communities *Patrick A. Kalilombe*   421

31 A Nicaraguan Example: The Alabaster Bottle – Matthew 26.6-13   436

32 An Indonesian Example: The Miraculous Catch – Luke 5.1-11   444

33 A South African Example: Jesus' Teaching at Nazareth – Luke 4.14-30   447

34 A Chinese Example: 'The Silences of the Bible' *K. H. Ting*   454

Afterword: Cultures, Texts and Margins: A Hermeneutical Odyssey *R. S. Surgirtharajah (Sri Lanka)*   457

Index of Scripture References   476

Select Index of Names and Subjects   481

Acknowledgements

This volume, like my previous ones, has been made possible by a great many people. I am grateful to Philip Law and Simon Kingston of SPCK, and Robert Ellsberg and Sue Perry of Orbis Books, the publishers, for their continued interest and confidence in my work; Dr Daniel O'Connor for help and advice whenever needed; Meline Nielson, Griselda Lartey, Helen Sorrell, Susan Abbott and Noor-el-Emam, the librarians at the Central Library, Selly Oak Colleges, for their helpfulness in locating and supplying materials; the Selly Oak students for their patience and understanding and more importantly their perceptive comments as we wrestled with these texts; all the copyright holders for their generous permission; and my wife Sharada, for often reminding me that scripture as understood by Christians may not do justice to written and oral sacred narratives of people of other faith traditions.

R. S. Sugirtharajah
Selly Oak Colleges
Birmingham

Publisher's Acknowledgements

We are grateful to the following for permission to reproduce copyright material:

The Asia Journal of Theology, India for ch. 24.
Biblical Interpretation, The Netherlands for chs. 23, 25 and 26.
Burns & Oates, Tunbridge Wells for ch. 15.
The Christian Study Centre and 'Women in Reflection and Action', Rawalpindi Cantt., Pakistan for ch. 13.
Christianity and Crisis, New York for ch. 20.
Christian Literature Society, Madras, India for ch. 10.
Commission on Theological Concerns of the Christian Conference of Asia, New York for ch. 6.
Concilium, The Netherlands for ch. 29.
Focus, Multan, Pakistan for ch. 28.
Hindu-Christian Studies Bulletin, Victoria, Canada for ch. 27.
In God's Image, Hong Kong for ch. 18.
International Association for Mission Studies (IAMS) Secretariat, Hamburg for ch. 22.
Jeevadhara, India for chs. 7 and 8.
Orbis Books, Maryknoll, New York for chs. 1, 3, 6, 9, 14, 15, 16, 17, 19 and 31.
The Pacific Journal of Theology, Fiji for ch. 12.
Plough Publications, Hong Kong for ch. 16.
SCM Press, London for ch. 4.
Semeia, Vanderbilt, USA for chs. 11 and 21.
Tao Fong Ecumenical Centre, Hong Kong for ch. 34.
Zed Press, London for ch. 6.

Introduction: The Margin as a Site of Creative Re-visioning

R. S. SUGIRTHARAJAH

There is at present an explosion of interest in Third-World biblical interpretation.[1] The present volume is a testimony to this. A few years ago, a proposal for an anthology of Asian, African, Latin-American, Caribbean and Pacific biblical interpretation, let alone a revised one, would have met with total incomprehension and would have been dismissed as presumptuous. There was a general scepticism in academic circles as to whether such a phenomenon existed, and even the publishers would have expressed doubts as to whether there were enough texts to make up a volume. There was a total lack of interest in and a failure to recognize the importance of Third-World biblical discourse. But this is no longer the case. There is on the one hand a greater awareness of the existence of the materials, and on the other hand a remarkable spurt of publishing activity by Third-World biblical scholars themselves.[2] More importantly there is a recognition that Third-World biblical interpretation holds a special hermeneutical promise because of its exclusive attempts to address the issues of struggle, marginality and colonialism.

The form of the revision of this volume was determined by the decision to include geographical regions such as the Caribbean and the Pacific, inadvertently left out of the previous volume; to offer a high profile to the emerging subaltern exegesis worked out by Indian dalits and the other indigenous people; to expand the cross-religious hermeneutics to include Christian-Buddhist inter-textual studies, and Christian-Chinese hermeneutics; and, in the case of Stanley J. Samartha and Naim Ateek, to use updated versions of their material.

MARGIN: A REDEFINITION

Before I introduce the volume, I would like to explain the choice of the word 'margin' in the title. Friends and critics have often queried it. Is not marginality a position of weakness and self-depreciation? When are you people going to move to the centre? Although it is tempting to move in from the periphery and find a place at the centre, whatever that centre may be, my intention is to stay firmly at the margin, but not to linger on the outskirts of Western scholarship as 'hewers of texts and drawers of book learning' as the Indian poet Rabindranath Tagore once cautioned us. Rather, the aim is to re-perceive the margin, as the Indian feminist and deconstructionist Gayatri Chakravorty Spivak has done – as a place pulsating with critical activity, a place alive with argument and controversy and a place of creative discourse. She sees the margin as a place of critical movement and full of interest. She writes: 'I would like to re-invent it as simply a critical movement rather than a de-centered movement'.[3] In the early days of textual criticism, it was in the margins that the great hermeneutical battles were fought, won and lost. It was Tyndale's marginal glosses even more than his text that created controversy. The marginal notes played a significant role in helping uninitiated readers to find their way into the texts. Moreover, innovation can be easier on the fringes of a culture, where the centre's hegemony is less fierce. Wary of the danger of 'marginality turning into separatism, and resistance hardening into dogma',[4] I would like to re-image the margin as a centre for critical reflection and clarification rather than as merely a site opposed to the centre or as a state of peripherality. I genuinely hope that this collection goes some way to capture this critical aspect of marginality and its problems.

EMERGENCE OF THE POST-COLONIAL READER/HEARER

Over the last two decades, the field of biblical studies has undergone a voluminous and far-reaching transformation. The arena is no more a homogenous place sustaining varied scholarly interests, but, to use a current metaphor, resembles an unregulated market-place, where all kinds of theories and methods are offered for public consumption. The importation of critical theory such as literary and social science methods, and the irruption of gender-specific and perspectival readings into the scene, have made the field scarcely recognizable. Amidst these ongoing changes, the current critical inquiry wrestles with 'historical', 'literary' and 'contextual' approaches to the Bible and passes through 'author-centered', 'text-centered' and 'reader-centered' phases.

It would be fair to say that this collection falls into the reader-response category. While acknowledging that this particular approach emerged out of specific Western contextual needs, we nevertheless share some of its presuppositions: that the meaning of the text is produced by mutual interaction between the reader and the text; that the reader engages the text and the text in turn engages the reader, and the meaning is the invention of the reader; that a specific meaning is perceived in the text by certain readers because of their particular social, cultural and religious location. The essays assembled here continue to highlight the hermeneutical attempts of the real and actual reader/hearer, or what I would like to call the post-colonial reader, and not the hypothetical or implied reader that recent literary theorists have been fondly concerned with. These are flesh-and-bone readers – minjung, dalits, indigenous people, male and female, professional and lay, standing within their own social location – oppressive, caste-ridden, patriarchal, multi-religious, and trying to make sense of their context and the texts. In doing so, they reinscribe and restate the concerns of the marginalized. What Bruce King said of the Commonwealth writers is equally applicable to Third-World biblical interpreters: 'They are deconstructionists, not out of the logic that led others from structuralism to post-structuralism, but from the experience of divided, uprooted, unassimilated lives; but they are also reconstructionists in that for those genuinely threatened by chaos the logic of survival requires some new order, even if only provisional.'[5] In spite of their different cultures, genders, races and regions, what holds these interpreters together is that they all emerge from a common experience of colonialism and neo-colonialism. It is this experience that makes them distinctly post-colonial and it is this experience which colours and determines their reading practice.

CONTENTS, CATEGORIES AND TABLES

Looking at the hermeneutical inputs of the Third World, it is evident that the conventional contents-format used by the publishing industry may not do justice to the multiple interests and relational character of these essays. The traditional categories worked out by academic scholarship are simply not applicable. There are relationships between these essays, and several of them are interconnected, embroiled in one another's questions, involved and linked, and thus the dividing line between them is far from exact. However, to meet as far as possible the conventions of publishing, the volume follows the format of the earlier edition by placing the essays under themes, acknowledging that this division is arbitrary and that several of these essays would be at home in more than one slot. The reader is encouraged to come up with his or her own contents categories.

Part One, 'Using the Bible: Reading Strategies and Issues', calls for an epistemic move from the ahistorical, objective, abstract, universal reading discourse which the academy diligently espouses for historical, subjective and context-specific readings. It calls for the abandonment of a homogenous reading for the celebration of diversity and plurality. These essays bring home the point that the Third World is not a single entity but is diverse and mixed. The differences, nevertheless, among its peoples need not broaden the gulfs between them; rather, they can be seen to offer a multiplicity of potentialities. This section includes three new entries – George Mulrain's proposal for a Calypso exegesis; Canaan Banana's controversial piece on rewriting the Bible and Stanley Samartha's updated version of his earlier piece.

Part Two, 'Re-use of the Bible: Subaltern Readings', has been radically revised to include the emerging suppressed voices of Indian dalits, women and indigenous people, who continue to be subjected to hermeneutical forgetting by mainstream biblical scholarship. The subaltern readings could be defined as a variety of voices engaged in retrieving narratives occluded or marginalized by society. The common denominator which links these various subjugated peoples is that they all have a hostile attitude towards the dominant culture. These essayists use both conventional historical-critical methods and indigenous reading practices to illuminate the texts. They demonstrate that, in spite of scepticism among certain Euro-American scholars, these methods can still be used as liberative tools. In other

4

words, as Edward Said would have put it, they use the 'same language employed by the dominant power, to dispute its hierarchy and methods, to elucidate what it has hidden, to pronounce what it has silenced or rendered unpronounceable'.[6] Interestingly the very method which was used to subjugate the subalterns is used by the subalterns themselves for their own emancipation. This section has been extensively altered, retaining only three items from the previous edition.

Part Three, 'The Exodus: One Narrative, Many Readings', demonstrates how a narrative segment, seen through the prism of different cultural, gender and social perspectives can yield itself to multiple meanings and multiple potentialities. The significant feature of this section is that the Exodus narrative, which is accorded a privileged status in the liberation hermeneutic, is challenged by a Palestinian (Naim Ateek) and a Native American (Robert Allen Warrior) for its colonializing potentiality in their own context. This section also contains a piece by Jean-Marc Ela, one of the very few African scholars outside South Africa who makes use of liberation hermeneutics for his theological enterprise.

The essays in Part Four, 'The Text and the Texts: Multi-faith Readings', illustrate how creatively the textual and cultural heritage can be used by those from a multi-faith setting to complement the biblical narratives. Once the Bible was projected as the metanarrative which adjudicated other peoples' texts and stories. Biblical criteria were used to assess their potential theological and spiritual value. The essayists here try to rectify this theological imperialism. They do not attempt to subsume other peoples' narratives in the biblical narratives, but rather, the biblical story is seen as one among many that are searching for truth. The effect of such endeavours is to undermine the religious intolerance and communal tension caused by claims of superiority and uniqueness of one faith tradition over another. This section has been substantially revised to include Christian-Buddhist inter-textual studies by George Soares-Prabhu and Seree Lorgunpai, Christian-Chinese hermeneutics by K. K. Yeo and Archie C. C. Lee, and also features a joint hermeneutical effort by a Christian, Israel Selvanayagam, and a Hindu, S. Gangadaran.

The final part, 'People as Exegetes: Popular Readings', endeavours to bring together the hermeneutical insights of people who are largely unrecognized and unknown in academic circles. As the examples show, peasants and housewives not only claim that the Bible is their book, but more significantly they have broken with dependency on others for their interpretations. In other words, they are no more the passive consumers but active producers of biblical interpretation. The question these inputs raise is whether there is any common ground for popular and academic reading to meet for mutual critique and transformation. This section retains all the previous essays, but includes a new one by Carlos Mesters.

A collection such as this which has liberation as the point of departure should be progressive in its use of language. Unfortunately, some of the essays use outmoded language which is insensitive to women, people of other faiths and indigenous people. This is largely due to the replication of the colonial vocabulary bequeathed to us, which was insensitive in such matters. Recently there has been a concerted effort among Third-World novelists and writers to appropriate the colonial language and deterritorialize it from its native context and use it as a strategy for subversion. It will not be long before biblical interpreters follow suit. In the meantime, the offending passages are all left untouched as historical markers of our hermeneutical journey as we strive towards a more inclusive and enlightened understanding of gender, race and culture.

An anthology like this will inevitably raise the question of why so and so was left out, or why so little representation from this or that region. The answer is that the field has become so vast, heterogeneous and amorphous that no one volume can do reasonable justice to the vast amount of literature now available. The texts included were chosen because I believe that they represent a distinctive position and reflect most adequately post-coloniality and its concomitant issues.

THE FUTURE SHAPE OF THIRD WORLD BIBLICAL DISCOURSE

Finally, a word about the future of Third-World biblical discourse. What is its future? Will it be seduced by the dominant scholarship? Will it lose its sharpness? Will it run out of issues and causes? I think the answer lies with the peoples of the Third World and the kind of deal they are likely to get in this rapid process of internationalization of markets, and how they are able to survive the imposition of Western commercial culture. It is from the future hopes and fears

6

of the people that biblical interpretation will receive both its authentication and its direction. At the same time, Third-World biblical inquiry also depends on the sharpness of its own critical practice. It is the critics, in Edward Said's view, who create 'the values by which art is judged and understood' and 'embody in writing those processes and actual conditions in the *present* (italics his) by means of which art and writing bear significance'.[7] In other words, all interpretative enquiries, including Third-World biblical discourse, depend on certain critical parameters and accountability. It is interesting that the emergence of liberation hermeneutics has coincided with the development of post-colonial theories and criticisms. These writings offer a sharp critique of Eurocentric assumptions, practices and concepts. The importance of such a critique for contemporary Western hermeneutics is seen in the growth of cultural studies in Western academies and the explosion in the publication of anthologies of post-colonial discourse.[8] There are striking affinities between Third-World biblical discourse and post-colonial theories, but they have hardly begun to interact or intersect. I think the future of Third-World biblical hermeneutics depends on a fruitful dialogue with these post-colonial critics and theorists who are trying to create a new critical tradition born out of the colonial experience.

In the meantime, the continuing task of the interpreter is to investigate and articulate the truth and to confront the powers that be. Put differently, this will continue to mean lending a voice for the voiceless, creating space for the marginalized, and providing visibility for those left at the periphery. Let me finish by quoting from Edward Said who has himself taken the role of advocacy seriously:

> Obviously you want to speak your piece where it can be heard best; and also you want it represented in such a way as to influence with an ongoing and actual process, for instance, the cause of peace and justice. Yes, the intellectual's voice is lonely, but it has resonance only because it associates itself freely with the reality of a movement, the aspirations of a people, the common pursuit of a shared ideal . . . Speaking the truth to the power is no Panglossian idealism: it is carefully weighing the alternatives, picking the right one, and then intelligently representing it where it can do the most good and cause the right change.[9]

NOTES

1 The term 'Third World' is used not in a numerical or geographical sense but as a socio-political designation of a people who have been excluded from power and authority to mould and shape their future. For the discussion of the term see first edition of this volume p. 3.

2 For instance, Grant LeMarquand has come up with 100 pages of bibliography on the use of the Bible in Africa. See *Interpreting the Bible in African Contexts: Minutes of the Glasgow Consultation*, Aug. 1994, p. 29.

3 Gayatri Chakravorty Spivak, *The Post-colonial Critic: Interviews, Strategies, Dialogues* (London, Routledge, 1990), p. 156.

4 Edward W. Said, *Culture and Imperialism* (London, Chatto and Windus, 1993), p. 63.

5 Bruce King, 'The Commonwealth Writer in Exile' in Anna Rutherford (ed.), *From Commonwealth to Post-Colonial* (Sydney, Dangaroo Press, 1992), p. 42.

6 Edward W. Said, 'Nationalism, Human Rights, and Interpretation' in Barbara Johnson (ed.), *Freedom and Interpretation: The Oxford Amnesty Lectures 1992* (New York, Basic Books, 1993), p. 198.

7 Edward W. Said, *The World, the Text and the Critic* (London, Vintage, 1991), p. 53.

8 Patrick Williams and Laura Chrisman (eds.), *Colonial Discourse and Post-Colonial Theory: A Reader* (Hemel Hempstead, Harvester Wheatsheaf, 1993); Bill Ashcroft, Gareth Griffiths and Helen Tiffin (eds.), *The Post-Colonial Studies Reader* (London, Routledge, 1995).

9 Edward W. Said, *Representations of the Intellectual: The 1993 Reith Lectures* (London, Vintage, 1994), p. 75.

PART ONE

Using the Bible: Reading Strategies and Issues

If we orientals are to achieve anything for ourselves, we must no longer permit the historical problems of the West to be foisted upon us. This is to reject a method of framing problems itself, the method presenting 'either-or' choices. Our own schema, too, is to be presented as a method of framing problems; this is a matter of tradition.

Choi In-hoon, in *A Grey Man*

1

Scripture and Scriptures

STANLEY J. SAMARTHA

In a multi-religious continent like Asia where scriptural texts abound, any claim for the supreme authority of one text is bound to face counter-claims. Samartha, who calls this chapter a 'transitional' one, contends that to face such claims, the task of hermeneutics is to work out a larger framework of neighbourly relationships within which the insights of different sacred texts can be related to each other for mutual enrichment, without denying their particularities.

This essay is from the author's *One Christ – Many Religions: Toward a Revised Christology* (Maryknoll, NY, Orbis Books, 1991), pp. 58–75.

Stanley J. Samartha, an Indian, was the first Director of the Dialogue Programme of the World Council of Churches, Geneva. He has written numerous articles on inter-faith matters and has edited and authored books on this theme. His monograph, *The Search for New Hermeneutics in Asian Christian Theology* (1987), explores further the issues related to biblical interpretation in Asia.

In a religiously plural world, a plurality of scriptures is to be expected. Where different religions respond differently to the mystery of life, and where the identities of different religious communities are mixed up with political and economic, social and cultural factors, the question of 'authority' becomes inescapable. What is the source of authority for the claims and counterclaims of different communities of faith? What happens when there is a clash of authorities in the larger community? The meaning, practice, and purpose of hermeneutics in a multiscriptural context has yet to be taken seriously by people concerned with interreligious relationships today.

Several questions arise in this connection. In a multireligious community there are different scriptures which are accepted as authoritative by their respective adherents. But can the authority of one scripture be extended to operate over other communities of faith who have their own scriptures? Who decides? Further, the notion of authority itself, particularly religious authority, is being questioned

11

today. In the West the Church had to develop its hermeneutics in response to developments in science, philosophy, historiography, and other secular movements. The Church in the West had no scriptures of other faiths to take into account. Therefore, its hermeneutics inevitably had to be a monoscriptural hermeneutics. Today, however, Christians in a multireligious world cannot ignore other scriptures that provide spiritual support and ethical guidance to millions of their adherents. Christian hermeneutics today has to respond to a double challenge, namely, from the side of scientific enterprise on one hand and the scriptures of neighbors of other faiths. The manner in which christo-logical affirmations are expressed in a multireligious society depends very much on the way in which the Bible, particularly the New Testa-ment, is interpreted in relation to other scriptures. Christologies developed in the monoscriptural situation in the West, in response to Western challenges, may indeed be helpful to Christians in Asia and Africa, but they cannot be 'normative' to them, because they have yet to develop new hermeneutics in a multiscriptural society.

THE PLURALITY OF SCRIPTURES

To Christians it is astonishing that neighbors of other faiths also have written scriptures. The notion that the Bible is the 'true' scripture and all other scriptures are 'false' is so stamped in the minds of many Christians that any discussion on scriptural authority becomes almost impossible.[1] It is therefore necessary to draw attention to different scriptures in the world which provide the living sources of authority to millions of people of other faiths.

The life of the people in Asia has been nourished for a few thou-sand years by the scriptures of religions other than Christianity. The Hindus have their *prasthana-traya* (triple canon) of the *Upanishads*, *Brahmasutra*, and the *Bhagavadgita*. The Buddhists have the *tripitaka* (the three baskets of the canon), and the Chinese have their classics of Confucianism and Taoism. Over and over again in the history of Asian people, when powerful renewal movements emerged, they were nourished by profound reinterpretations of their scriptures. It is the *Bhasyas* (commentaries) that have pointed out new directions to the *Sampradayas* (ways, traditions, movements) in India. Sankara and Ramanuja did not write treatises on theology but commentaries on the triple canon, bringing fresh meanings out of the texts. During

Stanley J. Samartha

more recent times, Radhakrishnan (1888–1975), the Indian philosopher president, in addition to his other works, produced his own translations and commentaries on the *Upanishads, Brahmasutra,* and the *Bhagavadgita.* During the days of India's freedom struggle, almost every Hindu nationalist leader – Tilak, Bhave, Gandhi, and many others – wrote commentaries on the *Bhagavadgita.* In fact, the *Gita* became the gospel of action supporting a *dharma yuddha* (righteous war) against the British.

During nearly a thousand years of Muslim presence in India, Pakistan, and Bangladesh, Muslim scholars of the Qur'an have produced important volumes on the interpretation and exposition of texts. Over the years these scholars have gained a reputation in the world of Islam that gives them recognition for their distinctive hermeneutic contributions to the interpretation of the Qur'an. In Indonesia, too, which has the largest Muslim population in the world, the work of Indonesian Muslim scholars has continued to nourish the lives of Muslims. Perhaps one should note that Islam, as a religion belonging to the Semitic family, is different in its approach to hermeneutics than the ancient religions of India and China.

Without sufficient information, it is difficult to make convincing observations about the religious situation in China. But there is no reason to believe that in spite of decades of Maoist ideology the classics of Confucianism, Taoism, and Buddhism have lost their hold on the hearts and minds of people. Confucius (born 551 BC deeply influenced the life and thought of the Chinese as a transmitter, teacher, and creative interpreter of ancient culture and literature. The Confucian classics, including the *Analects,* 'are not the canon of a particular sect but the literary heritage of a whole people.'[2] The book of *Lao Tzu,* translated into English as *I Ching,* the Book of Changes, goes back to the third century BC and is the foundation of Taoism. Although little is known of the two fathers of the sect, Lao Tzu and Chung Tzu, what is important is the book, which is 'one of the shortest, most provocative, and inspired works in all Chinese literature . . . the quietism, mysticism, and the love of paradox that distinguish this work probably represent very old strains in Chinese thought . . .'[3]

Buddhism originated in India, but in terms of its influence in China and Japan, the Lotus school is important. It is based on a text from North India, the *Saddharma Pundarika* or the *Lotus of the Good Law.* It is the interpretation given to this text by the great Chinese

13

monk Chih K'ai (or Chih-i, AD 538–597) that forms the basis of this school. He lectured for years on its written text, 'minutely examining every detail of language and subtlety of meaning, and giving special attention to the methods of religious practice embodied in the Lotus.'⁴ In recent years the Rissho-kosei kai, one of the most powerful new religious movements in Japan, is based on the *Lotus*, and a number of commentaries on it have been published recently in Japanese and English.

In devel oping new hermeneutics there are at least two considerations which Christians in a multireligious world cannot ignore. One is the attention given to the study of scriptures in the *original* languages, the meticulous attention given to texts, their interpretation in particular contexts, and the exposition of meanings (*artha, tatparya*) in the life of the people. Second, Christians must recognize that neighbors of other faiths in Asia, whether it is Hindu and Buddhist neighbors in India or Confucian, Taoist, and Buddhist in China, have developed their own hermeneutics in their own setting, without depending on external sources. For example, the hermeneutics of Buddhism developed in India in response to Indian situations was not uncritically accepted by China or Japan. One of the frequent objections raised by Confucianists and Taoists against Buddhism was: why should a Chinese allow himself to be influenced by Indian ways? Chinese Buddhists answered this question in various ways. Mou Tzu said:

> If a gentleman-scholar dwells in their midst, what business can there be among them? According to the Buddhist scriptures, above, below and all around, all beings containing blood belong to the Buddhist clan. Therefore, I revere and study these scriptures. Why should I reject the way of Tao, Shan, Confucius, and the Duke of Chou? Gold and jade do not harm each other. Crystal and amber do not cheapen each other. You say that another is in error when it is you yourself who err.⁵

According to official tradition, Buddhism reached China from India in the first century AD. Because of Chinese aversion to foreign languages, Buddhist texts were translated into Chinese. The book *Disposition of Error* or *Li-hoc-lun*, as it is known in Chinese, written probably during AD 420–587, appears to be an apologia for Buddhism. 'The author takes the stand that there is no fundamental conflict between the Chinese and Buddhist ways of life and that the great truths of Buddhism are preached in somewhat different languages, by Confucianism and Taoism as well.'⁶

Stanley J. Samartha

Hermeneutics as the disciplined study and interpretation of scriptures is neither recent in Asia nor the monopoly of Western biblical scholars. The question in Asia is not so much rules of interpretation as the perception of Truth or *Sat* or Reality or *Dharma* or the Tao itself. How Reality is to be perceived is a concern prior to questions of rules of interpreting the scriptures. To the Hindu *Sruti*, that which is heard is prior to and more authoritative than *Smriti*, that which is remembered and written down. The perception of Truth through *anubhaya* (inadequately translated as 'intuition' or 'experience') is basic to any knowledge to which the scriptures bear witness. The Sanskrit word for 'word' is *Sabda* (from which is derived *Sabda pramana*, one of the three Hindu criteria for interpretation), which means both *sound* (that which is heard), and *word* (that which conveys meaning). Thus by instantly attracting one's attention through hearing and in communicating a particular meaning through words, a relationship is established between the source of the word and the word itself. In the sacred syllable AUM, the sound produced by uttering it is as important, if not more, than the word itself. It overcomes the dichotomy between the knower and the known, between the subject and the object. Communication therefore becomes communion. 'He who knows the Brahman becomes the Brahman.'[7]

Confucius speaks of the unitary principle that runs through everything (*Analecta* IV, 15; XV,2). The teaching of *Lao Tzu* is based upon the way of Tao, the one great underlying principle that is the source of all being, which must remain essentially indescribable and known only through a kind of mystic intuition. 'The Tao that can be told of is not the eternal Tao: the name that can be named is not the eternal name . . . It is the Mystery of all mysteries! The door of all subtleties.'[8] The 'uncarved block' is a favorite figure in Taoism, referring to the original state of complete simplicity which is its highest ideal. *Lao Tzu* says, 'Truly a great cutter does not cut.'[9] There is an underlying mood or feeling or attitude which recognizes that true knowledge (*Satyasya Satyam* – the truth of the truth *Brihad.* I,16) is not a matter of exegesis of scripture but a transformation of the knowing subject. *Tarka* (logic) does not lead to truth. It is the person whose mind is purified through discipline who can *hear* or *see* the Truth. The essential point constantly affirmed is that hermeneutics by itself cannot yield truth in its fullness without purification of the mind, transformation of the heart, and discipline of the body.

HERMENEUTICS IN A
MULTISCRIPTURAL CONTEXT

A plurality of scriptures raises highly complex questions. The way in which a text becomes a scripture, the relation between 'spokenness' and 'writtenness', the manner in which a scripture functions religiously in the life of a community, and the notion and practice of authority itself are different within different communities of faith.

The notion of scriptural authority itself is understood differently by different religious communities. To most Hindus primary authority lies in that which is *heard*, not that which is *remembered* and written down. To the Buddhist, scriptures have an *instrumental* authority, like that of a boat that helps one to cross the river but which, after reaching the other shore, becomes unnecessary. It is sometimes said that to the Muslims the Qur'an is what Christ is to the Christians. The difficulty in that comparison indicates the striking differences in the notion of authority between the two. Although all Christians accept the normativity of the Bible, scriptural authority is understood differently in the Roman Catholic, Orthodox, and Protestant traditions. Within the Protestant tradition itself, not all accept the 'inerrancy' of the Bible. These differences mean that the criteria derived from one scripture cannot be applied to judge other scriptures. In addition to these is the fact that scriptures serve not just as sources for doctrinal formulations but also for personal devotion and the spiritual formation of the community. How does an oral tradition become a text and a text become scripture in the life of a community? Two examples may be given, one from the Hebrew and the other from the Hindu tradition.

Wilfred Cantwell Smith points out that originally the Song of Songs was a secular love song sung in taverns in the first century AD.[10] How then did it get a place in the Hebrew canon? Rabbi Solomon ben Isaac described it as depicting the love of God for the Jewish people. But for this, and the attribution of its authorship to Solomon, it probably would not have found a place in the canon. Bernard of Clairvaux interpreted it as the love of Christ for the Church. A modern commentary with very elaborate exegesis relates it to contemporary issues such as the correlation between love and death, women's liberation, and others.[11]

A more recent article (1986) brings out the connection between Eros and language, between the 'Pleasure of the Text and Text of

16

Stanley J. Samartha

Pleasure'.[12] In interpreting Origen's commentary on the Song of Songs, Miller points out that to Origen the Song of Songs was an *epithalamium*, a song sung before the bridal chamber, which then becomes 'a drama of love' in which the bride is described as *sponsa verbi*, the Bride of the Word who is espoused to Christ described as a *philtron*, 'a saving wound'. In this process, language and love are intimately related. 'Speaker and lover have been fused, and the reality over which the speaker-lover presides is linguistic.'[13] To Origen the Song of Songs was also mystical and contemplative. To contemplate is to desire, to long for the loved one, and words give expression to it. The name of love is the substance of language itself. Love seduces language. It hurts and wounds, and yet in the pain of wounding is also the pleasure of healing.

The manner in which the *Bhagavadgita* (hereafter the *Gita*, c. fourth century B C was used and interpreted through the centuries is a different example of the evolution of scriptural authority in a very different setting, namely, that of Hindus in India. Originally embedded in the epic *Mahabharata* very early in its history, it was lifted from the *Smriti* context (secondary authority) and placed among *Sruti* (primary authority). A striking change in its status took place by its being invested with higher authority. There are over 2,000 editions of the *Gita* in about seventy-five languages.[14] Sankara, (eighth century A D), the well-known teacher of *advaita*, interpreted the *Gita* not as a gospel of action but of *moksha*, release. Sankara subordinates the way of action and devotion to that of *jnana* (knowledge).[15] On the other hand, Ramanuja (twelfth century A D) interprets the *Gita* in a different way, emphasizing the devotional aspect of the book, drawing attention to a merciful God of grace who can be fully known only through love.[16]

A striking change took place in the twentieth century during India's freedom struggle against the British. The *Gita* was once again regarded as the gospel of action, this time for a *dharma yuddha*, a righteous war against the oppressive foreign power. Many political leaders such as Aurobindo, Tilak, Mahatma Gandhi, Bhave, and others have written commentaries on the *Gita*. Balagangadhar Tilak's commentary is one of the most outstanding in this connection.[17] To Tilak, Arjuna, the hero, was essentially a man of action, a *karma yogin*, and he interprets the message of the *Gita* to be an encouragement to act in such a way that one ultimately attains *moksha* through the way of action.

17

Radhakrishnan brought out his commentary of the *Gita* in 1948. It was dedicated to Mahatma Gandhi, who was assassinated that year.[18] By the time his book was published, political freedom in India had become a reality. Radhakrishnan's purpose in writing the commentary 'was to restate the truths of eternity in the accents of our time because it is the only way in which a great scripture can be of living value to mankind.'[19]

The latest book on the *Gita* by Krishna Chaitanya (1987) is a very different volume from others, in that it takes into account a far wider range of concerns, and is more acutely aware of the imminent disaster through nuclear holocaust and so seeks to bring out the message of the *Gita* to the inner anxieties of modern people. The book is illustrated with nineteen reproductions, five in color, of some of the most impressive works of Indian painters and sculptors, ancient and modern, as visual correlates of the themes of different chapters. Thus, 'hearing' the text and 'seeing' the paintings combine to produce a strikingly new 'integrative vision' of the message of the *Gita* very different from earlier works.

Thus scriptures function differently at different times within particular religious communities. In the case of the Song of Songs, a purely secular poem is gradually invested with sacred authority and, at different times, deeper meaning is read into it in different ways. In the case of the *Gita*, a scripture embedded in a source of secondary authority is lifted into a higher plane, and over the centuries, serves as the source of theological strength, spiritual solace, and ethical guidance.

Several points are involved in this process of a text becoming a scripture. There is obviously sensitivity and openness to new perceptions on the part of individuals. Unless individuals have the freedom and courage to bring out the new, no fresh developments can take place. Without Rabbi Solomon, the Song of Songs would have remained a secular song. The perception of the sacred in the secular, of divine love in human eros, is indeed a profound insight. Without Tilak's interpretation of the *Gita*, the freedom struggle in India would have probably remained purely political, without any spiritual, theological, and ethical undergirding. Further, the acceptance of individual insights by the community invests authority on new insights and interpretations. No text can function religiously in the life of the community unless the new interpretations meet the specific needs of a community at a particular time. An uncritical attachment to inherited notions may prevent a community from considering fresh interpretations. Thus people brought up in the notion that their scripture is 'the only true scripture' might refuse even to consider the suggestion that neighbors of other faiths cherish their own scriptures and are sustained and nourished by them.

But there is a third dimension in addition to individual sensitivity and community acceptance that should not be forgotten. This is what may be described as the transcendental element involved in all sacred scriptures. It may appear that in the case of the Song of Songs, because of its original secular character, this dimension is missing. But the whole Bible is witness to the divine initiative to which human beings respond and to which they bear witness in the scripture. In the case of the *Gita* this is more obvious, particularly because of the central importance of the vision of Krishna to Arjuna as the Lord of the whole universe. Thus in the history of religions an oral tradition becomes a text through a long process, and a text becomes a scripture, and provides not only *formal* authority but also *becomes* authoritative in new situations through new interpretations. The sensitivity and openness of individuals, the responsibility of the believing community to reject or accept new interpretations as authoritative, and the needs of the community as it faces the profound mysteries of life, birth and death, love and suffering, loneliness and companionship, time and eternity are all involved in this complex process. This means that the authority of one scripture cannot, and should not, be imposed on other scriptures.

LANGUAGE: 'SPOKENNESS' AND 'WRITTENNESS'

The connection between 'spokenness' and 'writtenness', along with the question of language, introduces another element into this discussion. Scriptures have played different roles in the religious life of different communities in history, sometimes within a particular religion. In Protestant Christianity in the West, the desire to look for an authority other than the Pope brought the authority of the Bible into greater prominence. Further, the invention of printing and the translation of the Bible into languages of the people gave them greater accessibility to the scriptures. When Western missionaries brought the Bible to multiscriptural Asia, the authority of the Bible that had been formulated against other authorities in Europe was set against the authority of other scriptures. This attitude, unfortunately, continues even to this day.

But the attitude toward written texts is very different in other religions. In cultures such as the Hindu and the Buddhist, even though scriptures were written very early, it was the recital and the hearing of the scriptures that operated as authority among the people. The profoundly *spoken* character of scripture in India, particularly the emphasis on the *mantra*, indicates this. What becomes important is not so much the rational intelligibility of the written texts but the power of the original Word (*Sabda*). The holiness of the words is intrinsic. One participates in it not just through reading and exegesis and interpretation but by reciting and hearing it.[20] This is by no means to minimize the importance of written scriptures that function religiously in the life of the people.

'Writtenness' introduces an element of rigidity into the freedom and fluidity of the spoken word. Between speech and writing a rupture takes place which can seldom be bridged by later readers. Writing, therefore, is 'a detour of speech'.[21] Writtenness also introduces a serious limitation on fluid, free-flowing speech by imposing a form, a structure of logical precision. Quite often, it misses the symbolic meaning that speech conveys. The scientific temper seeks precision and clarity and is therefore impatient with symbols and metaphors. It uses language as an instrument to define, control, and manipulate Truth, which is considered a liability to be overcome rather than a gift to be treasured.

'We dismiss realms of meaning beyond the literal either as confusion to be cleared up by logicians or as emotional embellishments to be kept in check,' remarks Paul Ricoeur, who goes on to say that for people in the West, it is hard 'to see scriptural language full as it is with figure, vision and myth, as having to do with Reality.'[22]

This note about the limitation of written words is meant as a caution against claiming final authority for the literalness of what is written, but it does not minimize the importance of scriptures. Hindu scholars have always emphasized the primary importance of the Word that is *heard* (*Sruti*) which, of course, is later on written down. The notion of separate individual letters forming a word and a cluster of words being shaped into a meaningful sentence introduces a profound sense of unity. The great *acharayas* (teachers) of Hindu *dharma* speak of *ekavakyatva* – 'one-sentence-ness' – that holds diverse elements together within itself.[23]

The particular formation of words and sentences in different religions and cultures indicates different ways of thinking about Truth and expressing it. There has been a great deal of discussion in India on the nature of language, the relationship between words and sentences, and the relationship between verbal and nonverbal words.[24] In the Hindu and Buddhist traditions there is a strong feeling that by merely reading texts and analyzing them one does move nearer Truth, that wisdom is not synonymous with knowledge, and that one should not too quickly identify wisdom and authority with written forms and techniques of communication.[25] Therefore to quote inadequately translated texts from a particular scripture without taking into account the original context in which it was spoken and impose it in place of other scriptures as the only true authority is neither charitable nor reasonable. This leads to a discussion of the manner in which Asian Christians are seeking to interpret the Bible as they live with neighbors of other faiths in a multireligious context.

THE QUEST FOR NEW HERMENEUTICS IN ASIA

At a time when scriptures cannot be regarded as the monopolistic possession of any one particular people but should be accepted as belonging to the heritage of the whole world, the hermeneutic question may be stated thus: How can the Bible, a Semitic book formed through oral and written traditions in an entirely different geographic, historical, and cultural context, appropriated and interpreted for so many centuries by the West through hermeneutic tools designed to meet different needs and shaped by different historical factors, now be interpreted in Asia by Asian Christians for their own people? In what ways does biblical authority help Asian Christians confess Christ in a multiscriptural context? Christians in Asia are heirs to a double heritage – that of the Bible and that of other scriptures. If this fact is taken seriously, Asian Christians could provide a bridge through which the insights of different scriptures might be shared in the larger community.

To enter this multiscriptural situation with the claim that the Bible 'is the only written witness to God's deeds in history'[26] is to cut off all conversation with neighbors of other faiths. This attitude makes it impossible for Christians to develop 'their own hermeneutics'. In a continent like Asia a claim for the supreme authority of *one* scripture can be met by a counterclaim for similar authority for *another* scripture. It ignores the relation between 'words' and 'events', spoken languages and written texts, the text and what or who is behind the text. 'Biblicism' should not be equated with being biblical. Further, the notion of 'correspondence' between contemporary situations and biblical situations fails to see the gap between then and now and results in alienating the text from both its own historical context and our context today. What if there are situations that obviously do *not* correspond to those in the present? Is the limited and narrow experience of Israel with its surrounding nations or one sermon by Paul to the Athenians sufficient grounds to pass heavily negative theological judgments on neighbors of other faiths in Asia today? One gets the impression that too often the search for 'similar situations' and 'applicability' of texts reduces 'the Kerygmatic content' of the Word of God to which biblical writings bear witness.

There are other trends in biblical interpretation in Asia which are more helpful in holding on to Christian commitment and developing new relations with neighbors of other faiths. The quest for new hermeneutics in Asia, although at present in its initial stages, is a significant movement. Too much should not be claimed for it. A comprehensive and systematic analysis and evaluation of the various trends in Asia is yet to be done.[27]

The concern in Asia here is not so much to formulate rules of interpretation as to bring out the insights, guideposts, and directions to which the Bible points, in order to illumine the path of Christian obedience in Asia today. The images, stories, and particular traditions of the Bible – carefully studied with considerable knowledge of the original languages and the formation of oral traditions and written texts – together with an understanding of historical contexts, form the basis of interpretations of God's Word for the life of the churches in Asia today. Some Asian theologians even seem to reject the formal authority of the Bible in order to come under the *living* authority of the Word. They point to a certain measure of plurality in the Bible, both in ways of knowing and defining the ultimate goals of life. Thus, for example, when two living religious traditions such as the Hindu and the Christian meet in the experience (*anubhaya*) of the interpreter, the *pramanas* (criteria for interpretation) of each tradition might help each other – by way of mutual criticism and mutual enrichment – encounter the reality behind the texts. So, too, in defining the ultimate goal of life salvation as *reconciliation*, with God or as the *realization* of God, the meeting of the two traditions – not in a formal academic way, but in the profound sharing of experiences (*anubhaya*) – should help the entry into 'new modes of being'. The meeting point or points between the Bible and scriptures of other faiths have yet to be discovered.

There are two related questions here. One is the plurality of languages into which the Bible has been translated in Asia; the other is the question of the nature of language itself. There is 'nothing more authentic than language itself . . . language itself is understanding.'[28] In the Bible, event and word are born together. They form a unity. The preachings of Jesus are language events. Once we recognize this, the gap between then and now, between biblical times and our times, is bridged because there is 'a merging of horizons'.

Asia is diversified into at least seven linguistic zones, the most that any continent can boast of.[29] Biblical languages are Hebrew and Greek. Almost *all* Asian theological writing is done in English, that is, a language other than the mother tongue of Asian people. Suppression or domination of the languages of a people is one of the most common and far-reaching methods of colonialism, with consequences that last for generations. The decolonization of speech is far more difficult than the decolonization of the land. Asian theologians and biblical scholars face a serious dilemma here. On the one hand, without using their own particular mother tongues, their encounter with the language events of the Bible can hardly be authentic. On the other, without using English, they cannot communicate with one another in the larger community of the Asian world.

Furthermore, a great deal of the preaching of the Word is done in the languages of the people. This is particularly true of a multilingual country such as India, where in a large number of village congregations the Word cannot be heard except through the mother tongue. The implications of preaching in the mother tongue for biblical interpretation and the manner in which theological training in English affects the minister's ability to communicate the message and encounter the language events of the Bible with the congregation have yet to be carefully studied.

There are other Asian theologians who, while based in sound biblical scholarship, move beyond its boundaries into the realm of symbols and images. They ignore the line of demarcation between biblical scholarship and theological reflection and move back and

23

forth across the boundaries with ease and sensitivity. To them these boundaries cease to be hindrances but become thresholds into the realm of meanings to be discovered where biblical realities and the life situations of Asian people meet in the inner experience of the interpreter. Almost all of them have had experience in teaching, and quite a few of them are still related to theological seminaries. Perhaps their large ecumenical experience enables them to lift images from the Bible and transpose them into Asian situations without doing violence to the text or the life situations of the Asian people.

Selecting a few among many such people is not easy. A certain representativeness, both geographical and confessional, has been kept in mind. Kosuke Koyama is a Japanese theologian well-known for his Bible studies. Choan-Seng Song, from Taiwan, combines a deep knowledge of Chinese classics with fresh Christian biblical insights. Mar Gregorios is a bishop of the Syrian Orthodox Church in India widely known for his Bible studies and other theological writings. He has also been one of the presidents of the World Council of Churches. D. S. Amalorpavadass is a Roman Catholic scholar in India well-known for his liturgical experiments in inculturation. He is one of the few Christian scholars who has given serious attention to the authority of nonbiblical scriptures. The concern here is not so much with the theological content of their writings as with their methodology of interpreting the Bible, although the two cannot strictly be kept separate.

Koyama's Bible studies are noted for the striking way in which he *contrasts* biblical images with images taken from contemporary life. One finds a methodology that is not always articulated but is implied in his writings.[30] Although a large number of his references are to Hebrew scriptural images, there is a certain christocentric emphasis in his writings, particularly those on the cross. He points out that we learn of Jesus Christ through studying the Bible, particularly the New Testament, identifying ourselves with the community of faith.[31] The 'crucified' mind is contrasted with the 'crusading' mind, the Good Friday mind with the Easter mind. The lunchbox and the briefcase have convenient handles to carry them; the cross has no handle to carry it.

There are other illustrations. The hand of Buddha is open; that of Lenin is closed (clenched fist); that of Jesus Christ is open, but pierced through with a nail.[32] In *Three Mile an Hour God*, Koyama contrasts the slowness of God in educating his people during forty years in the wilderness with the swiftness of modern technology. There is the technological straightness of the pipe and there is the natural 'curvedness' of the bamboo. A car is smooth, sleek, and fast. A bullock cart is rough, cumbersome, and slow. The wilderness to which God led the people of Israel is open on all sides; a modern city is closed on itself, without a sense of spaciousness. There is a 'tourist' approach and a 'pilgrim' approach to other people and other cultures. We need to move away from hostility to hospitality.[33] Most of these come from short, rather quick Bible studies presented mostly to Western Christian groups and are meant to convey a mood rather than demand sustained reflection. In a long Bible study entitled 'Adam in Deep Sleep', Koyama works on a dialogue between 'Adam awakened' and 'Adam in deep sleep' in the life of Asia.[34] K. C. Abraham, in his response to this study, which was presented to an Asian Christian consultation, remarks, 'I feel Dr Koyama's paper, with all respect to his creative contribution, is still basically Western. All the central categories and concepts are taken from Western thinkers . . . This is not a criticism but an observation!'[35] Koyama succeeds in conveying an Asian flavor to his Western hearers. His method is communication by contrast – contrast between biblical images and those in a technological Western society. Its possibilities for biblical interpretation in Asia need to be explored more critically where Christians live together with their neighbors of other faiths and ideological convictions.

Breaking away from literalist interpretations of the Bible, C. S. Song provides an important, perhaps more Asian, alternative to connect what is truly biblical with what is authentically Asian. He does this by going beyond the structures of languages to the meaning of symbols that provide openings into a transhistorical world. Meaningful selections from the Asian cultural heritage, particularly from Chinese – poems, stories, legends, myths, dramas, and proverbs – are placed alongside significant chunks of biblical material, challenging the imagination and touching the spirit of the readers, who are constantly invited to go beyond the written words to the symbolic meaning behind them. This is particularly true, for example, in his booklet *The Tears of Lady Ming* and the article 'Opening the Stone Gate of Religion with a Golden Key'. In the inner experience of the interpreters whose hearts and minds are opened to the meaning of symbols, the hermeneutical circle is closed, not short-circuited.[36]

A literalist interpretation of the Bible, according to Song, destroys the power and meaning of revelation. There cannot be 'a verbatim correspondence' between what is written down and what transcends history. 'Human language has to be stretched beyond its normal logic to capture something that transcends human rationality. Scriptures can thus be interpreted symbolically.'[37] One cannot become sensitive to the power of symbols without a spirit of 'transposition'. This is an important principle in Song's method of interpretation, which he elaborates on at considerable length. Transposition is 'a shift in space and time' from the biblical world to the Asian world, even 'a theological leap'. It is an effort 'to respond to that mysterious and powerful bond of life with which the compassionate God creates, redeems and recreates a family and a human community.'[38]

This calls for sensitivity and creative responses to vibrations coming from the depths of the human spirit that are outside the familiar realm of everyday life and may at first appear alien to our religious consciousness. Asia, with its vast number of peoples, religions, and cultures, demands a spirit of transposition 'and invites us to a hermeneutical and theological adventure'.[39] Song constantly notes that one has to go beyond the rules of interpretation to the heart of a self-revealing God who continues to redeem all people. Changes in present-day realities in Asia oblige us to reinterpret the Word of God afresh. Asian hearts need to be open to new insights as Asian Christians stand at the intersection where the Word of God and the reality of life in Asia constantly meet and react. 'The Christian Bible which follows God's search from the time of Adam and Eve to its culmination on the cross, gives us profound insights into God's work: the recovery of the human heart.'[40]

Mar Gregorios brings a distinctively Indian and Orthodox contribution to the quest for biblical interpretation in Asia.[41] He is very impatient with Western historical criticism of the Bible. Few people are so proud of their Indian heritage, so unmistakably Orthodox in their Christian commitment, and so unreservedly critical of the West and of Western Christianity as Mar Gregorios. It is easy to disagree with him, but difficult to ignore him. Europeans 'short-circuit' hermeneutics, remarks Gregorios. Instead of asking the question, 'How do I perceive reality and how can I improve the way I perceive it?' they ask, 'What are the rules to interpret the Bible and how do I improve my way of interpretation?'[42] This appears to be a little too harsh. But many Asian students, including Indians who have done their biblical studies in the West, are so trapped within the hedges of European biblical criticism that they are unable to move beyond their restricting limitations into the realms of original Asian theological reflection.

One should note that Asian religious traditions such as the Hindu and the Buddhist do not believe that one can develop a scriptural hermeneutic which will yield truth by itself. True knowledge is not the fruit of logical investigation or the exegesis of scriptures, but a transformation of the knowing subject. Gregorios connects this with the Eastern Orthodox tradition. Both Indian philosophy and the Eastern tradition, he says, generally hold the view that one can know reality only when one's whole life becomes pure. Gregory of Nyssa emphasizes the need to cleanse the mind and control the passions in order to 'see' God. The basic hermeneutic principle is that '*apatheia*' or a personality that is not only free from passions which dominate the mind and from all evil inclinations, but is also positively developed to conform to the image of God.[43] This emphasis on the discipline of the body, mind, and heart (*sadhana*) as a prerequisite to any hermeneutics is too often neglected by Asian Christians.

To this Gregorios adds two further points. One is the importance of tradition, that is, the ongoing life of the believing community within which scriptural interpretations take place. Community plays a much greater role in shaping our perceptions of truth than we imagine. His other point is the necessity to be open to the Spirit of God. Sharpening the intellectual tools of perception is only a minor part of hermeneutics. Being open to the Spirit is the major part. However, the moment we mention the Spirit of *God*, we must take into account the larger human community, particularly because in Asia the Christian community is a small part of a much larger multireligious and multicultural community. 'The Bible is an important element in the operation of the Spirit in the community. But we will certainly need to know more about the larger operation of the Spirit not only as a whole, and in fact in the whole universe, before we can understand what the Spirit is saying to the Churches.'[44]

This emphasis on tradition (*sampradaya*), which is the principle of continuity in the life of the Church, is accepted both by Orthodox and Roman Catholic scholars. Protestant scholars do not ignore this dimension, but their concern with biblical interpretations has been part of their quest for a source of authority independent of, or at least critical of, the authority of the institutional and hierarchical Church. This is understandable when one takes into account the history of the Church in the West during the Reformation and after. In Asia, however, with its many powerful religions, cultures, and scriptures, the story of the Bible has to be retold in a different context. When all the three major traditions of the Church – Roman Catholic, Orthodox and Protestant – are present in Asia, the *Christian* concern with the Bible has to be more ecumenical in its deepest sense. The dynamic interplay of scripture, tradition, and reason within the Christian Church should influence and be influenced by the hermeneutical struggle of neighbors of other faiths as well.

There are many Catholic scholars in Asia writing on the subject of biblical hermeneutics. Some tend to see it as a tool or instrument of theology. Biblical scholars are often regarded as technicians, selecting and sharpening the tools for the architects and engineers of theology. Thus Carlos H. Abesan remarks that 'theologians need the help of the exegetes and biblical scholars.' He speaks of different kinds of biblical scholars. Some, according to him, regard the Bible as 'an arsenal of incipient dogmatic truth'. Some see biblical study as 'a handmaid' to dogmatic theology. Others reconstruct the meaning of the Bible against its literary and historic contexts.

> Finally, there are the Biblical scholars, who, as they do vigorous exegesis, open each book of the Bible as they would different doors, and as they do, open up to themselves and to others a whole panorama in which to contemplate the whole history of salvation with its past and its promise for the future. These last are the *technicians* the theologians are looking for.[45]

The question inevitably arises: What is the authority of the Bible, not so much *against* as *in relation to* the authority of scriptures which are cherished and held in deep respect by our neighbors of other faiths, even as Christians cherish and respect the Bible? D. S. Amalorpavadass, the well-known Roman Catholic scholar in India, has given considerable attention to this question. There are also other articles by other scholars.[46] Protestant biblical scholars have not paid serious attention to this matter. The volume Amalorpavadass has edited is the fruit of a consultation which gathered together Roman Catholic, Orthodox, and Protestant scholars to consider this matter, although one must note that the Roman Catholics were the majority group that provided substance and direction to the discussion.

Amalorpavadass recognizes that the question of the authority and inspiration of non-biblical scriptures is important and urgent for the church in Asia. He prefers the term 'non-biblical' to 'non-Christian', because the latter has negative connotations. He points out that Christians are already using selections from non-biblical scriptures in their meditations, prayers, and sometimes even in the liturgy. The enrichment Christians receive from them is accepted. Further, in the growing experience of interreligious relations, the question of the authority of scriptures becomes increasingly important. It cannot be ignored any more. Christians in Asia should recognize that this is a new problem for the Church, because neither the early Church nor the Church in the West had to face this question as Christians do in Asia today. To the Church in the multireligious countries of Asia, the matter is even more important and urgent. He remarks, 'It seems that the Church in India is destined by Divine Providence to contribute as its specific share to the theology of the religious traditions of humankind, more specifically to that of non-biblical scriptures.'[47]

The notions of revelation and inspiration are changing within Christianity itself. One cannot therefore approach the scriptures of our neighbors with absolute notions of the exclusive inspiration of the Christian scriptures. The scriptures of any religious group are the objectification of the faith experience of that particular community. Therefore, scriptures have to be regarded not as an absolute creation, but an actualization, a re-creation of the experience. Inspiration can be meaningful only in the context of the faith experience of the believers.

In the statement that emerged out of the consultation, at which no less than thirty-two research papers were considered, two attitudes toward non-biblical scriptures are apparent. One is to regard them as preparing the way for Christ. Thus the Hindu scriptures, it is claimed, 'give us many openings into the mystery of Christ'. The mystical love of the *Bhagavadgita* foreshadows the love of Christ. If we can speak of 'the Unknown Christ of Hinduism', we can also speak of 'the half-known Christ of Islam'.

But this view is hardly new. It retains Christian scriptures as the norm and either uses other scriptures to justify its supremacy or co-opts them into its own structure in a patronizing way. Many people at the consultation expressed uneasiness about this position and argued for a theocentric approach rather than 'a Christomonistic' one. This attitude emphasizes that the mystery of God revealed in Jesus of Nazareth and attested to in the Bible is expressed in different ways in other religions such as Hinduism or Buddhism. Therefore, the scriptures of other religions should not be subordinated to the Christian but regarded as valid and authoritative to those who accept them, because they are based on their own particular faith experience.

Obviously, this whole question needs to be studied more carefully by Asian scholars in the years to come. Protestant scholars who have not given sufficient attention to this question need to grapple with this matter, together with their Catholic and Orthodox colleagues. Whether biblical hermeneutics is a separate and distinct discipline or whether it can benefit by sharing the general hermeneutical task with neighbors of other faiths is a matter that needs further discussion. In any case, this task cannot be done satisfactorily without accepting the fact that interreligious dialogue in Asia is no longer the concern of a few but part of the experience of the Church in Asia as a whole. Out of this experience and critical reflection on it, Christians should become sensitive to new insights and fresh perspectives. The Christian community can speak meaningfully of the inspiration of the scriptures of other religions only insofar as its experience of itself is no longer that of a closed group but of a community that is open and moving toward the formation of a new, wider community that would be as wide as God's economy of salvation.

SOME PRINCIPLES OF INTERPRETATION

In this discussion on scripture and scriptures in a religiously plural world, certain tentative conclusions may be noted here.

1. There is indeed a *plurality* of scriptures. This is a fact of history to be accepted, not a theological point to be discussed. This should be openly acknowledged by people of all religious traditions. Each particular tradition cherishes its own scripture, holding it as sacred and authoritative. To ignore this fact amounts to blindness and self-deception.

2. Scriptures *function differently* in the life of different religious communities. The manner in which an oral tradition comes to be written down, the ways in which a text becomes a scripture, and how a scripture functions religiously in the life of a believing community are all different, depending very much on cultural differences and historical circumstances. The notion and exercise of authority itself

is understood differently in different communities of faith. Therefore the criteria derived on the basis of one particular scripture cannot be used to pass judgment on other scriptures.

3. There are certain *exclusive* elements within each scripture leading to truth claims by each community of faith. Thus the *Gita* talks of many *avataras*; the New Testament speaks of Jesus Christ as 'the way, the truth and the life'; the Qur'an describes Mohammed as 'the seal' of the prophets; and the Torah is still waiting for the Messiah to come. These claims are important for the self-understanding and identity of each community of faith in the larger community. These should not be relativized, but accepted as legitimate *within* the boundaries of particular communities of faith. They cannot be extended to other faiths. How these claims based on scriptures are to be related to one another will become an important question. Premature conclusions made unilaterally by one community of faith would pre-empt discussions in a multireligious world.

4. The language of religion does not depend solely on *texts* but also on *symbols* that are not an end in themselves but point to something beyond that is deeper, larger, and more mysterious. The language of religion is a language of love and commitment. It would be most unwise to draw logical conclusions from the language of love. An exclusive claim expressed in religious language has the character of commitment, not of rejection. A negative judgment on other commitments based on one's own particular commitment is unwarranted. The relationship between different truth claims in the larger community is yet to be discussed. Charges of relativism should not be hurled against those who recognize other commitments in a religiously plural world.

5. In every living religion, scriptures are not just sources of doctrine, but also of personal devotion, spiritual sustenance, and help in times of trouble, perplexity, and suffering. Therefore the *devotional* use of *other* scriptures by people of a particular tradition should not be rejected or looked upon with suspicion. In the lives of many people, reading from other scriptures is enlarging horizons and deepening inner life without in any way disturbing, diluting, or betraying one's own commitment.

6. All life, including the religious, has a *pilgrim* character. We are always *on the way*. Every arrival is a point of departure, and every journey looks for a new destination. This means that scriptures should not be regarded as 'petrified texts' written once for all, or

31

that the entire religious life of humankind is limited to a continual hermeneutical exercise seeking to interpret texts handed over from the past. That would amount to ignoring the leading of the Spirit into new realms of truth and blocking the possibilities of new insights being recognized to sustain life on the way. The major religions in the world today, the Semitic and the Indian, originated in isolation from each other. The formation of particular scriptures and the development of the canon took place without reference to what was happening in other places and at other times among other people. Today, when the nations of the world are being drawn together as never before and people of different religious beliefs share a common destiny, the different scriptures should not be regarded as passport documents that divide different nationalities but as signposts that point to a more promising future.

In order to avoid any misunderstanding, it must be stated firmly and in as unambiguous terms as possible that the cumulative effect of these points does not in any way minimize or weaken the authority of the Bible for Christian life and thought, but puts it in a larger perspective that is theologically appropriate in a religiously plural world. The Bible remains normative for all Christians in all places and at all times, because it bears witness to God's dealings with the whole World and to Jesus Christ, his life and death, and resurrection, his deeds and teachings, thus providing the basis for Christian theological reflection. The dynamic interplay among the Bible, tradition, and reason – whatever the differences between Roman Catholics, Orthodox, and Protestant – is very much part of the Christian hermeneutical process in all situations. But to be 'biblical' it is not necessary to claim that every letter and word in the book is true or to ignore and condemn the scriptures of neighbors of other faiths. All christological reflections take place on the basis of the authority of the Bible and the strength of Christian tradition, which is the cumulative experience of the believing community in history. Today, however, in a religiously plural world, the interplay among scripture, tradition, and reason has to be far more dynamic and theologically imaginative than ever before.

NOTES

1   In my native language, Kannada, spoken by about 42 million people (1986) in the southern state of Karnataka, with a literary history of about 1,500 years, the title page of the Bible describes the book as *Satya Veda*, that is 'True Veda', implying that the four Vedas of the Hindus are false. The earlier edition in 1865 was printed in England, and the same title page was printed in the Indian edition in 1951.

2   Theodore de Bary, *The Sources of Chinese Tradition* (New York, Columbia University Press, 1961), p. 17.

3   ibid. See also Herrlee Glessner Creel, 'Literature', in *The Birth of China: A Survey of the Formative Period of Chinese Civilization* (New York, Frederick Unger Publishing Co., 1961), pp. 254ff. The *Book of Changes* was probably the first complete work of Chinese literature, p. 267. See also Peter N. Gregory, 'Chinese Buddhist Hermeneutics', *The Journal of the American Academy of Religion* 51 (1983), 231ff.

4   ibid., p. 350.

5   Quoted by de Bary, *The Sources of Chinese Tradition*, pp. 317–18.

6   ibid., p. 314. Quoted from *Hung-ming chi*, in *Raisho daizokvo* LII, 1–7.

7   *Lao Tzu, Mundaka*, III, ii, 9.

8   Quoted by de Bary, *The Sources of Chinese Tradition*, pp. 53ff.

9   ibid., p. 56.

10   Wilfred Cantwell Smith, 'Scripture: Issues Seen by a Comparative Religionist' (Claremont, Calif., Claremont Graduate School, 1985).

11   Marvin Pope, *Song of Songs: A New Translation*, with interpretive commentary (New York, Doubleday, 1977).

12   Patricia Cox Miller, 'Pleasure of the Text and Text of Pleasure', *The Journal of the American Academy of Religion* 2 (Summer 1986), pp. 241–56.

13   ibid., p. 242.

14   Krishna Chaitanya, *The Gita for the Modern Man* (New Delhi, Clarion Books, 1987), mentions that he himself has counted over 2,000 editions of the *Gita*.

15   Alladi Mahadeva Sastri, trans., *The Bhagavadgita with the Commentary of Sankaracharya* (Madras, Samata Books, 1897, 1985). See also V. N. Apte (ed.), Sankara's *Gitabhasya*, 34 (Bombay, Anandashram Sanskrit Series, 1936).

16   V. N. Apte (ed.), Ramanuja's *Gitabhasya*, 34 (Bombay, Anandashram Sanskrit Series, 1936), pp. 9ff.

17   See Balgangadhar Tilak, *Srimad Bhagavadgita Rahasya or Karma Yoga Sastra*, trans. Balchandra Sitaram Sukthankar (Pune, Arya Bhusana Press, 1936).

18   S. Radhakrishnan, *The Bhagavadgita* (London, Allen and Unwin, 1948), with an introductory essay, Sanskrit text, English translation and notes.

19   ibid., p. 6.

20   J. A. B. Van Buitenen, in Milton Singer (ed.), *Krishna: Myths, Rites*

and Attitudes (Honolulu, East-West Centre Press, 1984), pp. 35–36.

21 Jacques Derrida, *Writing and Difference*, trans. Alan Bass (Chicago, Chicago University Press, 1978), p. 280f.

22 Paul Ricoeur, *Essays in Biblical Interpretation* (Philadelphia, Fortress Press, 1980), p. 4.

23 Uma Shankar Joshi, *Book Review* 10 (1, August–December, 1985), p. 8f.

24 See Bimal Krishna Matilal, *Logic, Language and Reality* (Delhi, Motilal Banarasidas, 1985). The notion of a *vakya*, pp. 398ff., following Kumarila Bhatta, *Mimasa-Sloka vartikka codana-sutra* 2, verses 33–61 (Banaras, Chokadamba 1989). Panini (fourth century B C, the great grammarian, and Amarasimha (A D fourth century) have discussed the relation between metaphysical concepts and semantic forms and the ontological meaning of grammar.

25 J. M. Shukla (ed.), Bhartrahari's *Vakyapadiya* (Ahmedabad, Institute of Indology, 1984), is one of the basic works in Sanskrit on the philosophy of Word and Meaning. He identifies the word *Sabda* with *Brahman* and shifts the emphasis from grammar (*vyakarana*) to *tatparya* (meaning). See also Amanda E. Wood, *Knowledge Before Printing and After* (Delhi, Oxford University Press, 1985), pp. 183ff.

26 Saphir P. Athyal, in Douglas J. Elwood (ed.), *Asian Christian Theology* (Philadelphia, Westminster Press, 1980), p. 69.

27 For a preliminary investigation see S. J. Samartha, *The Search for New Hermeneutics in Asian Christian Theology* (Madras, CLS, 1987). See also S. Wesley Ariarajah, *The Bible and People of Other Faiths* (Maryknoll, NY, Orbis Books, 1989).

28 Samartha, *The Search for New Hermeneutics*, p. 233.

29 Aloysius Pieris, 'Toward an Asian Theology of Liberation: Some Religiocultural Guidelines', in Elwood, *Asian Christian Theology*, pp. 235–53. Also see 'Linguistic Heterogeneity', ibid., pp. 240ff., J. G. F. Collinson, 'Issues in the History of Biblical Hermeneutics: A Protestant Perspective', *The Indian Journal of Theology* 31 (314, July–December 1982), p. 335.

30 In addition to numerous articles, Kosuke Koyama has written the following books: *Water Buffalo Theology* (1974), *No Handle on the Cross* (1977), *Three Mile an Hour God* (1980), all published by Orbis Books, Maryknoll, NY. See also *Mount Fuji and Mount Sinai* (Maryknoll, NY, Orbis Books, 1985).

31 Kosuke Koyama, 'Theological Perspectives to Jesus Christ Frees and Unites', *North East Asia Journal of Theology* (March 1976), pp. 39ff.

32 Koyama, *No Handle on the Cross*, pp. 1f. 23f.

33 Koyama, *Three Mile an Hour God*, passim.

34 Kosuke Koyama, in Emerito P. Nacpil and Douglas J. Elwood (eds.), *The Human and the Holy* (Maryknoll, NY, Orbis Books, 1978), pp. 36–61.

35 ibid., p. 62.

36 Among C. S. Song's many books and articles, special mention must be made of the following. *Third-Eye Theology* (1979) and *The Compassionate God* (1982), both published by Orbis Books, Maryknoll, NY. *The Tears of*

Stanley J. Samartha

Lady Ming (Geneva, World Council of Churches, 1981, and Maryknoll, NY, Orbis Books, 1982). *Theology from the Womb of Asia* (Maryknoll, NY, Orbis Books, 1986). 'New China and Salvation History – A Methodological Enquiry', in S. J. Samartha (ed.), *Living Faiths and Ultimate Goals* (Maryknoll, NY, Orbis Books, 1974), pp. 68–89. 'From Israel to Asia: A Theological Leap', *Mission Trends* 3 (New York, Paulist Press, 1976), pp. 211–22. 'Opening the Stone Gate of Religions with a Golden Key', in C. D. Jathanna (ed.), *Dialogue in Community* (Mangalore, Karnataka Theological College, 1982), pp. 199–222.

37 Song, *Third-Eye Theology*, p. 103.
38 Song, *The Compassionate God*, p. xiii.
39 For a discussion on transpositional theology, see C. S. Song, *The Compassionate God*, pp. xiff. See also 'Transposition of Power', pp. 222ff. There are a number of illustrations where Song puts biblical selections alongside stories and poems from Asia. For example, 'The Cross and the Lotus', in *Third-Eye Theology*, pp. 101ff; a poem by a young widow in Vietnam entitled 'The First Tragedy', and Psalm 137; 'By the Waters of Babylon We Wept', a poem of Love by a Chinese woman poet, and parts of the Song of Songs, pp. 120f; a poem by a seventeen-year-old girl, Lai Leng Woon, from Singapore, entitled 'I Believe' and the heavenly chorus in the Book of Revelation, 5.12; 'Worthy is the Lamb that is slain . . .' p. 243.
40 Song, *Third-Eye Theology*, p. xi. See also 'The Hermeneutical Circle and *Active Theology*', pp. 8off.
41 See Mar Gregorios, 'Hermeneutics in India Today', *The Indian Journal of Theology* 31 (1982), 153ff. See also Mar Gregorios, 'Issues in the Hermeneutical Discussion in the West: Some Notes', ibid., pp. 156–65.
42 Gregorios, 'Hermeneutics in India Today', *The Indian Journal of Theology* 31 (1982), p. 153.
43 ibid., p. 12.
44 ibid., p. 155.
45 Carlos H. Abesan, SJ, 'Doing Theological Reflection in a Philippine Context', in Douglas J. Elwood, *Asian Christian Theology*, p. 94, italics mine. There are a number of other Roman Catholic scholars in Asia, particularly in the Philippines, Sri Lanka, Indonesia, and India writing on this subject to whom greater attention needs to be paid by Protestant scholars inhabiting the same *oikoumene*.
46 For example, Francis X. d'Sa, 'Christian Scriptures and Other Scriptures', *The Indian Journal of Theology* 31 (1982), pp. 236ff; P. M. Thomas, 'The Authority of Hindu Scripture', *The Indian Journal of Theology* 23 (1974), pp. 85ff. The Indian Roman Catholic journal, *Word and Worship*, has published many articles on the subject of nonbiblical scriptures. See also *Jeevadhara* 14 (80, March 1984). The whole issue is devoted to the theme, 'Bible and World Religions'. See articles there by E. C. John, 'Israel and Inculturation: An Appraisal', pp. 87ff; Lucius Neraparampil, 'Jesus and the Nations', pp. 136ff; Joseph Pathrapankal, 'Paul and his Attitude Towards the Gentiles', pp. 162ff. See also 'Indian Lines of Approach to the Bible', *Indian Theological Studies* 21 (September-December 1984). This volume has important articles

by Roman Catholic scholars in India on Hindu, Neo–Hindu, Buddhist, and cross-cultural hermeneutics. See especially 'Conclusions', pp. 398ff.

47   D. S. Amalorpavadass (ed.) 'Statement on Non-Biblical Scriptures' (Bangalore, 1976), p. 8.

2

Is There a Calypso Exegesis?

GEORGE M. MULRAIN

Dreams, visions, spirits, ecstatic dances and healings – the very issues dispar-
aged by Western interpreters as unscientific and deemed to be suitable
subjects only for psychologists and psychiatrists, have an important function
in Caribbean theologizing. The article below argues for the use of calypso,
a powerful medium in Trinidad, as a better way of engaging with biblical
texts than the application of scientific exegesis which, as a product of Western
enlightenment, may fail to grasp the cultural world and the hermeneutical
needs of the Caribbean peoples.

George M. Mulrain is a Trinidadian, currently serving as Methodist
Director of Mission Studies at Selly Oak Colleges, Birmingham, England.
He is the author of numerous articles on the interface of theology, Caribbean
culture and African cosmology, and of *Theology in Folk Culture: Theological
Significance of Haitian Folk Religion* (Frankfurt am Main, Peter Lang, 1984).

The question being addressed is this: 'Is there such a thing as a
calypso exegesis?' If indeed there is, then the further questions to
be asked are: 'What is the nature of it?' and 'What challenges will it
present to theology?'

EXEGESIS

Let us, first of all, establish what is meant by 'exegesis'. This word
could be rendered by three more familiar English terms – 'exposition', 'explanation', and 'interpretation'. Exegesis is taking a look
at Holy Scripture with the intention of having revealed to us the
underlying truth of God. To put it another way, exegesis is an exercise in God's revelation, so that through it, God's Holy Spirit may
be recognized as being at work. Indeed, when a passage of Scripture
is properly expounded, one ought to be in a position of knowing
more about the historical facts behind that passage and its context,
but more important still, its meaning for us today.

37

Scriptural exegesis then will facilitate revelation. My idea of revelation is that which points ultimately to God's supreme revelation of himself in Jesus Christ. I am aware that Scripture itself is considered to be but one of the tools of revelation. Scripture takes its place alongside salvation-history, nature, the Church and Christian tradition. But all veer towards the incarnation – God, in Christ; the Word become flesh. In dealing with such a topic as 'calypso exegesis', I am also mindful of the social conditioning of revelation.

Just as revelation varies, so too does exegesis vary with individuals and groups of people. When we study the Gospels, in the light of 'materialistic exegesis', we discover that it is important for us to know something about those who wrote them, and in whose interests they had been written. In so doing, we confront the issue of objective historiography, bearing in mind that the Bible itself was written from a biased point of view. Subjectivity is inevitable. This is true as far as interpreting the Scriptures is concerned, because exegetes are different, working as they do under different social and economic conditions. You have only to listen to some of the Latin American theologians of liberation to appreciate my point. Hugo Assmann, for example, has this to say:

> The 'word of God' is no longer some perduring, unchanging absolute, some eternal proposition that we accept as such before analyzing social conflicts and committing ourselves to the transformation out of historical reality. God's summons to us – God's word today – arises out of communal analysis of historical data and historical happenings as praxis. The Bible and Christian tradition as a whole do not address themselves directly to us in our present situation; instead they stand as a basic point of reference for us, indicating how God speaks to human beings in widely divergent contexts. Thus they can help us to see how God might be speaking to us in our present context . . .[1]

Listening to this theologian, one can immediately realize that what message he receives from a passage of Scripture will be vastly different from what will be transmitted to the person who views the Bible as *the* Word of God, fixed, addressing itself directly to all people, everywhere, regardless of race, colour, social, political and economic conditions under which they may live.

Dr Walter J. Hollenweger, during his time as Professor of Mission at Birmingham University, introduced his students to 'narrative exegesis'. Through this method, one is able to follow an excerpt from the Bible, and enter into the possible thought patterns of the narrator as well as the characters who present themselves, so that one has the advantage of looking at several points of view. Using his 'Conflict in Corinth'[2] as an example, we have the story interpreted not only from Paul, the author's point of view, but also from the possible angle of the listeners to Paul's letter. We may even enter into the minds of the slaves, or the high-ranking officials, as the case may be. The exegete who uses the narrative method is himself or herself limited in scope, selective, biased. Yet we are still able to derive from it that which we expect out of any passage of Scripture – historical data, context, and the word through which God would speak. What is more, the narrative tends to have a much wider appeal, not merely to the academic (as does literary theology) but to those who are not scholars, even to the illiterate.

Before we can arrive at any sensible decision as to whether or not there can be 'calypso exegesis', we must know something about 'calypso'.[3]

CALYPSO

A calypso is a narrative folk song which is common within the Caribbean region. It is a feature of an oral culture, which specializes in oral language, oral literature and oral music. It has traditionally been associated with the spontaneous outbursts into song which greet the tourists upon arrival in the island of Trinidad. Trinidad, 1864 square miles in area, home of the famous lake of asphalt or Pitch Lake, an oil-producing country, is popularly called the 'land of calypso'. Trinidad conjures up images of guitar-strumming ballad singers who entertain audiences with lyrics and rhythms that have emerged from the grass-roots. In other words, a calypso is not intended to be a sophisticated song, even though today it appeals to all classes of people. Its initial stages saw calypso associated with the working-class. Respectable, upper-class individuals did not sing calypso. They would be moved, literally, by its bouncy rhythm, but they felt that because of their social standing, they must suppress any urge to sing.

The calypso is a very powerful medium in Trinidad today. According to a former Prime Minister of the country, the late Dr Eric Williams, calypso is 'the use of song to comment on current happenings, to phrase social criticism, to convey innuendo'.[4] It is indeed so popular, that an estimated 500 are composed in Trinidad each year.

Naturally, very few such songs survive. Errol Hill, a well-known Caribbean writer, who has done much research on the calypso, has this to say:

> The calypso repertoire is as wide and varied as it is long. Patriotic songs, philosophic songs, songs in praise of human achievement or in dismay at human degradation, songs of protest and songs of crime and tragedy, of racial prejudice and pride, the whole spectrum of human experience is to be found in the calypso. It is at once a social document of the country's history, a compendium of the people's language, an archive of their music. It is an accurate indicator of the people's pulses on matters of national concerns.[5]

Hill suggests the eighteenth century as a probable period for its origins. 'Oral tradition has it that the first known Trinidad calypsonian or "shantwell" (Fr. *chanterel*) was Gros Jean, a professional singer attached to the retinue of Pierre Begorrat, one of the early French immigrants to the island who arrived from Martinique in 1784.'[6] Calypso is closely associated with Carnival, a pre-Lenten festival celebrated in Trinidad and other countries where the Roman Catholic Church predominates. In fact, during the eighteenth and nineteenth centuries, the masquerade bands (now an integral part of Carnival) used to be led by calypsonians. However, with the turn of the twentieth century, the calypsonian's role was restricted to singing. But as a singer, today's calypsonian conveys his or her message, not only in words, but to the accompaniment of comic mime.

As has already been stated, the calypso, or 'KAISO', has had humble beginnings, cradled in the folk culture of the simple people.

> The songs were addressed primarily to an unlettered working-class audience. They served as a newspaper and tabloid to convey information, offer commentary, and disseminate juicy gossip about the affairs of individuals belonging to all strata of society.[7]

It is so often the case that whenever initiative comes from the grassroots, the authorities try to suppress it. The story of calypso was no exception. But in spite of attempts to stifle this type of initiative, calypso has survived and flourished.

Calypso's origin is undoubtedly West African. Indeed, much of Trinidad's culture has been derived from that of Africa. Melville Herskovits in 1947 observed this predominantly African influence on calypso. He wrote:

Even though some of the music is cast in the mould of European folk tunes, and the words are in English, nothing of African purport or intent has been erased. For despite its non-African form, this musical complex can be regarded as nothing less than a retention of the purest type.[8]

However, since 1947, calypso has continued to evolve and today, apart from the predominance of African rhythm, one may detect other musical influences coming from Venezuela, Spain, France, Britain, Jamaica, India and China. This is in keeping with the cosmopolitan nature of the Trinidad population, which includes almost every conceivable ethnic group under the sun.

Calypso has developed over the years into a Caribbean phenomenon. It can hardly now be referred to as an 'idle' song. It has gained the respect of all classes of people. Much is due to the efforts of Trinidadian calypsonians: Kitchener, Spoiler, Melody, Sparrow, Chalkdust, Stalin, Rose, Shadow, et al. But Trinidad and Tobago can no longer claim the monopoly on calypso. The Antiguan carnival and the Barbados 'crop over' serve as reminders that calypso is a Caribbean phenomenon.

Calypso is more than just a song. It is a word denoting a type of culture, one in which the element of folklore is dominant. The Anansi stories are very popular, with the spider hero continuing to be a source of entertainment to all classes of people. Calypso has had a profound effect upon the mentality of people within the Caribbean region. As the calypso takes both serious and frivolous incidents in life and holds them up as a cause for laughter either through wit or satire, so too people tend not to take life too seriously. They are able, under the most trying and difficult situations, to laugh. When Hurricane Gilbert struck the island of Jamaica in September 1988, there were quite a number of songs produced about the incident. Some of the words in one of the most memorable ran as follows:

> Water come in a mih room
> Mih sweep out some wid a broom
> De lickle dog laugh to see such fun
> An' de dish run away wid de spoon.
> Unno see mih dish, unno see mih dish?
> Any body, unno see mih satellite dish?
> Mih dish take off like flyin' saucer,
> Mih roof migrate widout a visa
> Bedroom full up o' water . . .[9]

Caribbean people can still laugh good-humouredly when a government is oppressive or corrupt. Even on the cricket field, when other
nations approach the game with a seriousness and a firm determination to win, West Indian players indulge in calypso-type cricket –
stroking the ball to all corners of the field to the delight of the crowd.
It matters little that the team is facing possible defeat. The game must
go on for the amusement of the spectators. When the unfortunate
individual faces the prospect of terrible loss in a business deal, he
can still joke about it – he may even find a verse of some calypso
which is appropriate to his situation. Now this ability to laugh under
pressure is indicative of a basic theological concept, that God is
always providential. In spite of what happens, all things will work for
good. The Jamaicans have a popular saying: 'No problem!' The
Haitians constantly say in their Créole language: 'Bondié bon, oui',
that is 'Yes, God is good'.

Calypso has a political and prophetic function. The calypsonian
subtly challenges authority, just as Jesus challenged the leaders of
his day. Jamaican reggae fulfils roles traditionally associated with
Trinidad calypso. Just as we may speak about the therapeutic value
of music, so too we may refer to the liberating role of calypso. The
Caribbean is faced with the challenge of capitalizing as fully as possible upon the insights of calypso in liturgies, in Christian education
programmes and in scriptural exegesis, the focus of this chapter.

With these remarks about the nature of calypso, we turn our attention to the question: 'Is there such a thing as a calypso exegesis?'

A CALYPSO EXEGESIS

From what was suggested earlier on about material influences –
cultural, social and economic – upon one's interpretation of Scripture, it will be fairly obvious that my contention is that there *is* a
calypso exegesis. The culture of the exegete influences the exegesis.
As a non-European, I observe how European exegesis is culturally
conditioned. There are several calypsoes which vividly relate encounters between the living and the dead. In one such two lovers in a
cemetery are surprised when they hear a voice behind them:

> Mister, yuh brave,
> bringing yuh girl friend on top mih grave.[10]

The two race out of the cemetery, sometimes falling inside open tombs, encountering ghosts, meeting talking horses. The climax is attained in the calypso's last stanza:

> As I reach the street
> A tall gentleman I meet
> I was feeling so happy
> To tell him 'bout my fright in de cemetery.
> He said: 'I can understan'
> You're a wild young man
> But you are not to be blame
> When I was alive I was jus' de same.'

European and Caribbean people are both able to laugh at some of these lyrics. Perhaps the European laugh is provoked by the feeling that this sort of thing does not and cannot really happen. This is what the materialistic-oriented society has done to European thinking, that the spiritual realm including spirits and demons does not exist. So that when confronted with passages of Scripture like Paul's mention of the elemental spirits of the universe (Col. 2.8), the explanation is that these refer to the astronomical or astrological systems with which we are familiar. Fair enough! But with the reference in Ephesians (6.11–13) to the principalities and powers in the heavenly places, the tendency of the European exegete is to do his best to demythologize in order to 'make sense of' the Scriptures. By contrast, the calypso exegete, in his or her folk-cultured setting is aware of the possibility of interaction or communication between the living and the dead.

Calypso exegesis takes the spiritual realm and the demonic order very seriously. Where there are passages of Scripture in which Jesus exorcizes demons, the calypso exegete, though not unmindful of the possibility of psychiatric disorder, is not blind to the reality of demon possession. Bishop Lesslie Newbigin, well-known missiologist, relates how, as an Englishman, he was once conducting Bible study in an Indian village.[11] When it came to sections about Jesus' ministry of exorcism, he would fumble, stutter and apologize. While he struggled to give what he thought was a reasoned scientific explanation, one of the village leaders interrupted him. Why was he making such heavy weather of the passage? Thereupon he proceeded to rattle off a dozen or more exorcisms which had taken place in his village over the past weeks. The fact is, we are all conditioned by our culture.

We have not yet produced persons completely sensitive enough to be regarded as 'global citizens'.

But let us turn now and consider some more aspects of calypso exegesis.

Allusion was made earlier on to the multi-faceted nature of the calypso culture. Borrowing from other cultures, being influenced by so many other countries, means that calypso exegesis is itself multi-faceted. Themes such as God the Creator, the eternal Son and Spirit are of interest to the calypso exegete. A calypso exegesis does not disregard the ground covered by the systematic theologians. But there are other topics of interest. One which emerges constantly is that of freedom. The calypso, by its very nature, helps people to laugh in the face of terrible problems. This is in itself a liberating thing. Dr James Cone speaks, for example, of 'the ability of Black people to express the tragic side of social existence but also their refusal to be imprisoned by its limitations'.[12] This is part and parcel of the folk calypso culture, that people are conditioned not to let situations get them down. In fact, this is the keynote of its *folklore* which 'centres on the ability of the weak to survive through cunning, trickery and sheer deception in an environment of the strong and powerful'.[13]

Mention has equally been made of the difference between typical European exegesis of New Testament passages dealing with spirits, and the interpretation by people steeped in folk-culture. The latter are inclined to accept that there are lines of communication between the spirits and ordinary people. Consequently, dreams and visions constitute another important topic for calypso exegesis. In a Biblical context, it is accepted that God employs dreams and visions as one of the many ways in which he enters into communication with human beings and makes his will known to them. More than half a century ago, Alfred Guillaume made the point that

> probably a great many of the Biblical revelations must have come in sleep. Meditations on the spiritual, ethical, moral and political problems of the day coloured the prophets' prayers; and the verses which poured forth from their lips may well have shaped themselves in the night season when they took to rest. In what ways and by what means the prophets gained the conviction that they spoke with the authority of God we do not always know, but there can be no doubt that the importance ascribed to dreams in the Old Testament record of revelation cannot be overstated.[14]

As in the Biblical context, so it is with the calypso culture. God is known to reveal himself to people through dreams and visions. This fact may not be as striking among Christians within the denominations which have strong links with European Churches, but certainly among indigenous religious groups, like the Spiritual Baptists of Trinidad and Tobago[15], this divine revelation through dreams is commonplace.

A noticeable thing about calypso exegesis is its methodology. Since the predominant musical expressions within calypso culture concentrate on story-telling, it follows that narrative exegesis must be part and parcel of this culture. How is this story told? Of prime importance, it must be narrated in a language which is understood by all, and used by all. Taking Jamaica as an example, the official language is English, but in normal conversation, particularly among the working classes, 'patois' is used. An example of narrative exegesis in song is 'Blak-Up', Barry Chevannes' account of the happenings on the day of Pentecost. In Jamaican patois, the expression 'they are filled with new wine', or 'they are drunk', is rendered 'dem blak-up'. What the song says is that on the day of Pentecost the people were accused of being 'blak-up'. But it was the Spirit of the Lord which came down like fire, and all believers were caught up, in the Spirit, singing like a choir.

It goes without saying that calypso-type songs, using local language idioms, are an expression of calypso-exegesis. Another methodological tool of calypso exegesis would be the dance, which has not yet been as fully exploited as the songs. Many of the younger Christians of today are content to sing religious songs with local lyrics and bouncy rhythm, but as yet they feel inhibited where dancing is concerned. This avenue has still to be explored although it must be admitted that unconscious dancing usually accompanies singing and hand clapping during liturgical expressions among indigenous religious groups. If a survey were to be taken about the suitability of the various aspects of calypso exegesis, perhaps the majority would say 'that's okay for a youth group, but not for mature Christians'. In fact, story-telling, calypso singing and dance still have associations with the working-class. There is the unconscious feeling that they are not the tools for the educated, the sophisticated, the academic. So calypso exegesis, before it can come into its own, has a long road along which to travel.

The implications for theological training and scholarship are tremendous. For too long theology has been seen as a discipline only engaged in by academics and philosophers. That is why during my days as a theological student in Jamaica, I observed how some of the preachers at the University Chapel delighted in high-powered philosophical discourse at sermon time. Many students at worship were 'turned off' by this. No more of this academic stuff, please! We've had our fill of that throughout the past week in lectures! Rather, talk to us, talk to our hearts! Tell us God's story! This was the general cry. Students made their voices heard in the Worship Committee, and gradually changes were effected. Worship came alive, as creativity and imagination were injected into services. There were more conversational narrative-type sermons. Folk-services using guitars, drums and calypso songs were often experimented with, the result being that attendance increased by two hundred percent.

The theologians whom we train in the Caribbean, whether at the United Theological College in Jamaica, Codrington College in Barbados, or the St John's Vianney Roman Catholic Seminary in Trinidad, will have to be constantly reminded that our people belong to a folk culture. The oral tradition associated with our people has made us excellent conversationalists, if not excellent writers. Listen to how the average person in the Republic of Haiti prays and you recognize how intimate a relationship he or she has with God. God is as real as the person sitting, standing or kneeling next to them. Such prayers do not seek after excellence of literary style. Faulty grammar is not a sin. Their major concern is to talk – heart to heart – with God.

The big hurdle to be overcome before calypso exegesis can become commonplace in our theological seminaries is getting across to people the idea that theology must be engaged in by all God's people, the academics or the barely literate. It is an exercise for the ordained as well as the laity. The trouble with most theologians is that we are too stiff, cold, inhibited and as yet ill-equipped for the demands which will be made by a truly calypso-oriented exegesis. Perhaps we need a new awakening for empowering by the Spirit, so that new skills may be imparted which will enable our people to experiment further with calypso exegesis.

NOTES

1   Hugo Assmann, 'The Power of Christ in History: Conflicting Christologies and Discernment', in Rosino Gibellini (ed.), *Frontiers of Theology in Latin America* (London, SCM Press, 1980), p. 134.

2   W. J. Hollenweger, *Conflict in Corinth and Memoirs of an Old Man* (New York, Paulist Press, 1982).

3   A useful insight into calypso appears in the following book: Keith Q. Warner, *The Trinidad Calypso* (London, Heinemann, 1982).

4   Eric Williams, *History of the People of Trinidad and Tobago* (Port of Spain, Trinidad, PNM Publishing Co., 1962), p. 39.

5   Errol Hill, 'The Calypso', in Michael Anthony and Andrew Carr (eds.), *David Frost Introduces Trinidad and Tobago* (London, André Deutsch, 1975), p. 83.

6   ibid., p. 75.

7   ibid., p. 76.

8   Melville J. Herskovits and F. S. Herskovits, *Trinidad Village* (New York, 1947).

9   This was the creation of reggae singer Lloyd Lovindeer. His reference to 'dish' and 'visa' would be appreciated for their entertainment value. At the time, huge satellite dishes prominently placed on the roof-tops of houses were a common sight in the more affluent areas of Kingston. It was a time too when obtaining a visa to migrate to the United States involved standing from the early morning hours in long queues outside the Embassy.

10   The calypso, entitled 'Love in De Cemetery', was sung by Lord Kitchener.

11   This was revealed in one of his classes when Bishop Newbigin lectured in Mission at the Selly Oak Colleges, Birmingham, England.

12   James Cone, *God of the Oppressed* (London, SPCK, 1977), p. 22.

13   ibid., p. 29.

14   A. Guillaume, *Prophecy and Divination Among the Hebrews and other Semites*: Bampton Lectures 1938 (London, Hodder and Stoughton, 1938), pp. 213, 214.

15   cf. Eudora Thomas, *A History of the Shouter Baptists in Trinidad and Tobago* (Tacarigua, Calaloux Publications, 1987).

3

Women's Rereading of the Bible[*]

ELSA TAMEZ

The emergence of Euro-American feminist hermeneutics has raised important issues for biblical studies. Elsa Tamez, expanding on this, offers basic skills that are indispensable for a reading of the Bible from a Latin American woman's perspective.

This essay is from V. Fabella and M. A. Oduyoye (eds.), *With Passion and Compassion: Third World Women Doing Theology* (Maryknoll, NY, Orbis Books, 1988). Her books include *Bible of the Oppressed* (Maryknoll, NY, Orbis Books, 1982), *Against Machismo* (Oak Park, IL, Meyer Stone Books, 1987), and a volume of essays *Through Her Eyes: Women's Theology from Latin America* (Maryknoll, NY, Orbis Books, 1989).

Elsa Tamez is from Costa Rica and is on the staff of Seminario Biblico Latinamericano, in San Jose.

THE REDISCOVERY OF THE BIBLE

Not long ago, when the Latin American poor burst on the scene of church life in Latin America, the consciousness of a large number of people was stirred. The Bible took on new meaning. That book – read by many but until now assimilated through a safe, unidimensional interpretation controlled by a predominantly unchallenged way of thinking – became the simple text that speaks of a loving, just, liberating God who accompanies the poor in their suffering and their struggle through human history. This is not the only new development on our continent. On the contrary, it appears as one more breakthrough in a fast-growing movement in Latin America, a movement propelled mainly by the strong yearning of the poor for life. For multiple reasons and in many ways, the poor are today stronger than ever in their commitment. This is why we, in Latin America, speak of a new way of being church, of doing theology, of reading the Bible.

[*] Translated from Spanish by Alicia Partnoy.

48

A reading of the Scripture that truly liberates responds to the situation that has motivated the reading. It seems that, in a context of hunger, unemployment, repression, and war, creativity more than abounds in theology, hermeneutics, liturgy, and the pastoral field. At least this has been our experience. Both Catholic and Protestant grass-roots communities provide clear examples of the ways in which the Bible has been and still is being rediscovered. The study, discussion, and meditation based on the Word has become an integral part of the meetings of the Catholic grass-roots Christian communities. Everybody studies and discusses the Bible from the point of view of liberation. In the progressive Protestant communities, where the Bible has always been fundamental to the liturgy, hermeneutic keys have changed and the Bible has come to be read from the perspective of the poor. In both communities the Bible has been rediscovered.

Characteristically, their readings are strongly linked to the daily life of the members of these Christian communities. There is an unquestionable bridge between the life of the people of God in the Old Testament and that of Jesus' followers in the New Testament.

This reading of the Word from the point of view of the poor has been consolidated and has become so evident that Holy Scripture is regarded as a threatening or dangerous book by some sectors of society that do not share a preferential option for the poor. The sectors I mention might be either religious or secular, such as the government (particularly in countries where the National Security Doctrine is actively enforced). Some religious circles have even decided to avoid biblical discussions. Do they fear the Bible? The ancient book of Christianity has indeed become new and defiant when it is read from the perspective of the poor.

'HOWEVER . . . ,' SAY THE WOMEN

Despite this situation, women with a certain degree of female consciousness have started to raise some questions about the Bible. It is not that they don't feel included in the main liberation experiences of the Bible: the exodus and the historical role of Jesus. It is that women find clear, explicit cases of the marginalization or segregation of women in several passages of both the Old and the New Testaments. There are, then, differences between reading the Bible from the point of view of the poor and reading it from a woman's perspective. The poor find that the Word reaffirms in a clear and direct way that God is with them in their fight for life. Women who live in poverty, however, even when they are aware that the strength of the Holy Spirit is on their side, do not know how to confront the texts that openly segregate them. These texts sound strange and surprising to someone who is not familiar with the culture of the biblical world and believes in a just and liberating God.

This concrete problem has not been regarded as such until recently. First, the discovery of the Bible as 'historical memory of the poor' was greeted with great enthusiasm by both men and women. This discovery implied that it was necessary to discuss a significant number of biblical texts essential to the history of salvation from a new perspective, starting with those texts where the liberation of the oppressed is most apparent (Exodus, the Prophets, the Gospels). Up until now texts that segregate women have been disregarded and subordinated because the main criterion has been to experience God as a God of life who has a preferential option for the oppressed, including women. Second, only in recent years has a feminine consciousness gained some strength in the theological and ecclesiastical worlds. There have, of course, always been women who have openly questioned the church and theology. This is happening to an increasing degree in our days, especially with the upsurge of liberation theology and the proliferation of grass-roots Christian communities where women are the majority and their participation is key.

For several reasons this problem of the marginalization, or segregation, of women is harder to solve than it appears to be. One of the reasons is that our society is extremely sexist – a phenomenon that can be detected at both a tacit and an explicit level. Nor are grass-roots Christian communities free from this sexist ideology, which has deep historico-cultural roots that are hard to pull out in a single tug. To the extent that there is an easy correspondence between two cultures that marginalize women, it becomes even harder to discuss the biblical texts that reaffirm women's marginality.

Furthermore, it is a well-known fact that throughout history this correspondence of two patriarchal sexist societies has resulted in their mutual consolidation. On one hand, old-time antiwomen customs of Hebrew culture have been declared sacred; on the other hand, certain texts have consequently been held up as biblical principles to prove that women's marginalization is natural in daily life. It is in this sense that the Hebrew–Jewish lifestyle presented by the Bible is perpetuated precisely because 'thus is written the word of God.' This explains why the Bible has been used to reinforce the position of inferiority in which society and culture have placed women for centuries. Today this attitude is not so apparent as in the past, but in some churches it still manifests itself, albeit in disguise.

Something different takes place in grass-roots Christian communities. They react in different ways to difficult biblical texts. Sometimes they disregard antiwomen texts, at other times they juggle them to come out with a positive side or they soften the oppressive nature of the content. On other occasions they wisely simplify the problem by stating that those were other times, that reality should be different today, that God is a God of life and therefore he cannot favor discrimination against women.

Having experienced all of these attitudes in the context of different religious communities I have never taken this problem seriously. In truth, the problem would not be serious if everybody considered the Bible for what is really is: a testimony of a Judeo-Christian people with a particular culture, for whom holy revelation works always in favor of those who have least. Women would then feel included among the oppressed and they would contextualize those texts that segregate them. I believe this is what happens in many communities.

However, I have come to think that the problem is serious. Its seriousness comes, first, from the effects that these antiwomen biblical readings have produced on so many women and men who have internalized, as sacred natural law, the inferiority of women. Second, there is an inherent difficulty in interpreting texts that not only legitimate but also legislate the marginalization of women. Third, and this is mainly for Protestants, the problem is the principle of biblical authority as it is traditionally perceived. These are three difficulties that women are consciously confronting. Let us look at them in detail.

MYTHS, TEXTS, AND BIBLICAL AUTHORITY

After working with some biblical texts, like the famous narration in Genesis 3, it is easy to perceive that between the text and its current interpretation is a long series of ideologizing (or mythologizing) readings of this narration that are more harmful to women than the actual texts are.

Genesis 3 and the second account about creation have been the basis for creating a mythical framework that legitimizes women's inferiority and their submission to men. Myths – ideologies that distort reality – have been created based on these texts, not so much because of information contained in the story *per se*, but because of the conditions imposed by a society structured around men as its center; and by a particular way of reading the story, which places emphasis on its peripheral aspects; and by a story-telling technique that employs literal description and repetition as literary devices.

There are also other texts in which the example of a patriarchal culture has been brought in for a specific purpose. However, on many occasions, the readers of these texts have elevated the example to the category of divine law. The result is thus a legitimation and legislation, as if it were holy, of an order unfavorable to women.

Women are called, therefore, to deny the authority of those readings that harm them. It is here, then, that the collaboration of women experts in the Bible or of male exegetes with feminist perspectives is needed to reinterpret the texts, using a new hermeneutic approach.

Thus it would finally be possible for women to do a liberation-oriented reading of a text that for centuries had been used against them. However, on occasion there will be no other way to interpret the text except as a putdown of women. Its exegesis will show only the patriarchal ideology of the author, the commentator, the culture, and the historic moment in which the text was elaborated. This is the other Bible-related problem that women confront.

The tendency of some First World radical feminists to reject the Bible is, it seems to me, an exaggerated reaction. I think that by assigning too much importance to these peripheral texts, many leave aside the central message, which is profoundly liberating. From my point of view, it is precisely the Gospel's spirit of justice and freedom that neutralizes antifemale texts. A reading of the Bible that attempts to be faithful to the word of the Lord will achieve that goal best when it is done in a way that reflects the liberating meaning of the Gospel, even when sometimes fidelity to the Gospel forces the reader to distance herself or himself from the text. Therefore, a time has come to acknowledge that those biblical texts that reflect patriarchal culture and proclaim women's inferiority and their submission to men are not normative; neither are those texts that legitimize slavery normative. The rationale behind this statement is essentially the same as that offered by the Scriptures: the proclamation of the gospel of

Jesus calls us to life and announces the coming of the kingdom of justice.

German theologian Elisabeth Schüssler Fiorenza, who lives in the United States, proposes a new hermeneutic approach. She tries to reconstruct the beginnings of Christianity from a feminist perspective. Using this method she finds very interesting situations that explain women's active participation in the beginnings of the church. She also discovers contradictions in some of St Paul's writings, which eventually were used to promote the submission of women. From an exegetical point of view, this is one of the best and newest approaches to the Bible. We must admit that, for Third World women, this is an important contribution regarding the analysis of the text from a woman's point of view. However, it is likely that in some communities, mainly Protestant, it will be hard to accept the idea of questioning a biblical author, not to mention an apostle, as is the case with Paul.

This presents us with the third problem: the classic formulation of the doctrine of biblical authority. I shall refer here to Protestant churches because I know them a bit better.

Women with a certain degree of female consciousness, who move in conservative sectors, at times confront the difficulties of the principle implied in the idea of inspiration, namely, being without error, or God's word in a literal sense. I stress that they confront it *at times*, because, according to my experience, a curious phenomenon takes place in real life: there is a mismatch between belief in the traditionally formulated principle of biblical authority and daily-life practice. Women in both traditional and grass-roots Protestant churches have achieved an important degree of participation in the liturgy and other areas and – except in the case of extremely conservative churches – this has not been a problem even though it is clear to these institutions that St Paul called for 'women to keep silent' in church. The issue is not even under discussion; in practice there is a tacit acceptance of women's participation and an increasing recurrence of texts that suggest the active participation of women. However, in some more traditional churches, when a woman becomes dangerously active or threatening to those in powerful positions, aid is found in the classic Pauline texts to demand women's submission to men. It is in moments like these that some women do not know how to respond. This is because they either lack the proper hermeneutic tools or have a mistaken interpretation of the principle of biblical authority.

On the other hand, when at meetings of Christian women there

is an attempt to study texts such as Ephesians 5.22–4 or
1 Corinthians 14.34, the discussion frequently winds up on a dead-
end street. The conflict arises because women, although not in accord
with the texts nor practising such behavior in everyday life, yet do
concede at the same time that the Bible has all the authority of the
word of God. Thus they find themselves trapped within a framework
of literal translations, forgetting that the word of God is much more
than that.

This situation tells us that it is about time to reformulate the
principle of biblical authority, from the point of departure of our
Latin American reality. From a woman's perspective it is time to
look for new hermeneutic criteria, patterns that not only will help us
to handle patriarchal texts but also will illuminate our re-reading of
the whole Bible from a feminine perspective, even texts that do not
explicitly refer to women. I shall discuss now some matters that come
from my own experience.

GUIDES TOWARD READING THE BIBLE FROM A LATIN AMERICAN WOMAN'S PERSPECTIVE

Gaining distance and coming closer

To counteract myth-laden readings of biblical texts and to avoid the
risk of repeating the interpretations of other readers, I believe in the
importance of gaining distance from the text, mainly from those parts
that have been frequently read and therefore have become overly
familiar to our ears. When I say 'gaining distance' I mean picking
up the book and ignoring the interpretations that almost automatically
come to mind even before reading the actual text. To distance oneself
means to be new to the text (to be a stranger, a first-time visitor to
the text), to be amazed by everything, especially by those details
that repeated readings have made seem so logical and natural. It is
necessary to take up the Bible as a new book, a book that has never
been heard or read before. This demands a conscious effort that
implies reading the texts a thousand times and very carefully.

This way of reading is going to be conditioned by or embedded
in the life experience of the Latin American reader. Her or his
experiences must be very consciously taken into account at the time
of the reading. It is this experience, in the end, that will facilitate the

distancing of oneself from the all-too-familiar interpretation of the common suppositions in the text, and will help to uncover keys to a liberation-oriented reading. This is the process of coming closer to daily life, which implies the experiences of pain, joy, hope, hunger, celebration, and struggle. It is clear from this process of gaining distance and coming closer that in Latin America the Bible is not read as an intellectual or academic exercise; it is read with the goal of giving meaning to our lives today. In the confusing situation we find ourselves, we want to discern God's will and how it is present in our history. We think that the written word offers us criteria for discerning. Already this is a way of reformulating the principle of biblical authority.

The process I call 'gaining distance' and 'coming closer' is not only geared to finding a woman's perspective. Every Latin American reading of the Bible needs to shake off rote readings that cloud the text. We must approach it with questions coming from life. However, considering that a reading of the Scriptures from a woman's angle is very new for us, considering that it is mandatory to discern between 'macho' cultures and the gospel of life, the process of gaining distance from 'macho' readings and texts and coming closer to the experience of Latin American women gains relevance for all women.

The reading of the Bible with the poor as a point of departure

Every liberation reading from the perspective of Latin American women must be understood within the framework that arises from the situation of the poor. In a context of misery, malnutrition, repression, torture, Indian genocide, and war – in other words, in a context of death – there is no greater priority than framing and articulating the readings according to these situations. The poor (men, women, blacks, Indians) comprise the large majority, and it is because of their discontent that repression and mass killings generally take place. They are in a privileged place, hermeneutically speaking, because we conceive of the God of life and One who has a preferential option for the poor. Besides, the mystery of God's reign is with them because it has been revealed to them (Matt. 11.25). Therefore, a reading from a woman's perspective has to go through this world of the poor. This will be a guarantee that it has a core theme of liberation, and it will shed light on other faces of the poor, such as blacks and native peoples. This kind of reading will also give us methods to develop specific approaches to salvation in each of their situations.

Besides, this reading key, which has as a synonymous parallel 'God is on the side of the oppressed', is the key to cancel and disallow those – really very few in number – antiwomen texts that promote the submission of women to men and affirm the inferiority of certain human beings because of their gender.

It should be remembered that a reading of the Bible from the perspective of the poor is a hermeneutic key offered by the Scriptures themselves, mainly through 'events that create meaning' such as the exodus and the historical praxis of Jesus. Much has been said about this, and it is not my aim to discuss it more extensively here.

A clear feminist consciousness

To read the Bible from a woman's perspective, we must read it with women's eyes, that is to say, conscious of the existence of individuals who are cast aside because of their sex. This procedure includes not only women. Men who feel identified with this specific struggle might also be able to read the Bible from this approach. This simple step is fundamental to achieve a reading that attempts to include other oppressed sectors besides the poor. It is a stamp that will distinguish this reading from others that consider the oppressed in general.

This approach, as noted above, is recent in Latin America. Therefore, even we women are not entirely conscious of it yet. For this reason, our reading does not come out spontaneously, and a conscious effort is needed to discover new women-liberating aspects, or even elements in the text that other perspectives would not bring to light.

Women, as victims of sexist oppression, will obviously perceive with less difficulty those aspects that directly affect them. Their experiences, their bodies, their social upbringing, their suffering and specific struggles give them keys (insights) to this reading.

Some liberation theologians agree that to the degree women actively engage themselves as readers of Scriptures and participants in other theological activities they offer important contributions to exegesis, hermeneutics, and theology.

It must remain clear that when I speak of reading the Bible from a woman's perspective, I am not referring specifically to texts that mention female subjects, but to the whole Bible. It is here where an enriching contribution from a perspective long absent until now can be made.

The novelty of such readings comes from reflection on the experiences of women. Women, for example, due to their experiences of oppression, can pose new 'ideological suspicions' not only to the culture that reads the text but also to the heart of the text itself by reason of its being a product of a patriarchal culture. Furthermore, their 'ideological suspicions' are also applied to biblical tools, such as dictionaries, commentaries, and concordances, tools that are regarded as objective because they are scientific, but that are undoubtedly susceptible to being biased by sexism. This fact has been proved true by female exegetic scholars.

If to the oppression women endure we add the fact that they live a particular experience as women – in the sense that they are closer to vital processes, and have a unique stance in their view of the world – we shall see new contributions reflected in their readings (in recent years much has been discussed about women's identity).

In conclusion, the 'gaining distance' from and 'coming closer' to the Bible, the retrieval of liberation keys from the perspective of the poor, and a feminist consciousness are three basic skills indispensable to reading the Bible from a Latin American woman's perspective.

We are just taking the first steps. We are rediscovering new duties that will benefit Latin American women, and we are yearning to learn more. Consequently, this meeting in Mexico attended by Third World women from Asia and Africa, women who share concerns and hopes similar to ours, is for us an event of immeasurable value.

4

Marxist Critical Tools: Are they Helpful in Breaking the Stranglehold of Idealist Hermeneutics?

JOSÉ MIGUEZ-BONINO

Down through the history of interpretation, exegetes have used diverse external sources from philosophy and so on to illuminate biblical texts. Here is an attempt to use Marxist analysis to free biblical interpretation from its idealist imprisonment. It is a helpful method to awaken an interpreter to his or her context. Though Miguez-Bonino sees it as the 'best instrument' for social analysis, in some of his other writings he also draws attention to its shortcomings.

This essay first appeared in a pamphlet (*Holy Bible: The Politics of Bible Study*, issued by the Student Christian Movement, London, in 1974). For his further reflections on biblical hermeneutics, see his *Doing Theology in a Revolutionary Context* (Philadelphia, Fortress Press, 1975), pp. 85–105.

José Miguez-Bonino is an Argentinian and is one of the leading Protestant exponents of Latin American liberation theology.

The question of the title, given to me by the editor, is both puzzling and tempting. Marxism presents itself, whether as scientific analysis or as revolutionary theory and ideology, as a blunt negation (or overcoming) of religion in general and of the Christian religion in particular. The acceptance of a Marxist vision should logically result, therefore, not in the interpretation of the Biblical message but in its dissolution. On the other hand, Marx and his followers have offered an interpretation of the Christian religion and even of the Biblical (particularly but not exclusively the New Testament) writings. Is there anything in this interpretation which could help a Christian today to a better grasp of his own faith? Or, coming more specifically to our question: is there in the way in which Marx and some of his followers come to the interpretation of Christian origins and development anything that a Christian interpreter can learn when he faces the Scriptures? My subtitle tries to summarize my answer to this question. It is offered here very tentatively, as comments and questions to be discussed and pursued rather than as an elaborate analysis. And it is offered out of the concrete context of Christians who are engaged in the struggle for the liberation of man and society, and who are engaged in that struggle together with many Marxists in a common – though not undifferentiated – socialist commitment. It seems to me that, translated to the area of Biblical study, the Marxist insights are a powerful instrument to free interpretation from its idealist captivity. This is what I shall try to illustrate.

TRACKING DOWN 'IDEOLOGY': THE CRITICISM OF INTERPRETATION

It is well known that Marxism places religion in the area of ideologies – the intellectual constructions whose real significance is in the economic and social relations which they reflect (or hide). Among the criticisms that Marx directs against Christianity within this framework is the accusation that it provides religious sanction to the oppressive capitalist bourgeois system (in fact, that 'Christian principles' have justified all forms of exploitation and oppression). The concrete form to which he points is the Christian buttressing of the Prussian absolutist state.

Whatever qualifications one might have to make concerning this interpretation, I submit that 'ideological suspicion' is a fundamental critical tool for interpretation. I think the first application has to do with the 'history of interpretation' because, as a matter of fact, our study of the Bible is always placed within a stream of interpretations. We modify, correct, qualify, even reverse, 'meanings' which have already been given, traditioned, almost incorporated into the texts. It is, therefore, crucial to ask about the ideological presuppositions and functions which such interpretations may have had.

Marx said, for instance, that Protestant ethics had reflected the capitalist bourgeois ideology by substituting 'having' for 'being': man had to forgo all aesthetic, material and social enhancement of the self in order to work and save – 'the more you save . . . the greater will become your treasure which neither moss or rust will corrupt –

your capital'. We know that – although in a different way – Max Weber's sociological studies have borne out the operation (if not the reasoning) of this interpretation. But if this is so, should not we ask how has this affected Biblical interpretation? How has, in fact, Biblical interpretation dealt with the texts which relate being and having?

1 The first thing that comes to mind are Jesus' sayings about 'riches' and 'the rich'. Even a cursory look to Biblical commentaries in the Protestant tradition shows the almost uniform ideological train of thought: riches (in themselves) are good – therefore Jesus could not have condemned them as such, nor rich people as such – consequently the text must mean something else – this something else must be found in the 'subjective' sphere (intention, attitudes, motivations). Once this framework of interpretation is in operation, all texts gather around it in one coherent whole. Exegesis follows suit: Luke's version of the Beatitude of the poor, for instance, is interpreted through Matthew's 'in spirit'; this is in time disconnected from the prophetic-Psalmic relation of 'poor' and 'oppressed' or the whole is 'spiritualized' as devotion (humility before God). The ideological function of such interpretation is evident (however different the intention of the interpreter may have been), you can rest assured in your capitalist accumulation of wealth (or your attempt to reach it); religion (reverence for God) legitimizes and blesses your effort! The persistence of such ideological stereotypes is forcefully attested in the interpretation of such an honest and responsible exegete as J. Jeremias. He – perhaps correctly – argues that in the parable of the rich man and Lazarus, 'Jesus does not want to comment on a social problem'. But when verse 25 (Luke 16.19–31) poses the question of the reversal of the condition of the poor, Jeremias argues from the 'ideological supposition' and asks: 'Where had Jesus ever suggested that wealth in itself merits hell and that poverty in itself is rewarded by paradise?' To which, clearly, there are at least two answers that an interpretation free from the bourgeois presupposition could not have failed to see. One: that Jesus never speaks of wealth *in itself* or poverty *in itself* but of rich and poor as they are, historically. The 'in itself' abstraction is clearly a piece of liberal ideology. Second: a whole number of texts, or rather practically all texts dealing with the subject (with the exception of Matthew 13.12 and parallels if interpreted in this connection), point in the clear direction of this reversal, whatever explanation we may want to give them. Moreover, its relation to one

trend of the prophetic tradition – to which Jesus is evidently related in several other aspects of his teaching – makes it all the more clear. We reach the real ground of Jeremias' interpretation in the strange affirmation that 'Jesus does not intend to take a position on the question of rich and poor'.

2 A host of other examples could easily be given. The problem is not one of particular texts but of the total framework into which interpretation is cast. Once the 'mythical' cosmic dimension in which traditional interpretation had projected the Biblical story began to slip away at the advent of the modern world, the peculiar atmosphere of liberal bourgeois 'spirituality', individualistic and subjective, became normative for interpretation. Thus, historical and political events like the death of Jesus, the Parousia, or mission, were decoded out of their cosmic representation into an individualistic and inward 'existential' moment, experience or appropriation. A reinterpretation of the texts requires the explosion of the ideological straitjacket in which they have been imprisoned.

THE SOCIO-ECONOMIC MATRIX: THE CRITICISM OF THE SOURCES

Deeper than the discovery of the ideological functions of religion is Marx's understanding of it as the projection of man's 'misery', of his suffering from and protest against an unjust and oppressive world. In this line, Engels, Kautsky and others have understood the emergence of Christianity as the 'slave's' protest against oppression, finding a (substitutionary) satisfaction in the hope of an apocalyptic (and later otherworldly) vindication. Lately Ernst Bloch has called attention to the dynamism of that hope. A dynamism that can only find historic realisation when the religious 'heritage' is wrenched from its transcendent-mythical and incorporated into a historic-scientific (Marxist) projection.

We need not concern ourselves with the details of this interpretation. They suffer from serious historical oversimplifications and inaccuracies. Moreover, we must reject – even on Marxist grounds – all simplistic and mechanistic explanation of religion as a mere 'reflex' of economic conditions. The religious reality is a complex phenomenon which has its own laws and internal coherence. It would be ridiculous – though a wooden orthodox Marxism sometimes has tried it – to explain the biblical texts as a direct consequence of economic and social situations. But it is quite another thing to ask for the socio-economic matrix in which these texts were born. This is more than the already established determination of the *Sitz im Leben* in order to illumine a text. It is the question of whether and in what form a religious outlook which finds expression in texts expresses the socio-economic relations and circumstances of a given society.

1 The 'social' prophets offer a good illustration. Socially engaged and progressive Christians rightly appeal to them. Their scathing denunciation of exploitation and oppression, their condemnation of a religion which covers up injustice with ritual, their call to repentance and their announcement of judgement are all relevant to our present situation. But one may wonder whether the prophets can be so directly 'enrolled' for socio-economic revolution. As conservative exegetes are always ready to point out, most prophets are actually opposed to progress and change; they rather dream of a former (perhaps never existent) society in which every family freely cultivated its field, cared for its cattle and enjoyed a self-sufficient situation. In fact, sometimes they even go back to a pre-agricultural, nomadic ideal. The real crisis which prompts their message is the 'progress' to a more differentiated society in which class differences become accentuated and the structural class-relationships (landowner and labourer, producer and tradesman, the intermediation of business, and the corresponding political differentiations) take the place of face-to-face and intra-familial ones. Their prophecy is indeed 'the sigh of the oppressed creature' alienated in this change and 'the protest' of that creature. But it is cast in the form of an utopic projection of a previous real or imagined harmony.

What is the importance of this distinction? It is this: that unless we identify the utopian character of the prophetic projection, we run the risk (to which most 'progressive' interpretations succumb) of merely *moralizing* the prophetic message into a well-meaning admonition to those in power to repent and put an end to injustice. The real question posed by the prophetic message so understood is not how to translate into modern terms the prophetic demands. This can only result in a new set of idealistic principles. The question is: how can we, in the present historical conditions, give adequate expression to the prophetic protest against the disruption of human life created by the conditions of our capitalist society and how can we in the present historical conditions give adequate expression to the prophetic hope of a reintegration of human life and society in justice and solidarity?

2 Again, there is no need to provide many illustrations of the point we are trying to make. In one sense, what we are saying is that Biblical texts – like all texts – can be (and at one level must be) seen (as Marxism indicates) as an expression of the human misery and hope generated by the socio-economic conditions and finding expression in mythical or utopian projections. The 'eschatological reversal' of rich and poor to which we alluded previously, the thaumaturgic (healing) expectations and performances, the forms of communal solidarity which we find both in the Old and the New Testament, cannot be exempted from this level of analysis.

3 The previous affirmation will immediately prompt a question: is not God's reality and power evacuated in this interpretation? Because it seems clear that it is precisely in this 'mythical' or 'utopic' space where the Bible locates God's presence: God raises the Assyrian to punish Israel, he appoints Cyrus to bring his people back, he strikes down with sickness the wicked king. Jesus miraculously heals the sick, feeds the hungry, raises the dead – i.e. brings the signs of the coming Kingdom. A divinely ordained catastrophic event ushers in the new age. It seems to me that this question points to a deeper level of Biblical interpretation in several ways.

It is this question which helps us to see one peculiarity of the Biblical witness: its own tendency to historicize the space of God's intervention: thus, God judges and liberates 'in, with and under' historical, worldly events. Jesus relativizes his own role as thaumaturg by relating it to faith on the one hand and subordinating it to his message of the Kingdom on the other. Paul historicizes the eschatological expectation by demanding in the Christian community the reality of the eschatological reversal (no more woman and man, Jew or Greek, slave or master). Using the terms of the Marxist analysis: the Bible is not satisfied with expressing human misery, nor with other worldly or subjective realms – it announces, narrates and demands historical events which, at least in principle and initially, *overcome in reality* this misery. Biblical interpretation looks for the presence of these pointers not by denying the socio-economic matrix but by bringing it to light.

PRAXIS AND INTERPRETATION: WHAT IS THE 'TRUTH' OF THE BIBLE?

Are we really entitled to take the step indicated in the last paragraph? Is this not a dissolution of God's message into human activism, an unwarranted secularization of the Gospel? The answer to this question hinges on the understanding of the character of God's Word. If it is understood as a *statement* of what God is or does, then the mythical or utopian frameworks (or the subjectivistic inversion of reality of liberal hermeneutics) has the last word. But if the Biblical message is a *call, an announcement-proclamation (kerygma)* which is given in order to put in motion certain actions and to produce certain situations, then God is not the *content* of the message but the *wherefrom* and the *whereto*, the originator and the impulse of this course of action and these conditions. Then, *hearing* the message can mean no other than becoming involved in this action and this creation of conditions and situations. By defining an event as 'God's action', the Bible is not withdrawing it from history – even if the ideological framework used is mythical – but pointing to the divinely wrought and revealed background and power of the human action demanded. This is even so in the New Testament references to Christ's resurrection: mission, the new life, community, active love, are the human historical content of which Christ's resurrection is the ground and power.

1 In this perspective we are forced to transform our understanding of interpretation itself. Even in the Bible-study renewal which has been so significant for the SCM and the ecumenical movement, we have been used to the 'idealist' method of trying to establish the meaning of the text in the first place and then to relate it to our historical conditions and to listen to what the text will say to us. There are two misunderstandings in this procedure. The first is that it does not take seriously enough the fact that the text itself is an 'action', the record of an involvement in God's call. We are not faced with a naked divine word but with a human obedience or disobedience in which God's Word is made present to us. We enter into these courses of action.

But – and this is even more important – we always read the texts 'out of' a praxis and 'into' a praxis. As Christian citizens, workers, intellectuals, husbands or wives, we already have an 'enacted interpretation' of the text which will be confirmed, deepened, challenged or rejected in the confrontation – but which will set the terms of that confrontation. The relation between theory and praxis – to which Marxist thinking has called our attention – is by no means simple. It does not deny that any course of action already incorporates (conscious or unconscious) theoretical presuppositions. It underlines the importance of theoretical thinking which examines the practical course of action in terms of its relevance to the direction of the process and criticizes the theoretical presuppositions in terms of the development of the process. There is, in this respect, a constant relation between theory and praxis. We cannot and need not at this point enter further into this discussion. But we need to stress the importance of this basic understanding for Biblical interpretation.

2 Let me take an illustration from a very controversial person and situation in my continent: the Colombian priest Camilo Torres. When he reads in the Gospel: 'If you are offering your gift at the altar and then remember that your brother has something against you, leave your gift before the altar and go; first be reconciled to your brother, and then come and offer your gift' (Matt. 5.23–4), he asks himself – using all the tools of knowledge available to him: who is my brother who has something against me? Not merely in an individual and subjective sense but as a priest who belongs to a particular historical structure of religious and political power, as an intellectual who belongs to a group who has played a role in history, as a member of a (economically powerful and dominating) class. The answer is clear: the poor, the worker, the peasant, he 'has something against me'. Furthermore, what he has against me is objectively real – my action in the solidarity of the institution, the group, the class to which I belong is an oppressive action. Therefore, if I interpret the text as merely affecting my subjective interpersonal relation to those whom I know personally (within the circle of my relations) I am rejecting and denying the real estrangement. My interpretation in such a case is an ideological occultation, bound to the interests of my class. I can only read the text authentically from within the recognition of the class conflict in which my relation to the largest number of my brothers places me. The command to 'reconcile myself with my brother' can only be understood, therefore, as objectively demanding me to remove the objective alienation between my brother and myself.

We can perhaps question the course of action taken by Camilo

Torres as he moves into political action and finally into the guerrilla. But this discussion misses (or eludes) the point; Camilo reads the text in and out of the explicit recognition of his total involvement as an historical man and re-acts his praxis out of the total impact of the text on his involvement. He refuses to take refuge in a 'normative' course of behaviour which would be found in the text without exposing himself to it, without bringing to it his total present reality. Otherwise he might have been satisfied to fulfill the 'normative requirement' within the self-understood limits of his un-exposed and therefore unchallenged sociological condition (i.e. resolve the personal quarrel he may have had with a fellow-priest or a colleagueprofessor). And he refuses to let the command hover over the concrete historical circumstances in which his actions take place. Otherwise he might have been satisfied with an action of charity – which leaves the objective conflict untouched. Only by incorporating his action within a total 'praxis' in which the cause of 'offence' might be objectively removed could the reading of Jesus' word be actually 'heard.' Naturally, the relation between interpretation and praxis understood in this way, requires the use of all the analytical tools at our disposal – in the understanding of our present praxis, of the text and of the conditions for a new praxis. This is precisely the 'theoretical' work. And this is the only justification for doing theology . . . when it fulfills its task!

3 This is, in fact, the kind of theology that we meet in the Biblical 'reading of the Bible'. Modern scholarship has shown us, for instance, how the story of creation, or the exodus, is 'read' in the course of the tradition of Israel. When Deutero-Isaiah, for instance, tells the 'exodus' in chapter 35, he reads it as the exile who mourns in captivity far from the Promised Land and who waits for the return. The road in the desert, the springs of water, the power that comes to the weary, is *the new road* to the return from exile. He does not 'deduce' from the Exodus story a 'moral' for his time: he is invited to enter the exodus *now*, the first exodus as God's action is the *wherefrom* and the *power* of this call. This is what happens when people in the Third World receive today this same story. As a Latin-American theologian puts it: 'If our reading of the Biblical kerygma has any purpose, the "memory" of the Exodus becomes for us – oppressed people of the Third World – a provocative Word, an announcement of liberation. . . . It is our call to prolong the exodus, because it was not an exclusive Hebrew event but God's liberating

purpose for all peoples. In an hermeneutic line it is perfectly legitimate to understand ourselves *out of* the Biblical exodus and, above all, to understand it *out of* our situation as peoples living in political, social, economic or cultural "slavery"' (J. Croatto).

God's Word: the limitations of the tools

An interpretation which would limit itself to a Marxist analysis could not, certainly, make sense of what we have been saying, particularly in the last section. There is no 'wherefrom' and no 'power' in such interpretation, except in man's own action. Anything else is a human projection, the reification of relationships which man has not yet understood or wants to mystify. The Bible can – at best – record this dynamism of human action. Marxism gives it its real name. At this point no doubt there is a basic divergence. What for a Christian is the ultimate ground and power of his praxis is for an orthodox Marxist an ultimate alienation. This divergence cannot be solved in discussion or through argument. The faithfulness of his commitment is the only verification – not certain proof – that a Christian can offer for the reality of the source and the power which sustains it. But a few brief theological points may be in order for a Christian who intends to take seriously the critical tools that Marxism has developed.

1 The overcoming of an idealist interpretation, far from being a surrender to a materialistic conception of reality, seems to me – to use a Marxist analogy – placing the Biblical perspective 'back on its head'. Idealist interpretation, in fact, particularly in its modern subjectivist form, inverted the direction of the Biblical message by projecting the historical events of God's action into consciousness as subjective events. This is precisely the reverse of the Incarnation: while God's Word becomes history, idealist interpretation replaces history by words. God in the flesh is the rejection of the idealist resolution of objective conflict and liberation into subjective transactions.

2 God's Word – the power of the Risen Lord – is a dynamic reality. It cannot be tied down to the merely logical continuity of dogmatic formulae but it impinges creatively on historical circumstances. Jesus Christ is the same yesterday, today and for ever not in the static identity of a thing or a formulation, but in the dynamic

unity of his redemptive purpose working itself out within the conditions and possibilities of a human history which itself is in movement. As a normative witness of that purpose, the Biblical record has a 'reserve of meaning' which becomes concrete as men read it in obedience, within the conditions of their own history. To claim normativity for the sociological limitations of understanding and action of the eighth-century prophets or the first-century Apostles is to stultify the Word of God. This is certainly not to surrender to arbitrary interpretation. There is a direction and a congruity in God's purpose – and the tools of historical and literary criticism cannot be underestimated in helping to clarify this direction and congruity. But to look for a direct unmediated transposition is to deny the reality of the Holy Spirit.

3 'Discernment of the spirits' is not, therefore, a purely analytical process. Analytical processes (which are indispensable both in relation to the reading of the text and our relation to them) are assumed into and have their place within a synthetic act of commitment. Not the mere 'hearer' but only the 'doer' can understand God's Word.

5

The Case for a New Bible

CANAAN S. BANANA

The Bible has often conveyed mixed signals to the marginalized. They have the option of either rejecting the oppressive portions, or highlighting the passages that empower them. In the article below, Banana proposes a third option – revising the Bible and editing it and adding that which is not there to liberate the Bible and make it relevant for today: a rare proposal by an African theologian, though it has been on the hermeneutical agenda of Asian and feminist theologies for some time.

This article is reprinted from *Rewriting the Bible: The Real Issues*, I. Mukonyora and F. J. Verstraelen (eds.), (Gweru, Mambo Press, 1993), pp. 17–32. The book includes responses to the issues raised by Banana's proposal.

Professor Canaan Banana is an Honorary Professor in the Department of Religious Studies, University of Zimbabwe.

LIBERATE GOD FROM CAPTIVITY OF CULTURE

On 6th April 1991, in Hatfield, UK, I had the privilege of discussing the task of African (third world) theologians on the Middle East question. I observed that part of the problem was religious fundamentalism expressing itself in such ideologies as Zionism. During this discussion, the concept of re-writing the Bible was mentioned as a possible alternative to the exploitative situation in the Middle East. I challenged Christian scholars to seriously consider re-writing the Bible so that God can be liberated from dogmas that make God the property of ethnic syndicates.

My arguments cover:

1. A need to liberate the Bible from culture-specific world views;
2. How the Bible has been and continues to be used as an oppressive instrument;
3. A short review of the origin and development of the Christian Bible;

4. What a de-mythologized, liberated Bible might mean for humanity today; and
5. Is Christ the product of the Bible or the Bible the product of Christ?

LIBERATE THE BIBLE

I have used the phrase 're-writing the Bible'. That phrase seems to cause many people difficulties. Some suggest that I mean re-interpretation. Many want to know how the re-writing should be done and who should do it. I continue to maintain that re-writing is a necessary component to liberating the Bible. Some biblical scholars may think that such a task is unnecessary since the study of the Bible's origins and development, its significance within a particular faith stance, changes which happened over a period of centuries before the canonization of the Christian Bible, and the continuing revisions in the form of editing against newly discovered sources and/or contemporary demands (e.g. for a more inclusive language in English translations) is a continuing process. I do agree that much explanatory material is available in the field of biblical studies from which we can draw as we work with and interpret the Bible as pastors and religious people and as we study and meditate on the Bible as a source of guidance in our lives. However, none of this material – or very little of it – is incorporated in the Bible itself, and many people, therefore, are without it. The material contained in the Bible is but a small part of the whole gamut of God's revelation to humankind.

Other people suggest that the Bible is holy – sacred and divine – and therefore should not and cannot be changed in any way. Part of my challenge is to look again at the concept of 'divine inspiration'; how that developed and was used to prescribe not just the Bible but theology and doctrine also to a specified need. It is the sense of holiness – sacredness – which I see as a limiting factor rather than a freeing one. To suggest that the Bible is the sole source of God's revelation limits God and God's potential in the continuing creation of the world. Biblical scholars, for example, in pre-Christian times, set the canon for the Hebrew Bible and, as H. H. Rowley notes, established the Jews as 'the first people of the book, and prophetic inspiration became subservient to scripture and eventually disappeared'.[1] The early followers of Jesus refuted the claim that prophetic inspiration had died and argued that the Jewish scriptures were the 'vehicle of a true, but not final, revelation of God'. Holiness is a relative term. But the point I want to make here is that at certain times in the history of the development of the Bible, people considered additions – radical re-writing – as a continuation of God's revelation.

To maintain something as holy – sacred and divine – is a label and a concept people have about something they treasure. It is also a way to maintain the *status quo* and to develop an unthinking populace which continues to be at the mercy of the élite. Present and future generations must not be held hostage by dogmas and dogmatists who were themselves captives of their own parochial world. Holiness must not be confused with legitimacy. When human beings make claims that they are inspired by God and that arising from this so-called inspiration their utterances represent the voice of God, care should be taken so as not to mistake the voice of mortals for the voice of God.

This is not to say that God cannot speak through mortals, but it would be safer to be less dogmatic. When a group of religious people at any period in human history in any part of the world agree to give legitimacy to any matter, that sort of legitimation is not necessarily immutable. Room must always be left for further revelation and growth of understanding. It must be borne in mind that a large number of factors limit the revelation including the cultural environment in which particular communities find themselves. Holiness is a product of human imagination. To define certain areas as holy and by implication others as profane is indulging in a religious game of chess.

We must start from the assumption that all of creation is holy, an assumption which recognizes God's presence in all of creation. It is against this background that the concept of a holy land as confined to Palestine becomes nonsensical. Strictly speaking, there is no difference between the 'land of Israel' and Zimbabwe or any other land for that matter. The water from the Jordan River and that from the Zambezi are of similar importance. The fact that Jesus was baptized in the River Jordan was a pure accident of history. In the same vein, the prophets of Israel cannot be regarded as superior to the prophets from other lands. To afford these prophets a special status would be to limit God's power to reveal himself through other peoples of the world.

While I am increasingly aware of my position as a minority one, I am aware that I do not stand alone in suggesting the Bible needs something more for today's world. R. A. Kanzira of Uganda wrote,

The Bible is deficient. First of all, the Old Testament is nothing but Jewish mythology and legend; it's bits and pieces from Israel's history. The heart of the New Testament is the gospels. The gospels read like legend too on their confession 'according to . . .'. Legend, yes. The effectiveness of legends depends on the originality and creativeness of the narrator.[2]

Kanzira goes on to say: 'If the Bible, first the Old Testament, is to make sense, then it must be re-written or infused with world history into which humanity will not be divided into chosen and foreign. Justification of evils like Zionism will have no place in it.'[3]

Since the end of World War II, the ecumenical movement in Christianity has worked hard first of all to bring a sense of unity to the Christian fellowship. In more recent years, it has begun and expanded an inter-faith dialogue that seeks to bridge some of the misunderstandings and active diminishing of some cultures, people and religions by Christianity. Wesley Ariarajah, a Methodist minister from Sri Lanka and director of the Dialogue Sub-Unit of the World Council of Churches, has written a book entitled *The Bible and People of Other Faiths* (1985). In his foreword to that book, Dr Hans-Ruedi Weber, formerly director for biblical studies in the WCC, states:

The Bible is the record of a great dialogue. God's word – which both expresses and enacts the divine will – created the whole universe. The same creating, judging and promising word/event of God shaped the world of nations, one particular people, the person of Jesus, and the early church . . . To examine what dialogue means does indeed belong to the core of biblical studies. But it needs to be admitted that the biblical story concentrates mainly on God's dialogue with just one people, the people of Israel, and – through Christ – with the early church. It tells us little about the way in which other peoples, living in other cultures and epochs, were challenged by God and how they responded. In the biblical record, nothing is explicitly spelled out about what we might learn from such great teachers as Gautama Buddha or from such formidable prophets like Muhammed. To reflect biblically about God and the people of other faiths is therefore a difficult and risky enterprise.[4]

The traditions of liberation theologians from Latin America, Asia and Africa have issued and continue to issue a challenge of great import to the developed nations of the 'first' world. The basic challenge has been to enable Western/Northern nations to re-think theological and doctrinal assumptions about Christianity, to enable Christianity to be liberated from a bondage of social, political, economic and cultural oppression. A source for that challenge has been the Bible as it has been radically reinterpreted by people suffering at the hands of the oppressors. The strands of biblical thought used by liberation theologians frequently include an alternative or parallel tradition within the Bible: the tradition in which God sides with and suffers with and frees the captive, in which the demand for equitable justice – economically, socially and politically – is called for.

What has not happened fully in the move toward liberation is to free the Bible itself from an internal oppression. The voices of the people of the 'third' world are voices of God's revelation, inspired by God's Spirit. Why are they not reflected in the Bible, directly testifying to God's presence in their lives, in their time?

The challenge I am posing for Christians and all who ascribe to the present Bible is that we must expand the frontiers of archaeological research and excavation to encompass the entire universe. Religious shrines and traditions of the peoples of Asia, Africa, Europe, the Caribbean, and Latin America must surely be important sources of God's revelation. Nothing can be lost by studying how these peoples perceived and worshipped God in their own individual circumstances with the view of drawing from their rich heritage to broaden our understanding of God's activity in human history.

THE BIBLE AS AN AGENT OF OPPRESSION

Included in the Bible, both the Old and New Testaments, is a strand which establishes one people as a 'chosen' people. The sense of the early Israelites as God's chosen people became a justification for their conquering people in the land they viewed as the 'promised land' – promised to them by God as a reward for their faithfulness as a people of God and as a compensation for their suffering in slavery. The concept of chosenness carried over into the early Christian Church and its subsequent development, in the faith statements that unless a person acknowledged Jesus as the Christ, the Saviour, God's only Son, the person could not be considered as God's chosen. Even the language we use and the way in which we write certain words in capital letters visually reinforces the selectivity of God's people.

Christian church history is a saga of exploitation in the name of Christ, from the subjugation of the European tribes, to the crusades to redeem the Holy Land from the infidel, to the subjugation and exploitation of native people in the 'new world', to the colonization of Africa in the great mission thrusts of Western civilization. This history is long, sordid and deeply sad: the result of the use of the Bible as a justification for exploitation; the self-serving adoption of one group as 'superior' to another. In other words, it can be argued that the ideology of racism has its genesis in the Bible.

Thomas F. Gossett has discussed the theme of chosenness in the context of American history. To emphasize a commonly held attitude toward Native Americans, Gossett quotes the Revd Josiah Strong: 'Far from lamenting the gradual disappearance of the American Indian, . . . we should see in his extinction merely the reflection of the will of God in preparing the land for a better race.'[5] Gossett goes on to explain the theological and historical background to this statement:

> The troubles of the native peoples over the world – as vexing as they might be – were merely local manifestations of a cosmic process, the replacing of inferior with superior stock. Just as Strong was able to reconcile the theory of evolution, the struggle for existence, and the survival of the fittest with an optimistic Protestant theology, so he was able to view the ascendancy and decline of races as part of the providence of God . . . Likewise, the early English colonists had thought of themselves as a chosen people long before the laws of biology were invoked to justify their superiority. The Puritans frequently compared their relationship to God to that of the Israelites of old. In the American Revolution, the phrase was revived to induce patriotism among the colonists. After the war, the theme of an 'American Israel' formed the keynote of a sermon delivered in 1783 by Ezra Stiles, president of Yale. Two years later, Jefferson proposed that the seal of the United States should represent the children of Israel led by a pillar of light. In 1787, Timothy Dwight referred frankly to Americans as 'this chosen race'.[6]

Closer to home, we have seen the results of the Bible being used to designate one people superior to another through the separation of racial groups within a country. It is only recently that apartheid has been recognized as the heresy it is by some of those who helped to institute apartheid as the 'law' of the land – or their immediate descendants. The suffering imposed on the majority by the minority, the designation of less than full humanness, the justification of political and social and economic oppression and exploitation has its origins in the way the Bible has been used and in the material that rests within the Bible that allows such interpretations to be made.

The Bible has been and continues to be used to relegate women to a second class status in society, overlooking the liberating themes in the gospels in favour of the neo-legalism of Paul. Men – in the gender specific sense – wrote the parts which have been collected as the Bible. They reflect a male orientation to life, to the hierarchical system of society, to the father-ness of God.

Women often are not accepted in the Bible or they are regarded negatively. The emphasis seems to be more on Eve tempting Adam to sin, Lot's wife disobeying and being turned into a pillar of salt, women caught in the act of adultery, and attitudes which reinforce the 'typical' women's role of wife and mother. By contrast, Mary sitting at the feet of Jesus learning, the revelation of Jesus' nature as the messiah to the woman at the well, and the great news of the resurrection being revealed to the faithful women are less emphasized.

The Bible, moreover, frequently is quoted to keep major church bodies from ordaining women into professional ministry. Statements such as Paul's to the Corinthians exemplify this:

> As in all churches of the saints, the women should keep silent in the churches. For they are not permitted to speak, but should be subordinate, as even the law says. If there is anything they desire to know, let them ask their husbands at home. For it is shameful for a woman to speak in church (1 Corinthians 14. 34–35).

This is the kind of statement people seem to remember. And isn't it time that such thinking is changed to reflect women's full inclusion into humanity, even within the church itself?

THE BIBLE AS CANON

From the earliest times, the components which we recognize as the Bible were part of oral tradition. That which is in the Bible we know today reflects the events of the times in which they were created, written down from oral tradition to continue the remembrance of what had happened. Moreover, the process covered centuries, many editings and re-writings of the texts in order to fit new understandings of the past in relationship to the present.

The literature of the Old Testament reflects the political trials and successes of the ancient people of Israel. What is included in the section we know as the Old Testament was selected from a much larger body of national literature. R. H. Pfeiffer notes that passages were selected for 'their literary beauty or their nationalistic appeal, because they contributed to keep alive the nation and the worship of Jehovah'.[7] He adds that 'every sentence in the OT was profane literature before it became canonical sacred scripture'.[8] The decision as to what is sacred and worthy of canonization was a human decision of religious leaders.

Similarly, the New Testament was created to reflect the development of the Church and its doctrines in a particular time out of particular concerns. This point has been made by by F. W. Beare:

> The importance of the creation of such a canon of Christian scriptures cannot be too highly estimated, for in this one area the Church achieved a unity which proved able to endure through the schisms which rent her in the fifth century, the division of the Greek from the Western Church in the ninth century, and even the breakup of the Western Church through the Reformation movements of the sixteenth century.[9]

The first part of the Old Testament was not canonized until 621 BC with the discovery of the Deuteronomic Code. Though attributed to Moses as author, it was written by another person much later in Jewish history. The whole section which we know as either the Torah (Hebrew) or Pentateuch (Greek) was canonized around 400 BC. The value of this code is multidimensional: it provides a legal code for people of a particular time and place, it marks the end of the old religion of Israel and the beginning of Judaism and it marks the state of becoming a theocracy in which the Jews became a divinely chosen people, a kingdom of God on earth. The canonization of the Prophets and History occurred around 200 BC. The Writings were canonized in AD 90. The material in these latter sections was edited – re-touched – to reflect the deuteronomic writings. Pfeiffer observes, 'These retouches helped to change historical accounts which were objective into lessons from history, distorted according to the theory of divine retribution on earth.'[10] One of the important aspects of this process, I believe, is that the designation of 'sacred' scripture occurred at different times even though the materials were known, circulating and being used prior to canonization. It is also important to note that they were re-written – re-touched – to fit a specific perspective. For example, according to Pfeiffer, to become part of the Old Testament canon, a book had to 'possess a strong appeal of some kind to survive; it must have attracted readers for its religious, nationalistic or literary value.' Another condition for canonization after 200 BC 'was anonymous authorship'.

Pfeiffer demonstrates, moreover, that differences existed in the understanding of canonization.

> Palestinian Jews made a sharp distinction between inspired scripture and human writings; canonization was a solemn recognition on the part of the leaders and the people that certain books were divinely revealed to prophets . . . In Alexandria, on the contrary, the Jews tended to accept as scripture any writing in Hebrew or Aramaic which came from Palestine.[11]

The Bible known to the early Christians also differed. Jesus and his disciples used the Hebrew Bible, while Paul and his converts used the Greek (Septuagint) Bible. It was a long time before what we know as the New Testament was organized into canon. The Jewish canon was closed 'for all time' in AD 90 on the conviction that 'prophetic inspiration, the source of inspired scripture, had ceased – and presumably ceased forever – set aside the Law, the Prophets, and the Writings as a closed body of holy scripture, set apart from all other literature by its unique inspiration.[12]

The process for the canonization of the New Testament writings followed a similar pattern to that of the Jewish scriptures. Pfeiffer observes,

> Judaism was in danger of yielding to Hellenistic influence and Christianity to emperor-worship and other Roman practices, when they suffered cruel persecution under Antiochus IV Epiphanes (168–165 BC) and under Domitian, who ruled from 81 to 96. The death of the faithful and the safety of the apostates, which seemed to question the power and justice of God, moved noble dreamers to promise an imminent intervention of God to reward the martyrs and punish sinners after their death . . . Jews and Christians used the same remedy: both groups drew up an official list of inspired books and excluded from this list writings declared uncanonical.[13]

Many writings circulated during the early church times, all with various followings. A choice was made and some were included and some were not. The Bible was used differently in the Roman Catholic and Protestant traditions. Until the time of the Protestant Reformation, the Bible was printed in Latin, and until the time of the printing press, was not available to anyone other than church leaders. Since then, translations abound in most of the world's languages. Though the names of the books remain the same, translations do cause shifts in understanding from one world view to another.

The Christians rejected the Jewish understanding that prophetic inspiration had ceased, maintaining that in Jesus, the Christ, God's revelation reached a new peak. For Christians, the Old Testament was regarded as the inspired Word of God given for guidance, promising what was to come. Jesus seemed to see the Law as a first stage in progress and below the requirements of the kingdom of God. Paul identified the 'old testament' which was replaced by a 'new testament'.

My question is this: Has God's revelation finished? Is it not possible that there is more that needs to be added to (as well as subtracted from) the Bible as we know it today to make it relevant to our times and people?

LIBERATE CHRIST FROM THE BIBLE

My call for a new Bible has been taken by some to mean an attack on the person of Jesus. Just how anyone can draw that kind of conclusion baffles me. At no time in my arguments for a new Bible did I ever question the person of Christ. Now that the subject of Christ has been drawn into the controversy about the case for a new Bible, it is prudent to discuss how the call does or does not impinge upon the nature of Christ.

My argument that the Bible is a product of a specific culture does not necessarily deny the historicity of Jesus. However, it must be stressed that the entry of Jesus through a specific race, that of the Jews, was not by design but a mere accident of history. He could have been born among Asians, Africans, Europeans, etc. So, the humanity of Jesus is only important as a matter of convenience.

Jesus Christ is not a product of the Bible. He existed before the Bible; the Bible is a product of Jesus Christ. It is a document that tells us about Jesus' life and his saving grace. Let us not forget that most of what Jesus said and did is not recorded in the Bible. The Bible is but a bird's eye view of the life of the great man.

I must repeat, therefore, that while the Bible is an important source of God's revelation to humankind, it is by no means the only source. Christology is at the very centre of the Christian message. Many theologians have argued that Christ cannot be a captive of one specific culture. Whilst he communicates through the medium of culture, he is at the same time above all culture.

Albert Nolan in his book *Jesus before Christianity* sums up some of the misconceptions that have been propagated about Jesus.

> Many millions throughout the ages have venerated the name of Jesus but few have understood him and fewer still have tried to put into practice what he wanted to see done. His words have been twisted and turned to mean everything, anything and nothing. His name has been used and abused to justify crimes. Jesus cannot be fully identified with that great religious phenomenon of the Western world known as Christianity . . . nor can historical christianity claim him as its exclusive possession. Jesus belongs to all men.[14]

Leonard Boff raises a very fundamental question, 'What christological value can be attributed to the historical humanity of Jesus?' He quotes Bultmann as saying that the historical Jesus is irrelevant to christology: 'Concerning the life of Jesus, the *kerygma* (preaching) need only know that Jesus lived, and *that* he died on the cross. That there is no need to go beyond this is demonstrated by Paul and John each in his own way.'[15] The only aspect of interest to faith is that he existed. What really occurred, the historically objective facts, is of no interest. Boff argues that 'the present gospels are the products of a re-judaization of Christianity. The special task of Christology ought to consist in getting beyond the ethic of obedience, which has brought about so much evil in Christian history, and in de-judaizing Jesus' tradition.'[16] A distinction has to be made between Jesus and Christ since in Jesus the emphasis is placed on the humanity and genealogy that links Jesus with a specific culture. While the historical Jesus is not disclaimed and is an important evidence of his life on earth, the emphasis on Christ denotes a Supra-Christ, God incarnate superseding any and all forms of human limitation.

A LIBERATED BIBLE IN TODAY'S WORLD

One needs only to pick up a newspaper, listen to or watch the news to know that many divisions exist in our world today. The Middle East provides a critical example of divisions along religious lines. Christians, Jews and Muslims, who share history and who share an understanding of sacred scriptures out of common origins, continue to fight one another in order to achieve domination politically, socially, economically and religiously. The political divisions through-out the world are often exacerbated by the religious divisions as evidenced in calls for 'holy' wars where one religion, often from a sense of chosenness, labels other people as 'infidel', 'heathen', and 'pagan'. This is seen clearly in the establishment of a homeland for the Jews following World War II, which was carved out of someone else's territory. All acts such as these are justified by religious holy scriptures, including the Christian Bible, and are examples that haunt efforts to secure peace and equity in world problems.

The world is shrinking, not so much physically, as in the connec-tions people have with one another and the influences that are exerted. We are interdependent. The time for self-serving is over. As a Christian minister and as an African, I see the ways in which the Bible continues to be an oppressive and restricting instrument, maintaining the *status quo* rather than fully liberating all people. No matter how we emphasize the liberating and correcting strands within today's Bible, there remains the sense in which, unless one embraces the Christian concept of God, one is not fully a person of God. I think it is time to create a Bible that reflects the realities and possibilities of today's world.

A comparative study of religions, especially of religious sacred writings, reveals many points of commonality with regard to topics like creation, life and death, and tenets promoting a healthy and fulfilling life. To bring these together in some fashion would provide connections that could help heal the divisions that exist in the world. It has been stated earlier in this chapter that a function of the Bible was to unite the Christians against those things which divided them. So, too, do we today need a unifying element that will help our world to set aside our differences and learn to live together.

The people in the Bible – both Old and New Testaments – are people whose lives and faith response to God provide lessons for those who come after. Each culture has its record of those people. For Zimbabweans, Mbuya Nehanda, Mkwati, and other religious traditional leaders are people whose lives have opened new possibil-ities for us all. Each nation had its own organized religious traditions led by its own venerated priests. Mbuya Nehanda, as one of the leading spirit mediums in Central Mashonaland, fought relentlessly to defend her people's religious values against adulteration by foreigners. She died a martyr at the hands of British settlers on account of her own religious convictions. Her indomitable courage was immortalized in the hearts and minds of many young gallant Zimbabwean fighters for African heritage. It can be argued that Mbuya Nehanda and other traditional priests must be accorded an honoured place alongside leading religious leaders from other cultures such as Abraham of the Jewish tradition.

I must repeat here that logic requires us to recognize that, religiously speaking, there is no difference between Abraham and Mbuya Nehanda. Both were religious leaders in their own right. Who are we to argue that one was closer to God than the other? Let us leave that judgement to God. There are others throughout the world whose voices and experiences need to be collected into a source that reflects the plurality of religious experiences and expressions.

Archaeology, the study of the material remains of humanity's past, has made significant contributions to understanding the Bible. G. W. Van Beek notes that 'biblical events have been illustrated, obscure words defined, ideas explained, and the chronology refined by archaeological finds. To say that our knowledge of the Bible has been revolutionized by these discoveries is almost to understate the facts.'[17] While archaeology often confirms biblical history, it also points to discrepancies which must be considered.

Van Beek adds that archaeology provides a 'feeling of intimacy with the past' that enables the biblical scholar to transcend the barriers of time so that 'ancient man and ancient times become real to a degree that would be unattainable if he depended solely on the written word'. Archaeology is not limited to the area of the ancient near east. Archaeological investigations of many cultures throughout the world have been made. I see that intentional expansion into areas not yet investigated as well as using findings from these investigations will enlighten the quest for information about human religious studies. And the conclusions from this material and investigation can be used in re-writing the Bible, to add what is missing and to create a more universal Bible.

I have called for a re-writing of the Bible. This would include revision and editing to what is already there, but would also involve adding that which is not included. It is not a new task that I am calling for, not really. I see that a re-written Bible, one that is more universal, embracing the rich plurality of human experience in response to God, would be a more authentic and relevant document in today's world. I would hope that Christians, indeed religious persons of all faiths, will not react emotionally, but will consider and discuss the possibilities such a call provides each of us.

A Bible liberated from its oppressive limitations, a Bible liberated to be the freeing word of God as that is experienced world-wide by peoples of many traditions and faiths, would, I believe, enable humanity to more adequately fulfil our responsibility as a people of God. I agree with Letty M. Russell who, in response to the question 'what would it mean for the Bible to be a liberated word?' suggests that the Word of God is not identical with biblical texts and that liberation is an on-going process expressed in the *'already/not yet dynamic of God's action of New Creation.'*[18]

NOTES

1   R. H. Pfeiffer, 'Canon of the OT', *The Interpreter's Dictionary of the Bible*, vol. I, (Nashville, Abingdon, 1986), p. 506.

2   R. A. Kanzira, 'Was Jesus Christ a Failed Politician?', *Ugandan Daily*, 24 May 1991.

3   ibid.

4   Hans–Ruedi Weber, 'Foreword' (W. Ariarajah), in *The Bible and People of Other Faiths*, W. Ariarajah, (Geneva, WCC, 1985), p. ix.

5   Thomas F. Gossett, *Race: The History of an Idea in America* (New York, Schocken Books, 1965), p. 178.

6   ibid.

7   Pfeiffer, 'Canon of the OT', p. 500.

8   ibid, p. 499.

9   F. W. Beare, 'Canon of the NT', *The Interpreter's Dictionary of the Bible*, vol. I, p. 520.

10   Pfeiffer, 'Canon of the OT', p. 507.

11   ibid., p. 510.

12   ibid., p. 514.

13   ibid., p. 516.

14   Albert Nolan, *Jesus before Christianity* (London, Darton, Longman and Todd, 1977), p. 3, American edition: Orbis Books.

15   L. Boff, *Jesus Christ Liberator: A Critical Christology for our Time*, (Maryknoll, NY, Orbis Books, 1978), p. 9.

16   ibid., pp. 14–15.

17   G. W. Van Beek, 'Archaeology', *The Interpreter's Dictionary of the Bible*, vol. I, p. 204.

18   Letty M. Russell, 'Introduction: Liberating the Word', in L. Russell (ed.), *Feminist Interpretation of the Bible* (Oxford, Basil Blackwell, 1985), p. 17.

PART TWO

Re-use of the Bible:
Subaltern Readings

. . . we must realize that minority discourse is, in the
first instance, the product of damage – damage more
or less systematically inflicted on cultures produced
as the minorities by the dominant culture.

Abdul R. Jan Mohamed and David Lloyd

6

Jesus and the Minjung in the Gospel of Mark

AHN BYUNG-MU

Minjung theology is one of the most provocative and challenging theologies to emerge from Asia. As its starting-point for doing theology and reading the Bible, it takes the minjung, the people who are politically oppressed, socially alienated, economically exploited and kept uneducated in cultural and intellectual matters. Ahn Byung-Mu's piece is an example of such an enterprise. In this essay, he attempts to re-read 'the crowd' – the *ochlos* – in Mark's Gospel from the perspective of Korean minjung theology. His approach also demonstrates how historical–critical tools can be used to liberate biblical texts.

This article forms a chapter in a volume on minjung theology, *Minjung Theology: People as the Subjects of History*, edited by the Commission on Theological Concerns of the Christian Conference of Asia (Maryknoll, NY, Orbis Books, 1981; London, Zed Press).

Ahn Byung-Mu is one of the pioneers of minjung theology and has written extensively from a biblical perspective.

Although New Testament scholarship has focused a great deal of attention on the people who were the audience and the object of Jesus' teaching, not much attention has been paid to the social character of his audience. Consequently, the words and deeds of Jesus have been desocialized. Whom did Jesus address and what was the character of what he said? This question will clarify the historical character of Jesus' words. The social characteristics of the 'whom' can be clarified by investigating the economic, political, and cultural make-up of the people. To understand this subject more comprehensively we need to see the total social structure and the place of the people surrounding Jesus. This is what this chapter will seek to do on the basis of the editorial phrases in the Gospel of Mark and the words of Jesus himself.

OCHLOS IN THE GOSPEL ACCORDING TO MARK

From the beginning, the Gospel according to Mark mentions the crowds surrounding Jesus. Form critics view the editorial sections about the people surrounding Jesus as only the framework for the words of Jesus or for the kerygma that Jesus is the Christ. Therefore the people have been excluded and, as a result, a very important aspect has been lost.

In contrast to the approach of form critics, redaction critics consider the redactional framework important both for understanding the viewpoint of the author and the import of Jesus' sayings in context. However, surprisingly, these too have paid little attention to the audience of Jesus, preferring to concentrate on 'the theology' of the author as found in his redactional statements and redactional arrangements. Redaction critics also seem to have missed the point that the authors of the Gospels put so much emphasis on 'the people' because they considered the relationship between Jesus and the people to be crucial for understanding the identity and mission of Jesus. Therefore, while this paper will reflect essentially the approach of redaction criticism, it will pay greater attention to the reality of 'the people' and their relationship to Jesus.

As early as Mark 1.22 the crowd is mentioned, and it continually appears on the scene. At the beginning, 'the people,' or the third person plural, 'all', is used to refer to them. In this way attention is drawn to the people (Mark 1.22, 30, 32, 33, 37, 44, 45; 2.2). However, their identity does not become clear. This kind of descriptive method makes the readers pay attention to the social composition of the people. Eventually the concept which represents the many people (*polloi*) appears on the stage: this is *ochlos* (2.4). In the Gospel according to Mark, without counting the indicative pronouns, there are thirty-six occurrences of the word *ochlos*.[1] This indicates a definite intention in the use of the word.

Besides the frequency in the use of the word, there is another reason why our attention is drawn to this word. For we would normally expect the term *laos* rather than *ochlos* to be used for the people, since the term *laos* occurs far more frequently in the language of the biblical writers. The term *laos* is used around 2,000 times in the Septuagint. This word consistently indicates the people of Israel as the people of God.[2] However, in the Gospel according to Mark, there is no use of the word *laos* except in a quotation from the Old

Testament in 7.6 and in the words of the chief priests and lawyers (14.2).

Besides these two uses of *laos*, there is one occurrence of *plethos* as a noun, and 'the many' as an adjective, which do not describe any characteristic group (3.8).

It is certain that in the New Testament, Mark is the first writer to introduce the term *ochlos*. It does not appear in any New Testament writing before Mark, but the documents written after Mark, such as the other Gospels and Acts, contain this word many times, proving the influence of Mark. *Ochlos* appears three times in Revelation, which we know to have been written during the persecution of Christians (7.9; 19.1, 6). It is noteworthy that in the Epistles of Paul, which were written before Mark, this word does not appear even once.

All these facts indicate that we must pay close attention to Mark's use of the word *ochlos*. A comparison of the contexts and intentions of Paul's writings and those of Mark will indicate in a preliminary way Mark's predilection for this term.

The Epistles of Paul were written ten years before Mark's Gospel, that is, about AD 50–60. Paul's writings were intended to explicate the mission to the Gentiles and were addressed to the Gentile churches to exhort and to teach them the faith. These concentrate on Christology and soteriology, and therefore have an apologetic and a didactic character. For his purpose, Paul does not think it important to mention anything about the historical Jesus. In fact, he declares that he does not really want to know about the historical Jesus (2 Cor. 5.16).

In contrast, the Gospel of Mark was written when the Jewish War had already started, or when Jerusalem was already occupied in AD 70 (I believe the latter) and the Jews were being expelled *en masse* from the land of Judea.[3] Unlike Paul, Mark concentrates on the traditions of the historical Jesus. Although Mark's basic position is similar to that of Paul, namely, that Jesus is the Christ (the kerygma), his concern is to present the historical Jesus prior to the Resurrection. Hence the kerygmatic materials that were already established as the basis for Christology were insufficient. He uses other materials of a historical nature. Therefore, we cannot agree with Bultmann that Mark is only an expanded kerygma. Thus Mark, unlike Paul, is not apologetic, and neither is he interested in developing a Christology or a soteriology, which are abstract and idealistic. His descriptive style is simple and folksy, containing historical facts.

In the above comparison we can see certain factors that are related to our subject matter. Mark was in a different social situation from Paul's. Therefore, not only could Mark not accept the highly concentrated kerygmatic theology, but it seems he also consciously had to maintain a certain distance from Paul. Such a position made Mark move toward a historical rather than kerygmatic Jesus. Under such a premise, the term *ochlos*, which Mark introduces, has a very important function which was demanded by Mark's historical situation. During Mark's time, the Jewish people, including the Jewish Christians, were expelled from their land and were on the way to exile like lost sheep without a shepherd.

THE CHARACTERISTICS OF *OCHLOS* IN THE GOSPEL ACCORDING TO MARK

Normally, we would begin with a semantic and conceptual clarification of a term and then see how this is reflected in a writing. We are not going to follow this procedure. Rather, we will first determine the character of the *ochlos* by examining the occurrences of this term in Mark. By so doing we will reduce to a minimum the subjective interpretation of this term. We will later examine its semantic field and usage in other literature.

The characteristics of *ochlos*

1 Wherever Jesus went, there were always people who gathered around him. They are called the *ochlos* (2.4, 13; 3.9, 20, 32; 4.1; 5.21, 24, 31; 8.1; 10.1). In most instances, there is no clear reason as to why these people followed Jesus. They form the background of Jesus' activities.

2 These people were the so-called sinners, who stood condemned in their society. Especially at the beginning of his Gospel, Mark applies the term *ochlos* in a typical way to the tax collectors and sinners. As we shall show more fully later, Mark describes in this scene how the dogmatic legalists criticize Jesus for meeting with these people, who are the outcasts of society (2.13–17).

3 There are cases where they (the *ochlos*) are differentiated from the disciples (8.34; 9.14; 10.46). In some instances Jesus teaches only the disciples (4.36; 6.46; 7.17, 33). Thus it seems that Jesus

placed the disciples above the *ochlos*. However, we must note that Jesus often fiercely criticized the disciples.[4] On the contrary, there are no instances of Jesus rebuking the *ochlos*. Matthew and Luke either boldly suppress the criticism of the disciples or beautify Jesus' attitude toward the disciples. This fact should be remembered when we view the disciples as representatives of the church.[5]

4 The *ochlos* are contrasted with the ruling class from Jerusalem who attack and criticize Jesus as their enemy. The *ochlos* took an anti-Jerusalem position and were clearly on the side of Jesus (2.4–6; 3.2–21; 4.1; 11.18, 27, 32). In this connection, it is important to note that they were the minjung of Galilee.[6]

5 Because the *ochlos* were against the rulers, the rulers were afraid of them and tried not to arouse their anger (11.18, 32; 12.12; 15.8, 15). Accordingly, to get the *ochlos* on their side, the rulers had to bribe them. For instance, when Jesus was arrested the rulers are said to have given money to mobilize the *ochlos* – a fact which indicates the strength of the *ochlos*. However, the fact that they were mobilized in such a way does not mean that they were necessarily anti-Jesus, but that they could be manipulated.[7]

The attitude of Jesus toward the *ochlos*

1 'Jesus had compassion on them, because they were like sheep without a shepherd' (6.34). The expression 'sheep without a shepherd' comes from the Old Testament. Such an expression implies a tradition of criticism against the rulers, who had a responsibility to take care of the people (for example, Ezek. 34.5), as well as against the crowd, who were cursed with directionlessness because of their betrayal of Yahweh. The latter tradition, however, does not appear in the Gospels. In the prayer of Moses requesting a successor, he says, 'Please do not abandon the congregation of Yahweh like lost sheep without a shepherd' (Num. 27.17). Moses regards the *ochlos*, who were hungry and following him, as a crowd without leaders. At the same time, he seems to suggest that they were also alienated from the rulers.

2 After the brief narration in Mark 3.34 ('And looking around on those who sat about him . . .'), Jesus announces that they (the people) were his mother and brothers. Previously in verse 32, it is written, 'A crowd was sitting about him . . .' This editorial phrase specifically refers to the *ochlos*. The announcement indicates, on the one hand,

a deliberate extrication of Jesus from the ties and demands of kinship and, on the other, it announces that the *ochlos* are the members of a new community (family). This statement was not easily accepted in those days. Therefore, in Matthew we have *mathetai* (disciples) instead of *ochlos*, and in Luke it has been eliminated.

3 'As was his custom, Jesus taught the *ochlos*' (10.1; see also 2.13; 4.11–12; 7.4; 11.18). This means that the *ochlos* were fascinated with his teachings (13.18b). In Matthew and Luke the instances noted above of Jesus teaching the *ochlos* have either been partially eliminated or altered. Such alteration certainly weakens the position of the *ochlos* as the people whom Jesus taught and as the object of his teachings. Although the *ochlos* is not totally ignored in the other Gospels, there is evidence of the expanding authority of the apostles and the church.

Synthesis

Taking into consideration all these factors, we may state the following:

1 There is no evidence of a qualitative evaluation of the *ochlos*. In other words, there is no attempt to evaluate the *ochlos* either in terms of an established religious or ethical standard or in terms of a new ethic. (Mark 3.35 is patently a later addition.)

2 Those who were the *ochlos* gathered around Jesus and followed him: if Jesus was the *Wanderprediger*, they were the *Wanderochlos*. In 8.2 we see that they followed Jesus for three days without eating. This shows us that they had neither an established position in their society nor were they members of an identifiable economic class.

3 When we consider the fact that the *ochlos* are contrasted with the ruling class of that time and that Jesus was criticized for associating with the *ochlos*, it becomes evident that the *ochlos* were the condemned and alienated class.

4 Finally, there is a consistent attitude of Jesus toward the *ochlos*. He accepted and supported them without making any conditions. He received them as they were. He also promised them the future (the Kingdom of God). Such action was unacceptable to the leaders – the Pharisees and the Sadducees – and even to the religious groups who were anti-Jerusalem, i.e. the Essenes and the followers of John the Baptist.

THE COMPOSITION OF THE *OCHLOS* – THOSE WHO FOLLOWED JESUS

There are a variety of people who followed Jesus and about whom Jesus spoke. However, socially all these are seen as belonging to one social class, namely, the *ochlos*. In Mark 2.13–17, the *ochlos* is presented in a paradigmatic way, as we shall see in the following analysis.

Mark 2.13–17 can be divided into two parts: (1) verses 13–14 and (2) verses 15–17. The first part is concerned with the invitation 'Follow me!' addressed to Levi (14b); and the second focuses on the joy of sharing a meal in which Levi does not have a major role. These two parts were transmitted independently, as is particularly evident in Luke 5.29 where Luke clarifies the link Mark makes in 2.15a by saying that Levi invited Jesus and his disciples for a meal.

It is important to make a connection between these two passages without which it is not possible to see the significance of the two. If we keep the two separate, we do not really get the significance of Levi being a tax collector and the meaning of the meal also becomes vague. When we combine these two, the dinner becomes a joyful feast celebrating the fact that certain types of people were called to be the disciples of Jesus.

To make this connection, Mark does not rely simply on the connection he makes in 2.15a, which Luke amplifies. He perceives and states a more substantial connection in verses 13 and 15c, which scholars agree are Mark's own editorial compositions. In verse 13b Mark says that those who followed Jesus and listened to his teaching were 'the whole crowd' (*pas ho ochlos*); and in verse 15a he says that many tax collectors and sinners sat at the meal with Jesus and his disciples. In so saying, he sees the tax collectors and sinners as part of those who followed him. In other words, the 'many who followed him' are the very *ochlos* referred to in verse 13 (cf. 2.2–4).

The presence of the *ochlos* is what provides a substantial connection between these two parts, i.e. verses 13–14 and 15–17, and indeed provides the overall connection and background for Jesus' teaching and ministry. We will now turn to an examination of the composition of the *ochlos*.

The sinners and tax collectors already referred to are mentioned in the old so-called Q source (Matt. 11.19) and in Luke's special source. There is thus early and convincing agreement that 'tax collectors and sinners' were a part of the *ochlos*. In Matthew the category of prostitutes is also mentioned in 'tax collectors and prostitutes' (Matt. 21.32) so this category too formed a part of the designation 'sinners'. Although there are many references to the sick (fifteen times), to the hungry (16.34–5; 8.1ff), and to widows (12.41ff) who appear more often in Luke as part of the *ochlos*, the category 'tax-collectors and sinners' seems to be a more pervasive group in the *ochlos*. Hence, a clarification, in particular, of the concept of sinners and the social composition of tax collectors, identified in terms of their occupation, would provide us with a good idea of the contours of this amorphous group of people called the *ochlos*.

Sinners (*Hamartolos*)

There is no argument about the fact that Jesus associated with sinners. The question is who are the types of people called sinners, or what is the meaning of sinner?

A sinner in the Judaic tradition primarily signified one who is a criminal before God. Concretely, it is an overall designation for people who cannot accomplish the duty of the law. From the time the Pharisees appeared on the religious scene, the law of cleanliness, previously limited to the priests, was applied to the Israelites as a whole.[8] This raised a new problem *vis-à-vis* the classification of sinners.

In discussing this problem, Jeremias points out that the sinner in Jewish society was defined in two ways.[9] One was a publicly recognized criminal (offender against the law), and the other was a person in a lowly, i.e. a socially unacceptable, occupation as defined in those days. He differentiates these two and says that the latter was despised because of 'immoral conduct of life' or 'dishonorable occupation'. But the reason why the occupation made a person a sinner was because the occupation violated the law, either directly or indirectly, and not because of the occupation itself. These were persons who could not rest on the Sabbath day because of the character of their occupations (boatmen, shepherds, and prostitutes). Or, persons who were ill-smelling or those who had to handle things defined as impure (leather-makers, coppersmiths, and butchers). They were alienated and could not participate in worship. While drawing attention to these categories of sinners, Jeremias overlooked another important group. Even persons who could not fulfill the requirements of the law because of sickness or poverty were also designated sinners.

The notion that sickness was the result of crime was pervasive in
Judaism. Such a notion appears continually not only among the orthodox in the Old Testament (for example, Psalm 73, Job, etc.), but
also in the New Testament (John 9.1f). In particular, lepers, hemophiliacs, and the mentally ill were regarded either as unclean according to the law or as those upon whom the wrath of God had come.
These are not really criminals, but were forced into these situations
because of outside pressures and religious–social thinking. Poverty
also brought about this condition for it prevented people from keeping the Sabbath or the law of cleanliness.

These persons were different from those who violated the law on
purpose. But in effect they were also branded as sinners by the law
which upheld a particular system.

The tradition of the three Gospels views the scholars of religious
and civil law and the Pharisees as Jesus' antagonists. These understood sinners in terms of the categories given above. As we have
already noted, in Pharisaic thinking the label 'sinner' was applied
widely, especially to those who infringed the law of cleanliness, so
that the realm of the law was expanded. This brought about the
social alienation of those in humble occupations, the poor, and the
sick. Therefore, both persons defined according to their occupations
and those who were criminals were forcibly marginalized and alienated by the system. They were sinners because they violated the law
or could not adapt themselves to the system of the law. From this
standpoint, religious sin and social alienation were really two sides
of the same coin.

Tax collectors

Tax collectors are not included in the comprehensive category of
sinners, but are another conspicuous parallel category. As already
noted, the usage 'tax collectors and sinners' can be seen in the Q
source (Matt. 11.19), in the special source of Luke (15.1), and in
the Gospel of Mark.

If the tax collectors were regarded as Jesus' people (minjung), the
minjung cannot be limited just to politically and economically alienated people. For the tax collectors were agents of the Roman Empire
and cannot be characterized as the poor class. Mark dares to describe
the tax collector Levi as a person who could afford to give a dinner.
But there is a difficulty in characterizing tax collectors as a group

because among them too there were the rich and the poor. There was a class which received contracts from the Roman Empire to collect taxes and these exploited the people. There were also a number of others who worked under these people as their employees. Among the employee category, there were many people who worked part-time. All of them were treated as tax collectors in that society and were alienated. This can be seen in the fact that they were often referred to like Gentiles (Matt. 5.46–8; cf. 6.7, 32; 10.5).

When the anti-Roman movement eventually became a guerrilla movement, an attempt was made to get a general nationalist response. In order to do this the people rose in revolt at the time of a census for the purpose of tax-collection. They made Galilee their stronghold and made the refusal to pay taxes the beginning of their struggle. This fact indicates the general animosity towards tax collectors. Even in the Rabbinic tradition, they convicted the tax collectors and arrayed them with murderers and burglars.[10]

Why did Mark include them in the category of *ochlos*? First of all, it is precisely because of the tradition that Jesus associated with them (Matt. 11.9). The distinguishing character of this tradition about Jesus is that, no matter what, he unconditionally embraced the alienated and despised class in the community. It is clear that tax collectors were excluded not only by the nationalists, but also by the religious ruling class, landowners, and merchants. The tax collectors were denied the right to make offerings for the poor (Baba Qamma 10.1, 2), and they were not permitted as witnesses in the Judaic court (*Babylonian Talmud*).

Jesus' attitude to the tax collectors is implied in the saying 'those who are well have no need of a physician, but those who are sick; I came not to call the righteous, but sinners' (16b–17), which was given in answer to the question 'Why does he eat with tax collectors and sinners?' As already indicated, Jesus includes tax collectors with sinners and says that he has come to call the sinners.

Here it is necessary to note the meaning of *kalesai* (to call) in order to understand Jesus' attitude to tax collectors. Unlike Mark, Luke speaks of making one repent or the sinner who repents (Luke 15.7–10, 18). This idea is not present in Mark; and he uses the word *kalesai*, which is used to call one as a disciple.

Jesus shows this basic attitude also to other groups, that is, the ill, fishermen, women, and children. Though tax collectors were different in some respects from these people, they have something in common. They too were alienated from the system and were therefore despised. Taking into account the fact that Zealots were also included with tax collectors among Jesus' disciples (Mark 3.18), we know that Jesus' attitude toward the minjung was never limited to people who were politically oppressed.

The sick

In Judaism, sickness like other forms of ill fortune was considered to be punishment for sin. There are evidences of this notion also in the Gospels (cf. John 9.1; Luke 13.2; Mark 2.5, etc.). This idea became even more dominant when the Pharisees applied the law of cleanliness to the common people. Consequently, in particular, lepers, the mentally ill and hemophiliacs were also alienated. The sick appear many times in the Gospels, and in many cases it seems that they have already been deserted by their family and neighbors. The reason why the sick were socially alienated was because they were poor and their condition contrary to the law of cleanliness. They were thus also alienated on religious grounds. The belief that their unfortunate lot was punishment for crime made it possible to exclude them from the community.

Some people feel that, according to Mark 2.5b, Jesus also had such an idea, but this is wrong. Mark speaks of belief here, but he does not speak about the belief of the patient himself, but of the people who carried the sick person on their shoulders. There are two more cases like this (5.36; 9.23) where belief is seen as a precondition for healing. We must recognize the fact that here belief means pure trust, regardless of belief about redemption. If this text gives weight to the idea of absolution from sin, the advent of the Kingdom of God must be regarded as bringing liberation not just from sins but rather from the whole dominating system and from the ideas upon which it is founded.[11]

In this connection, we must take note of two things regarding the character of the healing story. One is that most of the sick had already left their dwelling-houses and were in the alienated situation of wanderers. The other is that, in most cases, Jesus sent them to their homes after curing them.

A good illustration of this character of the healing story, namely, the restoration of lost rights, occurs in those stories concerning lepers, who were typical of persons alienated by the law of cleanliness (cf. Bill. I, 474). Furthermore, lepers were isolated from places where others lived. Hence, an important aspect of the restoration is for the cured leper to show himself to the priest to prove that he is cured and to offer the sacrifice that Moses ordered. Except for cases where the sick were children (5.35ff; 7.24ff) and where healing stories have another purpose (3.1ff), Jesus says, 'Go back home!' or 'Go!' (2.11; 5.19; 5.34; 8.26; 10.52). The phrase in 5.19 that 'the cured man wanted to follow Jesus' emphasizes the fact that Jesus sent him home in spite of the fact that he wanted to remain with Jesus. The restoration here is different from 'to call him' (*kalesai*), which was a different process for the restoration of rights of people in the society.

SAYINGS IN MARK ABOUT JESUS' ATTITUDE TO THE *OCHLOS*

1 'I came not to call the righteous, but sinners' (2.17b). In this logion we have an indication of Jesus' basic attitude of love. We must not overlook in this logion the terms 'not' and 'but'. It cannot be interpreted as saying 'not only . . . but also . . .' Jesus never showed what may be called universal love. He loved people with partiality. He always stood on the side of the oppressed, the aggrieved, and the weak. This fact is clarified in the Q source, as for example in the parable in Luke 15.2ff (Q). It says, 'He leaves the other ninety-nine sheep in the pasture and goes looking for the one that got lost until he finds it.'

As we have already said, Mark views sinners as the *ochlos* and says definitely that Jesus came to the world for the *ochlos*.

Then it is necessary to clarify whether the sinners were defined from Jesus' standpoint or defined by the society. Luke, in using Mark, adds at the end 'who repent', so that they are sinners from the point of view of Jesus. The King James version adds this phrase to the text of Mark and understands it from Luke's standpoint. But 'who repent' is Luke's, not Mark's. However, Luke's understanding of 'sinners who repent' is clarified in Luke 15 in the parables of the lost sheep, lost coin, and lost son. The sinner who repents is the one who is lost and is returned to the place to which he or she belongs. Therefore Luke 15 also reflects in some measure Jesus' attitude to the *ochlos* as found in Mark. Hence, 'sinner' must be given the added prefix 'so-called'. For Jesus, those labeled sinners by the current ideology of the rulers were the victims who were robbed and oppressed.

2 'There is nothing outside a man which by going into him can defile him; but the things which come out of a man are what defile him' (7.15). This is Jesus' saying about the law of cleanliness. This logion reflects situational language related to verses 1, 2, 5, 14b, 15. The original meaning became unclear because of the insertion of verses 6–14, which are unrelated to the original content. When this section is bracketed out, the original speech shows a stand opposing the law of cleanliness as generalized in the Pharisaic system which, as noted above, alienated many people. Incidentally, the speech of Jesus opposes the absolute rule of cult over life. Most people have discussed this revolutionary declaration in terms of Judaism and anti-Judaism, but have not asked the question as to why he made it.

The situation which provided the background for this speech was that of the Pharisees and the scholars of law from Jerusalem criticizing Jesus' disciples for eating with unwashed hands. Eating with unwashed hands contravened the law of cleanliness. In Jewish society of that time, people who violated the law of cleanliness were branded as *'am ha'aretz*.12 In his editorial phrases (7.14a), Mark confirms the important fact that the hearers are the *ochlos*. They demonstrate their liberation from the system by disregarding the law of cleanliness which is a heavy burden on the *ochlos* – a fact which is confirmed in the saying in 7.15. Like this saying, the statement 'The sabbath was made for man, not man for the sabbath' (2.27) also is a declaration which liberates the people oppressed by the Sabbath law. In the Gospel of Matthew, it is for 'all who labor and are heavy-laden' (11.28).

3 The saying, in 9.37 and 10.13–15, requires respect for children. In 9.37 children are identified with Jesus and through him with God. In 10.13–15 he says that the Kingdom of God belongs to children. It is said that Judaism is the religion of adults because there is the responsibility to know the law and to keep it. In this situation women and children were treated contemptuously. There are many arguments about what the words 'with children' mean. In the context of the quarrel over who is higher or who is the first, Mark makes children the symbol of low persons (9.37). Mark 10.13–15 is the same because Jesus reacts to the bad attitude of the disciples toward the children. Luke (9.48) adds to the text of Mark the words 'for he who is least among you all is the one who is great' and indicates that

a child is the symbol of a person who is treated coldly by society. In fact, the children stand in common with the minority (*mikroi*).[13]

Bultmann considers Luke 17.1–2 to be the basic source reflecting this attitude of Jesus which was later Christianized by identifying 'little ones' with '*ton pisteuonton*' (believers) (Matt. 18.6–7). Kummel identifies the little ones with 'the poor in spirit' (Matt. 5.3). However, 'little ones' does not designate a modest attitude, but a social position. It is proper that they are understood in relation to the poor, the crying, and the hungry and as participants in the Kingdom of God. The attitude of Jesus to the children is similar to his attitude toward the crowd, *ochlos*.

THE LINGUISTIC MEANING OF *OCHLOS*

We have noted that Mark introduced the term *ochlos* into the New Testament and that he identified the followers of Jesus and the persons whom Jesus loved with partiality as the *ochlos*. We must now inquire into the linguistic tradition of this word. By so doing, we will be able to discover Mark's understanding of the meaning of 'min-jung'. We will focus on the characteristics of the minjung (people) mainly through an analysis of materials in Kittel's New Testament Dictionary.

Laos and ochlos

1 *Before the New Testament.* The Septuagint introduces the term *laos* into Jewish usage. It translates the Hebrew term '*am* as many as 2,000 times. In Greek sources it is mostly used to denote a national group and often means belonging to some ruling community. For example, the expression 'Pharaoh's *laos*' is found in Homer, Pindar, and Herodotus. The Septuagint reflects the meaning of 'national group', and this word especially indicates the Israelites who are referred to as '*am* in Hebrew. For non-Israelites the term *ethnos* is used in most cases. Of course, *laos* is used especially for 'God's people' ('*am*). Another characteristic usage of the Septuagint is that *laoi*, plural of *laos*, is used only 140 times, and it has the meaning of 'crowd' or *ochlos*. In this case, there is not the substantial meaning of *laos*. This is a significant characteristic, since ordinary common people hardly make an appearance in the use of *laos* in the Septuagint.

This tradition is also followed in Rabbinic documents. Usually, these documents employ *laos* also to designate non-Israelites, but the added description 'offended the law' differentiates them from the Israelites. Also epigraphic material from the Jewish diaspora often designates Israel as *laos*.

Compared with the use of *laos*, *ochlos* is used only about sixty times in the Septuagint. However, it does not occur in the ancient Old Testament documents, but in the documents of the later period. It is used to translate several Hebrew words, except *hamon*, which mean minjung. The common meaning of all these usages is 'the crowd'. But, it does not mean a particular social group or a member of a social group. Typical uses of the term are '*ochlos laou*' – a crowd of Israelites – or '*ochloi ethnou*' – a crowd of Gentiles.

After Pindar, the term *ochlos* appears in Greek documents referring to a confused majority or to the ordinary soldiers in a combat unit, but not to officers. It also refers to non-combat people who follow the army and perform menial duties. We must note that the anonymous people referred to as the *ochlos* are differentiated from the ruling class. The term *ochlos* refers to an ignorant crowd under a burden.

The Septuagint uses this Greek word with this general meaning of 'the mass'. As a descriptive term its precise meaning varies from context to context. It could mean 'insurgents', 'tactical troops', or just refer to the majority. It sometimes designates a crowd of children or women. Its usage in Rabbinic literature is not very different.

2 *Usage in the New Testament.* In the New Testament, unlike in the Septuagint, the term *ochlos* is used more often than *laos*. It occurs 174 times while the term *laos* occurs 141 times.

Looking at the use of the term *laos* in the New Testament, it occurs some 84 times in Luke, so that the majority of its uses are here. Luke seems to use it consciously since there are several aspects peculiar to his use of this term. First, quite often *laos* and *ochlos* are used interchangeably and carry the same meaning as *ochlos* in Mark. Second, Luke, however, seems to prefer the term *laos* for Israelites, though understood on the same lines as *ochlos* in Mark, to distinguish them from other national groups who are the *ethnoi* (Luke 19.47; 22.66; Acts 4.8; 23.5; etc.). This usage of *laos* betrays the influence of the Septuagint. It is worth noting in this connection that non-Christian Jews who oppress Christians are also called *ochlos* or *ochloi*. Third, the *laos* is in a situation of confrontation with those in power.

This is similar to the use of *ochlos* in Mark. However, sometimes, Luke takes the *laos* and the ruling class together: *presbuteroi tou laou*, the elders of the *laos* (Luke 22.66). Mark never uses the term *ochlos* in relation to the Jews of the ruling class.

By and large, it is Mark's use of the term *ochlos* for people that is distinctive in the New Testament and has even influenced Luke's use of *laos*. Besides this use of *laos* in Luke, other uses of this word in the New Testament are by and large in quotations from or allusions to the Old Testament and in the language of the rulers. References to Israel as the people of God also have *laos*, following the Septuagint.

Ochlos and the *'Am Ha'aretz*

In order to understand the meaning of *'am ha'aretz*, we should look not at its usage in the whole Old Testament but rather at its everyday use at the beginning of the first century BC.

Before the Israelites were taken into exile, this term designated landowners, aristocrats, etc. who were the upper class of Israelite society. However, the meaning of this word changed during the exilic and post-exilic periods. Once the leading members of the society were taken into exile, the ownership of the land passed to the common people, including the Samaritans, who were left behind. Thus, these became the *'am ha'aretz*.

However, this term became a pejorative and was used both in a religious sense and in a 'national sense for a low class of people as the people of the land', while the cream of the society was considered to be that which was taken into exile. From the time of Ezra onwards, it became a sociological term designating a class of people that was uneducated and ignorant of the law.

We must remember that it was during this time that Rabbinic Judaism was established; and it was Rabbinic Judaism that systematized the law and set up the social and religious system of its time. Defining the term *'am ha'aretz* in the way it did, Rabbinic Judaism made it refer to the poor and the powerless class which was despised and marginalized. According to Rabbinic Judaism, Jews were forbidden to marry the daughters of the *'am ha'aretz* or sit together with them at meals. This attitude was clearly evident during the time of Jesus.

In the *Babylonian Pesachim*, there are the following prohibitions concerning the *'am ha'aretz*. These are worth noting in relation to the *ochlos*. (1) They cannot be witnesses. (2) Their witness cannot be believed. (3) No secret is to be revealed to them. (4) They are not permitted to be the guardians of orphans. (5) They are not permitted to take charge of contributions for the poor. (6) No Jew is to travel with them.

As we have already mentioned, at least during the time of Mark, if not before, the *'am ha'aretz* designates a social status and indicates an object of contempt. It is close in meaning to *ochlos*. Geographically, Galilee symbolizes the *'am ha'aretz*. Mark selected the word *ochlos*, which was used in a negative sense at that time, to refer to the *'am ha'aretz* and took Galilee as the background to show the victims of the society of that time.

SUMMARY

1 Mark deliberately avoided the term *laos* and used the term *ochlos* to indicate the minjung. This is different from the people of God, who are those within the national and religious framework as defined by the Pharisees. It is also different from the *laos* in Luke, which refers to those who repent and become the new people of God. The minjung do not belong to either group, nor are they the baptized crowd. They belong to a class of society which has been marginalized and abandoned.

2 However, the term *ochlos* is not consolidated into a concept but is defined in a relational way, and is therefore a fluid notion. For example, the poor are *ochlos* in relation to the rich or the ruler. The tax collector is minjung only in relation to the Jewish nationalist establishment. Accordingly, a certain value or beautification cannot be attributed to the term.

3 The *ochlos* are feared by the unjust and powerful, but they are not organized into a power group. Therefore, we cannot regard them as a political power bloc; rather, they should be regarded existentially as a crowd. They are minjung not because they have a common destiny, but simply because they are alienated, dispossessed, and powerless. They are never represented as a class which has a power base. They yearn for something. In this sense, they are different from the people in the Gospel of John who sought to crown Jesus as a king. The *ochlos* in the Gospel of Mark follow Jesus, but they

do not force Jesus to conform to a course of action set up by them. In this sense they are different from the Zealots in Galilee. The Zealots, in their social character and position, have some things in common with the *ochlos*, but the Zealots have a clear purpose which the *ochlos* do not have.

4 Jesus sides with the *ochlos* and accepts them as they are without making any conditions. Jesus never rebukes these persons who are called sinners; rather he rebukes only those who criticize and attack the *ochlos*. (This reconfirms the statement in 2 above.)

5 Jesus does not give the impression that he intends to organize the *ochlos* into a force. He does not provide a program for their movement, nor does he make them an object of his movement. He does not forcibly demand anything from them. He does not ask to be their ruler or head. He 'passively' stands with them. A relationship between Jesus and the minjung takes place and then is broken. They follow him without condition. They welcome him. They also betray him.

6 In a word, Jesus informed the minjung of the advent of God's Kingdom. Significantly, Mark summarizes Jesus' preaching thus: 'The time is fulfilled, and the Kingdom of God is at hand' (1.15). This eschatological declaration announces that there is the creation of a new world as the old world ends. And this declaration gave the *ochlos* a new way and a new hope. Jesus struggled together with the suffering minjung on the frontline of this advent. In this sense, he is the Messiah – a viewpoint Mark reflects.

7 Jesus proclaims the coming of God's Kingdom. He stands with the minjung, and promises them the future of God. The God whom Jesus presented is not like Yahweh of the Old Testament who manifests a tension between love and justice. God's will is to side with the minjung completely and unconditionally. This notion was not comprehensible within the framework of established ethics, cult, and laws. God's will is revealed in the event of Jesus being with them in which he loves the minjung.

NOTES

1   J. Gnilka, *Das Evangelium nach Markus* in *Evangelsch-Katholischer Kommentar Zum Neuen Testament* 1 (Neukirchen, Neukirchen Verlag, 1978), p. 28.

2   H. Strathmann, 'Laos' in *Theological Dictionary of the New Testament* IV (Grand Rapids, MI, W. B. Eerdman's, 1967), pp. 29, 34.

3   Often chapter 13 of the Gospel of Mark is taken as the criterion for determining the date of the authorship of the Gospel, depending on whether one takes the account as a prophecy of the Fall of Jerusalem or as an expression of the reality after the Fall of Jerusalem. However, considering the situation of the *ochlos* as they appear in Mark – the four thousand people who followed Jesus for three days without food (Mark 8.1 ff) – I conclude that Mark 13 reflects the situation of the people of Israel, including Christians, who had been expelled from their homeland after the Jewish war. Even the expression in Mark 6.34 regarding Jesus' attitude to the five thousand, 'Jesus was moved with compassion as they were as sheep without a shepherd', is a reflection of the historical reality of the people.

4   Jesus mainly rebukes their ignorance, for example, their misunderstanding of the parables (4.13, 7.18), their unbelief during the storm (4.35– 41; 6.51 f), and their lack of understanding of Jesus' suffering (8.32 ff; 9.32; 10.32, etc.).

5   See especially Gnilka, p. 279.

6   The first to contrast Galilee with Jerusalem were E. Lohmeyer, *Galiläa und Jerusalem* (Gottingen, Vandenhock Ruprecht, 1936) and W. Marxen, *Mark the Evangelist: Studies on the Redaction of the Gospels* (Nashville, TN, Abingdon, 1969). But both simply note the contrasting characteristics of the two words in the light of the history of the church, and do not investigate the use of these words in terms of the socio-economic context.

7   The attempt to distinguish between the minjung of Galilee who stood by Jesus and the minjung of Jerusalem who turned against him – for example, Lohmeyer, *Galiläa* – is not tenable. The real intention of this attempt seems to be to beautify the minjung.

8   There is still much confusion about the identity of the Pharisees. This is because there is an opinion which puts Pharisees on the side of the minjung. The Pharisees originally came from the pietistic Chassidim, who fought in the Maccabean War. The Pharisees are known from the time of Simon of the house of Hasmon, who appointed himself as arch-priest and ethnarch in 140 BC. They popularized the law; therefore they conscientized the minjung. First they were in conflict with the royal family of Hasmon. But after the death of Jannai, their policies were accepted by the next ruler, who was Jannai's wife, Alexandra (76–67 BC). From then on their position changed, so that they became the defenders of the system. During the time of Herod the Great, they were in conflict with the regime, and ten Pharisees were even executed. However, after the death of Herod, they became part of the establishment. They were allowed to participate in the decision-making assemblies of the ruling regime centered around Jerusalem, i.e. the arch-

priest Hannas (AD 6–15), who was appointed by the Roman governor-general, Quirinus, AD 6–11. Therefore their role changed. From working for the minjung they now became inspectors enforcing submission to the establishment. At least, this is the way the Gospel of Mark presents the Pharisees. For example, they attacked Jesus and his disciples for their violation of rules concerning fasting (2.18), and their eating without washing their hands (7.15). These rules were made by the Pharisees, and therefore express the Pharisees' attitude about the minjung. Also they called themselves Pharisees in order to distinguish themselves, as elites, from the minjung.

9 J. Jeremias, *Jerusalem in the Time of Jesus* (London, SCM Press, 1969), pp. 303 f.

10 *Nedarim*, III, 4: *Bill.*, I, 379.

11 J. Schniewind and others understand this in a similar fashion, and John 9.2–3 also clearly indicates such an attitude.

12 See also discussion of *'am ha'aretz* in this paper.

13 Mark 9.42; Matt. 10.42; 17.2 (Q). Cf. R. Bultmann, *History of the Synoptic Tradition* (Oxford, Basil Blackwell, 1963), p. 84.

7

Yahweh the Defender of the Dalits: A Reflection on Isaiah 3.12–15

GEORGE KOONTHANAM

Indian Christian hermeneutics over a long period have engaged in a comparative exercise, looking at Sanskritic texts, the very texts which have been used to alienate the dalits (formerly classified as outcastes in the Indian caste system), and thus have overlooked the plight of these people. A significant feature of this article written from within the dalit movement, is that it draws hermeneutical implications from the writings of a Hebrew prophet.

This essay is from *Jeevadhara: A Journal of Christian Interpretation* 22 (128, 1992), pp. 112–23. This issue contains other examples of dalit biblical interpretation. *Jeevadhara* is a quarterly and is available from The Editor, *Jeevadhara*, Kottayam 686041, Kerala, India.

George Koonthanam is a member of the Missionary Congregation of the Blessed Sacrament, in Kerala, India. He is a biblical scholar and has published many articles on contextual hermeneutical issues.

> 3.12 My people – children are their oppressors, and women rule over them.
> O my people, your leaders mislead you,
> and confuse the course of your paths.
> 13 The LORD has taken his place to contend,
> he stands to judge his people.
> 14 The LORD enters into judgement
> with the elders and princes of his people:
> 'It is you who have devoured the vineyard,
> the spoil of the poor is in your houses.
> 15 What do you mean by crushing my people,
> by grinding the face of the poor?'
> says the LORD God of hosts.

Every prophet is a critic, but not every critic a prophet. A prophet may criticize and condemn at times the entire nation of Israel; but whenever he specifies certain groups, it is always those classes or individuals in the country who wield power, social, military or religious. Kings, priests, judges, generals and the rich fight against a prophet (Jer. 1.18), because they are the targets of his attack (Jer. 22.13–19; Mic. 3.1, 9–12; Amos 5.12; Hos. 4.4–10 etc.). In fact the beginnings of Israel's prophetic movement are usually traced back to the period of Samuel when power got centralized – and therefore absolutized – to such an extent, that one and the same person, namely Samuel, was exercising social, political and religious powers. When power is centralized, oppressive power-structures emerge. In a monarchical system such centralized power becomes a yoke. Prophecy, as God's voice, comes to the national stage precisely when the masses feel helpless in the stranglehold of oppressive centralized power. Every prophet therefore is bound to hurl diatribes at kings and their cronies. And the more crushing these power-structures, the more vehement a prophet's attack on them. In Israel the pre-exilic period was witness to oppressive power amassed in a monarchical structure. The valiant and virulent pre-exilic prophets who denounced this tyranny of power are therefore rightly called the prophets of the golden age!

We might be helped to understand and grasp the emotive thrust and spiritual framework of the prophets if we recall to mind that prophets are God-intoxicated persons. They are capable of holding in their hands the emotions that surge up in the heart of God. And the God experienced by the pre-exilic prophets is a morally outraged God. This God, who hears the cries of the oppressed (Exod. 3.7–9; 22.23–27 etc.), inspires the prophets so intensely that they get the experience of a God who roars like a lion (Amos 3.8), rends like a wild beast (Hos. 13.7–8), slays and blasts like a dynamite (Hos. 6.5; Isa. 9.8). The act of this God who avenges the poor on the criminal power-puffs is so really felt by the prophets in their proclamation that they with thorough matter-of-factness speak of God coming directly to judge (Isa. 3.12–15; Mic. 6.1ff; Hos. 4.1ff etc.).

George Koonthanam

GOD, THE DEFENDER OF THE POOR

In this context, Isaiah 3.12–15 merits special attention. This great prophet endowed with great cultural and educational clout belonged in fact to the uppermost social stratum of Judah. He was schooled in the imperial court theology of Jerusalem and therefore passionately loved the city, its traditions and its people. Yet, when he saw the pathetic plight of the defenceless classes, he called the citizenry of Jerusalem 'You rulers of Sodom, you people of Gomorrah' (1.10; cf. 1.17). These leaders are further branded as rebels, companions of thieves and lovers of bribes (1.23). The constellation and escalation of Jerusalem's sinfulness necessitated Yahweh's judgement on it. The Yahwist too, in his story of the tower of Babel, speaks of arrogance of power making imperative God's intervention (Gen. 11.1–9).

The LORD appears in Isaiah 3.12–15 as the defender of the poor, accuser and judge of the oppressors. In its present form the two originally independent units – 3.1–9 and 3.12–15 – build a coherent whole: vv. 1–9 describe how the LORD had punished Jerusalem and Judah for their sins, and then, with dramatic turn, the judgement scene opens out in vv. 12–15. This scene is introduced by accusation in v. 12 which necessitates Yahweh's appearance. Although there is mention of people, God's judgement is clearly on the ruling class (cf. 1.10). The term for rulers denotes in the Hebrew the equivalent of a taskmaster or a tormentor. They are branded as inept; to have such men as rulers is disgrace and punishment. The mention of elders shows how even the one-time tribal leaders, who used to be the voice and pulse of their respective tribes, and administrators of justice at the city gates, are now hand in glove with the princes who hold political and military power in the monarchical regime. Opportunism pointed out to the elders that making common cause with thieves in despoiling the helpless was a surer guarantee for a better future than being at the service of justice. The prophet does not mince words when speaking of Judah's princes: 'Your princes are rebels and companions of thieves. Everyone loves a bribe and runs after gifts. They do not defend the fatherless, and the widow's cause does not come to them.' (1.23).

The elders and rulers have not only abdicated their supreme duty of protecting the defenceless, but have become themselves oppressors, crushing the poor! The expression 'It is you who have devoured the vineyard' is perhaps itself a proverb, like the proverb in Malayalam which says 'The fence itself devours the crops'! Instead of guarding the vineyards, lest the shoots of the vines should be devoured by intruding animals, the elders and rulers of Judah plunder it. The Hebrew equivalent of the word 'spoil' usually refers to stolen goods, but here it may be the case of economic oppression legalized by unjust laws (10.1ff), judicial corruption, bribery etc. (cf. 1.23; 5.7; 8.20–23; Amos 3.10; 5.11–12 etc.).

The plight of the people is described in 3.15 as getting crushed or pulverized between upper and lower millstones. Such oppression smashes the body and crushes the spirit. What galls most in oppression is the painful and humiliating awareness of the crushed that they are totally helpless in the face of ruthless injustice perpetrated on them with full backing of corrupt power. And any and every human being with a modicum of humaneness would, on seeing the fate of the poor, make his own the words of Koheleth: 'And behold, the tears of the oppressed, and they had no one to comfort them! On the side of their oppressors there was power, and there was no one to comfort them.' (Eccles. 4.1–2).

THE GOD OF ISAIAH

Isaiah received his call in the year king Uzziah died, namely in 742 BC. Under Uzziah, who ruled from 783–742 BC, the kingdom of Judah made great economic progress unparalleled since the days of Solomon! But this economic boom was accompanied by social and religious decay. Economic and social disparities marred the face of the community of God's chosen people. The wealthy and the influential had unjust laws (Isa. 10.1–4) to legalize their latifundism (the amassing of big estates and properties) (Isa. 5.8; Mic. 2.2). Judges sold justice to the highest bidder (Isa. 2.23; 5.20; Mic. 3.9–11). Atrocities on the poor could be indulged in with impunity (Isa. 2.9; Mic. 3.1–4, 9–11). The arrogance of wealth was reflected in the life-style of the wicked (Isa. 3.16–4.1; 5.11–22; Amos 6.4–7). The oppressions of Egypt returned to Palestine, and the cry of the oppressed rose to God from his own vineyard (Isa. 5.7). An extravagant cult (Isa. 1.10–17) stood as a sort of whitewash over moral disintegration. Official religion both knowingly and unknowingly degenerated into cult-craft and projected a God who was not bothered about the misery of the poor. It was in such a situation of social apostacy and religious debauchery that Isaiah was sent out by Yahweh with a stunning experience of God's holiness and the shuddering awareness of its consequences upon a people of unclean lips (Isa. 6). No wonder then, Isaiah brings the God of holiness as avenger of the poor and judge over the oppressors. This God cannot calm down his nerves and conscience when the oppressed cry to him (Exod. 3.7f; 22.22–24, 26–27). He is the stronghold of the oppressed (Ps. 9.10); he is angered and outraged when the poor are crushed (Isa. 3.15); he will despoil those who despoil the poor (Prov. 22.22f). His concern for the poor is so great that he goes to the extent of identifying himself with them (Prov. 14.31; 19.17; cf. Matt. 25.40–45). Nay, he calls them 'my people' (Isa. 3.15; Ps. 72.2; Mic. 3.1–4), 'my sheep' (Ezek. 34.19).

In fact, going through the various epochs of salvation history, we never find any act of God in favour of the rich. The beneficiaries of the great saving acts of God are always the poor. He chose the patriarchal tribes of landless and rootless people to begin this great history. It was a band of oppressed slaves that he liberated from Egypt; he wandered with them in the wilderness, sharing their fate, feeding them, guiding them, chastizing them, but always as their God. During the monarchical period he thundered through the prophets as the voice of the silent agony of the oppressed masses. From Babylon he gathered the smitten remnant and brought them back to Palestine. In the fullness of time he clothed himself with flesh and walked on earth as the friend of the discriminated and marginalized sections of Palestine.

This God of the poor demands that all those who believe in him be Yahweh-like by championing the cause of the poor. True worship for Yahweh believers ought to consist in learning to do good, correcting oppression, defending the fatherless and pleading for the widows (Isa. 1.17). Believers in Yahweh should not seek him in and through cult, but in and through the struggle for justice (Amos 5.4–6, 14–15). The fruits that Yahweh expects from his beloved vineyard are justice and righteousness (Isa. 5.7). He makes his will as clear as daylight that he loves mercy, not sacrifice, knowledge of God rather than burnt offerings (Hos. 6.6). Israel will 'know' her God and be his beloved spouse only when she practises justice, righteousness, faithfulness, steadfast love and mercy (Hos. 2.19–20; 4.1). From times immemorial it has been revealed to Israel what is the good that Yahweh requires of her: it is nothing more and nothing less than to do justice and to love kindness, which alone can be termed walking wisely with the LORD (Mic. 6.8). The fast that Yahweh chooses is to liberate people from all forms of bondage, 'to share your bread with the hungry, to clothe the naked and to bring the homeless poor into your house' (Isa. 58.6–7). The community of his believers will be spiritually alive, not when they worship him, but when justice rolls down like water and righteousness like an everflowing stream (Amos 5.24).

Whenever Israel, in imitation of her neighbouring religions, forgot the practice of moral virtues – justice, righteousness, mercy, steadfast love and faithfulness – and indulged herself in cultic practices, she was reproached for it in the harshest possible terms (Isa. 1.10–17; Amos 5.21–24; Hos. 6.6; Mic. 6.1–8; Jer. 7.21–28; Zech. 7.1–14; cf. also Prov. 21.3; Sirach 34.18–22). The prophets' criticism of cult makes it abundantly clear, that in the practice of true religion, actions directed towards God are to be replaced by actions towards the poor. The priestly instructions in the Bible (e.g. Ps. 15; Ps. 24.3–6; Isa. 33.14–16), the description of a righteous man (Ezek. 18.6–9), the explanation how to amend one's life (Jer. 7.5–6), references to God's will in polemic against practices of piety (Zech. 7.9–10; Ps. 50; Ps. 51.16–17 etc.) and other similar themes emphasize how in the religion of Yahweh there is no substitute for mercy towards the poor. In the New Testament St James too makes it clear (James 1.27).

IDEAL REIGN

Nausea, repugnance and indignation over the present situation of crushing oppression and ruthless violence on the hapless masses churned up Isaiah's faith to hope for a new world with an ideal king. The story of Judah's kings from David and Solomon till Jotham, the king during the first period of Isaiah's prophetic ministry, was the story of betrayal. But the prophet who has strong faith in the dogma of the chosenness of the Davidic dynasty, sanguinely hopes for a shoot from the stump of Jesse (Isa. 11.1), namely, for a second David. This ideal king will give justice to the poor (the impoverished) and the meek (the oppressed) by slaying the rich and the oppressors (Isa. 11.4). The same hope is given in Isaiah 32.1–8, where the prophet looks to an ideal king who will rule in righteousness and whose princes will rule in justice. As a result the fools and knaves who are greeted as 'their Excellencies and their Honours' today by their sycophants will be put in their place, and the poor will have security and safety. Then the meek (the oppressed) and the poor (the impoverished) shall obtain joy in the LORD (Isa. 29.19–20). Authority is for service to the poor, and in order to serve Yahweh's poor, it is necessary for a God-fearing king to destroy the enemies of Yahweh and his people! Isaiah firmly believed that king and kingdom are integral to God's design of salvation for Israel. Yet, throne and king are for establishing and fostering steadfast love, faithfulness, justice and righteousness: 'then a throne will be established in steadfast love (*hesed*) and on it will sit in faithfulness (*emeth*) in the tent of David one who judges and seeks justice (*mishpāt*) and is swift to do righteousness (*sedaqah*) (Isa. 16.5; cf. 9.7 and Hos. 4.1; 2.19–20).

Who are the poor Isaiah talks about? The woe-oracle in 10.1–4 pronounces death on legislators who put laws into effect which oppressed three groups of people: the widows, the orphans and the needy. These three groups of people have no power in society and are therefore easily sinned against (Amos 4.1; 5.11; 8.4; Isa. 3.14), and are denied justice in the courts of law (Exod. 23.6–8; Amos 5.12; Isa. 10.2; Jer. 5.28). The widow has no husband to protect her, the orphans have no parents to take care of them, and the needy or the poor have no money to satisfy their needs. The people of God are exhorted to have a special concern for these groups. But it is the supreme duty of those among the people who hold authority to use their power which comes to them from their God-given authority, for giving justice to the defenceless classes (cf. Ps. 72.1–2; 12.14). Knowledge of God in the Old Testament signifies religion. A king who knows the LORD will give justice to the poor (Isa. 11.2–5). Jeremiah puts it in the form of a question, implying thereby that every believer in Yahweh ought to know this basic, fundamental truth, namely, to know the LORD is to give justice to the poor and needy (Jer. 22.16). The anchor of Jerusalem's court theology was the dogma of the Davidic covenant. Although this covenant is promissory in its wording (2 Sam. 7), Isaiah, a firm believer in this dogma, understands it conditionally when he exhorts Ahaz to believe (Isa. 7.9b). Jeremiah makes the survival of this dynasty explicitly conditioned on executing justice and righteousness which in concrete means concern for and partisanship with the defenceless classes (Jer. 22.1–5).

Proverbs played an important role in the education and training especially of kings and their officers. Isaiah received an excellent education in the wisdom schools of Jerusalem. This is manifested in his masterful use of the Hebrew language as well as in the high cultural level of his teachings. As a young pupil he received instruction in very clear terms on the obligations of power toward the defenceless (Prov. 22.22–23; 23.10–11; 29.14; 28.15; 31.8–9). These instructions forcefully drive home to the pupils that the poor have an avenger in God, and if the rulers oppress the poor, this God will come to judge them. This is what Isaiah pictures in 1.24–25; 3.12–15; 10.3. He exhorts the rulers (1.10) to defend the fatherless and plead for the widows (1.17); he pronounces woe – and thereby death, cf. 6.5 – on legislators who write iniquitous decrees (10.1); and he condemns evil rulers as murderers, rebels and companions of thieves (1.21–23). In all these texts the heart of the prophet aches for the helpless trio of widows (1.17; 1.23; 10.2), orphans (1.17; 1.23; 10.2) and the poor (3.14f; 10.2). The greedy land grabber exploits them (5.8), the unscrupulous legislators make laws to loot them (10.2) and the courts of law deny them justice (1.23; 5.20,23). Jerusalem, the joy of Isaiah's heart and the delight of his eyes, was once a faithful city, full of justice, and righteousness lodged in her; but the sins of her rulers made her a harlot, and murderers now lodge in her (1.21); nay, she is no better than Sodom and Gomorrah (1.10). The prophet from Nazareth too would one day have to shed bitter tears over the same city (Luke 19.41).

ISAIAH IN THE INDIA OF TODAY

The message of the prophets has its relevance today. Of all the various and varied oracles the prophets left us, their diatribes against those who oppress the weak are perhaps the most frighteningly relevant ones to our Indian situation. In the place of widows, orphans and the needy, we must put the dalits. Indignities that are being perpetrated on the dalits of India are certainly more heart-rending than those denounced by the eighth-century prophets of Israel. The helpless ones of our country are victims, not of injustice only, but of dastardly outrage. As in the days of the prophets, so also there is power on the side of the malefactors. Injustices suffered by the dalits are, broadly speaking, those relating to property-wage-money on one side and to body and person on the other.

Isaiah denounced legislators who kept on writing iniquitous

decrees in order to loot the defenceless classes. The rules, norms and conditionalities imposed on the poor nations by the blood-sucking G-7, the IMF, the multinationals and others, the traps they set and the pits they dig for the poor nations through GATT, IPR etc. can be left out in our reflections for focusing our attention more on the national scene than the international one; although these economic colonizers are the real and ultimate culprits who turn this world into a veritable hell for the vast majority of humans who populate it. On the national level, ordinances, laws, acts etc. are issued and passed galore in every session of the parliament. A good many of them aim at suppressing legitimate uprisings of exploited sections, or at exterminating them under the cry and camouflage of law and order. Projects and programmes by the hundred are not lacking in our country for helping the poor. But in order to receive the loans, subsidies, bonuses etc. from these apparently laudable and much touted schemes, the poor have to run from pillar to post, enervated by the maze of red tapes, and if, by a miracle, they get some help, by that time they will have spent an almost equal amount by way of bribes to the officers, from the door-keeper of the office to the greedy big shot who sits on top! Can we find conscientious judges anywhere in our country who feel free to pass honest and just verdicts when and where the interests of the ruling party or those of its members or fellow-travellers are implicated?

Denying justice to the poor is the unwritten motto of our judicial system. Felons with economic and/or political power can commit any crime in our country with absolute certainty to get acquitted in the courts, if at all these get charge-sheeted. For fear of brutal reprisals from the *goondas* and thugs of such criminals people do not dare to go to the courts to seek justice. When vandalism and mayhem are let loose in a village, the police will arrive only after the 'operation' is completed and then, their main concern will be to protect the political and social upper class vandals from the ire of the outraged poor! Or, these protectors of order and morality may themselves charge at the poor, making their miseries and ignominies even worse!

Prophets speak of crimes and atrocities on widows and orphans. Every day in our holy India so many *Harijan* women are being sinned against, be it in the form of flesh-trade, heavy loads and unjust quotas of work, rape, discrimination in wages, bride-burning, wife-beating and a hundred and one other forms of harassment, molestation, physical attack etc. Oppression of orphans, so vehemently denounced by the prophets, comes nowhere near the wide-spread practice of child-labour that thrives in our factories, estates, hotels etc. Many institutions with fine philanthropic names are often centres for stealing and trafficking in human organs, and in this devilish business, the victims are mostly poor children!

Bribes in the past used to be given to officers for inducing them to do what they were forbidden to do; today bribes and gifts are to be given for making the members of our civil force do their duty; often they openly and shamelessly ask for the amounts they themselves have fixed for each and every duty they do, big as well as small! Natural calamities like floods, earthquakes etc. are occasions for relief agencies and their workers to make good money. Amounts released for relief work end up in the pockets of officers. The spoil of the poor is indeed in the house of our politicians and pseudo-social workers (Isa. 3.14)!

The amassing of big estates and properties denounced by the prophets of the Old Testament serves just to make us laugh in our sleeves because the criminally huge landholdings of our politicians, religious institutions and church dignitaries, not to speak of conventional landlords, are so big as to defy any contrast or comparison with the former!

Where are the prophets in and for modern India? Do the Christian churches function as the conscience of the nation? In an unjust society, faith ought to be militant, although militancy does not necessarily imply use of violence, which none the less cannot be excluded if demanded by the thrust of faith and the urgency of the situation. If faith is awareness and commitment to God, then siding with the poor becomes the inescapable imperative of faith in today's context: for both Yahweh of the Old Testament and Jesus of the New Testament reveal to us a God who is defender of the oppressed and the neglected. Having faith in Jesus is identical with having the compassion and concern that he had for the poor. If so, the duty of the church would be neither social analysis nor theological synthesis to be dished out in erudite church documents, but to acquire and articulate sensitivity to the plight of the poor. Such articulation will not be a voice of conscientization of the poor, but the very voice itself of the poor expressing their pent-up frustrations and energizing them to struggle and fight without collapsing. Do we really have such a prophetic church in India?

The Indian church is authority-conscious *vis-à-vis* the Christian laity, and a coward *vis-à-vis* the political powers-that-be. First, the authority the church is conscious of is one that comes from above, in the fashion and arrogance of monarchical power. This stands diametrically opposed to the authority her founder spoke of (Mark 10.42–45) and demonstrated in a telling way (John 13.1–16). Authority in the Old Testament was for service to the poor (Jer. 22.16; Isa. 11.4–5; Ps. 72.2, 12–14; Prov. 31.8–9 etc.), because it was an authority that came from the God who hears the cry of the poor and avenges them (Exod. 3.7–9; 22.22–24, 26–27). Such God-given authority should be used for defending the defenceless against the offenders. We have a church that prolongs the agony of the masses by preaching submissiveness to the poor and generosity to the rich!

This policy and proclivity of the church comes from her sickening minority complex, preoccupation with interests, institutions and other sources of income, and a spineless dependence on the West. The prophets and their school of followers were minuscule minorities in their days; and precisely this made them supremely free in and for God. This freedom in God or rootedness in God in turn made them fearlessly free for and with God's people, the poor! They had no interests or institutions to safeguard, nor were they obsessed with money. Only those who build their palaces and cathedrals on the rock of mammon rather than on the rock of faith, are to be wary in their utterances, lest they antagonize or displease a government that can stop the inflow of foreign money! The same cowardliness and fear would make them toe the line of those who supply them with offices, prebends and patronage! Are we to seek anywhere else the reason why the church does not pronounce woe to the rich, so explicitly and emphatically done by Jesus? The poor, and only the poor, are God's people (Isa. 3.15; Ezek. 34.19; Ps. 72.2), for to them belongs the kingdom of God (Luke 6.20) and they, and they alone, can enter into it (Luke 18.25). A church that does not want to lose the crumbs that fall into her coffers from the table of the rich, a church that will be forced to tell her own conscience that she does not belong either to God or to his kingdom because of the mammon in her, opts to keep mum about this truth of God's kingdom!

A church, cushioned in poor India, owning assets that equal those owned by the industrial magnates of this country, and yet unashamedly waving a banner of 'service to the poor and commitment to national progress', will naturally and necessarily close herself into her own cocoon, lost in squabbles of rites, jurisdiction, wolf-crying in notions and beliefs and eager to avail herself of any and every opportunity to manifest subservience to the bossy high-ups in the West. The maximum that one can expect from this church is an occasional document on irrelevant thematics in bombastic pedantry! No wonder, then, that the palace theologians and mode-crazy spiritualists of this ecclesiastical industry, with full support and benediction from its snobbish and grade-conscious officials, practise and propagate from their five-star ashrams and colossal institutions, élitistic forms of worship, mental exercises, bodily postures etc. badged with fanciful names, proclaiming these as exercises and practice of prayer!

Isaiah 3.12–15 and other prophetic oracles of same or similar verve and vein were accusations, verdicts and the beginning of the execution of these verdicts, all in one; for a word that goes forth from the mouth of God shall not return to him empty (Isa. 55.10f)! God's verdict on unjust schemes of things that oppress his poor had its toll in history; but still the word and verdict of God needs further and further execution, because new forms and agents of oppression replace the old ones. The word of God does, and will continue to, march through contemporary history, shaking and shaping it, so that God's justice may give his people, the poor, the righteousness they so direly need. The church can either wake up to this urge of the hour or can feign bliss in the paradise of her fools!

8

Anti-Greed and Anti-Pride: Mark: 10.17–27 and 10.35–45 in the Light of Tribal Values

GEORGE M. SOARES-PRABHU

Along with minjung and dalits, the indigenous people (formerly known as tribals) form the subaltern section of Asian society. The dominant biblical interpretation, reared in Western Enlightenment values, has treated the corporate cultural and religious experience of the indigenous people as unimportant for theological reflection. The following piece is an attempt to evolve a hermeneutics for the indigenous people, using two of their pivotal cultural values which could offer an alternative model for a world driven by the greed of consumerism and the pride of caste and nationalism, the very values which according to the author resonate with biblical tradition – a tradition steeped in tribal ethos.

This essay, written by a sympathetic outsider, forms part of the theme issue of *Jeevadhara* 24 (140, 1994), pp. 130–50 entitled 'Tribal Values in the Bible'.

George Soares–Prabhu is on the staff of the Jana Deepa Vidyapeeth, Pune, India where he teaches New Testament. He has written widely on biblical interpretation and Indian hermeneutics in Asian and international journals.

One of the striking contradictions to be observed in India today is the astonishing difference between its political system, borrowed from the West, and its indigenous social structure. Politically India is a parliamentary democracy. Its government is based on the assumption of the equality of every citizen, who is guaranteed his or her fundamental rights. Socially India is predominantly a caste society. It is a hierarchical order of essentially unequal interdependent people, held together by a system of mutually interlocking duties (*Kula-jati dharma*), rather than a collection of autonomous individuals safeguarded by universal rights. The political system of India does

117

not grow out of its dominant religious ethos, but stands in marked opposition to it.[1]

The two systems, political and social (parliamentary democracy on the one hand and caste on the other), have existed together in an uneasy tension ever since India became an independent nation-state nearly half a century ago. It was then hoped that the first of these (parliamentary democracy) would lead to the gradual disappearance of the second (caste). Political democracy and the increasing 'modernization' of India, it was hoped, would result in growing egalitarian social attitudes, which would lead to the death of caste. This has not happened. If anything it is caste (stronger than ever) which threatens to swallow up parliamentary democracy, and has already influenced its working to such an extent that all politics today are caste politics.

The tension between the two systems has flared up occasionally in outbursts of caste and communal violence; for both caste and communal conflicts can, I suggest, be interpreted as reactions of traditional India to democratic, secular modernity. Caste atrocities are engendered by reactions of caste Hinduism to the threatened emancipation of the lower castes by parliamentary democracy; and communal attitudes are the defensive response of religious Hinduism to the threat of 'secularism'. These reactions are now surfacing into open conflict as 'secularists' defending the ideal of modern Western secular and democratic society confront 'fundamentalists', who, whatever lip service they may pay to democracy and human rights, are in fact clamouring for a political system that will give expression to the hierarchical order of caste. An autocracy based on caste, it seems to me, is as necessary an outcome of *Hindutva* as a theocracy based on the *Shariat* is always the outcome of Muslim fundamentalism. Ultimately, either democracy with its *homo aequalis* or caste and its *homo hierarchicus* must prevail.

THE SIGNIFICANCE OF TRIBAL VALUES

In this critical situation, it is heartening to remember that the notion of an egalitarian society is not wholly foreign to India. It is part of the self-consciousness of the sixty million of its tribal peoples (one seventh of its total population), whose identity is marked by their rootedness in land, and by the egalitarian social structure which derives from this. As Bosu Mullick comments in a splendid discussion of the identity of the indigenous peoples of India:

> The ideology of the indigenous peoples in India which has held them together till today has been based on their concept of regarding the earth as Mother, their symbiotic relationship with the environment and the animal kingdom; it has been rooted in their egalitarian principle of social system, and their sense of balance in the man-woman relationship and their respective social rights. Where there has been a deviation from this anchor of social ideology the people has been in the losing end. The quest of survival of the indigenous peoples demands a journey to the roots of this social ideology.[2]

Tribe and caste thus confront each other as two contrasting social systems both of which are indigenous to India; while the egalitarian liberalism which animates the political but not the social life of the so-called élite is not. This last is, in fact, an imported ideology, far more precarious than is generally supposed. Not only is its influence restricted to the 'convent-educated' middle classes (the products of British Empire and Christian Mission), but it is (even in these classes) skin deep. There can be little commitment to liberty, equality, and fraternity (the basis of liberal democracy) among people who experience others, and spontaneously react to them, as members of a graded caste hierarchy. So if parliamentary democracy has survived in India till now, it is not because of the secular liberalism of the middle classes (never an adequate and now a rapidly diminishing resource), but because of the inertia of an inherited post-colonial political system; and because inter-caste tensions between competing castes, and now a massive organized reaction of the lower castes against the domination of the upper castes, has prevented any dominant group emerging. Should such a group emerge, even under a saffron flag, and sporting a manifesto that spells the end of secular democracy, 'liberal' middle class India will, I suspect, have little difficulty in transferring its allegiance to it, provided it is assured of adequate supplies of Coca-Cola and Johnny Walker. For what has struck deep into the hearts of convent-educated India is Western consumerism, not Western liberalism.

The future of democracy and the values that it enshrines will depend, then, not on the liberalism of the middle class 'élite', whose ideological loyalties are quite inconstant and largely selfish, but on the growing awareness of the *bahujan* ('masses') that their future does not lie in perpetuating a caste system, which, for all the praise sometimes lavished on it by well-meaning Christian apologists, has not, as far as our experience goes, proved anything but oppressive and dehumanizing to the great majority of India's people. As the *bahujan* have begun to realize, the way to liberation does not lie in a return to stagnant immobility of a caste society, but in a movement forward to more egalitarian models, however 'Western' these may be. The hope of a more just society lies here. It is *mandal* ('community') that will prove the best bulwark against *mandir* ('temple') and all that it implies.

It is here that the awakening tribal peoples become significant. They bring a new element to India's political and religious consciousness: an indigenous experience of an egalitarian society. More importantly the egalitarian order of tribal society is rooted in basic values which Paulus Kullu in his article on 'Tribal Religion and Culture' has identified as 'anti-greed' and 'anti-pride'. 'For tribals', he writes, 'greed and pride are the capital "original" sins, because according to their creation myth, these were the sins which caused the mythical flood and the rain of fire, which are the symbols of death and destruction.'[3] Tribal values thus stand in sharp contrast to the 'pride' of the caste and the 'greed' of consumerism which largely determine the social oppression and economic exploitation, that define the brutal reality of Indian society today. The cultivation of these values is essential if Indian society is to be renewed.

Significantly, these values are precisely those which are given a significant place in the ethical teachings of Jesus. They are conspicuous gospel values whose biblical form and basis this article will explore. It will do this by examining (1) the rootedness of these values in the ethos of the Bible and (2) their formulation in the teaching of Jesus.

TRIBAL VALUES IN THE BIBLE

The values which undergird the ethos of tribal society are strikingly similar to those taught in the Bible. For the basic ethos of the Bible is that of a tribe.[4] 'Israel' began as a confederation of tribes, whose socio-political egalitarianism stood in sharp contrast to the hierarchical centralized rule of the Canaanite city states, which Israel eventually overwhelmed, either through conquest or peaceful immigration or popular revolt.[5] The social organization of Israel (whether inherited from its nomadic past or consciously built up by revolting 'peasants' reacting to the oppressive system of the city states from which they had freed themselves) has been well described by Gottwald as 'a self-governing association of self-sufficient free farmers and herdsmen constituting a single class of peoples with a common ownership of the means of production vested in large families'.[6]

This egalitarian, anti-greed, and anti-pride social order was sustained by Israel's unique religion, in which a single God, Yhwh, 'while conceived as the sole sovereign of the land in which Israel lived, was not defined primarily with reference to place, either land as a totality or particular locations within it but with reference to his rule over a people'.[7] Unlike the localized gods of the Canaanite city states with their highly consumptive cults and their powerful priesthood, Yhwh, whose cult was relatively non-consumptive of community resources and whose priesthood was without political power, did not legitimize a pyramidal social system apexing in a divine king, but guaranteed a community of equals. Yhwh's ownership of the land (the land is the Lord's) inhibited the differential accumulation of wealth that is the result of unrestricted 'private property'. Yhwh's absolute Lordship over his people prevented the emergence of totalitarian rulers, exercising absolute power. Yhwh's exclusive uniqueness as the one sole God of all Israel kept the community of socio-political equals together. As Gottwald has described it:

> The loosely federated egalitarian tribalism of Israel was symbolized and institutionalized at the most comprehensive level by a common cultic-ideological allegiance to monoYahwism . . . Yahwism as a social force was operative at precisely those critical points of common structural interest where the monarchic and aristocratic institutions of the Near East normally functioned to give hierarchic order and cohesion to societies – at the cost, however, of an enormous repression of human energies and values in the larger part of the populace. It was precisely social order achieved by human repression that Israel strove to resist at all costs and over against which it hoped to build an alternative social order that would be functional for the whole of the people.[8]

Israel's egalitarian social order was thus integrally related (in a relation of mutual interdependence) to its religion, with its absolute primacy of Yhwh, its concern for the weaker members of the tribe, and its aversion to the accumulation of wealth and the exercise of arbitrary power. That is why even when social and economic pressures (the threat of the Philistines, the need to manage a more sophisticated economy) led to the replacement of the federation of tribes by a monarchy,[9] Israel remained essentially different from the kingdoms around. It was leavened by elements of tribal egalitarianism and a concern for the weak members of the tribe; and was continually challenged by a prophetic tradition which drew its inspiration from the egalitarian ethos of tribal Israel. The close connection between Yhwh and the egalitarian structure of Israel as mutually dependent variables in the social structure of Israel, shows itself in the twin prophetic condemnations of idolatry and injustice. For Israel's prophets these were closely linked. Forsaking Yhwh led to injustice; practising injustice meant to forsake Yhwh. Yhwh continues, even during the monarchy, to be the sole owner of the land and the sole Lord of his people. Because of this absolute role of Yhwh, the king in Israel never enjoyed the divine prerogatives of his peers in Egypt, Assyria or Babylon. The Lordship of Yhwh inhibited exaggerated development of royal pretensions, and to an extent prevented massive accumulation of wealth. Tribal values continue to flourish in post-tribal Israel.

TRIBAL VALUES IN THE TEACHING OF JESUS

Such tribal values underlie I believe much of the ethical teaching of Jesus too. Jesus sees himself as standing within the prophetic tradition of Israel (Mark 6.4; Luke 13.33), and calls for the kind of religious and social renewal of his people that the prophets sought.[10] He too looked forward to an egalitarian community made up of people free from self-assertion and from greed. The kind of counter-culture envisioned by Jesus, it has been said, articulates the counter-cultural vision of peasant groups in pre-industrial agrarian societies everywhere. For here 'those who find themselves at the bottom of the social heap develop cultural forms which promise them dignity, respect and economic comfort which they lack in the world as it is. A real pattern of exploitation dialectically produces its own symbolic mirror image within a folk culture.'[11] Such counter-cultures, which are 'strikingly uniform' in a wide variety of little traditions in different parts of the world, have been described (at the admitted risk of oversimplification) as nearly always implying 'a society of brotherhood in which there will be no rich and poor, in which no distinctions of rank and status (save those between believers and non-believers) will exist'.[12] They imply, that is, an egalitarian, anti-greed and anti-pride society.

Peasant utopias like these do indeed come close to the kind of counter-culture envisaged by Jesus. But Jesus brings something radically new. A new experience of God, which allows him to rename Yhwh as *Abba*, leads to a radically new understanding of God and of society, that is to a new type of religion and a new form of politics. God is experienced not so much as 'holy' but as gracious and compassionate;[13] and people are experienced not just as members of an exclusive tribe, or a separated 'clean' caste, but as members of an open family, marked by a freedom from consumerism and an attitude of radical service.

This new understanding of God and of society, does not negate Israel's 'tribal' understanding of itself, but universalizes and radicalizes it. Israel's egalitarian social order and its legislation to maintain this (the prohibition of the sale of land outside the family, or the taking of interest on loans, regulations for the limitation of debtor-servitude and for the relief of the poverty-stricken) was restricted to Israel only. It did not apply to the gentiles, the 'outsiders' who did not belong to the 'tribe' (Lev. 19.17–18; Deut. 15.3). The concerns of Jesus reach out to all humankind. Israel's anti-greed and anti-pride was expressed in legislation and social protest which sought to control (without great success) the accumulation of private property (Deut. 15, Isa. 5, Mic. 2) and to prevent the setting up of a rigid hierarchy of status. Jesus called for a radical dispossession of goods (Mark 1.16–20; 10.17–23) and for a radical attitude of service (Mark 10. 42–45). The values of tribal society, its egalitarian acceptance of persons, its attitudes of anti-greed, and anti-pride, are thus brought to new levels of radicality in the teaching of Jesus as bonds of tribal and covenant loyalty are replaced by the bonds of agapeic love, and the solidarity of all humankind in Adam is restored at a wholly new level by the New Adam!

This is illustrated by several passages in the Gospels which describe the basic attitudes that must structure the community of his followers. I propose to reflect on two such passages from the Gospel of Mark, the story of the Rich Young Man in Mark 10. 17–27 and that of the request of the Sons of Zebedee in Mark 10. 35–45. Both passages are found in the section of the Gospel in which Jesus describes his 'way' of discipleship, contrasting it with other ways. They pinpoint two radical values of that way which correspond closely to the anti-greed and the anti-pride attitudes that structure tribal society.

A. Anti-Greed: The Call of the Rich Young Man (Mark 10. 17–27)

Mark 10. 17–23

V.17   As Jesus was setting out on his journey, a man ran up to him, fell on his knees before him, and asked him, 'Good Teacher, what must I do to inherit eternal life?'

V.18   And Jesus said to him, 'Why do you call me good? No one is good except God alone.

V.19   You know the commandments: "Do not murder, do not commit adultery, do not steal, do not give false testimony, do not defraud, honour your father and your mother."'

V.20   And he said to him, 'Teacher, all these I have kept since I was a boy.'

V.21   And Jesus looking at him loved him, and said to him, 'You lack one thing. Go, sell everything you have, and give to the poor, and you will have treasure in heaven; and come, follow me.'

V.22   At this word the man's face fell; and he went away sad, because he had great wealth.

For us who live in a society where conspicuous consumption is a sign of status (hence our extravagant celebrations of weddings, and ordinations to the priesthood), and is believed to be the source of all well being, Mark's story of the Rich Young Man can be a profoundly disturbing text.[14] It is the only story in the Gospels where a call of Jesus is refused, and where the cause of the refusal is noted quite precisely as the reluctance of the person called to give up his material possessions. The man who comes with such eagerness to learn about how to attain *moksha* and who greets Jesus as his *guru* with such profound respect ('a man ran up to him, fell on his knees before him and asked him, 'Good Teacher, what must I do to inherit eternal life?'), goes away sadly when invited by Jesus to sell his property and follow him ('At this word, the man's face fell; and he went away sad, because he had great wealth').

The contrast between the enthusiastic arrival of the man, who breaks into the story with verve ('a man *ran up* to him'), and his dismal exit ('he went away sad') is heightened by the extraordinary qualities (presumably) the young man reveals. He is no prodigal son 'squandering his wealth in wild living' (Luke 15.13). He has kept the commandments, and specifically those pertaining to interhuman justice ('all these I have kept since I was a boy').[15] He aspires to something more. He is obviously what vocation promoters of religious congregations today would call an 'ideal vocation'. Jesus certainly seems to think so. He looks at him, we are told, and loves him (v.21), that is, gives him a sign of his affection, the only time Jesus is said to do this in the Gospel of Mark.[16] The sign of love is to prepare the young man for the jolting words which follow. For now Jesus quite unexpectedly invites this highly rich, well behaved, respectable young man to sell all he has and join his disreputable band of itinerant disciples: 'You lack one thing. Go, sell everything you have, and give it to the poor . . . and come, follow me' (v.22).

In doing this, Jesus, as Fernando Belo points out, offers the young man 'a messianic reading of his practice'. That is, he evaluates his conduct in the light of the Kingdom.[17] Here, the ethic of the law he has been following is found to be inadequate. Whatever he may possess (in terms of material goods or moral merit), he lacks one thing, the freedom which comes to those who have experienced that God is good (10.18). To experience this he must give all that he has to the poor (who lack this!) and follow Jesus.[18]

But the young man's attachment to his possessions proves too much for this. Unlike the first disciples called by Jesus, who promptly leave their possessions, or their family, and follow Jesus (Mark 1.18–20), the young man, we are told, 'went away sad, because he had great wealth' (v.22). He cannot follow Jesus because he is unable to part with his possessions and break with his situation of social status and economic security. But such a radical break is essential for following Jesus. 'Leaving'/'following' are the dialectically related negative and positive moments of the appropriate response to every call to follow Jesus. For Jesus summons us out of our parochial loyalties to family, clan, tribe or nation into the new 'family of God', and invites us to leave the security offered by wealth, status or achievement to trust solely in God's providential care.

This risk the young man is unable to take. His inability comes from his attachment to money and the comfort, status and security it brings. Like our consumerism today this attachment must not be seen merely as an unfortunate personal disposition. It is the outcome of a system which has instilled and which continues to nourish it. As

Belo puts it: 'the dominant codes (his society – and of ours!) have gained the upper hand over him.'[19]

The story, then, climaxes in the invitation of Jesus (10.21), which breaks suddenly and sharply into the secure world of this well-intentioned young man, revealing its flawed fragility. 'You lack one thing. Go, sell everything you have, and give to the poor, and you will have treasure in heaven. Then come follow me' (v.21).[20] This saying, which certainly expresses the mind of Jesus, even if it may not go back to him in its present form,[21] links the following of Jesus to the renunciation of material possessions. There is no doubt that the immediate disciples of Jesus (like those of the Buddha) took this quite literally. They accompanied their master as itinerant teachers and healers: homeless (Luke 9.58), unattached to any family (Mark 3.31–35; Luke 9.59–62), unburdened by any possessions (Matt. 10.9–10), disdaining the protection of even sandals and staff (Matt. 10.10). According to the widely accepted thesis of Gerd Theissen, 'wandering charismatics' like these first disciples of Jesus, supported by small communities of local sympathizers, continued to be the mainstay of early Christianity long after the death of Jesus.[22] Until the emergence of the Hellenistic urban communities, which gradually took over the movement towards the end of the first century, early Christianity (and especially early Palestinian Christianity) was primarily a movement of 'wandering charismatics'. And it was among these first itinerant preachers of christianity, Theissen suggests, that sayings of Jesus (like the one in Mark's story), which call for a radical renunciation of home and possessions, found their appropriate setting.[23] Such drastic sayings were addressed to and preserved by the wandering charismatics and not by the local communities of the sympathizers who lived less radical lives within the normal structures of Judaism.

It is certainly true that the sayings of Jesus, calling for the renunciation of family and of possessions (the two main sources of security in the ancient world), were followed literally only by the close disciples who accompanied him on his preaching tours through Palestine; and, after his death, by the wandering charismatics who were largely responsible for the spread and maintenance of early Christianity. But it would be wrong to limit their relevance to these groups alone.[24] The sayings are addressed to all the followers of Jesus. For they do not merely prescribe concrete actions ('sell everything you have') which could be practised only by radical, élite followers, but they exemplify basic attitudes of freedom which are relevant to all. The story of the Rich Young Man in Mark's Gospel, as the commentary added to it shows, is not meant to be a mere reminder of the concrete instructions on discipleship that Jesus once gave, but an illustration of the kind of anti-greed attitude every reader of the Gospel, that is, every follower of Jesus, must have.

This attitude of anti-greed derives from and is constituted by three basic Gospel insights:

a) It is, first, an expression of Jesus' recognition (which he shares with founders of other religions) that riches are dangerous. This is brought out powerfully in the dialogue between Jesus and his disciples (10.23–27), which immediately follows the story of the Rich Young Man, and serves as an explanatory comment on it.[25] The dialogue is concentric, and centres on the striking aphorism of Jesus, surely one of the most memorable of his sayings, that it is easier for a camel (the largest animal Jesus knows) to go through the eye of a needle (the smallest opening known to him) than for a rich man to enter the Kingdom of God.

Mark 10.23–27

V.23 A   And Jesus looked around and said to his disciples, 'How hard it will be for the rich *to enter the Kingdom of God!'*

V.24 B   And the disciples were *amazed* at his words.

A   But Jesus said to them again, 'Children, how *hard* it is to *enter the Kingdom of God*'!

V.25 C   **It is easier for a camel to go through the eye of a needle than for a rich man to enter the Kingdom of God.**

V.26 B   The disciples were *even more amazed*, and said to each other, 'Then who can be saved?'

V.27 A   Jesus looked at them and said, 'For humans it is *impossible*, but not for God; all things are possible for God.'

The consternation that this flat assertion of the opposition between 'having riches' and 'entering the Kingdom of God' causes among the disciples (v.24; v.26), and Jesus' repeated, uncompromising, and indeed increasingly emphatic insistence on it (what is 'hard' in v.23 becomes 'impossible' in v.25 and v.27), shows us that the anti-greed attitude Jesus advocates is not a counsel of perfection addressed by Jesus to an élite group of his disciples (the wandering charismatics of the early Church or the Roman Catholic 'religious' today), but is an essential dimension of Christian discipleship itself. This becomes even clearer when we look at the second component of this attitude.

b) For the anti-greed attitude which Jesus requires is, secondly, also an expression of trust in the unique goodness of God, to which Jesus refers in the very first words he speaks in the story; 'No one is good except God alone' (10.17). This unique goodness of God is the unspoken presupposition of the whole story.[26] For the kind of renunciation which Jesus demands can make sense only to those who have learned to trust in the goodness of God so absolutely, that they can go out on a mission taking with them 'nothing for the journey except a staff – no bread, no bag, no money in (their) belts' (Mark 6.8); and who have stopped worrying about food, drink or clothing, so completely that they are as carefree as the birds of the air – not because they have (like 'poor' religious today) inexhaustible resources at their disposal, but because they are confident that God, their heavenly Parent, knows that they need these things and will take care of their need (Matt. 6.31).

c) Finally, such an anti-greed attitude is nourished by a concern for the poor. 'Go, sell everything you have', Jesus tells the rich young man, 'and give to the poor' (v. 21). This expresses Jesus' own option for the poor, so conspicuous in his life and teaching. For his life, we know, was lived out in a progressive identification with the needy and the outcast – an ongoing journey from the centre to the periphery, as Kosuke Koyama described it, which did not end until it reached the ultimate boundary of the Cross – beyond which no further movement was possible, for Jesus was here locally outcast and wholly poor;[27] and his teaching was a consistent proclamation of the 'privilege of the poor', to whom alone the good news is proclaimed (Matt. 11.5; Luke 4.18) and God's rule promised (Luke 6.20). But Jesus' instruction to sell all and give to the poor says more than this. Besides defining the option of Jesus, it also spells out the economy of God's rule. Its sell/give reminds us of the buy/give that structures the story of the multiplication of the loaves in Mark 6.35–44. 'Send the people away', the disciples advise Jesus, 'so that *they can go and buy* themselves something to eat' (v. 36). '*You give* them something to eat' replies Jesus (v. 37), replacing the consumer economy of the market with the anti-greed economy of sharing.[28]

Freedom from attachment to things, trust in the unique goodness of God and an effective concern for the poor are thus constituent elements in the anti-greed attitude which is implicit in Jesus' invitation to the rich young man. All three emerge from the foundational

Christian experience of God as Parent, which Jesus communicates to those who follow him (Matt. 11.25−27), and which becomes the basis of their Christian existence. The basic anti-greed attitude which they generate is therefore mandatory for every Christian. The attitude may find expression in various ways today, as it did in early Christianity where it showed itself in a radical renunciation of possessions among the wandering charismatics; in unostentatious almsgiving (Matt. 6.2−4), or a sharing of goods with needy members of the community (Acts 4.32), among the groups of local sympathizers. But in no case can a follower of Jesus dispense with this attitude, and pretend that Jesus' invitation to the rich young man has nothing to say to her or to him.

There is an in-built opposition in Christian discipleship to consumerism, to conspicuous consumption, to the satisfaction of our unbridled wants at the cost of the needs of others, to hoarding our possessions for ourselves instead of sharing them with those in need. Even more than the tribal ethos the Christian ethos is an ethos of anti-greed. However much they would like to do it, the followers of Jesus cannot serve both God and mammon (Matt. 6.24).

B. Anti-Pride: The Ambitious Request of the Sons of Zebedee (Mark 10.35−45)

Mark 10.35−45

V. 35 Then James and John, the sons of Zebedee, came to him and said:
'Teacher, we want you to do for us whatever we ask of you.'

V. 36 And he said to them,
'What do you want me to do for you?'

V. 37 And they said to him,
'Let one of us sit at your right hand, and the other at your left, in your glory.'

V. 38 But Jesus said to them,
'You do not know what you are asking.
Can you drink the cup that I drink, or be baptized with the baptism with which I am baptized?'

V. 39 And they said to him, 'We can.'
And Jesus said to them,
'The cup that I drink you will drink; and with the baptism with which I am baptized, you will be baptized;

V. 40 But to sit at my right hand or at my left is not for me to grant;

the places belong to those for whom they have been prepared.'

V. 41 And when the ten heard it, they became indignant with James and John.

V. 42 Jesus called them to him and said to them, 'You know that those who are regarded as rulers of the gentiles wield lordship over them, and their high officials exercise authority over them.

V. 43 But it shall not be so with you.
Instead, whoever wants to be great among you must be your servant,

V. 44 and whoever wants to be first among you must be slave of all.

V. 45 For the Son of Man did not come to be served but to serve, and to give his life as a ransom for many.'

The story of the Rich Young Man (10.17–27), which brings out the negative moment of Christian discipleship (not serving mammon), is balanced in Mark 10 by a second story, the Request of the Sons of Zebedee (10.35–45), which offers Jesus an occasion to speak about its positive moment (what it means to serve God). The anti-greed attitude taught by the first text is completed by the anti-pride attitude taught in the second.

Both these passages of the Gospel have a similar basic story/ instruction pattern. The story of an encounter between Jesus and someone who comes to him with a request (10.17–23 and 10.35– 40) becomes the occasion for instructions to the disciples on basic attitudes of discipleship (10.23–27 and 10.40–45). But the instructions of Jesus are linked to the introductory story more closely in the first passage than in the second. The lesson on the danger of riches (vv. 23–27), attached to the first story (vv. 17–23) is introduced by Jesus himself. His comment (v. 23) breaks into the painful silence that follows the sad departure of this 'failed vocation', and draws an obvious lesson from his failure. But the teaching on service (vv. 41– 45) added to the second story (vv. 35–40) does not follow immediately upon the request of the Sons of Zebedee. It is occasioned by the reaction of the other disciples to their request (v. 41). This introduces what might seem to be a new topic, but is not really so. For the two parts of the episode (vv. 35–40 and 41–45) are closely linked. The indignation of the disciples (v. 41) in the second part is, after all, occasioned by the ambition of the sons of Zebedee (v. 37) in the first; and the lesson Jesus gives to the ten on service (vv. 42– 45) is very closely linked to what he has told the sons of Zebedee about his martyrdom and theirs (vv. 38–39). Because the Son of

Man comes not to be served but to serve, his coming reaches its fulfilment in the laying down of his life as a ransom for many (v. 45). Service is fulfilled by martyrdom. The two themes of the episode are thus drawn together in the concluding saying of Jesus, which expresses, as possibly no other saying in the Gospels does, the essence of the *dharma* of Jesus which is also that of his disciples.

Still, the two parts of the passage, however closely joined,[29] do treat of two different themes. The request of the sons of Zebedee leads Jesus to speak of martyrdom, as his way to 'glory'; the indignation of the other disciples at their request leads to an instruction on service as the basic attitude of discipleship. It is this second section that I shall focus on, because it is here we best find the Gospel version of the tribal value of anti-pride that we are exploring here.

The section begins (v. 41) by describing the indignation of the ten disciples at the request made by the sons of Zebedee that they be given places of honour in the messianic Kingdom, which, they believe, is soon to be established, because Jesus is already on his way to Jerusalem (vv. 35–37). The indignation of the ten disciples would seem to be unwarranted, since Jesus has in fact refused the sons of Zebedee their request (v. 40) – after having elicited from them their readiness to follow him in martyrdom (vv. 38–39), and having predicted that they would in fact do so (v. 39).[30] But such niceties of narrative logic would not have bothered Mark or his readers. What interests them is how Jesus reacts to the crisis caused by the request of James and John, and to the currents of ambition simmering in the group of his disciples, that this crisis reveals. For the indignation of the ten at the self-serving request of the two brothers is, clearly, an indication of their own undisclosed ambition. They are angry that the sons of Zebedee should have foreclosed an honour that could have been claimed by others among them.

Jesus replies by explicitly contrasting the attitude towards the exercise of power which his disciples must have, with that which is found among earthly rulers; and by proposing his own life as a model for them. His discourse moves from 'the rulers of the gentiles' (v. 42), to 'you' (v. 43) and then on to 'the Son of Man' (v. 45). Earthly rulers 'wield lordship' (*katakyrieuousin*) and 'exercise authority' (*katexouslazousin*) over their subjects. That is, they dominate and exploit them to their own advantage.[31] This is not how the followers of Jesus must behave: 'It shall *not* be so with you.' Nothing could be more forceful than this flat, unadorned yet emphatic prohibition. The exercise of authority among his followers, Jesus says, cannot be like the dominating and exploitative lordship of the rulers of the earth, any more than their attitude to money can be like that of the worshippers of mammon. Once again, then, the followers of Jesus are faced with a choice. Just as they must choose between God and mammon ('you *cannot* serve God and mammon'), they must also choose, as Drewermann has put it, between Christ and Barabbas (Mark 15. 11)[32] – that is, between the way of God's rule and the way of earthly kings ('but it shall *not* be with you'). They must renounce, that is, not only the way of greed but the way of pride as well.

The reason Jesus gives for this is the example of his own life. He, the Son of Man, has come not be served but to serve. To be a servant (*diakonos*), then, is the highest ambition a follower of Jesus can have. Such an attitude stands in direct opposition to the attitudes of 'wielding lordship' (*katakyrieuein*) and 'exercising authority' (*katexousiazein*) shown by the rulers of the earth; and is completely congruent with the life-pattern of Jesus who has come not to be served (*diakonethenai*) but to serve (*diakonesai*), and to 'give his life as a ransom for many'. The followers of Jesus are called away from the pride of the 'rulers of the gentiles' to the anti-pride of Jesus, understood not as self-abasement but as fearless and active service.[33]

Three observations can be made about this attitude of anti-pride or service (*diakonia*) to which Jesus summons his followers:

a) The self-definition which Jesus gives us of his life and his mission, shows us what this attitude really means. To serve is not simply to do something helpful for others. It is to develop a standing attitude of radical self-giving, which will determine the shape of one's life. To serve is to lay down one's life, the way Jesus laid down his life not just at Calvary but all along his 'way' to the Cross, in ceaseless actions of self-giving love.

b) Serving therefore means sharing: sharing not only of what one has (this is only the first small step), but of what one is. The anti-pride to which Jesus summons his followers is thus the fulfilment of their anti-greed. Sharing of possessions leads to a sharing of self. The 'way' of Jesus leads us, therefore, from what Erich Fromm has called the mode of 'having' to the mode of 'being' – where 'having' and 'being' refer to 'two fundamental modes of existence, to two different kinds of orientation towards self and the world, to two different kinds of character structure, the predominance of which determines the totality of a person's thinking, feeling, and acting.'[34] The rich young man and the rulers of the gentiles live in the having-mode. For them to be is to have; that is, to possess things or control people. The more they have the more they believe they 'are'. Jesus invites his followers into a wholly different perception of things. He calls them to a counter-culture, in which to be is to love. One becomes more real and more alive to the extent one gives away all that one 'has' (not just one's material possessions but one's status, one's achievements, one's carefully constructed images of oneself as well), and risks living wholly out of the assurance of God's love.

c) Such dispositions of anti-greed and anti-pride are taught by Jesus not just as individual attitudes but as societal norms. Jesus was not concerned merely with the conversion of individuals, as New Testament scholarship until recently has consistently and wrongly taught, but with the transformation of society.[35] 'The subject supposed by Jesus' ethical teaching', as Ben Wiebe puts it, '. . . contrary to Weiss, Harnack, Schweitzer, Bultmann, Perrin and countless others, is not [primarily] the isolated individual person. It is Israel restored as a community of disciples.'[36] For as his election of the twelve disciples to symbolize the twelve tribes of Israel shows, the aim of Jesus was not leading individuals to 'heaven' (saving souls!), but the eschatological restoration of Israel, as a step towards the apocalyptic restoration of humankind.

Anti-greed and anti-pride are therefore not just individual virtues which Jesus demanded from those who wished to follow him. They are the structuring principles of the alternative community he sought to build. They are, therefore, meant to be community values. They are to be realized not just in individuals who strive to be 'poor' (Luke 6.20) and 'humble' (Matt. 5.3; 11.28) in the sense that has been explained above, but in the life style and functioning of the community as a whole. It is the whole Church (and not just a Mother Theresa in it) that must display conspicuously the tribal values of anti-greed and anti-pride as taught and lived out by Jesus. That is, it must demonstrate its poverty and its humility (its serviceability), as well as its option for the humble and the poor, in its transactions within the community (bishop–priest; priest–laity; men–women; rich–poor clean caste–dalit), as well as in its uncompromising prophetic stance towards the huge, immensely greedy, power-hungry, and status-conscious world outside. It is such anti-greed and anti-pride that are the true marks of the Church of Christ. For it is just these that make the Church the contrast community (the light of the world and the salt of the earth) that Jesus intended his community to be.

NOTES

1   Note Dumont's perceptive comment: 'On the whole, the essential form of the system [of caste] is of a hierarchical polarity. One might say that India has institutionalized inequality just as we [the West] are trying to do the same with equality. In the relation of two men, modern western society presupposes equality to the point that delicate situations are likely to arise where subordination is necessary. India on the contrary emphasizes inequality to the point that situations tending to equality are unstable and conflict is called for to solve them.' Louis Dumont, 'For a Sociology of India', *Contributions to Indian Sociology* 1 (1957), pp. 7–22[18].

2   S. Bosu Mullick, Edwin Jaydas, Anto Akkara and Anita Jaydas, *Indigenous Identity: Crisis and Reawakening* (Delhi, Navin Prakashan Kendra (ISPCK, 1993), pp. 8–9.

3   Paulus Kullu, 'Tribal Religion and Culture', *Jeevadhara* 24 (140) 1994, pp. 89–109.

4   The problems of applying the anthropological notion of 'tribe' (itself a highly ambiguous term) to the 'tribes' of the Bible is discussed in J. W. Rogerson, *Anthropology of the Old Testament* (Sheffield, JSOT Press, 1984), pp. 86–101. In spite of all ambiguities, the designation remains a convenient one. This 'predefinitional' term needs no doubt to be sharpened, but it does describe a basic culture common to groups widely separated in space and time. Robert Parkin, *The Munda of Central India: An Account of their Social Organization* (Delhi, OUP, 1992), p. 12, has shown how 'most of the tribes of central India, regardless of language, have systems of affinal alliance (cross cousin marriage) very similar to similar systems existing outside India – in South East Asia, ancient China, Australia, the Amazon Basin and parts of Oceania, some of which bear a very detailed resemblance to what is found in central India. Since these areas are sufficiently isolated to rule out historical contacts, these similarities can only be the result of more fundamental structural properties common to all.' It makes sense, then, to speak of a tribal culture, spread over space and time, even though awareness of the fuzziness of the term will make us wary of hasty comparisons.

5   Traditionally the settlement of Israel has been understood as the conquest of Canaan by 'all Israel' in a lightening campaign under Joshua (Josh. 1–12). Discrepancies in the biblical narrative itself (Josh. 13–19; Judg. 1), as well as conflicting archeological evidence, make this account of Israel's origins unlikely. Instead the settlement, it has been suggested, may have taken place either (1) by piecemeal conquest by various groups entering Canaan from different directions over a long space of time (Albright, Wright, Bright); or (2) through the peaceful sedenterization of semi-nomadic tribes in the uninhabited highlands of Palestine (Alt, Noth, Weippert); or (3)

through the revolt of the Canaanite peasantry against the military aristocracy of the city states, which controlled and taxed them, under the influence of a numerically small but ideological powerful group under Moses, which had escaped from Egypt and brought with them the cult of a liberating God (Yhwh) and the blue print of a new community (the Sinai covenant) which served to catalyse the revolt (Mendenhall, Gottwald). 'Israel' as a federation of tribes certainly did not exist before the settlement. Whether it was formed by the merging of nomadic or semi-nomadic tribes who had entered Canaan from outside, or was the result of a process of 'retribalization' through which the revolting peasants of Canaan created an egalitarian order in contrast to that of the city states they had overwhelmed, will depend on the theory of Israel's origins that one follows – cf. Marvin Chaney, 'Ancient Palestinian Peasant Movements and the Formation of Premonarchic Israel', in David N. Freedman and David F. Graf (eds.), *Palestine in Transition: The Emergence of Ancient Israel* (Sheffield, Almond Press, 1983), pp. 39–89; Norman Gottwald, *The Hebrew Bible: A Socio-Literary Introduction* (Philadelphia, Fortress Press, 1985), pp. 261–88.

6   Norman Gottwald, *The Tribes of Yahweh: A Sociology of the Religion of Liberated Israel, 1250–1050 BCE* (Maryknoll, NY, Orbis Books 1979), p. 613.

7   ibid., p. 614.

8   ibid., pp. 615–16.

9   On the emergence of the monarchy see *Semeia* 37 (1986) which has an excellent collection of articles on the sociological factors responsible for the rise of the Israelite monarchy.

10   Marcus Borg, *Jesus, a New Vision: Spirit, Culture and the Life of Discipleship* (San Francisco, Harper, 1987), pp. 150–71.

11   James C. Scott, 'Protest and Profanation: Agrarian Revolt and the Little Tradition', *Theory and Society* 4 (1977), 1–38; 211–246 [224] quoted in John Dominic Crossan, *The Historical Jesus: The Life of a Mediterranean Jewish Peasant* (Edinburgh, T. & T. Clark, 1991), p. 263.

12   ibid., p. 225.

13   Borg, *Jesus, a New Vision*, pp. 129–49.

14   Drewermann, *Das Markus Evangelium* 2 (Olten, Walter Verlag, 1990), p. 155.

15   The order in which the commandments are cited varies in the manuscript tradition. Some MSS follow the order of the Decalogue in the Masoretic text; others that in the LXX. The 'Do not defraud' (*me apostereses*) is not found in any version of the Decalogue. It may sum the demands of the ninth and tenth commandments, or it may as Gnilka suggests be an allusion to Sir. 4.1 which forbids us to 'defraud' the poor of their living, that is the poor labourers of their just wages – Joachim Gnilka, *Das Evangelium nach Markus*, 2 (Zurich, Benziger, 1979), p. 87.

16   cf. Robert H. Gundry, *Mark: A Commentary on His Apology for the Cross* (Grand Rapids, Eerdman's, 1993), p. 554; Rudolf Pesch, *Das Markusevangelium* 2 (Freiburg, Herder [HtKNT], 1977), p. 140.

17   Fernando Belo, *A Materialistic Reading of the Gospel of Mark* (NY, Orbis Books, 1982), p. 172.

18   Belo (ibid., 172) draws attention to the structural oppositions in the story: You *lack* one thing/whatever you *have* – the poor *lack*/whatever you *have* (give to them).

19   ibid.

20   As Gnilka p. 84 points out, Mark 10. 17–21 is a pronouncement story in form, and v.21 is its climactic saying.

21   For a good discussion of the tradition history of the passage see Pesch, *Das Markusevangelium*, p. 142.

22   Gerd Theissen, *The First Followers of Jesus: A Sociological Analysis of the Earliest Christianity* (London, SCM, 1978), pp. 1–14. Though Theissen's theory has found such widespread agreement among scholars that it is almost a consensus position today, it has been critiqued (1) for its exegesis by Wolfgang Stegemann, 'Vagabond Radicalism in Early Christianity? A Historical and Theological Discussion of a Thesis Proposed by Gerd Theissen', in W. Schottroff and W. Stegemann (eds.), *God of the Lowly: Socio-Historical Interpretations of the Bible* (Maryknoll, NY, Orbis Books, 1984), pp. 148–68 and (2) for its sociology by Thomas Schmeller, *Brechungen: Urchristliche Wandercharismatiker im Prisma Soziologisch Orientierter Exegese* (SBS 136) (Stuttgart, KBW, 1989). Stegemann rightly points to the absence of serious source-critical analyses in Theissen's use of gospel texts. In fact the 'cynic' interpretation of the Jesus movement he offers comes from sayings that do not go back to Jesus, but reflect the interpretation of evangelists, especially Luke. Schmeller notes that the wandering charismatics were much more varied in their function than Theissen makes them out to be, and exercised a much smaller role in the post-Easter Church than Theissen imagines. Both critiques are justified, but do not destroy the basic insight of Theissen's masterly synthesis.

23   ibid.

24   So too Schmeller (Brechungen, p. 105), who argues that after Easter all the sayings of Jesus, even the most radical, were given a new meaning that was relevant and binding on all Christians.

25   See George Soares–Prabhu, 'Good News to the Poor: The Social Implications of the Message of Jesus', in D. S. Amalorpavadass (ed.), *The Indian Church in the Struggle for a New Society* (Bangalore, NBCLC), pp. 609–26 [611–13] for a somewhat more detailed analysis of the text.

26   So too Drewermann, *Das Markus Evangelium*, p. 121–22.

27   Kosuke Koyama, 'Hallowed be Your Name', *International Review of Mission* 49 (1980–81) pp. 280–82.

28   Belo, p. 159.

29   Note the literary links binding the first part of the passage (vv. 35–40) with the second (vv. 41–45): *we wish* in v. 35 and *whoever wishes* in v. 44; *you do not know* in v. 38 and *you know* in v. 42.

30   This prediction, probably a *vaticinium ex eventu*, might conflict with the tradition in John 21.23, if the Johannine 'beloved disciple' is identified with the younger Zebedee. But this identification is by no means certain, cf. Pesch, *Das Markusevangelium* pp. 159–60; Gnilka, *Das Evangelium nach Markus* pp. 102–103.

31   Werner Foerster, *TDNT* 2, p. 575; 3, p. 1098.

George M. Soares-Prabhu

32 Drewermann, *Das Markus Evangelium*, p. 147.

33 Compare the parallel in Mark 23.11–12: 'The greatest among you will be your servant (*diakonos*); for whoever exalts himself will be humbled and whoever humbles himself (*tapeinosei*) will be exalted.' To 'humble oneself' is thus equivalent to becoming a servant. The much misunderstood 'humility' demanded by Jesus is not putting oneself down, but placing one's acknowledged gifts at the service of others.

34 Erich Fromm, *To Have or To Be?* (London, Abacus, 1979), p. 33.

35 cf. Gerhard Lohfink, *Jesus and Community: The Social Dimension of Christian Faith*, (Philadelphia, Fortress Press, 1984), p. 1–5; Ben Wiebe, 'Messianic Ethics: Response to the Kingdom of God', *Interpretation* 45 (1991) pp. 29–42.

36 Wiebe, 'Messianic Ethics', pp. 30–31.

9

The Syrophoenician Woman: Mark 7.24–30

HISAKO KINUKAWA

The core cultural values of the ancient Mediterranean world such as shame-honour, pollution-purity, patron-client, out of which the biblical narratives emerged have parallels in Asian culture. One such value, shame/honour, shores up racial exclusivism, single-group identity and one-nation theory, and this prompts Japanese theologian, Hisako Kinukawa, to look at her own context and the women who approached Jesus in Mark's Gospel. She sees in their experience a way forward in relationships with both Koreans who live in her country as resident aliens and the indigenous minority group in Japanese society.

This piece forms part of a chapter in Kinukawa's book, *Women and Jesus in Mark: A Japanese Feminist Perspective* (Maryknoll, NY, Orbis Books, 1994), pp. 51–65, in which her use of anthropological methods to look at the biblical period is a pioneering effort by an Asian biblical scholar.

Hisako Kinukawa is actively involved in women's groups in Japan. She is on the staff of Tokyo Women's Christian University.

CULTIC PURITY

The story of the Syrophoenician woman in Mark's Gospel begins with a plea for healing and ends with the success of the healing, but it is clear that the miracle is not reported for its own sake. The discourse between the woman and Jesus centers around eating bread, granted that 'eating bread' is a metaphor.

The story is preceded by long discourses with the Pharisees and some scribes concerning the fact that Jesus' disciples eat with unclean hands, purity in dietary activities (7.1–13), and a discourse with the disciples on personal defilement by things from within (7.17–23). Jesus openly undermined the purity laws and the traditions built up around them by citing phrases from Isaiah (29.13) and showing that recent traditions were making void God's commandment. Then Jesus gave his disciples additional teachings on internal and external sources of defilement.[1]

Restrictions on food and eating, which played a very important role in cultic purity and integrity of the holy (Lev. 11) could also be the major barrier between the Israelites and gentiles. Not only the length of the discourse,[2] but the emphatic pursuit of its main idea through different examples signify the importance of the theme in Mark's Gospel and suggest how deeply the Israelites were bound by their concept of purity, which was the cause of their exclusive attitude toward outsiders.

Jesus here again challenges the barrier-building between the pure and the unclean and negates an artificially warranted cultic purity. He has executed another boundary-breaking feat. Achtermeier points out that Mark's schematic intention is apparent here.[3] His perspective toward the mission to the gentiles may already be implicitly suggested in this section.

If the main obstacle to integrating the Jews and gentiles is removed, the concrete practice of accepting gentiles will follow.[4] So the next story may be a practical illustration of the liberation from the prejudice engendered by the purity laws. If Jesus leaves the land and the people who claim to be 'clean' and enters into an 'unclean' land, the definition of defilement will be put to the test and the tradition made void by Jesus himself. This is what Mark may have intended.[5] Apparently the story has absorbed Markan insights motivated by his redactional intentions for the community of faith of his time.

MARK'S CROSS-RACIAL COMMUNITY

The issue, however, has become intense for Mark, because he is writing his Gospel when gentiles already belong to the community of faith.[6] Mark has to be concerned about social separation and attitudes that would be very unbecoming for the new community.[7] Thus Mark's Gospel reflects the struggles being undergone in his community.

But we do not dare say that all these pericopes are the evangelist's inventive creations. The story of the Syrophoenician woman, which follows the record of these discourses, could have been detrimental to Mark's purpose, given his current situation. Yet he did not adjust his story accordingly. Therefore by depicting Jesus' interaction with the woman and his healing of a pagan gentile – the only example of this in Mark's Gospel[8] – the story may reflect much of Jesus' own attitude toward gentiles. We will see this later in detail. According to Taylor, the linguistic characteristics in the story suggest Aramaic tradition and Mark has adapted the story in the interests of gentile readers.[9]

By putting the story after Jesus' long discourse with the Pharisees and the scribes and then with his disciples over the purity laws, Mark lets Jesus withdraw from Jewish territory to gentile territory (7.24). 'From there he set out and went away to the region of Tyre.' Thus, Mark opens up the opportunity of Jesus' gentile itinerary and allows Jesus to avoid possible danger after he has dismissed the most important part of the traditional Jewish laws.[10]

There is much discussion among scholars about whether or not Jesus really crossed the border. There should have been nothing hindering Jesus from going any place, but it is another question whether Jesus actually intended a mission to the gentiles. We can see Jesus' perceptive and receptive attitude toward gentiles only from his interaction with the woman. Possibly the attitude shown in his words and deeds might have prepared the way for a gentile mission in the days to come.

> [Mark] wishes to illustrate the Lord's freedom from the purity regulations and to demonstrate that the apostolic mission to the gentiles was pre-figured in the earthly ministry; and he infers from the tradition's reference to the woman's Syrophoenician connections that the journey beyond Palestine was an excursion into the region of Tyre and Sidon – totally disregarding the possibility that she may have been thought of by the tradents as an *emigrée* resident in Galilee.[11]

In an age and culture that made a clear distinction between the holy land and the rest, the journey covering the entire gentile region surrounding Galilee from 'the region of Tyre' (7. 24) to 'the region of Decapolis through Sidon' (7. 31) is very symbolic. Tyre may be mentioned because the woman is a Syrophoenician, but since in the Old Testament Tyre is said to be proud and a threat to the Israelites and is always recorded with Sidon[12] (Isa. 23; Jer. 47.4; Ezek. 27, 28; Joel 3.4–8; Zech. 9.2) as polluted by materialism,[13] it is again very symbolic that Jesus dares to cross the border and go into the most despised, unclean territory.

All the places have already been mentioned (3.8; 5.20) in the

Gospel. Some, including Bultmann, reject the idea that the journey to the gentile territory could have been historical. It may be that in order to edit the healing miracles in the gentile cycle,[14] Mark added the two verses to 'provide a topological framework and connecting links, to show that Jesus' fame had spread beyond the border of Palestine, and to give a missionary coloring.'[15] Elisabeth Schüssler Fiorenza, too, finds the original location of the story in Galilee.[16] It should be said for certain that the horizon of Mark's worldview is expanded from that of Jesus' earthly mission as Mark tries to respond to the needs of gentile readers.

Many have also assigned the 'first' of verse 27 to Markan editorial work, because the 'first' weakens the impact and the comparison on which Jesus' rejection relies, but the remainder is assigned to the unitary composition.[17]

JESUS TRIES TO HIDE FROM THE CROWD: THE WOMAN'S UNEXPECTED BEHAVIOR

'And from there he set out and went away to the region of Tyre' (v. 24). Jesus seems to be seeking privacy. After a lengthy dispute with the Pharisees and the scribes that included a bold denunciation of their tradition on purity, his life may be in danger. Also, perhaps he is withdrawing to reflect upon his ministry.[18] He may be filled with sorrow for the hardness of people's hearts that makes their faith exclusive, and for his lack of success at proclaiming the good news in the heart of the temple-centered religion.

Seclusion from the crowd is repeatedly recorded in Mark's Gospel (1.35–39; 2.1; 3.20; 6.31, 45–46; 7.24; 9.30–31). In this particular case Jesus enters into a house, in line with the pattern in this Gospel that he never enters a synagogue to teach after his visit to Nazareth.[19] As usual, the seclusion is not successful. Somehow his fame has reached a gentile woman who comes to interrupt him.

As investigated so far, the story of the woman's encounter with Jesus is probably complete in verses 25–30, with verse 24 added by Mark. So the story begins with verse 25: 'But a woman whose little daughter had an unclean spirit immediately heard about him, and she came and bowed down at his feet.'

'Immediately' after the woman has heard of Jesus, she comes to him. What she has heard is not written, but probably she has heard something about Jesus as a popular healer, because she has a daughter with an unclean spirit. Though 'bowing down at his feet' may show one's inferior position in the social relationships in the patriarchal society, it is an action only accepted among men. Her bowing down is not considered to honor the status of Jesus as a male teacher.[20] On the contrary, it is a serious misdeed which brings disgrace on him. Women of the time are not expected to come out of their homes where they have their role, much less to make a plea in a public setting. There is some evidence that the contacts with Hellenism and Roman society may have given some impetus to an improved status for women.[21] But, generally speaking, her invasive solicitation would make a man lose his face in the culture of honor/shame. It is something very unusual for an anonymous woman, unknown and unrelated to the Jews, to dare to break his privacy. Nevertheless, she does.

She is introduced as 'a gentile, of Syrophoenician origin'. 'Syrophoenician' is used to distinguish 'Syrian-' from 'Carthaginian-' and 'Libyan-' Phoenicians. These designations reflect the nations of Jesus' own day. Matthew changes this to 'Canaanite', which was traditionally used to characterize local people hostile to the Jews. So racially she is Syrophoenician, but politically and socioculturally she is described as a gentile. Thus she is introduced not only as a non-Jew but also as a pagan by upbringing.[22]

Myers, who assumes that Jesus journeyed to the north beyond the border, sees here 'another Markan archetype, representative of the hellenized populations of the area.'[23] Others argue that such a detailed description of the woman should not occur in a place where almost everyone is gentile; it would be more suitable if the story were set in Galilee, a foreign place to her. Or it may be a way of letting the listeners to whom the miracle story is addressed know that she is not a Hellenistic Jew but a foreigner. She is presented as a gentile whom the traditions of the Jews have excluded and whom the community of Mark is to accept.[24]

It becomes clear that she is 'unclean' by birth, a foreigner and a female, and 'untouchable' because of her daughter who is possessed by an unclean spirit. She must know well as a woman of that culture and that time that she would defile Jesus and would be accused by his disciples. From the very fact that she dares cross her Rubicon, we can infer that she is on the verge of being desperate in her great need of help for her daughter. Daughters' issues are mothers' issues.

They are both thus triply polluted: foreign, female, and demon-possessed. She tries to be as polite as possible, but she is already far beyond the reserve she is expected to show. She is determined to encounter Jesus. 'She begged him to cast the demon out of her daughter' (v. 26).

JESUS' RESPONSE TO THE WOMAN

The phrase that follows her begging – 'And he said to her' – is very important in this story. It is naturally expected that a man put off by aggressive cries for help will turn away with anger in that patriarchal society. In addition, rabbis are prohibited contact with women. Matthew has Jesus giving her the silent treatment, as expected.

According to Mark, Jesus answers in two sentences: 'Let the children be fed first,' and 'for it is not fair to take the children's food and throw it to the dogs.' Most scholars have investigated the meanings and implications of the words 'first' and 'dogs' in his answer. Both words function to support Jewish superiority and define gentiles as second-class citizens, though 'first' may soften this tension by suggesting the possible existence of a 'second'.

In any case, Jesus' rebuff of her is understandable only if we pay attention to the social context of the culture of honor/shame. Jesus was expected to defend the collective honor of his people. And from the structural viewpoint we can see that the difficulty to be overcome in the story is increasing, since the miracle-worker himself becomes the obstacle. In this case another tension between different cultures is perceptible.[25]

Scholars suggest that 'first' is an editorial insertion by Mark, who had gentile readers in mind (cf. 'to the Jew first, and also to the Greek,' Romans 1.16).[26] Bultmann adds that the word 'weakens the comparison on which the argument of Jesus is based' and that the whole first sentence may be a later addition to Mark's text.[27] Burkill sees here the influence of Pauline teaching in Romans 1.16 and 11.11.[28] On the other hand, Taylor supports verse 27a as original, with the reason that it is what provokes the woman's witty reply in verse 28.[29] Belo asserts more positively that the first stage of Jesus' strategy aims at satisfying the Jews and the second at satisfying gentiles.[30]

There is no question that Jesus, as a Jew, started his ministry among the Jews. And his movement then became a sect of Judaism. Mark seems to think that the Jews have priority over the gentiles in hearing the gospel, the gentiles hearing the gospel only after Jesus' crucifixion (15.38–39 and 13.10). Yet, he wants to make clear that the mission to the gentiles is prefigured during Jesus' earthly ministry. He adds 'first' in 27a in light of the new second wave in the community of faith.[31] Therefore I conclude that Jesus' original answer lacked the 'first' and sounded very blunt to the woman.

The harshness continues in the latter half of Jesus' answer. The word used for 'dogs' is a diminutive indicating 'little dogs' or 'puppies'. There is evidence of Jewish writers describing gentiles as 'dog' though not as 'puppies', when they refer to their vices.[32] In the Bible the word is applied to 'unclean' persons such as gentiles and Sodomites (Deut. 23.18; Rev. 22.15). Taylor thinks that the use of 'puppies' rather than 'dogs' softens the apparent harshness of Jesus' answer by giving a gentler tone to his speech and showing that Jesus is speaking of household dogs. He suggests that this testifies to 'a tension in the mind of Jesus concerning the scope of his ministry, and that, in a sense, he is speaking to himself as well as to the woman. Her reply shows that she is quick to perceive this.'[33] Taylor goes beyond the text into analyzing the psyche of both Jesus and the woman.

Myers, in contrast, claims that Mark uses 'puppies' to express a traditional insult for the purpose of giving dramatic effect. He also quotes Theissen to say that the story both assumes and reflects the ethnic, cultural, and sociopolitical hostility between the Jews and their gentile neighbors.[34]

Others claim that 'puppy' is taken from a maxim, a proverb, or an epithet popular among the Jews.[35] Burkill, using form-critical analysis to trace back four evolutionary phases of the story, states that the oldest phase of the story reflects a time when the Jews were still enjoying the first prerogative. He sees no hint that 'there is some uncertainty in Jesus' own mind about the character of the divine purpose.'[36] Opposing Taylor's attempt to soften the harshness, he says: 'To call a woman "a little bitch" is no less abusive than to call a woman "a bitch" without qualification.'[37] According to his analysis, there was no need to soften any harshness until the gentiles began flowing into Mark's community of faith. His form-critical analysis gives some clues about how the story underwent crucial changes.

Nevertheless, says Burkill, the woman 'was able to indicate the shape of things to come. Her insight was foresight; she discerned in advance the Lord of the gentile churches, and duly received a miraculous award.'[38] Yet to go this far may well be speculation. For the moment, I will not try to clarify what 'puppy' means, but simply to take Jesus' phrase as the same kind of harsh expression in the woman's face as in the first half with 'first' being added later.

But other important words seem to have been overlooked by the scholars quoted above. Why does Jesus use 'allow' (in the second person singular imperative) and command her directly, instead of using 'let them be fed'? Why does he use the rather rough word 'throw' instead of 'give'? His language sounds defensive.

THE WOMAN'S PERSISTENCE

If any woman in a contemporary, individually oriented society were to hear such a response, she would become too angry even to remain there, preferring to endure her daughter's suffering rather than swallow such an affront. But this woman has been accustomed since birth to being subjugated and looked down upon; she has shouldered all sorts of grief and sacrificed herself for the honor of men. Having been taught to remain silent, hidden, and obedient all through her life, she only hears from Jesus what she is used to hearing. His response would not upset her. On the contrary, she must be well aware that merely her appearing there is defiling and goes against the accepted custom.

But she is also determined. That is why she can take him on and respond very actively. She is caught between life and death and she has to be aggressive if she and her daughter are to live. So she uses the same word that Jesus uses but in her own way. For her, to be a dog does not mean to be servile. She answers, 'Sir, even the dogs under the table eat the children's crumbs' (v. 28). For her, dogs are domestic animals. The way she uses the word shows that she thinks of them as cherished parts of the family. If the Jews had also used the word in this sense, the negative connotation would not have existed and the Jews would not have identified the gentiles with animals that they loved. The woman's response to Jesus indicates cultural difference in attitudes toward dogs. In any case, she is unexpectedly defending the right of her people.

Witherington is uncertain that the Jews in this period had domesti-
cated dogs, although he finds examples of the Jews playing with
puppies.[39] Francis Dufton has drawn our attention to the different
cultural backgrounds of the Jews and the gentiles: 'The Jews were
not pet-lovers. To them dogs were the dirty, unpleasant and savage
animals which roamed the streets in packs, scavenging for food.'[40]

If this is the case, it would have been quite natural for the Jews
to use the word to abuse gentiles, infidels, and, later, Christians.
Dufton even adds that 'the word was appropriate not only because
these people were despised, but also because they were outside the
house of Israel.'[41]

On the other hand, the woman is talking about dogs *inside*. If the
gentiles have a special fondness for dogs, children would enjoy giving
them tidbits from their tables. Thus we can also understand why
Jesus uses 'throw', which refers to bread for the dogs running outside.
The Jews need to 'throw' the bread from the window if they wish to
feed dogs.

It is clever of the woman to affirm Jesus' saying at first[42] and then
make full use of it to strike right back. She is intent on opening up
the impasse she is facing. All we know about her daughter is that
she has an unclean spirit and is very sick. In a society in which
women are men's property from birth to death and are valued by
giving birth to boys, girls are often regarded as a troublesome burden
to their families until they can be safely married off to a suitable
husband.[43] To accomplish this, fathers have to protect their virginity
and to prepare a large dowry. But this daughter cannot count on
following this process since she is sick and unclean, secluded and
ostracized. Apparently she has been left with her mother, or the
woman has been left with her daughter. In any case, it is the mother
who has to face adverse circumstances and carve a way out. The
woman who expected to be invisible becomes visible and acts; suppressing any feelings of fear and hesitation that she might have, she
knows they have little to lose and they must gain life.

Though many scholars, including women scholars, admire her wit
or uppityness, I do not think these qualities are the issue here. Rather,
a woman who is oppressed and held to be worthless, living in such
a patriarchal society and caring for her suffering daughter, is driven
into an impossible situation and cannot find any other solution than
to forget tradition, neglect social custom, and rush ahead recklessly
to Jesus. She can no longer turn back. She risks everything on Jesus.

This is her last resort. If she should be admired for anything, it is for her self-commitment in trust.

INTERACTION BETWEEN THE WOMAN AND JESUS

We are now ready to deal with the question of why Jesus' answer to the woman is extremely offensive. Metaphor or not, proverb or not, Jesus in fact compares her and her people to dogs and directly expresses his people's hatred toward them. Sharon H. Ringe correctly observes that there is no scene of domestic coziness here, with family and pets happily coexisting under one roof.[44]

Jesus, rejecting her plea point-blank, elbows her aside and tries to shake her off. 'Allow' at least indicates that Jesus is personally facing her. As Ringe says, he might 'be tired' or expressing 'the racism and sexism that characterized his society'.[45] We cannot tell why he answers so bluntly, but we do know that the gentile woman hangs on tenaciously and refuses to be shaken off.

Mark places the story after the long debate with Jesus' opponents and the long didactic conversation with his disciples. Jesus may wish to be left alone for meditation. He may be filled with sorrow and exasperation because he has to face the reality that the heart of the gospel has not reached his people. Why would he accept a gentile woman when he is so concerned about his compatriots? Or he might be wondering how this gentile woman could understand and accept him while his own circle is so obtuse. In the latter case, then, he paradoxically affirms her. And furthermore, the phrase 'Allow the children to be fed *first*' could mean that Jesus has in fact been open to the gentiles. He could be taking out his feelings on this gentile woman, using harsh words not because of her but because of his compatriots. Seen the other way around, Jesus could be attacking the lack of understanding and faith of his fellow Jews.

Jesus said to her, 'For saying that, you may go. The demon has left your daughter' (v. 29). His attitude seems to have changed from rejection to affirmation. She has made it clear to Jesus that Jesus should become Jesus and challenged him to cross another 'holy' barrier between Jews and gentiles: the racial barrier. As a Jew, Jesus is embedded in the social and cultural circumstances that may have made him hesitate to cross the border. In this context, she frees Jesus to be fully himself. Jesus, 'the boundary-breaker', may not have needed the encounter with her to cross the racial barrier, but certainly it is the woman that has created the opportunity for him to cross it and step over to her side. She has set the stage for him to act out his mission. She has enabled Jesus to see the situation in a different way and freed him to act in a way apparently blocked to him before.[46] Thus, the barrier between the Jews and gentiles has been opened.[47]

Scholars have made a variety of comments about this woman. (1) The intelligent retort of her argument prevails over that of Jesus. She 'wins' the contest.[48] (2) Her bold, assertive faith wins Jesus' favor and he grants her request.[49] This is woman's wit and persistence.[50] (3) Jesus interprets her persistence as 'faith' and tells her it has been effective.[51] (4) Her verbal riposte gives the twist to this story.[52] (5) Jesus endorses the woman's indomitable spirit.[53]

These are not appropriate when we read the story from the viewpoint of interactional relationship without which this story cannot be understood. Her intuition about who Jesus should be and Jesus' sensitivity to the marginalized are drawn into one vortex and create a mutual transformation.

Thus Jesus, crossing the boundary, allows himself to be 'defiled' and to become least in order to break through the exclusively group-oriented faith of his fellow Jews and redefine the community of faith in its radically new sense. The woman, along with her daughter, has been resurrected from death. The event clearly sets forth who Jesus is to be as the life-giving Christ. Jesus is motivated to act, inviting the gentile, the socially outcast, the materially poor, the sick, the oppressed, and the rejected into God's community, which has been occupied by the privileged people protected by their purity laws.

PARALLELS WITH JAPAN

I would like to point out some parallels between first-century Palestine and Japan on the issue of ethnic exclusivism and human rights claims.

The Israelites kept their ethnic identity and national integrity through holding to the laws and cultic traditions. It was very important, especially for men, to keep their family lineages pure. So they excluded foreigners from their ethnic borders in order to retain their purity of blood. Given their history, it might have been inevitable for them to live this way; geographically they were defenseless against foreign invasions and were invaded by one foreign power after another. Thus it also seems natural for Jesus as a Jew to defend his people and not to want to dilute their ethnic integrity.

Japan's Ethnic Exclusivism

Japan as a country is also known for its ethnic exclusivism, though the causes are different from those affecting the Israelites. Geographically the land of Japan, consisting of four main islands surrounded by almost four thousand small islands, is separated from any other country by the oceans. Even the nearest country, Korea, is at least ninety-three miles across the Japan Sea, which is very rough with storms and seasonal typhoons. Because of these geographical advantages, Japan has never been exposed to the threat of being conquered by other countries. In addition, the country is favored by mild climate.

Ethnically, there has been a myth, which is actually an illusion, that the Japanese people are a homogeneous race. This myth has given rise to the belief that it is important to maintain the purity of Japanese blood. It has also cultivated a spirit of homogeneous 'harmony' that functions only centripetally and goes hand-in-hand with the characteristics of the culture of shame: group-orientedness, dyadic personality, and gender-role difference. The result has been difficulty in accepting and respecting other people as they are, and in the colonized people and aborigines being deprived of their human rights. Ethnic homogeneity has been identified with superiority, connected with the religious concept of purity, and used by the authorities to exploit other peoples.

The 'Koreans Living in Japan'

The racial exclusivism of the Japanese has persecuted the seven hundred thousand 'Koreans living in Japan' – Ainus, Okinawans, and the outcast village people – as 'inside others'.[54] These people have been discriminated against and deprived of their right to live with their distinct cultures. They have been dealt with as if they were objects and treated as if they never existed. Ainus and Okinawans are aborigines who have been victimized throughout the course of history as a minority. 'Koreans living in Japan' and 'Chinese living in Japan' have a different history. They are the victims of the colonial invasions carried out by the Japanese military government between 1910 and 1945. They are those who were forced to leave their home countries and come to Japan as a cheap labor force, and their children who were born during and after the Second World War. During the war, it was claimed that they were all Japanese, and they were thus made to participate in the war in many degrading ways, one of the worst being the case of young girls who were taken to the battlefields to comfort Japanese soldiers.

These things were all done by the Japanese military government under the name of imperial commands. All kinds of exploitation of human rights were thus carried out by the divine will of the emperor. The power of this word, when directly connected with the divine power, wielded dictatorship. With the defeat of Japan, the Koreans, the Chinese, and all people in colonized Asian countries who had been claimed to be Japanese were liberated from the dictatorship of the Japanese military government. In 1910, only 780 Koreans lived in Japan, but in 1945 the Korean residents swelled to between 2,400,000 and 2,600,000. (So far about 300,000 Koreans have chosen to be naturalized as Japanese citizens.) Many Koreans and Chinese who were in Japan at the end of the war returned to their home countries, while many others remained in Japan because of the unsettled circumstances and for economic reasons. The new Japanese government unilaterally deprived these people of their Japanese citizenship. In addition, a last imperial edict was issued just a day before the new Constitution came into force. This edict has bound all the remaining Koreans and Chinese until today, drastically changing their destiny. Actually it took the form of an immigration control act, but it apparently aimed at maintaining public order by exercising strict control over the remaining Koreans, the number of whom reached more than 700,000. They were classified as 'inside others' without citizenship, voting rights, or social security.[55]

At present there are about 687,000 Koreans and 68,000 Chinese living in Japan, ninety percent of whom belong to the second or later generations without speaking Korean and knowing traditional Korean life. Since they speak, think, and behave just like Japanese, it is hard to tell from their appearance whether or not any given individual is a Korean living in Japan.

Despite this fact, under the Alien Registration Law they have been required as foreigners to carry their registration cards with their fingerprints. Criminals are the only ones required by Japanese law to be fingerprinted. Therefore when 'Koreans living in Japan' become sixteen years old and get their fingers printed on the registration cards they must always carry, they are made to feel like criminals. There have been many grass-roots movements against the finger-printing policy, among both foreigners and Japanese.[56]

Worst of all, exclusivism based on the myth of a single-race nation with pure blood had fermented among the Japanese people an idea that the Koreans represented an undeveloped, retrogressive, stagnant, and uncivilized society.[57] Thus they have been subjugated, dehumanized, and despised in every imaginable way. We Japanese people have failed to ask ourselves how we should relate to those who have a different and distinctive culture. Besides the poor legal supports, these people have had to suffer social discrimination as well as degrading treatment by Japanese citizens. It is a tragedy for both sides to live with such prejudice.

Like the people in the outcast villages, they had to conceal their identity by using Japanese names for a long time.[58] Recently more Koreans have dared to claim their identities as Koreans, but even in primary schools, children need a good deal of courage to claim their Korean names. Children, despised by their classmates, feel ashamed of themselves and afraid of being assaulted, isolated, and made 'inside others'.

The deep-rooted Japanese prejudice has caused most Koreans to hide themselves as if they were 'guilty'. Koreans themselves tend to accept negative self-images created without foundation. From an early age they have had it drummed into them that they are inferior humans. Eunja Lee claims that Koreans' distorted self-esteem must be recovered and reclaimed.[59] Although they speak, think, and behave like Japanese, the decisive difference lies in their experiences of all kinds of oppression and discrimination. Originally they did not come to Japan of their own free will but were forced to be Japanese, mercilessly exploited, and in the end granted no legal rights or support. Naturalization was also very difficult. Of course, it was natural for the Koreans to claim to be Korean, but they were also deprived of being able to identify themselves with their home country, Korea, after having lived in Japan for so many years.[60]

Where To Go From Here

Feminist theologians of Korea and Japan started an Annual Study Forum in 1988. Since the second Forum, Korean women living in Japan have also taken part in the group. Listening to stories shared by Korean women who have suffered from the hatred felt toward the Japanese that was long harbored deep in their hearts, and hearing stories shared by 'Korean women living in Japan' who have suffered from discrimination and exploitation, we Japanese women also suffer from the guilt of what the Japanese have done. Through sharing our pain and extending our apologies, the relations of hatred have turned into relations of forgiveness and reconciliation. From there, we began anew to reconstruct the parts of the history of exploitation that had been kept secret, so that we may do justice to those who have been victimized and forgotten. Through this process, we have been challenged to overcome the boundaries between us and built a new community of faith. 'Community' designates our living together in diversity. Here we have experienced a healing of our pain and guilt. A Korean woman theologian living in Japan claims,

> For Koreans living in Japan it is most important and urgent to be liberated from their distorted, negative self-images. For that purpose, we need to learn how to love ourselves in order that we may renew our alienated selves. In other words, asking who we are, we need to regain affirmative self-respect in ourselves. This identity construction process is not an easy one. It demands much struggle inside and outside of oneself.[61]

Only when we Japanese learn the truth about what has happened to the colonized and the victimized people in history, and how deeply ethnic exclusivism based on the religious concept of purity of blood has affected our mentality, can we attain a basis for regaining a right relationship with our neighbors of different cultures. On the basis of affirming and accepting each other as neighbors created in the image of God, we will be in the circle of Jesus' community of faith. Our struggle toward this goal has just started, and we realize that it will take a long time to overcome prejudice. Yet we are already walking in solidarity and in diversity toward building one true church. As Jesus dared to break down barriers by responding to the challenge by the Syrophoenician woman, churches in Japan are challenged to participate in breaking down barriers built around people's hearts.

NOTES

1   Gail R. O'Day, 'Surprised by Faith: Jesus and the Canaanite Woman', *Listening: A Journal of Religion and Culture* 24 (Fall 1989), p. 291; Ben Witherington III, *Women in the Ministry of Jesus: A Study of Jesus' Attitudes to Women and Their Roles as Reflected in His Earthly Life*, (Cambridge, University Press, 1984), p. 65; T. A. Burkill, 'Mark 6.31–8.26: The Context of the Story of the Syrophoenician Woman', *The Classical Tradition: Literary and Historical Studies in Honor of H. Caplin*, ed. L. Wallach (New York, Cornell University Press, 1966), pp. 331–32.

2   Karen A. Barta, *The Gospel of Mark* (Delaware, Michael Glazier, 1988), pp. 100–101.

3   Paul J. Achtermeier, 'Toward the Isolation of Pre-Markan Miracle Catenae', *Journal of Biblical Literature* 89 (1970), p. 288; Howard C. Kee, *Community of the New Age: Studies in Mark's Gospel* (Philadelphia, Western Press, 1977), p. 92.

4   Chad Myers, *Binding the Strong Man: A Political Reading of Mark's Story of Jesus* (Maryknoll, NY, Orbis Books, 1988), pp. 440–41.

5   O'Day, 'Surprised by Faith', p. 291.

6   Witherington, *Women in the Ministry of Jesus*, p. 63.

7   Marla J. Selvidge, *Women, Cult, and Miracle Recital: A Redactional Critical Investigation of Mark 5.24–34* (Lewisburg, PA, Bucknell University Press, 1990), p. 89.

8   Witherington, *Women in the Ministry of Jesus*, p. 63.

9   Vincent Taylor, *The Gospel According to St Mark* (London, Macmillan, 1953), p. 349.

10   Witherington, *Women in the Ministry of Jesus*, pp. 63–64.

11   T. A. Burkill, 'The Syrophoenician Woman: The Congruence of Mark 7.24–31', *Zeitschrift für die neutestamentliche Wissenschaft* 57 (1966), p. 35.

12   Some important manuscripts such as Sinaiticus, Alexandrinus, Vaticanus, and others add 'and Sidon' after 'Tyre' in verse 24.

13   O'Day, 'Surprised by Faith', p. 291; J. Duncan M. Derrett, 'Law in the New Testament: The Syro-Phoenician Woman and the Centurion of Capernaum', *Novum Testamentum* 15 (1973), pp. 163–64.

14   Myers, *Binding the Strong Man*, p. 204.

15   T. A. Burkill, 'The Historical Development of the Story of the Syrophoenician Woman (Mark 7.24–31): New Light on the Earliest Gospel', *Novum Testamentum* 9 (1967), p. 177.

16   E. Schüssler Fiorenza, *In Memory of Her: A Feminist Theological Reconstruction of Christian Origins* (New York, Crossroads, 1983), p. 137.

17   Rudolf K. Bultmann, *The History of the Synoptic Tradition*, tr. by John Marsh (Oxford, Basil Blackwell, 1972), p. 36; Achtermeier, 'Toward the Isolation', p. 287; Schüssler Fiorenza, *In Memory of Her*, p. 137; Burkill, 'The Historical Development', p. 177.

18   Fernando Belo, *A Materialist Reading of the Gospel of Mark* (Maryknoll, NY, Orbis Books, 1981), p. 145.

19   Rita Nakashima Brock, *Journey by Heart: A Christology of Erotic Power* (New York, Crossroad, 1988), pp. 86–87.

20   Myers, *Binding the Strong Man*, p. 203; also chapter 1.

21   Frederick J. Borsch, 'Jesus and Women Exemplars', *Anglican Theological Review*, Suppl. 11 (1990), pp. 29–30; Schüssler Fiorenza, *In Memory of Her*, pp. 106–110.

22   Burkill, 'The Syrophoenician Woman', p. 23; O'Day, 'Surprised by Faith', p. 291; Schüssler Fiorenza, *In Memory of Her*, p. 137; Taylor, *St Mark*, p. 349.

23   Myers, *Binding the Strong Man*, p. 203.

24   Gerd Theissen, *The Miracle Stories of the Early Christian Tradition* (Edinburgh, T. & T. Clark, 1986), p. 126; Burkill, 'The Historical Development', p. 172; Achtermeier, 'Toward the Isolation', p. 287.

25   Theissen, *The Miracle Stories*, p. 254.

26   Bultmann, *The History of the Synoptic Tradition*, p. 38; Taylor, *St Mark*, p. 350; Burkill, 'The Historical Development', p. 109; Myers, *Binding the Strong Man*, p. 203.

27   Bultmann, *The History of the Synoptic Tradition*, p. 38.

28   Burkill, 'The Historical Development', p. 109.

29   Taylor, *St Mark*, p. 360.

30   Belo, A. *Materialist Reading*, p. 145.

31   Burkill, 'The Historical Development', pp. 97–99, 114.

32   e.g. Rabbi Eliezer: 'He who eats with an idolator is like unto one who eats with a dog', etc. Quoted in Taylor, *St Mark*, p. 350; also O'Day, 'Surpised by Faith', p. 297.

33   Taylor, *St Mark*, p. 350.

34   Myers, *Binding the Strong Man*, p. 204.

35   O'Day, 'Surprised by Faith', p. 297; Derrett, 'Law in the New Testament', p. 172; Burkill, 'The Historical Development', p. 118; Witherington, *Women in the Ministry of Jesus*, p. 170.

36   Burkill, 'The Historical Development', pp. 112–13.

37   ibid., pp. 113–14.

38   ibid., p. 98.

39   Witherington, *Women in the Ministry of Jesus*, pp. 63, 70. See also Hermann L. Strack and Paul Billerbeck, *Kommentar zum Neuen Testament aus Talmud und Midrasch* (München, C. H. Beck'sche Verlagbuch handlung, 1956), vol. 2, p. 726.

40   Francis Dufton, 'The Syrophoenician Woman and Her Dogs', *Expository Times*, 100 (Aug. 1989), p. 417.

41   ibid., p. 417.

42   David Rhoades and Donald Michie, *Mark as Story: An Introduction to the Narrative of the Gospel* (Philadelphia, Fortress Press, 1982), p. 131.

43   Sharon H. Ringe, 'A Gentile Woman's Story', in *Feminist Interpretation of the Bible*, ed. Letty M. Russell (Philadelphia, Westminster Press, 1985), p. 70. See also the chapter on Sexuality.

44   ibid., p. 69.

45   ibid., p. 71.

46   ibid., p. 71.

47 Belo, *A Materialist Reading*, p. 145.

48 Schüssler Fiorenza, *In Memory of Her*, p. 137.

49 Burkill, 'The Historical Development', p. 91.

50 Taylor, *St Mark*, p. 351.

51 Belo, A. *Materialist Reading*, p. 145.

52 Myers, *Binding the Strong Man*, p. 204.

53 Rachel Conrad Wahlberg, *Jesus According to a Woman* (New York, Paulist Press, 1986), p. 16.

54 Sanjung Kan, 'Japanese Orientalism – Distortion Lurked in Internationalization of Japan', *Sekei* (Dec. 1988), p. 133.

55 Eunja Lee, 'Together with Our Neighbors', *Kyokai Hujin Rengo Tayori* 50 (26 May 1992), pp. 1–3.

56 The fingerprinting was abolished in 1993, but they are still asked to register their family names.

57 Kan, 'Japanese Orientalism', p. 137.

58 Aiko Utumi, 'To Live with Asian People', in Aido Utumi and Yayori Matui (eds.), *Laborers from Asian Countries* (Tokyo, Akasi Shoten, 1988), pp. 50–56.

59 Lee, 'Together with Our Neighbors', pp. 1–3.

60 ibid.

61 ibid., p. 1.

10

Water – God's Extravaganza: John 2.1–11

SR VANDANA

The historical–critical method is one among many of the tools applied to read the Bible, and its limitations are well-documented. In this essay, an Indian exegete employs an indigenous tool – the *Dhvani*, a Sankristic method of exegesis – to interpret Christian texts. The *Dhvani* method stresses the 'evocative', the 'beauty' of the passage, and its emotive grip on the hearer or the reader.

This piece is one of the many expositions of St John's Gospel from her book, *Waters of Fire* (Madras, The Christian Literature Society, 1981; New York, Amity House, 1988).

For examples of *Dhvani* interpretation by other Indian biblical scholars, see *Bible Bhashyam* 5 (4 December 1979). *Bible Bhashyam* is an Indian biblical quarterly published by St Thomas Apostolic Seminary, Vadavathoor, Kottayam 10, India.

Sister Vandana is a member of the Order of the Sacred Heart and has a great interest in Hindu spiritual tradition.

If it was in the waters of Jordan that Jesus chose to begin his public ministry by humbly going with publicans and sinners to be baptized, it was again through water that he performed the first of his 'signs'. It is one of the most charming stories in the life of Jesus. Mary, Jesus, and his disciples were invited to a wedding in Cana of Galilee. When wine – used liberally on merry-making occasions – gave out, it was Mary's presence that saved the situation. She turned to Jesus instinctively for help with the certainly of a true *bhakta* (a lover of God). When he seemed to refuse to do anything about it, with equal certainty and the equanimity of a *sthitaprajna* (one of steadfast wisdom),[1] she told the servants just to obey him. It was at this crucial point that Jesus used his 'creature' – water. He told them to fill six large water pots with water and they filled them to the brim. It was the best wine they had ever tasted. Thus through this miracle of water, he revealed his glory and his disciples believed in him.

1 WATER USED TO MANIFEST HIS GLORY

Water! An ordinary, everyday, familiar thing, usually taken for granted and unnoticed – except when found absent and needed. This the Lord used as an instrument to 'manifest his glory,' or 'He let his glory be seen' through it, 'and his disciples believed in him' (John 2.11, Jerusalem Bible translation). God often uses very ordinary things and lets his glory shine out through them. One is tempted perhaps to call water God's favorite creation! It may be worthwhile, then, to look at water in his first creation and then in St John's Gospel – as an aid to understanding better the miracle of Cana in Galilee.

2 WATER IN GENESIS AND ST JOHN

It is interesting to note that in the first half of John's Gospel, called 'the Book of Signs', the seven-day structure of the original creation story is imitated, culminating in this first manifestation of Jesus' glory.[2]

Three days later there was a wedding at Cana in Galilee (2.1), that is, three days after the meeting of Jesus with Philip and Nathaniel. The opening events of the Gospel, therefore, are contained within one week, of which almost every day is noticed.[3] That John 2.1 introduces an event that occurs on 'the third day' doubtless has yet another symbolism. But for our purpose, it is interesting to see how water is treated in the original creation story.

Water appears first in Genesis 1.2 as 'the raging ocean covering everything engulfed in darkness and the power of God moving over the waters on the first day'. On the second day God said, 'Let there be a dome to divide the water' (Gen. 1.6). On the third day God commanded, 'Let the water below the sky come together in one place, so that the land will appear . . . and he named the water sea' (Gen. 1.9–10). God had not yet finished with water. He said, 'Let the water be filled with many kinds of living beings. . . He blessed all and told the creatures that live in the water to reproduce, and to fill the sea . . . Evening passed and morning came – that was the fifth day' (Gen. 1.20–3). Thus on four out of the six days of creation, God dealt with water. 'From the waters is this universe produced.' No wonder we read this in the Vedas in the *Satpatha Brahmana* VI.8.2.4.

St John, while apparently alluding to the seven-day structure of the original creation story, shows the same predilection for water as God does – the way he uses it in a variety of circumstances through- out his narrative of Jesus' life – now as a 'venue' for his appearance, now for healing, now as a symbol of his life, now as a lesson in humility, now as signifying the pouring out of his Spirit. Here, in this his first miracle, Jesus used water as an instrument of his first 'sign'.

3 'THIS WAS THE FIRST OF THE SIGNS GIVEN BY JESUS' (JOHN 2.11)

In Israel, as in India, miracles and wonders were often looked for in prophets and saints, and were considered a seal of God on such men. There are many wonder-working '*Sai Babas*' found in the Old Testament.

In fact, the term *signs* comes from the Old Testament background in which it especially meant Yahweh's wonderful works in the Exodus story (Num. 14.11). 'However, what was meaningful about these wonderful deeds was not precisely that they were beyond natural causality, but that they had been worked by the God of Israel to reveal himself to his people. The "signs" of Jesus have exactly this meaning for John and only certain miracles are called "signs".'[4] The signs of Jesus constitute the miracles that reveal the nature of Jesus as the revelation of God: these are signs in the Johannine sense.[5] In transforming the waters into wine, this 'creative miracle' allowed us to see Jesus as the manifestation of God: 'we saw his glory . . . full of grace and truth' (John 1.14).

4 'AND THE MOTHER OF JESUS WAS THERE' (JOHN 2.2)

If water were an instrument Jesus used, he also used Mary. When he first manifested his glory, Mary was present, as she was there again at his death on the cross (John 19.25–27). Both these descriptions in

John 2 and 19 have several details in common, no doubt on purpose. And in both these events, together with Mary, water was present.

Mary and water have much in common. Mary, like water, was creature – ordinary, unnoticed, quiet, serviceable, lovely, and precious. As there can be no life without water, so God ordained that there would be no new life without Mary. In John, Mary is seen not only in her historical character but in her function in salvation history. The woman of the first creation was called 'Life' (Eve) because she was 'mother of all the living' (Gen. 3.20). Mary 'the woman' – as she will be called again at the foot of the cross – is mother of the new life; not only mother of the Word made flesh, but of all who live by his life. She is the figure of the Church – 'the New Eve'.[6] And although Jesus said his hour had not yet come, because of her intercession, he anticipates it and her petition is granted. Who can refuse a mother? And Mary is essentially mother.

In all ages and cultures people have sought God in a mother figure. Without making too facile connections, it is interesting to study similarities. Thus in the Vedas the waters are called 'mothers'. 'May the waters, the mothers, purify us!' The Lord is the Son of the waters, born of the waters. 'In the waters, Lord, is your seat' (Narayan, *Taittiriya Samhita* 1.2.2, *S.B.* VII. 4.1.6). Both a mother and a river are venerated with special love in India. The Ganges – the most sacred of all rivers – is always *Gangamata*. When crossing her, pilgrims in the ferries cry out, '*Gangamaya-ki-jai*'. *Arati* is done to her singing:

> Om jaya Gange-mata Ekhi Bar jto teri Sharangati ata, Yamkir tras mitakar paramgati pata.

> Hail to the Mother Ganges, He who comes to take refuge in you even once will cross the difficulties of death, and find the supreme heaven.

Ganga is called the 'refuge' of the *patita* – the fallen ones – as Mary is called 'Refuge of sinners', for did not the Lord, dispeller of all sins, dwell in her? There is a story of the goddess Ganga appearing before King Bhagiratha (who did austere penances to propitiate her) and saying, 'All the sinners of the world come to wash away their sins and purify themselves by immersing their sinful bodies in my holy waters. Where shall I wash the immense store of sins they deposit in my watery body?' Bhagiratha replied: 'O sacred mother, holy saints will bathe in the Ganges and will purge all sins away, for the Lord Vishnu (the all-pervading one), dispeller of all sins, dwells in their heart.' If Mary is, as we have seen, 'the mother of the new life', Gangaji is called 'the nectar of immortality that gives us salvation'. Over the radio recently I heard a song: *'Hamari zindagi, hamari roti, Gangajike dwara'* ('We receive life and bread through the Ganges'). She it is who gives to us life and bread, and Mary gives to us Jesus, who called himself our 'Life' and 'the true Bread of Life.' Some of the prayers addressed to the waters of the Ganga are reminiscent of prayers to the Virgin Mother:

> Who can describe, O Mother, thy glory and splendour? O, all powerful Mother of compassion and love!

Mary and water have yet something else in common. Waters of a river can be very silent, gentle, sometimes as still as a pool; they hardly seem to move, even though the river never ceases to flow from its source. They can be considerate, cautious as they pass by a rough rock. They are ever ready to give of themselves, to bathe or slake thirst, without ever objecting that too much is asked of them, without expecting a word of gratitude. They are a real example of *Nishkarma karma* that the *Gita* teaches; service without looking for any reward. They give what they have to give to those who ask or need their help, then pass on, silently, unnoticed, as unspectacularly as they came.

Mary was like that at the wedding feast in Cana – gentle, unobtrusive, quiet, yet able to secure a miracle from a seemingly reluctant son, with apparent ease through her softly spoken words and her unfailing trust. Lao-tse has said, 'The softest substance of the world goes through the hardest; softness and gentleness are the companions of life. There is nothing weaker than water, but none is superior to it in overcoming the hard, for which there is no substitute. Weakness overcomes strength and gentleness overcomes rigidity.'

Mary, like the waters, and like Dakshinamoorthy in Shankaracharya's Hymn, taught by her *maun vyakhya* (silent discourse). She noticed the need and embarrassment of the wedding party, as the wine came to an end. No one had asked her help, yet she went to her son and said gently, 'They have no wine' (John 2.3). Jesus answered, 'Woman' – which word in the vocative shows no disrespect, as many examples show (e.g. John 19.26 – 'You must not tell me what to do' (Good News Bible translation); 'You have no claims upon me yet' or 'My hour is not yet come' – his hour being his death and exaltation (John 7.30; 8.20; 12.23, 27; 13.1). 'What have I to do with you?' seems to draw a line between mother and son, especially as the words remind us of those used by demons to Jesus (Mark 1.24, 5.7; Matt. 8.29): 'You have no business with us yet.' But Jesus, as always, makes decisions only depending on his Father's will (cf. 6.38). He had refused, too, to act on his brothers' advice and instructions (John 7.6).

Without being deterred by the apparent rebuff, Mary told the servants what to do – in the words of John 2.5: 'Do whatever he tells you' – and slipped back into anonymity. She who had spent years listening to his word and pondering it in her heart knew the value of obedience. *Obaudiro:* from listening comes obedience. This had made her know her son and be sure of his unfailing love. She advised them simply to obey. She knew he would always do what was good, or rather, best.

And 'when the steward tasted the water' it was wine. Not only that, but in great abundance and the best they had! Each stone jar, we are told, could hold twenty to thirty gallons (John 2.6).

5 'THEY FILLED THEM TO THE BRIM'

Though we are not told – as we are in the miracle of the loaves – how much wine was 'left over', we may be sure there was some. Jesus, who could not refuse his mother, had told the servants, 'Fill the jars with water' – an apparently crazy thing to say and expect them to do. But they did and 'they filled them to the brim' (John 2.7). To the brim! Here we see the extravagance of water – and of love. God does nothing by half measures. Is Jesus not himself the *pleroma* of God, the plentitude, the *Poornam*? 'In him dwells the fullness of God corporeally' (cf. Col. 2.9; 1.19).

It is interesting that Schoonenberg bases his christology of the enhypostasis of the Word in the man Jesus, and of God's full presence in his human person, on these Pauline texts. Might one not say that Jesus, who was 'filled to the brim' with divinity, now sees the servants fill the stone pots 'to the brim', so that through this very human act of being present at a wedding and of sensitively saving an embarrassing situation, he could show forth the divinity, with which he was filled, to the full? One begins to see a new meaning – or a new interpretation – in the *Shanti* Path of the *Isa Upanishad*.

Poornamadah, Poornam idam
Fullness there (beyond); fullness here.

That is, the fully divine (there) is fully human (here). Christ, who is God's eternal Son, is seen by some modern theologians (like Schoonenberg) as being 'threatened to become dehumanized; the man in him risks being undermined to the benefit of the divine person'. John, in this miracle, however, shows Christ to be truly and utterly human, as we have seen. God in himself as God-made-man walking the earth, is seen living himself fully – to the full. 'Of his fullness we have all received grace upon grace' (John 1.16). The torrents of his grace flow freely on man – without 'let or stay', for God is generosity, and what better symbolism is there for this gracious and superabundant giving than waters released in abundance?

All through the Old Testament waters appear 'now real, now symbolic, now gentle and life-giving, now destructive and terrifying, now a trickle, now a torrent.' In Cana we see it as a torrent – freely given and flowing over. Water in the Bible is always freely given – from the first book to the last. In Genesis we read: 'When all was *Tohu-tohu* (a mess) – waters were created and flowed freely'. On the fifth day God said, 'Let the waters abound with life' and in Revelation we read, 'Let him receive the water of life freely – who thirsts – come!' The Garden of Eden had to abound in water. 'The desert mind, thirsting for beauty, must be told that there was water to make it a paradise, a couple of trees and the four-branched river. Even when sin becomes prevalent, waters are still abundant, and the floodgates of heaven are opened, but now to punish man.[7] Whether it is well water – or the rains sent by Yahweh – it is always in abundance – to show the greatness of his love. The floodwater covered the enemies of Israel as they tried to cross the Red Sea, until they sank into the depths like a stone: 'Horse and chariot he cast into the sea' (Exod. 15.1; 5). When Moses struck the rock, waters gushed forth in abundance – a figure, too, of the waters that would gush forth from the side of Christ and become 'waters of salvation', which Isaiah foretold we would draw with joy from the Saviour's fountains (Isa. 12.3).

The same superabundance is seen in the Gospels and in this miracle of Christ. For if Christ is the infinite self-expenditure of God,[8] was he not himself to be 'poured out like water' for our sake?

Ratzinger, speaking of an 'excess' of seven baskets mentioned in Mark 8.8, says:

One thinks at once of a related miracle preserved in the Johannine tradition; the changing of water into wine at the marriage feast at Cana. It is true that the word *excess* does not occur here, but the fact certainly does: according to the evidence of the Gospel, the new-made wine amounted to between 130 and 190 gallons, a somewhat unusual quantity for a private banquet![9] In the Evangelist's view both stories have to do with the central element in Christian worship, the Eucharist. They show it as the divine excess or abundance, which infinitely surpasses all needs and legitimate demands. In this way both stories are concerned, through their reference to the Eucharist,[10] with Christ Himself. And both point back to the law governing the structure of creation, in which life squanders a million seeds in order to save one living one, in which a whole universe is squandered in order to prepare at one point, a place for spirit, for man. Excess is God's trademark in his creation; as the fathers put it: 'God does not reckon his gifts by the measure.' At the same time excess is also the real foundation and form of the history of salvation, which in the last analysis is nothing other than the truly breath-taking fact that God, in an incredible outpouring of himself, expends not only a universe, but his own self, in order to lead man, a speck of dust, to salvation. So excess or superfluity – let us repeat – is the real definition or mark of the history of salvation. The purely calculating mind will always find it absurd that for man, God himself would be expended. Only the lover can understand the folly of a love to which prodigality is a law, and excess alone is sufficient.[11]

6 'THERE WERE SIX STONE WATER JARS STANDING THERE' (JOHN 2.6)

Stone was used because, according to Jewish belief, it would not contract ritual uncleanness, just as the Hindu Dharmashastra lays down which materials are considered pure and which not. The Jewish ritual provided for numerous purifications by water – as does the Hindu ritual. Hence the water jars were for ablutions customary among the Jews. But all these purifications were powerless to bring about effectively true purity of soul until the New Covenant. Hence Jesus' changing of water into wine is symbolic. At this wedding he foretells it when he changes water (destined for symbolic cleansing) into wine, which symbolizes both spirit (John 15.3) and the purifying word (John 13.10). John sees this changing of water into wine as the replacement of the weak elements of the Old Covenant by the rich wine of the New Covenant and Messianic Banquet.[12] It is interesting,

too, that Jesus says that his word and teaching will henceforth purify
– (rather than ritual washings) in the context of the vine (John 15).
The vine being 'pruned' means again purification. 'You are pruned
already by means of the Word I have spoken to you' (John 15.3).
To be truly purified by God does not mean mere external washings
laid down by rituals, but rather to enter into his word and teaching
that leads to self-emptying and death. At the washing of the feet of
his disciples, Jesus made this clear, though Peter took some time to
understand that by refusing to let Jesus wash his feet, he 'would have
no part' with him; he would cut himself off from our Lord's ministry
and glory if he did not share his outlook and accept the total mystery
of self-emptying – even unto love and service of his betrayers.[13]

The water pots at the wedding in Cana remind one, too, of the Indian
custom of water pots being piled up at the door of the house where the
wedding takes place. Pots with water, as with rice, earth, etc. are symbols of a new life – the *poorna kumbha* – the full pot – filled to the brim
– being a symbol of the fullness of life and joy. Laxmi, the goddess of
prosperity, often carries it in one of her four arms.

7 THE WINE

The wine, too, is symbolic – of joy, celebration, life, love, a new
creation, whether as Dodd thinks, the story of the Cana wedding
developed out of a parable, or whether, as F. E. Williams thinks, it
was based on Luke 5.33–39, together with the tradition of Jesus'
mother and brothers. In any case, says Barrett, it seems clear that
'John meant to show the supersession of Judaism in the glory of
Jesus.'[14] It is possible that in so doing he drew material from Dionys-
iac sources. 'There was an exact precedent for the benefaction of
Jesus in a pagan worship, doubtless known to some, at least, of John's
readers. The god Dionysius was not only the discoverer of wine, but
also the cause of miraculous transformation of water into wine (cf.
Euripides, *Bacchae* 704–7, etc.).[15]

So, too, in Vedic India, Soma – originally a plant – was raised to
the status of a god. The juice of this plant was offered three times
a day in a sacrifice – as wine is offered in the Eucharistic sacrifice.
If at Pentecost, the apostles, inebriated with the Divine Spirit, were
suspected of having drunk too much wine, the gods were often
thought to have been inspired by Soma. Thus Indra, for instance,

did great and extraordinary deeds. Believed to have grown on the Mujavat mountain, Parjnya the rain god is, interestingly enough, said to be Soma's father and the waters are his sisters.[16] We find Soma destroying towns, begetting gods, upholding the sky, prolonging mortals' lives. He is also the Lord of the tidal floods.[17] He is given all the attributes given to Indra.[18] For a Christian, wine, transformed into the Blood of Christ at a Eucharistic sacrifice, is believed to give immortality (life everlasting). He would find it interesting to read, in a Rig Vedic hymn (i.91), the prayer:

> And Soma, let it be thy will
> For us to live, nor let us die . . .
> Thou Soma, bliss upon the old,
> And on the young and pious men
> Ability to live, bestowest.

Christ fulfilled 'all the scriptures' (cf. Luke 24.27) and gave 'the best wine' – that inebriates one with love of God.

8 'THE SERVANTS WHO HAD DRAWN THE WATER'

Only the servants who had drawn the water knew from whence the wine had come. The steward and the bridegroom's friends were surprised that the best wine was kept to the last. Only the servants 'knew', for they had done the work of filling those huge water pots. Only those who labor, who taste, who experience personally, really 'know': 'I am the taste of water.' We read also in the *Bhagavad Gita*, 'I am the knowledge of those who know' (10.38) and again, 'I am the soul which dwells in the heart of all things' (10.20). 'He is the Lord of all, who is hidden in the heart of all things. Those who know him through their hearts and minds become immortal.'[19] Immortality is given to those who have the knowledge that comes from having drunk of this 'immortal nectar'. And only those who labor at 'drawing' from his heart, in the cave of their own hearts, in meditation, know from whence comes this best wine, which alone can satisfy man's thirst forever.

John, whenever dealing with water (as in 1.26; 3.25; 4.10; 7.38), shows it to be both purifying and satisfying of thirst. The Cana miracle illustrates, as already seen, 'at once the poverty of the old dispensation with its merely ceremonial cleansing and the richness of the new, in which the Blood of Christ is available both for cleansing (1.29) and for drink' (6.53). The initial reference is to the supersession of Judaism, but Bultmann is right to generalize: 'The water stands for everything that is a substitute for revelation, everything by which a man thinks he can live, and which yet fails him when put to the test.'[20]

CONCLUSION

And through water 'his disciples came to believe in him' (John 2.11).

Thus, by working this miracle of transformation with his humble creature water, Jesus 'manifested his glory'. 'The miracle of water made into wine may in itself not appear to be an apt indication of Christ's glory; however, it must be taken as John takes it, as the first of a series, all of which are related to the life that is to be found in the word of God.'[21] 'And his disciples came to believe in him' – through water turned into wine. And we, too, come to believe that the water of the self – the *ahamkar* or ego – if poured out in silent, unresisting surrender like Mary's – can become, at her word of intercession, the wine of the self, who dwells in the heart of all things.

> Be praised, my Lord,
> through sister water,
> for greatly useful, lowly,
> precious, chaste is she.
> (St Francis of Assisi)

NOTES

1   cf. *Bhagavad Gita* 2.54f.

2   B. Vawter, 'The Gospel According to John' in R. E. Brown *et al.* (eds.), *Jerome Bible Commentary* (London, Geoffrey Chapman, 1968), p. 424.

3   The sequence can be seen in John 1.29; 1.35; 1.39–42, 43 – four days.

4   John 2.11; 4.54; 6.14; 9.16; 12.18; also dealing with water, John 5.2– 9; 6.16–21 describe them in detail but do not call them 'signs', though they doubtless are.

5   ibid.

6   cf. the Woman of the Apocalypse 12, who is also the Mother of Christ and of the new Israel, where the vision of John is again by the imagery of Genesis.

7   T. T. Feeney, 'Waters of Salvation', *Bible Today* (March 1965), pp. 1097–1102.

8   J. Ratzinger, *Introduction to Christianity* (London, Search Press, 1971), p. 197.

9   cf. the use of the figure of an abundance of wine in Amos 9.13f; Hos. 14.7; Jer. 31.12; Enoch 10.19; Bar. 29.5.

10   C. K. Barrett, however, says: 'It remains quite uncertain whether any allusion to the Eucharist is intended': *The Gospel According to John*, introduction and commentary (London, SPCK, 1979), p. 189.

11   Ratzinger, pp. 197–198.

12   cf. L. Dufour, 'Water', in *Dictionary of Biblical Theology* (Bangalore, Theological Publications of India), p. 646.

13   ibid., p. 646.

14   Barrett, p. 188f.

15   ibid.

16   Rig Ved. X.34.1; IX.98.9.

17   Rig Ved. 88.24–25.

18   cf. Motilal Pandit, *Vedic Hinduism* (Allahabad, St. Paul's), p. 76.

19   *Svetasvatara Upanishad* 4.15, 17.

20   Bultmann, *The Gospel of John*, quoted by Barrett.

21   Vawter, p. 428.

11

The Implications of the Text of Esther for African Women's Struggle for Liberation in South Africa

ITUMELENG J. MOSALA

Among African theologies, South African theology has consistently argued for liberation as the starting point to do theology. Mosala, one of the leading proponents, argues here for a cultural-materialist biblical hermeneutics of struggle which he reckons in the context of South Africa requires the revolt of the reader – thus enabling the mutual liberation of the Bible and the oppressed communities. He re-reads the story of Esther and cautions the reader that before looking for any emancipatory potential in the story, one should scrutinize its feudal, patriarchal, tribal and class biases.

This essay is reprinted from *Semeia* 59 (1992), pp. 129–37.

Itumeleng J. Mosala teaches in the Department of Religious Studies, University of Cape Town, Republic of South Africa. He is the author of the much-quoted *Black Hermeneutics and Black Theology in South Africa* (Grand Rapids, Eerdman's, 1989).

INTRODUCTION

There exists a great deal of confusion concerning what exactly is meant by Liberation Theology. In part, the confusion relates to the use of terms, and in two different ways. First, there is the failure to distinguish between Liberation Theology and Theology of Liberation. Liberation Theology refers to the Latin American form of the Theology of Liberation. It is associated with the names of activist scholars such as Segundo, Gutiérrez, Assmann, Bonino, etc. By contrast, the term Theology of Liberation is generic and denotes a movement of Third World people involved in a struggle to break the chains of cultural-religious imperialism that help to perpetuate their political and economic exploitation.

The second form of the terminological confusion is conceptual, involving a discourse imperialism of a certain kind. At first sight, there may seem to be no distinction between this form of terminological confusion and the first. There is here a tendency to refer to all Third World theologies of the poor and oppressed peoples as Liberation Theologies, thus subsuming them under the Latin American version of the Theology of Liberation. This mistake is made mostly, though by no means exclusively, by white radical people who identify culturally more with the European descendants of Latin America than with Third World people. Cornel West raises the question of the political implications of this cultural preference of the political Left when he writes:

> For oppressed colored [black] peoples, the central problem is not only repressive capitalist regimes, but also oppressive European civilizing attitudes. And even Marxists who reject oppressive capitalist regimes often display oppressive European civilizing attitudes toward colored peoples. In this sense, such Marxists, though rightly critical of capitalism, remain captives of the worst of European culture. (1981: 256)

In addition to the confusion of terms, it is not being extreme to suspect a good deal of ideological distortion, that is, a deliberate misunderstanding that seeks to make a mockery of or to obscure things, in the face of which a simple apology for the Theology of Liberation would be grossly inappropriate. This is so not only because this theology has been in existence for so long that it is now an inescapable reality, but also because so many significant strides have already been made in developing it. In the case of South Africa, black theologians have been at work for more than a decade now wrestling with many issues of the nature, the method, the specific form, the epistemology, the sources and the goals of the Black Theology of Liberation. More recently, the question of the Black Feminist Theology of Liberation has emerged as a high priority on the agenda of Black Theology.

For the reason, therefore, of wanting to get on with business of *doing* Black Theology as opposed to simply *apologizing* for it, as well as for the reason of giving priority to a Black Feminist theological discourse, I have chosen to address the topic of the implications of Esther for African women's struggle for liberation in South Africa.

READING THE BIBLE IN SOUTH AFRICA

That the Bible is a thoroughly political document is eloquently attested to by its role in the apartheid system in South Africa. No other political or ideological system in the modern world that I know of derives itself so directly from the Bible as the ideology of apartheid. The superiority of white people over black people, for example, is premised on the divine privileging of the Israelites over the Canaanites in the conquest texts of the Old Testament.

For this reason, in South Africa, all manner of theological sophistry has been produced by way of countering this embarrassing use of the Bible. The dominant opposition discourse against this way of using the Bible has been the liberal humanist one. The key character-istic of this oppositional perspective has not been its fundamental disapproval of the conquest texts of the Old Testament. Rather, this model concurs with the conservative model in its approval of the conquest texts, but disagrees with the apartheid ideologues' interpret-ation of them.

Thus in effect a biblical hermeneutics of textual or authorial col-lusion/collaboration, rather than one of struggle or revolt, dominated the debate concerning the reading of the Bible. Increasingly, there-fore, biblical appropriation in South Africa became alienating to Blacks as their reality constantly contradicted their supposed inclusion in the biblically-based love of God.

Consequently, the struggle of the 1960s, which led to the exile, imprisonment and banishment of many Blacks and their organiza-tions, notwithstanding God's love for them witnessed to in the Bible, produced a crisis in black people's self-insertion in the story of the Bible. The rise of Black Theology, which, like its counterpart – Liberation Theology – in Latin America, grounded itself in the liber-ation stories of the Bible, signified black people's discursive attempt to deal with this crisis. This new reading of the Bible by black people themselves in the light of the struggle for liberation would attempt to argue that liberation and not conquest or oppression was the key message of the Bible.

Black Theology and Liberation Theology's biblical hermeneutics was a product of a crisis situation and not of a revolt on the part of the readers. In South Africa it was not until the post-1976 period, when black people seem to have looked death in the face and come to terms with it in their struggle against the forces of apartheid, that revolutionary reading practice became an integral part of the social insurgency of the black masses and a necessity of the organic location of its subjects in the context of that insurgency.

The new and developing biblical hermeneutics of liberation differs from the liberal humanist tradition in that it represents a theoretical and not simply a moral mutation from ruling class hermeneutics. Such new reading of the Bible, particularly in the context of South Africa, would concur with Terry Eagleton when he says, in support of what in literary criticism has come to be know as the 'Revolt of the Reader' movement:

> That readers should be forcibly subjected to textual authority is disturbing enough; that they should be insultingly invited to hug their chains, merge into empathetic harmony with their oppressors to the point where they befuddledly cease to recognize whether they are subject or object, worker, boss, or product is surely the ultimate opiate. (1986: 182)

A study of Esther's relevance for African women's liberation struggle will need to take into account the tradition of the revolt of the reader that is becoming part of Black Theology's liberation praxis. Not only will this hermeneutics refuse to submit to the chains imposed on it by the biblical exegetes of apartheid, or those of the liberal humanist tradition including its Black and Liberation Theology versions, but it will contend against the 'regimes of truth' (West 1985: 120) of these traditions as they manifest themselves in the text of the Bible itself.

THE BIBLICAL SCHOLARSHIP OF ESTHER

Most studies of the book of Esther are preoccupied with questions of its religiosity, canonical status, historicity and purpose. The problem with these studies is not that they address themselves to these questions but that they rely heavily on the text itself not only for information but also for the theoretical frameworks with which the text must be interpreted. Thus most works simply retell the story, assess the obvious irreligiosity of the text and confirm the book's own confession of its purpose.

Traditional scholarship does, however, raise crucial issues which a biblical hermeneutics of liberation cannot ignore. Norman Gottwald, for instance, addresses the question of the plot of the story, 'replete with dramatic reversals' (561) which it is important to note in order to understand the rhetorical devices employed by the dominant ideology of the text. It is also crucial to observe concerning the historicity of the book that:

> The archaic placement of the story in the Persian court is accomplished with considerable knowledge of its inner workings and customs, but there are so many historical inaccuracies and improbabilities that the work cannot be taken at face value. The story may draw on memories of conflicts over Persian policies toward the Jews in which the Jews serving in the imperial court were involved, but the actual setting of the narrator is in the Maccabean–Hasmonean era. This is indicated by several lines of evidence: the intensity and bitterness of the Jewish–Gentile conflicts in the book which are pictured as 'fights to the finish', the lack of external references to the book until late Hellenistic times, and the very late appearance of Purim as a recognized Jewish festival. (Gottwald: 562)

Historical-critical scholarship provides these insights which cannot be ignored by newer exegetical and hermeneutical methods. It must be noted, however, that traditional scholarship consistently fails to draw the ideological implications of its historical and literary studies. This is because it is often in ideological collusion with the text. A criticism that sets itself the task of serving the cause of human liberation must overcome this limitation. For as Eagleton rightly argues:

> The task of criticism . . . is not to situate itself within the same space as the text, allowing it to speak or completing what it necessarily leaves unsaid. On the contrary, its function is to install itself in the very incompleteness of the work in order to *theorize* it – to explain the ideological necessity of those 'not-saids' which constitute the very principle of its identity. Its object is the unconsciousness of the work – that of which it is not, and cannot be, aware. (1976: 89)

AFRICAN WOMEN'S STRUGGLE FOR LIBERATION

The hermeneutical weapons of struggle of African women must of necessity issue out of the specificity of their praxis within what Cornel West calls the process of 'critical negation, wise preservation, and insurgent transformation of the black lineage which protects the earth and projects a better world' (1985: 124).

In the South African situation black women's struggle takes at once the form of a gender, national, and class struggle. The oppression and exploitation of black women operates at all those levels. What is more, these dimensions of African women's struggle span different historical periods and social systems, each of which has inflected this struggle in particular ways.

Contemporary African women are products of pre-capitalist semi-feudal, colonial and settler-colonial monopoly, capitalist, racist, social systems, on the one hand, as well as of heroic anti-sexist, anti-colonial, anti-racist and anti-capitalist struggles in South Africa, on the other hand. At different times and in different ways aspects of these processes and struggles were dominant or subservient in determining who African women were and how they would wage their struggle.

Thus, given this complex nature of African women's struggle, a biblical hermeneutics arising out of such a struggle can hardly be simplistic. It is rather akin to the program that West suggests for revolutionary black intellectuals. He writes:

> The new 'regime of truth' to be pioneered by black thinkers is neither a hermetic discourse (or set of discourses), which safeguards mediocre black intellectual production, nor the latest fashion of black writing, which is often motivated by the desire to parade for the white bourgeois intellectual establishment. Rather it is inseparable from the emergence of new cultural forms which prefigure (and point toward) a post-Western civilization. (1985: 122)

A hermeneutics of liberation which is envisaged for an African women's struggle will be at once a human, African and feminist hermeneutics of liberation; it will be *polemical* in the sense of being critical of the history, the devices, the culture, the ideologies and agendas of both the text and itself; it will be *appropriative* of the resources and victories inscribed in the biblical text as well as its own contemporary text; it will be *projective* in that its task is performed in the service of a transformed and liberated social order (for these terms, see Eagleton 1981: 113).

READING THE TEXT OF ESTHER

A Feudal-Tributary Text

The social formation implied by the text of Esther is clearly a kind of feudal or tributary system. Chapter 1 describes the social and political topography in the Persian Empire which patently presupposes the tributary mode of production; a hierarchical political structure with the monarch – *melek* – at the head of the royal ruling class, followed by the chiefs and governors (*śārîm*) still within the ruling nobility (vv. 1–3); then follow the non-royal ruling class factions, some of whom may be properly designated middle class, the influential sector – probably by virtue of its property ownership – advisors and people of high office (*gĕdôlîm, hăkāmîm* and *yōšĕbîm*, vv. 5, 13–14). The Queen (*malkâ*) is of course a member of the royal nobility, but even in a fairly straightforward descriptive text like chapter 1 her insertion into the ruling class is gender-structured (vv. 10–11), in that mention of her necessitates the royal summoning of seven eur ьchs, symbolizing the private property character of the sexuality of the king's wife. In fact, the fundamental problematic of this chapter as indeed of the whole text of Esther is the *gender structuring of politics*.

The feudal social relations of the Persian Empire as articulated in this text reflect two forms of oppression and exploitation. The one form is present by its absence; it is represented by the 'not-said' of the text. This form of oppression is signified in the verses of chapter 1 that describe the use to which the surplus production of the economy was put. In typical feudal and tributary fashion, surplus was squandered on non-productive luxury goods and a luxurious life-style among the ruling classes. None of it was invested in productive activities or technologies in order to enable development to take place. More importantly, verses 5–9, which describe this wasteful expenditure of the economic products, simultaneously function to obscure the social relations of production on which this consumptionist practice is premised. It mystifies the fact that behind these luxurious goods and extravaganza lie exploited, oppressed and dispossessed peasants, serfs, and sub-classes. This text, which is otherwise excellent in its provision of socio-economic data, is eloquent by its silence on the conditions and struggles of the non-kings, non-office holders, non-chiefs, non-governors and non-queens in the Persian Empire.

The second form of oppression is patriarchy. This specific kind of oppression is an inherent part of the structure of feudal society. This central thrust of the book begins, in chapter 1, with the question of the anti-patriarchal revolt of Queen Vashti. The text's agenda is spun around the view, generated by the text itself and representing its dominant ideology, that the audacity of one woman unleashed the political possibilities reflected approvingly in the rest of the book. All this, however, is located in and refracted through a feudal social-structural arrangement, producing a thoroughly feudal text.

African women, who are themselves products and victims of past feudal legacies and are presently historical subjects in the context of transformed but pervasive tributary/feudal practices under capitalism, understand the specificity of this form of oppression. Further, they recognize that this oppression cannot simply be subsumed under other kinds of oppression such as capitalist or colonial oppression. For this reason the revolt of Queen Vashti represents a form of struggle with which an African biblical feminist hermeneutic of liberation must identify. It does not accept the implicit condemnation of Vashti by the text, and eschews the technique whereby her revolt is used as a reason for the rise of an apparently more acceptable queen. This identification is possible only on the basis of a biblical hermeneutics of struggle.

A Survival Text

The book of Esther builds its story around the memory of very difficult times under colonial exile. The specific lesson it seeks to draw attention to revolves around the struggle for survival. In particular, two forms of survival are accented in this story: cultural and national survival. Needless to say, these two types of survival are inseparable, though not identical.

The material conditions of the practice of survival presupposed by the text are political powerlessness, economic exploitation, cultural and national alienation. The text proposes its own solution. It suggests a pure survival strategy, which is not underpinned by any liberative political ideology. According to this solution Esther gets incorporated into the feudal haven of the king, Mordecai is appointed an administrator in the colonial political machinery and later an even higher honor is given him. Through the co-operation of these two figures the rest of the oppressed Jewish community manage to survive the odds against them, and in fact find themselves in a position where they outpace the Persians at their own game.

The price that the oppressed pay for this turn of events favorable for them is at least two-fold. First, the oppressed must be seen to have bought heavily into the dominant ideology in order that their survival struggle should find approval. In chapter 9 this ideological capitulation is expressed in three terse but powerful repetitious statements: v. 10, 'However, there was no looting'; v. 15, 'But again, they did no looting'; v. 16, 'But they did no looting'. This principle of upholding the sanctity of property over the life of people is well known as part of ruling class ideology. The final chapter of the book of Esther exposes the politics of this ideology when it summarizes the thrust of its discourse:

> King Xerxes imposed forced labor on the people of the coastal regions of his empire as well as on those of the interior. . . Mordecai the Jew was second in rank only to King Xerxes himself. He was honored and well-liked by his fellow-Jews. He worked for the good of his people and for the security of all their descendants. (10.1, 3)

Second, in this book the survival of the group is achieved first and foremost by the alienation of Esther's gender-power and its integration into the patriarchal structures of feudalism.

A Patriarchal Text

More than being a feudal and survival discourse, the book of Esther is a patriarchal text. There are at least three objections that a biblical hermeneutics of liberation must raise against it. These three are related to each other and to the questions raised in relation to the text's feudal and survival character.

First, the text's choice of a female character to achieve what are basically patriarchal ends is objectionable. The fact that the story is woven around Esther does not make her the heroine. The hero of the story is Mordecai who needless to say gives nothing of himself for what he gets. Esther struggles, but Mordecai reaps the fruit of the struggle. African women who work within liberation movements and other groups will be very familiar with these kinds of dynamics. A truly liberative biblical hermeneutics will struggle against this tendency.

Second, the book of Esther sacrifices gender struggles to national struggles. In the name of the struggle for the national survival of the Jewish people it disprivileges the question of gender oppression and exploitation. The matter of the subsumption of some struggles under others is a serious issue of discourse imperialism. In the book of Esther this problem is especially unacceptable given the purely nationalist character of the national struggle. The Maccabean-Hasmonean revolution which probably underlies the nationalist struggle of the text of Esther is known to have replaced Greek Hellenism with Jewish Hellenism.

Third, the discourse of Esther suppresses class issues, including the class character of cultural practices. The feast of Purim, for example, which represents the principal cultural benefit of the Esther revolution, is not located in class terms in such a way that proper ideological choices can be made about it. In this it is very much like many cultural practices that seem inherently autocratic in the demands they place on their people.

CONCLUSION

This essay has tried to take seriously Elisabeth Schüssler Fiorenza's critique of what she calls the biblical 'hermeneutics of consent' (15 and *passim*). In taking this critique seriously it has argued for the need for a cultural-materialist biblical hermeneutics of struggle. Such a hermeneutics will raise questions of the material, ideological and cultural conditions of production of the text. It is argued here that it is only when such questions are raised that the political issues affecting nations, women, races, age groups, and classes will receive proper treatment in the interpretation of the Bible.

The conviction that I have articulated elsewhere must be reiterated here, namely, that oppressed communities must liberate the Bible so that the Bible can liberate them. An oppressed Bible oppresses and a liberated Bible liberates (Mosala: 193).

REFERENCES

Eagleton, T. (1976), *Criticism and Ideology: A Study in Marxist Literary Theory* (London, New Left Books).
— (1981), *Walter Benjamin: Or Towards a Revolutionary Criticism* (London, Verso).
— (1986), *Against the Grain: Essays 1975–1985* (London, Verso).
Gottwald, N. (1985), *The Hebrew Bible: A Socio-Literary Introduction* (Philadelphia, Fortress Press).
Mosala, I. J. (1989), *Biblical Hermeneutics and Black Theology in South Africa* (Grand Rapids, Eerdman's).
Schüssler Fiorenza, E. (1984), *Bread Not Stone* (Boston, Beacon Press).
West, C. (1981), 'The North American Blacks', in S. Torres and J. Eagleson (eds.), *The Challenge of Basic Christian Communities: Papers from the Inter-*

national *Ecumenical Congress of Theology, February 20-March 2, 1980, São Paulo Brazil* (Maryknoll, NY, Orbis Books), pp. 225–227.

— (1985), 'The Dilemma of the Black Intellectual', *Cultural Critique* 7, pp. 109–124.

12

The Gospel of Economy from a Solomon Islands Perspective

LESLIE BOSETO

Christians in Asia, Africa and Latin America are alienated from their own culture partly at the insistence of the missionaries, who not only denigrated their culture but also warned them not to apply their own cultural insights to open up the biblical texts. This essay reverses that axiom and shows how the reclamation of indigenous cultural insights can illuminate the biblical narratives.

This essay is reprinted from *The Pacific Journal of Theology* Series 2, 8 (1992), pp. 79–84. It is available from South Pacific Association of Theological Schools, PO Box 2426, Government Buildings, Suva, Fiji.

Leslie Boseto, a former Bishop of the United Church of Papua New Guinea and the Solomon Islands, is currently working from his village. He has written extensively on Pacific Theology and contextual hermeneutics.

From my reading of the four Gospels, Jesus of Nazareth is an economist, evangelist, social worker, politician, pastor, professor, physician, prophet, servant, counsellor, and more. He is the whole caring and loving concern of God for the whole world. In that light, I want to share with you some thoughts about a gospel of economy related to Solomon Islands culture. We can learn much from our traditional cultures concerning the God-given Good News which our ancestors treasured for hundreds of years before the written words about Jesus were introduced to our shores by those belonging to foreign cultures.

Our ancestors had many altars for worshipping their gods similar to the people of Athens in Acts 17.22–23. Although we may call our ancestors worshippers of untrue gods, it is clear that their gods were very close to them. They were not far away. Because of their awareness of the closeness of their gods, our people were obedient and reverent to any being who was supreme, more powerful, more holy, pure, righteous and truthful than the members of their human communities. It was from this local awareness of the presence of the one mightier and holier than themselves that God had already prepared and led our ancestors, as he prepared and led the people of Israel (see Amos 9.7).

It is from this understanding of God the Creator who had already given us 'wisdom and worthy customs', as expressed in the preamble of our national constitution, that we in the Solomons can make a major contribution to the subject of the gospel of economy.

GOSPEL, ECONOMY AND CREATION

Gospel and economy belong together. Both good news (gospel) and economy are related to creation. Our ancestors located their gods in creation. Their gods resided in the rivers, the mountains, valleys, reefs, trees, and so forth. They were not far away and above us in heaven.

In the same way, the one God who is present in creation gives us a choice between good or bad news, a choice between blessing or curse, between life or death. But this choice depends very much on our good or bad relationship with our Creator. This relationship is interrelated with the environment and other people. God speaks from the environment, not from heaven. This was what Moses experienced in Exodus 3 when he saw that the bush was on fire: God's voice came from the bush itself. God called Moses from the peopled earth, not from heaven (see Exodus 3.7–12).

Moreover, the good news we can choose to receive is good news of and for the people who are economically poor, politically oppressed and racially alienated, like those alienated within the house (tribe) of Pharoah in Egypt. Both the universal *presence* and the *location* of God in creation, which make us aware of God's closeness, permeate our understanding of good news as a gospel of economy.

AN UNDERSTANDING OF ECONOMY

The word 'economy' comes from two Greek words: *oikos*, which means house or household, and *nomos*, which means rule, law or custom. Together they refer to the management or stewardship of a household. An economist is a steward. It is from this definition of the word 'economy' that we see the importance of the role which the steward or manager of the household undertakes. In our Solomon

Islands' understanding of the household, we see all members of our extended families belonging to one household. They usually belong to one area or section of the village. Everyone in the household must be loved, taken care of, fed and recognized. The father or uncle, who are expected to be the chief stewards of the household, must think more about the members of their family, clan or tribe than about themselves. Everyone must be given a place for shelter. Everyone must be given a piece of land for gardening. In other words, the resources from land and sea which are available to sustain the household must be shared or distributed for everyone's survival. This is a gospel of sharing and distribution within the household.

Within every island in the Solomons there are many households. Each household has a steward or manager. Each household is the base for our human security and survival. This concept of the household also extends to members of the same language group. The security network of *won-tok* (one-talkism) is God's gift to us in the Solomons. If one member of this extended household is sick or hungry or even dying, his or her *won-toks* have a special concern for helping that person. Our ministers or priests can go and visit and pray, but the actual sacrifices made for sustaining and comforting the needy member come from his or her cousins, brothers, sisters and *won-toks*.

From this understanding of the human base of the many households of each island, we can also say that every island is itself a household. Every chief, every politician, every church leader, every community leader is a steward of the whole island – the whole household. This is where sharing of human and material resources becomes essential in any given island context.

Let us also remember that our philosophy of life can never be compartmentalized into a dualism of secular and sacred, material and spiritual, rich and poor, women and men. Our whole life's existence and survival depends on the interrelatedness, interdependence and interrelationship of the whole of life. It is at this point that we in the Solomons cannot afford to work denominationally and politically independent of each other. Because our gospel is rooted in our ideology and theology of the wholeness and oneness of life, anything that separates, isolates and privatizes us from our human base of *won-tokism* is a foreign concept.

It is therefore time for each of our island-households to mobilize economically and utilize our God-given resources for the sake of *all* our people. Even though we talk about *won-tokism* and one family as our God-given base, the growing reality now is that through inter-island marriages we have had to welcome members of different households, of different families and clans to our island-household base. Today we talk not only about the family base and the island base of our household, but also about our national-household of the Solomon Islands – and even beyond.

GOD THE SUPREME ECONOMIST

One of our central biblical texts is John 3.16: 'For God loved the world so much that he gave his only son, so that everyone who believes in him may not die but have eternal life.' The whole world is the household of God. The Psalmist says, 'The world and all that is in it belong to the Lord. The earth and all who live on it are his. He built it on the deep waters beneath the earth and laid its foundations in the ocean depths.' (Psalm 24.1–2) If God from the beginning created the whole universe and this particular planet, then God is the Owner, Giver and Sustainer of life and all things therein.

God's love for the whole household (the world) means that he is neither distant nor removed from creation, but is actually involved in it. God has a great plan for managing the whole world. This plan is not spiritual and unseen, but publicly manifested. This manifestation came to fullness when the Word became Flesh and lived amongst us, full of grace and truth. Before the birth of the One whom God sent, Mary saw what this great divine economist was coming to do: to put in order, in proper relationship, all the members within the whole world-household (Luke 1.46–55). It is clear from the Scriptures that God the Economist's plan for the salvation of the whole world is that everyone must be fed, cared for, recognized, accepted, empowered, and nurtured to live for others.

Yet many people today want to rape our mother-earth for their own use, for their own benefits, without recognizing our real cousins, brothers and sisters within the one world-household. The Owner-Manager of the world loves the whole world. God not only created the earth but cries out not to spoil the earth (1 Kings 3.26). The great divine Economist did not come to judge the world but to be its Saviour. Those who accept this – God's plan of love for the world-household – experience eternal life, which is God's love (1 Cor. 13.8; 1 John 4.12).

Leslie Boseto

BEING CO-CREATORS AND CO-STEWARDS

Our ancestors could perceive whether or not their relationship with their gods was right. Tragedy and calamity were the result of their disobedience or rebellion against their gods. Hence it was the duty of the key leaders (priests and politicians) to try to maintain a right relationship with their gods. Victory, blessings and prosperity were the results of their faithfulness to the expectations of their gods. They continued to seek the gods' forgiveness and power in order to maintain a right relationship to the gods and blessings for the people under their care. From this understanding of the interrelatedness of faith and action we see that men and women who know the will of God and do God's will today are co-creators and co-stewards with the God of the Bible, our Creator.

Jesus of Nazareth came to recognize, release and empower ordinary people's potentialities to be used for each other in their given locality and contextual situation. Incarnation means to contextualize and inculturate the economics (stewardship) of resources for the equitable benefit of the whole population of any given community.

With the incarnation the invisible heart of God was no longer hidden from the world. Jesus said: 'I do not call you servants any longer, because a servant does not know what his master is doing. Instead I call you friends, because I have told you everything I heard from my Father' (John 15.15). Knowledge about loving people, caring for people, being in solidarity with each other, loving our neighbours as ourselves – this knowledge is no longer hidden from us. The motivating factor behind God's purchasing power is his love, which enables God to accept and forgive us in our weakest and most powerless situations.

God in Jesus Christ has overcome racial, economic, religious, educational, political and cultural boundaries and barriers by applying his purchasing power of love. The author of Hebrews 1.1–3 acknowledges that God spoke through our ancestors, but his concern revealed through these ancestors was finally manifested through the gift of his own Son, the only true likeness of God's own being, sustaining the universe with his powerful Word. This powerful Word became a human being in action.

A POSTSCRIPT ABOUT GOD'S PARTNER ECONOMISTS

We must not end without acknowledging the often neglected economic power that works along with God to maintain the survival of our people in the Solomon Islands. This power is our faithful, untiring women. They continue to work extremely hard to produce and share resources from their gardens, as well as from their God-given skills, energies and loving care. I have come to learn more and more from our women's perseverance and sacrifice as they participate in God's overall plan for sustaining our island households.

Because of our economic base in the human household, women are able to make a major contribution to the overall economy of our country. May they continue to be empowered by the Mother of Jesus' openness and willingness to be a co-creator and co-steward with God in his universal plan for the salvation of the whole world.

Finally, let us all, men and women, pray for and empower one another in a new way. May every member of our household learn in a deeper way the concern of God for the totality of life.

13

The Equality of Women: Form or Substance (1 Corinthians 11.2–16)

CHRISTINE AMJAD-ALI

This essay is one of the first examples of women's exegetical reflection from Pakistan available in English. Christine Amjad-Ali's paper is among several presented at a 'Women in Reflection and Action' group meeting held in Multan, Pakistan, in April 1989. At this ecumenical gathering, Pakistani women concerned with the situation of women both within the Church and within their country, looked together at Paul's first letter to the Corinthians, especially the section on women's head covering, to help them focus on the issue of women and culture.

For Christine Amjad-Ali's piece and for other examples of hermeneutical reflections by the women of Pakistan on the contentious relationship between gospel and culture, see *Dare to Dream: Studies on Women and Culture with Reference to 1 Corinthians 11.2–16* by 'Women in Reflection and Action', ed. Christine Amjad-Ali. This monograph is available from Christian Study Centre, PO Box 529, Rawalpindi Cantt, Pakistan.

The passage from Paul's first letter to the Corinthians, 11.2–16, is a peculiarly appropriate starting point for a discussion on women and culture for at least two reasons. First, Paul's own arguments and the situation of the Corinthian Christians, already reflect – from their own context – the seemingly impenetrable mixture of tradition, religion and culture which seems to surround any discussion of women and culture. Second, this passage itself has become part of the religious tradition which often determines the culturally acceptable roles open to Christian women.

My paper basically tries to clarify what Paul says in this passage and to draw out some possible implications both for our discussions of 'women's issues' and for our behaviour as women.

1 CORINTHIANS 11.2–16[1]

2   I commend you because in all things you remember me and, just as I transmitted to you, you keep the traditions.

3   And (*de*) I want you to know that the head (*kephale*) of every man (*aner*) is Christ and (*de*) the head of a woman is [the] man and (*de*) the head of Christ is God.

4   Any man who prays or prophesies having [something] down over the head (*kephales*) shames his head,

5   but (*de*) any woman who prays or prophesies with the head uncovered (*akalypto*)[2] shames her head – because it is one and the same thing as it being shaved.

6   For if a woman does not cover [herself] (*katakalypto*), let her also cut off [her hair].

7   For, on the one hand, a man ought not to cover up his head since he comes into being (*hyparchon*)[3] as the image and glory of God; but the woman, on the other hand, is the glory of man.

8   For man is not out of woman but rather woman out of man. Because also man was not created for the sake of the woman, but rather woman for the sake of the man.

9   Because of this the woman ought to have authority (*exousia*)[4] upon the head for the sake of the angels.

10   However (*plen*) neither woman is without man, nor man is without woman in the Lord.

11   Since, just as the woman [was/is] from the man, so the man [was/is] for the sake of the woman. And all things [are/were] from God.

12   Judge for yourselves: Is it fitting for an uncovered woman to pray to God?

13   Does not nature herself teach you that on the one hand if a man wears long hair it is a dishonour for him; but on the other hand, if a woman wears long hair it is a glory for her,

14   because the hair is given instead of (*anti*) a covering (*peribolaion*).

15   But if any one seems to be obstinate we have not any other custom than this, and neither do the churches of God.

INTRODUCTION

This passage in Paul is extremely difficult to understand for at least three reasons. First, the language is obscure. Paul uses at least five different ways of speaking about the head covering. In verse 4, in referring to men, he speaks in a roundabout way of something 'falling

186

down over' the head. In verse 5, he talks of women who are 'uncovered' (*akalypto*), and verse 6, 'covered' (*kalyptra*), using slightly different words, both of which are related to the usual word for a woman's veil (*kalyptra*), but he never actually uses this term. In verse 9, he speaks of a woman having 'authority on the head', which presumably refers, in a symbolic way, to a head covering, but this is not the usual expression, and was probably coined by Paul. In verse 14, Paul speaks of a woman's hair acting as, or replacing, a covering (*peribolaion*), a very general term that could refer to any encircling material such as, for example, a fence (or a turban?). Verse 14 is very strange, in fact, because it seems almost to contradict what Paul has previously said. If a woman's hair is given as a covering, why does she need to cover (veil) her covering (hair)?

Second, it is not at all clear why Paul brings up the subject at all. What was going on in Corinth? A number of issues in 1 Corinthians are addressed by Paul in response to questions from the Corinthians; they are marked by the introductory phrase 'Now concerning such and such' (e.g. 1 Corinthians 8.1, 'Now concerning food offered to idols . . .'). But 1 Corinthians 11.2–16 is not of these sections. The Corinthians did not address any question to Paul concerning the proper dress for women; Paul himself brought the issue up. Nor is it clear what was happening in Corinth that Paul objected to. Some commentators[5] have argued that Paul is not interested in *head coverings*, but rather *hair styles*. He objects to men and women having long unbound hair in worship. It is further suggested that the Corinthians adopted this hair style to show that they were Spirit-inspired prophets, who spoke in an ecstatic frenzy, in imitation of the devotees of pagan mystery cults. Paul, on this hypothesis, wants men to keep their hair short and women to keep theirs bound up. However, there is no evidence in 1 Corinthians 11 that this is the problem. Paul does not suggest the Corinthians are in danger of being mistaken for pagan initiates (contrast, for example, his discussion of eating sacrificed meat, where Paul is quite open about the possibility of the Christian being drawn into idol worship, or 'weaker' Christians thinking that this is what is happening). And while 'binding up the hair' could be what is referred to in two of Paul's references (v. 4 and v. 14), two of the other three clearly speak of 'covering' (*kalypt* the root means 'covered' or 'hidden'; *apocalypse* is from the same root and means 'revealed' or 'un-covered'). Also, having 'authority on the head' suggests putting something on the head, not just binding up the hair.

Other commentators[6] suggest that the Corinthian women led worship with their head uncovered as a deliberate way of asserting their equality to men. Paul objected to this practice not because it affirmed women's equality with men (which Paul accepted), but because it obliterated the sexual distinctions between women and men (which Paul considered basic to human personality). That women led worship in Corinth with their heads uncovered does seem to me to be the point at issue. But I am doubtful that there was a specific, theological, conscious rationale behind this practice. Paul gives theological (and other) reasons for the counter-practice he wants to introduce, but he does not explicitly combat any alternative theology. Again, it is instructive to compare his discussion of eating food offered to idols. Here Paul clearly engages the Corinthian theological justification, that is, that 'all things are lawful' and 'idols have no real existence' (see 10.23, 8.4).

Third, this passage is difficult to follow because we are not at all sure of what the customs of head covering generally were. High-class urban women seen to have worn elaborate hair styles, with the hair piled on top of the head and held there with pins, decorated with jewels and perhaps veils of some sort. Lower-class and working women, however, cannot have worn such styles, which were impractical except for the leisured class. One guesses that lower-class women probably plaited their hair, and perhaps wrapped the plait round the head. There is, however, no way of knowing – poor women are not the subjects of sculptures or paintings. Did urban women of any class cover their heads when they were out in public? One does not know. Urban men (especially those influenced by Rome) went short-haired and clean shaven. Greek and Roman men do not seem to have used head coverings. But Greek urban culture is not the only culture at issue. There is the question of Jewish practices, both the Jewish community in Palestine and the Jewish communities in the Greek cities. It is probable that Jewish practice allowed women less freedom than was customary in the Greek cities. Philo and Josephus (two famous Jewish writers from this period) both speak of the ideal situation as that where women are enclosed in the inner house and see no one but their immediate relatives. Again this may well be a class-specific ideal. As in Pakistan, *purdah* (veil) is the ideal mostly for the urban lower-middle-class – it is impractical for lower-class women who have to work, and it is often rejected by upper-class women whose wealth allows them a greater freedom. It may also have been an urban phenomenon. However, the gospel stories, largely set in the countryside, suggest a greater interaction between men and women.

The question of Jewish male head coverings is even more interesting. Jewish practice now – like Muslim practice – is that men *should cover* their heads while praying. There is no reason at all to think this is a recent innovation. Further, long hair has not normally been considered shameful in Jewish tradition (think of Samson), and one guesses that among Palestinian Jews – as among most eastern groups – men normally wore a head covering, for protection from the sun if for no other reason. Thus when Paul appeals to nature and custom, one has to ask which custom he is appealing to.

To sum up, not only is it difficult to work out what Paul is saying, we are not at all sure why he is saying it, what is going on at Corinth, and what the customary practices are. Nevertheless, this passage is very important because it has been used (and is still used) to supply a norm for both male and female dress in worship, and, because of the way Paul argues, seems to be paradigmatic for the way 'women's questions' are discussed in the Church.

PAUL'S ARGUMENT

1 What he does not say

Before analysing what Paul says it is very important to see what he does not say, and to avoid reading things into the passage that are not there. In this passage Paul clearly assumes that women will lead in worship just as men lead in worship. He is not saying that women should not lead worship, only regulating what they should wear. This is important. In our Christian culture women are in the habit of covering their heads whenever someone (else) reads from the Bible, prays or preaches, and this is often justified on the basis of 1 Corinthians 11. Paul, however, is talking about what a women should do when *she* reads the Scriptures, prays or preaches. He uses exactly the same words about men's activity as about women's ('If a man prays or prophesies . . . ; If a woman prays or prophesies . . .'). There are passages in the New Testament that say women should not lead in church, but *this passage takes for granted that women will lead worship services.*

2 The argument from religious tradition

Paul begins and ends his discussion with a reference to 'the traditions' (v. 2) and Christian traditional practices (what the other Churches do, v. 16). He wants the Corinthians to follow his teaching in this matter because it is 'traditional'. The question is 'whose tradition?'

Head covering of women probably follows Jewish practice, and it may or may not match certain areas of Greek culture. It certainly goes against the Corinthian Church's local practice. (It is worth asking how Paul knew of the practice, in any case. My guess is some of the more conservative – perhaps Jewish – members complained privately. Again it may be that the Corinthian practice offended middle-class sensibilities.) Paul wishes to introduce Jewish culture for women and Greek culture for men, but he baptizes both in the name of religious tradition.

3 The argument from creation (vv. 3–12)

The theological justification for the practice Paul wants to introduce at Corinth comes from a hierarchical reading of the creation story found in Genesis 2. It is significant, in the first place, that Paul uses the Genesis 2 creation story. The Genesis 1 story speaks of the equality in creation of men and women ('God created man in his own image, male and female he created them'), and would not have served Paul's purpose here. The fact that Paul starts from Genesis 2 shows that Paul is justifying his practice through scripture – scripture is not the cause of his practice. In the Genesis 2 story God first creates the male (thus God is the 'source' or 'head'[7] of the man) who is thus the image and glory of God. The woman, however, 'comes out of' the man – being created from his rib. Thus her source is the man, and she is his glory. (Interestingly, Paul does not use the word 'image' in reference to women, perhaps because Genesis 1 clearly states that woman as well as man is the image of God. Paul cannot contradict this so he simply ignores it.)

This reading of Genesis 2 is first given by Paul in the hierarchical summary of verse 3. The implications are drawn, equally for men and women, in verses 4 and 5. (Why – even granting Paul's premise that a woman's head is the man – it should shame her head to be uncovered, I do not know. Nor do I know why it shames the man's head to be covered.) It is clear, however, that Paul is not equally concerned about men's and women's behaviour, since he rather irrelevantly brings in the question of women shaving their heads. What he seems to be saying is that women who do not cover their heads are no better than prostitutes.

From Genesis 2, Paul argues that women are not the same as men, they are subordinate to men, and therefore when they exercise leadership within the Church they ought to show that they acknowledge this God-created differentiation by 'having authority on the head' (v. 10). Having 'authority on the head' is therefore either a symbol that, despite the God-given order of creation, within the Church women have a legitimate leadership role; or a symbol that, despite the fact they exercise leadership, women recognize their God-given subordination. They must do this also for the sake of the angels. Again this phrase is far from clear. It could mean that women should take care that the angels – who are the guardians of proper order – are not offended. Or it could be a reference to a Jewish tradition that blamed the Fall on the mating of the angels (the sons of God) with the daughters of men (cf. Gen. 6.1 and 6.2). The women in this view must cover their heads so as not to tempt the angels to sin.

Finally, Paul draws back a little from the subordination he has been teaching. In verses 11 and 12 he argues that 'in the Lord', that is, in the Church, or the New Creation, women are not subordinate to men. Women and men are interdependent. However, in my view, the damage has already been done. Paul has argued that women are subordinate to men *from creation*. If he had argued that women's subordination was a result of the Fall, then to say that women and men are equal in Christ would be to affirm the restoration of God's creation which Christ's ministry effects. But Paul does not do this. He acknowledges the functional equality of men and women 'in the Lord', in terms of leading worship, but he also acknowledges the validity of traditional beliefs about the subordination of women, and justifies these beliefs theologically through an interpretation of Scripture. He, therefore, allows women to *function* as the equals of men, but even as they are doing this he wants them to *symbolically acknowledge* that they are in fact subordinate to men. Women may break the cultural stereotypes by being leaders in the Church, but they must not break the forms and symbols which give shape to these stereotypes.

4 The argument from 'nature'

Paul finally appeals to the Corinthians' own sense of what is 'natural' or proper. As always, in practice what is 'natural' is culturally defined, although the assumption is usually that it is a universal value. The question is again, which culture? There is nothing 'naturally' either good or bad about covering the head in worship. The problem with Paul's whole argument is that he has reified a cultural practice.

IMPLICATIONS FOR OUR OWN CONTEXT

It seems to me that what Paul does in 1 Corinthians 11 is rather similar to what Benazir Bhutto does [in 1989]. The Prime Minister *functionally* disregards the traditional, cultural and religious understanding of the subordination of women, which is current in Pakistan, and is the leader of the country. On the other hand, in an effort to avoid criticism from conservative quarters, she *symbolically* acknowledges and validates the traditional view that women are subordinate. This is seen, for example, in her very visible deference to the dress code; she dresses far more conservatively than most women of her class – for example, Begum Nusrat Bhutto. The question is how long one can keep the symbols while transforming the substance. Jesus said that one cannot put new wine in old wine skins, because the wine will break the skins and both skins *and* wine will be lost. My fear is that the skins will remain, but the wine will go stale.

This is certainly what happened in the case of women's leadership in the Pauline churches. Paul acknowledged the equality of men and women 'in the Lord', but he wanted to preserve the cultural symbols of deference and subordination, presumably in order not to give offence. Within a few years, however, the theological argument from creation, which Paul used to enforce the covering of women's heads when they led in worship, had became the justification for shutting women out of all leadership roles. Women were to keep silent in church. Women could not teach or have authority over men. Women must be submissive to their husbands, calling them 'lord'.

My question about women's dress in Pakistan – especially in the context of the Church – is what is the dress meant to symbolize? If it is simply a cultural expression of reverence for the holy, why don't our men also cover their heads (which would be culturally appropriate also)? My fear, however, is that we are not just following Pakistani culture, we are also following western missionary culture, and that we cover our heads for the reasons Paul gave: to acknowledge our acceptance of our cultural position of subordination.

In my view, we cannot hope to manifest the *substance* of what it means to say we – as women – are created in God's image if we hold on to the *forms* which symbolize the belief that we are created as secondary beings, for the glory of man, and not in the image of God. The task for us is to find those forms which will express our human identity in ways which are culturally appropriate.

NOTES

1   I have given below my own translation of this passage from the original Greek in order to bring out fully the problematic issues of this passage. I have therefore given the original Greek in parentheses in order to clarify the issues.

2   *Akalypto* means 'uncovered'; it is closely connected with *kalyptra* which means 'woman's veil' – or, more exactly, 'head covering'.

3   This is a slight overtranslation; *hyparchon* can simply mean 'is', but it is not the usual word for 'is'. Presumably Paul used it because it does have overtones of origination.

4   The word in Greek (*exousia*) means 'authority'; it is not an idiomatic expression for 'veil'. Presumably Paul means something like 'the woman ought to have a symbol of authority [i.e. a head covering] upon the head'.

5   Notably E. Schüssler Fiorenza, *In Memory of Her* (New York, Crossroad, 1983), p. 227.

6   See, for example, R. Scroggs, 'Paul and the Eschatological Women', *Journal of the American Academy of Religion* 41 (1972), pp. 283–303.

7   In Greek, 'head' can have the metaphorical meaning 'source' – as in 'the head of a river', but not the meaning 'ruler', which it has, for example, in English. However, concepts of origin can also lead to concepts of subordination.

14

Racial Motifs in the Biblical Narratives

CAIN HOPE FELDER

While Latin American liberation theology has persuasively introduced the questions of class and ideology into the hermeneutical debate, the black theologies of North America and Africa have added the questions of race and culture. This article is an attempt to highlight the racial motifs in the Christian Scriptures and their importance for interpretation.

This piece is from his book, *Troubling Biblical Waters: Race, Class, and Family* (Maryknoll, NY, Orbis Books, 1989).

Cain Hope Felder is Professor of New Testament Language and Literature at Howard University, Washington DC.

The Bible contains different, even conflicting, traditions about the precise location of ancient Sheba, although the evidence suggests that Sheba was in or very near Black Africa. The Old Testament may lack details on the race or ethnicity of the celebrated Queen of Sheba, but there are sufficient ancient extrabiblical witnesses that favour her Black identity.

We now take up the larger questions of race and racism – not in relation to a particular biblical figure, but as it pertains to a wide range of biblical narratives. We do not find any elaborate definitions or theories about race in antiquity. This means we must reckon with certain methodological problems in attempting to examine racial motifs in the Bible. Ancient authors of biblical texts did have color and race consciousness (they were aware of certain physiological differences), but this consciousness of color and race was by no means a political or ideological basis for enslaving or otherwise oppressing other peoples. In fact, the Bible contains scarcely any narratives in which the original intent was to negate the humanity of Black people or view Blacks unfavourably.

The specific racial type of the biblical Hebrews is itself quite difficult to determine.[1] Scholars today generally recognize that the biblical Hebrews most probably emerged as an amalgamation of races rather than from any pure racial stock. When they departed from Egypt, they may well have been Afroasiatics. To refer to the earliest Hebrews as 'Semites' does not take us very far, since the eighteenth-century term does not designate a race, but a family of languages embracing Hebrew, Akkadian, Arabic, and Ethiopic (*Gé'ez*).[2] The language of 'burnt-face' Africans, for example, is as equally Semitic as the language of the Jews or the Arabs.[3] This reaffirms our earlier contention that sophisticated theories about race and the phenomenon of racism are by-products of the postbiblical era. Consequently part of the task in this chapter is to construct an interpretive framework for a range of biblical attitudes about race and to determine implications for the problem of racism and ethnocentrism that still bedevil both Church and society in many nations today, including those of the Third World.

Although the Bible primarily presents sociopolitical entities that are differentiated as empires, nations, and tribes, there are important ways in which the subject of race acquires particular significance. In the Bible, two broad processes related to racism may be operating. First there is the phenomenon of 'sacralization'. By this we mean *the transposing of an ideological concept into a tenet of religious faith in order to serve the vested interest of a particular ethnic group.* Second is the process of 'secularization' or *the diluting of a rich religious concept under the weighty influence of secular pressures (social or political).*[4] In secularization, ideas are wrenched from their original religious moorings and fall prey to nationalistic ideologies. These often cultivate patterns of ethnocentrism and even racism, which in turn can have harmful effects on certain racial groups who are scorned and marginalized.

RACE AND SACRALIZATION IN THE OLD TESTAMENT

Several Old Testament passages are quite suitable as illustrations of sacralization, and as such, require a new kind of critical engagement. First, we shall consider the so-called curse of Ham (Gen. 9.18–27), which rabbis of the early Talmudic periods and the Church Fathers at times used to denigrate Black people. Later Europeans adopted the so-called curse of Ham as a justification for slavery and stereotypical aspersions about Blacks. Second, we shall discuss the fascinating narrative about Miriam and Aaron, who object to Moses' Ethiopian wife (Num. 12.1–16). Third, our attention will focus on the Old Testament genealogies that contributed to the Israelite and ancient Jewish perception that they constituted a most divinely favored people ('race'). Fourth, we shall take up the biblical notion of election (chosen people) as it develops as an explicit theme in the Old Testament and changes in the New Testament.

Our first example of sacralization is found in some of the earliest Jahwist ('J') traditions of the Old Testament. It is Genesis 9.18–27, which has achieved notoriety in many quarters because it contains the so-called curse of Ham. Technically, the passage should follow directly after the 'J' passage that concludes the flood narrative (Gen. 8.20–2), since critical investigations have shown that Genesis 9.1–17, 28, 29 represent the much later Priestly ('P') exilic tradition.[5] The great significance of Genesis 9.18–27 is not that it contains the so-called curse of Ham, which technically does not take place at all. Rather, these verses make it clear that, to the mind of the ancient Israelite author, 'the whole post-diluvial humanity stems from Noah's three sons.'[6] On Genesis 9.19, Claus Westermann remarks:

> The whole of humankind takes its origin from them [Shem, Ham, Japheth] ... humanity is conceived here as a unity, in a way different from the creation; humanity in all its variety across the earth, takes its origin from these three who survived the flood. The purpose of the contrast is to underscore the amazing fact that humanity scattered in all its variety throughout the world comes from one family.[7]

Once the passage established this essential aspect of human origin (vv. 18, 19), it continued by providing what appears to be a primeval rationale for differences in the destinies or fortunes of certain groups of persons. Certainly, as one scholar notes, 'from a form critical viewpoint Genesis 9.20–7 is an ethnological etiology concerned with the theology of culture and history.'[8] This observation alerts us to the theological motives in verses 20–7 that have implications for definite interpretations regarding culture and history. It is this development that most clearly attests to the process of sacralization, where cultural and historical phenomena are recast as theological truths holding the vested interest of particular groups.

A word about the literary form of this narrative is important. In general, the narrative passages of Genesis 1–11 concern themselves with the matter of 'crime and punishment; this is particularly evident in the ('J') narratives.'[9] Westermann informs us that these narratives have antecedents and parallels in ancient African myths: 'It is beyond dispute that African myths about the primeval state and biblical stories of crime and punishment in J correspond both in their leading motifs and in their structure.'[10]

With respect to Genesis 9.18–27, the crime is Ham's seeing the nakedness of his drunken father, Noah, without immediately covering him. In error, Ham leaves his father uncovered (an act of great shamelessness and parental disrespect in Hebrew tradition) while he goes to report Noah's condition to Shem and Japheth, his brothers (v. 22). Ham's two brothers display proper respect by discreetly covering their father (v. 23). When Noah awakens (v. 24), the problems begin. Noah pronounces a curse – *not* on Ham, but on Ham's son Canaan, who has not been mentioned before. Noah also blesses Shem and Japheth, presumably as a reward for their sense of respect.

If one attempts to argue for the unity of the passage, inconsistencies and other difficulties abound. To illustrate, Ham commits the shameless act in verse 22, but Canaan is cursed in verse 25. In 9.18, the list of Noah's sons refers to Ham as being second, but in 9.24, the text – presumably referring to Ham – uses the phrase, Noah's 'youngest son'. Also, the mentioning of Canaan as cursed in verse 25 raises the possibility (albeit untenable) that Noah had a fourth son, named Canaan.

Then too, uncertainties about the precise nature of Ham's error result in a fantastic variety of suggestions, which range from Ham's having possibly castrated his father, attacked his father homosexually, committed incest with his father's wife, or having had sexual relations with his own wife while aboard the ark.[11] The matter was far less complicated: Ham violated a vital rule of respect. Many of the difficulties within this passage find a solution if we allow the possibility that the original version of Genesis 9.18–27 only referred to Ham and his error, and a later version of the story – one motivated by political developments in ancient Palestine – attempted to justify Shem's descendants (Israel) and those of Japheth (Philistines) over the subjugated Canaanites.[12]

While admitting that it is Ham who shows disrespect to Noah but Canaan, Ham's son, who is cursed, Westermann asserts:

The same person who committed the outrage in v. 22 falls under the curse in v. 25. The Yahwist has preserved, together with the story of Ham's outrage, a curse over Canaan which could be resumed because of the genealogical proximity of Canaan to Ham. Those who heard the story knew the descendants of Ham as identical with those of Canaan.[13]

In Westermann's view, Ham *was* cursed and presumably not just Canaan, but all the other descendants of Ham cited in Genesis 10.6: Cush, Egypt, and Put (Punt).

Although I disagree with Westermann's contention that Ham was, *in effect*, cursed in Genesis 9.18–27, he helps us see that the ambiguity of the text can lead Bible interpreters to justify their particular history, culture, and race by developing self-serving theological constructs. In one instance, the Canaanites 'deserve' subjugation; in another instance, the Hamites 'deserve' to be hewers of wood and drawers of water.

Whether or not sacralization was actually part of the original narrative, we have much evidence in the Midrashim (AD fifth century), where Noah says to Ham: 'You have prevented me from doing something in the dark (cohabitation), therefore your seed will be ugly and dark-skinned.'[14] Similarly, the Babylonian Talmud (AD sixth century) states that 'the descendants of Ham are cursed by being Black and are sinful with a degenerate progeny.'[15] The idea that the blackness of Africans was due to a curse, and thus reinforced and sanctioned enslaving Blacks, persisted into the seventeenth century.[16] Even today, in such versions of Holy Scripture as *Dake's Annotated Reference Bible*, one finds in Genesis 9.18–27 a so-called 'great racial prophecy' with the following racist hermeneutic:

> All colors and types of men came into existence after the flood. All men were white up to this point, for there was only one family line of Christ, being mentioned in Luke 3.36 with his son Shem . . . prophecy that Shem would be a chosen race and have a peculiar relationship with God. All divine revelation since Shem has come through his line . . . prophecy that Japheth would be the father of the great and enlarged races. Government, Science and Art are mainly Japhethic. . . . His descendants constitute the leading nations of civilization.[17]

Another instance of sacralization confronts us quite early in the Old Testament, within the genealogies of the descendants of Noah. It is especially useful to consider the so-called table of nations (Genesis 10) in conjunction with the much later genealogical listing of

1 Chronicles 1.1–2.55. On the one hand, these listings purport to be comprehensive catalogs. All too often they have been erroneously taken as reliable sources of ancient ethnography. Critical study of these genealogies illuminates theological motives that inevitably demonstrate a tendency to arrange different groups in priority, thereby attaching the greatest significance to the Israelites as an ethnic and national entity greater than all other peoples of the earth.

At first glance, Genesis 10 appears to be a single listing of ancient nations. However, biblical criticism has for some time demonstrated that Genesis 10 represents a combination of at least two different lists, separated by centuries: Jahwist ('J') and Priestly ('P').[18] In fact, the fusing of different traditions in Genesis 10 doubtlessly accounts for the difficulty in locating the land of Cush, and determining the relationship between Cush and Sheba or the differences between Seba and Sheba. Genesis 10.7 mentions Seba as a son of Cush, and Sheba is a grandson of Cush. Here the text clearly is identifying the descendants of Ham (*ham*). Then in Genesis 10.28, the text introduces an anomaly, mentioning Sheba as a direct descendant of Shem, not Ham. Furthermore, since the initial Samech (*s*) of *seb'a* is the equivalent of and interchangeable with the Hebrew Shin (*s*) in old South Arabic,[19] one could argue that Genesis 10 offers us two persons named Sheba as descendants of Cush, but only one person by that name as a descendant of Shem. In any case, it is not clear that the table of nations as it stands does not have the motive of delineating sharp ethnic differences between the ancient peoples of Africa, South Arabia, and Mesopotamia. The true motive lies elsewhere.

Rather than an objective historical account of genealogies, the table of nations in Genesis 10 is a theologically motivated catalog of people. The table not only ends with the descendants of Shem, but does so in a way consciously stylized to accentuate the importance of his descendants.[20] About this, the author of the genealogy in 1 Chronicles 1.17–34 is most explicit; of all the descendants of the sons of Noah, Shem's receive the most elaborate attention. Thus the most primitive 'J' listing of the nations is theologically edited centuries later according to the post-exilic Priestly tradition, in order to establish the priority of the descendants of Shem. Centuries later, a further elaboration takes place, as found in the genealogies of 1 Chronicles. In this long progression, the theological presuppositions of a particular ethnic group displace any concern for objective historiography and ethnography. The descendants of Noah not related to Shem become increasingly insignificant and are mentioned only when they serve as foils to demonstrate the priority of the Israelites.

The subtle process being described may consequently be called sacralization, because it represents an attempt on the part of one ethnic group to construe salvation history in terms that are distinctly favorable to it, as opposed to others. Here, ethnic particularity evolves with a certain divine vindication, and the dangers of rank racism lie just beneath the surface. While the genealogies do not express negative attitudes about persons of African descent, as my colleague Gene Rice has noted, it is important to clarify an aspect of his judgement in light of the way in which sacralization expresses itself in these genealogies. Consider Rice's remarks:

> Genesis 10 has to do with all the peoples of the world known to ancient Israel and since this chapter immediately follows the episode of Noah's cursing and blessing, it would have been most appropriate to express here any prejudicial feelings toward African peoples. Not only are such feelings absent, but all peoples are consciously and deliberately related to each other as brothers. *No one, not even Israel, is elevated above anyone else and no disparaging remark is made about any people, not even the enemies of Israel* [emphasis mine].[21]

Rice's contention that the genealogies do not elevate Israel above anyone else must be qualified. After all, Genesis 10.21–31 becomes the basis for amplifying the descendants of Shem and Judah (1 Chron. 2.1–55) as the distinctive *laos tou Theou* (LXX 'people of God'). Thus the entire genealogies are construed theologically to enhance the status of a particular people, and this is sacralization.

Numbers 12 attests all too well to the way individuals can quickly move from a sacred ethnic stance to racism of the worst sort. In Numbers 12.1, Moses' brother and sister castigate him for having married a Cushite woman (*hāʾišā hacū šiʿt*). Several factors point to the probability that the offensive aspect of the marriage was the woman's Black identity. In the first place, this is clearly the view expressed in the wording of the Septuagint: *heneken tēs gunaikos tēs Aithiopissēs* ('on account of the Ethiopian woman').[22] Secondly, in the selection of the rather odd punishment that God unleashes on Miriam (v. 10), it can hardly be accidental that leprosy is described vividly as 'leprous, as white as snow'. Quite an intentional contrast is dramatized here: Moses' Black wife, accursed by Miriam and Aaron, is now contrasted with Miriam, who suddenly becomes 'as white as snow' in her punishment. The contrast is sharpened all the more because only Miriam is punished for an offense of which Aaron is equally guilty. The LXX witness, together with these exegetical considerations, point strongly to the probability that more than arrogance is at issue in this text. Also involved is a rebuke to the racial prejudice characterized by the attitudes of Miriam and Aaron.

God's stern rebuke of Miriam's and Aaron's incipient racial prejudice is a perennial reminder of the extraordinarily progressive racial values of the Bible in comparison to the hostile racial attitudes in the medieval and modern period.[23] At the same time, however, the Numbers 12 narrative exposes the inherent difficulties of any quick generality about the racial implications of sacralization that appear when early traditions assume, through years of refinement, an ethnic particularity that marginalizes groups outside the Torah, 'The Land of Israel' (*'ereș Israēl*), and the Covenant.

For theological reasons, the process of sacralization in the Old Testament largely remains racially ambiguous, especially with specific reference to Black people. The distinction the Old Testament makes is not racial. Rather, the Hebrew Scripture distinguishes groups on the basis of national identity and ethnic tribes. All who do not meet the criteria for salvation as defined by the ethnic or national 'in-groups' are relegated to an inferior status. It is therefore surprising to many that Black people are not only frequently mentioned in numerous Old Testament texts but are mentioned in ways that acknowledge their actual and potential role in the salvation history of Israel. By no means are Black people excluded from Israel's story, as long as they claim it (however secondarily) and do not proclaim their own story apart from the activity of Israel's God.

Extensive lists of Old Testament passages that make favorable reference to Black people are readily accessible.[24] There are many illustrations of such provocative texts. Isaiah 37.9 and 2 Kings 19.9 refer to Tirhaka, king of the Ethiopians. This ancient Black Pharaoh was actually the fourth member of the Twenty-fifth Egyptian Dynasty that ruled all of Egypt (730–653 BC).[25] According to the biblical texts, Tirhaka was the object of the desperate hopes of Israel. In the days of Hezekiah, Israel hoped desperately that Tirhaka's armies would intervene and stave off an impending Assyrian assault by Sennacherib. More than a half-century later, another text would refer to 'men of Ethiopia and Put who handle the shield' (Jer. 46.9). The Old Testament indicates that Black people were part of the Hebrew army (2 Sam. 18.21–32) and even part of the royal court. Ebedmelech takes action to save Jeremiah's life (Jer. 38.7–13) and thereby becomes the beneficiary of a singular divine blessing (Jer. 39.15–18). The dominant portrait of the Ethiopians in the Old Testament is that of a wealthy people (Job 28.19; Isa. 45.14) who would soon experience conversion (Ps. 68.31; Isa. 11.11, 18.7; Zeph. 3.10). The reference to 'Zephaniah the son of Cushi' (Zeph. 1.1) may indicate that one of the books of the Old Testament was authored by a Black African.[26]

ELECTION AND SACRALIZATION IN THE BIBLE

Israel's particularity loses much of its subtlety as the dubious concept of her election (*bāḥar*) begins to gain a firm footing in the Old Testament. Certainly, traces of the idea of Israel's chosenness and personal, special relationship with her deity were present in 'the pre-Jahwistic cult of the ancestors', but the explicit concept of Jahweh's loving preference for the people of Israel develops relatively late.[27] The theologically elaborated belief that Jahweh specifically chose Israel above all other nations does not become a matter of religious ideology – and therefore an instance of sacralization – until the period of Deuteronomistic history toward the end of the seventh century BC (Deut. 7.6–8, 10.15; Jer. 2.3; compare: Isa. 43.20, 65.9).[28]

Regardless of the theological structure that attempts to support the Deuteronomistic concept of Israel's election, ambiguities engulf this concept of election. Horst Seebass, for example, insists that even among the Deuteronomistic writers, Israel's election 'only rarely stands at the center of what is meant by election.'[29] According to him, *bāḥar*, as a technical term for Israel's election, always functions as a symbol of universalism. It represents Israel in the role of 'service to the whole'.[30] Seebass is representative of those who want to de-emphasize the distinctive ethnic or racial significance of the concept in Israel's self-understanding during the Deuteronomistic period.[31]

The ethnic and racial ambiguities involved in the concept of Israel's election seem to persist. The ambiguity does not result from the fact that a universalistic history is presupposed by the biblical writers who advance the Old Testament concept of Israel's election. Rather, the ambiguities stem from the nature of the presupposed universalism. Gerhard von Rad points out that in the Deuteronomistic circles, the chosenness of Israel attains a radical form and its universal aspect is at best paradoxical.[32] Perhaps the real paradox resides in the notion that Israel's divine election seems to lead inevitably to sacralization, with the people of Israel as an ethnic group at the center. Certainly, the Deuteronomistic authors struggle to demonstrate Jahweh's affirmation of the Davidic monarchy and, more importantly, Jahweh's selection of Jerusalem as the center of any continuing redemptive activity.[33] Although the people of Israel exhibit no extraordinary attributes or values by which they objectively merit Jahweh's election, there later develops an elaborate doctrine of merit, by which those who know and follow the Torah attempt to prove their worthiness as the chosen people.

Despite the absence of any inherent superiority of the people of Israel, the concept of election becomes inextricably bound up with ethnic particularity. Accordingly, the people of Israel claim the status of being pre-eminently chosen. They thereby claim to possess the Law, the Covenant, and a continuing promise of the land and the city as the 'in-group'. At the same time, all who stand outside the community or apart from the supporting religious ideology of election are relegated to the margins of Israel's 'universal' saving history. Other races and ethnic groups may, of course, subscribe to Israel's religious ideology and derive the commensurate benefits. But the criteria for such subscription always seem to be mediated through the biases of an ethnic group reinforced by elaborate genealogies and the transmission of particular legal religious traditions.

This entire development typifies the process of sacralization, and it is striking to see the different treatment of election in the New Testament. George Foot Moore provides us with a glimpse of the New Testament conception of election when he asserts that, 'Paul and the church substituted an individual election to eternal life, without regard to race or station.'[34] However, such an assertion oversimplifies New Testament ideas about election. Rudolf Bultmann provides us with a more helpful understanding of the New Testament in this regard. He argues that in the New Testament, 'the Christian Church becomes the true people of God.' In Bultmann's view, the New Testament no longer concerns itself with a pre-eminent ethnic group, that is, *Israēl kata sarka* (1 Cor. 10.18), but with the Israel of

God (Gal. 6.16), without any exclusive ethnic or racial coordinates.[35]

In contrast to the Deuteronomistic usage of the Hebrew term *bāḥar*, the New Testament never presents the Greek verb *eklegomai* or its nominal derivatives *eklektos* ('chosen') and *eklogē* ('election') in an ethnically or racially exclusive sense. Paul wants to maintain a certain continuity with aspects of Israel's election, but that continuity is neither ethnic nor cultic (Rom. 9.11; 11.2, 11, 28, 29). For Paul, corporate election can include some Jews, but it must also embrace Gentiles (Rom. 11.25; Gal. 3.28; 1 Cor. 12.13); being 'in' and 'with' Christ becomes the new *crux interpretum*. In Paul's view, God *chose* the foolish, weak, and low (1 Cor. 1.27, 28). For James, God *chose* the poor who are rich in faith (Jas. 2.5). For Matthew, God calls many, but *chooses* only the few (Matt. 22.14). The new universalism and unity to be found in the Christian Church expresses itself further within the context of 'God's chosen ones' in the following sequence of thoughts:

> There is neither Jew nor Greek, there is neither slave nor free, there is neither male nor female; for you are all one in Christ Jesus (Gal. 3.28).
>
> For by one Spirit we were all baptized into one body – Jews or Greeks, slaves or free – and all were made to drink of one Spirit (1 Cor. 12.13).
>
> Here there cannot be Greek and Jew, circumcised and uncircumcised, barbarian, Scythian, slave, free man, but Christ is all, and in all (Col. 3.11, 12).

The only New Testament text that refers to Christians as 'a chosen race' (*genos eklekton*) is 1 Peter 2.9. Yet, in this text, the phrase is manifestly metaphorical. 1 Peter 2.9 depends very heavily on the wording found in LXX Isaiah 43.20, 21, but the ethnic particularity implied in the Old Testament text has fallen away entirely in 1 Peter.[36] Throughout the New Testament period (which extends well into the second century), 'the elect' become the Church as the new Israel. Matthew is even more specific, because the elect represent the faithful few in the Church who accept the call to the higher righteousness and the doing of the will of God. In either case, these New Testament perspectives eliminate all ethnic or racial criteria for determining the elect.[37]

Cain Hope Felder

SECULARIZATION IN THE NEW TESTAMENT

Ambiguities with regard to race in the New Testament do not appear within the context of what we have defined as sacralization. The New Testament disapproves of ethnic corporate election, or 'Israel according to the flesh'. In fact, the New Testament offers no grand genealogies to sacralize the myth of any ethnic or national superiority.

If one is to explore the subject of racialist tendencies in the New Testament, one may turn to a different phenomenon: the process of secularization. How did the expanding Church – in its attempt to survive without the temporary protection she derived from being confused with Judaism – begin to succumb to the dominant symbols and ideologies of the Greco-Roman world? We will see how the universalism of the New Testament diminishes as Athens and Rome substitute for Jerusalem as the alleged new centers of God's redemptive activity.

The early Christian authors' understanding of the world barely included sub-Saharan Africa. They had no idea at all of the Americas or the Far East. These writers referred to Spain as 'the limits of the West' (1 Clem. 5.7; Rom. 15.28); they envisioned the perimeter of the world as the outer reaches of the Roman Empire.[38] For New Testament authors, Roman sociopolitical realities, as well as the language and culture of Hellenism, often determined how God was seen as acting in Jesus Christ. Just as Old Testament Jerusalem came to represent the pre-eminent holy city of the God of Israel (Zion), New Testament authors attached a pre-eminent status to Rome, the capital city of their world.[39]

It is no coincidence that Mark, the earliest composer of a passion narrative, goes to such great lengths to show that the confession of the Roman centurion brings his whole gospel narrative to its climax.[40] For his part, Luke expends considerable effort to specify the positive qualities of his various centurions.[41] There is even a sense in which their official titles symbolize Rome as the capital of the Gentile world, for their incipient acts of faith or confessions (according to Luke) find their denouement in the Acts 28 portrait of Paul, who relentlessly proclaims the *kerygma* in Rome. The immediate significance of this New Testament tendency to focus on Rome instead of Jerusalem is that the darker races outside the Roman orbit are for the most part overlooked by New Testament authors.

For lack of more descriptive terminology, this process may be

205

called secularization. Here, sociopolitical realities tend to dilute the New Testament vision of racial inclusiveness and universalism. Early traditions are accordingly adapted at later stages in such a way as to expose an undue compromising of a religious vision and to show how secular sociopolitical realities cause religious texts to be slanted to the detriment of the darker races.

Perhaps one of the best illustrations of this process of seculariz-ation is Luke's narrative about the baptism and conversion of the Ethiopian official in Acts 8.26–40. On the surface, this is a highly problematic text. One wonders immediately if the Ethiopian finance minister is a Jew or Gentile. One also wonders about the efficacy of his baptism and whether it constituted or led to a full conversion to Christianity. Probably the best survey of the problems posed by this story is that by Ernst Haenchen, who entitles the story 'Philip Con-verts a Chamberlain'.[42] According to Haenchen, Luke is intentionally ambiguous about the Ethiopian's identity as a Gentile or Jew. Luke merely appeals to this conversion story to suggest 'that with this new convert the mission has taken a step beyond the conversion of Jews and Samaritans.'[43] The story itself derives from Hellenistic circles and represents for Luke (in Haenchen's view) a parallel and rival to Luke's account of Cornelius, the first Gentile convert under the auspices of Peter.[44] Haenchen detects no particularly significant racial difficulties posed by Acts 8.26–40. For him, Luke merely edits this Hellenistic tradition to conform to his own theological design.

Certainly those who tend to exclude Black people from any role in Christian origins need to be reminded that a Nubian was possibly the first Gentile convert.[45] Nonetheless, Luke's awkward use of this story seems to have certain racial implications. Notice that in Acts 8.37, the Ethiopian says, 'See, here is water! What is to prevent my being baptized?' A variant reading immediately follows in some ancient versions of the text: 'And Philip said, "If you believe with all your heart, you may [be baptized]." And he [the Ethiopian] replied, "I believe that Jesus Christ is the Son of God."'[46] Whether or not one accepts this variant reading as an authentic part of the text, it is clear that the Ethiopian's baptism takes place in the water without reference to a prior or simultaneous descent of the Holy Spirit (com-pare John 3.5; 1 John 5.6–8).

By contrast, Luke provides an elaborate narrative about Cornelius' conversion and baptism (Acts 10.12–48), at the end of which, the Holy Spirit descends and the baptism by water follows. Furthermore,

Peter's speech (Acts 10.34–43) indicates a new development in which Gentiles are unambiguously eligible for conversion and baptism. Given the importance of the Holy Spirit's role throughout Luke–Acts as a theological motif, Luke's narrative about Cornelius' baptism gives the distinct impression (perhaps unwittingly) that Cornelius' baptism is more legitimate than that of the Ethiopian.

This by no means suggests that Luke had a negative attitude about Black people. One need only consider the Antioch Church's leadership presented in Acts 13.1 to dispel such notions. There Luke mentions one 'Symeon who is called the Black man' (*Symeōn ho kaloumenos Niger*). The Latinism 'Niger' probably reinforces the idea that Symeon was a dark-skinned person, probably an African.[47] Luke's vision was one of racial pluralism in the leadership of the young Christian Church at Antioch (Acts 11.26). In no way is it important or useful to attempt to show, on the basis of any of the traditions in Acts of the Apostles, that the first Gentile convert was a Nubian rather than an Italian or member of any other ethnic group. This would be absurd, given the confessional nature of the entire Luke–Acts work, which does not come to us as objective history. But Luke's editorializing does result in a circumstantial de-emphasis of a Nubian (African) in favor of an Italian (European) and thereby enables some Europeans to claim or imply that Acts demonstrates some divine preference for Europeans.

Luke is not innocent in all of this. His possible apologetics for the Roman official Theophilus, as well as the great significance he attaches to Rome as the center of the world, betrays the subtle way in which Luke's theology fell prey to secular ideological ideas.[48] In the last third of the first century, the Church generally struggled to survive in an increasingly hostile political environment. Luke, not unlike other New Testament writers of this period and after,[49] perhaps seeks to assuage Rome by allowing his theological framework to be determined by the assumption of a Roman-centered world.[50] In this process of secularization, the Lukan vision of universalism is undermined. Fortunately, this is not Luke's only message. We must remember that the New Testament's final vision of the holy remnant (Rev. 7.9) is consistent with Luke's notion of racial pluralism as reflected in the leadership of the Church of Antioch (Acts 13.1). Both texts indicate that persons of all nations and races constitute part of the righteous remnant at the consummation of the ages.

Secularization in the New Testament needs much fuller

exploration in terms of its racial dimensions. At one level, it highlights a certain ambiguity of race in the New Testament. At another level, it confronts us with a challenge to search for more adequate modes of hermeneutics by which the New Testament can be demonstrated as relevant to Blacks and other people of the Third World, even as it stands locked into the socioreligious framework of the Greco-Roman world. Of all the mandates confronting the Church today, the mandate of world community predicated on a renewed commitment to pluralism and the attendant acknowledgement of the integrity of all racial groups constitutes an urgent agenda for Bible scholars and laity alike. It is an agenda far too long neglected in the vast array of Eurocentric theological and ecclesial traditions that continue to marginalize people of color throughout the world today.

NOTES

1   R. E. Clements, 'Goy', in G. J. Botterweck and H. Ringgren (eds.), *Theological Dictionary of the Old Testament*, vol. 2 (Grand Rapids, Mich., W. B. Eerdman, 1974–84), pp. 426–9.
2   S. D. Goitein, *Jews and Arabs: Their Contacts Through the Ages* (New York, Schocken Books, 1964), pp. 19–21.
3   F. M. Snowden, Jr, *Blacks in Antiquity: Ethiopians in the Greco-Roman Experience* (Cambridge, Mass., Harvard University Press, 1970), pp. 118–19: '*Aithiops* ("burnt-face"): the most frequent translation of CUSH found in the LXX, designating usually Africans of dark pigmentation and Negroid features, used as early as Homer (*Odyssey* 19, pp. 246ff). While *Aithiops* in ancient biblical and classical texts refers specifically to Ethiopians, the term also identifies Africans, regardless of race.'
4   G. A. Buttrick (ed.), 'Election', *The Interpreter's Dictionary of the Bible*, vol. 2 (Nashville, Tenn., Abingdon Press, 1962), p. 77. G. E. Mendenhall employs the term *secularization* in this sense.
5   C. Westermann, *Genesis 1–11: A Commentary* (Minneapolis, Minn., Augsburg Publishing House, 1984 (1974)), p. 459.
6   ibid., p. 482.
7   ibid., p. 486.
8   G. Rice, 'The Curse That Never Was (Genesis 9.18–27)', *The Journal of Religious Thought* 29 (1972), p. 13.
9   Westermann, p. 47.
10 ibid., p. 54.
11 Rice, pp. 11–12; Westermann, pp. 488–9; E. Isaac, 'Genesis, Judaism and the "Sons of Ham",' *Slavery and Abolition: A Journal of Comparative Studies* 1 (1 May 1980), pp. 4–5.

12   Rice, pp. 7–8, suggests that the passage contains two parallel but different traditions – one universal (Gen. 9.18–19a; cf. 5.32; 6.10; 7.13; 10.1; 1 Chron. 1.4) and the other limited to Palestine and more parochial (Gen. 9.20–7, and seems presupposed in 10.21).

13   Westermann, p. 484.

14   Rice, pp. 17, 25.

15   See E. Isaac, ibid., p. 19.

16   Rice, p. 26, n. 116.

17   F. Jennings Dake, *Dake's Annotated Reference Bible* (Lawrenceville, Ga., Dake Bible Sales, 1981 (1961)), pp. 8, 9, 36, 40. One of my African seminarians, who had been given *Dake's Annotated* by fundamentalist American missionaries, innocently presented me with a gift copy for study and comment!

18   M. Noth, *A History of Pentateuchal Traditions*, trans. W. Anderson (Chico, Calif., Scholars Press, 1981), pp. 21–3, 28 and the translator's supplement, pp. 262–3; Eissfeldt, *The Old Testament: An Introduction* (New York, Harper & Row, 1965), p. 184.

19   Buttrick, 'Sabeans', in *Interpreter's Dictionary*, 4, p. 311.

20   The postexilic Priestly ('P') redaction accounts for the order Shem, Ham, Japheth (omitting Canaan) in Genesis 10.1 as well as for the inversion of this order in the subsequent verses, e.g. Genesis 10.2 the sons of Japheth; Genesis 10.6 the sons of Ham; and Genesis 10.21 'To Shem also, the father of all the children of Eber (Hebrew).'

21   Rice, p. 16.

22   Contra B. W. Anderson's note in *The New Oxford Annotated Bible* (RSV, p. 179: 'The term Cushite apparently [*sic*] includes Midianites and other Arabic peoples (Hab. 3.7).'

23   Isaac, pp. 3–17.

24   S. Hable Sellassie, *Ancient and Medieval Ethiopian History to 1270* (Addis Ababa, United Printers, 1972), p. 96; R. A. Morrisey, *Colored People and Bible History* (Hammond, Ind., W. B. Conkey Company, 1925); E. Ullendorff, *Ethiopia and the Bible* (London, Oxford University Press, 1968), pp. 6–8.

25   Snowden, pp. 115–17; C. Anta Diop, *African Origin of Civilization: Myth or Reality?*, trans. M. Cook (New York and Westport, Conn., Lawrence Hill, 1974 (1955)), pp. 220–1; Sir A. Gardiner, *Egypt of the Pharaohs* (New York, Oxford University Press, 1974 (1961)), p. 450.

26   C. B. Copher, '3,000 Years of Biblical Interpretation with Reference to Black Peoples', *The Journal of the Interdenominational Theological Center* 13 (2, Spring 1986), pp. 225–46.

27   G. von Rad, *Old Testament Theology*, 2 vols., trans. D. M. G. Stalker (New York, Harper & Row, 1962), vol. 1, p. 7; vol. 2, p. 322.

28   ibid., 1, pp. 118, 178; Botterweck and Ringgren (eds.), 'Bāchar', *Theological Dictionary of the Old Testament*, vol. 2, p. 78; Buttrick, 'Election', *Interpreter's Dictionary*, vol. 2, p. 76.

29   Botterweck and Ringgren (eds.), 'Bāchar', vol. 2, p. 82.

30   ibid., p. 83.

31   Buttrick (ed.), *Interpreter's Dictionary*, vol. 2, p. 79; G. F. Moore,

Judaism, vol. 2 (Cambridge, Mass., Harvard University Press, 1932), p. 95; cf. Rashi's Commentary, *Deuteronomy*, pp. 56, 195.

32 von Rad, vol. 1, pp. 178, 223.

33 Botterweck and Ringgren (eds.), 'Bāchar', p. 78.

34 Moore, p. 95.

35 R. Bultmann, *Theology of the New Testament*, vol. 1 (London, SCM Press, 1965 (1952) and New York, Scribner's, 1952), p. 97.

36 (LXX) Isa. 43.20 *to genos mou to eklekton* = M.T. *ʿammi běḥiri*.

37 W. Bauer, *Eklektos: A Greek-English Lexicon of the New Testament*, trans. and ed. W. E. Arndt and F. W. Gingrich (Chicago, University of Chicago Press, 1957), p. 242.

38 In 1 Clem. v.7, 'the limits of the west' (*epi to terma tēs duseōs*) designates Spain (of Rome). K. Lake (trans.), *Apostolic Fathers*, vol. 1, Loeb Classical Library (Cambridge, Mass., Harvard University Press, 1975), p. 16. Cf. E. Käsemann, *Commentary on Romans*, trans. and ed. G. W. Bromiley (Grand Rapids, Mich., W. B. Eerdman, 1980), p. 402.

39 Luke's Acts of the Apostles outlines this scheme quite decidedly: Jerusalem (Acts 2), Antioch (Acts 12), Athens (Acts 17), and Rome (Acts 28). See W. G. Kümmel, *Introduction to the New Testament*, rev. English edn., trans. H. C. Kee (Nashville, Tenn., Abingdon Press, 1973), p. 164ff.

40 V. Taylor, *The Gospel According to St Mark* (New York, St. Martin's Press, 1966), p. 598; W. H. Kelber (ed.), *The Passion in Mark* (Philadelphia, Pa., Fortress Press, 1976), pp. 120n, 155, 166.

41 The good reputations of the centurion in Luke 7.2ff and Cornelius the centurion in Acts 10.1, 22 are intentional designs by Luke. F. J. Foakes Jackson and K. Lake, *The Acts of the Apostles*, vol. 4 (Grand Rapids, Mich., Baker Book House, 1979), p. 112; E. Haenchen, *Acts of the Apostles: A Commentary* (Oxford, Basil Blackwell, 1971), pp. 346–9.

42 Haenchen, p. 309.

43 ibid., p. 314.

44 ibid., p. 315. Similarly, M. Hengel, *Acts and the Ancient History of Earliest Christianity* (Philadelphia, Pa., Fortress Press, 1980), p. 79.

45 Foakes Jackson and Lake, vol. 4, p. 98. Irenaeus (AD 120–202) reports that the Ethiopian became a missionary to 'the regions of Ethiopia'; Epiphanius (AD 315–403) says that he preached in Arabia Felix and on the coasts of the Red Sea. Unfortunately, there are no records of Ethiopian Christianity until the fourth century.

46 Irenaeus cites the text as if the variant reading is part of the text (*Adv. Haer.* iii.12.8). A. Roberts and J. Donaldson (eds.), *The Ante-Nicene Fathers* (Grand Rapids, Mich., W. B. Eerdman, 1981), vol. 1, p. 433. See also *The Western Text*, *The Antiochian Text*, and *Textus Receptus*; the English AV includes v. 37. Jackson and Lake, *Acts*, vol. 4, p. 98, suggest that the principal significance of v. 37 is 'perhaps the earliest form of the baptismal creed. It is also remarkable that it is an expansion of the baptismal formula "in the name of Jesus Christ", not of the trinitarian formula.'

47 C. S. C. Williams, *The Acts of the Apostles* (New York, Harper & Row, 1957), p. 154. 'Simeon the "Black" may have come from Africa and may possibly be Simon of Cyrene.' Haenchen, *Acts of the Apostles*, p. 395, n. 2,

reminds us that 1 Corinthians 12.28ff. lists first apostles, prophets, and teachers as persons endowed with *charismata*, and these constituted a charismatic office in Pauline churches.

48   Luke 1.3; Acts 1.1. See H. Conzelmann, *The Theology of St Luke*, trans. G. Buswell (New York, Harper & Row, 1960), pp. 138–41; R. J. Cassidy, *Jesus, Politics and Society* (Maryknoll, NY, Orbis Books, 1978), pp. 128–30.

49   Notably the pastorals and 1 Peter; cf. Romans 13.1–5.

50   It should be noted, however, that the extent of the political apologetic element in Luke–Acts continues to be at the storm center of New Testament debate. See Cassidy; R. Cassidy, *Society and Politics in the Acts of the Apostles* (Maryknoll, NY, Orbis Books, 1987); D. Juel, *Luke–Acts: The Promise of History* (Atlanta, Ga., John Knox Press, 1983); J. T. Sanders, *The Jews in Luke–Acts* (Philadelphia, Pa., Fortress Press, 1987).

PART THREE

The Exodus: One Narrative, Many Readings

In such a world, systems of meaning are elicited by contexts, by the nature (and substance) of the listener. In *Brhadaranyaka* 5.1., Lord Prajapati speaks in thunder three times: 'DA DA DA'. When the gods, given to pleasure, hear it, they hear it as the first syllable of *damyata*, 'control'. The anti-gods, given as they are to cruelty, hear it as *dayadhvam*, 'be compassionate'. When the humans, given to greed, hear it, they hear it as *datta*, 'give to others'.

A. K. Ramanujan

15

A Latin American Perspective:
The Option for the Poor in the
Old Testament

GEORGE V. PIXLEY AND CLODOVIS BOFF

This piece is an attempt to situate the Exodus story in its historical setting
and at the same time to draw out insights for contemporary concerns, namely
that the liberating act has significance not only for the Hebrews, but for all
the oppressed of the world.

Pixley teaches in Nicaragua; Boff is a Servite priest from Brazil. This is
the opening chapter of their book, *The Bible, The Church and the Poor* (Maryknoll, NY, Orbis Books, 1989; Tunbridge Wells, Burns & Oates, 1989).

For an extended and a fuller exposition on Exodus, see George V. Pixley,
On Exodus: A Liberation Perspective (Maryknoll, NY, Orbis Books, 1987).

1 INTRODUCTION

This chapter seeks to establish just who the God of the Bible is.
This might not seem necessary, as the question of who God is could
seem to have been settled by the common understanding of our
Western culture. God is the one perfect being, all-powerful and
all-wise, creator of heaven and earth, whose goodness and justice
never fail. But common understanding, in this as in so many other
things, is deceptive. The long history of conflicts between Christians
in Latin America has taught us that the common confession of one
God hides different, and even opposing, ways of envisaging this
all-powerful and all-wise creator God. The Bible takes great care to
identify the God it speaks of, and does so using categories other
than our common understanding. To simplify somewhat, but without
distorting the matter in essentials, we can say that the God of the
Bible is the God who led Israel out of Egypt and who raised Jesus
Christ from the dead. This is the God who created heaven and earth,
and this is the God whose perfection we have to postulate.

There is no reason to dispute the Western philosophical affirmation that for God's love to be perfect, it has to be universal. But this does need some qualification. The biblical narratives tell us that the concrete expression of this love favoured the slaves in Egypt and Palestine, and the poor of Galilee. God's love for Pharaoh was mediated through God's preferential love for the Israelite slaves. In the same way, God's love for the scribes and Pharisees was mediated through God's love for and solidarity with the fishermen and women of Galilee. And so the God whom the Bible calls creator of heaven and earth takes on specific characteristics.

So, having, we hope, established the importance of asking who the God of the Bible is, let us approach the question through the introduction to that admirable synthesis of law that we know as the Decalogue: 'I am Yahweh your God who brought you out of the land of Egypt, out of the house of slavery. You shall have no gods except me' (Exod. 20.2–3).[1]

The words are so familiar to us that we hardly pay attention to them, yet they contain affirmations that are far from obvious at first sight. In the first place, the God Yahweh displays a polemical tone with regard to other possible gods. The text neither denies nor affirms that there are other gods. Their existence or non-existence is not the case at issue. What is at issue is that *you*, Israelite, to whom the law is addressed, must base your justice on the prohibition to worship them or ask them for favours. In other words, any god who has not brought you out of the house of slavery cannot be your God.

All the commandments dealing with just conduct among people – 'honour your father and mother ... you shall not kill ... you shall not steal', etc. – are presented as the direct and personal commands of *this* God, who 'brought you out of the land of Egypt, out of the house of slavery'. There is nothing to show that it had to be this way; at least, there is nothing in the common understanding of Western culture that would indicate this. But let us look at the text a little more closely:

(a) 'I am *Yahweh* your God.' The proper name Yahweh serves to ensure that those gods who cannot or will not save Israel from the house of slavery in Egypt cannot hide under the generic term *god*. It is not possible to make definite assertions about the origin of the name Yahweh.[2] Nevertheless, the Elohist and priestly traditions, two of the three great narrative traditions in the Pentateuch, agree in placing the revelation of this divine name within the context of the exodus. In the Elohist tradition, Yahweh revealed his proper name to Moses in the desert at the time he was persuading him to undertake the liberation of his enslaved people (Exod. 3.14–15). In the priestly tradition, he revealed his name to Moses still in Egypt as a confirmation of his will to set the slaves free (Exod. 6.2–6). Both traditions coincide in having God already known to the patriarchs Abraham, Isaac and Jacob, though they did not know God's *name*. This was revealed only to the prophet who was to lead Israel in its liberation. So the name Yahweh asserts the singularity of God as liberator.

(b) 'I am Yahweh *your* God.' Because he brought Israel out of the land of Egypt, out of the house of slavery, Yahweh is the God of Israel. This liberation establishes a relationship of exclusive dependence on Yahweh. Yahweh cannot be adored except by those who confess themselves slaves liberated from the slavery in Egypt. To understand this, we have to be careful not to be confused by the patriarchal traditions. This *your* does not indicate a previous relationship independent of the liberation. The exodus formed the people of Yahweh. According to Exodus 12.38 (from the Yahwist tradition), 'people of various sorts' (*erev rav*) joined the Israelites on the march, showing that the unity of Israel had to be constituted on the basis of the exodus. What was ordained for the Passover shows how the nation was defined:

> No alien may take part in it. . . Should a stranger be staying with you and wish to celebrate the Passover in honour of Yahweh, all the males of his household must be circumcised: he may then be admitted to the celebration, for he becomes as it were a native-born. But no uncircumcised person may take part (Exod. 12.43, 48).

In other words, for Yahweh to be *your* God, you have to unite yourself to those who are celebrating their liberation from slavery. And no one who shows solidarity with the liberated people, demonstrating it through the circumcision of his foreskin, will be excluded from the community that celebrates its liberation from Egypt. In Israel's later practice, things were not that simple, but this expresses an intention: Yahweh is *your* God.

(c) 'I am Yahweh your *God*.' Theology in the Old Testament is not organized round dogmatic themes. Strictly speaking, the Old Testament includes no Creed defining the nature of God. Its theology is narrative, and the great majority of the books that make up this collection of writings recognize the foundational character of the story of the exodus. Efforts at generalizing about the nature of God are based on this story:

> Yahweh your God is God of gods and Lord of lords, the great God, triumphant and terrible, never partial, never to be bribed. It is he who sees justice done for the orphan and the widow, who loves the stranger and gives him food and clothing (Deut. 10.16–18).

The God of the exodus account is a God who heard the cries wrung from the slaves by the slave-drivers of Pharaoh and so came down to set them free and lead them to a land flowing with milk and honey. Moses, the man chosen to lead this project, had gained his credentials by risking his high social position by killing an Egyptian who was maltreating a Hebrew (Exod. 2.11–15). So the exodus account clearly shows that justice means taking sides with the oppressed. The Yahweh of the exodus takes the part of the oppressed. From this our text draws the theological principle that God's impartiality makes God love the orphan and the widow with preference. Curiously, but nevertheless logically, not making exception of persons means making a preferential option for the oppressed in a situation of oppression.

These initial observations show that Yahweh, the God of the Bible, is characterized by his preferential option for the oppressed. The remaining sections of this chapter will examine some of the principal witnesses of the Bible concerning the way in which they appropriated this Yahweh God of the exodus. We need to remind ourselves here that the Bible is not one continuous work, but a collection of writings originating at different periods. This diversity of origin is also shown in the different ways it takes up the basic themes of Israel's tradition. Yahweh's option for the oppressed, as an integral element in the exodus narrative, which has a foundational character for Israel, exercised a basic influence over virtually all the books of the Bible (the notable exception being Proverbs, which we shall examine in due course as an expression of the teaching of 'wise men'). Our examination will seek to bring out the different shades with which God's preferential option for the impoverished and oppressed is presented.

2 THE EXODUS REVEALS YAHWEH AS LIBERATOR GOD: THE TEXT AND THE SOCIAL CONTEXT IN WHICH IT WAS PRODUCED

In the account of the exodus from Egyptian slavery under the inspiration of Yahweh and the leadership of Moses, Israel narrates its origins as a people and confesses that it owes these to Yahweh and is, in consequence, the people of Yahweh. Although the events narrated are earlier than the formation of Israel as a nation with its own language and identity, the account presupposes the existence of this nation. It is an 'official' account; and, like the official accounts of any nation explaining its origins, it hides some elements while revealing others. We therefore need to have some idea of the social history of Israel, the context in which the account was produced. So in this section we begin by reconstructing the probable origins of Israel, and go on to examine the exodus narrative and what it tells us about Yahweh and his choice of a nation for himself, showing how the social changes that came about in Israel altered the way in which the foundational events were understood.

Israel first appeared on the historical scene around the end of the thirteenth century BC. The name features on the stele of Merneptah, king of Egypt, in the context of his campaign in Palestine in 1208 BC. Although this text tells us no more than the existence of Israel in Palestine at this date, later texts tell us that it originated in the central mountains of Palestine, which, till the thirteenth century, had been the least populated area of Palestine. There is an extensive correspondence between the Egyptian court and the kings of Canaan, dating from the fourteenth and thirteenth centuries. Letters from Tel-el-Amarna indicate that the centres of population were the coastal plain and the valley of Yezreel, which crosses the mountain range by Mount Carmel. These were precisely the areas Israel did not control at the time of its origins, which is significant. Another important fact derived from these letters is that Egypt was unable to maintain stable control in Palestine, owing to continuous wars among the kings of the cities.

According to its own traditions of the early period, as recounted in the Book of Judges, Israel consisted of various peasant groups scattered around the mountain areas. The valleys and plains were controlled by hostile tribes, whose material culture was superior to that of the Israelites (they possessed horses and carts).

Around 1200 BC, archaeology shows a vital transitional point in the material culture of Palestine, the introduction of iron tools. This must be the major factor leading at just this period to the clearing of mountain areas previously unserviceable for agriculture, producing the population shift that brought together groups who were to make up the nation of Israel.

All these facts are explained by the thesis that Israel arose in the thirteenth century BC from a process of internal migration in Palestine. Families and clans that had previously lived on the plain and in the valleys fled from the endless wars to seek a new life in country that had become cultivatable through the introduction of iron tools. This movement is illustrated in the biblical tradition of the migration of the tribe of Dan from the cities of Zorah and Eshtaol to the extreme northeast of Galilee (Judg. 17–18). These migrations also had a social effect. Those who migrated were peasants; not only did they escape the political conflicts; they also escaped the tributes they had previously paid to the lords of the cities. In their new hill areas they did not build cities because they were not city people. Archaeological excavations have produced cases of cities destroyed at this period and rebuilt on a smaller scale, with humbler materials. This diminution of urban life can be explained by the incursion of peasant groups coming up from the plain. If this is the demographic origin of the clans that were to make up the nation of Israel, then one can talk of a movement of migration/uprising.[3]

These peasant groups were joined around 1200 BC by a group that came from Egypt, where it had carried out an uprising and an exodus into the desert under the leadership of Moses, a prophet of the God Yahweh. Their rebellion had been provoked by King Rameses II (1290–1224 BC), whose construction projects had placed an intolerable burden on the peasant population of Egypt. The social system obtaining in Egypt is described in Genesis 47.13–26: the people lived in their own villages and with their own families, but all the land belonged to the state and its produce was subject to a tax imposed by the Pharaoh. This was the same 'Asiastic' system as in Palestine, aggravated by the fact that the Egyptian state was far more powerful. The Hebrews who came out of Egypt understood that their success had been due to Yahweh, their God, being with them. The coincidence of this experience with that of the clans of Israel was noteworthy, and the clans gradually came to accept Yahweh as their God. The exodus of the Hebrews came to be the founding history of Israel.[4]

So the material basis of confession of faith in Yahweh was the diffuse peasant movement arising from the particular conditions in Palestine in the fourteenth and thirteenth centuries BC. Israelite society was made up of small villages organized by ties of blood relationship into families, clans and tribes. At the beginning, they had neither cities nor kings. The arrival of the Hebrew group gave the movement a political and social consciousness, the axis of which was confession of Yahweh as their only king.[5] The laws given on Sinai lent coherence to the movement and a consciousness of the group's difference from the 'Canaanites' who dwelt in the cities, subject to human kings and worshipping Baal. The Israelites spoke the language of Canaan (see Isa. 19.18), from where they had come. The telling of the exodus and their confession of faith in Yahweh gave weight to their consciousness of being different from the inhabitants of the valleys and the cities. They were the people of Yahweh and had no kings 'like the other nations' (1 Sam. 8.5).

Reflecting on the importance of their movement, the tribes of Israel gradually came to see its universal significance, and to recognize Yahweh as God *tout court*, not simply as the God of Israel. One tradition held that Yahweh had promised Abraham: 'All the tribes of the earth shall bless themselves by you' (Gen. 12.3). Deutero-Isaiah (sixth century) proclaimed that Israel, the servant of Yahweh, would be a 'light to the nations' (Isa. 49.6). So some biblical texts give universal value to the Israelite experience that God is a saviour of the oppressed. Logically, Israel also came to confess Yahweh as creator of heaven and earth. It also saw in Yahweh a companion to those who wander the face of the earth without a home, a God who gave them land in which to settle.[6] And so the people of Israel came to understand that the Yahweh of the exodus was the one God who governs all nations. This is the historical thesis we follow here.

After this brief reconstruction of the origin of Israel, let us turn to its founding text, the account of the exodus. The book of Exodus, like the whole of the Pentateuch of which it forms part, was not finally completed till the fifth century BC, eight hundred years after the events it recounts. During these eight centuries, several major changes took place in the life of Israel:

(i) For two hundred years, Israel existed as a loose grouping of clans and tribes of peasants, surrounded by cities under monarchical regimes, generally hostile to Israel (with some exceptions, such as Gibeon and Shechem).

(ii) Around the year 1000 BC, the attacks from the cities forced Israel to create its own monarchical state, which lasted some four hundred years.

(iii) After the destruction of the capital (587 BC), the Jewish people organized themselves as a religious nation led by a priestly caste, under the tolerant suzereignty of the Persian empire.

As the account of the exodus is the founding document of Israel, it was naturally revised in each of these three epochs. The final text of the book of Exodus contains elements from each of these revisions. So it is a text made up of superimposed layers, with differing interpretations of those events in Egypt in the thirteenth century BC.

The earliest stage of the account, probably exclusively oral, calls the people of the exodus 'Hebrews'. This term did not originally denote a race, but was a designation given to various groups in several localities from Egypt to Mesopotamia. Such people were mercenaries, nomads, rebels; the name denoted the fact that they were not integrated into the broader framework of society, were outside the general rule of law.[7] When the exodus narrative was the foundational text of the Israelite tribes, the experience in Egypt was read as that of a group of peasants who had rebelled and placed themselves outside Egyptian law. Those who heeded the call of Yahweh and Moses to undertake a struggle that would set them free from slavery in Egypt were, therefore, 'Hebrews', 'people of various sorts' who decided to break with the Egyptian legal system, under which they had to hold their flocks, lands and bodies at the king's disposition.

The central feature of the account for the tribes of Israel was the part played by Yahweh in their liberation. They did not read the exodus as a secular revolutionary movement. Yahweh was on their side and guided the movement through his prophet Moses. The fact that they succeeded in escaping from their enforced serfdom despite the powerful Egyptian army showed that God, who took the side of the poor in Egypt, was the true God.

With the establishment of the monarchical state in Israel, the exodus narrative was taken up by the official scribes and converted into a national epic, together with the ancient traditions concerning the patriarchs Abraham, Isaac and Jacob. This process of adapting the Israelite traditions for the ends of the new monarchy probably took place at the court of Solomon. This produced the written version of the traditions that exegetes call the Yahwist version (known as 'J'), the earliest writings that survive as part of the Pentateuch.

At this period, when the state was seeking to create a consciousness of national identity built up round the Davidic dynasty, it had to re-read the exodus as a national liberation struggle. The children of Israel, according to this re-reading, had been enslaved in Egypt after settling there to escape the famine in their own land of Canaan. A perverse king took advantage of their presence as guests, and the struggle that followed was between Egyptians and Israelites. The Israelites conceived the plan of 'returning' to the land of Canaan. In this way the account ceased to describe a social movement within Egyptian society and replaced it with a struggle between peoples, in which Yahweh took the side of Israel. Israel was an exploited people, but more importantly, it was the people of Yahweh, and this from before the time of its exploitation in Egypt. This is the emphasis in the Yahwist version:

> Go and gather the elders of Israel together and tell them, 'Yahweh, the God of your fathers, has appeared to me – the God of Abraham, of Isaac, and of Jacob; and he has said to me: I have visited you and seen all that the Egyptians are doing to you' (Exod. 3.16).

The children of Israel are shown as having a relationship with Yahweh going back to the time of their ancestors who lived in Canaan. They are his people and this is the reason Yahweh intervened to rescue them from their slavery. In this way the exodus lost a large part of its challenging content and could become useful for the monarchical aim of creating a national consciousness.

On the basis of this re-reading of the exodus, a theological reflection on the election of Israel as the special people of God was developed in the late monarchical period (seventh century BC):

> If Yahweh set his heart on you and chose you, it was not because you outnumbered other peoples: you were the least of all peoples. It was for love of you and to keep the oath that he swore to your fathers that Yahweh brought you out with his mighty hand and redeemed you from the house of slavery, from the power of Pharaoh king of Egypt (Deut. 7.7–8).

The exodus changes from Yahweh's option for the oppressed to being an inscrutable favour conferred by Yahweh in fulfilment of his promises to the patriarchs. This does not mean that the memory of the favour enjoyed by the poor in Yahweh's eyes was lost, but it was carried on as part of a thought-process that enhanced Yahweh's special relationship with his people dating from commitments entered into with the patriarchs.

The final re-reading of the exodus further overlaid the revelation of Yahweh as the liberator God who showed his preference for the oppressed. This is the reading made by the priests in the sixth century BC, when Judah existed as a national group within the Persian empire, internally led by the priestly caste. This re-reading could not quite efface the privilege of the poor, but it changed the emphasis so as to exalt the greatness of Yahweh. The following is an example:

> Yahweh said to Moses, 'See, I make you as a god for Pharaoh, and Aaron your brother is to be your prophet. You yourself must tell him all I command you, and Aaron your brother will tell Pharaoh to let the sons of Israel leave his land. I myself will make Pharaoh's heart stubborn, and perform many a sign and wonder in the land of Egypt. Pharaoh will not listen to you, and so I will lay my hand on Egypt and with strokes of power lead out my armies, my people, the sons of Israel, from the land of Egypt. And all the Egyptians shall come to know that I am Yahweh when I stretch out my hand against Egypt and bring out the sons of Israel from their midst' (Exod. 7.1–5).

In the earlier layers of the account, the blows delivered against Pharaoh were to force him to let the Hebrews go. Every time Pharaoh hardened his heart, Yahweh visited a fresh plague on him so as to soften it. In the priestly re-reading, the marvels have another purpose: to demonstrate the greatness of Yahweh. This is why Yahweh himself hardens Pharaoh's heart so as to give himself new opportunities of showing his greatness.

In this priestly re-reading of the exodus, the desire to show the greatness of Yahweh has grown to such an extent that it obscures – though it cannot completely erase – Yahweh's predilection for the poor and oppressed. So Yahweh's option for the slaves and their liberation, the inspiration of pre-monarchical Israel, was gradually weakened in later re-readings. The original vision was kept in prophetic circles.

3 COULD ISRAEL HAVE KNOWN CLASS CONSCIOUSNESS?

Discussion of the origins of Israel as coming about through an uprising/migration and repudiation of the structures of domination personalized in the kings of the surrounding peoples raises a doubt: are we not imposing on these early years a level of social consciousness that could not have existed two thousand years before Christ? This is a legitimate concern, and needs examination.

Obviously, there were no 'social sciences' either in Canaan or in Egypt in the thirteenth century BC. So there was no possibility of making a 'scientific' analysis of the structure of society and the dynamics of its reproduction. Hence if we raise the above question with reference to a kind of social consciousness grounded in social-scientific analysis, the reply has to be affirmative.

So let us put the question differently. Was it possible for groups of peasants in Canaan to arrive at a realization that their interests as peasant groups were being threatened by their subjection to the king of their cities – Dor, Megiddo, Bethshean? In a stable society, even though the king sequestered a large portion of agricultural produce and required significant labour quotas for state works, it is highly unlikely that a peasant class which had never known any other way of life would have hankered after alternative lifestyles. Furthermore, the king was not regarded as a man, but as a god, on whom they were dependent for such essentials as sun and rain.

Nevertheless, Canaan in the fourteenth and thirteenth centuries BC was going through a critical phase in the Egyptian domination, reflected in the continual wars among the kings of its cities. Such a situation would lead to each village undergoing changes of overlord, besides interruptions to its crop production. One god/king would take the place of another as 'benefactor' responsible for giving life to the people of one place, without any internal change taking place within the people themselves. These changes would create the possibility of thinking of alternatives to the system of domination by kings. The peasants, well organized in large families on the local level, could come to realize that their interests were not identical with those of the city which demanded a quota of their produce. The presence of nearby virgin land, even if not as fertile as that of the plain, would have completed the process of 'conscientization' concerning the possibility of an alternative to their traditional subjection.

In Egypt, conditions that could have led to an alternative conscious-ness among the peasants were different. Here there was only one state, and it was a very strong state, with a very convincing religious underpinning. Conditions for a consciousness of oppression were created by the excessive exploitation of the peasant base of society for funerary constructions. It was natural to attribute these excesses of exploitation to abuses by the king's henchmen, which the king would correct if he knew the wrong being done his servants. That is, exploitation in itself would not have produced an alternative consciousness. As long as everyone continued to believe in the supreme god, whose goodness was shown in the richness of the country, irrigated every year by the flood waters of the great river Nile, the social structure was very secure. There was no alternative cultivatable land in the region. No one suggested the possibility of an alternative, and the wrongs suffered by a particular group of workers were a very localized incident compared to the overall riches of a land blessed by heaven.

Here, consciousness of an alternative must have come principally from an outside element introduced, undoubtedly, from the East, in the form of the God Yahweh, who appeared on the holy mountain. Yahweh had presented himself as a God of the poor, promising their liberation. It seems certain that very few peasants in the land of Egypt were prepared to receive such a message, though the conditions of exceptional oppression produced by the construction works of Rameses II would have led some to this extreme. So a small group of 'Hebrews' gathered round Moses, determined to understand their withdrawal from society as a repudiation of the oppression they now associated with Pharaoh, demystified for them by their acceptance of the God who had appeared to Moses with the promise of another land flowing with milk and honey.

NOTES

1 Biblical quotations are taken from the Jerusalem Bible, adapted occasionally in accordance with the authors' own references to the original Hebrew and Greek.

2 J. Severino Croatto, 'Yavé, el Dios de la "presencia" salvífica: Exod. 3.14 en su contexto literario y querigmático', *Revista Bíblica* 43 (1981), pp. 153–63.

3 Though there are antecedents on the insurrectional theory of the origins of Israel, the definitive work is N. K. Gottwald, *The Tribes of Yahweh: A Sociology of the Religion of Liberated Israel 1250–1050 BCE* (Maryknoll, NY, Orbis Books, 1979).

4 For a detailed examination of the texts, see G. V. Pixley, *On Exodus: A Liberation Perspective* (Maryknoll, NY, Orbis Books, 1987).

5 See Judges 8.22–3, and for an interpretation, G. V. Pixley, *God's Kingdom: A Guide for Biblical Study* (Maryknoll, NY, Orbis Books, 1981).

6 A good reading of the Pentateuch in the light of lack of land for Israel

can be found in J. Severino Croatto, 'Una promesa aún no cumplida: La estructura literaria del Pentateuco', *Revista Bíblica* 44 (1982), pp. 193–206.

7   Much has been written on Hebrews/*'apiru*. See G. E. Mendenhall, 'The *'Apiru* Movements in the Late Bronze Age' in *The Tenth Generation: The Origins of the Biblical Tradition* (Baltimore, John Hopkins University Press, 1973), pp. 122–41; M. L. Chaney, 'Ancient Palestinian Peasant Movements and the Formation of Premonarchic Israel' in D. N. Freedman and D. F. Graf (eds.), *Palestine in Transition: The Emergence of Ancient Israel* (Sheffield, Almond Press, 1983), pp. 39–90.

16

A Korean Minjung Perspective: The Hebrews and the Exodus

CYRIS H. S. MOON

A biblical scholar from Korea sees parallels between the social history of the Korean minjung and the Hebrews.

This chapter is reprinted from the author's book, *A Korean Minjung Theology: An Old Testament Perspective* (Maryknoll, NY, Orbis Books, 1985).

Cyris H. S. Moon is a professor of Old Testament studies and has published papers on political history and the sociology of hermeneutics.

At the outset, we should note that the Old Testament is a collection of writings by scribes, priests, and other learned people from a society dominated by a patriarchy. The *minjung* of the Old Testament did not participate in writing these documents. Therefore, these writings portray the world from the perspective of men and royalty. From the vantage point of the rulers, they describe events and activities engaged in primarily by men (such as war, cult, and government). However, the Old Testament is also filled with stories of liberation. So although the *minjung* of the Old Testament could not and did not write their own aspirations and biographies of suffering and oppression, there is ample evidence of the liberation movement of the *minjung* in the Old Testament.

The first such movement that comes instantly to mind is that of the exodus, which took place in the thirteenth century BC. The Hebrews, during the reign of Rameses II,[1] were being forced to serve as slaves under the repressive rule of the Egyptians. Moses emerged as the liberator of the Hebrews and brought about the confrontation between himself and the Pharaoh that eventually led to the Hebrews' liberation. In order to appreciate the enormousness of this achievement, we must first focus our attention on the object of Moses' concern: the Hebrew slaves, the despised, the powerless, the outcasts, and those who had no rights at all. Indeed, Moses' greatness lies in his identifying himself with these people in order to liberate them.

The word *habiru* (which is often equated with the word 'Hebrew' and is also spelled *apiru* or *habiru*) is a term that can be traced to records in the second millennium BC in Egypt, Babylonia, Syria, and Palestine; it appears frequently also in the oldest extant tablets and written records. The nature and identity of the *habiru* have been the subject of considerable literature, for the term provides a clue to who the *minjung* of that time were. The 1976 supplementary volume of *The Interpreter's Dictionary of the Bible* describes the *habiru* as mercenary soldiers, people under treaty, and prisoners of war.[2] Other sources suggest that they were outlaws, outcasts, and those who stood outside the dominant social system. At any rate, they most certainly were rebels standing in defiance of the prevailing social or power structure.[3] The *habiru*, therefore, were part of the *minjung* of their time, driven by their *han* (grudge or resentment)[4] to act against what they felt to be injustices imposed on them by those in power.

The social system in Egypt was a strict bureaucracy within which the functions of the various classes were strictly regulated. The structure of the state was largely dependent on four influential factors: the king, his civil servants, the army, and the priests. These were the dominating groups which exerted their power over everyone else, particularly the Hebrews.

Apart from the individuals who were closely connected with some of the basic institutions of the country, there were two more groups of people. The first group consisted of the free citizens, that is, the peasants and tillers of the land. These individuals, though free in the technical sense of the word, were actually bound to the soil they worked, often living on a starvation level. And then, apart from the free population, there was a large group of slaves spread throughout the land.

There were three types of slaves: those who worked as the personal property of individuals, those who worked as state-owned property on public works or military projects, and those who were temple slaves. How they were treated varied according to times and circumstances, but if the members of the lower class of free citizens were referred to as 'children of nobodies', one can well imagine in what regard a slave was held. In short, the slaves were the lowest class of people, and under the oppressive Egyptian system, they suffered total and brutal exploitation.

Despite the fact that the Hebrews suffered this complete loss of their rights and freedom, Moses had difficulty in persuading them to act toward achieving their liberty. According to Exodus 3.1–14, he had to make them realize that they had to escape from Egypt in order to be a liberated people. This is important, for one would think that because the Hebrews had suffered an oppressed life, they would realize that the only way to liberation was to trust God and Moses and act accordingly. However, it seems that they did not have this kind of trust. As a result of such a long and cruel oppression by the Egyptians, the Hebrews had developed the mentality of slaves. This is one way rulers can prevent rebellion before it begins: they break the spirit of their slaves by driving them more severely and depriving them of tolerable living conditions. As the people are deprived of their humanity, they are subordinated. It is not difficult to see why a completely dominated people, who are reduced to being concerned only with eating the food distributed regularly by the ruler, would not want to risk escape from the protection of the ruler and make a long journey to a virtual wasteland.

In this way, the Exodus narrative points out an important fact: Yahweh cannot be the sole actor in the movement for liberation. Rather, humanity is invited to act as a partner with God. People are to assist in the restoration of their own rights which have been infringed upon, a concept which differs from the idea that the fulfillment of all human history is carried out under God's sovereignty alone. The writers of Exodus stress that if oppressed people are to obtain liberation, they must – with God's aid – confront the pharaohs of the world: in order for the Hebrews to participate in the struggle for their human rights, they had first to realize that it was Pharaoh who had infringed upon their rights and that their struggle had to begin with a direct confrontation with Pharaoh. Thus, the third chapter of Exodus says that Moses was ordered to confront Pharaoh in order to help the Hebrews escape from slavery.

At the same time, the writers of Exodus did not presume to say that the Hebrews deserved to receive God's protection and the restoration of their human rights. Rather, their liberation was the result of God's gracious action. Thus Exodus reveals what anyone who participates in the struggle for liberation comes eventually to realize: God is on the side of the oppressed and downtrodden and will always give encouragement and protection to them. In fact, some of the first words with which God is introduced to Moses in the Exodus narrative indicate that God is concerned with the *minjung*. In Exodus 3.7 God states: 'I have seen indeed the affliction of my people which are in Egypt.' God relates not just in a general way as the creator of human beings, but as concerned with a specific oppressed people to whom Moses stands in a special relationship.

In the Hebrew text of Exodus 3.7 the verbal construction of the form 'I have seen' makes the 'seeing' an emphatic process. Furthermore, the little phrase 'which are in Egypt', instead of the simpler 'in Egypt', seems to show an incongruent situation: God's *minjung* are in Egypt when they should be in the promised land. At this point it should be remembered that the Hebrews must have regarded the promised land as a kind of never-never land, and to the question 'Whose people are you?' they would very likely have answered: 'Do you not see that we are Pharaoh's people?' Thus, it is significant that even while the people did not call themselves Yahweh's people, Yahweh immediately thinks of them as 'my people'. In other words, God owns them long before they own God.

Moreover, when in Exodus 3.6 the encounter between God and Moses is linked to the patriarchs, the faithfulness and reliability of God are emphasized. God is not one to change God's mind or to forget; God stands true to God's promise. In Exodus 3 God is revealed as a liberator first, as one who would liberate God's *minjung* from bondage and settle them in a land of their own. This liberation is also connected with a religious purpose which is clearly stated in Exodus 3.12: 'God said, "But I will be with you; and this shall be the sign for you, that I have sent you; when you have brought forth the people out of Egypt, you shall serve God upon this mountain."'

Apart from the revelation of God in this personal and historical sense, we have at this encounter between God and Moses a further statement (Exod. 3.14) concerning God's personal self, a statement which stands unique even in the pages of the Old Testament. It furnishes us with the only explanation of the name Yahweh, a name which is used more than six thousand times in the Old Testament. When we consider the meaning of the name Yahweh as given to Moses in the striking phrase 'I am who I am', two factors seem to emerge clearly. On the one hand, the words strike us as mysterious, enigmatic; they seem to conceal more than to reveal; on the other hand, considering the situation in which they were spoken, they are meant to reassure, to make real the presence of God.

'I am who I am' tells us indeed that we are face to face with a

God whose being is beyond comprehension, beyond human intellect which would seek to define God within certain categories of thought. The essential Being of God cannot be understood by reference to human beings or nature, for God stands outside time and space and God's Being is beyond cause and effect. The infinite and eternal, that which transcends our realm altogether, is implied in the statement 'I am who I am.' Yet this Being of God is not expressed in a form which could make God synonymous with the idea of the infinite or eternal, for Being is linked here to the personal 'I'. God is not to be understood as an impersonal force behind the universe; rather God is revealed as a personal Being. As the eternal 'I am' (the phrase could also be rendered 'I shall be who I shall be'), God makes history indeed, for this transcendent God is revealed as being actively present within the realm of human experience. The phrase 'I am who I am' stresses the truth of both the transcendence and the immanence of God. God's Being is not only 'throned afar', but God is also the God of justice and compassion who is a very helpful presence in time of oppression and trouble. And it is obvious that the revelation of the name of God given to Moses has the purpose of assuring him and the Hebrews of the very real presence of God who will act justly for the liberation of the *minjung*. 'I am who I am' should be understood in the sense of 'you can take my presence as a guarantee for action on your behalf for the cause of justice and compassion.' Thus, with the assurance of Yahweh, the Hebrews began to make their freedom march, crossing the Red Sea and the wilderness. And after many years of wandering, they finally found themselves in Canaan, the promised land.

As the contextual situation of this Exodus motif is reconstructed, parallels between it and Korea come to light. For instance, Koreans, like the Hebrews, suffered for years under the domination of ruthless governments and foreign oppressors. In order to see these parallels more clearly, let us now turn briefly to a short history of the Korean people.

According to tradition, Korean history dates back to 2333 BC when Tangun, the son of a bear, founded Korea. In early history it appears that tribal communities developed and matured into three states: Koguryo in the north, and Silla and Paekche in the south. It was during this era, the Three Kingdom Period (57 BC–AD 668), that Korean recorded history began. It was also during this period that Buddhism was first introduced into Korea by the Chinese.

By 668, with the help of the T'ang Dynasty in China, the state of Silla had unified Korea. However, in the latter part of the ninth century, the power of the Silla Dynasty began to weaken steadily. There were several reasons for this decline. The hereditary nature of the government positions had resulted in a ruling élite which was restricted to members from a few clans. These family factions were constantly vying for power and influence; this weakened the central government.

Out of all this political chaos a new leadership finally emerged. In 918 Wan Kon defeated his opponents and founded the Koryo Dynasty. He immediately instituted several new ordinances and changes. One such change was in the system of land ownership. It was declared that all property was to belong to the government, the high officials, and the Buddhist priesthood. During this period, Buddhism reached its height of power. This was due to the fact that the aristocracy supported Buddhism, as it promised happiness for the ruling class and Buddha's protection for the king. The priests gradually became powerful landowners, and their influence on political decisions greatly increased. Toward the end of the fourteenth century, Buddhist priests controlled much of the national economy and became *de facto* rulers in many areas.

From 1219 to 1392 the country was in deep trouble. In 1219, the new Mongolian leadership in China invaded Korea and Koryo became a tributary state. In the midst of this political turmoil, many of the ruling élite and Buddhist priesthood began to exercise their power ruthlessly. This led to excessive exploitation of the *minjung,* especially the peasantry, which in turn resulted in rebellion and unrest.

Because of these problems, the government desperately tried to institute several reform programs. These programs had a two-fold purpose: one, the revitalization of the nation after almost a century of Mongol domination and, two, the elimination of the social and political abuses of the *minjung* for which the Buddhist priesthood was held responsible. The persons initiating the reforms were the Confucian scholar-officials, those who had obtained their positions by passing the civil service examinations.

In 1392, Yi Songgye, the newly risen military leader, overthrew the Koryo Dynasty, thus founding the Yi Dynasty. Yi immediately turned the new administration over to the classical scholars, who then instituted numerous reform programs. All of the estates were confiscated and redistributed to those who had been loyal to Yi Songgye. In addition, Buddhism was deemed unacceptable as the official religion; Confucianism, or more accurately Neo-Confucianism, was substituted for it. There were several reasons for this change. Toward the end of the Koryo period there was a definite deterioration in the moral and spiritual leadership of the Buddhist priests. As they grew wealthier and more powerful, they also became more corrupt. Thus, in order for the new dynasty to retain its position and increase its power, it was imperative that the Buddhists lose their influence and power. The administration confiscated all temple property and forbade all Buddhist activities. Not surprisingly, this change received wide support. An anti-Buddhist movement had already started in the late Koryo years as a result of the resentment generated by the priests' manipulation of power and wealth. Thus the switch from Buddhism to Neo-Confucianism was, for most of the *minjung*, a welcome change. However, as it turned out, this shift to Neo-Confucianism was not beneficial to the *minjung*, for basically two social strata emerged. They were the *yang ban* (the ruling class people) and the *xiang rom* (the slaves, the landless peasants, the powerless, and the lower-class people).

The Korean Confucian scholars believed that the universe was comprised of two forces which were manifested in light and darkness, heaven and earth, male and female. These forces were called *Yang* and *Yin*. According to the scholars, *Yang*, which symbolized heaven, was superior to *Yin*, symbolizing earth. As long as this natural hierarchy was obeyed, the human world and the cosmic order would be in balance, and society would be in harmony and peace. If this hierarchical system was disrupted, a state of barbarism and chaos in which human desires would be uncontrolled would result. Thus, according to the Confucianists, a harmonious and orderly society could exist only when the *minjung* had served their superiors, the *yang ban*. The Confucianists also taught that the female was created especially for the purposes of procreation and of giving pleasure to the male. Thus, they insisted upon the inferiority of women, placing them in the same class as slaves.[5] *Xiang rom* and women were the *minjung* of the time.

During the reign of King Sungjong (1469–94), the classical scholars emerged as a new force, and the number of the ruling class increased. This was followed by the reign of King Kusanghaegun (1608–23), during which many independent middle-class farmers and wholesale dealers also became part of the ruling class. Yet the two distinct classes remained evident until the end of the Yi Dynasty in 1910. In this kind of socio-economico-political context Protestant Christianity was introduced to Korea in the year 1884.

Dr Horace N. Allen was the first Protestant missionary (co-worker) to come to Korea. A member of the Presbyterian Mission Board, he brought courage, vision, and devotion with him in his desire to be a partner with the Koreans to work for the extension of God's kingdom. However, one of the policies of the Yi Dynasty toward the West at that time was *choksa chongwi* ('expel the wrong and defend the right'). This policy was evident in a series of persecutions of the Catholics (who came to Korea in 1784) and in an uncompromising closed door policy toward the Western powers.[6] Therefore, Dr Allen arrived in Korea through the 'back door' of the American legation, which appointed him the legation doctor. With his Western medical skills he gradually gained the favor of the royal family and laid a foundation for future mission work. On April 5, 1885, Rev. M. G. Underwood, a Presbyterian missionary, and Henry Apenzeller, a Methodist missionary, and his wife joined Dr Allen. As time passed, the missionary community grew and carried out a considerable amount of medical work.[7]

A landmark occasion for the American Protestant mission was the opening of a school for girls in 1885. The opportunities that the missionaries made available through education were both for girls (who were still considered to be inferior creatures) as well as boys of the *minjung*. The sons of the *yang ban* were not attracted to the schools.[8]

Meanwhile, because Christian evangelism was still banned, the work of the American mission had to be done among the *minjung*, and it had to be secret and underground work. The early missionaries tried to gain the favor of the government, being cautious and patient in doing their work to gain the confidence of the government and the people. They were very busy, for, on the one hand, the missionaries were using the good offices of the American legation while, on the other hand, they were slowly penetrating the lower class, that is, the *minjung*, of the Korean society.[9]

During this period the missionaries made a major breakthrough. Discovering that *Hangul*, the Korean vernacular script, was being despised and neglected, they picked it to study and to use to communicate to the *minjung* of Korea. Thus the medium through which they worked was the language of the *minjung*, while Chinese was the official written language of the Korean officialdom and the *yang ban* class. Using this medium encouraged and facilitated the contact of the Christian message and of its missionary bearers with the *minjung* in Korea. This was the beginning of the process of rehabilitating the language of the Korean *minjung*.[10]

Next, the Bible was translated into *Hangul*. The translation of the New Testament began in 1887, and by 1900 the entire Bible was translated into the Korean vernacular. Other books and tracts were also published; the circulation of these and of the Bible became the most effective strategy of the missionaries in spreading the gospel of Jesus Christ.

In January 1893, the early Protestant missionaries adopted a very significant mission policy, which was called the 'Nevius Method'. The four articles of the policy were outlined as follows:

1 It is better to aim at the conversion of the working classes than that of the higher classes.

2 The conversion of women and the training of Christian girls should be a special aim, since mothers exercise so important an influence over future generations.

3 The Word of God converts where humankind is without resources; therefore it is most important that we make every effort to place a clear translation of the Bible before the people as soon as possible.

4 The mass of Koreans must be led to Christ by their own fellow countrymen; therefore we shall thoroughly train a few as evangelists rather than preach to a multitude ourselves.[11]

During the latter years of the Yi Dynasty there were also many important political events that took place. Much social unrest and many political revolts by the *minjung* against the ruling class occurred. Among them, one event deserves special attention. That is the *Tonghak* Rebellion. Among the *yang ban* class the buying and selling of government positions was a common practice. Then, anyone who purchased an official position could generally reimburse himself through extortion. Taxes and levies were increased by local and national governments until they reached three or four times the legal rate. Extravagance, licentiousness, and debauchery were the order of the day at the court. The suffering *minjung* could no longer remain silent. In 1895, the *Tonghaks*, a group mostly comprised of poor peasants, rose in rebellion in the south.[12] This *Tonghak* Rebellion had both religious and political significance. In many ways, it represented the first indigenous, organized *minjung* movement in Korea. Through struggle against the feudal social system in Korea and armed with the ideology 'humanity is heaven', the oppressed *minjung* began to define themselves as subjects, rather than objects, of history and destiny.

Also during the Yi Dynasty, bands of armed peasants called *Hwal-bindang* rose up in every part of the country. The social ideal that they possessed came from a story written by Ho-Kyun about Hong Kil Dong. Ho-Kyun was a *chungin* (member of the social class between the ruling *yang ban* class and the commoners). He wrote this popular story in the *Hangul* so that the *minjung* could read it easily. The story was told and retold and was most popular during the Yi Dynasty, when the ruling powers were making the *minjung* suffer most.[13]

The story of Hong Kil Dong is as follows. An alienated social hero named Hong Kil Dong leaves home and joins a group of bandits because he cannot fulfill his life's ambitions and goals in the existing society. Collecting a gang around him he names it *Hwalbindang* (party to liberate the poor and oppressed). The hero of the story attacks the rich and distributes wealth to the poor *minjung*. This creates great social disturbances. Finally, the hero is persuaded by his father to leave the country, and he goes off to an island called Yuldo, which is his paradise. It is characterized by the absence of social and class divisions.

With its picture of a messianic kingdom, the novel prompted a new social vision among the people. Just like the hero in the story, the *Hwalbindang* in Korea were concerned with national rights and equality of all. Driven by the desire to eliminate the gap between the rich and the poor, they too robbed the rich in order to help the poor.[14]

Meanwhile, after the crushing of the *Tonghak* Rebellion (1895) by the government, the countryside was wide open for missionary penetration. Missionaries went deep into the countryside and made contacts with the *minjung* who were associated with the *Tonghak* movement. Christianity was then accepted by the *minjung* as a tool for fighting for justice, equality, and human rights. Christianity became a politically oriented faith and a religion of hope and power for the oppressed and suffering *minjung.*

During this period the major emphasis of Korean Christianity was to achieve equality of human beings and to assure human rights and social justice for the Korean people. The *minjung* became enlightened and inspired, and they were stirred up against the administration and illegal acts of government officials. An important part of the Korean Christian movement was the 'common meeting', at which a cross section of the *minjung* voiced their common concerns.[15] The common meetings also engendered a new *minjung* leadership. For instance, after attending the meetings a butcher (whose occupation was classified as *xiang rom*) named Park Song-chun became a Christian and later went on to lead the Butchers' Liberation Movement from 1895 to 1898 and to become one of the founding members of the Seungdong Presbyterian Church in Seoul.[16] These common meetings spread throughout the countryside. Since the missionaries had to travel to reach the *minjung*, they had to train more Korean Christian leaders who could go with them. Thus Dr Samuel A. Moffett founded a theological institution (which is now the Presbyterian College and Seminary) in 1901.

The missionaries gradually ceased to be pioneers and to preach directly to the *minjung*. They became organizers or managers, directing and supervising the Korean Christians' evangelical enterprise. They would make occasional trips into the countryside, visiting newly established churches and administering sacraments. The Korean churches used the *Hangul* Bible widely as a very important tool for evangelizing Korea. The Bible became the greatest factor in evangelization. The Korean churches derived their power, spirituality, great faith in prayer, and liberality from the fact that all the churches were saturated with a knowledge of the Bible. Bible study and training classes constituted the most unique and most important factor in the growth of the Korean churches.[17]

The *minjung* in Korea responded to the Christian message. The motives and reasons for the response, in great measure, were to improve their social and political condition. This was true particularly after 1895. Certainly the Christian message gave some hope to the *minjung*, the outcasts. Political oppression was another cause of the increase in believers. The *minjung* felt that they had reached the summit of misery.

The year 1905 was a fateful year for the Korean people. That year Korea lost its independence and became a protectorate of Japan. The treaty of the protectorship robbed the kingdom of Korea of its diplomatic rights to deal with foreign powers, for the Japanese established the office of governor-general under the Korean king to control the Korean government. For the Korean people this meant that their historical situation now provided a new external focus. Independence and the expulsion of Japanese power from Korea became the main concern of the Korean people.[18]

In the political arena, Korean Christians were not exempt from a sense of national crisis and national humiliation, and they harbored an intense anti-Japanese feeling. The missionaries also felt keenly the estrangement between the Koreans and the Japanese which seemed to presage a general uprising. However, they not only understood the hopelessness of fighting against the Japanese imperial army, but also foresaw the danger of making the young Korean churches a political agency. It seems that missionaries were successful in depoliticizing the Korean Christians through mass revival meetings. The main features of the several Protestant revival meetings held in 1907 were the confession of sins after a sermon convincing the people of their sins, loud prayers, and various forms of collective emotional expressions. These revival meetings brought a deep sense of fellowship among Christian communities and a moral transformation of individual lives. However, the Christian message was no longer geared to the social and national crisis of the Korean *minjung*, but was limited to the rigid and narrow definition of salvation of the soul. The Korean Christians' aspiration for national liberation was completely ignored, and the missionaries' tight control of the Korean Christian communities stifled the dynamism of the autonomous communities which could have responded better to the historical predicament.

August 29, 1910, was a day of national humiliation for the Korean people. This was the day that Korea was formally annexed to Japan. The Korean people lost their country and became enslaved *minjung* subjected to the Japanese military rule. The Yi Dynasty formally ended and the right of government was transferred to the Japanese emperor.

The Japanese government strongly infused the policy of Japanese ultranationalism into Korea. According to that policy, all values and institutions came under the imperial authority of the emperor. Hence, the government, the military, business, and all truth, beauty, and morality were linked to the institution of emperor. The infamous Education Rescript was an open declaration of the fact that the Japanese state, being a religious, spiritual, and moral entity, claimed the right to determine all values. This was the spirit of Japanese national policy. It was combined with the doctrine of the divinity of the emperor, a belief championed by the Japanese military, which was the holy army of the emperor and which had launched the mission of bringing the 'light of the emperor' to Korea.[19]

For the Korean Christians, political neutrality was not possible whether they were in the churches or outside of them. The oppression, exploitation, and alienation by the Japanese government of the Koreans became extraordinarily cruel. Physical tortures and imprisonments were common practices. Living under the oppressive Japanese rule meant inevitable suffering for powerless Koreans, the *minjung* of the time.

Under the extreme conditions of political oppression, economic exploitation, social alienation by a foreign regime, and internal control by the missionaries, the Korean Christians had no positive outlet to express their feelings and aspirations other than in dreams, but dreams were powerful forces for the people's historical self-understanding. In their dreams, Korean Christians found the God of the Exodus most meaningful for their historical condition. For example, a preface to a Sunday school lesson from this period states:

> The Book of Exodus is written about the powerful God, who liberated the people of Israel [which would have been interpreted as meaning the Korean people] from suffering and enslavement and made them the people who enjoyed glorious freedom; God appeared as Yahweh before Israel, and as the whole and just God. God exists by himself and of himself, God has sympathy, and God is the Saviour. Exodus is the book of the miracle of God's liberation of the people of Israel from the power of Pharaoh [the Japanese emperor] with God's power. God has saved Israel first and established it as holy. This book is a foreshadowing of the redemptive love of Jesus in the Gospels and of God's power that cleanses; that is, the miracle of the grace shown forth.[20]

The struggles of the Korean Christians for independence and social justice were persistent despite the regulation concerning meetings (1910) and that concerning guns and explosives (1912). The continuing efforts of the Korean Christians became the spiritual backbone of the March First Independence Movement of 1919. From 1896 to 1898 many intellectuals, merchants, and industrialists had organized the Independence Association. With the help of the *minjung* who participated in the *Tonghak* Rebellion in 1895, the Independence Association formed a society which later provided two main leaders of the March First Independence Movement. These people had the consciousness of the struggle of the *minjung* for liberation. Perhaps this movement was the broadest in scope of the *minjung* liberation movements. Of the people who constituted the movement, 48 percent were peasants, 22 percent were Christians, and 30 percent were ordinary men and women in their twenties. Christians provided much of the leadership of this movement. Unfortunately, the March First Independence Movement was crushed by the Japanese imperial army.

The missionaries in this period were products of early twentieth-century fundamentalism, and their only concern was the 'salvation of souls'. Also, in order to do their mission work, they found it necessary to collaborate with the Japanese authorities. However, these relationships changed as World War II approached and began, and toward the end of World War II, the missionaries were expelled from Korea, leaving the Korean churches to carry on their mission by themselves. We may characterize the Korean Church between 1920 and 1945 in the following manner: (1) It lacked a historical consciousness. (2) It yielded to the enforcement of worship at the Japanese shrine (Shintoism). (3) It was under the sway of fundamentalistic dogma and imported theology. (4) It became a captive to those who were striving for ecclesiastical authority. This was the period of the 'Egyptian Captivity' of the Korean Church's history.

The Koreans did not see their liberation until the end of World War II in 1945. It was at this time that they finally were liberated from the rule of the Japanese emperor who, like Pharaoh, had exploited them to the utmost. Thus, the Exodus Model parallels the Korean experience in many ways. The *minjung* of Korea, like the Hebrews, had to assume responsibility and strengthen their awareness of the depths of their bondage in order to rise up against the system in rebellion. In other words, the *minjung* in Korea were actively participating in the process of their own liberation, fully aware that God stood with them and for them.

Furthermore, in the context of the Exodus event, the *minjung* can be clearly understood as a force that stands in opposition to the powerful. The *minjung* are the oppressed who have their rights infringed upon by rulers. They are 'uprooted people' who have no national identity or legal protection and who are considered to be slaves. In Korea, the pattern of slavery, like that experienced by the Hebrews in Egypt, was not questioned and was considered reasonable by those who benefited from the social system. A slave society had long been accepted as the natural and unchangeable order of things. In both Egypt and Korea, while the government leaders regarded the subjected people as a most important element in their economy, they never considered giving them fair compensation for their work. Finally, the Hebrews, being the objects of God's liberation, cried out to God for liberation from the oppressive and unjust Egyptian society. These cries reflected the same aspirations as those of the *han*-ridden *minjung* in Korea.

NOTES

1   There is no agreement among the scholars who take the view that the exodus took place in the thirteenth century BC as to who the actual Pharaoh was when Moses liberated his people from Egypt. Some believe that Rameses II was the Pharaoh of the oppression as well as that of the exodus, and there are those who date the exodus as being during the time of Maniptah, the son of Rameses II. The problem lies in the Old Testament reference to the death of the Pharaoh from whom Moses had fled. If we assume that it was Sethi I who initiated the oppression, then we would have some difficulty in accounting for Moses' stay of forty years in Egypt and an equal stay in Midian before returning to liberate his people near the end of Rameses II's reign. Of course, it has been suggested with some plausibility that the period of forty years is often taken as a round figure to describe a generation, and that the actual figure would be much lower, say twenty-five years. Even though we are not able to solve the chronological problem satisfactorily, the reign of Rameses II seems to be at the time of Moses' challenge to Pharaoh.

2   M. C. Astour, 'Habiru, Hapiru', in *The Interpreter's Dictionary of the Bible*, supplementary volume (Nashville, Abingdon Press, 1976), pp. 382–5.

3   M. L. Chaney, 'Ancient Palestinian Peasant Movements and the Formation of Premonarchic Israel', in D. N. Freedman and D. F. Graf (eds.), *Palestine in Transition: The Emergence of Ancient Israel* (Sheffield, Almond Press, 1983).

4   For a more detailed study on *han*, see S. Nam-dong, 'Towards a Theology of *Han*', in *Minjung Theology*, ed. CTC-CCA (Maryknoll, NY, Orbis Books, 1983), pp. 55ff.

5   R. Yong-jin Moon, 'A Study of the Change in Status of the Korean Woman from Ancient Times through the Yi Period' (dissertation, Emory University, Atlanta, 1982), pp. 4–16.

6   K. Yong-bock, 'Korean Christianity as a Messianic Movement of the People', in *Minjung Theology*, p. 81.

7   ibid.
8   ibid.
9   ibid.

10   ibid., p. 82.
11   ibid., p. 83.
12   C. Chai-yong, 'A Brief Sketch of Korean Christian History from the Minjung Perspective', in *Minjung Theology*, p. 75.
13   K. Yong-bock, 'Messiah and Minjung', in *Minjung Theology*, p. 188.
14   ibid.
15   C. Chai-yong, p. 76.
16   ibid.
17   K. Yong-bock, 'Korean Christianity', p. 86.
18   ibid., p. 88.
19   ibid., p. 95.
20   W. L. Swallen, Preface to *Sunday School Lessons on the Book of Exodus* (Seoul, Religious Tract Society, 1907).

17

A Black African Perspective: An African Reading of Exodus

JEAN-MARC ELA

To read the Exodus in Africa means to enter into solidarity with individuals and groups who are refused the dignity of being human, to denounce the abuses of established systems, and to intervene to protect the weak, as Moses did.

This chapter is taken from the author's book, *African Cry* (Maryknoll, NY, Orbis Books, 1986).

Jean-Marc Ela is a Cameroonian and worked among the Kirdis in North Cameroon. He is on the staff of the Department of Sociology, University of Yaoundé, Cameroon.

What is the message of the Book of Exodus today for so many millions of Africans in their religious, cultural, political and socioeconomic situations? What can men and women in black Africa who seek deliverance from political and economic oppression look for in a reading of Exodus? This is a towering question facing us. I shall examine it here.

It is not difficult to see the import of this question. Our faith in the God of revelation cannot be lived and understood abstractly, in some atemporal fashion. It can only be lived through the warp and woof of the events that make up history. Faith will grapple with the tensions and conflicts of global society. It runs into the crucial questions and urgent aspirations of all women and men. The praxis of the Christians struggling in situations of injustice must be reckoned with in any effort to understand the living faith. We must reflect on this activity, bring it into confrontation with the gospel, and make explicit the theological intent it expresses.

Ultimately, the sense of revelation will need to be understood in history through the situations and experiences by which the word of God makes itself heard. After all, theology is nothing but a reflection fashioned of the stuff of living experience. One extracts the current meaning of God's word from a point of departure in the historical understanding that human beings have of themselves and the world. Theology is a labor of deciphering the sense of revelation in the historical context in which we become aware of ourselves and our situation in the world. We must respect this hermeneutic function of theology, remembering that the enterprise it supposes is that of the Bible itself. The Bible in the life of God's people never was anything but a reflection on, a resumption of, the basic meaning of the biblical message and the promise of salvation at the heart of the happenings and the history being lived out by the people of God.

We are called today to understand ourselves in the light of a living revelation, to understand the profound sense of the situations and events that we experience, to read the word of God in the world. History, then, including the history of the life of the Church, must be the locus *par excellence* of theological research and reflection. And so we must renounce any discourse on the exodus that we might generate *in absoluto* without taking into consideration our own concrete, vital context. In other words, from a point of departure in the center of vital interest and in view of the historical experiences and questioning that mark the life of our peoples, we must overcome the temporal distance between us and the exodus and lay hold of the meaning that God seeks to impart to us by means of this key event in salvation history.

And so the questions arise. In the colonial or neocolonial situation that has marked Christianity in Africa, is Exodus not a book terribly absent to us? And is the reason for this absence not that the message it delivers calls into question not only a certain theology but also an ecclesiastical praxis, a worship, and a spirituality?

The God of missionary preaching was a God so distant, so foreign, to the history of the colonized peoples. Exploited and oppressed, they find it difficult to identify this God with the God of Exodus, who becomes aware of the situation of oppression and servitude in which the people find themselves. The primary role of the Bible, and of the Old Testament in a special way, in African religious movements is to express the reaction and revolt of African Christians within the institutional churches in which the despised, humiliated human being lives a relationship to God under the rubric of absence.

The God of the Old Testament, the God of the Promise, continually shows human beings a future of hope, which enables them to criticize the existing situation. God summons up from within the hoping consciousness of the human being a nonconformity with reality. In short, God carries human beings forward, toward a future characterized by a new reality. But in the official churches, God's divinity has been posited in a changelessness, an immutability, an impassibility such that the history of human beings is effectively abandoned to its own devices, deprived of the capacity to appear as the locus of manifestation of God's action. If the God of preaching, when all is said and done, is simply the God of the theodicies, that is, of Greek metaphysics, then God is nothing but a supreme, eternal idea, having no connection with anything that happens on earth, where human beings live their lives. Devoid of any openness to the world, God cannot become involved in the human drama, for God cannot compromise the divine purity in any historical becoming.

My point is this: the God proclaimed to the African human being in the precise context of the colonial situation is a God who is a stranger to the times, indifferent to political, social, economic, and cultural occurrences, having no prospect of involvement such as would necessarily be implied in the Promise. At most, the God of the Christian churches in the times of colonization commanded adaptation and submission to the existing order of things. At the First Vatican Council, did not a group of missionary bishops beseech Pope Pius IX to release the black race from the curse of Ham? A like request is not only perfectly logical in a theology of established disorder; it implies a praxis that accepts a ready-made world, accepts the status imposed on the colonized peoples and justified by a popular theology that interprets the condition of the black race as a punishment from God.

It is scarcely surprising, then, that the missionaries did not seek to spell out the biblical notion of the salvation they claimed to be bringing to the African. In the mind of most African converts, being saved meant going to heaven. Missionaries failed to point out that in the Bible the notion of salvation is shot through with that of liberation, and that salvation (or liberation) is expressed at once as present and future. Salvation is indeed the object of hope, but it has a present dimension as well. To be saved means to be delivered now, to be liberated already, from the forces of alienation that enslave persons.

By contrast, the Church, by its silence or by hiding behind an apolitical disguise, reinforces and legitimates dependency. It fails to enunciate the sociohistorical dimensions of salvation and hope. In thrall to a religious anthropology that sees the human being only as a soul to be saved, the Church has consolidated a state of misery by teaching the colonized peoples contempt for earthly values. A prayer frequently recited in Christian assemblies, in village and town, went as follows: 'I ask thee not for earthly riches and happiness. I ask thee but for one thing: Give me thy grace and I shall learn to condemn the joys of this world.' The notion of religion as the opium of the people, one might conclude, is not devoid of foundation here.

In the colonial situation that has marked imported Christianity, mission has undergone a systematic distortion. Globally the Christian message has been cut off from its political extensions, which give it its human, concrete meaning. Where world and society are concerned, missionaries have not generally sought to raise up rousers and doers, leaders of men and women, liberators, but have trained passive Christians, persons to be treated as minors. It would have been difficult for missioners emerging from the colonial seminary to teach anything calculated to impugn the situation of colonial dependence. In the missions the privatization of Christianity reached its zenith. The colonized peoples never had a complete view of Christianity. Bereft of a historical, critical sensitivity that would relate the salvation message to the particular context of colonial domination, the Church kept Africans in line with taboos and sanctions instead of launching them into the historical adventure of liberation – where, precisely, the living God is revealed.

If the exodus has any meaning for us, it will be first and foremost in its capacity to illuminate the living relationship between revelation and history. The central event through which God is revealed by intervening in people's history is the exodus. God utters the divine being definitively in the action by which God snatches the people from the servitude of Egypt, and leads them, with mighty hand and outstretched arm, to the very land of Canaan, the land of the promise Abraham has received: 'When Israel was a child I loved him, and out of Egypt I called my son' (Hos. 11.1). Deuteronomy capsulizes Israel's religion thus: 'We were once slaves of Pharaoh in Egypt, but the Lord brought us out of Egypt with his strong hand' (Deut. 6.21).

Israel's liturgy is shot through from beginning to end with the memory of the exodus. The core, as we know, is the Feast of Passover – no longer a feast of returning spring, such as neighboring peoples celebrated – but a commemoration of the flight from Egypt (see

Exod. 12.12–14). The Jewish religion is steeped in the memory of the Passover. The whole psalter seems driven by Miriam's refrain after the passage through the sea (Exod. 15.21–2). There is no psalm without an echo of *In exitu Israel de Egypto . . .* (see Pss. 105, 66, 78). Indeed, for Israel the entire Bible is simply a rereading of the exodus, when the people of the covenant became aware of the crucial moment when God genuinely created them as a people.

Thus the exodus theme is a commonplace in prophetical preaching. Hosea speaks of leading Israel back to the desert to 'speak to her heart' (see Hos. 2.16–17). Ezekiel transforms his memory of the espousal of the exodus to a promise of a wedding (Ezek. 16). The Song of Songs, so rich with reminiscences of the exodus, is a foretaste of the end of the ages, when Jesus of Nazareth will assume the divine name of the exodus to manifest that in him all revelation is accomplished (John 8.28). The Christ appears in some way as the burning bush, out of which the name of God is communicated to human beings (see John 17.26). This appearance of Christ, wherein the story of the burning bush receives its fuller sense, sheds light on the meaning of the exodus. In the logic of revelation, the word of God develops by a projection into a future that had been awaited throughout the past. In the first great deeds of God, a messianic hope will discern the proclamation of the crowning action to consummate God's revelation in history.

Thus the state of things toward which history is moving is something that mythic time or cosmic cycles could never produce: the full and real accomplishment of divine promises is only partially realized at a given moment in history. In this perspective, the exodus, in which God, in a first moment, has created a people by the first convenant, will be a presage and presentiment of a future event that will be a second exodus. Thanks to the prophets, Israel comes to realize that the liberation from Egypt does not exhaust God's promise. Second Isaiah proclaims to the exiles a liberation that will be as a new exodus (Isa. 43.16–21; 52.4–6; 41.17–20). Cyrus restores freedom to God's people, but this liberation does not yet fulfill expectations. All of these partial realizations, far from quenching hope, only sharpen it. In other words, the capital event, in which God – in a conflict where God triumphs over the forces of slavery and death, symbolized by Egypt and its Pharaoh – bestows on Israel existence as a free people (Ezek. 16.3–9), is not the fulfillment of the promise, but a partial accomplishment and reiteration of the promise.

Such an event refers to a future of God in history, then. More precisely, it refers not to the God who is, but to the God who comes, and whose promise is never exhausted by its historical realizations. Ultimately the basic meaning of the exodus is bestowed by the revelation of a God who personally 'owns' the future. Revelation is not mainly a doctrine, but a promise, which remains to be verified in its realization in the future of the world. Thus it unceasingly opens out upon the future of a new creation, a new exodus. God's revelation in history always comports a horizon of the future, in which the divine design will be accomplished in its fullness. Out beyond events having the value of a sign, a more distant perspective appears, that of the end of the ages. Israel thus appears ever the people to whom God addresses the divine word, to be sure; but Israel is also created by this word, which endlessly bears this people toward a future – inasmuch as the promise of salvation in its plenitude constitutes the essential kernel of God's word, the thing that awakens hope in the human being.

We must seek the meaning of the God of the exodus in light of the fact that the fulfillment of the promises is the locus of intelligibility of revelation as a whole. When we interpret the divine name of the exodus in a dynamic perspective, we understand that, in giving the divine name, God is not content with showing that the divinity is not a being turned inward upon itself. God is actually turned toward human beings, the subject of personal relationships, to the precise extent that it is God's intervention in history that will say that God is God. But God does not designate the divinity as 'I am' in order to say that the divine being abides and subsists in the midst of events (Isa. 40.6–8); rather, God's word is immutable and was, is, and will be *revealed* in history. Through the exodus event, God is revealed in the history of the promise. Deliverance from servitude in Egypt is an event that illuminates the language of the promise: it is an act of fidelity on the part of God. In a word: in the exodus, God is revealed under the formality of promise.

God's revelation is still bound up with history, through the happenings in which Israel's faith deciphers the intervention of the hand of God, through events that are the vessels of the future by reason of God's promises with which they are intertwined. Just so, we see, the divine name of the exodus not only unveils the mystery of God's personhood, but is at the same time a name to be used on a journey, a name revealing God in the direction of the future, a name of promise to show forth, in the darkness of an unknown future, what it is that can be relied upon. It is in an event to be awaited, and not only in reference to an earlier event already known, that God is made known. As Moltmann says so well:

> The God of the exodus [is] a God of promise and of leaving the present to face the future, a God whose freedom is the source of new things that are to come... His name is a wayfaring name, a promise that discloses a new future, a name whose truth is experienced in history inasmuch as his promise discloses its future possibilities.[1]

The God who reveals the divine name shows thereby that God is not a force of nature whose epiphany signifies the eternal processes of life and death. God is a God concerned to orient the human being not toward the perpetual recommencement of the cosmic cycle, but toward a future constituting the goal of all of the human being's history. When all is said and done, the God who reveals the divine name is the God of hope in the future of an irreversible movement and a radical novelty. The exodus is the event *par excellence* reread by the people of God and commemorated by them in precise function of its revelation to them of who God is. In referring the human being to a future of God, the divine name of the exodus becomes a call of hope.

In a perspective in which the history of human beings is of value for God, who gets involved in that history and fulfills the divine promise there, we cannot posit the happiness of human beings, justice and freedom, reconciliation and peace, in a beyond having no connection with the realities and situations of the present world.

It is impossible to speak of hope without recalling that social and temporal reality is the locus of God's interventions and revelation alike. There God proposes to human beings a collective project of communion and oneness. Hence not only are liberation movements, mobilizing the collective aspirations, the locus where we are to read the history of the promise, but we must know, too, that God's revelation, in ongoing fashion, calls for the transformation of the world. Charged with a message of hope, God's revelation protests the present in order to actualize the future. God's revelation gives birth to a people who are witnesses to the promise. Their corresponding task is to do something new in history. Ultimately, revelation stirs up a community in exodus, whose mission is not only to live in expectation of the fulfillment of the promise, but also to promote the historical transformation of the world and of life.

Of necessity, the revelation of the God of the exodus enables us to renounce the temptation to short-circuit time and history. It enables us to rediscover the importance of the future and the depth of the present moment. It constrains us to assume historicity and thus to rethink the divine message in the space where the economy of solidarity characterizing God's designs on men and women and their world is being realized. In obedience to God's promise, we are to discern and prepare the roadways to the future. A grasp of the mystery proper to the God of the exodus arouses us to react against a flight to the future that would disregard the historical now. The God of the promise invites us to make history the locus of the progressive fulfillment of the promises.

Thus God's revelation not only has the purpose of illuminating and interpreting the existing reality of the world and of human beings; it also introduces a contradiction into present reality and thus initiates a dynamism whose thrust is toward the definitive fulfillment of the promise. In the perspective of divine revelation, the world itself is on a journey. It is impossible to speak of the promise, of its radical openness to the future, and at the same time to consider the world a self-enclosed system, a perfect order, or a ready-made reality. The fact is that history's end is not yet here. History is the tension between promise and fulfillment. Accordingly, knowledge of God is always provisional – and impossible without a transformation of the world. In other words, if the world is not yet a theophany, if reality is still open to the future, our true situation is still ahead of us. Thus we are at once on the way toward the God who comes and on the way toward a world as it ought to be, in conformity with the final fulfillment of the promise. Revelation in its plenitude coincides with the end of the process of transformation of the world. In short, the expectation of another world calls for another kind of world.

For millions of Africans, the signs of a world in quest of freedom and justice are too evident not to attract the attention of churches that boast the Judaeo-Christian revelation or claim that the message of the exodus occupies a central place. How many illiterate people are paralyzed today by their ancestral (and modern) fears in societies in which the accumulation of new knowledge operates according to the model of an élitist culture? Ignorance is not limited here to an inability to read and write. It extends to the functioning of political institutions, to the mechanisms of economics, to the laws of society. In the face of the manifold harassments and blind bullying of which they are the victims, the illiterate African rural masses are ignorant of the very law designed to protect them. Their very fear of defending themselves, even when they know they are in the right, itself constitutes a stumbling block, one from which many human groups need to be liberated.

In any breach with situations of servitude, a first step will be to promote a mentality of active solidarity. Of course no such mentality can exist without an inventory of the factors or mechanisms of oppression. No change is possible without an awareness of injustices such as will render them intolerable in the mind of the people. Ultimately, in raising up leaders for a determinate community who will perform the function of prophets in that community, the group will receive a 'word' from which it can draw the strength to forge ahead. There must be individuals to take up the questions and traumas of a group and awaken the group to injustices from within and injustices from without. Certain individuals must decide to speak, in the conviction that many in the group are aware of their suffering.

In any community, village or city neighborhood, the prime interest in reading the Book of Exodus is to rescue the majority of African Christians from ignorance of the history of liberation. After all, this text is about nothing else. Moses is not sent to Egypt to preach a spiritual conversion, but to lead Israel 'out of the house of slavery'. In this escape God is revealed as the unique, matchless God. In today's world changes do result from liberation movements, and Africans must not be kept from knowing that, in our age, living communities are struggling for respect for their rights.

A knowledge of the history of today's liberation movements will spur on communities held down by fatalism and resignation. It will be crucial to remember that through this history God's spirit is at work, toiling internally for the transformation of the world, in view of the fact that injustice and domination, with contempt for men and women and the violence all these things engender, constitute a key aspect of the sin of the world.

Accordingly, a reading of the Book of Exodus in Africa today demands that the Christian churches attempt to solve the problem of the interrelationship between the proclamation and education of faith and projects that will permit local communities to move from servitude to freedom. More radically, in a cultural context marked by the theme of withdrawal or estrangement from God as recorded in most African mythic traditions, how will it be possible to create any space for a desire of the living God apart from liberation experiences? What can supply a starting point for the proclamation of the word of God to human beings in a cultural universe in which, as for the Kirdi of North Cameroon, God has been killed, abandoning men and women to misery, suffering, and death? In the African churches where, all too frequently, a moralizing instruction has influenced generations of Christians, a reading of Exodus can help recall that God utters the divine being in history. It is precisely the place of Exodus in the Bible that obliges us to question ourselves concerning our forms of celebration of salvation in connection with all of the enterprises of human promotion. In other words, how may God's benevolent interventions in human history be recalled from within an experience of life, of joy and freedom, of sharing and communion – all concretely signified in the life of local communities? Must faith and salvation, and the Church itself, be imprisoned in purely religious matters? Salvation comes from God, to be sure; but must one experience it outside the concrete history of a people? Or should we rather receive it in the context in which people live, taking account of their creative effort to construct a future that will be different from their past, a past so cruelly marked by slavery and domination? In Africa, where these situations form an integral part of the collective memory, one cannot shut Christianity up within the limits of a religion of the beyond.

If the Church's mission is before all else a supernatural one, it can scarcely proclaim the One who fulfills the revelation of the cloud-wrapped God of the exodus without including, in its perceptions and its awareness, the concrete life of human beings, institutions and structures, social categories and ideologies – because these can all promote or paralyze the ascent of the daughters and sons of God. In this view, should the churches not confront today's Pharaohs and demand that they allow the people of God speech, decision, and freedom? Will it be enough to continue to run schools and hospitals, dispensaries and orphanages, all manner of charitable activities, or rather will it be in order to prioritize the assumption of the new aspirations of all of the disinherited by bringing the problems of women and men crushed by injustice into religious education, religious formation, and prayer?

In short: by entering into solidarity with the individuals and groups who are refused the dignity of being human, are the churches not called upon, on the one hand, to rediscover the function of Moses and the prophets as the spokespersons of the oppressed and collectively denounce the most crying abuses of the established systems, and, on the other hand, to intervene at all levels of the social system to protect the weak and the little from the arbitrary will of the great? The churches of black Africa ought to distinguish themselves in this role by the quality of their reflection and ought to be able to count on a laity committed to the process of transformation and change of society.

Beyond the shadow of a doubt, a reading of the exodus is a must in the Christian communities of Africa today. As the oppressed of all times have turned to this primordial event, thence to draw hope, we shall never come to any self-understanding without ourselves taking up that same history and discovering there that God intervenes in the human adventure of servitude and death to free the human being. The exodus event is the grid permitting the deciphering of human history and the discovery of its deeper sense – that of an intervention of God revealing the divine power and love.[2]

NOTES

1   J. Moltmann, *Theology of Hope: On the Ground and the Implications of a Christian Eschatology* (New York and Evanston, Harper & Row, 1967), p. 30.

2   As his public life opens (see Luke 4.16–21), Jesus quotes a text of Isaiah (ch. 61), the latter being what is called an 'actualisation de l'Exode' – a recovery of the exodus event for the present. Jesus was steeped in the tradition of the exodus and the prophets. This tradition permeates the Old Testament from beginning to end. For the witnesses of revelation, the exodus was the prototype both of God's action and of the action God expected of the people.

18

An Asian Feminist Perspective:
The Exodus Story
(Exodus 1.8–22, 2.1–10)

AN ASIAN GROUP WORK

This piece is refreshingly different from the other essays in Part Three. For one thing, it is not a formal discourse on the narrative, but a skit centred around some lesser-known characters of the Exodus; for another, it is not written by an individual, but by a group of women.

In the hermeneutical tradition of the West, the biblical documents are studied in silence and it is assumed that only the printed word can communicate the authentic meaning. What this feminist reflection goes on to show is that hermeneutics can use not only philosophical tools, but also the medium of performing arts to unlock the biblical narratives. It further reiterates the point that interpretation can be a meaningful communal activity.

This skit was produced by a group of Indian women – Cresy John, Susan Joseph, Pearl Derego, Sister Pauline, Mary Lobo, Sister Margaret and a Korean, Lee Sun Ai, at the Human Liberation Workshop held in Bombay, May 1988, and is reprinted from *In God's Image* (September 1988). *In God's Image* is a feminist quarterly and it is available from The Editor, *In God's Image*, Kiu Kin Mansion, 568 Nathan Road, Kowloon, Hong Kong.

SCENE I

The house of Moses's mother. A Hebrew home – not lavish in any way.
Time: Afternoon 1–3 p.m.
Cast: Moses's mother Jochebed
       Miriam
       Susannah (another mother)
       Hannah
       Shiprah (midwife)
       Puah (midwife)

JOCHEBED: Shalom, sisters, Shalom. There is much to thank our God. Yahweh has protected us and our leaders out of difficulties in this land of slavery.

HANNAH: To think that we came as a privileged minority in the time of our father Joseph and now we are slaves bereft of our herds and cattle and lands.

JOCHEBED: We have been strong through it all. Our days have not been easy, but God has been faithful. We are not in any easier times. But God has given us wisdom. It has grown through the experience of pain and as women we can unite and have courage. In solidarity is our wisdom. We must preserve ourselves and have faith. In this way we praise Jehovah our God, the source of our life, wisdom and hope. Let us share our stories . . .

SUSANNAH: Our stories are not sweet. Wherever I turn my eyes and ears there is only pain and suffering. Yesterday Judah came home from the building site, bruised badly having been beaten by the foreman. He was in such pain while I cleaned his cuts with wine and oil. I have never seen Judah so close to cursing God. (*She sighs*) This morning he could barely stand, but he had to go back to work. Amos was with him. But before leaving, Judah told me to keep the water boiling when he returns because he expects to be injured further. The foreman, he said, seems more interested in killing the wounded than getting bricks made. It seems almost as though it doesn't matter that the city of Rameses should be built. What matters to our Egyptian lords is that we should all be finished.

JOCHEBED: But Susannah, why did this foreman do this to Judah again?

SUSANNAH: For no good reason. Judah made beautiful bricks without straw. Pharaoh's new scheme is merely to disable and demoralize our men in their place of work. But our men are producing miracles. Our people have a power from God, from above.

HANNAH: It is not just our men who are facing tribulations. Our women and children are also going through difficulties. My Egyptian mistress orders me around, always finding more work when I finish my share at the end of the day. I come home when it is dark. Sometimes she sends me to her husband who uses me and then spits in my face and I have to return home totally unable to help mother in the housework – knowing always that one of our men will never take me as I am. I am afraid to leave – because it will mean public flogging. Death seems easier.

SUSANNAH: (*Putting her arm around Hannah*) How our children suffer!

JOCHEBED: (*Deep sigh*) Yes. Their suffering breaks my heart more than anything. Our husbands work in the building site; we work in their homes as servants and yet our income is not enough for our livelihood. My Aaron . . .

SUSANNAH: Yes, I heard about what happened to him. How is he today?

HANNAH: What happened to Aaron?

SUSANNAH: He also went to the work site. Towards the end of the day, a couple of days ago, while carrying bricks, he stumbled and the bricks fell on his feet. How is he today?

JOCHEBED: He had to go to work this morning. He is still limping.

(*Two midwives enter*)

PUAH: Sisters, there's bad news, bad news.

SHIPRAH: Bad news for our people.

JOCHEBED: Sit, Puah. Sit, Shiprah. Tell us what the trouble is.

PUAH: We were both summoned to Pharaoh's palace this morning.

SHIPRAH: Pharaoh has ordered us to kill all the Hebrew male children at birth.

JOCHEBED: Oh my God, my God. Would that God will help us.

SUSANNAH: Why did you bring her this news like this? Lie down. Don't panic. You need to keep from worrying. When is your baby due?

JOCHEBED: Any time now, really. And I am sure this will be a boy. The way he kicks! This child is very different from Miriam. We must plan a strategy to get out of this. Puah and Shiprah, have you any ideas? What did you do? Were there any babies born this morning?

PUAH: Yes, two male Israeli babies – such strapping young ones and five Egyptians.

HANNAH: Tell us, what did you do?

SHIPRAH: Puah and I took the Israeli births.

JOCHEBED: Did you kill the babies?

SHIPRAH: No. God have mercy. We did not.

SUSANNAH: God bless you. Does Pharaoh know?

SHIPRAH: Yes, while I was coming home, Pharaoh summoned me. And I told him that the babies were born before we reached the women. But we thought we should come and inform you. We felt you sisters should know Pharaoh's plan.

PUAH: We can only fulfil our role in giving life and helping it live, not in killing it.

SUSANNAH: But why does Pharaoh want to kill our boys and not our girls?

PUAH: They are afraid that the numbers of our men are increasing. They are afraid that if our men increase and become strong, they may rebel and go to war.

SHIPRAH: Our girls, of course, can become their concubines, domestic servants and slaves.

JOCHEBED: By killing our men they will slowly destroy the only trade we have now – of brick-making. They will finish the line of our mothers Sarah and Rebecca and of our father Abraham. They will annihilate us as a people. We will have no identity.

SUSANNAH: and HANNAH: Oh God, have mercy on us all!

PUAH: We must go. Pharaoh may have set spies on us.

SHIPRAH: Yes, we must go.

HANNAH: Be strong, sisters. Peace to you and us.

SUSANNAH: I must go too. (*Draws Miriam to herself and strokes her head*) Take care of your mother, girl. If there is any need, come and tell me. (*Embraces Jochebed*) Shalom. Be at rest.

SCENE II

The market place. Jochebed and Susannah and Leah are walking down. Puah and Shiprah walk hastily to them.
Cast: Jochebed
      Susannah
      Leah
      Shiprah
      Puah
      Soldiers

PUAH: (*Drawing Jochebed aside*) Let us go home. We have more news for you.

Shiprah talks to the other women and they draw their skirts and veils and scuttle away to Jochebed's house

(*Jochebed sits resting with her feet up. Miriam brings a bowl of water and towel for each of them to wash their feet*)

PUAH: Pharaoh summoned us again.

SUSANNAH: Again?

JOCHEBED: Why? When?

SHIPRAH: This morning. He was angry because he got a report that we did not kill three male Jewish babies.

SUSANNAH: What did you say?

SHIPRAH: We told Pharaoh that the Hebrew women are so strong that they delivered their babies before we arrived to assist.

JOCHEBED: Praise God for giving you wisdom.

SUSANNAH: You were not treated badly, were you?

PUAH: Pharaoh's men kicked us and threatened to kill us if we would not follow Pharaoh's command.

JOCHEBED: The power of Yahweh be with you and protect you.

SHIPRAH: Don't worry about us. But we must make plans. We think we should train some more Hebrew women who can act as midwives so that we do not come to each delivery. But that will take time. Before that we must plan about you, our dear Jochebed. We must find a way to save your baby if it is a boy.

(*Sound of banging on the door. The door opens ajar. Soldiers enter*)

SOLDIER: So Puah and Shiprah, you are on another lifesaving mission, are you?

SHIPRAH: No. We were here to dine.

JOCHEBED: Jehovah is mightier than Pharaoh. He is the defence of the weak.

SOLDIER: There is a new decree then, women, for Yahweh to work with. The great Pharaoh says that all the newly born baby boys must be thrown into the river Nile. (*Points to Jochebed with a stick*) Anyone who disobeys will bring death to the entire household. (*Steps out grinning*) May your gods have wisdom to meet the wisdom of the Pharaoh of Egypt.

(*Out in the street. The gong is sounded and the decree announced while the women listen. Miriam is clinging to the skirt of her mother*)

JOCHEBED: (*Taking Miriam in her arms*) It is a death sentence to

259

my baby. The death sentence is on me and my family, on all Hebrew babies and families. God have mercy. Have mercy.

SUSANNAH: and PUAH: (*Going up to Jochebed and holding her*) Be brave, Jochebed. Be strong. Let us think of ways to save the baby – to save you and your family.

PUAH: You are the last of the Hebrew women that are to have babies this season. For some weeks now there aren't others.

SUSANNAH: Yes, we must do what we can.

PUAH: Leah, you have been very silent. You haven't said a word. What have you been thinking?

LEAH: I was thinking about the Princess. How different she is from her father.

SHIPRAH: Yes, I heard she is very kind and very good to her Hebrew slaves. I also heard rumours in the palace that she isn't pleased with Pharaoh's decree.

LEAH: Yes, that's true.

PUAH: I have an idea. The Princess comes to the river to bathe every Thursday, does she not?

LEAH: Yes.

PUAH: You are also very close to her, Leah. She loves you because you have been her nurse since she was young. You can influence her, can't you?

LEAH: Into what?

PUAH: Into saving Jochebed's baby if he is a boy.

LEAH: I can try.

SHIPRAH: Jochebed, don't go out of the house any more so that the day of the birth is not known. Either Puah or I will be with you all the time. After the baby comes, if Leah has found favour with the Princess, we will hide the baby in the bulrushes in a basket and have Miriam hide to watch. If the Princess finds favour towards the baby, who knows what can happen.

LEAH: Yes, we can try.

JOCHEBED: All this seems like a dream. It all sounds too good to be true. May Yahweh have mercy on me and on this child. If my baby is a son and he is spared, Yahweh must have a purpose for him. If he lives I live. If he dies I die.

SUSANNAH: He will live.

JOCHEBED: The Princess may find him and may even kill him.

LEAH: Jochebed, be strong. You have charged us to be strong through many things. Trust God and remember his faithfulness to Sarah when he returned Isaac alive and honoured her womb.

SUSANNAH: Yes, Sister, be strong. We will meet again and plan further, but Leah, go and do all you can.

SCENE III

The palace. The Princess getting ready for a walk by the river. Leah and the Princess are talking while she dresses the Princess.
Cast: Princess Zephartiti
   Leah
   Maidens

PRINCESS: Leah, you have been very quiet and sad these past few days. What is disturbing you?

LEAH: Your majesty, I am grieving with my people.

PRINCESS: It has shaken me to see how my father has passed these commands. But Leah, tell me, Puah and Shiprah are not following those insane commands of my father.

LEAH: In most cases the babies have lived and been born before the nurses got there. But things are getting more and more difficult for them.

PRINCESS: In my case I have longed for a child and it hasn't been possible, and there is no heir to the throne. So my father has now chosen to build a city in his name with the blood of others for posterity to remember him.

LEAH: The Pharaoh is wise. In so many ways he has been good, but when he sees a Hebrew something happens to him. We became slaves in the days of his father. So why should he persecute us now?

PRINCESS: He is afraid, more afraid of your God. Your cattle grew stronger than ours and multiplied so well. So he was forced to take them over, and now that they belong to us they are no longer virile. The same thing with your fields: when you gave up your tenancy, the fields became fallow. It is mysterious. But perhaps my father doesn't realize that it is important to work with you and to win fame with love rather than with hate.

LEAH: True, your highness. But now shouldn't you go to the river for your walk? The sun will be setting soon and then it may be too late.

PRINCESS: Leah, you have been a mother to me, speak your heart to me when you need to. Do not ever be afraid. (*Pats Leah lovingly*) Let us go.

SCENE IV

Walking beside the river – the Princess and her entourage. The maidens walking beside the Princess, fanning her, and some of them clean the river of bulrushes and prepare a place for her to sit.
Cast: Princess
     Leah
     Maids – 5
     Miriam
     Baby in a basket
     3 soldiers
     Jochebed

PRINCESS: The evening is beautiful. Leah, it is a better day to bathe than to walk. Prepare for it, Leah; have the sentries posted further.
LEAH: Yes, your majesty. (*She instructs the soldiers and the maidens. The Princess begins to undress. Just then a baby cries. Princess stops*)
PRINCESS: Who's that, Leah? (*Baby cries*) It is a baby, Leah. Where is it? Look for it, women.

(*They begin looking through the bulrushes with the Princess. She comes across the basket and the baby*)

PRINCESS: Leah, it is a Hebrew baby boy! He is beautiful! Just so beautiful! And only a few days old.
LEAH: Yes, your highness. It must be somebody's child, hidden for the fear of Pharaoh.
PRINCESS: Draw him here.

(*They draw out the crying baby and hand him over to the Princess. The baby is comforted*)

LEAH: He chooses you, Princess.
PRINCESS: I choose him too. He will be saved from my father's wrath. But he must be nursed. Is there a wet nurse among the Hebrews?

A MAID: Your highness, there is a little Hebrew girl that's peeping out of the bulrushes.

PRINCESS: Bring her to me. Leah, she must belong to this baby.

LEAH: Perhaps.

(*Maid comes with Miriam. Miriam is very frightened*)

PRINCESS: Come here, girl. Don't be afraid. (*Draws Miriam to herself*) Do you know of a wet nurse among your Hebrew women?

MIRIAM: Yes, your highness.

PRINCESS: Then go and bring her here at once.

MIRIAM: Yes, your highness. (*She runs out*)

PRINCESS: I am sure she is his sister. (*She is rocking the baby in her arms*) I will call him Moses because I drew him out of the water. The gods must be his protector for him to find favour with the Princess of Egypt. He must be a special baby. Leah, how I have longed for a child! I feel so fortunate to receive this gift.

(*Miriam comes running and stares aghast while the Princess kisses the baby. Jochebed follows her. Her eyes open wide in surprise. Jochebed falls at the Princess's feet*)

JOCHEBED: Your highness – you called for me.

PRINCESS: Woman, can you nurse my child?

JOCHEBED: Yes, your highness. (*Eyes filling with tears*)

PRINCESS: Take this child. His name shall be Moses. Nurse him for a while. Bring him to me each day and let no harm come to him. Leah, give this woman all she needs from my kitchen – fruits and milk and good food. Let her not lack in any way. Woman, he is mine. Yours, only to care for now. Remember he is to be prince.

JOCHEBED: Yes, your highness.

PRINCESS: (*Kisses the baby. Removes her ring and chain and puts it around the baby. Gives him to Jochebed*) Be wise, woman. Be very careful. Go now.

JOCHEBED: (*Bows*) Yes, your highness.

(*Jochebed leaves with Moses close to her bosom and Miriam trailing behind*)

PRINCESS: There could not be a better caretaker or nurse than his own mother.

(*Leah is silent but surprised*)

SCENE V

Pharaoh's palace. Sentries are around him. Pharaoh is pacing.
Cast: Pharaoh
Sentries
Princess

PHARAOH: What news of the Hebrews?

SOLDIER: All's well at the building sites. They are flogged and they are working hard.

PHARAOH: Sure. Sure – but have the Hebrew babies been killed?

SOLDIER: Your majesty, in that regard, there is some confusion in the land.

PHARAOH: Confusion – what confusion?

SOLDIER: I hesitate, your majesty.

PHARAOH: Your hesitation will cost you your life. Speak of what you know.

SOLDIER: Surely you will not be angry with the Princess.

PHARAOH: The Princess? What has she done?

SOLDIER: Your majesty, she has saved a Hebrew baby out of the water.

PHARAOH: What?

SOLDIER: It is true. While she was bathing in the river. I was her guard. I saw this happen. It has created quite a stir in the Hebrew camp.

PHARAOH: Send for her immediately.

(*Soldier bows and leaves*)
(*Princess enters*)

PHARAOH: Zephartiti, you have defied the orders of the Pharaoh of Egypt?

PRINCESS: What have I done?

PHARAOH: You have saved a Hebrew boy when you should have ordered to have him killed –

PRINCESS: Oh, so you do have your spies on me, do you?

PHARAOH: What you do is told me by the gods.

PRINCESS: Strange gods these, that give us opposite commands.

PHARAOH: Find a better reason for your sin.

PRINCESS: The gods have not deemed to give me a child in spite of all the feasts and sacrifices I have offered.

PHARAOH: That is because of your rebellious nature. Is that why you have defied the justice of Pharaoh?

PRINCESS: Do you call the killing of babies – the shedding of innocent blood, destroying life, the very gift of the gods – justice?

PHARAOH: How can you justify yourself? You have prevented my orders from being carried out.

PRINCESS: Father, your orders were to throw the babies into the water to die. That order was carried out. But your decree did not say that the babies could not be rescued.

PHARAOH: Foolish woman. These are the follies of a female mind. Bring me the baby and I will have him killed.

PRINCESS: Then you go against your own decree. As well as against my protection for the baby. He wears my insignia – he is my heir.

PHARAOH: (*Pacing restlessly*) Damn the gods!

PRINCESS: Father, have you ever thought what would happen if you let this baby grow up in the palace and be educated as a king? He is strong and beautiful. Think of what will happen when they see a Hebrew worshipping our gods, chief of whom is Pharaoh. Their God will be insulted.

PHARAOH: (*Pondering*) You propose to have a friend in the enemy's camp. You plan to have a Hebrew Pharaoh – worshipping me. (*Laughs*) Ha ha.

PRINCESS: I will enforce that he grows up in the wisdom of Egypt.

PHARAOH: Yes, I think it will be a new and stronger bondage in their slavery. You can have the child.

PRINCESS: So I will keep him. I will not forget your wishes.

PHARAOH: I see that, occasionally, the wisdom of the line of Pharaohs shines through your natural darkness as a woman. Go with my blessing. (*To the sentry*) Revert the decree. There is no need to kill the babies any more.

(*Princess leaves after kissing the Pharaoh's ring. Sentry also goes out*)

SCENE VI

The Princess walks into her palace. Leah is pacing restlessly. She stops short as she hears the Princess entering.
Cast: Princess
        Leah
        Maids

PRINCESS: Leah.

LEAH: Your majesty.

PRINCESS: Leah, your God must be powerful – he saved my baby. The Pharaoh has already changed his mind and the decree has gone out that your children may live – sons and daughters. Go immediately – bring my baby to me with his mother. She can stay here; he will grow up in this palace just like the Pharaohs.

LEAH: Really, your majesty?

PRINCESS: Hasten, Leah. Don't waste time – today before the sun sets he should be here.

CONCLUSION

This is an episode in the history of a people whose women refuse to accept the verdict of the male oppressor – in this event the Pharaoh. Instead, women gather in solidarity to save and protect life. The role of the princess, Pharaoh's daughter, is that of a woman, who, irrespective of her nationality and class, saves a child from the water. Linked together as women, Pharaoh's daughter joins the ranks of women in the triumph of life over death. The conspiracy of the midwives and Leah in saving the male babies and not adhering to Pharaoh's edict is a heroic witness to the strength of women. Every woman is close to life and loves her child. Woman is Life and Love. The killing of the male baby is ironic of the two-edged sword that patriarchy has in itself, namely, in male power is also death!

19

A Palestinian Perspective:
Biblical Perspectives on the Land

NAIM S. ATEEK

This essay is a reminder that a biblical paradigm which is liberative and life-enhancing in one context may be hostile, hurtful and unhelpful and act as a colonizing agent in another. This Palestinian example shows the unsuitability of the first Exodus story for that context and calls attention to the often forgotten second Exodus which speaks of a greater realism and a new understanding of the land and the indigenous people. Though this essay was written before the Israeli-Palestinian accord, the point Ateek tries to make still holds good.

This piece forms a chapter in Naim S. Ateek, Marc H. Ellis and Rosemary Radford Ruether (eds.), *Faith and the Intifada: Palestinian Christian Voices* (Maryknoll, NY, Orbis Books, 1992), pp. 108–16.

Naim S. Ateek describes himself as an Arab, a Palestinian Christian, and a citizen of the state of Israel; he is a Canon of St George's Cathedral, Jerusalem. In his *Justice and Only Justice: A Palestinian Theology of Liberation* (Maryknoll, NY, Orbis Books, 1989), he employs a liberation hermeneutic to work out a theology for his people, the Palestinians.

The 1967 war was a great turning point in the Israel-Palestine conflict. Religion in Israel caught up with the Zionist dream and appropriated it in a special way. The state of Israel gradually became the servant of religion, and religion became the servant of the state. The political had become inseparable from the religious claims to the land.

Anywhere else in the world a conflict like ours would be considered a political one. A people, living in their own country, are overrun by a group of people who come from outside. These outsiders are determined to take over the country. They are stronger and equipped to do so. Such an act is a violation of the political and human rights of the indigenous population; it has no special religious significance. Arbitration, therefore, should be based on international law.

267

But in Israel-Palestine today, the Bible is being quoted to give the primary claim over the land to Jews. In the mind of many religious Jews and fundamentalist Christians the solution to the conflict lies in Palestinian recognition that God has given the Jews the land of Palestine forever.[1] Palestinians are asked to accept this as a basic truth. Any settlement that is not based on such a foundation is seen as contrary to the promises and covenant of God with the Jewish people.

Today this kind of abuse of the Bible and of religion is precisely the religious argument presented by most religious Jews and fundamentalist Christians. Therefore, Palestinian Christians must tackle the issue of land from a biblical perspective, not because I believe that the religious argument over the land is of the *bene esse* of the conflict, but because we are driven to it as a result of the religious-political abuse of biblical interpretation.

I would like to begin by calling attention to some of the abuses of the Bible which we frequently encounter. Recently a document came my way, prepared by some Anglican fundamentalist, on the issue of the land. This person wrote:

> a) I counted that on 109 occasions the Old Testament refers to the land as given or promised to the Jewish people. b) In addition, on a further 36 occasions, it states that God swore a solemn oath to give them the land. c) And on a further 15 occasions, the land is promised 'forever'. d) So strong is the emphasis on this in the Old Testament that it is clear that the people and the land are very deeply and closely associated. If the two are separated something is seriously wrong.

Later in the document this person concludes that since God swore an oath that the land is an eternal possession of Israel, though they did not deserve it, 'Would it not be strange if God decided against fulfilling his strong and numerous promises to Israel about the land? If God breaks such promises, how reliable is he in other promises?'

This is only one sample of the way some of these fundamentalists argue. Any look at the Old Testament shows how often the issue of the land is mentioned. A mere count of the word 'land' in the Old Testament (without any study of context) shows that the three Hebrew words most often translated 'land', *adamah, erez,* and *sadeh,* appear in the text of the Old Testament more than fifteen hundred times. By comparison, in the New Testament the two Greek words that are most often translated as 'land' are *agros* and *ge,* and they appear forty-one times.

One cannot deny at all that there is a great difference between the outlook of the Old Testament and that of the New Testament on the issue of the land. The issue of the land is very much bound up in the life of the people of the Old Testament. The same is not true for the New Testament. I would, therefore, like to submit the following points:

1. The Old Testament makes it very clear that the land belongs to God.[2] There are a number of references in the Old Testament that God is the owner of the land. In one place in the Torah the divine claim to the land is so emphasized that the Israelites are regarded as strangers and foreigners themselves: 'Land will not be sold absolutely, for the land belongs to me, and you are only strangers and guests of mine' (Lev. 25.23; see Jer. 16.18).

Another emphasis is that the Israelites were not supposed to defile the land. In Jeremiah it becomes clear that the defilement of the land had actually taken place, 'But when you entered you defiled my country and made my heritage loathsome' (Jer. 2.7). Those who live in the land must, therefore, obey the owner. Disobedience of God defiles the land. When the land is defiled, it would thrust its inhabitants out (see Lev. 20.22; Deut. 4.25–26, 28.63; Jos. 23.15–16).

Furthermore, we know from the Old Testament that the God who was thought to be one among many gods (Ps. 95.3) and then the greatest God above other gods, was eventually perceived as the only one God, Creator of the world (Ps. 96.5, 97). God was no more the owner of the land of Palestine, but the owner of the whole world. The whole world becomes sanctified because it is God's world and because God dwells in it. 'To Yahweh belongs the earth and all it contains, the world and all who live there' (Ps. 24.1).

I believe that the lesson God has tried to teach the ancient Hebrews all along is the importance of understanding God's promises. The Bible witnesses to the misunderstood promises of God. Chosenness, which was intended to be a responsibility for service, was understood as a privilege to hoard. From one point of view the first exile from the land was meant to shatter the people's narrow concept of God and the land. They had to learn that God existed without the land and outside of it. They needed to learn that God is concerned about other people besides themselves.[3] The exile was meant to help them mature in their understanding of God. One observes that some post-exile prophets put the emphasis on the people who are returning rather than on the land itself. Second Isaiah made the remarkable discovery that the promise of God to the people after the exile was not about land and nationhood, but about the outpouring of God's Spirit on the people.

> For I shall pour out water
>   on the thirsty soil
> and streams on the dry ground.
> I shall pour out my spirit
>   on your descendants,
> my blessing on your offspring,
> and they will spring up among the grass,
> like willows on the banks of a stream (Isa. 44.3–4).

If the people are going to be a light to the nations, then they have to be the carriers of that blessing, rather than hoarding it. Unfortunately, the lesson of the exile was never fully learned; the people were easily swayed by fanatics to adopt a narrow view of the land, which led to the destruction of the nation in 70 CE. Again, the people were given another chance to learn the lessons of history and of the period extended to eighteen hundred years. We observe, sadly, that many Jews have not been willing to learn the lesson that it is wrong to put one's heart on the land. To do so is to invite disaster and another exile.

In other words, within the pages of the Old Testament itself there is a developing understanding of God and the land. There is a movement, mostly in a zigzag way, from a narrow concept of God and the land to a broader, deeper, and more inclusive concept.

2. The second point that one observes in the Old Testament regarding this whole issue of the land has to do with the exodus. In fact, the Old Testament talks about two exoduses. The first is the one that took place when the children of Israel came out of Egypt. The second happened when the exiles returned from Babylon in the sixth century BCE. Most of us are very familiar with the first exodus. Its dramatic stories are very well known to many people: the plagues against the Egyptians, the dramatic escape from Egypt into Sinai, the forty years in the wilderness, the invasion of Canaan, the battle of Jericho, the command of God to annihilate all the inhabitants, and many other exciting stories people enjoy and cherish about the wonderful acts of God for his people.

Very few people know about the second exodus. It is more quiet. It is significantly less dramatic than the first. Yet some of the prophets like Jeremiah thought that it would be a greater event than the first exodus.

> So, look, the days are coming, Yahweh declares, when people will no longer say, 'As Yahweh lives who brought the Israelites out of Egypt,' but, 'As Yahweh lives who led back and brought home the offspring of the House of Israel from the land of the north and all the countries to which he had driven them, to live on their own soil' (Jer. 23.7–8).

When one compares the two exoduses, it is amazing that the first had all the negative attitudes toward the indigenous peoples who were already living in the land. Every time they are mentioned, the language is very hostile. They are supposed to be displaced or destroyed. There is no room for them in the land among the chosen people of God to whom the land was promised. The second is totally different. One gets the feeling that the returning exiles reflected greater realism. They were much more accepting of the people around them. In fact, one of the greatest passages that comes to us after the exile is from the prophet Ezekiel, who was speaking the word of the Lord to the people:

> You must distribute this country among yourselves, among the tribes of Israel. You must distribute it as a heritage for yourselves and the aliens settled among you who have fathered children among you, since you must treat them as citizens of Israel. They must draw lots for their heritage with you, among the tribes of Israel. You will give the alien his heritage in the tribe where he has settled – declares the Lord Yahweh (Ezek. 47.21–3).

This is an amazing change in the approach to the indigenous population. There is an amazing switch from the hostile language of Joshua. Here there is a clear indication that, after the exile, when the second exodus took place, there is a new understanding of the relationship to the land. There is an acceptance of the changes of history. Certain demographic changes had taken place, and the prophet pronouncing the word of God exhorts the people to accept these changes and to share the land with those who are living on it.

It is difficult to understand why Jews have not emphasized the pragmatic nature of the second exodus, and why so much emphasis has been placed on the first war-like exodus, with its violent and bloody treatment of the indigenous people. We also see that, in the twentieth century, instead of living up to the ideal and realism of the second exodus, many have tried to draw their inspiration from the first. This is, indeed, a tragedy. The 'third exodus' has glossed over the second, which expresses a greater understanding of the world. It has clung to the first, which reflects a more primitive concept of God and the world.

Part of the problem, as I perceive it, has to do with the central position of the Torah in Judaism. Although the Torah has in it the seed of a broader concept of God, much of it is narrow and reflects an exclusivist understanding of God. The book of Deuteronomy, for example, has made it impossible for a good Jew to live outside the land. Yet, we know that Jews had to live outside the land during the first and second exiles. In the nineteenth century some Jews in the Reform Movement were ready to break away from the landbound faith and emphasize the prophetic and ethical demands of the Jewish faith. Unfortunately, these have been swamped by Zionism. The tragedy is that there is very little use of the great prophetic material and its insistence on God's demand for justice. The tragedy today is that both the Jewish and Christian fundamentalists have received their inspiration from the vocabulary of the first return to the land, rather than from the spirit of the second return. The first saw the indigenous inhabitants as wicked people who should be slaughtered and displaced. The second saw them realistically as people who should share the land. The returning exiles, in fact, were happy to accept a very small territory between Bethel and Hebron.

3. Any student of the New Testament is struck by the observation that the New Testament as a whole is not preoccupied with the issue of the land as was the Old Testament. Some scholars have suggested that in the process of writing the gospels there was a tendency to depoliticize them in order to decrease any tension between Christians and the Roman Empire. Others feel that the evangelists intentionally were de-Zionizing the tradition. There are other reasons scholars offer as they debate such phenomena. It seems to me, however, that the lack of interest in the land stems from the very nature of the gospel and its basic difference from an Orthodox Jewish outlook.

I believe that the gospels reflect genuinely and faithfully the message of Jesus. Some scholars have tried to suggest that Jesus was a revolutionary, that he was a Zealot. But I am convinced, as some scholars have argued, that Jesus, who knew very well the position of the Zealots, rejected it, and consciously chose to go in another direction.[4] The third temptation in Matthew 4, which speaks about gaining authority over the kingdoms of this world by following the ways and strategy of the devil, is, I believe, the attractive message of the Zealots that Jesus considered and was confronted with but, early in his ministry, rejected. It faced him at other junctures, but he was able to resist it. It is clear, therefore, that the gospel writers, as well as other New Testament writers, have remained faithful to the basic message of Jesus. The land was of very little significance to them.

In this regard there is a difference between a New Testament view and a later Church's view of the land. In some places in the New Testament, the land, Jerusalem, and the Temple are viewed critically and negatively.[5] One way to illustrate this is by looking at the four places in Jewish life that had an ascendant order of significance: the land of Palestine, Jerusalem, the Temple, and the Holy of Holies. At Jesus' death the veil of the Temple was rent from top to bottom; that is, the way between the holy place and the Holy of Holies was now opened. The way between God and humans has been opened in Jesus Christ. Thus the Holy of Holies has lost its significance for the Church. The Temple was destroyed in 70 CE and, in the minds of Christians, was no longer needed. Jesus himself had predicted its destruction. At one time he talked about his body as a temple, when he said, 'Destroy this temple and in three days I will raise it up' (John 2.19).

So, for Christians, Christ takes the place of the Temple. Paul talks of Christians as constituting the temple of God where the spirit of Christ dwells in them (1 Cor 3.16). Again, he is calling attention to the significance of people who carry the witness of God by the Spirit in their life, rather than the witness of a geographical place. Furthermore, the city of Jerusalem was also destroyed in 70 CE by the Romans. Jesus himself predicted its destruction and wept over it because it did not know 'the things that make for peace' (Luke 19.42). The whole land of Palestine did not seem to be of great significance, because there is no more holiness in one area of the world than in another, but now there is the holiness and presence of Christ. So the New Testament message transcends the land, Jerusalem, and the Temple. The significance and holiness of place had been replaced by the significance and holiness of one person, Jesus Christ.

As one reflects further on this subject, it is important to emphasize two important points. First, the ministry of Jesus was very much preoccupied with the concept of the kingdom of God. In fact, the kingdom of God implies Jesus' radical understanding of God's relationship with the world. It is the true corrective for any misunderstanding of God's concern for one land. The kingdom of God stresses the reign of God in the hearts and minds of people, whoever and wherever they are. This is not dependent on one place or one region. It is dependent on faith. Where Christ is acknowledged as Lord, there God reigns. The concept of the kingdom of God, therefore, shatters any narrow concept of the land. I believe that Jesus' frequent use of the term, *kingdom of God*, was an intentional way to lift people's ideas and thoughts from a concentration on the land to the universality of God and of God's reign. This becomes an inclusive concept, and it fits the whole spirit and ethos of the New Testament.[6]

Second, the New Testament is concerned with the spreading of the gospel into the whole world. The narrow concept of the land has been replaced by a worldwide vision of God's concern for all people and in every country of the world. What started in the land in the birth, ministry, death, and resurrection of Christ must now be transported to every other place under the sun. The gospel must move from the vicinity of Jerusalem and reach the capital of the Roman Empire. The parameters have been expanded. The dimensions of the gospel have shattered the geographic focus on the land of Palestine. God's love for the world in Christ encompassed all people (see John 3.16, 1.12; Gal. 3.26–29; Eph. 3).

Later in the life of the Church the land started again assuming greater significance. The Church, after all, lives in the world. Geography is significant because of the incarnation. 'The Word became flesh and dwelt among us' (John 1.14). Christ was born in Bethlehem. He grew up in Nazareth. He was baptized in the Jordan River. He ministered to people around the Sea of Galilee. He suffered, died, and was resurrected in Jerusalem. The Church was born on Pentecost in Jerusalem. The land gradually started assuming greater significance for the Church, because the Church lives in history and because God in Christ had taken history very seriously. And Christians from early centuries made pilgrimage to the land, because the land hosted the Holy One. Recent studies have shown that this gradual shift in Christian attitudes to the land did not begin to take hold of Christians until after Constantine.[7]

What does all this have to do with the whole issue of the land today in the Israel-Palestine conflict?

1. Admittedly, Jews have come to understand their identity as being very much bound up with the land. Many of them today who

emphasize this link from a religious understanding see no room for the Palestinians in the land. It is important to confront such groups with the challenge of a deeper investigation and study of their own Bible to discover that their own tradition has provided answers to such a dilemma by accepting sharing the land, or even the option of living away from the land and still maintaining faithfulness to God. We must encourage the more open understanding of God and the land as it is found in the Bible, rather than the more narrow and limited view.

One gets the impression today that the state of Israel denies history. It pretends that there was no history in Palestine between 135 CE and 1948 CE. This is very clear when you visit the Israeli Museum. Every period of Israelite history is well covered except the period between 135 and 1948, as if nothing happened in between. In Ezekiel 47 we hear the prophet say to the people, 'Do not deny history. There are now other people who are living on the land, and they have a right to it.'

2. For Palestinian Christians the conflict over the land of Palestine is not a religiously motivated conflict. It is true that Palestinian Christians cherish and pride themselves on the fact that they live in the land where Jesus was born, died, and was resurrected. Such a historical fact has great significance for many of them. At the same time, this is not the reason which is paramount when they defend their right to the land. For most of them the land is their *watan*, their homeland. This is the land of their birth. It is the land which God, in his wisdom, has chosen to give them as *watan*; in the same way as God has chosen to give you your own *watan*. They are fighting to maintain the God-given right to their own land. Any *watan* is a responsibility given by God to all the people of that land and country. It is not that they own their country, for in the final analysis God is really the owner as God is the owner of the whole world. But because they have been given the land, they have a responsibility before God. They would like to live in dignity as human beings on their land and as good stewards of it.

3. It seems to me that many Israeli Jews must come to accept the fact that, in order to live their religious faith, they do not have to have an exclusive political control of the whole of Palestine. In one sense, even at the height of Solomon's reign, there were certain parts of Palestine not under Israelite control.[8] Palestinians would like to assure Jews that, just as it is important to have a continued physical

presence of Christian and Muslim communities in this land, it is equally important to have a continued presence of a Jewish community. But, in the same breath, we must emphasize that, in order to be living in the land and to fulfil our religious duties here, we do not need an exclusive political control over it all. The challenge before us is a challenge that would hammer out a new understanding of our relationship to the land. We can achieve a full expression of our religious life by sharing the land. Once this principle is affirmed, justice is not far off, and peace and reconciliation will become a welcomed reality.

NOTES

1 Much has been made of the words *for ever*, especially as pronounced by both fundamentalist Christians and Jews. But the Hebrew words *'ad 'olam* do not necessarily carry a literal meaning that deals with an unending duration of time. Sometimes it only applies to the length of a person's life (Deut. 15.17). The words reflect a Semitic Eastern expression that contemporary Middle Eastern people still use to reflect a lengthy period of time but not an indefinite period. This is surely the meaning of the words in 1 Samuel 1.22. See Dewey M. Beegle, *Prophecy and Prediction* (Ann Arbor, Pryor Pettengill, 1978), p. 183; see also William W. Baker, *Theft of a Nation* (West Monrow, La., Jireh Publications, 1982), pp. 84–86.

2 Naim S. Ateek, *Justice and Only Justice: A Palestinian Theology of Liberation* (Maryknoll, NY, Orbis Books, 1989).

3 This point is eloquently expressed in the story of Jonah and God's concern for the people of Ninevah, that is, the Assyrians, who were one of the deadliest enemies of ancient Israel and Judah.

4 See John Yoder, *The Politics of Jesus* (Grand Rapids, Eerdman's, 1972).

5 I am heavily indebted to the excellent work of W. D. Davies, *Gospel and Land* (Berkeley, University of California Press, 1974).

6 Even the words of Jesus, 'The kingdom of God is within you', reflect this same view. People carry within them the seed of the kingdom in their faithfulness and obedience to God. It is no more the land as locus but the people.

7 See P. W. L. Walker, *Holy City, Holy Places: Christian Attitudes to Jerusalem and the Holy Land in the Fourth Century* (Oxford, Clarendon Press, 1990).

8 Parts of the western coastal area were not part of Solomon's reign.

20

A Native American Perspective: Canaanites, Cowboys, and Indians

ROBERT ALLEN WARRIOR

Like the last essay, this exegetical discourse throws a different light on the Exodus story and points out its inappropriateness as a model for liberation for all contexts and all people. Here is an attempt by a member of the Osage Nation of American Indians, who reads the Exodus from the perspective of the Canaanites and discerns parallels between the humiliated people of biblical times and his own people in the history of America, and draws out implications for hermeneutical reflection and political action.

This essay appeared in *Christianity and Crisis* 49 (12, 1989). *Christianity and Crisis* is an American journal of Christian opinion. The address is: 537 W. 121 St. New York 10027.

Robert Allen Warrior is a New York correspondent for the *Lakota Times*, published in Rapid City.

Native American theology of liberation has a nice ring to it. Politically active Christians in the US have been bandying about the idea of such a theology for several years now, encouraging Indians to develop it. There are theologies of liberation for African Americans, Hispanic Americans, women, Asian Americans, even Jews. Why not Native Americans? Christians recognize that American injustice on this continent began nearly five hundred years ago with the oppression of its indigenous people and that justice for American Indians is a fundamental part of broader social struggle. The churches' complicity in much of the violence perpetrated on Indians makes this realization even clearer. So, there are a lot of well-intentioned Christians looking for some way to include Native Americans in their political action.

For Native Americans involved in political struggle, the participation of church people is often an attractive proposition. Churches have financial, political, and institutional resources that many Indian activists would dearly love to have at their disposal. Since American

Indians have a relatively small population base and few financial resources, assistance from churches can be of great help in gaining the attention of the public, the media, and the government.

It sounds like the perfect marriage – Christians with the desire to include Native Americans in their struggle for justice and Indian activists in need of resources and support from non-Indians. Well, speaking as the product of a marriage between an Indian and a white, I can tell you that it is not as easy as it sounds. The inclusion of Native Americans in Christian political praxis is difficult – even dangerous. Christians have a different way of going about the struggle for justice than most Native Americans: different models of leadership, different ways of making decisions, different ways of viewing the relationship between politics and religion. These differences have gone all but unnoticed in the history of church involvement in American Indian affairs. Liberals and conservatives alike have too often surveyed the conditions of Native Americans and decided to come to the rescue, always using *their* methods, *their* ideas, and *their* programs. The idea that Indians might know best how to address their own problems is seemingly lost on these well-meaning folks.

Still, the time does seem ripe to find a new way for Indians and Christians (and Native American Christians) to be partners in the struggle against injustice and economic and racial oppression. This is a new era for both the Church and for Native Americans. Christians are breaking away from their liberal moorings and looking for more effective means of social and political engagement. Indians, in this era of 'self-determination', have verified for themselves and the government that they are the people best able to address Indian problems as long as they are given the necessary resources and if they can hold the US government accountable to the policy. But an enormous stumbling block immediately presents itself. Most of the liberation theologies that have emerged in the last twenty years are preoccupied with the Exodus story, using it as the fundamental model for liberation. I believe that the story of the Exodus is an inappropriate way for Native Americans to think about liberation.

No doubt, the story is one that has inspired many people in many contexts to struggle against injustice. Israel, in the Exile, then Diaspora, would remember the story and be reminded of God's faithfulness. Enslaved African Americans, given Bibles to read by their masters and mistresses, would begin at the beginning of the book and find in the pages of the Pentateuch a god who was obviously on their side, even if that god was the god of their oppressors. People in Latin American base communities read the story and have been inspired to struggle against injustice. The Exodus, with its picture of a god who takes the side of the oppressed and powerless, has been a beacon of hope for many in despair.

GOD THE CONQUEROR

Yet, the liberationist picture of Yahweh is not complete. A delivered people is not a free people, nor is it a nation. People who have survived the nightmare of subjugation dream of escape. Once the victims have been delivered, they seek a new dream, a new goal, usually a place of safety away from the oppressors, a place that can be defended against future subjugation. Israel's new dream became the land of Canaan. And Yahweh was still with them: Yahweh promised to go before the people and give them Canaan, with its flowing milk and honey. The land, Yahweh decided, belonged to these former slaves from Egypt and Yahweh planned on giving it to them – using the same power used against the enslaving Egyptians to defeat the indigenous inhabitants of Canaan. Yahweh the deliverer became Yahweh the conqueror.

The obvious characters in the story for Native Americans to ident-ify with are the Canaanites, the people who already lived in the promised land. As a member of the Osage Nation of American Indians who stands in solidarity with other tribal people around the world, I read the Exodus stories with Canaanite eyes. And, it is the Canaanite side of the story that has been overlooked by those seeking to articulate theologies of liberation. Especially ignored are those parts of the story that describe Yahweh's command to mercilessly annihilate the indigenous population.

To be sure, most scholars, of a variety of political and theological stripes, agree that the actual events of Israel's early history are much different than what was commanded in the narrative. The Canaanites were not systematically annihilated, nor were they completely driven from the land. In fact, they made up, to a large extent, the people of the new nation of Israel. Perhaps it was a process of gradual immigration of people from many places and religions who came together to form a new nation. Or maybe, as Norman Gottwald and others have argued, the peasants of Canaan revolted against their feudal masters, a revolt instigated and aided by a vanguard of escaped slaves from Egypt who believed in the liberating god, Yahweh. Whatever happened, scholars agree that the people of Canaan had a lot to do with it.

Nonetheless, scholarly agreement should not allow us to breathe a sigh of relief. For historical knowledge does not change the status of the indigenes in the *narrative* and the theology that grows out of it. The research of Old Testament scholars, however much it provides an answer to the historical question – the contribution of the indigenous people of Canaan to the formation and emergence of Israel as a nation – does not resolve the narrative problem. People who read the narratives read them as they are, not as scholars and experts would *like* them to be read and interpreted. History is no longer with us. The narrative remains.

Though the Exodus and Conquest stories are familiar to most readers, I want to highlight some sections that are commonly ignored. The covenant begins when Yahweh comes to Abram saying, 'Know of a surety that your descendants will be sojourners in a land that is not theirs, and they will be slaves there, and they will be oppressed for four hundred years; but I will bring judgment on the nation they serve and they shall come out' (Gen. 15.13,14). Then, Yahweh adds: 'To your descendants I give this land, the land of the Kenites, the Kenizzites, the Kadmonites, the Hittites, the Perizzites, the Rephaim, the Amorites, the Canaanites, and the Jebusites' (15.18–21). The next important moment is the commissioning of Moses. Yahweh says to him, 'I promise I will bring you out of the affliction of Egypt, to the land of the Canaanites, the Hittites, the Amorites, the Perizzites, the Hivites, and the Jebusites, a land flowing with milk and honey' (Exod. 3.17). The covenant, in other words, has two parts: deliverance and conquest.

After the people have escaped and are headed to the promised land, the covenant is made more complicated, but it still has two parts. If the delivered people remain faithful to Yahweh, they will be blessed in the land Yahweh will conquer for them (Exod. 20–23 and Deut. 7–9). The god who delivered Israel from slavery will lead the people into the land and keep them there as long as they live up to the terms of the covenant: 'You shall not wrong a stranger or oppress him [*sic*], for you were strangers in the land of Egypt. You shall not afflict any widow or orphan. If you do afflict them, and they cry out to me, I will surely hear their cry; and my wrath will burn, and I will kill you with the sword, and your wives shall become widows and your children fatherless' (Exod. 22.21).

WHOSE NARRATIVE?

Israel's reward for keeping Yahweh's commandments – for building a society where the evils done to them have no place – is the continuation of life in the land. But one of the most important of Yahweh's commands is the prohibition on social relations with Canaanites or participation in their religion. 'I will deliver the inhabitants of the land into your hand, and you shall drive them out before you. You shall make no covenant with them or with their gods. They shall not dwell in your land, lest they make you sin against me; for if you serve their gods it will surely be a snare to you' (Exod. 23.31b–33).

In fact, the indigenes are to be destroyed:

> When the Lord your God brings you into the land which you are entering to take possession of it, and clears away many nations before you, the Hittites, the Girgashites, the Amorites, the Canaanites, the Perizzites, the Hivites, and the Jebusites, seven nations greater and mightier than yourselves, and when the Lord your God gives them over to you and you defeat them; then you must utterly destroy them; you shall make no covenant with them, and show no mercy to them (Deut. 7.1,2).

These words are spoken to the people of Israel as they are preparing to go into Canaan. The promises made to Abraham and Moses are ready to be fulfilled. All that remains is for the people to enter into the land and dispossess those who already live there.

Joshua gives an account of the conquest. After ten chapters of stories about Israel's successes and failures to obey Yahweh's commands, the writer states, 'So Joshua defeated the whole land, the hill country and the Negeb and the lowland and the slopes, and all their kings, he left none remaining, but utterly destroyed all that breathed, as the Lord God of Israel commanded.' In Judges, the writer disagrees with this account of what happened, but the Canaanites are held in no higher esteem. The angel of the Lord says, 'I will not drive out [the indigenous people] before you; but they shall become adversaries to you, and their gods shall be a snare to you.'

Thus, the narrative tells us that the Canaanites have status only as the people Yahweh removes from the land in order to bring the chosen people in. They are not to be trusted, nor are they to be allowed to enter into social relationships with the people of Israel. They are wicked, and their religion is to be avoided at all costs. The laws put forth regarding strangers and sojourners may have stopped the people of Yahweh from wanton oppression, but presumably only after the land was safely in the hands of Israel. The covenant of Yahweh depends on this.

The Exodus narrative is where discussion about Christian involvement in Native American activism must begin. It is these stories of deliverance and conquest that are ready to be picked up and believed by anyone wondering what to do about the people who already live in their promised land. They provide an example of what can happen when powerless people come to power. Historical scholarship may tell a different story; but even if the annihilation did not take place, the narratives tell what happened to those indigenous people who put their hope and faith in ideas and gods that were foreign to their culture. The Canaanites trusted in the god of outsiders and their story of oppression and exploitation was lost. Interreligious praxis became betrayal and the surviving narrative tells us nothing about it.

Confronting the conquest stories as a narrative rather than a historical problem is especially important given the tenor of contemporary theology and criticism. After two hundred years of preoccupation with historical questions, scholars and theologians across a broad spectrum of political and ideological positions have recognized the function of narrative in the development of religious communities. Along with the work of US scholars like Brevard Childs, Stanley Hauerwas, and George Lindbeck, the radical liberation theologies of Latin America are based on empowering believing communities to read scriptural narratives for themselves and make their reading central to theology and political action. The danger is that these communities will read the narratives, not the history behind them.

And, of course, the text itself will never be altered by interpretations of it, though its reception may be. It is part of the canon for both Jews and Christians. It is part of the heritage and thus the consciousness of people in the United States. Whatever dangers we identify in the text, the god represented there will remain as long as the text remains. These dangers only grow as the emphasis upon catechetical (Lindbeck), narrative (Hauerwas), canonical (Childs), and Bible-centered Christian base communities (Gutierrez) grows. The peasants of Solentiname bring a wisdom and experience previously unknown to Christian theology, but I do not see what mechanism guarantees that they – or any other people who seek to be shaped and moulded by reading the text – will differentiate between the liberating god and the god of conquest.

IS THERE A SPIRIT?

What is to be done? First, the Canaanites should be at the center of Christian theological reflection and political action. They are the last remaining ignored voice in the text, except perhaps for the land itself. The Conquest stories, with all their violence and injustice, must be taken seriously by those who believe in the god of the Old Testament. Commentaries and critical works rarely mention these texts. When they do, they express little concern for the status of the indigenes and their rights as human beings and as nations. The same blindness is evident in theologies that use the Exodus motif as their basis for political action. The leading into the land becomes just one more redemptive moment rather than a violation of innocent peoples' rights to land and self-determination.

Keeping the Canaanites at the center makes it more likely that those who read the Bible will read *all* of it, not just the part that inspires and justifies them. And should anyone be surprised by the brutality, the terror of these texts? It was, after all, a Jewish victim of the Holocaust, Walter Benjamin, who said, 'There is no document of civilization which is not at the same time a document of barbarism.' People whose theology involves the Bible need to take this insight seriously. It is those who know these texts who must speak the truth about what they contain. It is to those who believe in these texts that the barbarism belongs. It is those who act on the basis of these texts who must take responsibility for the terror and violence they can and have engendered.

Second, we need to be more aware of the way ideas such as those in the Conquest narratives have made their way into Americans' consciousness and ideology. And only when we understand this process can those of us who have suffered from it know how to fight back. Many Puritan preachers were fond of referring to Native Americans as Amelkites and Canaanites – in other words, people who, if they would not be converted, were worthy of annihilation. By examining such instances in theological and political writings, in sermons, and elsewhere, we can understand how America's self-image as a 'chosen people' has provided a rhetoric to mystify domination.

Finally, we need to decide if we want to accept the model of leadership and social change presented by the entire Exodus story. Is it appropriate to the needs of indigenous people seeking justice and deliverance? If indeed the Canaanites were integral to Israel's early history, the Exodus narratives reflect a situation in which indigenous people put their hope in a god from outside, were liberated from their oppressors, and then saw their story of oppression revised out of the new nation's history of salvation. They were assimilated into another people's identity and the history of their ancestors came to be regarded as suspect and a danger to the safety of Israel. In short, they were betrayed.

Do Native Americans and other indigenous people dare trust the same god in their struggle for justice? I am not asking an easy question and I in no way mean that people who are both Native Americans and Christians cannot work toward justice in the context of their faith in Jesus Christ. Such people have a lot of theological reflection to do, however, to avoid the dangers I have pointed to in the Conquest narratives. Christians, whether Native American or not, if they are to be involved, must learn how to participate in the struggle without making their story the whole story. Otherwise the sins of the past will be visited upon us again.

No matter what we do, the Conquest narratives will remain. As long as people believe in the Yahweh of deliverance, the world will not be safe from Yahweh the conqueror. But perhaps, if they are true to their struggle, people will be able to achieve what Yahweh's chosen people in the past have not: a society of people delivered from oppression who are not so afraid of becoming victims again that they become oppressors themselves, a society where the original inhabitants can become something other than subjects to be converted to a better way of life or adversaries who provide cannon fodder for a nation's militaristic pride.

With what voice will we, the Canaanites of the world, say, 'Let my people go and leave my people alone?' And, with what ears will followers of alien gods who have wooed us (Christians, Jews, Marxists, capitalists), listen to us? The indigenous people of this hemisphere have endured a subjugation now a hundred years longer than the sojourn of Israel in Egypt. Is there a god, a spirit, who will hear us and stand with us in the Amazon, Osage County, and Wounded

Knee? Is there a god, a spirit, able to move among the pain and anger of the Nablus, Gaza, and Soweto of 1989? Perhaps. But we, the wretched of the earth, may be well advised this time not to listen to outsiders with their promises of liberation and deliverance. We will perhaps do better to look elsewhere for our vision of justice, peace, and political sanity – a vision through which we escape not only our oppressors, but our oppression as well. Maybe, for once, we will just have to listen to ourselves, leaving the gods of this continent's real strangers to do battle among themselves.

PART FOUR

The Text and The Texts: Multi-faith Readings

We explain the fact that the Milky Way is there by the doctrine of creation, but how do we explain the fact that the Bhagavad Gita is there?

Wilfred Cantwell Smith

21

Discovering the Bible in the Non-biblical World

KWOK PUI LAN

For many centuries the Christian Scripture has been taken as the norm to judge other, non-biblical cultures. Seldom do biblical scholars and others feel the need to rediscover the Bible through the issues raised by people whose lives are not shaped by the biblical vision. Kwok Pui Lan, a Chinese biblical scholar, questions the rigidity of the biblical canon and its universal truth-claims, and offers a proposal for interpreting the Christian Scripture in a religiously plural world and from a woman's perspective.

Kwok Pui Lan is one of the prominent Asian theologians and has written numerous articles in various journals. This article is reprinted from *Semeia* 47 (1989).

Kwok Pui Lan is a member of the faculty at Chung Chi College, Chinese University of Hong Kong, Hong Kong.

'To the African, God speaks as if He [sic] were an African; to the Chinese, God speaks as if He [sic] were a Chinese. To all men and women, the Word goes out over against their particular existing environment and their several cultural settings.' Thus spoke T. C. Chao, a Protestant theologian from China.[1] The central *Problematik* of biblical hermeneutics for Christians living in the 'non-Christian' world is how to hear God speaking in a different voice – one other than Hebrew, Greek, German or English.

Christianity has been brought into interaction with Chinese culture for many centuries, but the Christian population in China never exceeded 1 percent. Since the nineteenth century, the Christian missionary enterprise has often been criticized as being intricately linked to western domination and cultural imperialism. Chinese Christians have been struggling with the question of how to interpret the biblical message to our fellow Chinese, the majority of whom do not share our belief.

In fact, this should not only be a serious concern to the Chinese, but a challenge to all Christians with a global awareness, and to biblical scholars in particular. For two-thirds of our world is made up of non-Christians and most of these people are under the yoke of exploitation by the privileged one-third of our world. The interpretation of the Bible is not just a religious matter within the Christian community, but a matter with significant political implications for other peoples as well. The Bible can be used as an instrument of domination, but it can also be interpreted to work for our liberation.

This paper attempts to discuss some of the crucial issues raised by the interaction of the Bible with the non-biblical world. My observation will be chiefly based on the Chinese situation, with which I am most familiar, drawing also upon insights from other Asian theologians. I shall first discuss biblical interpretation in the context of the political economy of truth. The second part will focus on biblical interpretation as dialogical imagination based on contemporary reappropriation of the Bible by Asian Christians. Finally, I shall offer my own understanding of the Bible from a Chinese woman's perspective.

BIBLICAL INTERPRETATION AND
THE POLITICS OF TRUTH

Biblical interpretation is never simply a religious matter, for the processes of formation, canonization and transmission of the Bible have been imbued with the issues of authority and power. The French philosopher Michel Foucault helps us to see the complex relationship of truth to power by studying the power mechanisms which govern the production and the repression of truth. He calls this the 'political economy' of truth:

> Each society has its regime of truth, its 'general politics' of truth: that is, the types of discourse which it accepts and makes function as true; the mechanisms and instances which enable one to distinguish true and false statements, the means by which each is sanctioned; the techniques and procedures accorded value in the acquisition of truth; the status of those who are charged with saying what counts as true.[2]

Foucault's analysis leads me to examine the power dynamics underlying such questions as: What is truth? Who owns it? Who has the authority to interpret it? This is particularly illuminating when we try to investigate how the Bible is used in a cross-cultural setting.

Who owns the truth? In the heyday of the missionary movement of the late nineteenth century, John R. Mott, the chief engineer of what was called the campaign of the 'evangelization of the world in this generation', cried out:

> The need of the non-Christian world is indescribably great. Hundreds of millions are today living in ignorance and darkness, steeped in idolatry, superstition, degradation and corruption. . . The Scriptures clearly teach that if men are to be saved they must be saved through Christ. He alone can deliver them from the power of sin and its penalty. His death made salvation possible. The Word of God sets forth the conditions of salvation.[3]

Mott and others saw the Bible as the revealed Word of God which had to be made known to all 'heathens' who were living in idolatry and superstition. The Bible was to be the 'signifier' of a basic deficiency in the 'heathen' culture. This is a western construction superimposed on other cultures, to show that western culture is the norm and it is superior. It might be compared to the function of the 'phallus' as a signifier of the fundamental lack of female superimposed on women by men in the male psychological discourse.[4] It is not mere coincidence that missionary literatures describe Christian mission as 'aggressive work' and western expansion as 'intrusion' and 'penetration'.

The introduction of the Bible into Asia has been marked by difficulty and resistance mainly because Asian countries have their own religious and cultural systems. The issue of communicating the 'Christian message in a non-Christian world' was the primary concern of the World Missionary Conference in 1938. Hendrik Kraemer, the key figure in the Conference, acknowledged that non-Christian religions are more than a set of speculative ideas, but are 'all-inclusive systems and theories of life, rooted in a religious basis, and therefore at the same time embrace a system of culture and civilizaton and a definite structure of society and state.'[5] But his biblical realism, influenced much by Karl Barth's theology, maintains that the Christian Gospel is the special revelation of God, which implies a discontinuity with all cultures and judges all religions.

This narrow interpretation of truth has disturbed many Christians coming from other cultural contexts. T. C. Chao, for example, presented a paper on 'Revelation' which stated: 'There has been no time, in other words, when God has not been breaking into our human world; nor is there a place where men have been that He [*sic*] has not entered and ruled.'[6] Citing the long line of sages, moral teachers of China such as Confucius, Mencius and Moti, he questioned, 'Who can say that these sages have not been truly inspired by the spirit of our God, the God of our Lord Jesus Christ? Who can judge that the Almighty has not appeared to them in His [*sic*] Holy, loving essence and that they have not been among the pure heart of whom Jesus speaks?'[7]

In this battle for truth, many Chinese Christians reject the assumption that the Bible contains all the truth and that the biblical canon is rigidly closed. Po Ch'en Kuang argued in 1927 that many Chinese classics, such as Analects, Mencius, the Book of Songs and Rites are comparable to the prophets, the Psalms, and the Book of Deuteronomy of the Old Testament.[8] Since the Bible contains the important classics of the Jewish people which preceded Jesus, he could see no reason why the Chinese would not include their own. Others such as Hsieh Fu Ya[9] and Hu Tsan Yun[10] argue that the Chinese Bible should consist of parts of the Hebrew Bible, the Christian Bible, Confucian classics, and even Taoist and Buddhist texts! For a long time, Chinese Christians have been saying that western people do not own the truth simply because they bring the Bible to us, for truth is found in other cultures and religions as well.

Who interprets the truth? Another important issue in the political economy of truth concerns who has the power to interpret it. In the great century of missionary expansion, many missionaries acted as though they alone knew what the Bible meant, believing they were closer to truth. The Gospel message was invariably interpreted as being the personal salvation of the soul from human sinfulness. This interpretation reflects an understanding of human nature and destiny steeped in western dualistic thinking. Other cultures, having a different linguistic system and thought form, may not share similar concerns. As Y. T. Wu, a Chinese theologian, notes, 'Such terms as original sin, atonement, salvation, the Trinity, the Godhead, the incarnation, may have rich meanings for those who understand their origins and implications, but they are just so much superstition and speculation for the average Chinese.'[11]

More importantly, this simplistic version of the Gospel functions to alienate the Christians in the Third World from the struggle against material poverty and other oppressions in their society. But in the name of a 'universal gospel', this thin-sliced biblical understanding was pre-packaged and shipped all over the world. The basic problem of the so-called 'universal Gospel' is that it not only claims to provide the answer but defines the question too! The American historian William R. Hutchison rightly observes that: American missionary ideologies at the turn of the century shared the belief that 'Christianity as it existed in the West had a "right" not only to conquer the world, but to define reality for the peoples of the world.'[12] If other people can only define truth according to the western perspective, then Christianization really means westernization! Chinese Christians began a conscious effort to redefine what the Gospel meant for them in the 1920s, as a response to the anti-Christian movement which criticized Christianity as 'the running dog of imperialism.' Chinese Christians became collectively aware that they had to be accountable to their fellow Chinese in their biblical interpretations, not just to the tiny Christian minority. They tried to show that biblical concepts such as 'agape' were compatible to 'benevolence' in Chinese classics and that the moral teachings of Jesus were comparable to the teachings of the Confucian tradition. As foreign invasion became imminent, the central concern of all Chinese was national salvation and the gospel message, too, became politicized.[13] Y. T. Wu, for example, reinterpreted Jesus as 'a revolutionary, the upholder of justice and the challenger of the rights of the oppressed'[14] in the mid-1930s, anticipating the kind of liberation theology that developed decades later. These attempts of indigenization clearly show that biblical truth cannot be pre-packaged, but that it must be found in the actual interaction between text and context in the concrete historical situation.

What constitutes truth? The last point I want to consider briefly concerns the norm by which we judge something as truth. Here again, Chinese philosophical tradition is very different from the west in that it is not primarily interested in metaphysical and epistemological questions. On the contrary, it is more concerned with the moral and ethical visions of a good society. The Neo-Confucian tradition in particular has emphasized the integral relationship between knowing and doing. Truth is not merely something to be grasped cognitively, but to be practised and acted out in the self-cultivation of moral beings.

For most Chinese, the truth claim of the Bible cannot be based on its being the supposed revealed Word of God, for 99 percent of the people do not believe in this faith statement. They can only judge the meaningfulness of the biblical tradition by looking at how it is acted out in the Christian community. Some of the burning questions of Chinese students at the time of foreign encroachment were: 'Can Christianity save China?', 'Why does not God restrain the stronger nations from oppressing the weaker ones?', 'Why are the Christian nations of the west so aggressive and cruel?'[15] These probing questions can be compared to what Katie G. Cannon, an Afro-American ethicist, has also asked: 'Where was the Church and the Christian believers when Black women and Black men, Black boys and Black girls, were being raped, sexually abused, lynched, assassinated, castrated and physically oppressed? What kind of Christianity allowed white Christians to deny basic human rights and simple dignity to Blacks, these same rights which had been given to others without question?'

The politics of truth is not fought on the epistemological level. People in the Third World are not interested in whether or not the Bible contains some metaphysical or revelational truth. The authority of the Bible can no more hide behind the unchallenged belief that it is the Word of God, nor by an appeal to a church tradition which has been defined by white, male, clerical power. The poor, women, and other marginalized people are asking whether the Bible can be of help in the global struggle for liberation.

BIBLICAL INTERPRETATION AS DIALOGICAL IMAGINATION

To interpret the Bible for a world historically not shaped by the biblical vision, there is need to conjure up a new image for the process of biblical interpretation itself. I have coined the term 'dialogical imagination' based on my observation of what Asian theologians are doing. I will explain what this term means and illustrate it with some examples of the contemporary use of the Bible in Asia.

Dialogue in Chinese means talking with each other. It implies mutuality, active listening, and openness to what the other has to say. Asian Christians are heirs to both the biblical story and to our own story as Asian people, and we are concerned to bring the two in dialogue with one another. Kosuke Koyama, a Japanese theologian, has tried to explain this metaphorically in the title of his book, *Mount Fuji and Mount Sinai*. He affirms the need to do theology in the context of a dialogue between Mount Fuji and Mount Sinai, between Asian spirituality and biblical spirituality.[16] Biblical interpretation in Asia, too, must create a two-way traffic between our own tradition and that of the Bible.

There is, however, another level of dialogue we are engaged in because of our multi-religious cultural setting. Our fellow Asians who have other faiths must not be considered our missiological objects, but as dialogical partners in our ongoing search for truth. This can only be done when each one of us takes seriously the Asian reality, the suffering and aspirations of the Asian people, so that we can share our religious insights to build a better society.

Biblical interpretation in Asia must involve a powerful act of imagination. Sharon Parks[17] shows that the process of imagination involves the following stages: a consciousness of conflict (something as not fitting), a pause, the finding of a new image, the repatterning of reality, and interpretation. Asian Christians have recognized the dissonance between the kind of biblical interpretation we inherited and the Asian reality we are facing. We have to find new images for our reality and to make new connections between the Bible and our lives.

The act of imagination involves a dialectical process. On the one hand, we have to imagine how the biblical tradition which was formulated in another time and culture can address our burning questions today. On the other hand, based on our present circumstances, we have to re-imagine what the biblical world was like, thus opening up new horizons hitherto hidden from us. Especially since the Bible was written from an androcentric perspective, we women have to imagine ourselves as if we were the audience of the biblical message at that time. As Susan Brooks Thistlethwaite suggested, we have to critically judge both the text and the experience underlying it.[18]

I have coined the term 'dialogical imagination' to describe the process of creative hermeneutics in Asia. It attempts to capture the complexities, the multi-dimensional linkages, the different levels of meaning in our present task of relating the Bible to Asia. It is dialogical, for it involves a constant conversation between different religious and cultural traditions. It is highly imaginative, for it looks at both the Bible and our Asian reality anew, challenging the established 'order of things'. The German word for imagination is *Einbildungskraft*, which means the power of shaping into one.[19] Dialogical imagination attempts to bridge the gap of time and space, to create new horizons, and to connect the disparate elements of our lives in a meaningful whole.

I shall illustrate the meaning of dialogical imagination by discussing how Asian theologians have combined the insights of biblical themes with Asian resources. We can discern two trends in this process today. The first is the use of Asian myths, legends and stories in biblical reflection. The second is the use of the social biography of the people as a hermeneutical key to understand both our reality and the message of the Bible.

For some years now, C. S. Song, a theologian from Taiwan, has urged his Asian colleagues to stretch their theological minds and to use Asian resources to understand the depths of Asian humanity and God's action in the world. He says: 'Resources in Asia for doing theology are unlimited. What is limited is our theological imagination. Powerful is the voice crying out of the abyss of the Asian heart, but powerless is the power of our theological imaging.'[20] To be able to touch the Hindu heart, Buddhist heart, the Confucian heart, we have to strengthen the power of theological imaging.

C. S. Song demonstrates what this means in his book, *The Tears of Lady Meng*,[21] which was originally delivered in an assembly of the Christian Conference of Asia. Song uses a well-known legend from China, the story of Lady Meng, weaving it together with the biblical themes of Jesus' death and resurrection. In one of his recent books, *Tell Us Our Names*, Song shows how fairy-tales, folk stories and legends, shared from generation to generation among the common people, have the power to illuminate many biblical stories and other theological motifs. Song reminds us that Jesus was a master storyteller who transformed common stories into parables concerning God's Kingdom and human life.[22]

The use of Asian resources has stimulated many exciting and creative ways of re-reading the scriptures. A biblical scholar from Thailand, Maen Pongudom, uses the creation folk-tales of the Northern Thai to contrast with the creation story in Genesis, arguing that people of other faiths and traditions share certain essential ideas of creation found in the biblical story.[23] Archie Lee, an Old Testament scholar from Hong Kong, uses the role of the remonstrator in the Chinese tradition to interpret the parable of Nathan in the context of political theology in Hong Kong. His creative re-reading of the stories from two traditions shows that 'story has the unlimited power to capture our imagination and invite the readers to exert their own feeling and intention.'[24]

Asian women theologians are discovering the liberating elements of the Asian traditions as powerful resources to re-image the biblical story. Padma Gallup reinterprets the image of God in Genesis 1.27– 8 in terms of the popular Arthanareesvara image in the Hindu tradition which is an expression of male/female deity. She argues that 'if the Godhead created humans in its image, then the Godhead must be a male/female, side-by-side, non-dualistic whole.'[25] I myself have used Asian poems, a lullaby, and a letter of women prisoners to interpret the meaning of suffering and hope.[26] I have also used the story of the boat people in Southeast Asia to re-appropriate the theme of the diaspora.[27]

In her observations concerning the growing use of Asian resources in theologizing, Nantawan Boonprasat Lewis, a Thai woman theologian, makes the following perceptive remarks:

> The use of one's cultural and religious tradition indicates the respect and pride of one's heritage which is the root of one's being to be authentic enough to draw as a source for theologizing. On the other hand, it demonstrates a determination of hope for possibilities beyond one's faith tradition, possibilities which can overcome barriers of human expression, including language, vision, and imagination.[28]

The dialogical imagination operates not only in using the cultural and religious traditions of Asia, but also in the radical appropriation of our own history. We begin to view the history of our people with utmost seriousness in order to discern the signs of the time and of God's redeeming action in that history. We have tried to define the historical reality in our own terms and we find it filled with theological insights.

In Korean *minjung* theology, Korean history is reinterpreted from the *minjung* perspective. *Minjung* is a Korean word which means the mass of people, or the mass who were subjugated or being ruled. *Minjung* is a very dynamic concept: it can refer to women who are politically dominated by men, or to an ethnic group ruled by another group, or to a race when it is ruled by another powerful race.[29] The history of the *minjung* was often neglected in traditional historical writing. They were treated as either docile or as mere spectators of the rise and fall of kingdoms and dynasties. *Minjung* theology, however, reclaims *minjung* as protagonists in the historical drama, for they are the subject of history.

Korean theologians stress the need for understanding the corporate spirit – the consciousness and the aspirations of the *minjung* – through their social biography. According to Kim Yong Bock: 'The social biography is not merely social or cultural history: it is political in the sense that it is comprehensively related to the reality of power and to the "polis", namely the community. . . . Social biography functions to integrate and interrelate the dimensions and components of the people's social and cultural experiences, especially in terms of the dramatic scenario of the people as the historical protagonists.'[30]

The social biography of the *minjung* has helped Korean Christians to discover the meaning of the Bible in a new way. Cyris H. S. Moon reinterprets the Hebrew Bible story through the social biography of the *minjung* in Korea. He demonstrates how the story of the Korean people, for example, the constant threat of big surrounding nations, and the loss of national identity under Japanese colonialization, can help to amplify our understanding of the Old Testament. On the other hand, he also shows how the social biography of the Hebrew people has illuminated the meaning of the Korean *minjung* story. Through powerful theological imagination, Moon has brought the two social biographies into dialogue with one another.[31]

The hermeneutical framework of the *minjung*'s social biography also helps us to see in a new way the relationship between Jesus and the *minjung*. According to Ahn Byung Mu, the *minjung* are the *ochlos* rather than the *laos*. In Jesus' time, they were the ones who gathered around Jesus – the so-called sinners and outcasts of society. They might not have been the direct followers of Jesus and were differentiated from the disciples. They were the people who were opposed to the rulers in Jerusalem.[32] Concerning the question of how Jesus is related to these *minjung*, theologian Suk Nam Dong says, in a radical voice, '[T]he subject matter of *minjung* theology is not Jesus but *minjung*. Jesus is the means for understanding the *minjung* correctly, rather than the concept of '*minjung*' being the instrument for understanding Jesus.'[33] For him, 'Jesus was truly *a part of* the *minjung*, not just *for* the *minjung*. Therefore, Jesus was the personification of the *minjung* and their symbol.'[34]

Social biography can also be used to characterize the hopes and aspirations of the women, as Lee Sung Hee has demonstrated.[35] The question of whether Jesus can be taken as a symbol for the women among the *minjung* has yet to be fully clarified. Social biography is a promising hermeneutical tool because it reads history from the underside, and therefore invites us to read the Bible from the underside as well. Korean *minjung* theology represents one imaginative attempt to bring the social biography of *minjung* in Korea into dialogue with the *minjung* of Israel and the *minjung* in the world of Jesus. It shows how dialogical imagination operates in the attempt to reclaim the *minjung* as the center of both our Asian reality and the biblical drama.

LIBERATING THE BIBLE: MANY VOICES AND MANY TRUTHS

After this brief survey of the history of the politics of truth in the Chinese Christian community and a discussion of dialogical imagination as a new image for biblical reflection, I would like to briefly discuss my own understanding of the Bible. I shall focus on three issues: (1) the sacrality of the text, (2) the issue of canon and (3) the norm of interpretation.

Sacrality of the text. The authority of the Bible derives from the claim that it is the Scripture, a written text of the Word of God. However, it must be recognized that the notion of 'scripture' is culturally conditioned and cannot be found in some other religious and cultural traditions, such as Hinduism and Confucianism. This may partly account for the relative fluidity of these traditions, which can often assimilate other visions and traditions. These traditions also do not have a crusading spirit to convert the whole world.

Why has the Bible, seen as sacred text, shaped western consciousness for so long? Jacques Derrida's deconstruction theory, particularly his criticism of the 'transcendent presence' in the text and the logocentrism of the whole western metaphysical tradition offers important insights. In an earlier volume of *Semeia* which focuses on 'Derrida and Biblical Studies', the editor Robert Detweiler summarizes Derrida's challenge to biblical scholarship:

> The main characteristic of sacred texts has been their evocation and recollection of sacred presence – to the extent that the texts themselves, the very figures of writing, are said to be imbued with that divine immanence. But Derrida argues that such a notion of presence in writing is based on the false assumption of a prior and more unmediated presence in the spoken word; this spoken word in the religious context is taken to be none other than the utterance of deity, which utterance is then reduced

to holy inscription in and as the text. For Derrida, however, written language is not derivative in this sense; it does not find its legitimacy as a sign of a 'greater' presence, and the sacred text is not rendered sacred as an embodiment of an absolute presence but rather as the interplay of language signs to designate 'sacred'.[36]

The notion of the 'presence' of God speaking through the text drives us to discover what the 'one voice' is, and logocentrism leads us to posit some ultimate truth or absolute meaning which is the foundation of all other meanings. But once we recognize the Bible is one system of language to designate the 'sacred', we should be able to see that the whole biblical text represents one form of human construction to talk about God. Other systems of language, for example, the hieroglyphic Chinese which is so different from the Indo-European languages, might have a radically different way to present the 'sacred'. Moreover, once we liberate ourselves from viewing the biblical text as sacred, we can then feel free to test and reappropriate it in other contexts. We will see more clearly the meaning of the text is very closely related to the context and we will expect a multiplicity of interpretations of the Bible; as Jonathan Culler says, 'meaning is context-bound but context is boundless.'[37]

The issue of canon. Canonization is the historical process which designates some texts as sacred and thus authoritative or binding for the religious community. This whole process must be analyzed in the contest of religio-political struggles for power. For example, scholars have pointed out that the formation of the canon of the Hebrew Bible was imbued with the power-play between the prophets and priests. The New Testament canon was formed in the struggle for 'orthodoxy' against such heresies as Marcionism and Gnosticism. Recently, feminist scholarship has also shown how the Biblical canon has excluded Goddess worship in the Ancient Near East and that the New Testament canon was slowly taking shape in the process of the growing patriarchalization of the early church.

The formation of the canon is clearly a matter of power. As Robert Detweiler so aptly puts it: 'A Text becomes sacred when a segment of the community is able to establish it as such in order to gain control and set order over the whole community.'[38] This was true both inside the religious group as well as outside of it. Inside the religious community, women, the marginalized and the poor (in other words, the *minjung*), did not have the power to decide what would be the truth for them. Later, when Christianity was brought to other cultures, the biblical canon was considered to be closed, excluding all other cultural manifestations.

As a woman from a non-biblical culture, I have found the notion of canon doubly problematic. As my fellow Chinese theologians have long argued, Chinese Christians cannot simply accept a canon which relegates their great cultural teachings and traditions to the secondary. As a woman, I share much of what Carol Christ has said; 'women's experiences have not shaped the spoken language of cultural myths and sacred stories.'[39] Women need to tell our own stories, which give meaning to our experience. As Christ continues, 'We must seek, discover, and create the symbols, metaphors, and plots of our own experience.'[40]

I have begun to question whether the concept 'canon' is still useful, for what claims to safeguard truth on the one hand can also lead to the repression of truth on the other. A closed canon excludes the many voices of the *minjung* and freezes our imagination. It is not surprising that feminist scholars of religion are involved in the rediscovery of alternate truths or the formulation of new ones. Rosemary R. Ruether's book, *Womanguides*, is a selection of readings from both historical sources and modern reformulations that are liberating for women.[41] Elisabeth Schüssler Fiorenza's reconstruction of the early Christian origins borrows insights from non-canonical sources.[42] Carol Christ describes women's spiritual experiences from women's stories and novels.[43] Black women scholars such as Katie G. Cannon[44] and Delores Williams[45] have also emphasized black women's literature as resources for doing theology and ethics. These stories of the liberation of women as well as other stories from different cultural contexts must be regarded as being as 'sacred' as the biblical stories. There is always the element of holiness in the people's struggle for humanhood, and their stories are authenticated by their own lives and not the divine voice of God.

The norm for interpretation. Since I reject both the sacrality of the text and the canon as a guarantee of truth, I also do not think that the Bible provides the norm for interpretation in itself. For a long time, such 'mystified' doctrine has taken away the power from women, the poor and the powerless, for it helps to sustain the notion that the 'divine presence' is located somewhere else and not in ourselves. Today, we must claim back the power to look at the Bible with our own eyes and to stress that divine immanence is within us, not in something sealed off and handed down from almost two thousand years ago.

Because I do not believe that the Bible is to be taken as a norm for itself, I also reject that we can find one critical principle in the Bible to provide an Archimedian point for interpretation. Rosemary Ruether has argued that the 'biblical critical principle is that of the prophetic-messianic tradition', which seems to her to 'constitute the distinctive expression of biblical faith'. This is highly problematic for three reasons: (1) The richness of the Bible cannot be boiled down to one critical principle. Ruether often makes comments like 'God speaks through the prophet or prophetess . . . the spokesperson of God . . .'[46] as if the utterance of God is the guarantee of the one principle. Here again we discern the need for 'absoluteness' and 'oneness' which Derrida questions. The *minjung* need many voices, not one critical principle. (2) The attempt to find something 'distinctive' in the biblical tradition may have dangerous implications that it is again held up against other traditions. (3) Her suggestion that this critical principle of the Bible can be correlated with women's experiences assumes that the prophetic principle can be lifted from the original context and transplanted elsewhere. She fails to see that the method of correlation as proposed by Tillich and Tracy presupposes the Christian answer to all human situations, an assumption which needs to be critically challenged in the light of the Third World situation today.

Conversely, I support Elisabeth Schüssler Fiorenza's suggestion that a feminist interpretation of the Bible must 'sort through particular biblical texts and test out in a process of critical analysis and evaluation how much their content and function perpetuates and legitimates patriarchal structures, not only in their original historical contexts but also in our contemporary situation.'[47] The critical principle lies not in the Bible itself, but in the community of women and men who read the Bible and who, through their dialogical imagination, appropriate it for their own liberation.

The communities of *minjung* differ from each other. There is no one norm for interpretation that can be applied cross-culturally. Different communities raise critical questions to the Bible and find diverse segments of it as addressing their situations. Our dialogical imagination has infinite potential to generate more truths, opening up hidden corners we have failed to see. While each community of *minjung* must work out their own critical norm for interpretation, it is important that we hold ourselves accountable to each other. Our truth claims must be tested in public discourse, in constant dialogue with other communities. Good news for the Christians might be bad news for the Buddhists or Confucianists.

The Bible offers us insights for our survival. Historically, it has not just been used as a tool for oppression, because the *minjung* themselves have also appropriated it for their liberation. It represents one story of the slaves' struggle for justice in Egypt, the fight for survival of refugees in Babylon, the continual struggles of anxious prophets, sinners, prostitutes and tax-collectors. Today, many women's communities and Christian base communities in the Third World are claiming the power of this heritage for their liberation. These groups, which used to be peripheral in the Christian Church, are revitalizing the Church at the center. It is the commitment of these people which justifies the biblical story to be heard and shared in our dialogue to search for a collective new religious imagination.

In the end, we must liberate ourselves from a hierarchical model of truth which assumes there is one truth above many. This biased belief leads to the coercion of others into sameness, oneness, and homogeneity which excludes multiplicity and plurality. Instead, I suggest a dialogical model for truth where each has a part to share and to contribute to the whole. In the so-called 'non-Christian' world, we tell our sisters and brothers the biblical story that gives us inspiration for hope and liberation. But it must be told as an open invitation: what treasures have you to share?

(I am grateful to Kesaya Noda for editing the manuscript and to the Asian Women Theologians, US Group, for mutual support and challenge.)

NOTES

1 T. C. Chao, 'The Articulate Word and the Problem of Communication', *International Review of Mission* 36 (1947), p. 482.

2 M. Foucault, *Power/Knowledge: Selected Interviews and Other Writings 1972–1977*, ed. C. Gordon (New York, Pantheon, 1980), p. 131.

3 J. R. Mott, *The Evangelization of The World in This Generation* (New York, Arno, 1972), pp. 17–18 (reprinted from the original 1900 edition).

4 J. Lacan and the 'echoe Freuidinne, *Feminine Sexuality*, ed. J. Mitchell and J. Rose (New York, W. W. Norton, 1982), pp. 74–85.

5 H. Kraemer, *The Christian Message in a Non-Christian World* (Grand Rapids, Mich., Kregel, 1956), p. 102.

6 Chao, p. 42.

7 ibid., p. 43.

8 Po Ch'en Kuang, '*Chung-Kuo ti chiu-yueh*' (Chinese Old Testament), *Chen-li yu Sheng-ming (Truth and Life)* 2 (1927) pp. 240–4.

9 Hsieh Fu Ya, '*Kuan-hu chung-hua Chi-tu-chiao Sheng-ching ti pien-ting wen-ti*' ('On the issues of editing the Chinese Christian Bible'), in *Chung-hua chi-tu-chiao shen-hsueh lun-chi (Chinese Christian Theology Anthology)* (Hong Kong, Chinese Christians Book Giving Society, 1974), pp. 39–40.

10 Hu Tsan Yun, '*Liang-pu chiu-yueh*' ('Two Old Testaments'), in *Chung-hua chi-tu-chiao shen-hsueh lun-chi*, pp. 67–71.

11 Y. T. Wu, 'The Orient Reconsiders Christianity', *Christianity and Crisis* 54 (1937), p. 836.

12 W. R. Hutchison, 'A Moral Equivalent for Imperialism: Americans and the Promotion of Christian Civilization, 1880–1910', in *Missionary Ideologies in the Imperialist Era: 1880–1920*, ed. T. Christensen and W. R. Hutchinson (Aarhus, Aros, 1982), p. 174.

13 Ng Lee Ming, 'The Promise and Limitations of Chinese Protestant Theologians, 1920–50' (*Ching Feng*, 21 and 22, 4 and 1, 1978–9), pp. 178–9.

14 Wu, p. 837.

15 ibid., p. 836.

16 K. Koyama, *Mount Fuji and Mount Sinai: A Critique of Idols* (Maryknoll, NY, Orbis Books, 1984), pp. 7, 8; London, SCM Press, 1984).

17 S. Parks, *The Critical Years: The Young Adult Search for a Faith to Live By* (San Francisco, Harper & Row, 1986), p. 117.

18 S. Brooks Thistlethwaite, 'Every Two Minutes: Battered Women and Feminist Interpretation of the Bible', in *Feminist Interpretation of the Bible*, ed. L. M. Russell (Philadelphia, Westminster Press; Oxford, Basil Blackwell, 1985), p. 98.

19 Parks, p. 113.

20 C. S. Song, *Theology from the Womb of Asia* (Maryknoll, NY, Orbis Books, 1986), p. 16.

21 C. S. Song, *The Tears of Lady Meng* (Geneva, WCC, 1981).

22 C. S. Song, *Tell Us Our Names: Story Theology From An Asian Perspective* (Maryknoll, NY, Orbis Books, 1984), p. x.

23 M. Pongudom, 'Creation of Man: Theological Reflections based on Northern Thai Folktales', *East Asia Journal of Theology* 3 (2, 1985), pp. 222–7. See Part Four of this volume.

24 A. C. C. Lee, 'Doing Theology in the Chinese Context: The David–Bathsheba Story and the Parable of Nathan', *East Asia Journal of Theology*, 3 (2, 1985), pp. 243–57. See Part Two of this volume.

25 P. Gallup, 'Doing Theology – An Asian Feminist Perspective', in *Commission on Theological Concerns Bulletin* (Christian Conference in Asia, 4, 1983), p. 22.

26 P. Ian Kwok, 'God Weeps with Our Pain', *East Asia Journal of Theology* 2 (2, 1984), pp. 228–32.

27 P. Ian Kwok, 'A Chinese Perspective', in *Theology by the People: Reflections on Doing Theology in Community*, ed. S. Amirtham and J. S. Pobee (Geneva, WCC, 1986), pp. 78–83.

28   N. Boonprasat Lewis, 'Asian Women's Theology: A Historical and Theological Analysis', *East Asia Journal of Theology* 4 (2, 1986), p. 21.

29   Y. Bock Kim, 'Messiah and Minjung: Discerning Messianic Politics over against Political Messianism', in *Minjung Theology: People as the Subjects of History*, ed. by the Commission on Theological Concerns of the Christian Conference of Asia (Maryknoll, NY, Orbis Books, 1983; London, Zed Press, 1983), p. 186.

30   Y. Bock Kim, 'Minjung Social Biography and Theology', *Ching Feng* 28 (4, 1985), p. 224.

31   See C. H. S. Moon, *A Korean Minjung Theology: An Old Testament Perspective* (Maryknoll, NY, Orbis Books, 1985).

32   A. Byung Mu, 'Jesus and the Minjung in the Gospel of Mark', in *Minjung Theology: the Subjects of History*, pp. 140–1. See Part Two of this volume.

33   S. Nam Dong, 'Historical References for a Theology of Minjung', in *Minjung Theology: People as the Subjects of History*, p. 160.

34   ibid., p. 159.

35   S. Hee Lee, 'Women's Liberation as the Foundation for Asian Theology', *East Asia Journal of Theology* 4 (2, 1986), pp. 2–13.

36   R. Detweiler, 'Introduction', *Semeia* 23 (1982), p. 1.

37   J. Culler, *On Deconstruction: Theory and Criticism After Structuralism* (Ithaca, Cornell University Press, 1982), p. 128.

38   R. Detweiler, 'What is a Sacred Text?', *Semeia* 31 (1985), p. 217.

39   C. P. Christ, 'Spiritual Quest and Women's Experience', in *Womanspirit Rising: A Feminist Reader in Religion*, ed. C. P. Christ and J. Plaskow (San Francisco, Harper & Row, 1979), p. 230.

40   ibid., p. 231.

41   R. R. Ruether, *Womanguides: Readings Towards a Feminist Theology* (Boston, Beacon Press, 1985).

42   E. Schüssler Fiorenza, *In Memory of Her: A Feminist Theological Reconstruction of Christian Origins* (New York, Crossroad, 1983; London, SCM Press, 1983).

43   C. P. Christ, *Diving Deep and Surfacing: Women's Writers on Spiritual Quest* (Boston, Beacon Press, 1980).

44   Katie G. Cannon, 'Resources for a Constructive Ethic in the Life and Work of Zora Neale Hurston' *Journal of Feminist Studies in Religion* 1 (1985), pp. 37–51.

45   D. Williams, 'Black Women's Literature and the Task of Feminist Theology', in *Immaculate and Powerful: The Female in Sacred Image and Social Reality*, ed. C. W. Atkinson, C. H. Buchanan and M. R. Miles (Boston, Beacon Press, 1985).

46   R. R. Ruether, 'Feminist Interpretation: A Method of Correlation', in *Feminist Interpretation of the Bible*, p. 117.

47   E. Schüssler Fiorenza, 'The Will to Choose or to Reject: Continuing Our Critical Work', in *Feminist Interpretation of the Bible*, p. 131.

22

Inter-faith Hermeneutics: An Example and Some Implications

R. S. SUGIRTHARAJAH

This essay addresses the question of using the Christian Scripture in a multi-faith context, and the need for biblical scholars to be sensitive to the people of other faiths in their interpretative task. Conversion is one of the key theological issues in a religiously pluralistic world, and among other things it causes cultural and religious dislocation and resocialization. Taking a cue from Latin American liberation hermeneutics, the texts that are associated with what is commonly known as Paul's conversion experience are looked at from a multi-faith point of view. The essay also points out the implications and new possibilities offered by such a re-reading, and sets out some ground rules for multi-faith hermeneutics.

This essay was first presented at the British New Testament Conference, Bristol, 1989, and was subsequently published in *Misson Studies* 7 (1, 1990) – a journal of the International Association for Mission Studies, available from IAMS Secretariat, EMW, Mittelweg 143, D-2000 Hamburg, West Germany.

The fact that we in Britain live in a multi-faith context is an existential reality of our times. This has been increasingly recognized by the media, politicians and church people. But the key question is how seriously have biblical interpreters taken into account the people of other faiths in their exegetical cogitations.

Biblical interpretation in a multi-faith context should be aware of at least two things. One, it must be sensitive to the scriptural texts of other faith communities and the spiritual sustenance they provide for many of their adherents. Mahatma Gandhi, so sympathetic to the person and teaching of Christ, nevertheless regarded the *Bhagavad Gita* as 'the supreme book for the knowledge of Truth' affording him invaluable help 'in times of distress'.[1] He also held the view that 'many things in the Bible have to be reinterpreted in the light of discoveries – not of modern science – but in the spiritual world in the shape of direct experiences common to all faiths'.[2]

Second, Christian scriptural interpreters should be conscious that their literary output is likely to reach a wide audience which is not necessarily exclusively Christian. Wilfred Cantwell Smith has been warning Christian interpreters that in their theologizing they should not only take note of Hindu, Buddhist and Muslim scholars who are 'equally intelligent', 'equally devout' and 'equally moral', but also be conscious of a prospective readership which is likely to include Buddhists, or those who have Muslim husbands or Hindu colleagues.[3]

The task then for a biblical interpreter is not only to discover how to live as a member of a multi-faith society, but also how to interpret the scriptural texts taking note of the presence and the spiritual intuitions of people of other faiths.

One way of facing the situation is to take a cue from the Latin American liberation theologians and re-read some of the biblical materials in the light of the multi-faith context. Recently the Latin American liberation theologians have been vigorously arguing for a re-reading of the biblical texts from the perspective of the poor. In doing so they have given a new meaning to the phrase 're-read'. It means more than to read again or to re-interpret. It means to take a fresh look at the data and read anew and reformulate the message. It means investing the text with new meanings and nuances.

There are a number of passages that one could subject to such a re-reading. I would like to have a re-look at the narratives which are commonly used to understand Paul's change of mind, traditionally known as his conversion.

Before that, we need to look briefly at the matter of religious conversions and the deep theological and sociological questions they raise.

In the religiously pluralistic context of India, religious conversion means a shift from one religion to another, but also more importantly, from one community to another. Therefore conversion to Christianity means not only experiencing, relating to and realizing the ultimate reality in a totally different way, but also stepping into an utterly strange social and religious milieu. It is a change of outlook and an orienting of one's life to a different focal point, but it also means leaving one's own cultural heritage and joining a Christian community whose style of worship and church structure follows western cultural patterns. Therefore conversion raises many theological issues. Among them are: (a) Is one religion superior to the other?

(b) What aspects of culture and social life should a convert be encouraged to preserve? (c) In what ways should he or she be helped to make use of his or her rich tradition to interpret the new faith? and (d) Should one leave one's own cultural social tradition entirely in accepting another faith? The words of Y. D. Tiwari, a Brahmin convert who became a Christian, echo these questions:

> When I decided to be baptized, I did not think that I was 'leaving' Hindu society. I thought I was adding something anew, something glorious to my Hindu heritage. I wanted to continue to live with my parents, to co-operate with other Hindus in social service work, to visit the temple etc. I was like the early Christians who met daily at Solomon's porch in the temple. Soon I discovered that this was not possible.[4]

PAUL'S EXPERIENCE: TWO APPROACHES

Paul's spiritual experience on the Damascus highway – Acts 9.1–9, 22.4–16 and 26.9–19, and his assumed reference to it in Galatians 1.11–17 – have been exegeted in many ways. Scholarly energies have been spent looking at these texts historically, philologically, psychologically, and of course, theologically. Basically there are two approaches to these texts and they can be summed up as the Conquest approach and the Reorientation approach.

The Conquest approach

The Conquest approach sees Paul's experience in terms of conversion and commissioning him to preach Christ to the gentiles. He is conquered by Christ and he is sent to conquer others for Christ. This approach neatly bifurcates Paul's life – Saul, the fanatical Pharisee bent on persecuting the followers of the Jesus movement, and Paul the Christian, equally fanatical about preaching his newfound saviour to the gentiles. F. F. Bruce captures the essence of this approach:

> With astonishing suddenness the persecutor of the church became the apostle of Jesus Christ. He was in mid-course as a zealot for the law, bent on checking a plague which threatened the life of Israel, when, in his own words, he was 'apprehended by Christ Jesus' (Philippians 3.12) and constrained to turn right round and became a champion of the cause which, up to that moment, he had been endeavouring to exterminate,

dedicated henceforth to building up what he had been doing his best to demolish.[5]

The Conquest approach functions at two levels. Theologically, it tends to project a Paul who is deeply dissatisfied with the arid spirituality of his own faith. His own tradition, the Judaism of his day, is seen as outmoded and legalistic. Romans 7 is taken to be Paul's autobiographical reflection on his inability to fulfil the requirements of the Jewish law. Missiologically, this approach sees his conversion as a warrant to take the Christian message to all parts of the world. In essence, the Conquest approach sees Paul's conversion from the Christian Church's apologetical and propagandistic point of view.

The Reorientation approach

This approach tries to rehabilitate Paul within Judaism and sees his turning point not as conversion, but as call – a call to a specific task, in the fashion of the Hebrew prophets. Krister Stendahl is the main exponent of this position.[6] This view does not see Paul as changing from one religion to another, but as changing from one of the Jewish sects to another. Therefore Paul's earlier life is not perceived as one of dejection and spiritual impoverishment. Instead, he is seen as a person who was proud of his traditions, his people and their calling. Put differently, Paul's life is not the case of a person without faith finding his way to God, nor of a person who is dissatisfied with his own faith, but rather of a person who gets a new understanding of his task.

This approach emphasizes two things. Firstly, it stresses Paul's call as a call to a particular assignment, and secondly, it detects prophetic character in his call. Krister Stendahl's words sum up these concerns:

> If, then, we use the term 'Conversion' for Paul's experience, we would also have to use it of such prophets as Jeremiah and Isaiah. Yet we do not speak of their conversion, but rather of their call. Paul's experience is also that of a call – to a specific vocation – to be God's appointed apostle to the Gentile.[7]

From a multi-faith perspective both these approaches are insensitive to the people of other faiths. Both see Paul's so-called conversion from a mission and proselytization point of view. The difficulty with such an exegetical approach is that it envisages confrontation with the people of other faiths. It sees its task in terms of conversion of people who are not within the Christian-fold. While one plans for an open aggressive propaganda of the Christian gospel, the other opts for a soft, covert operation. Under this second approach, the prophetic vocation is seen in terms of purifying and castigating evil elements in other faiths.

A third way: Dialogical approach

In the multi-faith context, there is another way of exegeting the data that is linked with Paul's experience. That is, the Dialogical approach – an approach which acknowledges the validity of the varied and diverse religious experiences of all people and rules out any exclusive claim to the truth by one religious tradition. In this approach, every religion is worthy of love and respect. All religions contain liberative as well as oppressive elements and the hermeneutical task is to enlist the liberative aspects to bring harmony and social change to all people. It is from this perspective I invite you to look at the biblical datum.

Traditionally, scholars have used two sources – Luke's account and Paul's own meagre recollections. It is from the accounts of Acts that one gets the popular images of Paul's conversion – supernatural voice, blindness, companions, etc. Paul's letters are virtually silent about these and it would be difficult to construct a conversion scenario from them. Moreover, one has to cull it from his letters which are in fact essentially concerned with other matters, his apostolic status and authority, his integrity, the practical problems of his communities and the non-arrival of the End.

Paul's letters, namely the ones accepted by the majority of scholars – 1 Thessalonians, Galatians, 1 and 2 Corinthians, Philemon, Philippians and Romans – do not suggest that he agonized over his past or that he rejected his own tradition. Rather, they claim that he was blameless (Phil. 3.6); he was proud of his Jewish calling and in religious fervour he was well ahead of people of his time (Gal. 1.14).

Interestingly, Paul does not use the traditional vocabulary that is normally associated with the process of conversion. He does not use the noun form of 'conversion' (*epistrophe*) or 'forgiveness' (*aphesis*) or the verb *ahienai*. There are three places where he uses 'repentance' (*metanoia*) or 'repenting' (*metanoun*), but on all these occasions they refer not to his own experience but to that of others who have already accepted Christ (Rom. 2.4; 2 Cor. 7.9–10, 12.21).

If one were to look for a word that epitomizes Paul's change of perspective, it is Transformation – *metamorphosis*. In his letter to the Romans he wrote, 'Do not be conformed to the world, but be transformed by the renewal of your mind' (12.2). The vocabulary and the imagery of transformation is evident in his letter to the Philippians as well. In chapter 3 he speaks about his transformation and reformation into the body of Christ – 'becoming him in his death', *symmorphosis*, verse 10. One of the exciting pictures Paul paints of becoming a child of God is that of transforming from the state of slavery into the state of sonship (Rom. 8.15–17). His hope for the Roman Christians is that they, too, will be conformed (*symmorphosis*) to the image of the Son (8.29).

Naturally, the question then arises as to what caused this radical transformation in Paul's life. Paul, in his letter to the Galatians, says that the gospel he preaches comes from 'the revelation of Jesus Christ' (1.12). In the next verse he goes on to say that this disclosure caused him to change from his 'former life in Judaism'. It was this revelation that opened up new horizons for Paul. But Paul nowhere tells what the content or the nature of this revelation was. It is here where one has to deal with conjectures.

What then was 'the revelation of Jesus Christ' which transformed Paul? The meaning of the genitive 'of Jesus Christ' is very ambiguous. It could mean either that Jesus was the agent through whom Paul received the revelation, or that Jesus was the content of the revelation, namely, that he was the Messiah. The majority of scholars tend to concur with this latter reading. But I would like to agree with George MacRae that Jesus as the Messiah was not central to Paul's gospel.[8] Incidentally, Paul does not use 'Messiah' in the sense of a title.

I would like to opt for the other reading which points to the revealing aspect of Jesus Christ, which may give us a clue to unravel the reason for Paul's radically rethinking his 'former life in Judaism'. Paul by his own admission was a Pharisee, and as such he was brought up in the understanding that God was holy. This notion of God as a holy One emerged in Judaism as a strategy during the exile and continued to dominate Jewish thinking till the time of Jesus. The Torah, too, was interpreted from the perspective of holiness. Marcus Borg writes:

'Holiness' became the paradigm by which the Torah was interpreted. The portions of the law which emphasized the separateness of the Jewish people from other peoples, and which stressed separation from everything impure within Israel, became dominant. Holiness became the *Zeitgeist*, the 'spirit of the age', shaping the development of the Jewish social world in the centuries leading up to the time of Jesus, providing the particular content of the Jewish life.[9]

Marcus Borg goes on to show that Jesus on the other hand advocated a different kind of holiness:

Instead, he proposed an alternative path grounded in the nature of God as merciful, gathered a community based on that paradigm, and sought to lead his people in the way of peace, a way that flowed intrinsically from the paradigm of inclusive mercy.[10]

Jesus, as an initiator of a revitalization movement within Judaism, opened up another aspect of the God of Israel – God as merciful and compassionate. Jesus was not handing down a new tradition. He was simply reiterating a forgotten aspect of God – that he was merciful and gracious (Exod. 34.6) – and as a consequence Jesus was urging his contemporaries to show solidarity and compassion towards one another. 'Be merciful, even as your Father is merciful' (Luke 6.36). Jesus' healing miracles, his acceptance of the marginalized of the time – the sinners, tax-collectors and the women – was an indication that (a) God's mercy was available to the very people who were cut off by the pharisaic interpretation of the law, and (b) that this was available without any intermediaries such as the law or the temple. It is not unreasonable to surmise that it was Jesus' retrieval of the availability of God to people without any mediating agencies which caused Paul to rethink his 'former life in Judaism'. It was Jesus' announcement of God's generosity to the people who are not normally within the pharisaic pale that contributed to his death. It is this death which becomes Paul's gospel, because in this death God demonstrated that he had abolished the impediments and the powers that dominate human life. It was Jesus' words and actions that prompted Paul to retrieve neglected elements in the tradition and transformed his thinking so that he preached a gospel of salvation which is available to all.

This Dialogical approach, which sees Paul's experience as transformation, offers new possibilities in a multi-faith context.

First, it changes the understanding of what conversion is. Paul's experience shows that conversion can take place within a religious tradition itself. Conversion does not necessarily mean changing from one religion to another. It can mean a conversion to a new dimension of one own's faith. One can be rooted in one's tradition and yet learn more and be open to its forgotten aspects. Peter is another case in point. When we talk about the Cornelius–Peter episode, we always refer to the conversion of Cornelius. What we often overlook is that Peter too was converted. It was a rude shock to him, as it was to Jonah before him, that God's grace knows no bounds and extends to outsiders who are not normally recipients of such love.

Second, this approach views the people of other faiths differently. It does not see them in terms of mission and conversion, but accepts them unconditionally without the requirement of ritual purity. One of the key issues that Peter, Paul and those who met at Jerusalem faced was not inculcation of Christian ideas into gentile minds but incorporation of them into the fellowship. It was to this end that Paul became the apostle to the gentiles – to accommodate them as God's people.

Third, it points to the fact that any spiritually transforming experience is not something that is private, subjective and emotional. But it involves praxis and engagement. Paul's experience underlines not only the solidarity of the believer with Christ, but his/her ethical obligation to walk in the newness of life (Rom. 6.4). This means imitating Paul by sharing maximum solidarity with people who are theologically, socially and economically marginalized.

SOME IMPLICATIONS AND SOME LESSONS

General

1 There is no universal interpretation of a text. All interpretations are contextual and tentative. A text becomes authoritative and sacred when it has contextual quality.

2 Biblical texts are not static or final. They possess a reservoir of meanings and nuances. When one particular meaning fails to meet the need of a community, one can always choose other meanings or other texts that can speak to the situation meaningfully and imaginatively. It is here one can learn from the hermeneutical principles of Hindus and especially how they handle the story of Rama. The story

of Rama is told in the epic called *Ramayana*. But this story is told in a variety of ways within India and also in South Asia. Harry M. Buck has shown how different nationalities (Indians, Sri Lankans, Malaysians, Indonesians) and various sectors of community (women, students, non-brahminical castes) reject the bits that fail to meet their needs and project narratives that continue to excite and speak to their situation.[11] In other words, the community chooses to re-tell the episodes that empower them to meet new demands.

3 There is no value-free exegesis. All interpretations are biased. Bultmann himself has said that there is no pre-suppositionless exegesis. The Form-critical school has always insisted on the *sitz im leben* of a text. The Latin American liberation theologians point out the importance not only of the context of the text but also the *sitz im leben* of the interpreter. All interpreters bring their own academic, ideological and religious biases into their interpretation. Karl Barth in his preface to the English edition of the commentary on Romans wrote, 'No one can, of course, bring out the meaning of a text (*auslegen*) without at the same time adding something to it (*einlegen*).'[12]

4 How then do we overcome our own prejudices? One way is to engage in communitarian exegesis. It is an exercise in which the community of the faithful – lay and professional, male and female, oppressed and oppressor, adults and children, Blacks and Whites – read the text in a dialectical relationship, each questioning, correcting and enabling the other. This way the pre-suppositions of one community are mutually challenged and critiqued by the other. It is an enterprise in which the questions posed by one section of community preoccupied with their context are read along with the critical reflections on the text with a view to seeking the truth together. In this way biblical scholars are compelled to come to grips with the problems of the ordinary people. Biblical scholars tend to withdraw from the harsh realities of social problems by taking refuge in the biblical past or, to use the words J. C. Beker, they tend to wander into the hinterland of archaeology. A good example of communitarian exegesis is the hermeneutical engagement of the peasants of Solentiname with Ernesto Cardenal.[13]

SOME GROUND RULES FOR MULTI-FAITH HERMENEUTICS

1 Calling names

Christians traditionally divide their scripture into two sections and call the first thirty-nine books the Old Testament, and the last twenty-seven the New Testament. What Christians regard as the Old Testament is held by the Jews to be their sacred scripture. The popular assumption among Christians is that the Old Testament is spiritually and morally somewhat inferior and obsolete, whereas the New Testament is superior and theologically up-to-date. But such a view, as history shows, reflects the very hostile, anti-Jewish stance that we commonly find among Christians.

The customary understanding that the new covenant of the Christians (NT) supersedes the old covenant (OT) is no longer tenable. The books of the new covenant have their own share of theologically and spiritually dubious elements – for example subjugation of women and complacency about slavery. The Jews do not like their sacred scripture to be treated as old. The two adjectives 'Old' and 'New' give the impression that one is outdated, archaic and no longer applicable, and the other is recent, interesting and relevant. As historical writings, both are ancient, belong to the distant past, and are products of an alien culture.

Therefore, when using sacred writings in an inter-faith context, one cannot speak of them in a way that exalts one and denigrates the other, but must allow each to be unique and speak on its own terms. In order to value the integrity of these scriptures, we might call the first thirty-nine books the Jewish Scriptures, or the Canonical Scripture of Israel or the Sacred Scripture of Israel, and the last twenty-seven books could be referred as the Canonical Literature of the Jesus Movement, or the Sacred Writings of the Early Followers of Jesus or the Canonical Writings of the Jesus Movement.

2 Place of other scriptures

Christians can no longer claim with Tertullian that 'I possess the Scripture and I am the only one to possess it'. In the present hermeneutical task Christian interpreters cannot ignore the religious texts of other faith communities. In the past, biblical concepts were taken as a yardstick to evaluate other scriptural traditions. For example, the Johannine understanding of Incarnation was viewed against the *Gita's* concept of *Avatar*, and the latter was judged inadequate and limited. Or the biblical notion of Grace is compared with Saiva Siddhanta's view of *Arul* (Grace) and it is critiqued for its impersonal nature. Similarly, other scriptural traditions are judged defective for their lack of a salvation history model.

A proper hermeneutics should go beyond these tendencies and look for what these religious texts are trying to convey, and understand them on their own terms rather than pre-judge them. All scriptures seek to tell in their own way the story of how they understand the mercies of God and the mysteries of life. Of course there is a radical diversity in the form and content of their stories. Traditionally Christians have insisted that their story is superior and more valid than the others. Christians may tell their story differently, but they cannot claim that theirs is the only story. In fact, these stories belong to all humankind. The fact that the Tamil classic *Tirukural* is claimed by different religions proves the point of its catholic nature. *The Tirukural* – a book of wisdom sayings, and speaks about God, righteousness, right praxis, etc. – is used by Saivites, Jains and Buddhists and it is called *Pothumarai* – Common Scripture. In one of the Father Brown stories, 'The Sign of the Broken Sword', Father Brown remarks, 'When will people understand that it is useless for a man to read his Bible unless he also reads everybody else's?'

3 Wisdom tradition

Probably one way to initiate multi-faith hermeneutics is to retrieve the Wisdom tradition. The strength of the Wisdom tradition is that it is universal. It is not confined to one culture or a nation. This tradition acknowledges that if wisdom is spirit, it is not restricted to Israel alone but embraces the whole world (Wisd. 1.17) and finds expression in all peoples and all lands. 'In the waves of the sea, in the whole earth, and in every people and nation I have gotten a possession' (Sir. 24.6).

The other positive feature of the Wisdom tradition is its ability to borrow freely and modify materials from other cultures and sources. The Synoptic Gospels record at least 100 proverbial and aphoristic sayings of Jesus. C. E. Carlston has shown that not all of them were from rural Palestine and that one can detect the influence of wider

Hellenistic culture.[14] The undue concentration on the distinctive features of Jesus' teaching not only diverted attention from the aphoristic elements in his sayings, but also encouraged a dim view of other cultures. The bracketing of Jesus' message with that of other sages is not to minimize his importance, but to point to the creative possibilities of the commonly held universal elements in his message. These common elements should provide starting points to engage in multi-faith hermeneutics in a way that the traditional missionary view that Christians have the superior truth, does not. An African proverb says that it is through other people's wisdom that we learn ourselves, and no single person's understanding amounts to nothing. While acknowledging the distinctiveness of each tradition, the role of the interpreter is to bring out the common elements in them. Three recent examples of such an attempt are Ishanand Vempeny's work on the *Bhagavad Gita* and the New Testament;[15] A. C. Amore's exegetical study of the Buddhist scriptures and their influence on the message of Jesus,[16] and John Eaton's comparative reading of the Wisdom spirituality of the Hebrew scriptures in the context of world religion.[17]

Finally, the task of interpretation is not merely description but engagement. The goal of biblical interpretation is not only understanding of the biblical text, but ultimately enacting it. The meaning of a text is discovered not only through reflection upon it, but also in concrete social action based upon it. The primary concern of an interpreter lies not only in transforming social inequalities, as the Latin American liberation theologians are vigorously reminding us, but also in bringing racial and religious harmony among peoples of different faiths.

NOTES

1 C. F. Andrews (ed.), *Mahatma Gandhi: His Own Story* (London, George Allen & Unwin, 1930), p. 31.

2 M. K. Gandhi, *Christian Missions: Their Place in India* (Ahamedabad, Navjivan Press, 1941), p. 159.

3 W. C. Smith, *Religious Diversity*, ed. W. G. Oxtoby (New York, Harper & Row, 1976), p. 9.

4 Y. D. Tiwari, 'From Vedic Dharma to the Christian Faith', *Religion and Society* 10 (3, 1963), pp. 117–18.

5 F. F. Bruce, *Paul: Apostle of the Free Spirit* (Exeter, Paternoster Press, 1980, rev. edn), p. 74.

6 See his *Paul Among Jews and Gentiles* (London, SCM Press, 1977), pp. 7–23.

7 ibid., p. 10.

8 G. MacRae, 'Messiah and Gospel', in *Judaisms and their Messiahs at the Turn of the Christian Era*, ed. J. Neusner *et al.* (Cambridge, Cambridge University Press, 1987), p. 171f.

9 M. Borg, *Jesus a New Vision: Spirit, Culture and the Life of Discipleship* (San Francisco, Harper & Row, 1987), p. 87.

10 M. Borg, *Conflict, Holiness and Politics in the Teaching of Jesus* (New York, Edwin Mellen Press, 1984), p. 199.

11 H. M. Buck, 'Rama and the Asian World' *World Faiths Insights* 9 (Summer 1984), pp. 27–36.

12 K. Barth, *The Epistle to the Romans* (London, Oxford University Press, 1933), p. ix.

13 E. Cardenal, *Gospel in Solentiname*, vols 1–4 (Maryknoll, NY, Orbis Books, 1982).

14 C. E. Carlston, 'Proverbs, Maxims, and the Historical Jesus', *Journal of Biblical Literature* 99 (1, 1980), pp. 87–105.

15 I. Vempeny, *Kṛṣṇa and Christ: In the Light of Some of the Fundamental Themes and Concepts of the Bhagavad Gita and the New Testament* (Pune, Ishvani Kendra, 1988).

16 A. C. Amore, *Two Masters: One Message: The Lives and Teachings of Gautama and Jesus* (Nashville, Abingdon Press, 1978).

17 J. Eaton, *The Contemplative Face of the Old Testament in the Context of World Religions* (London, SCM Press, 1989).

23

Two Mission Commands: An Interpretation of Matthew 28.16–20 in the Light of a Buddhist Text

GEORGE M. SOARES-PRABHU

This essay is an exercise in inter-textual study of two missionary commands – one Christian (Matthew 28.16–20) and the other Buddhist (Mahavagga 1.10–11.1). In this comparative analysis George Soares-Prabhu uses the Buddhist text to illuminate the Christian. In doing so, he draws out the similarities and differences, continuities and absences in these ancient texts and uses such a cross-religious reading to question the traditional triumphalistic exegesis of the Matthean passage.

This article is reprinted from *Biblical Interpretation: A Journal of Contemporary Approaches* 2 (3, 1994), pp. 264–82. This issue is a thematic volume on Asian biblical interpretation, entitled, 'Commitment, Context and Text: Examples of Asian Hermeneutics'.

As important for the Asian theologian as what Juan Luis Segundo has called the 'liberation of theology'[1] has been the postmodern liberation of biblical exegesis. Critical biblical exegesis has been 'liberated' from the strait-jacket of the historical critical method to which it was, since its origins, tightly confined; and it is this liberation which has made an Asian interpretation of the Bible possible. Historical criticism emerged as part of the great intellectual revolution of sixteenth and seventeenth century Europe in which the modern world was born.[2] It became a part of the dominant ideology of the modern West, and till about thirty years ago was the only method of biblical interpretation recognized as legitimate by the academy. With its pretended objectivity (which tried to emulate the objectivity of the natural sciences), and its precise, univocal understanding of the meaning of a text (which it identified with its 'authorical meaning', what the author intended to say), historical criticism aimed at being a rigorously 'objective' method. It purported to disclose the one true meaning of a text through the skilful use of its precisely crafted philological, grammatical and historical tools, without being influenced in any way by the concerns of the interpreter. By bracketing out these concerns, the method aspired to be a universally valid, 'scientific' method, without cultural particularity or denominational bias. Like modern science, the method admitted no cultural variants. It was always and everywhere the same.

As long as historical criticism remained the dominant method of biblical exegesis one could, therefore, no more attempt an 'Asian' interpretation of the Bible than one could hope to elaborate, say, an Asian physics. The *application* of a biblical text (that is, the spelling out its 'significance' for the reader) might differ from place to place. But its *exegesis* (the disclosure of its 'meaning') would always follow the standard procedures of historical criticism. Attempts at a contextualized interpretation were dismissed by historical critics as uncritical 'readings' (*lectures* in French), which might serve pastoral purposes, but had no place in the serious, 'critical' exegesis of the academy.

THE LEGITIMACY OF AN ASIAN INTERPRETATION

The situation is very different today, because historical criticism is no longer the dominant model of biblical exegesis in a postmodern world. It has been dethroned by new developments in philosophical hermeneutics, and a new postmodern climate which has given up the 'positivistic ideal of a scientific realm freed from all interpretation',[3] which used to be the *mythos* or the unifying narrative of the modern world.

New developments in hermeneutical theory have recognized the fact that a text (1) because of its linguistic structure, enjoys *semantic autonomy*, that is, has a 'textual meaning' (what the words of the text actually say), which is not limited by what the author may have intended; and (2) because of the natural polysemy of language, has a *surplus of meaning*, that is, is open to different interpretations by different readers.[4] The 'true' meaning of a text, then, is not some fixed 'authorial meaning', buried in the codes of the text, but the trajectory of meaning which emerges from the interaction of the text with a succession of readers each of whom brings his or her own pre-understanding to the text and reads it from a specific place.[5] And while philosophical hermeneutics has given us this new understanding of a text, a new climate of postmodernism has effectively challenged the modern *mythos* of 'an analytic-referential gaze that looks on the world and constitutes it as an object for an autonomous perceiving subject.'[6]

Because of this, the focus of biblical exegesis has been steadily shifting from the author to the text, and from the text to the reader. An exclusively author-oriented historical criticism made way for text-immanent structuralist and literary critical methods (especially the New Criticism) in the sixties; and is now making room for reader-response and post-structuralist approaches, in which the reader 'produces meaning "intertextually" on the basis of a multiplicity of signs, both written and un-written, which impinge upon him [*sic!*] in his world.'[7] If historical criticism was the exegetical method appropriate to the post-Enlightenment, 'modern' age, a radical pluralism of exegetical methods with particular emphasis on the role of the reader seems to be the characteristic feature of postmodern exegesis. For in postmodern interpretation, as in philosophical hermeneutics (of which it appears to be the literary *avatar*), a text is not seen as an 'object' already possessing a meaning but as a linguistic network inviting a reader response.[8] Its meaning is potential. To use the image proposed by Roland Barthes, 'a written text is like a musical score; just as a musical score becomes music only when it is performed, a written text produces meaning only when it is read.'[9]

But the role of the reader in the postmodern reading of a text goes further yet. In the hermeneutical conversation between text and reader, each interprets the other. All reading can therefore be said to be the reading of a 'bilingual' text, so that 'When a given text is read, simultaneously another text is also read, namely, the reader, or better put, the life experience of the reader of the text.'[10] In this process of mutual interpretation the life experience of the reader has a privileged role. This is the place where the interpretative process takes place, and from which it must begin. For the reader is both (to speak intertextually) the 'space on which all the quotations that make up a writing are inscribed'[11] as well as (to speak hermeneutically) the pole from which any genuinely dialogical conversation between text and reader must begin. For, as I have suggested elsewhere, only a reading which takes off from the concerns of the interpreter can set going a proper hermeneutical circle, which will relate text to life.[12] A reading which starts from the text, whether it be a diachronic investigation of its tradition (historical criticism) or a synchronic exploration of its surface or deep structures (literary criticism or structuralism) will always remain text-bound. It may set up some sort dialogue between reader and text (each new historical or literary insight leading to others), but the dialogue will always circle around the narrow confines of the text. It will yield more and more information about the text, but will never relate it to the concerns of the carefully insulated reader. It is only when an interpretation starts off from the reader's concerns that it evokes a response from the text which affects the reader's situation; and this gives rise to new questions that set a genuine hermeneutical circle in motion. That is why 'it is this sort of inter-textuality, proceeding *from* the life-experience text of the interpreter *to* the text in question, which has taken on such overarching importance in the so-called "postmodern" approach to literary texts.'[13]

Postmodernism thus gives great importance to the role of the reader in the interpretation of a text. The reader it has in mind is not the indeterminate 'implied reader' of narrative criticism, who does not really take us out of the 'neutral' world of the text,[14] but the 'real reader' who reads the text from a concrete socio-historical situation, and immediately relates it to the concerns of the real world. Methods of reader-response criticism which focus on the implied reader (the 'reader in the text') suffer, it seems to me, from several limitations. They (1) succumb to the 'intentional fallacy', that is, they locate the meaning of the text in the intention of the author, which is supposedly revealed by the implied reader for whom the author writes; they (2) ignore the creative role of the real reader in producing the meaning of the text;[15] and they (3) so decontextualize the text which is being interpreted, that they neutralize its significance. As Wilhelm Wuellner has noted: 'The very theories we (in the First World, or members of a patriarchial culture) promote about textually encoded readers as heuristic devices for the interpretation of normative texts can consciously or unconsciously perpetuate the cultural and sexual imperialism which at best, we readily disavow, or at worst, readily disregard.[16]

This postmodern recognition of the role of the real reader legitimizes an Asian reading of the Bible. It allows, indeed invites, the Asian reader to read the Bible with an Asian pre-understanding, inspired by Asian concerns and drawing on an Asian life-experience enriched by the enormously rich and vital religious traditions of Asia. It is by reading the Bible in this way that the Asian reader will enter into a hermeneutical dialogue with the text, and so disclose its specifically Asian meaning(s). 'Asian Christians', as Kwok Pui Lan has said, 'are heirs to both the biblical story and to our own story as Asian people, and we are concerned to bring these two into dialogue with one another.'[17]

THE PROBLEMS OF AN ASIAN INTERPRETATION

To start off this dialogue between the biblical story and the Asian story might seem easy enough. What, after all, could be more natural than for an Asian to read the Bible with Asian eyes? In practice, however, such an Asian reading is fraught with difficulties. These come from the complexity of the Asian situation and the contingencies of its history.

1. The Alienation of the Asian Reader

Most of Asia has been colonized by the West and bears the economic and psychological scars of its colonial history. The Christianity practised by two per cent of its people is a colonial Christianity whose doctrine, ritual and ethics were developed in the West to respond to Western concerns and show little sensitivity to the entirely different sensibilities of Asian cultures. To speak of South Asia alone (the only area of Asia with which I am familiar), Christian theology is still taught in doctrinal formulae couched in the universal context-free categories of Greek philosophy, in a culture (predominantly Hindu) where explanations and moral judgements are context-sensitive not context-free.[18] Christian ethics offers norms for the behaviour of persons construed as isolated self-sufficient individuals, in a culture where the human person is 'dividual rather than individual', that is, is experienced as connected to others through permeable ego boundaries that allow a constant interchange of substance ('in the voice travelling from mouth to ear, in cooking and sharing of food, or in other more evident transactions'[19]); and where the sense of self is the We-self of the extended family or the caste group rather than the I-self of the West.[20] And Christian spirituality proposes therapies for personal growth, in a culture where the aim of religious discipline is not to strengthen the ego through the development of 'human potential' or the 'proliferation of mental structures as unifiers of reality', but to dismantle it 'until only pure consciousness remains'.[21] There are obviously great differences between a traditional Christian and Asian self-understanding, so that a dialogical interaction between them is far from easy.[22]

The result is that an Asian Christian inevitably reads the Bible from a situation of great alienation.[23] Unlike a Hindu reading of the Vedas, or a Buddhist reading of the Pali Canon, an Asian reading of the Bible is never a 'natural' reading, taking place spontaneously within a living tradition. It has always to be a deliberate strategy, a forced and somewhat artificial exercise, a reading against the grain, a challenge to church orthodoxy or academic parochialism.

2. The Complexity of the Asian Situation

What sort of strategy, then, must an Asian reader of the Bible adopt to overcome such alienation? The answer is by no means clear, for Asia is an extra-ordinarily complex differentiated society. It is, culturally, the most complex of the continents, and supports an astonishing variety of religions and cultures. It is not easy, then, to identify the 'Asian story' which is to be brought into a mutually illuminating relationship with the story of the Bible through a creative act of the 'dialogical imagination'.[24] The culture of South Asia is evidently not that of East Asia, and within each of these immense cultural worlds there is a great diversity of cultural forms. Louis Dumont speaks of 'the sort of nightmare of perpetual diversity that haunts the naive observer' of Indian culture, even while postulating the existence of a pan-Indian civilization based on a hierarchical system of caste, which, he believes, underlies and makes sense of all this diversity.[25] But holistic explanations of Indian or Asian culture, like that of Dumont, tend to be reductionist. They favour the 'great tradition' of the urban literate élites, embodied in the classical literature of a culture, as against the varied, regional, orally transmitted 'little traditions' of the rural villages. The Asian story they offer is a distorted story which leaves out 'the unreflective many' who are the main constructors of a people's history.[26]

STRATEGIES FOR AN ASIAN INTERPRETATION OF THE BIBLE

Awareness of the great diversity of Asian society will prevent the Asian interpreter from striving after the elusive goal of a single all-purpose Asian method of interpreting the Bible. The basic method of Asian exegesis, the use of the dialogical imagination to relate reader and text so that each interprets the other, will take different forms in different situations. Because Asia as a whole is defined, as Aloysius Pieris pointed out long ago, by its overwhelming poverty (which specifies its Third Worldness) and its multifaceted religiosity, (which marks its specifically Asian character in the Third World), there will be, I suggest, at least two main approaches to an Asian interpretation of the Bible. One will read the Bible primarily in the light of Asia's poverty, the other in the light of its religious traditions. Corresponding roughly to these concerns one can think of two strategies of interpretation. The first of these will confront the Bible with Asian social concerns, which are best expressed in what C. S. Song has called 'the stories of broken Asian humanity'.[27] The second will relate it to the texts of the great Asian religions. One can best interpret the Bible in Asia by relating it intertextually to Asia's living stories or Asia's religious texts.

These two strategies are obviously not exhaustive, nor are they to be practised in isolation from one another, for the concerns to which they (roughly) correspond interpenetrate. Biblical reflection on the stories expressing Asia's broken humanity, takes place in the context of the dominant non-Christian religiosity of Asia, and cannot ignore Asian religious texts. And biblical reflection on Asian religiosity cannot be restricted to confronting the Bible with religious *texts* only, since the religiosity of the great mass of the Asian peoples is expressed in unwritten traditions. The stories that we bring to the Bible will be stories not only of Asia's broken humanity but also of Asia's religious quest.

In the Asian context, the basic concern which will determine our 'matrixing' of these Asian stories and texts with the Bible will be liberation, for this is, in different ways, the primary goal of both the biblical and the Asian religions, besides being Asia's most urgent social need. Interpreting the Bible in its postmodern Asian context must always, therefore, be liberative. But it can be liberative in at least three different ways. The liberation that interpreting the Bible brings to its Asian context can be (1) the liberation of Asian religions – not excluding Christianity – from the pre-critical dogmatism which still plagues them, and is a source of the malevolent fundamentalism that keeps irrupting in so many parts of Asia today. Critical exegesis achieved this in modern Europe, and its 'enlightenment' needs to be extended to traditional Asia too. That is why historical criticism is needed in Asia today in an ancillary role, though it must not go on to become the sole or dominant method of an Asian exegesis. Critical exegesis must take a further step to engage (2) in the prophetic critique of Asian reality that will foster the social liberation of Asia's marginalized people from their overwhelming poverty, social oppression and patriarchy. This will lead to an Asian theology of liberation emerging not from the Bible alone but also from the stories and texts of Asian religions that are read with it. And these two liberations must (3) be completed by a third, that spiritual liberation of the individual from the bondage of inordinate attachments, which is the primary goal of the non-Semitic religions of Asia. Here, it is the reading of the Bible that must be illuminated by the Asian religious texts and stories which are brought to it, so that it begins to reveal the biblical way to the 'disinterested action' (*nishkāma karma*) of the Bhagavadgita (2.47; 4.18–20), or to that unshakable 'calm' (*sāntam*), like that of a deep lake clear and still, which in the Dhammapada (6.7; 7.7), is the mark of the 'saint' (*arhant*). For without such spiritual freedom, attempts at other kinds of liberation will inevitably end in further bondage. The 'enlightenment' of Kant must be completed by the enlightenment of the Buddha, the liberation of Marx with the 'liberation' (*moksha*) of the Gita.[28] It is to achieve a dialectical interplay of these three freedoms that we attempt Asian interpretations of the Bible, by relating it to Asian stories and Asian texts.

Several attempts have been made to interpret the Bible by relating it to the stories of Asia's broken humanity or Asia's religious quest.[29] There have been a few, sporadic attempts at interpreting biblical texts with the help of texts from other Asian religious works.[30] There has even been an extraordinary venture to write a commentary on a biblical book (1 John) in the style of a *bhāshya*, that is, a classical Indian commentary on a religious text.[31] But, to my knowledge, what has not been attempted as yet is a detailed and systematic comparison of parallel biblical and Asian scriptural texts. I attempt to do this here by offering a rather hurried comparison of two 'mission commands', one from a Christian, the other from a Buddhist scripture, in the hope that such a comparison might help us to an Asian understanding of the Christian text. This particular technique is as yet largely unexplored, and may open doors to new understanding of biblical texts.

TWO MISSION COMMANDS

The mission command or the so-called 'great commission' of Matthew 28.16–20 is one of the best known texts of the New Testament, justly esteemed for its meticulously constructed form, and highly valued for its rich theological content, by exegete and missiologist alike.[32] Recent discussion on the form of the text (and indirectly on its meaning) has been well summed up by Gerhard Friederich, in an extensive and judicious survey,[33] and need not be repeated here. What has not been observed in the extensive study of the text is the remarkable similarity it shows to a parallel from the Buddhist tradition, that is to a 'mission command' given by the Buddha to his first followers, as narrated in the Mahavagga, a section of the Vinaya texts of the Pali Canon.[34] It is to comparison of these two mission commands, Christian and Buddhist, that we now turn.

Matthew 28.16–20	Mahavagga 1.10–11.1
28.16 Now the *eleven disciples* went to Galilee, to the mountain to which Jesus had directed them. 17 And when they saw him they worshipped him; but some doubted	1.10 At that time there were *sixty-one Arahats* in the world.
A	**A**
18 *And Jesus came and said to them, 'All authority in heaven and on earth has been given to me.*	1.11 *The Lord said to the Bhikkus, 'I am delivered, O Bhikkus, from all fetters human and divine.*
(cf. Matt. 5.13–16)	***You, O Bhikkus, are also delivered from all fetters, human and divine.***
B	**B**
19 *Go therefore and make disciples of all nations,*	*Go now, O Bhikkus, and wander for the profit of many, for the happiness of many, and out of compassion for the world,* for the good, profit, and happiness of gods and human beings.

baptizing them in the name of the Father and of the Son and of the Holy Spirit,

Let not two of you go the same way.

20 *teaching them to observe all that I have commanded you*; (cf. Matt. 5.48)

Preach, O Bhikkus, the dhamma, which is good in the beginning, good in the middle and good in the end, in the spirit and in the letter. Proclaim a consummate, perfect and pure life of holiness. . .

C

and lo, I am with you always, to the close of the age.'

C

And I will go also, O Bhikkus, to Uruvela, to Senanigama, in order to preach the dhamma.'

1. The Contexts of the Mission Commands

The two texts belong to very different literary contexts. The mission command in Matthew concludes a coherent, carefully constructed narrative about Jesus. It 'concludes' this narrative and does not merely end it. Its meticulously formulated verses bring Matthew's story of Jesus to a climatic end, and open out its significance to a future which reaches to the 'end of the age'. They also give us a compact summary of the Gospel, which draws together its christological (28.18), ecclesiological (28.19–20a) and eschatological (28.20b) threads into a text whose theological density rivals that of the prologue of John (1.1–14).

By contrast, the mission command of the Mahavagga is part of a loose collection of traditions, put together to serve as 'rules of discipline' for the Buddhist monastic community. These 'Vinaya texts' contain regulations, interspersed with illustrative and aetiological stories about the Buddha. The mission command that is being studied is from one such story. It belongs to a section (Mahavagga 1–24) which gives a continuous account of the life of the Buddha from the time of his enlightenment to the conversion of his two most important disciples, and contains the 'oldest version accessible to us now and, most probably, for ever, of what the Buddhist fraternity deemed to be the history of their Master's life in its most important period.'[35]

In a sense, then, the section of the Mahavagga from which the mission command has been taken forms a sort of 'gospel' within the great collection of the Vinaya texts. But its mission command does not form the conclusion to this 'gospel', as does the mission command in Matthew. Rather it is one of several incidents in a crucial period of the life of the Enlightened One to which no special importance is given. Its proper analogue in the Gospel of Matthew would be not the 'great commission' of the Risen Lord in Matthew 28, but the mission discourse in Matthew 10. But the mission discourse in Matthew 10 has no explicit mission command. Or one might say, perhaps, that its mission command is in fact the 'great commission' of Matthew 28. For, in spite of their chronological separation, the mission instruction of Matthew 10 and the mission command of Matthew 28 belong together. They are linked by Matthew's mythic understanding of time and by the paradigmatic role he assigns to the twelve disciples as representatives of the Christian community. Properly understood, even the literary contexts of the two mission commands may not be so different as might at first sight appear.

But however different their literary contexts, the two mission commands have the same life-context. Both define the missionary task of the respective communities to which they are addressed. This amply justifies their intertextual study. For, in such a study 'the texts that really matter are those intertexts which have been used in comparable contexts. Birth stories for example point to other birth stories, and so do apocalyptic texts',[36] and so too, we might add, do mission commands. We can proceed, then, to compare the two texts, for the light that one can throw on the other.

2. The Form of the Mission Commands

Such a comparison shows that the two mission commands are strikingly similar in form. Both have the same tripartite structure. They (A) begin with a grounding of the mission in the authority of the sender. They then (B) proceed to spell out the mission, which in both cases involves teaching, the communication of religious doctrine and praxis. And they both (C) conclude with a return to the sender whose presence in one form or the other accompanies those who are sent.

This remarkable similarity of form between texts which are certainly independent of one another, warns us against the obsessive search for Jewish or Hellenistic models, which, as Friederich's survey shows, has in fact dogged the study of Matthew's text.[37] Matthew 28. 16–20 functions as a 'mission command', and this automatically imposes on it a basic structure, which is determined by the exigencies of its function, and which is, therefore, common even to mission commands deriving from such widely different cultural contexts as India in the third century BCE and Syria in the first century of our era. That Matthew has elaborated this basic, innate pattern to produce a finely crafted conclusion to his Gospel is evident. That he needed a model for this may, in view of its formal similarity with the mission command of the Buddha, be doubted.

3. The Content of the Mission Commands

If the form of the two commands is the same, the content is markedly different. Two major differences appear from a first glance at the parallel texts. The liberation of the *bhikkus* (Buddhist monks) mentioned in the Buddhist text has no parallel in Matthew; the command to baptize in Matthew has no parallel in the Buddhist text. This observation can serve as the starting point of our comparative study, which when pursued through the three parallel stages of our texts, reveals the following significant points.

(a) Where, in Matthew, the mission command is grounded solely in the authority of Jesus ('All authority in heaven and on earth has been given to me'), in the Mahavagga it is based not only on the liberation of the Buddha himself ('I am delivered . . . from all fetters, human and divine'), but, equally, on the similar liberation his followers have achieved ('You, O Bhikkus, are also delivered from all fetters, human and divine'). The Buddhist mission rests as much on the experience of the *bhikkus* he sends, as it does on the authority of the Buddha himself. It is because the *bhikkus* have, like the Buddha himself, attained enlightenment, that they can now, out of their own personal experience, proclaim the *dhamma*.

This need for such 'enlightenment' (in Christian terms, for 'conversion') on the part of the missioner is not explicitly stated in the command of Matthew. As a result, the mission command has often been taken as a heteronomous decree, a sort of a military commissioning (the 'great commission'), which imposes the 'duty' of proclaiming Christ on all true followers of Jesus. Reluctant Christians are whipped through guilt into a frenzy for mission. But attention to

the Buddhist intertext adverts us to the fact that those who are sent
to make disciples are themselves, 'the eleven disciples' (Matt. 28.16);
that as such they represent Jesus (Matt. 10.42), because they share
in his life-experience of suffering and of glory (Matt. 10. 24–25;
19.20); that as 'light' and 'salt' they are to make disciples not just by
teaching and baptizing, but by the infectious witness of a genuine
Christian life (Matt. 5.13–16); and that their mission proceeds from
a transforming encounter with the Risen Lord, expressed as but
not really amounting to a command.[38] The Buddhist intertext thus
reminds us that the Christian mission, for all its christological
grounding, also presupposes the 'enlightenment' of those who are
sent.

(b) Both the Christian and the Buddhist mission commands
include a summons to teach. The command in Matthew mandates
the disciples to teach all that Jesus has commanded them, once again
revealing the christological focus of the text. The Buddha commands
his *bhikkus* to preach the *dhamma*. If this *dhamma* is the way to a
'perfect and pure life of holiness', so too is what Jesus has commanded. For the teaching of Jesus, Matthew has told us, invites us to
be 'perfect as the heavenly Father is perfect' (Matt. 5.48). Obviously
'perfection' will not be understood in exactly same way in the different traditions from which the two texts come. Christian love (*agāpē*)
is not Buddhist freedom (*nirvāna*). But there is a convergence
between them, for the Buddhist ideal of absolute freedom implies
unlimited compassion; just as the Christian goal of unconditional love
leads to perfect freedom. The ideal of the free and the compassionate
person stands as the desired goal of both traditions. The radical
difference, not clearly indicated in our text but possibly implied in
the Trinitarian formula for baptism which Matthew gives, is that a
person becomes free and loving as part of a community of disciples
among Christians, whereas he or she is liberated as an isolated individual in Buddhism.

(c) Both mission commands aim at the ultimate liberation of
humankind, but they express this aim in very different ways. In the
Buddhist mission this aim is quite explicit. The monks are sent out
'for the profit of many, for the happiness of many, and out of compassion for the world'. The aim of mission is, expressly, the welfare
of all, indeed not only of humankind, but of all other beings in the
world as well. Mission for the Buddhist is an expression of that
'passionate desire for the welfare of all beings' (*sarvabhūta-hite-*

ratāh), which the Bhagavadgita (5.25; 12.4) posits as a significant attribute of the liberated human being.

This is much less clear in Matthew. Here there is no mention of the welfare of the 'nations' to whom the disciples are being sent. They are referred to merely as objects of mission, those who are to be made disciples of Jesus. That is why the mission command contains an injunction (not found in the corresponding Buddhist text) to baptize them, that is, to bring the 'converts' through a rite of initiation into a distinct social group. Such 'baptism' implies, of course, the welfare, indeed the supreme welfare, of the people baptized. But this is not explicit in the text and can easily be forgotten. The 'great commission' can then become a call to an aggressively selfish mission, a form of 'conquest', in which the numerical growth of the missionizing church or the political interests of its colonial patrons, becomes more important than the welfare of the evangelized peoples. Mission then ceases to be an act of service and becomes a sinful exercise of institutional survival, expansion, or power. Reflection on the Christian mission to the Americas, whose fifth centenary was 'celebrated' in 1994, will remind us of how easily this can happen.[39] Once again the Buddhist intertext draws our attention to a dimension of the Christian text (all mission must be for the good, the profit, the happiness of the world and human beings) that is not explicitly expressed in it and can easily be overlooked.

(d) The mission command in Matthew is conscious of the universality and plurality of mission. Mission is expressly addressed to 'all nations' of the plural Hellenistic world. Though the Buddhist mission is even more universal than the Christian one (no creature is excluded from its scope) it is more conscious of the unity of humankind than of national differences within it. It does not distinguish between 'nations', but between 'gods' and 'human beings'. The urgency of mission is expressed in the (for the Christian) unexpected instruction, 'Let not two of you go the same way.' This might suggest, in contrast to the pair-wise sending by Jesus of twelve disciples in Mark (6.7) or of seventy disciples in Luke (10.2), a deliberately non-communitarian mission. But it probably indicates no more than a maximum deployment of forces to reach the largest number of places in the shortest possible time.

(e) Both the Christian and the Buddhist mission commands end with a promise. The promise is theologically significant in the mission command of Matthew, which promises the disciples the supportive presence of Jesus during their mission until 'the end of the age'. The christological and eschatological dimensions of the text are here particularly evident. These are wholly lacking in the mission command of the Buddha, who merely promises his *bhikkus* to go out, just like them, to preach the *dhamma*. His presence fulfils at best an exemplary function.

CONCLUDING REFLECTIONS

Much more could be inferred from a closer study of these two parallel texts, so similar in form but expressing religious traditions that are so strikingly different. For two very different world-views underlie the surface differences of the two mission commands that have been noted. But this paper is not meant to present a comparative study of Christianity and Buddhism. It has a much more limited aim: to provide an example of an Asian interpretation of the Bible by comparing a familiar biblical text with a 'parallel' from the Buddhist tradition. The comparison has proved, I believe, illuminating. It has highlighted significant elements of the biblical text, and lit up its dark corners. Elements in the biblical text not found in its Buddhist intertext have stood out strongly; other elements, conspicuous in the Buddhist intertext but not mentioned in the Gospel, have been shown to be implicit in it.

What has emerged as the most striking feature of the mission command in Matthew is its christological character. It is the Risen Lord who dominates the text from end to end. By contrast the role of the Buddha in the mission command of the Mahavagga is over-shadowed by that of the *dhamma*. It is the *dhamma*, 'good in the beginning, good in the middle and good in the end', which is the centre of the text, and both the Buddha and his *bhikkus* place themselves at its service.

But because of its christological concentration the mission command in Matthew tends to neglect, on the one hand, the dispositions of the missionaries sent by the Risen Lord, and on the other, the welfare of the people to whom the missionaries are sent. That is why the command can and has sometimes become the occasion for a mission more preoccupied with aggrandizement of the missioner rather than the welfare of the missionized. The Buddhist intertext with which it is 'matrixed' draws attention to these 'gaps' in our text.

It helps us to arrive at a more rounded interpretation of the mission command in Matthew, by pointing to elements implicit in it, which, though explicit elsewhere in the Gospel, could be overlooked in an over-focused, atomistic reading of the text.

Attempts – such as this first, hesitant venture – at interpreting the Bible through a 'wider intertextuality' that links biblical texts with texts from the other religious scriptures promise, then, to be a fruitful source for a richer understanding of the Bible.

NOTES

1   Juan Luis Segundo, *The Liberation of Theology* (Maryknoll, NY, Orbis Books, 1975).

2   For an exposition and a critique of the origins and presuppositions of historical criticism see George Soares-Prabhu, 'The Historical Critical Method: Reflections on its Relevance for the Study of the Gospels in India Today', in M. Amaladoss, G. Gispert–Sauch and T. K. John (eds.), *Theologizing in India* (Bangalore, Theological Publications in India, 1981), pp. 314–67. An abbreviated version of this article has appeared as 'Towards an Indian Interpretation of the Bible,' *Bible Bhashyam* 6 (1980), pp. 151–70. I have there argued that in spite of its immense productivity (reflecting doubtless the hyper-productivity of its social world), and its spectacular successes in individual cases, the method as a whole tends to be (1) historically ineffective in that it comes to no really conclusive results; (2) theologically sterile because it offers few interpretations of biblical texts that are at all relevant for the life of the Christian community today; and (3) hermeneutically naive in its assumption that it is ideologically neutral. Today, as Gary Phillips notes: 'The peaceful days of exegesis understood as a straightforward disinterested philological exercise are long past; the fantasy has been dispelled that traditional historical exegesis is neither theoretical nor ideological. Non-theoretical, non-ideological exegesis has never existed except as a romantic construct, itself an ideological imposition on the way exegetes were taught to represent to themselves what it is they said and did.' See 'Exegesis as Critical Praxis: Reclaiming History and Text from a Postmodern Perspective', *Semeia* 51 (1990), pp. 7–49 [12].

3   David Tracy, *Plurality and Ambiguity, Hermeneutics, Religion, Hope*, (San Francisco, Harper, 1987), p. 47.

4   For the hermeneutical model of text interpretation presupposed here see Paul Ricoeur, *Interpretation Theory: Discourse and Surplus of Meaning* (Fort Worth, Tex., Christian University Press, 1976), pp. 25–44; Severino Croatto, *Biblical Hermeneutics: Towards a Theory of Reading as the Production of Meaning*, (Maryknoll, NY, Orbis Books, 1987), pp. 13–88; Raimundo Panikkar, 'The Texture of a Text: In Response to P. Ricoeur', *Point of Contact*, 5 (April-May 1978), pp. 51–64.

5 'What we see', as Elisabeth Schüssler Fiorenza has said, 'depends on where we stand. One's social location or rhetorical context is decisive of how one sees the world, constructs reality or interprets biblical texts.' See 'The Ethics of Biblical Interpretation: Decentering Biblical Scholarship', *JBL* 107 (1988), pp. 3–17 [5].

6 Phillips, 'Critical Praxis', p. 13.

7 James Voelz, 'Multiple Signs and Double Texts: Elements of Intertextuality', in Sipke Draisma (ed.), *Intertextuality in Biblical Writings: Essays in honour of Bas van Iersel* (Kampen, Kok, 1989), pp. 27–34 [27].

8 Temma F. Berg, 'Reading In/To Mark', *Semeia* or, 48 (1989), pp. 188–206; 'Readers read to expose themselves to the flickering significance of the text, and, in the process, organize texts according to patterns preinscribed in their (un)conscious' [89].

9 Roland Barthes, *S/Z* (Paris, Seuil, 1975), pp. 35–7, quoted in B. van Iersel, 'The Reader of Mark as Operator of a System of Connotations', *Semeia* 48 (1989), pp. 83–114 [83]. This, in fact, has been the traditional Asian way of reading a religious text. A text is read not for what it may have originally meant (for religious texts in Asia are nearly always anonymous, with no historical context in which they can be properly located), but for the significance it now has for a particular readership. Mahatma Gandhi's non-violent interpretation of the Bhagavadgita is read alongside Lokmanaya Tilak's opposite, militant interpretation, as complementary valid understandings of the text. For what ultimately matters is the transformative effect of a text rather than its conceptual 'meaning'.

10 Voelz, 'Multiple Signs', p. 32.

11 Roland Barthes, *Image, Music, Text* (New York), p. 146, quoted in Voelz, p. 27.

12 I have argued the point in some detail in an unpublished paper 'Commitment and Conversion: A Biblical Hermeneutic for India Today' (1988).

13 Voelz, 'Multiple Signs', p. 33.

14 Bernard C. Lategan, 'Coming to Grips with the Reader in Biblical Literature', *Semeia* 48 (1989), pp. 3–17. As Lategan points out: 'The real author, when writing, is reaching out for the implied reader (as no other reader is present at this moment). The real reader, when reading, is reaching out for the implied author (as no other author is present) ... Real authors can address only what they imagine or intend their readers to be; real readers can reach the real authors only via the implied authors, that is, they have to figure out what the real authors are getting at by concentrating on the clues and signals given by the encoded authors' [10]. This is an insightful analysis, but it supposes, questionably, that the goal of interpretation is the recovery of 'what the real author is getting at', that is, of the authorial meaning of the text.

15 As Temma Berg ('Reading', p. 202) reminds us: 'The reader is in and not in the text. The reader can never be separated from the texts that surround him, partly because "reader" and "text" are interchangeable signs, but also because the reader is an active producer of what she reads.'

16 cf. Wilhelm Wuellner, 'Is There an Encoded Reader Fallacy?', *Semeia* 48 (1989), pp. 41–54 [49].

17 Kwok Pui Lan, 'Discovering the Bible in the Non-Biblical World', *Semeia* 47 (1989), pp. 25–42 [30] and chapter 21 of this book.

18 A. K. Ramanujan, 'Is There an Indian Way of Thinking? An Informal essay', *Contributions to Indian Sociology* 23 (1989), pp. 41–58.

19 John Leavitt, 'Cultural Holism in the Anthropology of South Asia: The Challenge of Regional Traditions', *Contributions to Indian Sociology* (n.s.) 26, no. 1 (1992), pp. 3–49 [11], referring to McKim Marriott, 'Hindu Transactions: Diversity without Dualism', in Bruce Kapferer (ed.), *Transactions and Meaning: Directions in the Anthropology of Exchange and Symbolic Behaviour* (Philadelphia, Institute for the Study of Human Issues, 1976), pp. 109–42.

20 Harold Coward, 'Human Nature in Yoga and Transpersonal Psychology', *Religious Studies Review* 18 (1992), pp. 100–102 [101], reviewing Alan Roland, *In Search of Self in India and Japan* (Princeton, University Press, 1988).

21 ibid.

22 For an unusually good comparative study of the two world-views see Francis X. D'Sa, *Gott der Dreieine und der All-Ganze, Vorwort zur Begegnung zwischen Christentum und Hinduismus* (Düsseldorf, Patmos, 1987).

23 See George Soares–Prabhu, 'From Alienation to Inculturation: Some Reflections on Doing Theology in India Today', in T. K. John (ed.), *Bread and Breath: Essays in Honor of Samuel Rayan* (Anand, Gujerat Sahitya Prakash, 1991), pp. 55–99.

24 Kwok, 'Discovering the Bible', p. 31.

25 Louis Dumont, 'For a Sociology of India', *Contributions to Indian Sociology* 1 (1957), pp. 7–22 [33]. The classic work in which Dumont spells out the unifying ideology underlying Indian civilization is his *Homo Hierarchicus: The Caste System and its Implications*, 2nd edn (Delhi, Oxford University Press, 1988). Here an essentially hierarchical understanding of persons and society based on a system of ritual purity/pollution, very different from the radical egalitarianism (the *homo aequalis*) of modern Western society, is posited as the basic structure of Indian society. While the pervasiveness of caste in India cannot be denied, it is doubtful whether the great regional differences that obtain in the sub-continent can be explained in terms of *homo hierarchicus* alone.

26 Leavitt, 'Cultural Holism', pp. 12–20. The categories of the 'great' and 'little' traditions were formulated by Robert Redfield in his seminal study of peasant societies, *Peasant Society and Culture* (Chicago, University of Chicago Press, 1956). Anyone acquainted with peasant societies will be wary of reconstructions of biblical history which depend heavily on literary sources, without sufficient awareness of how unrepresentative such sources (expressions of the 'great tradition') can be of the real lived culture (the 'little tradition') of the people. A study of the literary output in India today, for instance, would suggest that nearly half its people speaks English. In fact, English is spoken by less than five per cent of the population belonging to a tiny upper class élite. Westernization in India is demographically insig-

nificant, and culturally skin-deep – as was, I suspect (*pace* Martin Hengel), Hellenization in first century Palestine.

27 C. S. Song, *Theology from the Womb of Asia* (Maryknoll, NY, Orbis Books, 1986), p. 146.

28 Jon Sobrino, *The True Church and the Poor* (London, SCM Press, 1984), pp. 10–15, distinguishes two phases of the Enlightenment, represented by Kant and Marx. The first, Kantian phase, which sought 'the liberation of reason from all authority', has been the inspiration of modern Western theology. The second, Marxian phase, which looked for societal liberation from 'the wretched conditions of the real world', has inspired Latin American liberation theology. I suggest that a third dimension of freedom, liberation from inordinate attachments, so central to Asian religions and so strikingly needed in a consumer society, which deliberately cultivates what the Bhagavadgita (2.70) calls 'desirers of desires' (*kama-kami*), would be the contribution of an Asian exegesis of the Bible.

29 See Chung Hyun Kyung, *Struggle to be the Sun Again: Introducing Asian Women's Theology* (Maryknoll, NY, Orbis Books, 1990); and Choan-Seng Song, *Third-Eye Theology* (Maryknoll, NY, Orbis Books, 1979). These are excellent examples of Asian theology not only in their content but in the personal, imaginative and experiential idiom they use.

30 See Sister Vandana, *Waters of Fire* (Bangalore, Asian Trading Corporation, 1989) a remarkable study of the water symbolism in the Gospel of John in the light of the Hindu scriptures. (See chapter 10.)

31 See H. Sharma and S. Hemraj, *Karuṇākarīyam Updeśāmṛtam* (*The First Letter of John in Sanskrit*) (Ranchi, Satya-Bharati, 1987). This is a unique and authentic *bhashya* (commentary in the classical Indian style) in English, but based on a Sanskrit translation of 1 John.

32 See David Bosch, *Transforming Mission: Paradigm Shifts in Theology of Mission* (Maryknoll, NY, Orbis Books, 1991), pp. 56–7.

33 Gerhard Friederich, 'Die formale Struktur von Maat 28.18–20', *ZTK* 80 (1983), pp. 137–83.

34 The text from the Mahavagga is cited from the translation of T. W. Rhys Davids and Hermann Oldenberg, published as *Vinaya Texts, Part 1* in the Sacred Books of the East series vol. 13 (Varanasi, Motilal Banarsidas, reprinted 1968), pp. 112–13.

35 Rhys Davids and Oldenberg, *Vinaya Texts*, p. 73, n. 1.

36 Willem Vorster, 'Intertextuality and Redaktionsgeschichte', in Sipke Drairma (ed.), *Intertextuality in Biblical Writings: Essays in honour of Bas van Iersel* (Kampen, Kok, 1989), pp. 15–26 [21].

37 Friederich, 'Die Formale Struktur', pp. 137–62.

38 Like its 'love-commands' the 'mission-commands' of the New Testament are not strictly commands. Neither love nor mission can (if genuine) be made to order. Both are variant expressions of the same spirit which takes hold of the follower of Jesus when he or she encounters the Risen Lord. The variant 'mission commands' described by Matthew (28.16–20), Luke (22.44–49) and John (20.21–23) – the mission command in Mark (16.9–20), is not part of the original Gospel – are redactional formulations which

express in terms of the theology of each evangelist an essential but unthemat-
ized dimension of the Easter experience.

39   See the issue of *Concilium* 1990/6 on '*1492–1992:* The Voices of
the Victims' (ed. L. Boff and V. Elizondo); also *Missiology* 20–2 (1992) on
'Christopher Columbus: Five Centuries of Colonization.' The 'discovery' of
America, as Ignacio Ellacuria has pertinently remarked, turned out to be a
discovery of 'the true character of Spain, of Western culture and of the
Church of that time' – see his 'Fifth Centenary of Latin America: Discovery
or Cover Up?', *Social Action* 42 (1992), pp. 40–50. The celebration of this
event in 1992, and the very different reactions it inspired, turned out to be
an equally revealing 'discovery' of the theologians and church people who
reacted to it! It is significant that nothing comparable to the violence of the
Christian colonial mission (inspired presumably by the great commission of
Matthew), darkened the benign spread of Buddhism all over Eastern and
Central Asia. However similar the two mission commands we have been
studying, their *Wirkungsgeschichte* has been strikingly different, and this difference needs to be reflected on.

24

The Book of Ecclesiastes and Thai Buddhism

SEREE LORGUNPAI

Western biblical scholarship not only controls the interpretation but also determines the selection of texts for interpretation. Thailand provides an example of such hegemonic dominance, where the missionary translators accorded a low priority to the Book of Ecclesiastes which resonates with some Buddhist texts. The article below tries to reclaim the book and use it as a possible basis to enter into dialogue with Buddhists.

This essay is reprinted from *Asia Journal of Theology* 8 (1) 1994, pp. 155–62, which is available from c/o BTESSC, PO Box 4635, 63, Miller's Road, Bangalore, India.

Seree Lorgunpai, from Thailand, is a post-graduate student at the University of Edinburgh, currently completing a doctorate in inter-textual study of Hebrew and Buddhist scriptures.

The world is becoming smaller with the progress of modern technology. People from different parts of the world are quickly informed about events happening on the other side of the world. This is made possible by the media, especially television and radio. This kind of modern communication is supposed to be a helpful means of mutual understanding among people from different cultures, but such is not always the case. It depends entirely on the person who conveys the information. For example, in May of 1994 the pro-democracy movement took to the streets of Bangkok to demonstrate against the unelected Prime Minister, General Sunchida Kraprayu. The peaceful demonstration became violent and many people were killed when the military used force against the demonstrators. This violence was stopped almost immediately by the intervention of the king of Thailand. When many saw General Sunchida kneel and bow down in front of the king on British television, they thought that General Sunchida had repented. Actually, it was not his repentance that made him bow down in front of the king, but the fact that any Thai who

339

seeks the king's audience has to bow down before the king. Cultural differences make people perceive the same information differently.

SIMILARITIES BETWEEN ECCLESIASTES AND BUDDHISM

The book of Ecclesiastes is often thought to be one of the strange books in the Old Testament by Western Christians. But when Thais read this book they feel at home because they find teachings common with Buddhism. When missionaries began to translate the Bible into the Thai language they started with the New Testament and then the Old Testament. The book of Ecclesiastes was almost one of the last books to be translated, perhaps because the translators were not aware of the similarity between it and Buddhism or because they just chose to ignore this connection between them. Even now Ecclesiastes is not used as much as it should be; it is mostly used in Thailand at funeral services. This book should be used more often, especially on occasions of interreligious dialogue.

Many scholars think that certain of Qoheleth's perceptions found in Ecclesiastes are different from the general beliefs of the Old Testament. And therefore such scholars work hard to identify the sources of Qoheleth's ideas. Some find relationships between the teachings in the book of Ecclesiastes and the wisdom literature in ancient Near East or Greek philosophy. Dillon, however, feels strongly that Qoheleth was acquainted, and to some extent imbued, with the doctrines of Gautama Buddha.[1] Though Dillon's thesis may not be right – and there is no external evidence that supports his view – the similarity between Ecclesiastes and Buddhism is quite obvious.

This similarity may arise from the universality of human experiences or from ideas that were carried by merchants from region to region such as through the Silk Route. This route had existed since the early years of the Han dynasty (206 BCE to 220 CE and had served as a trading link between China and the cultures to the west.[2] Dahood makes the intriguing observation, which he does not work out, that Ecclesiastes' vocabulary is full of commercial terminology. Terms such as 'advantage or profit' (*yithrôn, yôther,* and *môthar*), 'toil' (*'amal*), 'occupation, business' (*'inyan*), 'money' (*keseph*), 'portion' (*cheleq*), 'success' (*kishrôn*), 'riches' (*'osher*), 'owner' (*ba'al*), 'lack, deficit' (*chesrôn*), are among those used. The overall picture delineated in Ecclesiastes suggests a distinctly commercial environment.[3] Another possible point of contact could have been through the untiring efforts of zealous missionaries sent by the great Indian emperor, Ashoka, who reigned from 269 to 237 BCE.[4]

A number of comparative studies between Buddhism and Christianity have been done by various scholars, but not many have compared the Old Testament with Buddhism, at least until recently, when John Eaton wrote a book, *The Contemplative Face of Old Testament Wisdom*, published in 1989. His book covers quite a wide range of materials. Eaton mentions Buddhism under the section on India. Nevertheless, he does not use any specific examples of Buddha's teaching in his book. Another scholar who sees links between the wisdom tradition of the Old Testament and another eastern tradition is Graham Ogden. In his commentary on Qoheleth, he sets aside an excursus to compare Chinese wisdom with biblical revelation. He points out that in terms of methodology, both Israelite and Chinese wisdom traditions adopt the same 'observation-reflection' approach which is so typical of Qoheleth.[5] Any Buddhist who wants to reach enlightenment also needs to reflect on his past and learn to meditate about life. Both Eaton and Ogden are quite general in their study. What I want to do is to be more specific by comparing the teachings in Ecclesiastes with the teachings of Thai Buddhism. Before doing this, to help those who do not know much about Thailand or Buddhism, I will give some necessary background information.

BUDDHISM IN THAILAND

Thailand is a Buddhist country, and about ninety-five per cent of Thais call themselves Buddhists. Buddhism in Thailand is Theravada Buddhism. Another important school of Buddhism is Mahayana. The main doctrinal difference between the two seems to have been the means of attaining Buddhahood; the Theravada school maintains the strict observance of the Buddhist ascetic, but the Mahayana school holds that Buddhahood already dwells within, and only needs developing.[6] It is almost impossible to separate Buddhism from Thai culture. To help Thai people understand Christianity, we need to find common areas of belief when communicating the Christian faith to them. Ecclesiastes is the best book to be used as a point of contact. When Thai people read Ecclesiastes they find many familiar concepts. For example, the so-called 'vanity' theme which is also a prominent subject in Thai Buddhism.

The Hebrew root (of the word vanity) occurs in the Old Testament about seventy-eight times, but occurs in the book of Ecclesiastes alone thirty-eight times. That means nearly fifty per cent of its usage in the Hebrew Bible is in the book of Ecclesiastes, though the book has only twelve chapters. When this Hebrew root is translated into the Thai Bible, a Buddhist term *anitjung* is used. When this term is used by Thais it usually refers to things that are unstable, impermanent, and cannot be relied on. Buddhists are taught to think that everything in this world is *anitjung*. If Ecclesiastes was separated from the Christian Bible and handed to Thai Buddhists to read, they might consider it to be a Buddhist book. If we look in detail, certainly we will find some differences, but generally, there are a number of similarities. I will not give a comprehensive list of the similarities, but I have tried to select a few topics that are relevant for our purpose.

THE TWO AUTHORS

The beginning of Ecclesiastes is interesting for a comparison of the two traditions. I do agree with most scholars that this book was not written by King Solomon, but the autobiographical section (2.1-11), does remind many readers of King Solomon or at least to feel that the author is well-to-do. Similarly, the founder of Buddhism was the Buddha whose family name was Gautama (or Gotama), and his personal name was Siddartha. His father was Suddhodhana, an aristocratic Hindu chieftain, and his mother's name was Mahamaya. The young prince was brought up in princely luxury. At the age of sixteen he married a beautiful wife. From that time on for about thirteen years he led a life of luxury and domestic happiness. Eventually the prince drove through the streets of the city, in a gaily decorated chariot, and he saw some unpleasant scenes: an old man with grey hair tottering out of a hut dressed in nothing but rags; a sick man twisting his body about in the dust, groaning and moaning and gasping for breath; and a corpse being carried by a crowd of people who were weeping and wailing. After these experiences, he began to think about the mystery of life. He realized the sorrow which is present in the life of all people, and he felt despair, pain, and sorrow. Later he used the term *dukkha*, loosely translated as 'suffering,' to express this fact of human life. Both the founder of Buddhism and the author of Ecclesiastes confronted crises in life, though they were very wealthy and did not experience suffering themselves. What they had seen in the world bothered them greatly. Siddartha gave up his life of luxury and left the palace to seek out the truth of life. Finally he found an answer and became the enlightened one. Qoheleth might not have given up all his wealth, but he has put his struggle down in the book of Ecclesiastes.

SUFFERING AND ITS CAUSES

After his enlightenment, the Buddha preached his first sermon to the five ascetics who had been his companions. In this sermon, the first Noble Truth is that suffering or *dukkha*, the Pali word, is a universal fact. The word *dukkha* has a deep philosophical meaning; it includes the ordinary meaning of suffering such as misery, distress, despair, agony, suffering of body and mind. But it also means change, emptiness, imperfection, conflict. Qoheleth, the author of Ecclesiastes uses his powerful motto 'futility of futility, all is futility', to introduce his audience to this reality of life. The Hebrew term used by Qoheleth means 'futility'. This includes unfairness, injustice, a lack of any 'real' progress, lack of satisfaction, unpredictability, fruitlessness, etc. Both the Buddha and Qoheleth recognize the bad side of human destiny, and they present it quite vividly.

The Buddha clearly points out that the cause of suffering is desire. People seek for self-satisfaction through things that they can cling to, because they do not know the nature of all things, that they are impermanent. Qoheleth does not point out exactly what the cause of suffering is, but he uses many examples of unfulfilled desire to show how futile human life is. For example, he is in anguish because he must leave his property to the man who comes after him, who may be a wise man or a fool (Eccles. 2. 18–19). In another example, there is a man who has no one, neither son nor brother, yet there is no end to all his toil. His eyes are never satisfied with riches, so that he never asks, 'For whom am I toiling and depriving myself of pleasure?' (Eccles. 4.8). Qoheleth thinks more in terms of what people should get from the time and energy they have invested in something.

The Buddha suggests that there is a state in which there is complete freedom from suffering and bondage. This state is called

Nirvana. In a chapter on 'Koheleth's Philosophy of Life', Dillon states that 'happiness is a chimaera, birth a curse, death a boon, and absolute nothingness (*Nirvana*) the only real good.'[7] Dillon seems to think that Qoheleth has the same goal as Buddhism. But I am not convinced that Qoheleth would seek absolute nothingness. At one point he suggests that 'there is nothing better for a man than that he should eat and drink, and find enjoyment in his toil' (Eccles. 2.24). Not all Buddhists in Thailand hope for *Nirvana*; they just hope for the better future in this life or the next rebirth. Many of them think *Nirvana* is an unattainable aim.

The Buddha declares that there is a way that leads to *Nirvana*. It consists of eight duties or principles of conduct and so it is known as the Noble Eightfold Path. It is also known as the Middle Way because it is the way between the extremes of self-indulgence and self-torture. Qoheleth agrees with Buddha that self-indulgence is not the way, because he himself had tested all kinds of pleasure and found out that they are futility (Eccles. 2.1–11). Qoheleth does not give specific steps for his audience to follow to reach the happy state, but he does give more general practical advice. He also has the idea of the Middle Way for he suggests that 'Do not be too righteous, do not be over-clever; why should you be ruined? Do not be too wicked, and do not be a fool; why should you die before your time?' (Eccles 7.16–17). His suggestion may be based on his observation that 'in the place of justice wickedness is there, in the place of righteousness wickedness is there' (Eccles 3.6). Qoheleth seems to point out that in reality, we hardly find true justice. Therefore we should not expect too much from judicial systems, but at the same time we should not disregard judicial systems, because somehow the wicked will be punished.

Buddhism does not teach that man has an eternal, indestructible soul. Instead Buddhism says that there is 'no-soul' (*an-atta*). According to Buddhism, there is no permanent self; what we see about ourselves is only an illusion created by a combination of physical and mental forces. Qoheleth does not state clearly whether soul exists permanently or not but he is questioning a newly emerging view that soul is immortal. He asks 'who knows if the spirit of human beings goes upward and the spirit of animals goes downward to the earth?' (Eccles. 3.21).

Buddhism teaches that our mind, body and all the world are subject to the principle of conditional causality. This principle operates by the law of *karma* (Sanskrit) or *kamma* (Pali). The law of *kamma* is used as a means to explain why we are the way we are; there must be something about us that relates to the past. What we sow we shall reap. No God can interfere with this law. Even prayers, ceremonies, rites, and offerings cannot alter this law. As long as we are not able to destroy our desire completely, we will be controlled by the law of *kamma*. The chain of existence will continue as long as there is desire for existence. Qohelet does not think that our situation is controlled by the law of *kamma*; he insists that our situation is controlled by God. He says 'For the man who is good in his presence, he (God) gives wisdom and knowledge and happiness, but to the sinner he gives the work of gathering and collecting to give to the one who pleases God' (Eccles. 2.26). According to Qoheleth, God's plan is final, for he says that 'I know that everything God does will be forever. It is impossible to add to it and it is impossible to subtract from it. God has made it in order that they will fear him' (Eccles. 3.14).

Buddhism teaches men and women to trust themselves and summon their powers within them to achieve their goals in life. People must work out their own salvation by their own efforts. For their better future they should accumulate merit, for example: alms-giving to the monks or to the poor, abstaining from all immorality, protecting others from harm, and so on. In a modern example, one of the prominent politicians in Thailand, Mr Chamlong Srimuang, whose determination brought the Sunchida government to collapse, claimed that he had abstained from a sexual relationship with his wife. As a Buddhist layman he was successful in overcoming sexual desire. In contrast, Qoheleth does not think that we can do anything to change our fortune, because he sees that the righteous and the wicked will come to the same end, that is to die. Therefore he suggests we should make use of our time in this world when we still have opportunities to do so, because we do not know what will come after.

Qoheleth does not talk about life after death. He concentrates more on life in the present until death. Though he saw much injustice in this world, he did not lose hope in living on. Though at times he though that the aborted child and the dead were better off than the living in the sense that they do not face the suffering this world (Eccles. 4.2; 6.3), at other times he thinks the living are still better than the dead, because there is hope for the living (9.4–5). The living person can enjoy life, which Qoheleth sees as a gift of God. He comments, 'Go to it then, eat your food and enjoy it, and drink your wine with a cheerful heart; for already God has accepted what you have done. Always be dressed in white and never fail to anoint your head. Enjoy life with a woman you love all the days of your allotted span here under the sun' (Eccles. 9.7–9).

THE *ARAHANT* AND THE SAGE IN HEBREW TRADITION

In Buddhism, believers are grouped according to their ability to suppress their desire or according to the level of their wisdom. A person who is neither attached to the world nor repelled by it, has successfully suppressed lust, hatred and delusion and developed detachment, loving kindness and objectivity is called *arahant* or 'the perfect one'. An *arahant* is the one who has attained the fourth or highest stage in the realization of *Nirvana*. An *arahant* continues to live and work in the world and inspire others until, after death, he or she is born no more. Only a few Buddhists are able to become *arahant*, but there are a lot of Buddhist men who dedicate themselves to become Buddhist monks or *bhikkus* – beggars. A monk in *Theravada* tradition is expected to live a life of utmost simplicity, owning no personal property, or money, and is supposed to get his food only by begging, so that he can have more time to study the Buddhist scriptures and to teach laymen the way to reach *Nirvana*.

Toward the end of the book of Ecclesiastes, Qoheleth is called 'the wise' and he also has a role of teacher, because he taught the people knowledge (12.9,11). The Hebrew term used in this context is normally translated 'the wise men'. It has quite a broad meaning in the Old Testament. Whybray would not accept the wise men as a professional class in Israelite society because he points out that the term is never used as the title of any person or as the designation of any group of persons in any narrative in the historical books or in Isaiah or Jeremiah which refers to the court or the administrative establishment.[8] Crenshaw does not agree with Whybray. He points out that the 'existence of a body of literature which reflects specific interests at variance with Yahwistic texts in general seems to argue strongly for a professional class of sages in Israel.'[9] Ben Sira argues in Sirach 38.24–39.11, that the sages in Israel have more free time than other occupations, therefore the sages can afford to concentrate upon intellectual pursuits. A sage in Proverbs is like a true father,

so he could appeal for personal trust and sincere respect (Prov.
23.26). The Hebrew tradition of the fatherly sage and spiritual director lived on in Jesus ben Sira who was the master of a 'house of
research' (*bet midrashi*).[10] This house was always open to the untaught
to enter and lodge and receive the discipline of learning, the yoke of
training, discovering the life of dedicated work, mercy and the praise
of God (Ecclus. 51.23–30).

Both Buddhism and the wisdom tradition in Israel to which
Qoheleth belonged, place a strong emphasis on wisdom, and in both
there is a specific group of people who dedicate themselves to learn
the truth.

From what has been said, we can see that both Qoheleth and the
Buddha who lived in the different parts of the world had similar
experiences of human suffering. Both of them were seeking for the
truth, responding to similar circumstances and pursuing similar
paths, but each of them came to different conclusions. The Buddha
suggests a way to *Nirvana* by denying one's own desire and working
for one's salvation. Qohelet encourages us to enjoy life in this world
while we still have a chance and accept life as a gift from God,
because God is the one who controls everything and we cannot know
what is going to happen in the future. So, while there are obviously
differences between them, we can see that there are also significant
areas of common ground between Buddhism and Qoheleth. And in
the future possibly these areas could be used to facilitate mutual
understanding between Thai Christians and Thai Buddhists and to
provide modern scholars with another approach to the interpretation
of the book of Ecclesiastes.

NOTES

1 E. J. Dillon, *The Sceptics of the Old Testament* (London, Isbister and
Co., 1895), p. 122.

2 Roderick Whitefield and Anne Farrer, *Caves of the Thousand Buddhas:
Chinese Art from the Silk Route* (London, British Museum Publications, 1990),
pp. 9–10.

3 Dahood, *Canaanite-Phoenician Influence in Qoheleth* (Rome, Pontifico
Instituto Biblico, 1952), pp. 51–2.

4 Lynn De Silva, 'Buddhism', *A Guide to Religions* (Delhi, ISPCK,
1987), p. 136.

5 Graham Ogden, *Qoheleth* (Sheffield, JSOT Press, 1987), p. 217.

6   Christmas Humphries, *Buddhism: An Introduction and Guide*, (London, Penguin Books, 1990), p. 45.

7   Dillon, *The Sceptics*, p. 111.

8   R. N. Whybray, *The Intellectual Tradition in the Old Testament* (1974), p. 17.

9   James L. Crenshaw, *Old Testament Wisdom: An Introduction* (London, SCM Press, 1982), p. 28.

10   John Eaton, *The Contemplative Face of Old Testament Wisdom* (London, SCM Press, 1989), p. 26.

25

The Rhetorical Hermeneutic of 1 Corinthians 8 and Chinese Ancestor Worship

KHIOK-KHNG YEO

In his attempt to reverse the missionary condemnation of ancestor worship as idolatrous, Yeo rereads the Corinthian passage with its special attention to rhetorical strategies. Thus he engages in what he calls the twin task of hermeneutics – to prevent cultural isolation and to help resurrect the power of Paul's rhetoric and theology.

This essay is reproduced from *Biblical Interpretation: A Journal of Contemporary Approaches* 2(3) 1994, pp. 294–311.

K. K. Yeo is a Malaysian, currently on the staff of the Alliance Bible Seminary in Hong Kong. He is one of the editors of *Jian Dao: A Journal of Bible and Theology* and is presently working on a book on Chinese biblical hermeneutics.

Christian missionaries have used 1 Corinthians 8 to deal with the issue of ancestor worship in Chinese church history. Missionaries such as William Martin, Young Allen, and Timothy Richard took a compromising and tolerant position – a minority position. Most missionaries, both Protestants and Roman Catholics,[1] prohibited the ritualistic practice of ancestor worship on the grounds that ancestor worship is rooted in filial pietism, a religious exercise in which the Chinese are unintentionally offering food to idol-demons instead of to their ancestors. Since worship is to be rendered to God alone, for 'God is One' (1 Cor. 8.6), can one say that ancestral worship is idolatry? How are we going to suggest alternative responses from Paul's rhetoric and theology in 1 Corinthians 8? How are we going to imitate Paul rhetorically?

Because of the significance of ancestor worship in Chinese culture and the lack of Christian response to this issue,[2] this paper seeks to respond from a rhetorical-hermeneutical perspective. Thus, the purpose of this paper is twofold: first, it seeks to observe how Paul interacts with the Corinthians rhetorically over the issue of idol meat;[3] second, the paper attempts to transmit the hermeneutical implications of Paul's rhetoric for a new audience – the Chinese pietists who are steeped in the belief in and practice of ancestor worship.

PAUL'S RHETORICAL INTERACTION WITH THE CORINTHIANS

A rhetorical study of 1 Corinthians 8 would begin with the reconstruction of the rhetorical situation.[4] The three interlinking issues that are relevant to the rhetorical analysis of this pericope are: (1) the social environment which gives rise to the dissensions and their theologies; (2) the occasion for eating idol meat (temples, marketplace, homes or social clubs); (3) the audience hypotheses and their identities: the knowledgeable 'gnostics' and the 'weak conscience' ones. Here I will focus on the identities of the 'strong' and the 'weak'. The 'strong' are the proto-gnostics who are influenced by the Hellenistic Jewish thought prominent in the Wisdom tradition and the writings of Philo.[5] These proto-gnostics hold that knowledge is divinely given by God or by his consort Sophia to make one wise, righteous or perfect.[6] These gnostics believe they are undefileable by the idols because of the knowledge they have (8.1) and their belief that 'an idol is nothing in the world' (8.4b). The weak, however, abstain from eating the idol meat because: (a) they believe that idols are real; (b) their past association with idols convinces them that idols are real and that to eat idol food now is to relapse into the previous guilty experience. The gnostics want to demonstrate their divine knowledge, their power and spirituality. The weak refuse to eat the idol food because their experience informs them that eating idol food will defile their bodies and thus betray Christ. For Paul, the questions arising out of this conflict of *stasis* concern knowledge (theology) and love (ethics). As we will see, the best approach for Paul is not to judge, or to praise or blame one party, but to 'talk it over' with them.

Rhetorical Disposition of 1 Corinthians 8

The genre of 1 Corinthians 8 is deliberative and has the following rhetorical structure: (a) the *exordium* of 8.1a in which Paul secures the attention of his audience and hints at the desired goal of his rhetoric; (b) Paul states clearly the desired goal of the discourse by which he desires to persuade/dissuade in the *propositio* (or thesis) of 8.1b: 'Knowledge puffs up, but love builds up'; (c) In the proof (or *confirmatio*) of 8.2–10, Paul advances his argumentation regarding what is honorable, edifying, and right as he, the rhetor, speaks for the many voices of the congregation; (d) In the epilogue (or *peroration* or *conclusio*) of 8.11–13, Paul restates with all possible force factors that are alluded to in the *exordium* and factors that are adduced or developed in the proof for the purpose of urging the audience into the right course of understanding and action. The response of Paul in verses 10–13 reveals his view that knowledge without love is destructive to the weaker brothers and disastrous to the salvific work of Christ. Verse 13 is an exhortation by personal example to the gnostics (i.e., the knowers in the congregation), who have no other choice but to practise their knowledge with love for their brothers/sisters.

Rhetorical Techniques Used in Argumentation

Vv. 1–6: 1 Cor. 8.1–3 reminds the audience of chapters 1–4, of the contrast between the knowers and Christ. In the light of the distinction between 'spiritual' ($\pi\nu\varepsilon\upsilon\mu\alpha\tau\iota\kappa\acute{o}\varsigma$ and 'unspiritual' ($\psi\upsilon\chi\iota\kappa\acute{o}\varsigma$) in 1 Corinthians 2, the former claim to have a gnosis that the latter do not possess. That is, $\pi\acute{\alpha}\nu\tau\varepsilon\varsigma\ \gamma\nu\omega\sigma\iota\nu\ \acute{\varepsilon}\chi o\mu\varepsilon\nu$ ('we all have knowledge') is used by the gnostics to claim knowledge for themselves exclusively. In v. 7 Paul clarifies that $o\dot{\upsilon}\kappa\ \pi\alpha\sigma\iota\nu$ ('not all') have the knowledge the gnostic congregation claims to have. The Corinthian gnostics claim that 'we know that we all have knowledge'. But Paul quotes them and considers himself as one of the 'we' in $o\ddot{\iota}\delta\alpha\mu\varepsilon\nu$ ('we know') used by the Corinthians. The 'we' Paul uses is inclusive of himself and the weak in the community.

By partially quoting the Corinthians' slogan in the first five verses, Paul has gained strong footage in his persuasion. It is a way of gaining attention from the audience also, letting them know their argument has some validity. But Paul does not just quote, he also clarifies. In

8.1b for example, he states his position: ἡ γνῶσις φυσιοι, ἡ δε ἀγάπη οἰκοδομει ('knowledge puffs up, but love builds up'). Note that γνῶσις and ἀγάπη are not exclusive of each other, but this antithetical parallelism indicates a contrast in the fundamental understanding between Paul and the Corinthian gnostics. The contrast between φυσιοω ('puff up') and οἰκοδομέω ('build up') is significant. φυσιοι ('it puffs up') is a kind of inflating, boasting with the purpose of putting down or hurting, 'against one another' (as indicated in 1 Cor. 4.6, κατα του ἑτέρου. This thesis (8.1b) pinpoints the heart of the matter: puffing up in knowledge or building up with love.

'Love' is the positive quality which describes one's inclusive and mutual relationship with God and with other people through the death of Christ. Love therefore is a willed relationship which demands that one be considerate for another's benefit without any boasting, inflating, or destructive motive.[7] Paul persuades by attempting to alter (in 8.2–3) the static cognitive argument of the gnostics into a dynamic affectional relationship, from knowledge of God to being known by God. Paul gives the gnostics' view a correction: 'knowing' in the sense of self-edification means that one does not really know; but if one is known by God as God elects and redeems, one really knows.

In v. 5a, Paul paraphrases (he does not quote) the argument of the Corinthian gnostics and smoothly extends it with a hymn in v. 6. The Oneness-Lord-Creator God is affirmed by both the audience and the rhetor. But the cosmological and redemptive motifs of the person Jesus Christ appear in the hymn in a subtle way. An initial look at the creed in v. 6 suggests the idea that it merely reinforces the gnostics' argument. It is in fact purposely used to set up the Pauline argument of creation *and redemption*; Paul's argument is 'God created all, he is one; but note Christ redeems all. Therefore do not be a stumbling block!'

V. 7: In v. 1 the gnostics assert that they have γνῶσις. Here Paul says οὐκ ἐν πασιν ἡ γνῶσις ('not all have the knowledge'). Vv. 1 and 7 sound contradictory. But rhetorically they are not: in v. 1 Paul accepts the gnostics' claim of knowledge, whereas in v. 7 he explains to them that not all have the knowledge they claim.

Vv. 8–9: In the light of the reconstruction of the gnostics' theology of knowledge and monotheism, I surmise that the gnostics' edification campaign for the weak is probably a strategy to persuade the weak to eat idol food so that they might overcome their weak conscience. In that sense, βρῶμα ἡμᾶς παραστήσει τῷ θεῷ ('food will bring us to God'). However, Paul reverses their argument by adding οὐ before the παραστήσει. Paul has shown already the negative effect of idol food on the weak in 7b. Now in 8b he elucidates his reasoning on the effect of βρῶμα to the gnostics: οὔτε ἐαν μὴ φάγωμεν ὑστερουμεθα, οὔτε ἐαν φάγωμεν περισσευομεν ('we are no worse off if we do not eat, and no better off if we do').

The final self-justification by the gnostics for their course of action is seen in the word ἐξουσία they use in v. 9. For the gnostics, knowledge means the right to act in freedom, because freedom is self-realization in the realm of the divine (monotheism). For Paul, however, love is the giving up freely of one's right for the sake of the other because of the creative and redemptive works of God and Christ (monotheism).

Vv. 10–13: The key word of the gnostic argument is ἐξουσία ('authority/right'), but Paul formulates the result of their ἐξουσια: ἐξουσία ('right') without ἀγαπη ('love') equals πρόσκομμα ('a stumbling-block'). To convince them fully of his logos (argument), Paul is going to use the following rhetorical devices:

(a) A rhetorical question,[8] which includes a pedagogical dialogue in v. 10, with the change from a plural to a singular 'you', σε.[9] Paul also seems to be turning to an imaginary interlocutor.[10] The rhetorical technique is probably not a diatribe. In any case, the function of the rhetorical question is twofold: it recapitulates the issue discussed above; and it acts as *proserotonta*, i.e., it puts questions as to the rhetorician's strongest point and the opponent's weakest point.[11] According to hellenistic rhetorical tradition, the use of an interlocutor in a rhetorical question depicts and exposes the 'moral contradiction'[12] of the opponents, in this case, the gnostics. This persuasion is reinforced by the fictional interlocutor, who lends a degree of detachment from theoretical prejudices, thus adding an objective judgment to the rhetor's argument. The pedagogical use of the question in vv. 10–11 evokes irony and forces the audience to accept the rhetor's persuasion; thus indicating the pastoral sensitivity of Paul as a missionary.

(b) A serious didactic tone follows the rhetorical question. The answer to the rhetorical question is clear: a brother with a weak conscience will not be built up. So Paul draws the conclusion from their action in v. 11. The conclusion entails, however, a reluctant respect for their behaviour: the knowledge of the gnostic is destructive!

(c) The *conduplicatio* of their action, its purpose being to amplify or appeal to action,[13] is given in v. 12, which shows beyond a shadow of doubt that their knowledge alone is not enough; it can end up as sin against Christ, and that is not love. If Christ died for the brethren out of love, how can they sin against their brethren? That is the biggest mistake one can make in having knowledge.

(d) While the audience ponders the right course of action (though by now they are convinced by Paul's argument), the rhetorician exemplifies personally what he would surely do (in v. 13). The personal example Paul gives in v. 13 is more than a guide to the Corinthians; it is a forceful way of saying '*μιμηταί μου γίνεσθε καθὼς κἀγὼ Χριστοῦ*' (11.1: 'Imitate me as I am imitating Christ'). Implied in v. 13 is the right to eat; but the primary concern is that one's action will result in the 'eternal trapping'[14] (*σκανδαλίζει* of others, the direct opposite of one's intention. The radical nature of the Gospel – love – is manifested in Paul's response. Love cannot be merely stated; it must be demonstrated, demonstrated in the rhetoric of Paul and in his exemplary conduct (in the last verse).

In short, Paul seems to agree with the factual knowledge of the gnostics about monotheism (cf. 10.26); but he cares for the conscience, the instinctual knowledge of the weak. He counters arrogance with love, clarifies partial knowledge with conviction, and turns abstract theory into a real-life issue of caring for the weaker members of the community. And that is a rhetoric of knowledge practised in love.

Pauline Rhetoric in 1 Corinthians 8 as a Whole

Paul's rhetorical style is dialogical. It functions well in a polemical situation such as that in Corinth. Meeks rightly draws upon the insight of Bakhtin to argue that Paul's rhetoric is not dialectical but 'polyphonic'.[15]

First, Paul identifies with the most dominant and articulate voice of the Corinthian community, which is the 'we' voice in 8.1 and 4. After asserting and granting the validity of their claim to possess knowledge in 8.1–4, Paul then relativizes their assumed superiority in 8.7, 8 and 9. Also, by using 'we' in the first four verses, Paul is certainly including the 'weak' who are left out; this 'we' is used therefore to create a community discourse among the Corinthians; the weak in conscience are probably weak in rhetoric. This community discourse is one of the Paul's intentions as we hear the voice of the weak in vv. 7–9, and 11 with the help of Paul, their spokesperson. Pauline rhetoric therefore fosters a more inclusive community.

This community discourse is intentional in the Pauline rhetoric in 1 Corinthians 8. Paul's rhetoric of knowledge and love, in short, creates a rhetorical process whereby all parties can talk and listen to one another for the sake of edification. The result of such community discourse is that the weak are taught by Paul to be eloquent and the gnostics are taught to edify others. The way they can all grow up is to listen to each other's voices.

IMPLICATIONS OF PAUL'S RHETORIC FOR THE CHINESE CONTEXT

A Cross-cultural Hermeneutic: An Interpathic Understanding

Has Pauline rhetorical interaction with the Corinthians concerning idol food in 1 Corinthians 8 any affinity with the practice of ancestor worship in Chinese culture? If there is any relevance and relation, it is in the *hermeneutical implications* of the rhetorical analysis of 1 Corinthians 8 for ancestor worship. The task of hermeneutics is to prevent cultural isolation and to help resurrect the power of Paul's rhetoric and theology. Thus, 1 Corinthians 8 can provide us with insights and paradigms for how to interact with the Chinese Christians who are sincere filial pietists.

Before addressing ancestor worship hermeneutically at both the contextual and indigenous levels, there is a prior task which serves as a bracket between exegesis and hermeneutics. This task concerns the interpathic nature of cross-cultural understanding of a particular issue. The approach of 'interpathy',

> is an intentional cognitive envisioning and affective experiencing of another's thoughts and feelings, even though the thoughts rise from another process of knowing, the values grow from another frame of moral

reasoning, and the feelings spring from another basis of assumptions. In interpathic caring, the process of 'feeling with' and 'thinking with' another requires that one enter the other's world of assumptions, beliefs, and values and temporarily take them as one's own.[16]

Our interpathic exercise will focus on the values the filial pietists ascribe to ancestor worship.

Ancestor Worship and Hsiao: Cosmic and Spiritual value

Ancestor worship is rooted in the ethics and spirituality of '*hsiao*' ('filial piety'). The word '*hsiao*' is made up of two radicals: an old person and a child, perhaps denoting the responsibility of a child in bearing or supporting the old person. Why is this responsibility of the child conceived by the Chinese to be both spiritual and ethical?

Hsiao Ching ('The Classics of Filial Piety') says that 'filial piety is the first principle of heaven, the ultimate standard of earth, the norm of conduct for the people. The people ought to follow the pattern of heaven and earth, which leads them by the rightness of the heavens and the benefits of the earth to harmonize all under heaven' (chap. 7). Here the dialectic between cosmology and anthropology, between metaphysics and ethics, between universe and family, are conceived and symbolized in Chinese thinking. In other words, this dialectical thinking is a typical Chinese or Confucian worldview, which I will name the value of *Tao Te* ('the Way and the Moral'). *Tao* is the relationship with the cosmos, *Te* is the relationship with humanity.[17] The *Tao* denotes the actualization of the self in harmony with the cosmic and spiritual realm; the *Te* denotes the actualization of the self in wholeness with the social and ethical realm. Filial piety encompasses these two notions together. In other words, filial pietists seek selfhood and cosmic harmony, and hence the value of *Tao Te*. Since the virtue of filial piety is central and well-developed in Confucius' thought, I will locate his metaphysical and ethical values of filial piety as concretely as possible, most notably in his understanding of the 'transcendence/immanence' *T'ien* (Heaven).

The book Confucius (551–479 BCE loved, *The Book of Odes*, says: '*T'ien* gave birth to the multitude of people; where there is a thing, there is a principle; that is why people hold to rightness and like this natural, beautiful virtue' (*Ta-ya*, III: 3, 6; 505 and 541). This religio-philosophical understanding of human life assumes that all humans come from *T'ien* the Creator; and that morality is derived from *T'ien*. A similar concept of this 'transcendence/immanence' *T'ien* is expressed in the *Analects*. This concept is best summed up by a Confucian scholar, Donald L. Alexander, who argues that Confucius' religious-metaphysical understanding of ultimate reality is couched in the bi-polar conception of *T'ien*; and out of that conception comes Confucian metaphysics and ethics. The *Tao* of *T'ien* ('the heavenly principle/way') is the way of the Heaven which not only gives birth to people but continues to regenerate and sustain them. The transcendence is best known in the immanence. Furthermore, Confucius seeks to popularize and democratize that way of Heaven to all people so that all can cultivate selfhood and attain the wholeness of life.[18]

Confucianism emphasizes filial piety as one of the central teachings in the more immanent realm while seemingly neglecting those aspects in the transcendent realm. In philosophical understanding, the immanent aspect is seen as the expression of the transcendent aspect. Therefore, filial piety is regarded not merely as human responsibility, but also as a spiritual or heavenly-ordained way of life.

When Confucius is asked what is the greatest virtue, he replies: 'Filial piety is the first principle of heaven, the ultimate standard of earth, the norm of conduct for the people. The people ought to follow the pattern of heaven and earth, which leads them by the rightness of the heavens and the benefits of the earth to harmonize all under heaven' (*Hsiao Ching*, 7). This virtue is promoted by Confucius as a means to restore harmony in the midst of the political disintegration, social unrest, intellectual anarchy, and moral disorder of his age. Confucius' ingenuity here is to portray to the people the whole vision of life; that is, familial values, social values, and other immanence values are actually transcendental values. This vision is summed up in *Hsiao Ching*, 9 in a hierarchical mode:

> Human beings excel all other beings in heaven and earth, and of all human actions, none is greater than filial piety. In the practice of filial piety, no aspect is greater than paying due respect to one's parent, and in paying respect to one's parent, none is greater than venerating him as a mediator of God *T'ien*.

The *Hsiao Ching* says that 'The relation and duties between parent and child thus belong to the Heaven-conferred nature' (*Hsiao Ching*, 9). The virtue of filial piety, which underlies the practice of ancestor worship, is therefore rooted in the cosmic and spiritual value systems of Confucius.

Social values: Personhood and Selfhood

Not only is filial piety a virtue that is endowed by Heaven, *Hsiao Ching* continues, 'The son derives his life from his parents, and no greater gift could possibly be transmitted ... Hence, the one who does not love his parents, but loves other people, is called a rebel against virtue; and he who does not revere his parents, but reveres other people, is called a rebel against propriety' (*Hsiao Ching*, 9). This proverbial saying expounds the social values of ancestor worship which are delineated in the following intricately interrelated tenets: (a) Personhood in individuation as practised in *jen* and *li*;[19] and (b) Selfhood actualization as practised in the dynamic dyadic social relations.

Personhood in Jen and Li

The importance of ancestor worship for the filial pietists is demonstrated in the Confucian notion of selfhood and personhood cultivation. The whole of Confucius' philosophy can be summed up succinctly in his words, 'to demonstrate illustrious virtue, renovate the people, and rest in the highest excellence.'[20] Confucius regards filial piety as the root of all virtues. When Tseng Tsu asked Confucius 'Is filial piety the highest of all the virtues possessed by a great sage?' Confucius replies: 'There is nothing so great in the world as a human being, and there is nothing so great in a man as filial piety' (*Hsiao Ching*, 1). But Confucius also regards *jen* as the fountain-head of all virtues. Thus, he advocates that all should actualize the mandate of *T'ien* by committing ourselves to *jen*[21] because what makes human beings human is *jen*.[22] In other words, the will of God for any community is to practise a lifestyle of love.

Filial piety then is the first concrete step in actualizing *jen* in a person. In this respect, *Hsiao Ching* notes that 'The effect of education upon the minds of the people was well-known to the good emperors of old. They made all people love others by loving their parents first.' (7) Mencius extends the practice of *jen* even further: 'The superior man should love his parents and be lovingly disposed to people in general; and he should also be kind to all living creatures' (Mencius 7.45).

Filial piety is the root of all virtue together with *jen*, and filial piety is related to *li* (propriety) also. Confucius observes that 'Parents, when alive, should be served according to *li* (propriety); when dead, they should be buried according to *li* (propriety); and they should be sacrificed according to *li* (propriety)' (*Analects* 2.5).

How is the cultivation of personhood related to *jen* and *li*? It is possible that one loves another merely for the sake of ritual; and this is what Confucius warns against: 'Merely to feed one's parents well ... even dogs and horses are fed' (*Analects* 2.7). That means that merely to fulfil the obligations of *li* is superficial what is essential is a higher principle, and that is *jen*. So *li* without *jen* can degenerate into formalism or insensitivity (cf. *Analects* 3.3). Therefore, *li* must be grounded in *jen*.[23]

Selfhood in Dyadic Social Relations

Confucius includes in his idea of liberal education or wide culture not only book-learning but also ritual and cultural practice which reinforce the interaction of the self with the larger community (from self to home to society to nation to the world). That constant reinforcement serves as a process of self-cultivation if it is practised in a spirit of loyalty, filiality, brotherhood, discipleship and so forth (*Analects* 1). The parent-child relationship is the basic one in selfculti-vation. Hsieh Yu-Wei rightly observes that

> With genuine and comprehensive love toward one's own parents, in its developing process, one may naturally learn to be benevolent to all living creatures, affectionate toward humankind as a whole, loyal to one's country and to the duties of a free citizen, faithful in keeping obligations, righteous in action, peaceful in behaviour, and just in all dealings.[24]

Hsiao Ching declares that 'It is filial piety which forms the root of all virtues, and with it all enlightening studies come into existence'(1).

Family Values: Preservation and Support

Ancestor worship also seeks to promote the continuity of lineage and family in terms of identity. Thus the responsibility of the children and grandchildren, particularly the eldest son and the grandson, is to perform ritual services to the ancestor. Ancestor worship is 'a cult that contributed substantially to the integration and perpetuation of the family as a basic unit of Chinese society.'[25]

The social functions of ancestor worship are many. Among them are the following: (1) It provides an occasion for the reunion of the family; thus, the ancestral shrine (*she*) is the meeting place of the family; (2) It provides economical, social and psychological support to bereaved families.[26] Ahern, for example, emphasizes the economic motivation for ancestor worship from her studies in Taiwan.[27] The ancestor's property provides the economic stability for the descendant, but also shows the prosperity of the ancestor; (3) Socially, the cult of ancestor worship is therapeutic in coping with 'the emotionally shattering and socially disintegrating event of the death . . .'[28] The meal with the dead is conceived as a common meal both with the dead and the living. Meyer Fortes says that 'Food dependence is from the moment of birth the vital bond that unites child to parent. To share a meal is, as is well-known, an expression of amity and trust. . .'[29] The form, time, and place of meals are fixed, as for example in ancestor festivals;[30] therefore a meal ritual shows not only mutual dependence but also the trust and affection of living and dead.

Conflictual Values of Ancestor Worship

So far, the approach through interpathic research has made use mostly of the philosophical and some of the religious traditions. The mythological sources for ancestor worship, coupled with the religious practice of the little tradition, often portray different values that contradict (thus are in conflict with) the idealized values of the great tradition.[31] The fear and myth of ancestor worship are real and substantial in the value systems of the filial pietists. To categorize more concretely what the fear and myth are, one needs to understand (a) the Chinese belief in spirit/god, ghost, and ancestor; and (b) the practice of geomancy (*fung shui*).

Many filial pietists do look for supernatural power in the deceased parents or ancestors for blessing, guidance, protection from evil, or forgiveness from wrongs. So in popular culture or the little tradition there is another philosophical understanding of ancestor worship which is over-clouded with superstitious baggage and bondage.

The superstition concerning the ancestor becoming a haunting ghost originated from a very ancient Chinese belief that there are three categories of spiritual being: ghosts (*kui*, or evil spirits), gods (*cieng-sin*), and ancestors (*kong-ma* or *co-kong*). One has a different attitude towards each of them: 'One propitiates (*ce*) *kui*, but honors (*hok-sai, kieng-hong*, or *pai*) gods'[32] and ancestors. Gods, ancestors, and *kui* are all thought of by the masses as former human beings. Living humans inhabit the *yang* world, the others the *yin* world or *im-kan* ('prisons of the earth'). The Chinese believe that a human being becomes a person when the spirit (*hun*, that comes from heaven) and the soul (*p'o*, that comes from the earth) enter the body. The spirit and the soul will return to heaven and the earth respectively while the body decays upon a person's death. But the spirits and the souls have powers beyond those of humans, and they are mediators between human beings and supernatural beings.

Many Chinese worship their ancestors for their supernatural power, often for selfish reasons. Moreover, they worship out of fear because they believe that when the souls and the spirits return to their descendants' homes, they need to be well taken care of through sacrifice and divinations. Otherwise they become ghosts or *kui* (literally 'returning') who will haunt people.[33] Good ghosts called 'spirits' will bring blessing and wisdom to their descendants; evil ghosts called *kui* will bring bad luck, disaster and torments. An infant that dies prematurely is believed to be a reincarnation of or possessed by the evil spirit.[34] Thus, dying infants are never sacrificed to and seldom remembered.

One of the ways to deal with the fear of the curse of barrenness from past ancestors is through geomancy. The technique is to relocate the grave to a better site involving mediation by shamans between the living and the dead, or employing shamans and intermediaries to manipulate fate or circumstances as much as possible. De Groot seems to overemphasize that in a patriarchal society of authority and respect, absolute obedience and worship of the dead 'signifies that family ties are by no means broken by death, and that the dead continue to exercise their authority and to afford their protection.'[35]

A PAULINE RESPONSE

How one ought to respond to such practices in the light of Christian faith continues to create an impasse in missiological practice to this day. To advise the Chinese not to offer food and not to eat the food in ancestor worship may be implicitly advising them not to love their parents, not to practise love, and ultimately not to be Chinese. Yet the fear and myth of this practice carries with it a conflictual side. In this section I will attempt to construct a Pauline response by using the rhetorical insights of Paul in 1 Corinthians 8.

First, in 1 Corinthians 8 Paul never resorts to absolute prohibitions concerning idol meat eating. To begin from the prohibition would contradict the 'in-Christ' gospel he so preached. The gospel of Christ is not a right/wrong ethical system. Therefore for the missionary to preach the gospel with prohibitions – however wrong the audience's practice is – contradicts Paul's rhetoric and the very nature of the gospel he proclaimed. Paul rarely corrects sub-Christian or non-Christian behavior by prohibition.[36] To do so would 'turn ethical response into legal obligation.'[37] In short, Paul's strategy is to deal with the more basic issue of the nature of the gospel, since our existence is qualified always by the fact that Christ the Sophia is the Creator and Redeemer of us all (8. 6). None is superior or better or more righteous than the other even if we are 'in-Christ'.

Second, Paul would affirm that prohibition alone, unless being informed by knowledge and practised in love, is unwise.[38] I will deal with the 'practised in love' clause later. Here I want to focus on the 'informed by knowledge' clause. Though Paul does not totally accept the viewpoint of the Corinthians, he does (a) begin his argument from their slogans or points of view, and (b) affirm some of their beliefs. The strategy of point (a) draws the audience on to common ground with the responder, as we have discussed above. The strategy of point (b) allows them to feel accepted. Both strategies keep them open for dynamic community discourse. But both strategies required him to be knowledgeable of the audience's belief and arguments.

In order to formulate a responsible attitude to the Chinese ancestor worship issue, one needs an interpathic understanding of the issue and the values of the practice. This is a necessary step towards being 'informed by knowledge' as one suggests a viable response. In other words, to advise the Chinese not to practise ancestor worship or not to offer food to ancestors is implicitly advising them not to be Chinese, not to love their parents, not to practise love, etc.

Third, Paul is sensitive to the needs of the audience as he interacts with them for example, the need of the strong to be less overbearing, and the need of the weak to be more eloquent. The needs of the Chinese pietists are likewise real and varied. This is where the gospel of Christ can grant them hope, freedom, and salvation. We observe that most filial pietists do look for supernatural power in deceased parents or ancestors, for blessing, guidance, protection from evil, or forgiveness of wrongs. Much is done out of fear and bondage. Many Chinese filial pietists are living in fear of the supernatural power of the ancestors, who might punish them if they either do not worship or worship inappropriately. Others worship with manipulative motives. Here, the gospel of the Lord summarized in 8. 6 can be indeed Good News to the fearful filial pietists: 'there is one God, the Father, from whom are *all things* and for whom we exist, and one Lord, Jesus Christ, *through whom* are all things and through whom we exist.'

Fourth, however one interacts with the pietists concerning ancestor worship, one needs to learn from Paul, whose rhetoric is not only informed by knowledge but also 'practised with love'. Paul's rhetorical techniques and strategies are shaped and influenced by the classical rhetoric of his day; even more, his rhetoric is guided and controlled by the gospel of love. Paul's rhetoric in 1 Corinthians 8 could have been strictly judicial and could have provided absolute imperatives about what the Corinthian Christians are supposed to do regarding the eating of idol meat. Instead, we see a rhetor with pastoral sensitivity to both the strong and the weak for mutual and social edification. Paul's rhetorical strategy is wisdom practised with *jen*, demonstrating the gospel he believes in.

I believe that the gospel of Christ is the gospel of love which cares for one's relationship with God in Christ as expressed in one's relationship with one's neighbours. In other words, seeking to draw the Chinese closer in relationship to the Christian God by issuing imperatives is to begin at the wrong point. Such presentation of imperatives as divinely ordained, without respect for an individual's needs and context, is not an act of love. Also, ancestor worship is a Chinese 'gospel of love' for the ancestors by showing respect and love for them. One has no right to criticize this practice just because it is shaped by a different culture. In fact, understanding ancestor worship from the perspectives of its cosmic, spiritual, social, and family values, one cannot but affirm and encourage its practice. Whatever view one holds concerning ancestor worship, I am convinced that the next point speaks to the heart of Paul's response.

Fifth, the Pauline response establishes a deliberative, community discourse and does not attempt to give an easy answer of 'yes' or 'no'. Such a response will create an ongoing process of interaction as all parties commit themselves to that rhetorical event. The Pauline response is more concerned with the process than with the answer. This is not to say that Paul's theology has no content. It only means that to absolutize Paul's theology in 1 Corinthians 8 (especially without observing the rhetorical context) is inadequate. It also means that without a rhetorical understanding of his argument, one will misappropriate his theology. My attempt to create a discoursed community in this paper is seen in the dialogical rhetoric I analyze in 1 Corinthians 8 (part one) and in the way I need to listen to the Chinese pietists (hence interpathic understanding in part two) before I give a response. The use of rhetorical criticism of 1 Corinthians 8 reveals that both the gnostics and the 'weak' are being nurtured in love as they participate in the community discourse.

A rhetorical analysis of 1 Corinthians 8 is necessary and helpful because it helps to overcome the traditional focus on the content of Paul's theology alone. This rhetorical analysis has focused on and appreciates the way Paul approaches the issue within the Corinthian historical context, and has viewed Paul's theology or ethics in light of and in relation to his rhetoric. My hope is that this provides the means to construct an indigenous theology that speaks beyond the original historical context. What Paul explicitly says in 1 Corinthians 8 and 10 is not *necessarily* universal, absolute, and applicable to all in all situations. But with a broader understanding of rhetorical-hermeneutical study, which takes the twentieth-century audience and situation seriously, I believe the Bible can be appropriated and addressed to new audiences and situations. Maybe it is in this type of combined exegesis-hermeneutic that we can say that the Bible is eternal and life-changing.

The analysis of 1 Corinthians 8 reveals that Paul's theology is expressed in the rhetoric of knowledge and love. Paul's theology and rhetoric suggest to the global community that all traditions can participate in the interpretive process whereby the uniqueness of each is differentiated, affirmed, and esteemed, while the commonalities of all are shared, identified, and celebrated. The purpose of Pauline rhetoric is to encourage the confluence of traditions to the edification of humanity and to the glory of God.

NOTES

1   Protestant missionaries were represented, for example, by those of the China Inland Mission between 1807 and 1860.

Other Protestant missionaries holding the same position prior to 1860 include Walter Henry Medurst and John L. Nevius, and even present-day mainline Protestant churches in Asia take this line. Cf. Ro Bong-rin (ed.), *Consultation on Christian Response to Ancestor Practices, Christian Alternative to Ancestor Practices* (Taichung, Taiwan, Asia Theological Association, 1985), pp. 45–80; W. A. P. Martin, 'The Worship of Ancestors – a Plea for Tolerance', *Records of the General Conference of the Protestant Missionaries of China Held at Shanghai* (1890), pp. 619–31; idem, 'How Shall We Deal with the Worship of Ancestors?' *Chinese Recorder* 33 (1902), pp. 117–19; and idem, 'The Worship of Confucius: Is it Idolatry?' *Chinese Recorder* 34 (1904), pp. 92–93.

The Jesuits represented by Matteo Ricci held the compromising position towards ancestor worship at the end of the sixteenth century. But the seventeenth century Dominicans and Franciscans held the opposing view which (coupled with the issue of the translation of 'GOD') eventually led to the proscription of their missionary work (in 1720). For more on the various responses to ancestor worship, see Henry N. Smith, 'A Typology of Christian Responses to Chinese Ancestor Worship', *Journal of Ecumenical Studies* 26 (1989), pp. 628–47.

2   Most of the Christian scholarly material is mentioned in note 1.

3   The first part of the discussion is a summary of a larger section in my Ph.D. Disseration, see 'Rhetorical Interaction in 1 Corinthians 8 and 10: Potential Implications for a Chinese, Cross-cultural Hermeneutic', Ph.D. dissertation (Evanston, Northwestern University, 1992), pp. 282–332.

4   ibid., pp. 117–241.

5   ibid., pp. 189–241.

6   cf. Wisd. 7.17, 10.10; Philo, *Quod Deus* 92; Op. 70–71.

7   cf. Rom. 13.10, 14.15; 1 Cor. 14.1; Gal. 5.13; Phil. 2.1–3.

8   cf. Heinrich Lausberg, *Handbuch der literarischen Rhetorik: Eine Grundlegung der Literaturwissenschaft*, 2nd edn, 2 vols (Munich, Max Heuber, 1973), 1.379–84.

9   B, F, G, and latt lack δέ. But it is more likely for the copyist to omit rather than insert it. So B. M. Metzger, *A Textual Commentary on the Greek New Testament* (London/New York, United Bible Societies, 1971), p. 557.

10   For interlocutor in Rhetoric, see Chaïm Perelman, *The New Rhetoric and the Humanities: Essays on Rhetoric and its Applications* (Dordrecht, Holland; Boston, D. Reidel Publishing Co., 1979), pp. 30–40; idem, *The Realm of Rhetoric* (Notre Dame University Press, 1982), pp. 15–16.

11   As discussed by Aristotle, *Rhetoric* 3.18.

12   cf. Stanley K. Stower, *The Diatribe and Paul's Letter to the Romans*, SBLDS 57, (Chico, Scholars Press, 1981), p. 110.

13   cf. *Rhetorica Ad Herennium*, 4.28.38.

14   See G. Stählin, 'Σκάνδαλον, σκανδαλίζω', *Theological Dictionary of*

Voices from the Margin

the New Testament, vol. 7 (1971), pp. 339–343; Liddell and Scott, *Greek-English Lexicon*, s.v. 'σκάνδαλον'.

15 Wayne A. Meeks, 'The Polyphonic Ethics of the Apostle Paul', *Annual of the Society of Christian Ethics* [Knoxville] (1988), p. 18.

16 David W. Augsburger, *Pastoral Counseling Across Cultures* (Philadelphia, Westminster Press, 1986), p. 29.

17 cf. Chae-Woon Ng, 'Filial Piety in Confucian Thought', *North-East Asia Journal of Theology* 18 (1982), p. 40.

18 Sung-Hae Kim, 'Silent Heaven Giving Birth to the Multitude of People', *Ching Feng* 31 (4, 1988), pp. 195–6.

19 On the differences between *jen* and *li*, see Ng, 'Filial Piety', pp. 37–8.

20 'The Great Learning' 1.1. The naming of that way of life as philosophy, ethic or spirituality is itself an intellectual controversy. T'ang Chun-I for example explains that 'love and respect for one's parents, is not biological but is moral, being based on a sense of obligation or a debt of gratitude, and is therefore spiritual.' (Charles A. Moore, (ed.), *The Chinese Mind: Essentials of Chinese Philosophy and Culture* (Honolulu, University Press of Hawaii, 1971), p. 186).

21 Milton M. Chiu, *The Tao of Chinese Religion* (Lanham, University Press of America, 1984), pp. 191–2.

22 Translated variously as human-heartedness (E. R. Hughes), benevolence (Derk Bodde), benevolent Love (H. H. Dubs), humane, human-at-its-best, goodness (A. Waley), humanity, virtue (H. G. Creel), human-relatedness, charity, humanity (W. T. Chan), morality, etc. Cf. Fung Yu-lan, *A History of Chinese Philosophy*, tr. Derk Bodde (Princeton University Press, 1952), pp. 69–73.

23 This is what Tu Wei-ming means by 'the primacy of *jen* over *li* and the inseparability of *li* from *jen*.' See his '*Li* as Process of Humanization', *Philosophy East and West* 22 (1972), p. 188.

24 Moore, *The Chinese Mind*, p. 174.

25 C. K. Yang, *Religion in Chinese Society* (Berkeley, University of California Press, 1967), p. 29.

26 cf. Yang, *Religion*, pp. 31–8, on the social functions of ancestor worship: for the benefit and salvation of the soul, for the protection of the living from the dead, for the expression of grief, for reassembling the family group and reasserting family status.

27 Emily M. Ahern, *The Cult of the Dead in a Chinese Village* (Stanford University Press, 1973), p. 121: 'an adult man who is a direct descendant of the lineage ancestors and who has married, sired male children and handed sown property to his sons is a paradigm of the person with a right to have his tablet placed in the hall.'

28 Yang, *Religion*, p. 29.

29 Meyer Fortes, 'An Introductory Commentary', in William H. Newell, (ed.), *Ancestors* (Hague/Paris, Mouton Publishers, 1976), p. 11.

30 cf. Francis L. K. Hsu, *Under the Ancestor's Shadow: Kinship, Personality, and Social Mobility in China* (Stanford University Press, 1971), pp. 182ff.

31 The conflictual value is similar to the discrepancy or inconsistency

366

between the operative, conceived and desirable values proposed by Charles W. Morris; see his *Varieties of Human Value* (Chicago University Press, 1956), pp. 9–12.

32   Stephan Feuchtwang, 'Domestic and Communal Worship in Taiwan', in Arthur P. Wolf, (ed.), *Religion and Ritual in Chinese Society* (Stanford University Press, 1974), p. 107; similarly Hsu, *Under the Ancestor's Shadow*, pp. 144–5.

33   Milton M. Chiu, *The Tao of Chinese Religion* (Lanham, University Press of America, 1984), p. 343.

34   Therefore, dead infants are often not remembered ritually, nor buried with the coffin.

35   J. J. M. de Groot, *Religion in China* (American Lectures on the History of Religions), (New York/London, Knickerbocker Press, 1912), p. 178.

36   G. D. Fee, '*Εἰδωλόθυτα* Once Again: An Interpretation of 1 Corinthians 8–10', *Biblica* 61 (1980), p. 197.

37   ibid., p. 197.

38   ibid., p. 196.

26

The Chinese Creation Myth of Nu Kua and the Biblical Narrative in Genesis 1–11

ARCHIE C. C. LEE

Lee's essay is an example of extra-textual hermeneutics – an approach which tries to go beyond the canonical scriptures and normative texts and employs stories, fables and folk traditions such as are common to Asian people. The task here is to place them vividly alongside biblical narratives and draw out the hermeneutical implications. This article highlights the hermeneutical dilemma faced by Asian Christians as they struggle to come to terms with the imported biblical stories and the indigenous Asian stories.

This article appeared in *Biblical Interpretation: A Journal of Contemporary Approaches* 2 (3) 1994, pp. 312–24.

Archie C. C. Lee is Chairman of the Department of Religion, Chinese University of Hong Kong. He is also the Dean of Programme for Theology and Cultures in Asia. His current research interest is in cross-textual hermeneutics in an Asian context.

THE CREATION OF HUMAN BEINGS

It is said that when the heaven and the earth were separated there was no human being. It was Nu Kua who first created human beings by moulding yellow earth. The work was so taxing that she was very exhausted. So she dipped a rope into the mud and then lifted it. The mud that dripped from the rope also became human beings. Those made by moulding yellow earth were rich and noble, while those made by dripped mud were poor and low.[1]

This is one of the oldest Chinese creation myths on the origin of the human race. Through the female creator, Nu Kua, who is portrayed as a potter, Derk Bodde takes a passage in a datable book, *T'ien Wen* ('Nu Kua had a body; who formed and fashioned it?'), as an indicator of the knowledge of Nu Kua's fashioning activities among people of Chou times (c. 1776 BCE.[2]

Human beings are conceived as being made from the yellow earth, so a close link between humanity and the earth is clearly underlined. It will be noticed that the biblical narrative in Genesis 2 makes a similar point with regard to the relationship between humanity and the earth. In Genesis 2 the Hebrew word used for humanity in a collective sense is '*adam*' and that for the ground is '*adamah*', obviously a wordplay.

Though the above Chinese tale does not mention explicitly the close link between humanity and the earth, the concept of the Chinese race being born from and growing out of the yellow soil/ earth is presupposed. Strong attachment to the land in particular and to nature in general was viewed in ancient times as an essential ingredient for a full human existence. (The close link between human beings, the cosmos and nature is also clearly spelled out in the creation myth of Pan Ku.[3] Upon his death, Pan Ku's body decomposed to form the universe and the parasites from his body turned into human beings.)

In comparison with the biblical text, the Chinese narrative lacks the divine dimension. Genesis tells of God's breathing into the nostrils of Adam the breath of life. This Nu Kua text has a greater anthropocentric emphasis. In other Chinese philosophical articulations the transcendental or divine aspect of humanity is asserted more explicitly. The Book of Rites states that humanity consists of 'the benevolent virtue of Heaven and Earth, the cooperative union of *Yin* and *Yang*, the joint assembly of ghost and spirit, and the finest breath contained in the Five Elements.'[4] The 'finest breath' or *Ch'i* is the cosmic force or vital force of human life. *Ch'i* has to be in union with the body in order that human life can function in harmony, peace, and health. The synthesis of these materialistic and spiritualistic dimensions of life are much sought in Chinese religious practices, especially in Taoism.

The creation myth of Nu Kua represents not only an anthropogonic view of the origin of human beings but also a sociogonic propagation that supports the social hierarchy of a class distinction between the noble and the common people, as well as the rich and the poor. Such a myth most probably originated with the people at the top of the hierarchical social structure, who surely would have benefited from its propagation.[5]

The sociogonic concern of the myth associated with Nu Kua is further developed in another version depicting the social disorder of ancient times and the contribution of Nu Kua in combating conflict and overcoming chaos:

> Turning back to ancient times, the Four Pillars were shattered and the Nine Provinces dislocated. The sky did not cover [the earth] completely; nor did the earth uphold [all of the sky]. Fire roared with inextinguishable flames, and waters gushed forth in powerful and incessant waves. Ferocious animals devoured the good people, and birds of prey snatched away the old and weak. Thereupon, Nu Kua fused together stones of the five colours with which she patched up the azure sky. She cut off the feet of the turtle with which she set up the Four Pillars. She slaughtered the black dragon in order to save the Land of Chi. She piled up reed ashes with which to check the flooding waters.
>
> When the azure sky was patched up, the Four Pillars set up straight, the flooding waters dried up, the Land of Chi made orderly and the cunning wild animals exterminated, the good people thrived.[6]

Though the creation narratives associated with Nu Kua do not mention any cosmogonic themes, the above account of the collapse of the social structure together with a complete breakdown in the universe ushers in the concept of the role of Nu Kua as recreating the damaged universe and its social harmony as well as the cosmic order. The universe was in great chaos as the four pillars that upheld heaven were destroyed. The classical destructive and chaotic forces, unextinguishable fires, untamed waters, and wild animals that would always bring death and threat to human life on earth, were all at large on the earth. In a word, the earth was then in tremendous chaos and threatened with total destruction.

Such a situation of destruction and disorder is described in the book of Jeremiah as the opposite or reverse of creation:

> I saw the earth, and it was without form and void; the heavens and their light was gone. I saw the mountains, and they reeled; all the hills rocked to and fro. I saw, and there was no man, and the very birds had taken flight. I saw, and the farm-land was wilderness, and the towns all razed to the ground, before the LORD in his anger (Jer. 4.23–26, NEB).

The Chinese narrative, on the other hand, does not give the cause for all the destruction. However, it would be natural for a reader of *Huai Nan Tzu* ('Writings of Prince Huai Nan') to associate a piece of myth found in Chapter 4 with the description of chaos before Nu Kua recreated the universe:

A long time ago Gonggong (Kung Kung) fought with Zhuanxu (Chuan-hsu) for the throne. In his rage he knocked his head against Buzhou Mountain, breaking this pillar of the sky and causing one corner of the earth to collapse. The sky tilted towards the northwest; therefore the sun, the moon and stars moved in that direction. As the earth sank in the southeast, all the waters and muddy contents of the rivers flowed south-eastwards.[7]

This Kung Kung story of cosmic warfare, though providing an explanation for the collapse of the pillar of heaven, does not account for the devastating situation of total chaos and destruction of the earth, is the case in the Nu Kua story. Its intention is rather aetiological, explaining the origin of the meteorological and the geographical features of China. It was very unlikely that the combat between Kung Kung and Chuan-hsu provided the cause for the cosmic collapse and social disaster which Nu Kua was to deal with and to rectify in her re-creation. In *Huai Nan Tzu*, the cosmic struggle of Kung Kung and Chuan-hsu is independent of the Nu Kua story, and in the book of *Lieh-tzu*, the Nu Kua story comes before the Kung Kung story, which destroys the logical sequence and denies a connection between them.[8]

The consequence of Nu Kua's reordering of the universe is a great peace and harmony on earth enjoyed by humanity:

[The people responded to] the amenity of spring, the canicule of summer, the rotting of autumn and the indigence of winter. They slept in their pillow squares and rush mats ... At that time, they would go to rest carefree and calm, and arise with a serene unblinking gaze ... In their rustic simplicity they all enjoyed harmony ... At that time, of the wild birds and animals, insects and reptiles, there were none that did not sheathe their claws and store away their venom and poison, and none that displayed predatory and voracious dispositions.[9]

We may recall the same kind of harmony and seasonal order after the restoration in the flood story of Genesis: 'As long as the earth endures seedtime and harvest, cold and heat, summer and winter, day and night shall not cease' (8.22).

The repairing and patching up of the azure heaven, the drying up of the flood waters and the re-setting and straightening up of the four pillars of heaven are acts of re-ordering and re-creation. Unlike the biblical account of the flood (Gen 6–8), no one is held responsible for the disaster in the Chinese myth. The flood story in Genesis is characterized by the notion of moral corruption and human violence (6.11–12). God's sending of the flood was taken as a punishment aiming at the extermination of humankind and the destruction of the earth.

> And God saw that the earth was corrupt; for all flesh had corrupted its ways upon the earth. And God said to Noah, 'I have determined to make an end of all flesh, for the earth is filled with violence because of them; now I am going to destroy them along with the earth' (6.12–13).

The concern of the Chinese story is the achievement of Nu Kua in her combat with chaos. It is really a reorganization story. The description of social harmony and order in human life, as well as peacefulness in the animal world, resembles the eschalotogical vision of Isaiah, especially the change in the nature of the wild animals: 'The wolf and the lamb shall feed together, the lion shall eat straw like the ox; but the serpent – its food shall be dust!' (65. 25). Though such a shift of animal dispositions, as well as wild animals storing away their venom and poison, were not particularly attributed to Nu Kua, she did create a harmonized natural order, and was also praised for her contribution to human history.

Nu Kua was remembered as a matchmaker who instituted the marriage rite, and she was also honoured and respected by local traditions in China as a patroness of matrimony and protector of family life. Numerous Han stone reliefs which have been unearthed depict Fu Hsi, the 'Chinese Adam', and Nu Kua with human heads and serpent body. Their tails are interwined with one another. A carpenter's square is held in Fu Hsi's hand while Nu Kua has a compass. In some of the stone carvings, there is a body in between the couple. This latter feature represents their role in the procreation of human beings.

The Genesis 2 account also expresses the aetiological intention of tracing the ordination of marriage to continue the human race, with Yahweh implicitly referred to as the patron of marriage (Gen 2.18–24).[10]

Huai Nan Tzu places Nu Kua together with the highly acclaimed legendary cultural hero and mythical sovereign of ancient China (c. 2953–2838 BCE, Fu Hsi.[11] After the Han dynasty, Nu Kua was gradually connected with Fu Hsi, and she came to be presented as either his wife or sister. In the conclusion of the Nu Kua story, *Huai Nan Tzu* praises the meritorious achievement of Nu Kua together with Fu Hsi. They were glorified and honoured by being raised to heaven.

> They reached to the Nine Heavens above and touched the Yellow Clay below. Their fame was celebrated by later ages, and their glory pervaded the Ten Thousand Things. They rode the thunder chariot, using winged dragons as the inner pair and green dragons as the outer pair. Drifting aimlessly, they led the ghosts and spirits and ascended the Nine Heavens, and remained reverently silent in the presence of the Great Ancestor.[12]

The ascension of Nu Kua and Fu Hsi to heaven is a clear example of human beings being accredited with divinity of their merits. While in heaven, they continue to embody the way to true humanity and follow the unchanging course of heaven and earth. Tao is conceived of as the ultimate origin of heaven and earth as well as the mother of all creatures and the ten thousand things.

The above story of Nu Kua and Fu Hsi is narrated in the context of the author's description of ancient utopias in the book of *Huai Nan Tzu*.[13] To him, the utopia of Nu Kua and Fu Hsi is even superior to that of Huang Ti, who according to tradition, is portrayed as an exceptionally good human ruler who was in consequence honoured and transformed into the greater ancestor of the Chinese people and their culture.[14]

DIVINE-HUMAN CONTINUUM VS. COMPLETE SEPARATION

The ascension of Nu Kua to the highest heaven is an example of human beings being transformed into divinities in ancient China. According to the Greek understanding of the concept of euhemerization, gods and demigods in myths were originally actual, historical human beings. Nu Kua in *Huai Nan Tzu* was perceived as a female human ruler, who assisted Fu Hsi in governing the ancient world and who by her superb accomplishments of re-establishing cosmic harmony and social order was transformed into a goddess.

The traditions associated with Nu Kua, however, are not that straightforward, as traces and fragments incorporated into other ancient writings had her portrayed as a supernatural figure with a snake body and a human head or a divine being whose sex was not definitely specified in the earliest times.[15] In *Shuo Wen*, from the second century, she was represented as a female deity or sage woman.

'Nu Kua was a divine woman of antiquity, she was transformed into the ten thousand things.' Charles Le Blanc, in commenting on the role of Nu Kua in Chapter 6 of *Huai Nan Tzu*, sees her marvellous work in repairing the collapsed heaven as of cosmic dimensions and concludes that

> we have a double process of euhemerization taking place here. First an euhemerization process (as sinologists understand the term) whereby Nu Kua, who was originally (we may presume) a goddess, is transformed into a True Man (or True Woman), and a second process of euhemerization (as Euhemerus understands the term) whereby Nu Kua is transformed into a goddess.[16]

It is quite interesting to observe from the above description that Nu Kua is seen in Chinese tradition as both a human being who is raised to be a goddess, and a divine being becoming an empress or female ruler of the ancient times. Nu Kua was one of the human emperors in the prehistorical period. Her sex has been changed to female in Chinese historical writing since the Han dynasty. This is not an exceptional instance of a double process of euhemerization for, in the Chinese mind, there has not been a sharp distinction between divine and human. The continuum between them exists and is accepted in popular belief.

There are numerous Chinese stories and folk-tales which depict divine beings who are sent by the heavenly court to the earth to carry out missions for the heavenly council. These divine beings incarnate in human forms and take up various roles in society. They participate in human affairs or intervene in the historical process. In Taoist tradition, Lao Tzu is conceived of as pre-existent and he has descended into the world in different roles, in various generations, either to impart the Taoist teachings and to deliver Taoist books to the world, or to act as political adviser to the emperor.[17]

In addition to divine beings descending into this world, Chinese religious traditions also advocate the ascension to heaven of historical figures of great accomplishment. Popular religious beliefs have it that important sages and heroes of the people acquired divinity or immortality and ascended to heaven. Ge Hong's *Shenzian zhuan* ('Biographies of Spirit Immortals') and *Baopuzi* ('Book of the Master who Embraces Simplicity') contain stories of ascension. *Feng Shen Yen I* narrates tales of human beings canonized as gods and becoming famous celestial generals.[18] The above characteristics in Chinese religion and mythology of the divine-human relationship present a problem to Judeo-Christian tradition which maintains a sharp distinction between the divine and the human. The monotheistic assertions in the Bible, especially in the Old Testament, just do not allow any room for the breaching of the boundary between God and humanity.[19] The concept of human beings becoming God cannot be reconciled with the monotheistic God though there is a divine element or 'image' of God in human life.[20]

In Christian understanding, the mystery of God incarnating to take up human flesh in the historical figure of Jesus is not to be repeated in the historical process. Therefore, if incarnation is a once and-for-all event, the notion of human beings becoming divine is not only an impossibility but also a rebellious idea.

The Yahwistic account of creation in Genesis 2–3 intends to communicate the major theme of human existence in relation to God the creator. The two trees (Gen. 2.9), the fruits of which are forbidden to Adam and Eve, represent the two aspirations of human beings – a longing for knowledge and a quest for immortality. We are told that when the first human couple ate the fruit of the tree of knowledge, their eyes were opened and they became like God. It is admitted by God in the text: 'See, the man has become like one of us, knowing good and evil; and now, he might reach out his hand and take also from the tree of life, and eat, and live forever' (Gen. 3.22). The tree of knowledge has made human beings become like God, but the tree of life will grant them immortality or eternal life which, according to Ancient Near Eastern understanding, is reserved for the gods only. That means that the mark of divinity is immorality, while the portion of human beings is death. In the Adapa story, humanity lost the opportunity to achieve immortality. The Gilgamesh Epic of the ancient Sumerians sets itself the task of investigating this issue, and the conclusion is definitely that only the gods can live forever and the days of human beings are counted. When Gilgamesh experienced the death of his friend, he set out upon his earnest quest for everlasting life. He was constantly told by all those he met on his journey that the quest would only end in despair:

> Gilgamesh, whither are you wandering? Life, which you look for, you will never find. For when the gods created man, they let death be his share, and life withheld in their own hands. Gilgamesh, fill your belly – day and night make merry, let days be full of joy, dance and make music day and night. And wear fresh clothes, and wash your head and bathe. Look at

the child that is holding your hand, and let your wife delight in your embrace. These things alone are the concern of men.[21]

A similar quest and struggle are put forward by Qoheleth:

> True, the living know nothing. There are no more rewards for them; they are utterly forgotten. For them love, hate, ambition, all are now over. Never again will they have any part in what is done here under the sun. Go to it then, eat your food and enjoy it, and drink your wine with a cheerful heart; for already God has accepted what you have done. Always be dressed in white and never fail to anoint your head. Enjoy life with a woman you love all the days of your allotted span here under the sun, empty as they are: for that is your lot while you live and labour here under the sun (Eccles. 9.5–9, NEB).

The limited duration of human life is acknowledged by Qoheleth, who perceived death as a major blow to human life (Eccles. 2.14–17; 8. 8; 9.1–5).

The Genesis story is worthy of special attention:

> When the people began to multiply on the face of the ground, and daughters were born to them, the sons of God saw that they were fair, and they took wives for themselves of all that they chose. Then the Lord said, 'My spirit shall not abide in mortals forever, for they are flesh; their days shall be one hundred and twenty years (Gen. 6.1–3).

The first two verses reveal the interaction of the 'sons of God' and human creatures. The 'mixed marriages' result in a special breed of beings – Nephilim, the heroes that were of old, warriors of renown (6. 4). The mixed marriages resulted in the blurring of the distinction between the divine and the human. Yahweh intervened to punish human beings, although the whole event was not of human initiative but that of the sons of God. The narrative has an aetiological motif of accounting for the existence of giants of old. The myth in Genesis 6.1–4 is not a fragment but a unity whose intention is to affirm the created order which has been threatened by the union of the divine beings and human creatures. It is a reorganizational myth which puts its major emphasis on the sharp distinction between God and human beings. Humanity is punished by the transcendent God who imposes limited duration to life on earth.

The same intention to reaffirm the sharp distinction between God and human beings is also seen in the story of the Tower of Babel (11.1–9) which comes after the flood story. The narrative in Genesis 11.1–9 has an element of irony as a device to contrast human deeds and divine response. Humanity wishes to go up to express its 'intention to ascend to heaven and thus to become as God'.[22]

> The people said:
> 'Come, let us make bricks . . .
> Come, let us build ourselves a city, a tower with its tops in the heavens and
> let us make a name for ourselves.' (11.3–4)
> God said:
> 'Come, let us go down, and confuse their languages there . . .' (11. 7)

The text adopts an 'aural' chiasmus in contrasting the construction work of the people and the destruction work of God:

> Come, let us build (*lbn*)
> Come . . . let us confuse (*nbl*).[23]

It is also to be noted that the story begins with the whole earth (*kol ha'ares*) having one language and with the people's fear of being scattered, but ends with God confusing the people's languages and scattering them over the face of all the earth (*kol ha'ares*). Fokkelman concludes his discussion on the Tower of Babel with the following observations: 'It is one of the pillars of biblical theology that the earth has been given to man (*sic*) and that the heavens are God's private domain, the place of his throne and his hosts. The two planes do not meet; they are essentially different and each other's opposites.[24]

The idea of the separation of heaven and earth to prevent direct communication and interaction of the divine and the human is, however, also found in ancient China. A mythic tale from *Kuo–yu* ('Narratives of the States') tells of an ancient God commissioning Governor Chung and Governor Li to eliminate the *axis mundi*, the cosmic mountain that connects heaven and earth, because the frequent going up of human beings and coming down of the gods confused the cosmic order and human beings became lax in morality. It was then reported that: 'Chung lifted heaven up, Li pressed earth down.'[25]

This tale really intends to convey the necessity of *cultic* communication between heaven and earth, the divine and the human realms; direct communication is no longer a possibility and human beings have to rely on the shaman who acts as mediator and in whose presence alone can worshippers communicate with the gods.

In subsequent developments in Taoist and popular religions in China, there has been a great emphasis on the self-cultivation of individuals to achieve union with the Tao of heaven and earth and to reach out for the *Ch'i* (cosmic force or vitality of life) which will nurture the physical body. The Taoist quest for longevity of life affirms the value of the physical body, and immortality is therefore not restricted to the soul or spirit. Skills in both spiritual and physical exercises which aim at attaining harmonious union and integration with nature, and the strengthening of the body and mind, have developed in Taoism. There are ritualistic and alchemical practices which may contribute to our understanding of human life in relation to the divine and the ultimate. Chinese theological discourse cannot claim to be relevant and comprehensive if these resources are deliberately neglected or rejected as evil and pagan.

CONCLUSION

This investigation into the creation myth of Nu Kua is an attempt to understand a particular Asian religious and cultural resource in the theological terms of the Genesis creation story. It is commonly held that the concern to account for the origin of human beings and the order of the universe is a common human quest. These concerns allow us to look into the relationship between human beings, the creator and the cosmos.

Nu Kua in Chinese tradition is the fashioning deity who created human beings. Her major achievement, however, lies in her re-creating the collapsed world and the damaged universe. It is her accomplishment, in reorganizing the cosmos and in providing a harmonious society for human beings, that allowed her to be elevated to the highest heaven and united with the Tao of heaven and earth.

This Chinese concept of human beings becoming gods, and of the incarnation of gods in human form in history, presents a theological challenge to the monotheistic faith of Christian theology. It is a challenge that Asian Christians, nurtured in their own cultural and religious heritages, cannot afford to ignore.

From the perspective of the aspiration of humanity for transcendence and the constant quest for immortality of eternal life, we may come to appreciate the same human yearnings that are expressed, though fragmentarily, in the biblical text and perhaps more strongly in the culture and world-views of the Ancient Near Eastern people. Scholars often seem to maintain that Israel did not possess anything different in terms of world-view from that of the ancient Near East. What distinguishes Israel from her surroundings was not her world view but her faith in the sovereignty of God, the relationship between God and humanity, and God's saving acts in the history of Israel. In reading the Genesis creation stories, especially Genesis 1, Christians and scholars usually reduce the world view to a doctrine of creation.[26] The world view is simply not being taken seriously. Von Rad therefore poses the crucial question: 'Can one so easily distinguish between the faith of Israel and her world view?'

In doing our theology with Asian resources, especially using Asian creation myths in our theological constructions, can we take seriously but selectively the elements common to our own cultural text and the biblical text? What about beliefs that are directly in opposition to those of Christian theological tradition? There are world views which cannot easily, if at all, be reconciled with the theology of creation which we derived from the biblical text and have developed in the doctrine of creation in the West. The issue of the universe being the body of the creator, as is conveyed in the creation myth of Pan Ku, and the idea of a close unity between the divine and the human (that human beings can somehow become 'gods' as well as that human beings can await the coming of the divine into our life) are significant topics for investigation in Asian theological endeavour.

NOTES

1 *Tai-ping yu-lan* ('Taiping Anthologies for the Emperor').

2 Derk Bodde, 'Myths of Ancient China', in Samuel Noah Kramer, (ed.), *Mythologies of the Ancient World* (New York, Doubleday, 1961), p. 389.

3 An article by the present author on the creation myth of Pan Ku is to be published in A. G. Auld, (ed.), *Understanding Poets and Prophets, Essays in Biblical Interpretation for George W. Anderson* (Sheffield, Sheffield Academic Press, 1993), pp. 186–98.

4 Milton M. Chiu, *The Tao of Chinese Religion* (Lanham University Press of America, 1984), p. 173. *Yin* and *Yang* refer essentially to the female and male dimensions of reality respectively. The Five Elements are metal, wood, water, fire and earth. On *Yin, Yang*, Five Elements and *Ch'i* (breath/energy), which are basic concepts in Chinese religious culture, see the discussion by Milton Chiu, pp. 146–66, 185.

5 For a discussion of the relation between myth and society, see Bruce Lincoln, *Myth, Cosmos and Society* (Cambridge, Harvard University Press, 1986), ch. 7.

6 Milton M. Chiu, *The Tao*, pp. 158–60.

7   Wangdao Ding (tr.), *100 Chinese Myths and Fantasies* (Hong Kong, Commercial Press, 1988), p. 37.

8   Bodde, 'Myths', pp. 387–8.

9   Charles Le Blanc, *Huai Nan Tzu: Philosophical Synthesis in Early Han Thought* (Hong Kong University Press, 1985), p. 160.

10   On the role and position of the women in Gen. 2–3, see John A. Bailey, 'Invitation and the Primal Woman in Gilgamesh and Genesis 2–3', *JBL* 89 (1970), pp. 137–50.

11   Le Blanc, *Huai Nan Tzu*, p. 157, note 148.

12   ibid., p. 162. The Great Ancestor 'refers to the originator or progenitor of all things', p. 162, note 182.

13   ibid., p. 163.

14   Charles Le Blanc gives a detailed description of the age of Huang Ti in comparison with that of Fu Hsi and Nu Kua, *Huai Nan Tzu*, pp. 164–70.

15   *Tien Wen* in *Ch'u T'zu* and *Shan-hai Ching*. For English translation of *Tien Wen* ('Questions on Heaven'), see David Hawkes, *Ch'u Tz'u, The Songs of the South: An Ancient Chinese Anthology*, (Oxford, Oxford University Press), 1959), p. 51.

16   Le Blanc, *Huai Nan Tzu*, p. 169.

17   There are texts in the Taoist canon that portray the incarnation of Lao Tzu. See also the discussion and translation of *Hsi Sheng Ching* ('The Scripture of Western Ascension') by Livia Kohn, in *Taoist Mystical Philosophy* (Albany, New York, State University of New York, 1991), pp. 57–80.

18   For discussion of religious influences on Chinese folk-stories, see Liu Ts'un Yan, *Buddhist and Taoist Influences on Chinese Novels* (Wiesbaden, Kommisionsverlag, 1962). On Taoist gods and immortals, see ch. 7.

19   An exception to this is the case of Enoch in early Jewish literature – a human being who was 'canonized' without death.

20   Robert A. Ogden Jr. discusses the issues of the absence of differentiation and the enforcement of regulations in respect of the divine-human relationship in *Atrahasis*, and he compares the latter with Genesis 1–11 in his article 'Transformations in Near Eastern Myths: Genesis 1–11 and the Old Babylonian Epic of Atrahasis', *Religion* 11 (1981), pp. 21–37.

21   Jacobsen Thorkild, 'Mesopotamia,' in Henri Frankfort et al. (eds.), *The Intellectual Adventure of Ancient Man* (Chicago University Press, 1946), pp. 210–11.

22   Zri Adar, *The Book of Genesis* (Jerusalem, The Magnes Press, 1990), p. 45.

23   J. P. Fokkelman, *Narrative Art in Genesis* (Amsterdam, Van Gorcum, Assen, 1975), p. 15.

24   ibid., pp. 16–17.

25   Bodde, 'Myths', p. 391.

26   G. Von Rad, 'Some Aspects of the Old Testament World-view', *The Problem of the Hexateuch and Other Essays* (London, SCM Press, 1966), pp. 144–45.

27

The Communion of Saints: Christian and Tamil Śaiva Perspectives

S. GANGADARAN AND ISRAEL SELVANAYAGAM

This essay is a rare piece of hermeneutical enterprise in which a Hindu and a Christian, long-time partners in Hindu-Christian dialogue in South India, seek to rectify a misconception perpetuated by Christian apologetics that the Hindu faith is individualistic, private and solitary, that its weakness is its lack of any cohesive body of corporate believers. In their examination of Śaiva texts and references to the communion of saints in the New Testament, the authors demonstrate a remarkable heritage of belief in the communion of saints in the Tamil Śaiva tradition, though it differs from that of the Christians.

This article is reprinted from *Hindu-Christian Studies Bulletin* 5 (1992), pp. 13–19.

S. Gangadran, a Śaivite, is on the staff of Madurai–Kamaraj University, Madurai, South India. He also teaches Śaiva Sidhantha philosophy at Tamilnadu Theological Seminary, Madurai.

Israel Selvanayagam is Professor of Religions at Tamilnadu Theological Seminary. Both have jointly and independently published on Hindu-Christian issues.

Discussions on saints normally focus on the nature and meaning of sainthood. While apostles, church fathers, martyrs and people of outstanding dedication are considered as saints in Christian tradition, the Vedic sages and gurus are taken as counterparts in the Hindu religious tradition.[1] But mostly significance is attached to their individual worth, charisma and exemplary life. However, the communion of saints is a significant phenomenon in the New Testament and its resemblance seems to lie more in the wandering saints of the regional *bhakti* traditions of Hinduism (c. 500–700 CE than in the Vedic sages and gurus. Particularly the theological significance attached to the communion of saints in Tamil Śaiva scriptures is remarkable.

Although the canonical leaders or teachers of Śaivism (*nāyaṉārs*) are well acknowledged for their devotional experience and their contribution to Śaiva Siddhanta,[2] the theological significance of the communion of saints remains an undeveloped theme.

'I believe in the communion of saints', is part of the creeds used in the Christian tradition. This belief has both general and specific connotations. It has close association with the preceding belief in the holy catholic Church occurring in the creeds. The idea of the communion of saints along with the community of Christians organized in the form of the Church has been seen as very unique in relation to, for example, the Hindu religious tradition. In India, it is no less a person than P. D. Devanandan, one of the pioneers of the inter-faith dialogue in this century, who points out how 'except perhaps in the more renascent movements, Hinduism has never thought in terms of congregational worship, where a corporate body of believers approaches God in a sense of togetherness and with the idea of seeking to know and do his will. The conception of the Church is therefore a rock of offence to the Hindu believer.'[3] Devanandam is right in his emphasis on church as a transforming community which is unique to Christianity. But his opinion of the absence of a corporate body of believers in traditional Hinduism needs to be questioned. Is there no sense of togetherness in approaching God to know and do his will in Hinduism? Is the concept of the Church really a rock of offence to the Hindu believer?

One of the fruits of inter-faith dialogue is the realization of important ideas which have been hidden in a faith tradition. The writers of this chapter, long-time partners in the pilgrimage of Śaiva–Christian dialogue, realized at a certain point that the phenomenon of the communion of saints found in the Tamil Śaiva texts needs to be highlighted in the light of what the Christian tradition has understood and made thematic concerning this notion. Although the Śaiva communion of saints cannot be identified with the Christian Church, a study of its significance may help to recover it at least to a limited extent. This discovery is important because the fact that Hinduism is an unorganized religion often appears to be a hindrance in the pursuit of inter-faith co-operation for social transformation.

The following reflections are preliminary in nature and need to be developed further. We confine ourselves to the most important references to the communion of saints found in the New Testament and in the twelve canonical books of Tamil Śaivism. The references are given as they appear without thematic classification. A summary at the end will highlight the fundamental aspects of the communion of saints in Christian Tamil and Śaiva traditions.

'I BELIEVE IN THE COMMUNION OF SAINTS'

The belief in the communion of saints in the Christian creeds was originally inserted to denote the unity of the living and the dead in the Church. In this connection in the Roman Catholic Church, there was the practice of offering prayers to the dead canonized saints who were believed to be the mediators. But the reformers and the Protestant Church denounced this practice, emphasizing that Christ alone was the mediator between God and humankind. Today the communion of saints in most Christian traditions is taken to mean primarily the sacramental fellowship through baptism and the Eucharist. Secondarily, it is interpreted in terms of the unity of the Church as an instrument and model for the wider fellowship and unity (*Koinonia*) of the whole inhabited earth (*Oikumene*). It is difficult to find a doctrine of the communion of saints spelled out in the Bible. However, the relationship of God with a fellowship or community and his special presence in it is an important theme occurring in the Bible in relation to different aspects of the Christian faith. The following references are taken as examples.

As a people the Israelites were consecrated to God as a nation of priesthood and holiness (Exod. 19.5); so also were the Christians (1 Pet. 2.9). By partaking of God's holiness the creatures are called to be holy (Heb. 12.10). In this sense the Christians are called saints in the New Testament (2 Cor. 1.1). Being holy has the significance of spiritual relationship with God and moral character of life. More remarkably it implies that mutual sanctification too takes place in a family and in a Church (1 Cor. 7.14; Eph. 5.22–33). According to the New Testament the Christian believers are united with Christ through baptism (Rom. 6.3f; Eph. 2.5f) and participate in the blood and body of Christ in Eucharist (John 5.56; 1 Cor. 10.16); they have fellowship with God through his Son Jesus Christ (1 Cor. 1.9) and the Holy Spirit (Phil. 2.1; 2 Cor. 13.14); participate in the ministry to the 'saints' (fellow Christians) (2 Cor. 8.4); and more significantly participate in Christ's sufferings (Phil. 3.10). They are built up as

one body. The true Christians are so tightly united as to abide in
the love of the Father and the Son, just as the Father and Son abide
in one another and are only one (John 14.20; 15.4, 7; 17.20, 23;
1 John 4.12). It is their privilege to have a share in the resources and
fellowship of the Church and equally it is their responsibility to give
a share for the common upliftment. The glorious future (1 Thess.
4.17; 1 Pet. 5.1) is given as a foretaste in the communion of saints.

Biblically speaking it is not enough to say that God is omnipresent.
Of course, God's presence is unlimited. But he is actively present
where people suffer politically, socially and economically as the history of Exodus amply shows. Further, he is the God who moves
about the dwellings of his people (2 Sam. 7.6). The temple was
supposed to help realize God's presence in a community but it could
never domesticate him. The position of the early Church in this
regard could be seen not only in their gathering for worship in any
place but also in that they emphasized the link between people's
unity and God's favour as we read in Matthew 18.19. Following this
verse Jesus says, 'wherever two or three gather in my name I am in
their midst.' It is not out of place to recall that the risen Christ
appeared to his disciples when they were together and the Holy Spirit
was poured down manifestly in the fellowship of believers. They are
the living temples of the Spirit (1 Cor. 6.19). Therefore it is biblical
to say that the sanctity of the Church lies in the unity of the people.
This communion and unity is theologically significant in terms of
God's active presence and his aim to create a united humanity using
the communion of saints, i.e. the Church, as an instrument and
model.

THE COMMUNION OF SAINTS IN THE TAMIL
ŚAIVA TRADITION

Devotees as groups appear in the twelve canonical books of Tamil
Śaivism. Here we see them in order of the books. Devotees (*aṭiyavar*)
are those who have love in their heart. The Lord resides in the
place of goodness and broadmindedness (*Nallūr Perumanam*). In his
Tevāram, Jñāna Sambandar says that those who adore his feet and
perform service will be rid of their suffering (*entai iṉaiyati ettuvār,
tun puru vārallar toṇṭ uceyvāre* – p. 44).[4]

It is to be noted in this connection that Saint Jñāna Sambandar gave release to all the devotees who came to his wedding at Nallūr Perumanam. By the grace of God, fire of knowledge appears and Jñāna Sambandar enters the fire of knowledge after all the devotees enter the fire with his newly wedded wife.[5]

Jñāna Sambandar in the verse describes Śiva's saving act of Mārkandeyar from Yama, the Lord of death.[6] He observed that having known this fact, the representatives of Yama are afraid of coming near the devotees of the Lord.

The devotees engage in service contemplating Śiva as one who drank poison and having Uma as his consort. God prevents suffering for these devotees (p. 66). The devotees worship the feet of Śiva for many days thinking that the Lord will redeem them and remove suffering from these devotees (p. 66). God is easily accessible to the devotees, but is not accessible to the celestials (p. 66f). Many singing devotees adore the dancing Lord with love (p. 67). The devotees who excel by their service praise the Lord with songs (p. 95).

Jñāna Sambandar is emphatic in his *Tirukkallil* decade that the devotees are not to be insulted on any account. This verse expresses the reverence with which the devotees are to be adored (p. 790). He says that the devotees who wear sacred ash, drink intoxicating drinks, the devotees of the Lord at Kallil, are not to be insulted. Only ignorant people speak ill of the devotees. If the devotee wants knowledge and the consequent release, penance and consequent weakness of the body are not the way. The devotee has to worship the Lord at Tiruvalanjuli with the help of the hymns of Sambandar. In this way the devotee can attain knowledge and release (p. 544).

The devotees will not have diseases, will not be affected by wicked *karmas*, even the Lord of death will leave the devotee, and the supreme Lord gives the devotees refuge. They become devotees of the devotee of the Lord (p. 790). Even heaven is not important for the devotees of the Lord who wear Koṇṛai flowers (p. 56). If one serves the devotee of the devotees, the spotless way of reaching God becomes easy (p. 991). The devotees worship the Lord at Tiruppugalūr with their songs, with flowers, water and offerings and they always hear the praise of the Lord without interruption (p. 806). The ancient devotees of the Lord at Tiruppadiripuliyur break new ground and destroy old *karmas* (p. 1257). God is the light which transcends the light of the word. The God is to be found in the heart of the devotees (p. 727).

Appar, also known as Tirunāvukkarasar, observes that good merit accrues to a person as a result of serving the devotees of a faultless devotee of the Lord (v. 5142).[7] He also exhorts us to worship and serve the devotees of the Lord, to mingle with them and avoid those who do not serve the Lord (v. 5658).

Saint Sundarar calls God as 'Lord, my father, the respectable Lord who has accepted me as his devotee for many (seven times seven, i.e., forty-nine) births... Let me be the devotee of the devotees of the LORD' (v. 7762). He also observes: 'I am your servant and you have complete control over me and I become your servant of my own accord' (v. 8789). It is remarkable that it was Sundarer who wrote the short hagiography of saints which was further elaborated by others.[8]

Māṇikkavācakar's *Tiruvācakam* is the most popular devotional text of the Tamil Śaiva tradition, forming the eighth of its twelve canonical books. The whole poem of *Tiruvācakam* centres around the conversion experience of Saint Māṇikkavācakar that occurred quite unexpectedly when as a minister in the Pāṇḍya Kingdom on a trade trip he met Śiva in the form of a guru. Remarkably the guru was seated surrounded by a host of saints, and this scene transformed the poet to the core. He enjoyed the fellowship of these saints for a period, forgetting his kingdom and trade. But when they were taken up he could not bear the feeling of separation and this he recalls repeatedly in his poem (e.g., 27.10).[9] However, he had the opportunity of joining the fellowship of the Śaiva saints in different places, particularly in *Tillai* (Citamparam), the centre of Tamil Śaiva tradition. Here was dwelling the 'all-glorious' company of Śiva who gained grace to go with him and mingled in perfect union with him (2.128–132). Māṇikkavācakar's association with the communion of saints made him mention it in relation to God's special identification with them, the place of *śakti*, the consort of Śiva in modelling this communion and to the experience of devotees here and hereafter.

Śiva dances in the midst of his perfect saints (42.14). He rejoices amid those that fold adoring hands (1.9). Though he is supreme and transcendent with uncanny nature and capricious authority he is near to his servants (6.86, 87) from whom he never departs (6.100). The praises of the devotees surround him (1.94, 95).

Māṇikkavācakar very strikingly sees the union of the goddess with Śiva as an exemplary model. She is the chief servant who surrendered all her power to Śiva by marriage. Along with her Śiva steps into the ancient huts (i.e. temples), so that their image may be a perpetual inspiration for the communion of saints (20.30; 5.291, 292). They dwell within each other and in turn both dwell in saints. The following lines are graphic in this regard:

> The Mistress dwells in midmost of Thyself;
> Within the Mistress centred dwellest Thou;
> Midst of Thy servant if Ye Both do dwell,
> do me Thy servant over give the grace
> Amidst Thy lowliest servants to abide ... (21.1–3)

Elsewhere the poet describes the joy of this multi-dimensional communion:

> Here those who wash away their sin are gathered around;
> This swelling tank is our Queen and King
> We entering plunge and plunge again, our shells round;
> Our anklets tinkling sound; our bosoms throb with joy;
> The wave we plunge in swells, plunge into lotus-crowned
> flood and joyful bathe ... (7.50–52)

This song of maidens well represents the ecstatic fellowship of the saints who are united with Śiva and the goddess, who is the paradigm for faithful devotion to and union with God.

The saints are the loving ones (*anpar*) who have gained cessation of all their bonds (5.57; 32.21). They are the blessed ones (*celvar*), praising God always (1.95). Since Śiva is united with them their life is chiefly characterized by great freedom by his grace. Māṇikkavācakar sings:

> The King of all! He came, and made me, too, his own;
> Henceforth I'm no one's vassal; none I fear!
> We've reached the goal; with servants of his saints
> In sea of bliss we evermore shall bathe. (5.119, 120)

Like their supreme master the saints enjoy social freedom and spontaneity transcending the society of kin and caste. They sustain the life of each other always smiling, rejoicing and singing Śiva's sacred names (21.33–36).

Since Māṇikkavācakar gained a new life in the midst of a host of saints, his association with the communion of saints helped him not only to keep the devotion dynamic but also to foresee his life after death with creative imagination. The poet is ever grateful to Śiva for causing him to enter the band of devotees (1.43; 6.106, 107). The devotees he saw at the time of his conversion were a stimulating factor. Therefore, the saint asks Śiva to show once again the band of his devotees (21.32). Further, the fellowship in this world foreshadows a great communion of saints in heaven where the 'ancient saints' stand around the throne of Śiva (21.14). He prays:

The saints around thee, where Thou and they in happy sport
   commingled, ever dwell.
That I may thither rise to join the band,
Our only Bliss, in grace, O bid me come. (21.27, 28)

Those who have gone ahead, Māṇikkavācakar says, have reached the Lord's grace and his feet (32.59; 24.13, 14). So he too hurries to be with them:

Midmost of Thy devoted ones, like them in mystic dance to move;
Within thy home above to gain wish'd entrance, lo I eager haste! (5.41,
   42)

Thus for Māṇikkavācakar, from the beginning up to the ultimate goal of his religious life, the communion of saints provides a basic component of meaning of this life.

In the ninth *Thirumurai* we have a decade by Sundanar which is called *Tiruppallāṇṭu*. The second song in this decade (290)[10] describes:

Those who have hard mind (not melting mind) do not come near the Lord; those who have melting mind and are real devotees come quickly. The devotees live by giving and receiving.

The devotees receive the grace from the Lord and give their body, belongings, and even their lives to him. Here the term 'giving and receiving' has a significant meaning. It primarily signifies giving his love to him and receiving grace from him. It also signifies giving and receiving the grace of God among the devotees. In this sense it shows the importance of the communion of saints and also shows the way in which the devotees of the LORD should live. The term 'entering the temple as a group' in this *Tiruppallāṇṭu* verse is also significant. The saints live as a group praising the grace of the Lord, and the communion of saints is the expression of God's grace.

In the tenth book of *Tirumantiram* we find the section called 'the praise of the devotees'. The author makes a distinction between the mobile God (the devotee) who is released from bondage, and the immobile God who gives grace residing in temples. He says that if we give something to the immobile God in the temple, that will not reach the mobile God. But if we give something to the mobile God, it automatically reaches the immobile God, for God is the indwelling spirit behind all the devotees (1857).[11]

The eleventh *Tirumurai* is a collection of many poets and poet-esses.[12] Kāraikal Ammaiyār, who is the forerunner of the bhakti movement representing the female saints, talks about Śiva and his devotees. She is one of the sixty-three classical *Nāyanārs* of Śaivism. She has sung with outpouring devotion. She says, 'Oh! Ignorant mind! Consider always performing worship as your goal.' Here per-forming worship is specifically referred to as worship of the devotees. She also advises us to be away from those persons who do not think of Śiva as a person who has the Moon as his garland. The Moon requests the pardon of Śiva after expressing regret for his misdeeds. Śiva gives the Moon proper status by having him on his head like a garland. This shows that God gives his devotees pardon when they repent for their misdeeds.

Kāraikal Ammaiyār not only praises Śiva, but also emphasizes the importance of the devotees of Śiva by asking the devotee to desist from the company of persons who do not worship Śiva with the Moon on his head. This is comparable to the twelfth sutra of the *Śivajñāa Bodham*, one of the fourteen philosophical texts of Śaiva Siddhanta, where Meykandar asks us to wash the impurity of spiritual darkness (*ānava mala*) and to be with the company of devotees. The devotees should consider the faultless nature of Śiva's devotees and images which are in the temple giving grace to the devotees as Śiva himself.

In the introduction (*Pāyiram*) to the *Tiruttoṇṭar Purāṇam*, the last book, Sekkilār talks about the assembly of Saints (*puṇitar peravai –* 4).[13] The Śaiva devotees worship the Lord having the Moon on his head and sing his praise. The assembly of the devotees enjoy the grace of the Lord through the songs of Śaiva leaders, i.e. the saints (*Nāyanārs*). Sekkilār praises the assembly of the holy people and prays to God for the success of the assembly of holy men in this world. He emphasizes the important characteristics of the devotees. He says that clinging on to the feet of Śiva who rides on the bull (standing for righteousness), the devotees renounce all attachment to the world (980).

So far we have glanced through the canonical books of Tamil Śaivism pointing out the significance of the communion of saints. Further we may consider the historical monuments of the corporate living of saints. The Devasiriyan Hall in the Tiruvarur temple is the historical monument which reminds us about the emergence of *Tiruttoṇṭa togai* by the initiative of Viranmenda Nāyanār. It is the practice in the Śaiva tradition to remember the saints particularly on their days of release and pay obeisance to them in veneration.

The mutts are the historical monuments of the corporate living of Śaiva saints and their service. Tirujñāna Sambandar Mutt at Madurai, for instance, brings to memory the saint who stayed in Madurai when he defeated the Jains in argument and established the supremacy of Śaivism during the reign of Pandya King Nedumā-ran. There are literary indications about royal patronage extended to the saints in the Tamil country.

Tiruppugalur Velakurichi Mutt is said to have been established by Appar when he stayed there along with a devotee during his last days performing service in the temple. In Tiruperundurai temple we have a place where Śiva came as a preceptor to guide Māṇikkavācakar for his spiritual enlightenment. Tillai or Cidambaram is the place where three thousand brahmins called *Tillaivāl atanār* (brahmins residing in Cidambaram) have the hereditary right of managing the Naṭarāja temple there. Even though we do not have three thousand priests now, we have more than three hundred priests who perform service in the temple.

It is remarkable that the communion of saints in the Tamil Śaiva tradition transcended caste and colour. Although a number of saints had a brahmanic background, once they joined the band of Śaiva devotees, they stopped exercising any caste identity. We have a number of instances of brahmins receiving grace and blessing from the non-brahmin saints. The communion of saints provided an alternative to caste-ridden society. However, one may wonder at the decline of the corporate spirit and social dimension exhibited by the communion of saints. Perhaps the penetration of brahminic values such as the āgamic ritual tradition and individual liberation contrib-uted to the decline of the saints' movement. It is beyond the scope of this essay to investigate the reasons for this development, which is an important area for further study.

While the present-day Śaivas celebrate the heritage of the saints, they do not feel compelled to recover the institution of the com-munion of saints. One reason may be the extraordinary catholicity of the pan-mythic Hindu faith to accommodate all living things and beings, from a blade of grass to a celestial God, without bothering about a particular group. However, it should be recognized that a few attempts have been made to revive the spirit of corporate living of devotion and service to people. Kuṇṭrakkuṭi Aṭikal, for instance, started a forum called *Deivīkapperavai* (Association of the Divine-oriented) and is working among the rural masses surrounding his mutt. Other Śaiva mutts may also be inspired to follow suit. However, such developments continue to depend on the charisma of a few individuals like Kuṇṭrakkuṭi Aṭikal. For more visible forums, therefore, it is left to the present Śaiva devotees and scholars to highlight and propagate the idea of the communion of saints.

CONCLUSION

It is not true to say that Hinduism is totally individualistic. While the brahmanic Hinduism developed a social stratification on the basis of caste, the bhakti traditions formed fellowship of saints around the image of God. The Tamil Śaiva tradition has a remarkable heritage of the communion of saints. Although they cannot be fully identified with the idea of the communion of saints in the Christian tradition, they have a similar theological significance.

Although God is present everywhere, he is actively present in the fellowship of his devotees as evident in the two traditions. God's grace and intimacy is closely related to this fellowship. The sacraments of baptism and Eucharist help the Christian saints to realize and celebrate this grace while the symbols of three horizontal lines on the forehead and holy ash on other parts of the body signify grace and liberation for the Śaiva saints. The saints in the formative period of the traditions become both models to be imitated and objects to be venerated (except in Protestant Christianity where veneration of saints is discouraged). Service is an important element in the communion of saints. It takes place within the fellowship and outside. But the major difference is that the Christian Church as the extension of saints and the body of saints in the sense of being forgiven and santified by God through the mediation and model of Jesus Christ has continued to exist in an organized form. But in the Śaiva tradition there is no such continuity saving occasional fellowships and gatherings by the effort of charismatic individuals. However, it is always a possibility to recover the idea of the communion of Śaiva saints and to give it shape through the formation of fellowships and congregations not necessarily following the Christian Church model.

Voices from the Margin

The communion of saints in the Christian tradition appears to have a universal appeal. It is often emphasized that the Church, despite all its pitfalls, must not only provide a model community of love, justice and unity but also be an instrument to achieve it. The Śaiva saints also speak of Śiva as the God of all, and call all people to a liberated life and fellowship through his grace that he especially manifested through his devotees. But the unique Śaiva voice is not often heard because of its integral place in the complex pan-mythic tradition of Hinduism. The idea of the communion of saints may prove to be a point of continuing dialogue between Christians and Śaivas.

NOTES

1 See Robert L. Cohn, 'Sainthood' in Mircea Eliade (ed.), *The Encyclo-paedia of Religion* (New York, Macmillan, 1987), vol. 13, pp. 1–6.

2 See Indira Viswanathan Peterson, '*Nāyanārs*', in Eliade, (ed.), pp. 13f.

3 Robin Boyd, *An Introduction to Indian Christian Theology* (Madras, CLS, 1975), p. 198.

4 *Moovar Tevāram* (Kasi Tiruppanandal Mutt, 1968), p. 44. (As verse order is inconsistent we give the page no.)

5 *Periyapurāṇam, Tirujñāna Sambandarpurāṇam*, 3155 and 3156, (Śaiva Siddhanta Maha Samajam, 1950). (*Periyapurāṇam* was written by Sekkilar giving the hagiography of saints).

6 *Moovar Tevāram*, p. 65.

7 *Tevāram, Andankalmurai*, (Mayilai Ila Maruganar, 1953), vol. 2.

8 Sundarar is one of the leaders of Śaivism (*Nāyanār*) who composed the decade *Tiruttoṇta togai* which gives a short note of the sixty-three devotees of Śaivism (63 individual devotees and nine groups of devotees like those who wear sacred ash, who praise devotees through devotion, who are born in Tiruvarur etc.).

Nampiantar Nampi expands this decade into a work of 100 stanzas called *Tiruttoṇtar Tiruvantāti*. Sekkilar expands this work into a grand epic of Śaivism (*Tiruttoṇtar Purāṇam*, also known as *Periyapurāṇam*) consisting of 4287 stanzas. Sekkilar says that the reason for the emergence of Sandarar is to give *Tiruttoṇta togai* to our world.

Viranmindar, one of the 63 devotees, was from Kerala. He wanted to renounce the world by clinging on to the feet of Śiva and had concern for the devotees of Śiva. When Sundarar went to worship Śiva in the temple of Tiruvarur, he did not recognize the assembly of devotees in the Devaseriyan Hall at Tiruvarur temple. Viranmindar saw the failure of Sundarar in not recognizing the importance of the devotees and considered Sundarar as 'one of non-consequence' (*puragu*). Viranmindar thought that even though Sundarar himself was one of the leaders of Śaivism, his failure of not giving importance to the assembly of devotees could not be treated lightly.

It is interesting that Viranmindar considers even Śiva, who gave importance to Sundarar who in turn did not recognize the importance of the
assembly of devotees, as 'one of non-consequence'. After realizing the view
of Viranmindar, Sundarar paid respect to the assembly of devotees and then
composed *Tiruttoṇṭa togai*. Lord Śiva helped Sundarar to start with the first
line. '*Tillaivāl antanartam aṭiyārkkum aṭiyār*' (I am the devotee residing in
Tillai).

Sekkilar describes the life history of Sundarar in the beginning, middle
and end of *Tiruttoṇṭar Purāṇam* and thus Sundarar is the hero of this epic.

9   G. U. Pope, *The Tiruvācagam or 'Sacred Utterances' of the Tamil Poet,
Saint and Sage Māṇikkavācakar* (Oxford, Clarendon Press, 1900). The first
number in this section indicates the poem and the second the line.

10   *Onpatām (ninth) Tirumurai* (Dharmapura Adheenan, 1969).

11   *Tirumantiram* (Thiruvatuthurai Adheenan, 1987).

12   *Patinorām (eleventh) Tirumurai*, (Kasi Tirruppanandal Mutt, 1963),
p. 20.

13   *Periyapurāṭam* (Madras, Śaiva Siddhanta Mahasamajam, 1950). Verse
numbers given.

28

On Developing Liberation Theology in Islam

ASGHAR ALI ENGINEER

This essay has been chosen to show how people of other faiths use their sacred texts to respond to the questions of poverty and oppression, and seek to work out a theology of liberation in their own terms. The implications of this for inter-faith dialogue are incalculable.

The essay is taken from *Focus* 6 (3, 1986), a Pakistani quarterly, and is available from Pastoral Institute, GPO 288, Multan, Pakistan 60000.

Asghar Ali Engineer is the Director of the Institute of Islamic Studies, Bombay, India. He has published articles on communalism, Islamic theology, etc.

INTRODUCTION

I propose to throw light on developing liberation theology in Islam. If we do not treat the Islamic theology as developed by the 'ulama' during the medieval ages to suit their time and conditions as sacrosanct, immutable and unalterable, as is often assumed, Islam, in my opinion, has great potential for lending itself to develop liberation theology. Liberation theology, it must be understood, is much more than rational theology.

Rational theology views the religious teachings and institutions in the light of reason and advocates freedom of reinterpretation of the scriptural text. It has great appeal for the modern élite as, more often than not, rational theology subserves the ends of this élite. However, this rational approach may not appeal to the masses as they hardly feel any need for rational theology. In the present social structure which imposes severe constraints on the economic as well as intellectual progress of the masses and compels them to remain backward, a rational or book view of religion with its transcendental complex does not enthuse them. In this state of backwardness, what appeals to them is folk religion with its attendant rituals. Religion, in this form, serves their psychological need to bear the hard conditions of life, miseries which would be difficult to bear without such a psychological prop.

However, liberation theology does not confine itself to the arena of pure and speculative reasoning: it widens its scope to become a most powerful instrument for emancipating the masses from the clutches of their masters and exploiters and inspires them to act with revolutionary zeal to fight against tyranny, exploitation and persecution. Thus liberation theology enables them to change their condition for the better and transforms religion into a powerful instrument of militant struggle and revolutionary change.

HISTORICAL GENESIS OF ISLAM

Islam has great potential for developing a liberation theology. The historical genesis of Islam can help us understand its revolutionary potential. Mecca, birthplace of Islam, was a centre of international commerce at the time of its origin. There had emerged on the social scene of Mecca powerful merchants specializing in complex international financial operations and commercial transactions. Due to these developments, the institution of private property which was absent in the tribal society began to consolidate itself. The rich merchants had formed intertribal corporations to carry on and monopolise trade with the regions of the Byzantine empire and accumulated profits without distributing a part of it to the poor and needy of their tribes. This went against the tribal norms and caused social malaise in Mecca.

The Prophet felt the acute social tensions developing in the Meccan society due to the widening gap between the rich and poor and the violent conflict it could lead to if these tensions were not resolved. He addressed himself to the powerful merchants of Mecca and exhorted them not to hoard their wealth but to take of the poor, orphans, and the needy. The Meccan verses revealed to the Prophet sharply condemn the practice of accumulation of wealth and warn the Meccan merchants of the dangerous consequence which will follow if they do not spend their wealth in the way of Allah. It is said in one of the Meccan verses:

395

[Woe unto] who has gathered wealth and sedulously hoards it, thinking that their riches will render them immortal!

By no means! They shall be flung to the destroying flame. Would that you knew what the destroying flame is like. It is Allah's own kindled fire, which will rise up to the hearts of men. It will close them from every side, in towering columns (Qur'an, 104.2–9).

And again: Wordly affluence has made you oblivious [of consequences] until you come to the graves.

But you shall know, you shall before long come to know. Indeed, if you knew the truth with certainty, you would see the fire of hell: you would see it with your very eyes. Then, on that day, you shall be questioned about your joy (Qur'an, 102.1–8).

Thus we see that in the verses quoted above hoarding of wealth and wordly affluence is condemned in no uncertain terms. Significantly, in the latter verse it is said that preoccupation with the piling up of wealth makes one oblivious of all the consequences until they meet their graves. It is further predicted that if they remain preoccupied with joys of life they would soon see hell fire (i.e. people's wrath who are deprived of their just and legitimate share), and they would certainly be confronted with this wrath and then they will be questioned about their joys.

It was primarily for this reason that the powerful merchants of Mecca opposed the Prophet and became his sworn enemies. These were the vested interests the Prophet had to fight against in Mecca. First, the Meccan rich offered inducements to the Prophet if only he stopped preaching his egalitarian doctrine. The Prophet refused to compromise with the rich and so they began to severely persecute him. The Meccan rich, who also commanded the leadership of the society (there was no regular government or state machinery as such in Mecca at that time) like the rich in any other society, were not much perturbed with the religious doctrines preached by the Prophet. They were seriously concerned with the socio-economic consequences of his teachings and the attack he launched on their wealth and privileges. The Qur'an attacked their power, which was a result of concentration of wealth and monopoly of trade established by them.

It can thus be seen that the Prophet initiated a process of profound change in Arabian society which brought about the downfall of the powerful vested interests which had emerged on the Meccan scene. The Prophet of Islam was seriously concerned with the fate of the downtrodden in Mecca and this concern burst forth in the verses revealed during this period. Some of the terms often used in the Qur'an will have to be redefined while developing liberation theology in the light of this consideration. Islam naturally began as a religious movement and these terms, therefore, have acquired deep religious connotations. However, Islam, as pointed out above, was not only concerned with the spiritual, but also equally with the worldly side of life. It took the project of establishing a just society here on earth quite seriously and repeatedly emphasized this approach.

SOCIO-ECONOMIC PERSPECTIVE

The terms we are referring to will, therefore, have to be seen in a socio-economic perspective also. A liberation theology cannot confine these terms to their religious connotations only; they must be reinterpreted to bring out their socio-economic import. Islam gives a concept of society which is free of exploitation, oppression, domination and injustice in any form. Also, it emphasizes progress and change in harmony with the laws of God who is merciful and just. The God of Qur'an, it must be remembered, is not only merciful but is also mighty and powerful. He approved of those oppressed avenging themselves.

THE QUR'ANIC CONCEPT OF JUSTICE

The true qur'anic spirit would make it necessary to devise new institutions other than mere almsgiving to ensure social justice. Socialist concepts and institutions come much nearer to this qur'anic spirit. In a socialist economy distributive justice is as much important as production of wealth. According to the qur'anic concept of justice it is the producers who have the right of ownership over the wealth produced by them. It is very clearly stated in the Qur'an that no one shall bear the burden of others (Qur'an 53.38). It is a clear denial of the right of extracting labour without fully compensating for it as is sanctioned by feudal or capitalist systems in one form or the other. The Qur'an also says that man shall get what he strives for (Qur'an 53.39). Both the above qur'anic verses put together are clear enunciation of the principle of ownership of wealth based on one's labour.

In other words, Islam does not recognise ownership based on exploitation of labour by way of appropriation of surplus labour or by way of speculation and future trading in commodities. It is in this spirit that speculation and future trading in commodities has been categorically banned in Islam. Liberation theology, needless to say, would give great emphasis to the principle of ownership based on labour or work – a principle which has been neglected by medieval theology.

PRIVATE PROPERTY IN ISLAM

This brings us to the most important question of right of private property in Islam. The traditional theologian considers the institution of property as sacred and inviolable. An Islamic conference held in Mecca in 1976 opposed the concept of nationalization as against the teachings of Islam. It emphasized man's trusteeship of natural resources and of social and economic institutions. State intervention in their view should not extend beyond supervising the economic growth for realization of ideological objectives. However, taking the true spirit of Islam into account, the 'ulama' are not justified in treating private property *per se* as sacred: 'Those who do oppress [others] will come to know by what a [great] reverse they will be overturned' (Qur'an 26.227).

The God of the Qur'an also declares his sympathy in no uncertain terms in favour of the oppressed and the weak:

> And we desired to show favour unto those who were oppressed in the earth, and to make them leaders of mankind and to make them inheritors [of this earth] (Qur'an 27.5).

When the Qur'an categorically condemns oppression and injustice, its concern for the social health and egalitarian social structure cannot be denied and hence the qur'anic terms would have, apart from religious import, socio-economic connotations also. Thus a condemnatory term like *kafir* would not only connote religious disbelief, as is the case in traditional theology, but would also imply obstruction in the creation of a just and egalitarian society free of all forms of exploitation and oppression. Thus a *kafir* is one who does not believe in God and actively opposes with all his might an honest attempt to restructure a society in order to eliminate concentration of wealth, exploitation and other forms of injustice.

Kufr (disbelief) would not be determined, as far as liberation theology is concerned, by more formal denial of faith in God; one who formally professes faith in God but indulges in accumulation of wealth by exploiting others and goes in for conspicuous consumption while others starve in the neighbourhood would also commit *kufr*, and thus incur the displeasure of God. The Qur'an says in one of the Meccan suras:

> Have you observed him who belies the religious? It is he who turns away the orphan and does not urge others to feed the poor. Woe to those who pray but are heedless in their prayer; who make a show of piety and obstruct the needy from necessities (Qur'an 107).

Thus it is clear that those who profess their faith in religion and make show of their piety but deprive the orphans and destitutes of their rights are not real believers. Thus to be a believer or a true Muslim one has to act in a way so as to create a just society that takes care of the orphans, the destitute and the needy. The medieval theologians emphasized giving of alms but a liberation theologian in a modern society would interpret it to mean creation of a just society. A property acquired by exploitation, speculation or by any means other than by one's own labour cannot have any sanction in Islam.

There are clear traditions of the Prophet prohibiting share cropping or owning the land which is not cultivated by the owner himself. All the standard works on *hadith* (traditions), that is, *Muwatta* of Iman Malik, Sahih Bukhari, Sahih Muslim, etc., have included a number of traditions of the Prophet against giving the land on share cropping or on rent. These traditions have been narrated by six companions of the Prophet who are considered highly reliable. According to a tradition in Sahih Muslim narrated by Jabir bin, 'Abdallah the Prophet said that one who possesses land should cultivate it himself, and if he is unable to do so he should give (that portion of the land or whole piece of land which he cannot cultivate) without taking any compensation.'

TAWHIDI SOCIETY

The other central concept of Islam is *tawhid* which, as far as traditional theology is concerned, means 'unity of Godhood'. *Shirk* (i.e. associating another with Allah) has been strongly condemned by the

Qur'an. Liberation theology, while accepting the concept of the unity of Godhood, strives to broaden the scope of *tawhid*. *Tawhid* in liberation theology implies not only unity of God but also unity of mankind in all aspects. The *mujahiddin* of Iran are engaged in a liberation struggle and they are giving new interpretations to the qur'anic concepts like *tawhid*, *kufr*, etc. A truly *tawhidi* society is one which ensures complete unity among mankind, and for that it is necessary to create a classless society. Unity of Godhood must ensure complete unity of society and such a society cannot admit of any division, not even class division. There cannot be true solidarity of the faithful unless all racial, national and socio-economic divisions are done away with. Thus such a concept of *tawhid* acquires primary importance in developing liberation theology. Class divisions would imply domination of the strong over the weak. Such a domination is the very denial of the creation of a just society.

REINTERPRETING THE QUR'AN

These are some of the most important considerations in reinterpreting the Holy Qur'an for developing a liberation theology of Islam.

The Qur'an, it is important to note, opposes in categorical terms all oppressive establishments. Most of the prophets mentioned in it are from amongst the masses and fight against tyrants and oppressive rulers. The prophets came from among the people, not from among the rulers of ruling establishments. The Qur'an declares:

> It is he who has sent forth apostles from amongst the people to recite to them his revelations, to purify them, and to impart to them wisdom and knowledge of the scripture . . . (62.2).

It is made quite clear by the Qur'an that apostles are selected from amongst the people themselves and they impart wisdom to them and guide them to fight against oppression and exploitation. The prophet Moses is projected by the Qur'an as a liberator of the Israelis who were being oppressed by Pharaoh. The Israelis were the oppressed and weak *mustad'ifun* on earth. Moses was the man of the people who fought for their liberation from the oppressive establishment.

Another important concept in Islam is that of *jihad*, which literally means 'struggle'. This concept also needs to be reinterpreted in the context of liberation theology. A propounder of liberation theology has to emphasize (as the Qur'an does) to wage struggle (*jihad*) for eliminating exploitation, corruption and *zulm* (wrongdoing, tyranny) in all their varied forms and this struggle will continue until these corrupting influences are completely eliminated from the earth. The Qur'an declares unambiguously:

> And fight them until persecution is no more, and religion is all for Allah. But if they cease, then Lo: Allah is seer of what they do (8.39).

Thus it is very clear that Allah desires that the faithful fight until persecution ceases on earth. And seen in a proper context, the real import of 'religion is all for Allah' is the creation of a society where there would no more be persecution and exploitation of man by man. It is the basic duty of every believer to wage struggle until this divine objective is realized.

The Qur'an does not approve of people sitting idly by when others are being persecuted. It says:

> Why should you not fight for the cause of Allah and of the weak among men and of the women and the children who are crying: 'Our Lord! Deliver us from this town of which the people are oppressors! Oh, give us from thy presence some protecting friend! Oh! give us from thy presence some defender!'

It is thus clear that the Qur'an wants the faithful to fight for the cause of the weak among men, women and children who pray to be delivered from the clutches of the oppressors. And it must be noted that to fight for this cause is to fight for the cause of Allah. The Qur'an also makes it clear that an oppressor cannot be entrusted with the leadership of the people even if he belongs to the progeny of a prophet. When the prophet Abraham is told that he would be appointed the leader of the people he inquires about the status of his offspring. He is told in no uncertain terms that this covenant does not include the wrongdoers:

> 'And of my offspring (will there be leaders)?' He said: 'My covenant includes no oppressors' (Qur'an 4.75).

Thus the whole emphasis of the Qur'an is on liberation of mankind from exploitation and oppression. The liberation theology in Islam derives its strength from such qur'anic injunctions. Those who do not fight for the liberation of the oppressed and the weak cannot claim to be really faithful by mere profession of faith verbally. The Qur'an says:

Do men imagine that they will be left because they say, 'We believe' and will not be tested (in action). Lo! We tested those who were before you (29.2).

The prophetic tradition also says that 'the best form of *jihad* is telling the truth in the face of tyrants'. Today most of the Muslim countries happen to be in the Third World and are exploited by imperialist forces. Thus it would be their duty to wage struggle against the imperialist forces and it is in this light that the struggles of the peoples of Palestine, Iran and other countries should be seen. Liberation theology would urge every Muslim to fight against exploiters and oppressors within the country they belong to, and outside the country by joining hands with all anti-imperialist forces.

THE REAL AND THE POSSIBLE

A perceptive observer of the social scene knows that there is always tension between the real and the possible. A traditional theology tries to resolve this tension by compromising with the real and coming to terms with it. As against this, liberation theology seeks to intensify tension between the real and the possible by putting greater emphasis on the possible and by waging struggle against that which exists today in order to bring it closer to the possible. The attainment of the possible, liberation theology emphasizes, can be brought about by increasing degrees of freedom both for individuals and collectively (a group, a community or a nation), reducing economic exploitation (by socializing instruments of production, prohibiting accumulation of wealth, severely penalizing practice of usury, creating appropriate institutions to ensure satisfaction of basic needs of all the people, etc.), waging unceasing struggles against those who have a vested interest in maintaining the *status quo* and interpreting the qur'anic injunctions in such a way as to ensure continuous progress of humanity. Liberation theology is, therefore, essentially the theology of the possible.

Liberation theology stands for unity of mankind and does not admit of any division based on caste, creed, class or race. It continuously strives to achieve this unity by eliminating all such differences. Even the differences based on religion are more apparent than real. The Qur'an says:

For each we have appointed a divine law and a way (of worshipping). Had Allah willed he could have made you one community. But that he may try you by that which he has given you. So vie with one another for good deeds (5.15).

Thus the real emphasis is on good deeds and on the ways of worshipping (which may differ from community to community). Liberation theology also lays a good deal of emphasis on justice, which is one of the most important qur'anic doctrines.

CONCLUSION

Thus justice is of primary importance for liberation theology in Islam. One must not be carried away by passions as it would lead to oppression (*zulm*), injuring the cause of justice which Islam upholds so dearly and, therefore, liberation theology also has to make it a matter of central concern. The traditional theologians have, more often than not, remained preoccupied with metaphysical questions and *ibadat* (prayer, fasting, etc.), relegating the question of social justice and this worldly existence to a secondary position. Liberation theology seeks to re-emphasize the central concern of Islam with social justice and its fundamental emphasis on liberating the weaker sections and the oppressed masses and radically restructuring society to eliminate all the vested interests, which would ultimately lead to the creation of a classless society which is the real purpose of *tawhidi* society. It is needless to point out that liberation theology is opposed to the fundamentalist movement as it seeks to re-emphasize traditional issues and seeks to give new lease of life to traditional theology without concerning itself with the problems of the modern world.

PART FIVE

People as Exegetes: Popular Readings

'What do you understand about St John's Apocalypse?' the friar asked the chandler. 'At what university did you study? At the loom I suppose? For I understand that you were nothing but a poor weaver and chandler before you went around preaching . . . I have attended the university of Louvain, and for long studied divinity, and yet I do not understand anything at all about St John's Apocalypse. That is a fact.' To which Jacob answered: 'Therefore Christ thanked his heavenly father that he had revealed and made it known to babes and hid it from the wise of the world, as it is written in Matthew 11.25.' 'Exactly!' the friar replied, 'God has revealed it the weavers at the loom, to the cobblers on the bench, and to bellow-menders, lantern-tinkers, scissors-grinders, brass-makers, thatchers and all sorts of riff-raff, and poor, filthy and lousy beggars. And to us ecclesiastics who have studied from our youth, night and day, God has concealed it.'

Taken from Christopher Rowland, in
Biblical Interpretation 1 (2) 1993, p. 229

29

A Brazilian Example: 'Listening to What the Spirit is Saying to the Churches'. Popular Interpretation of the Bible in Brazil

CARLOS MESTERS

Popular interpretations of the Bible have been sidelined by the mainstream for the lack of rationality in their reflections and the absence of a discursive approach in their outputs. This article, which comes out of the author's long involvement with base Christian communities, demonstrates that people who read the Bible in the context of struggle can offer a paradigm which can enrich academic reading.

This article first appeared in *Concilium* 1 (1991), pp. 100–11. The translator is Francis McDonagh.

Carlos Mesters, a professionally trained biblical scholar, has become renowned for his involvement with ecclesial base communities in Brazil and bringing them to wider attention. His books include *Defenseless Flower* and *God, Where are You? An Introduction to the Bible*, both published by Orbis Books.

A FACT WHICH SHOWS THE DIRECTION

It happened during the first meeting of the Bible course. There were about twenty-five people present. On the wall was the sentence 'God is love'. The priest asked, 'Who wrote that?' 'I did,' said Maria. 'Why did you write it?' 'I thought the wall looked very empty.' 'Why did you choose that sentence?' 'I thought it was beautiful.' 'Where did you find it?' 'I made it up myself. I thought that's the way we have to live as Christians!'

Then the priest said, 'Let's open our bibles at the First Letter of

St John, chapter 4, verse 8.' It took a little while for everyone to find the text. He asked Maria to read the verse. She said, 'Whoever fails to love does not know God, because *God is love.*' It was the first time in her life that Maria had opened the Bible. She got a shock. She didn't expect to find inside it the sentence she had written on the wall. She discovered that, without her knowing it, the word of God was already present in her life. She was so delighted and happy that she hardly slept that night. The next day her bible was full of scraps of paper marking pages. During the night she had found other familiar phrases.

There are many other simple, ordinary facts like this. They point to the direction of popular interpretation: the gradual discovery that the word of God is not only in the Bible, but is also and primarily present in the lives of *all* those who are trying to live faithfully. The Bible awakens people, reveals and confirms to them that our God is God-with-us, today, here, on the onward march and in the struggle of the poor. The Bible is the source of new attitudes.

In this article the expression 'popular interpretation' refers only to the way the Bible is read by the poor in their ecclesial base communities. There are other ways of reading the Bible among the people; for example, that of the poor in the Pentecostal movements. I shall talk only about what I have got to know and see at first hand. Nevertheless, my horizon is limited. I am only aware of what is happening in some Brazilian communities.

SOME DETAILS OF THE HISTORY OF POPULAR INTERPRETATION

Popular interpretation didn't come from nowhere. Its roots are lost in the past. In the course of the years three aspects have come to stand out, one after the other.

1. Getting to know the Bible

The desire to get to know the Bible prompted many people to read it more frequently. Let us recall some facts which set this process in motion: 1. The renewal of exegesis, which began in Europe, created a new interest in the text and its content; 2. The three papal encyclicals on the Bible encouraged Catholic exegetes to be more open and use the sciences to discover the historico-literal meaning; 3. The wide dissemination of the conclusions of exegesis and the use of the missal in the vernacular brought the Bible closer to the people.

In Brazil this movement of renewal was limited to the middle classes. What helped to bring the Bible to the poorest was the missionary energy of the Protestant Churches. Many Catholics started to read the Bible in order to be able to answer the Protestants and so overcome their inferiority complex. Gradually, especially after the Great War, this closed and polemical mentality relaxed and the way was open for the discovery of the novelty of the word of God.

In the course of these years, slowly, from within this renewed interest in the Bible, there grew up a new concept of *revelation* which is of great importance for an understanding of popular interpretation. In this God did not only speak in the past; he continues to speak today!

2. Creating community

Just as the word of God began to become familiar, it began to produce its fruits. The first fruit was to bring people together and create community. These are some of the facts which contributed to the people's taking this new step in reading the Bible: 1. People's Bible Weeks throughout the country spread the knowledge accumulated by the exegetes; 2. The distribution of the Bible in the language of the people: in Brazil alone there are more than ten different translations, and more than a million Bibles are printed each year; 3. Scarcity of clergy led some bishops to entrust the administration of parishes to nuns, which, in practice, placed greater stress on the celebration of the Word; 4. In the liturgical renewal and in the celebrations of the Word, the people gradually rediscovered a favourable environment for reading and interpreting the Bible; 5. Millions of Brazilians, relying on the Bible, found the courage to break with the almost absolute authority of the clergy. They abandoned the Catholic Church and joined Pentecostal communities; 6. In reaction to the rapid growth of the Pentecostal groups, in some places catechists were trained to go around the villages and gather people together for biblical catechesis.

In the course of these years, from this community ferment, there gradually grew up a new concept of *interpretation* which helped people to understand popular interpretation better. Interpreting the Bible ceased to be thought of as the transmission of information exclusively by the exegete who has studied for the purpose, but a community activity to which all should contribute, each in his or her own way, including the exegete.

3. Serving the people

The year 1968 was the year of the world revolution of youth, the military coup in Brazil, the meeting of the Latin American bishops' conference at Medellín, and the systematization of the theology of liberation. It was also the time when this new step in popular interpretation became more clearly visible.

The community born of the word of God is meant to be a source of blessing for *all* peoples (cf. Gen. 12.3). Faithfulness to the word calls on us to take a step beyond knowledge and community concerns, towards the people. It is here, in the service of the people, that the difference and the novelty of popular interpretation begins to become visible.

The following are some of the historical factors which led the people to take this qualitative step forward in the way they read the Bible: 1. The abandonment of the poor, condemned by the social and cultural system to the status of 'ignorant' and 'inferior'. No one took them seriously or knew them by name. In the community, however, they received names and a history; 2. The military coups of 1964 and 1968 subjected the people to repression, led to persecution of leaders and exposed the failure of left-wing 'vanguardism'. Many leaders disappeared among the people and began more consistent base-level work; 3. After some initial hesitations, the official Church became a source of criticism of the military regime. It welcomed and gave shelter to the popular movement, which in this way acquired a strong religious motivation; 4. The see-judge-act method, used especially by Catholic Action, explained and disseminated the new vision of revelation, namely: God is speaking today; 5. The Second Vatican Council and the bishops' conference assemblies of Medellín and Puebla. The Medellín conference was a reinterpretation of Vatican II for Latin America based on a critical view of the economic, social, political and religious situation; 6. The history of Latin America itself: with tacit cover from the Church, Christians killed millions of Indians and blacks and destroyed native cultures. The captivity of the blacks and Indians was worse than the captivity in Babylon; 7. The new instruments of pastoral action in the service of the poor were inherently ecumenical: CIMI (defending Indians), the Pastoral Land Commission (defending land) and the Workers' Pastoral Commission (defending the rights of workers).

All these factors influenced and still influence the way the poor read the Bible. There are communities which, motivated by reading the Bible, place themselves at the service of the people and enter the struggle for justice. Other communities emerge directly out the struggle and, as a result of that struggle, begin to read the Bible.

Without money or ability to read books *about* the Bible, the poor read the Bible by the only criterion they possess, their faith lived in community and their lives of suffering as an oppressed people. Reading the Bible in this way, the poor discover within it the obvious truth which they did not know or which was hidden from them for centuries, namely: 1. a history of oppression like their own today, with the same conflicts; and 2. a liberation struggle for the same values which they pursue today here in Brazil: land, justice, sharing, fraternity, a decent life.

The Bible comes to be seen as the mirror or 'symbol' of what they live today. It is at that point, from this new connection between the Bible and life, that the poor make the discovery, the greatest of all discoveries: 'If God was with that people then, in the past, then he is also with us in this struggle we are waging to free ourselves. He hears our cries.' It is the discovery of God-with-us, the heart of Scripture. This is the seed of the theology of liberation. The Bible is the source of a liberated mind.

In the course of these years, out of this attempt to serve the people, there emerged a new way of looking at the Bible and its interpretation, namely: the Bible is no longer a strange book, but *our book*, 'described in writing to be a lesson for us' (I Cor. 10.11), the mirror of our history, or 'symbol', as the fathers said. The aim of interpretation is no longer to interpret the Bible, but to interpret life with the help of the Bible.

To conclude. What before was distant has now come near. What before was mysterious and inaccessible has now become human and begun to become part of the everyday texture of the life of the poor. And not only that: along with the word of God, God himself has drawn near. This is the Good News which the poor are taking it on themselves to spread across the country. If anyone thirty years ago had made a prophecy and given an exact description of all that is happening here among the poor in connection with the reading of the Bible, no one would have believed them. 'This is Yahweh's doing, and we marvel at it' (Ps. 118.23).

THE INTERNAL DYNAMIC OF THE PROCESS OF POPULAR INTERPRETATION

In the rural areas of the state of Minas Gerais there is an evangelization movement. Its initial concern was to initiate a process of participation and transmit to the people the new knowledge about the Bible and faith. The political dimension of the service of the people was almost absent. When they were criticized because of this, the leaders of the movement said, 'If the word of God has a political dimension, it will appear in the people's action. What we're interested in is fidelity to the word.' And in fact the political dimension has appeared with great strength in recent years, and the apologetic concern has disappeared. Today the movement has between 5000 and 6000 groups.

The fact shows that there is an internal dynamic in the process of popular interpretation. *Getting to know the Bible* leads to *living together as a community*. Living as a community leads to *service of the people*. This *service* in turn leads to a *deeper knowledge*, and so on. It is an endless dynamic. It constantly starts again from the beginning, and becomes ever deeper.

It is not that important which of the three aspects is the starting-point of the process of interpretation. This depends on the situation, the history, the culture and the interests of the community or group. What is important is to understand that any single aspect is incomplete without the other two.

1. Getting to know the Bible

The way the people read the Bible never remains abstract study. They immediately create a community environment of song and prayer in which the Spirit acts. After a careful reading, 'the veil is taken away' (cf. 2 Cor. 3.12–17), and they discover the connection between the text and the present situation.

2. Creating community

The community rises from the word like a river from its source. Because of this it always returns to listen to and meditate anew on the word which brought it into being. It is fidelity to that word which leads the community to go beyond its own boundaries and defend the lives of the people.

3. The service of the people

In the last few years the communities have embarked on the service of the people. They have thrown themselves fully into the popular movement and have not been afraid to make party political options in the name of their commitment to the gospel. Now, however, this very political activity is calling for a deeper knowledge of the biblical text and a more intense living out in community of the spirituality of liberation.

Generally, in all communities, some people identify more with one of the three aspects and others with one of the others. This produces healthy tensions. If there is an atmosphere of dialogue, a balance is created which encourages and enriches the interpretation of the Bible and prevents it from becoming one-sided. The three aspects are connected with each other in a dynamic unity: one grows out of another, depends on the other and leads to the third.

At the same time, each of the three is exposed to the temptation and risk of closing in on itself and excluding the other two. In other words, all is not always harmony. Very often the process of popular interpretation is tense and full of conflict. There is always a risk of narrowness and regression.

THE DANGER OF NARROWNESS AND REGRESSION

When a community reaches its goal in one of these three aspects (knowledge, community and service), some members, from fidelity to the word, want to move forward, to take another step. Others, in the name of the same fidelity, oppose this opening. It is a moment of crisis and also a moment of grace. It is not always the group which wants to advance that wins.

In the Church all religious movements use the Bible, even the most conservative. Usually all that they do is motivated by the Bible. The fundamentalist movements, in the name of the Bible, oppose interpretation and openness to society. In some places bible groups which have closed in on themselves and on the Bible have become the most conservative groups in the parish. The poorest of the poor are not in the ecclesial base communities, but in the Pentecostal movements, the great majority of which, for the time being, follow a fundamentalist line.

It is not enough to spread the Bible among the people and think that the word of God on its own will do the rest. Read in isolation, out of the context of the community's faith and service of the people, the Bible is ambivalent and can be manipulated fairly easily. It can become a reactionary book which ends up giving legitimacy to false idols, oppressive ideologies and wars: the extermination of the Indians in Latin America, the slave trade with Africa, the Vietnam war, etc.

There can be a closing in on the opposite side, too, though it is much less frequent. As the community grows and achieves a clearer political understanding and a deeper commitment to service, it may shut itself up in service to the people, in the social and political dimension, and think that the communal and the personal, study, prayer and mysticism, no longer have anything to contribute to the onward journey. There can be absorption in the communal, in mysticism, in the charismatic movement. There can also be absorption in liberal, or even progressive, study of the ancient text. These sorts of absorption are tragic, because none of the three aspects alone reaches the full meaning of Scripture.

Even in the interpreter's personal life there can be these risks of absorption and regression. What is important in overcoming these temptations inherent in the process of popular interpretation is to be able to create and maintain an atmosphere of dialogue in the community, in which the human word has freedom of movement, without censorship. Where the human word has freedom of movement, the word of God is fruitful and creates freedom.

Despite these dangers, the facts show that the people are able to find the knack of mixing the Bible with life and removing its ambivalence. In a very poor community in a remote rural area of the state of Espírito Santo, the people read the text which forbids the eating of pork and concluded: 'Through this ban God is trying to teach us today that we should eat pork.' These were the arguments:

God's concern is the people's life and health. In the Old Testament, in that desert, eating pork was dangerous. The lack of water caused disease and damaged people's health. So God ordered a ban on pork. But today we know how to treat this meat. Besides, all we have to feed our children with are these pigs. If we didn't use them, we'd be damaging their health. That's why, today, God is telling us to eat pork.

Why do some communities achieve this openness and others not? The following fact may help with the reply. In the first stage of a bible course in the same state of Espírito Santo, almost all the questions were about disputed biblical questions: Adam and Eve, the Garden of Eden, the beast of Revelation, the flood, and so on. During that year the diocese came to give more attention to very specific problems of the people: housing, land, health. This had an effect on the second stage of the course, a year later. Those disputed questions no longer held the same interest. Other questions came up, this time connected with the reality of the people's life, both in the Bible and today.

THE METHOD OF POPULAR INTERPRETATION

The method one adopts in reading and interpreting the Bible is much more than a set of techniques and dynamics. It expresses, actualizes and transmits a particular vision of the Bible and revelation. That is why not just any method will do. The three aspects we looked at earlier are also characteristics of the method used by the poor in reading the Bible. They are like the three apexes of a triangle.

1. Serving the poor – starting from real life
The poor bring their real-life problems with them into the Bible. They read the Bible in terms of their lives. They have in their minds the situation of the people they want to serve. In the *mirror* of the Bible they meet the reflection of their own lives. The produces in them a certain *familiarity* with the Bible.

2. Creating community – starting from the community's faith
The poor read the Bible with eyes filled with the faith of the community which tells them, 'The Bible is God's word. Jesus is alive and present among us.' Reading becomes a community activity, a prayerful activity, an act of faith. The poor recreate, without a label and without the name, in a new and updated form, the centuries-old

practice of the *lectio divina*. The Bible is seen as the community's book, *our* book, things 'described in writing to be a lesson for us' (1 Cor. 10.11). This creates a certain *freedom* in them.

3. Getting to know the Bible – respecting the text

The poor read obediently, that is, they have a deep respect for the text. Sometimes this obedience resembles fundamentalism. They are straightforward people, without much critical sense, and open themselves to listen to what God has to say, ready to change their lives and fight, if he demands it. What comes through here is an attitude of *fidelity* on the part of people who not only hear the word, but also seek to put it into practice.

Freedom

Spirit = Prayer

Creating community = Faith

LISTENING
TO GOD
TODAY

Real life   Studying the text

Serving the people   Getting to know the Bible

Familiarity   *Fidelity*

The triangle diagram helps to illustrate what we have just discussed. Each of the three apexes has its own characteristics and requirements in the process of interpretation. When the Bible is read, the three interact to contribute to the common objective, *listening to God today*.

United and acting in conjunction, the three criteria constitute what might be called the spirituality of popular interpretation, its trade-mark. The three are always present, in one way of another, when the poor read the Bible. If one of them is forgotten, some person or a group will always point this out.

THE NOVELTY AND SCOPE OF POPULAR INTERPRETATION

The interpretation the poor make of the Bible contains a novelty of great significance for the life of the churches. It is a gift of God, a breath of the Spirit. It is an ancient novelty from the distant past which revives some basic elements of tradition.

1. The purpose of interpretation is no longer to seek information about the past, but to illuminate the present with the light of God-with-us. It is to interpret life with the help of the Bible.
2. The leader of the interpretation is no longer the exegete. Interpretation is a community activity in which all take part, including the exegete, who has a special role. Because of this it is important to keep in mind the faith of the community and look for a *common meaning* accepted by the community.
3. The social position from which interpretation is carried out is that of the poor and marginalized. This changes the approach. Very often, for want of a more critical social awareness, the interpreter falls victim to ideological prejudices and unknowingly uses the Bible to legitimize an anti-human system of oppression.
4. A reading which connects the Bible with life is necessarily ecumenical and liberating. To call a reading ecumenical does not mean that Protestants and Catholics discuss their differences in order to reach a common conclusion. This may be a result. The most ecumenical thing we have is the life God has given us. This life is being threatened, destroyed. An ecumenical reading means interpreting the Bible to defend life and not to defend our religious institutions and denominations. In the present situation of the Latin American people a reading which defends life has to promote liberation.
5. This illustrates the difference from European exegesis. The greatest problem for us in Latin America is not that faith is endangered because of secularization, but that life is in danger of being destroyed and dehumanized. What is worse is that the Bible is in

417

danger of being used to legitimize this situation with the name of God, just as in the time of the kings of Judah and Israel, tradition was being used to legitimize idols. Popular interpretation identifies, exposes and denounces this manipulation.

6. The connection between the Old and New Testaments is beginning to be seen with different eyes. Our people's cultures are *our* Old Testament. They have to be seen, not as aberrations to be corrected by the message of the New Testament, but as *our* promises and *our* law to be put into effect and fulfilled by the Good News of Jesus.

7. The method and the dynamic used by the poor in their meetings are very simple. They do not generally use rational, discursive language, built up out of arguments and reasoning. They prefer to tell stories and use similes. It is a language which works through associations of ideas, the primary concern of which is not to *produce knowledge* but to *produce discoveries*.

PROBLEMS, DIFFICULTIES AND CHALLENGES

Not everything is positive. There are many problems and weaknesses. Some have no solution; others are already being solved. There are problems in each of the three angles of the triangle. Let us look at some of them.

1. Life and people

1. Hunger and destitution. It is difficult to talk about the Bible to someone who is hungry and lacks the bare necessities of a human life.
2. Lack of time. Work and the difficulties of life prevent people from taking part in bible groups.
3. Lack of money. A bible is expensive, and many people cannot afford one.
4. Illiteracy. Will we be able to create a 'Bible of the poor'?
5. The people's silence. Having been silenced for centuries, they have an inferiority complex.
6. Town and country. The Bible emerged from a rural culture; what relevance does it have to today's big urban conglomerations?

7. People and exegesis. Both have their problems: how can we create an exegesis which helps to solve the people's problems?

2. Community and faith

1. Authoritarian leaders who refuse to dialogue: they oppress others while talking about liberation.
2. The departure of millions for Pentecostal groups produces an apologetic and polemical attitude; where are our communities failing?
3. Lack of training for priests to help the poor to interpret the Bible; the demand is greater than the supply, and the Church was not ready to meet so many requests.
4. Conflicting interpretations within the Church disorientate the people.
5. In the past the clergy kept control of interpretation; now the *expert* may create a new dependence. How can we respect the faith of the simple?
6. Many people try to tar the liberating dimension of popular interpretation with the brush of Marxist subversion. How can we combine gratuitousness and effectiveness in the struggle for liberation?
7. In the current ecclesiastical climate there is an urgent task to be performed to legitimate popular interpretation in terms of tradition and scholarship.

3. Text and Bible

1. The great variety of translations makes it difficult for people to memorize and ponder on the word.
2. Fundamentalism is an attitude which interferes with the connection between the Bible and life; liberation from the grip of the letter is the first step towards liberation.
3. The many study guides have the advantage of keeping a group going in difficult times, but may create dependence and kill creativity.
4. In their enthusiasm the people don't pay much attention to the literal meaning; how can we avoid this subjectivism without falling into literalist exegesis?

5. More and more, practice makes one feel the need for a more solid theoretical base.
6. The difficult and strange language keeps the Bible remote from the lives of the people.
7. How are we to reveal to the poor the 'biblical' dimension which has existed in their lives for centuries?

It is very difficult to make a complete and exact survey of all that is happening among the poor in connection with the interpretation of the Bible. The ordinary people don't worry about recording what they do. The poor don't write books, don't cite authors, and don't use bibliographies. Many of those who participate in this biblical movement are barely able to read. As a result what the people do, when described either by themselves or by someone else, seems not to have much substance. The same is true of this article. It doesn't cite authorities or consult books. The document it consulted is the people themselves, scattered in their communities.

30

A Malawian Example: The Bible and Non-literate Communities

PATRICK A. KALILOMBE

Re-reading of the Bible assumes literacy. But how does one use the Bible in a non-literate context? A Malawian tries to provide some hermeneutical clues as to how to tackle this problem.

This essay is the revised version of the paper presented at the International Congress on Africa and the Bible, August 1988, Cairo.

Bishop Patrick Kalilombe is the Director of the Centre for Black and White Christian Partnership, Selly Oak Colleges, Birmingham, UK.

African theology, as the Ecumenical Association for African Theologians (EAAT would want to practise it, must be a tool for human liberation in obedience to the Word of God as revealed in the Scriptures. This is why EAAT's inaugural declaration indicated as the first source of theology the Bible and Christian heritage, saying:

> The Bible is the basic source of African theology, because it is the primary witness of God's revelation in Jesus Christ. No theology can retain its Christian identity apart from Scripture... Through a re-reading of this Scripture in the social context of our struggle for our humanity, God speaks to us in the midst of our troublesome situation.[1]

But it is not just any use of the Bible that serves the purposes of liberation. As Mesters has reminded us: 'The Bible is ambiguous. It can be a force for liberation or a force for oppression. If it is treated like a finished monument that cannot be touched, that must be taken literally as it is, then it will be an oppressive force.'[2] In the past the Bible has often been invoked in such a way as to legitimize the most obvious social, economic or political injustices, to discourage stirrings of revolt against oppressive or discriminatory practices, and to promote attitudes of resignation and compliance in the face of exploitative manipulations of power-holders.

Even today there seems to be an intensified invasion of certain types of biblical interpretation which can only be characterized as simplistic and distracting. They centre so much on the spiritual and interior needs of the people that the connection between the Word of God and the realities of every day becomes secondary, almost irrelevant. Ominously this kind of biblical faith is being promoted with particular effect in countries of the Third World; that is, precisely among those peoples for whom the facts of material deprivation, violations of human rights and sheer exploitation are the most pressing concerns. In such circumstances the Bible is hardly a credible liberating power, and can even become a tool for continued enslavement.

It is, however, in these same areas of the Third World that special efforts are currently being made to discover and employ the power of the Bible for people's full liberation. There are conditions for this liberating force to come out. Advocates of liberation theology have been studying, as a matter of urgency, this question of the use and misuse of the Scriptures, acknowledging that what might be called a 'political' reading of the Bible is not only legitimate, but highly desirable.[3] These investigations are useful and enlightening. And yet they are at such a level of scholarly sophistication that it is not immediately evident how useful they can be when we consider the problems of biblical usage by ordinary people engaged in the project of liberation at the grass-roots.

Liberation theology is of practical use only in the measure in which it is practised by these ordinary people; otherwise it remains a merely intellectual activity indulged in by comfortable academics. By the same token a liberative handling of the Bible becomes effective only when the people themselves are practising it in their own struggle. It is necessary, therefore, to examine carefully how the people at the grass-roots actually use the Scriptures and how this use can relate to their liberation.

THE SPECIAL PREDICAMENT OF THE NON-LITERATE

When Mesters warns against the possible oppressive use of the Bible, it is clear that the central issue is that of interpretation: what meaning do we give to the text of the Scriptures? This assumes that the biblical text is itself available to the people and can therefore become the object of interpretation.

My interest is with a more radical situation. What happens when the text of the Bible is not available, or when its availability to one section of the community is controlled and regulated by another section? This is the case when part of the community is illiterate and cannot therefore have direct contact with the written Word of God. Such people are at the mercy of their literate neighbours if they wish to know what the Bible has to say.

Those who can read and write are in a position to share with their less fortunate brothers and sisters the contents of the Holy Book. But they have also the possibility of withholding parts of the contents and distorting what they report from the Bible. They may choose to share only some sections and leave out others, according as they themselves judge good or opportune. They could very well leave out those parts that they think useless, ambiguous, or dangerous. This is not simply a matter of quantity. It is also a question of interpretation. What the readers of the text choose to share is determined very much by their own judgement, interests, or objectives. The illiterate hearers have very little scope of judging for themselves. Therefore their understanding of God's Word and their capacity to reflect on it and use it for their own lives are to a large extent controlled by others.

When, then, we discuss the importance of the Bible for doing theology in Africa, we are raising some quite vexing questions. This theology is meant to be a liberating tool, especially for those who are underprivileged or oppressed. In our developing countries the illiterate are surely among such disadvantaged people. What possibility is there for them to take an active and fair part in hearing the Word of God and reflecting on it in the light of their own experience? Are they reduced to having others do theology for them? Such questions are of special relevance in a continent like Africa.

LITERACY AND ILLITERACY IN AFRICA: EXAMPLE OF MALAWIAN CATHOLICS

It is important to remember that, in general, Africa is largely non-literate. In more than half of the countries less than half of the population above fifteen years of age know how to read and write, and in about all the countries literacy among the female population is far below that among the male.[4] Let it be said in passing that this last fact is, as far as religion is concerned, of tremendous consequence since in general the more active and practising members in any community are often women. And in many communities, especially among matrilineal people, the female role (mother, sister, grandmother) is most decisive as far as religious development and practice are concerned. It is legitimate, therefore, to assume that African life is, in general, less literate and more oral, auricular, and visual.

Christianity would normally be expected to be influenced by this factor. Only where literacy has been seen as in some way a precondition for membership in the Church would one expect the majority of believers to belong to the literate sector. This has been the case for most Protestant churches in Africa. If that constitutes an advantage as far as contact with the Bible is concerned, it also spells out the danger of a serious constraint in evangelization: only those with a certain degree of modern education will feel at home in the Church. In other words, conversion and fidelity to the Christian faith would be conditioned by acceptance of modern culture. That certainly leaves out a large part of the African population, those people who for one reason or another have not had the chance of a meaningful education and live largely within the confines of traditional life. This is the case for many people in the rural areas; and even in urban and semi-urban areas the proportion of people who live a non-literate culture is greater than one might be led to imagine.[5]

I am less acquainted with communities where literacy is preponderant, and where therefore the use of the Bible as written word presents no special problem. My experience has been mainly with communities for whom reading and writing were peripheral in daily life: in acquiring and communicating knowledge and in passing on information. Among them there were admittedly persons who had been to school and could read and write more or less fluently. One hoped that more schooling would become available to them; and indeed heroic efforts in education were being made in these areas. Still, for the time being, their ordinary way of life was not dependent on literacy. When we imagine such people using the Bible for their Christian life, for 'doing theology at the grass-roots', are we just dreaming? Is there no way these people can come into real contact with the Scriptures?

I shall take the case of my own country, Malawi; and more

precisely, I am thinking of the Catholic population there. Although statistics indicate that 49.9 per cent of the population above fifteen years of age are literate,[6] among Catholics this percentage would be too high. For reasons that are due mainly to history, the Catholic Church in Malawi has been successful mainly among the more traditional and less Westernized communities. As Linden pointed out: 'On the whole their [Catholic missionaries'] converts came from the edges of African society, the marginal men and late-comers to Nyasaland [former name of Malawi] like the immigrant Alomwe and Sena.'[7]

A large proportion of Malawian Catholics are therefore either illiterate or semi-literate, and belong to the oral tradition rather than the literary one. As such, the Bible as written word still remains unfamiliar and marginal to their life as believers. When you watch Catholics going to church or to other services, very few will be carrying literature of any kind. A few may be bringing along their hymn and/or prayer-books, or perhaps a catechism or some devotional book. But hardly any will be carrying the Bible, not even the New Testament text! They know in advance that the standard Catholic service does not require the general faithful to read written texts for themselves. Why is this so?

The historical fact of a majority of non-literate members has been reinforced by what seems to be traditional Catholic practice. In standard Catholic ideology the faith expression of believers and their practical response to God's Word do not derive directly from the Bible, but from the teaching authority of the Church: the *magisterium*. It is understood, of course, that the *magisterium* itself is informed by the Scriptures, and to that extent the faith of the believers rests in the final analysis on the authority of the Bible. But the Bible is read and interpreted, not necessarily by each individual believer, but within the 'Tradition' of the Church. Sometimes this ideology has been unfairly and incorrectly expressed, as though for Catholics the faith derives from two distinct sources: the Scriptures *and* Tradition. The more correct way of putting the matter is this: faith derives from God's revelation, and this revelation reaches us through the Bible within Tradition. Vatican Council II, in its Constitution on Divine Revelation, has attempted to express more satisfactorily the relation between these two complementary aspects of God's revelation. 'Sacred Tradition and Sacred Scripture', it says, 'make up a single deposit of the Word of God, which is entrusted to the Church'.[8]

Whether or not this Constitution has succeeded in shedding new light around the Reformation contention about *Sola Scriptura* is a different matter which is not our direct concern here. What comes out clearly, however, is the crucial importance of two elements: Tradition and Community. The need for Catholics to read Scripture *within Tradition* makes this Tradition the *practically* decisive hermeneutical authority. If this principle is taken to its bitter logical conclusion, it would be quite normal for the believers to be satisfied with Tradition's presentation of the Scriptures without the necessity to read and examine personally the letter itself of the Bible. The biblical witness, content, selection, and interpretation would come to them through the various organs whereby Tradition addresses itself concretely to the believer. Such are, for example, the catechism, the pronouncements of the *magisterium* (Pope, Councils, Bishops, Synods, etc.), the liturgy (including rituals, preaching, hymnody, iconography . . .), and indeed also popular piety and devotions. Here lies the special power of Catholic faith, but also the source of problems which we shall need to examine later on.

Until quite recently direct contact with the Bible was a rare phenomenon among Catholics, certainly among the ordinary faithful in Malawi. Since Vatican II things have begun to change, and it is fair to say that heroic efforts are being made to bring the Scriptures to the people.[9] Since the coming of the use of vernacular languages in the liturgy, more and more biblical texts are heard by the faithful at Mass and other services. In many areas, as complete Bibles or portions of Scripture become available to the faithful, suggestions for daily Scripture readings are being proposed, often with accompanying aids of an exegetical or spiritual nature. The possibility, then, for a widespread contact with the Scriptures is now there in Malawi.

THE CRUCIAL PROBLEM: BRINGING THE BIBLE TO NON-LITERATE PEOPLE

But does this solve the problem of the use of Scripture among our Catholic faithful? Not automatically. The crucial point is that even here the methods being used assume largely a literary culture which the majority of the people are not accustomed to. For a people of a non-literate way of life, the mere availability of the written Word is not enough to bring the Scriptures into their life. The Word of God must first become 'incarnated' in their own specific way of hearing and responding. In other words: the Bible needs to come to them in non-literate ways.

In communities where reading and writing are marginal ways for learning, communicating, assimilating knowledge and values, and expressing them, there exist other media which are, for those people, much more familiar and effective. *Hearing* appropriately formulated inputs and *seeing* culturally adapted messages take the place of reading as means for taking in and assimilating information and knowledge. To match the value of the ever-present written text (to which the readers can always return if they forget), non-literate people employ mnemonic devices like *repetition* or *variation* of analogous visual aids. In order to interpret and apply to life what is being taken in, they have such potent tools as *acting, retelling* in their own words, or *responding* through gestures or emotion-filled expressions. Through these appropriate methods, messages and instructions are passed around, selected, interpreted and evaluated, and then assimilated so that they influence people's lives.

There is no reason why the Bible could not be made to reach the non-literate through these ways with the same efficacy that the written word reaches the literate. If all of them cannot read the Bible text for themselves, they surely can hear it read to them, provided care is taken to make this reading as effective as possible. In a community of mostly illiterate folk there might be two or more who are able to read. By reading out the text to the group these few would enable their brothers and sisters to hear the Word ('Faith cometh by hearing, and hearing by the word of God': Rom. 10.17). Reading out or 'proclaiming' the Scriptures could thus become a value ministry for the few literates among our people. If need be, the readers would be requested to repeat the text or parts of it for the benefit of the audience. In our modern times when such technical instruments as tape-recorders are no longer rarities even in the remote villages, much use can be made of recorded biblical tapes. Our Moslem neighbours know this only too well: have you not heard hoisted loudspeakers blaring out recorded Qur'anic surahs from up the mosque tower in the market-place? Christians could learn to make such a resourceful use of these modern devices.

Reading out biblical texts could very easily become a new version of the traditional art of the story-teller. Our people do enjoy story-telling: children and adults alike. In all sorts of formal (ritual, courts) or informal occasions people are ever eager to hear *nkhani* (story or narrative). They crowd around the public place where cases are being tried; they surround the newly arrived visitor who brings fresh news and messages from relatives or friends, or who simply describes the wonders of faraway places and peoples; they regale one another with wise sayings, parables, fables or riddles. The spoken and heard word is very central. It fulfils the functions of newspapers, reviews, books, or advertisements in literate communities. That is why the radio has become a favourite toy in the villages. The Bible would come effectively to the non-literate if the skills of the spoken word were used judiciously, and if the power of this word were put at the service of the Scriptures.

The role of music and singing in non-literate societies is likewise great. Often the song accompanies dancing, but it should not be thought of simply as a means of entertainment. Singing serves to express interior sentiments, to underline and reinforce values, to praise or to ridicule, to exalt or to debase. In ritual and religion, singing is often used as a means of arousing and communicating appropriate attitudes of mind and soul. As with the spoken word, so also the incantation has effective power. The song is also a vehicle of information and teaching, all the more effective because it is easy to remember and to reproduce. In traditional rituals singing was a favourite tool for instruction, for admonition, and for passing on traditional lore: history, customs, or the art of living.

With a bit of imagination, singing could be used for bringing the Bible to the people. A lot of the Scripture text was originally for singing – for example, the psalms and the numerous canticles and hymns which scholars discover in various books of the Bible (Revelation seems to be full of them). Our hymn-books offer quantities of fine hymns. Some of them are more or less directly biblical in origin and inspiration. But a large number are not. This is principally because in standard congregational practice the hymns are simply a commentary on, or an accompaniment or reinforcement of, the Bible text that is supposed to be read during the service. But where reading is not possible, or is marginal, why should the song itself not replace the reading of the written word?

Important texts would be put to music (e.g. the Beatitudes, the Sermon on the Mount, the parables). Thus the singing itself could constitute a direct contact with God's Word, thus abolishing the unfair discrimination whereby the Bible is unduly restricted to the literate. In sessions for Christian instruction, and even in bible discussion groups, the song could thus serve as the Scripture text. There are enough gifted people in the local congregations for whom composing tunes is not a problem. All they need is to be given the Bible text. One can imagine a special ministry for such people whereby they could gradually build up a home-made repertoire of biblical portions in local music.

The part played by the *visual media* in non-literate societies should also be taken into account. Much information and many important messages circulate through what people are able to see and to handle. Students of the so-called African art are wont to say that the objects that Western sensibility classifies as 'art' are actually very functional tools in the society, be they sculptures, paintings, pottery, vestments and 'ornamentation', architecture, and even weapons and utensils. They are not there simply as an embodiment of the aesthetic spirit. First and foremost they are saying something and are meant to produce useful results for the needs of the community. As with the gestures and words that are usually associated with these objects, we are dealing here with 'symbols', understood in the strong sense of conventional signs which are meant to effect what they signify. Symbolism is a central force in non-literate societies. The visual object, by virtue of the evocative and associational power of its shape, design, texture and colours, becomes a medium for expressing values, recalling stories, fables or parables, and often also for evoking meaningful history.

Christian churches still need to learn to exploit the vast resources of our people's visual media in the religious field. The schools, especially at the primary level, have always recognized the importance of visual aids. Just as much contact with the Bible can be established through hearing (e.g. tapes), so also can the eyes capture what the Scriptures are saying through words. A picture depicting a biblical scene is able to bring the message quite powerfully to those who are unable to read. Often the illustrations in a book convey the essential points of the text. Paintings, sketches, statues, or artistic arrangements in the place of worship have been used traditionally for more than mere decorative purposes: they were often the textbook of the illiterate. How much biblical instruction could be done with the help of slides, videos or films for non-literate audiences! In recent years catechetical centres have been providing material of this kind. The biblical apostolate should make more use of such visual aids.

EXPLOITING LOCAL RESOURCES

There is, of course, the objection that this type of material is often prohibitively expensive, and in many cases there is need for sophisticated equipment which simple people would neither possess nor be in a position to handle efficiently. And again, some material is foreign and ill-adapted for use among Africans. That is sometimes true. Well-meaning people, when they set out to meet the needs of non-literate communities, tend to introduce resources that have to be sought from outside. This is not helpful: it simply prolongs, often even aggravates, the dependence of these disadvantaged people on outside help.

But there is no reason why locally available resources should not be exploited. Simple, ordinary material, which the people use in their daily life, can be easily turned into effective illustrations for biblical communication. The people are able to attach didactic value to what they possess. They do not need exotic equipment for that. They can resort to the various symbols in their culture which express values and meanings in line with the biblical message: symbols of birth, life, death, purification, joy, humility. These can be used anew to stand for one or the other biblical message.

In this connection the symbolic value of colours, insignia, or ritual objects comes to mind. If the people themselves establish this connection between their culture and the Bible, there can slowly grow up an inventory of visual symbolism through which the Bible message can be interpreted, evoked and made use of. At any rate, it is counter-productive to create the impression that progress is being made because the local needs are being met with 'modern' means.

HOW TO INTERPRET AND APPLY
THE BIBLICAL MESSAGE

Through auditory and visual media, biblical material is able to be taken in by people who are not of a written tradition. The objective, however, is not simply to receive and take in what Scripture offers. As they receive the Bible message, the people should at the same time have the capacity *to react* to the input, to *interpret it*; that is, give it their own understanding, and then to *apply it* to their life as believers. This is a decisive stage, for it is only in this way that the non-literate actually do their own theologizing with the means that are familiar to them. They allow the Word of God to meet and challenge their ordinary experience. In ways and idioms proper to their culture, they take the initiative to reflect on this Word, asking themselves what it means to them. They evaluate its significance and relevancy to their lives, and then apply it.

There are several ways whereby non-literate people appropriate and interpret inputs. One of these is *repeating in their own words* what they hear, see or experience. The exercise of re-telling or putting in one's own words forces the person to say what in the input was worth retaining. It is therefore an exercise in personal *selection* of the meaningful: for in a given input not everything is equally relevant to everyone. By the same token it is an exercise in *interpretation* and assessment of value: for one remarks and retains only those points that are significant for one (personal) reason or another.

The value of retelling is enhanced when several people *exchange and discuss* what they have retained singly. By so doing they enlarge the extent of the meaningful, one person's points being enriched by points from the others. At the same time this makes possible mutual challenges and criticism. Questions will come as to whether one heard correctly or missed out on an important point. There will be questions about the real meaning of this or that word or expression. And then there is the wider area of discussion about how the biblical message applies to individual or common living. By engaging in a discussion of this type the group is actually constructing their 'theology': a reasoned reflection on their experience in the light of God's Word.

Another powerful means of selecting, interpreting and applying inputs is what we may call *drama* or re-enacting. When the audience proceeds to act out what they have taken in, they inevitably select what struck them, and automatically express *why* and in what way it struck them. By reproducing it through drama they are also applying the meaning to their familiar world in familiar idiom. Even when only one part of the community does the acting, while the others look on, there is possibility of mutual exchange and 'discussion'. The reactions of the onlookers can be affirmative, interrogatory, encouraging, reinforcing (e.g. through applause), or, on the contrary, cool, disapproving, or indifferent. It has been said that the preaching in some churches, where the congregation is expected to manifest its response, is a version of this kind of drama. It is not the preacher alone who interprets and expresses the message. Through their responses and reactions, the 'audience' take part in directing the content, affecting the flow of delivery, and giving it shape. This too is a group-type of theologizing.

In this context of a religious gathering, another effective way of interpreting and applying God's Word is *prayer*. When people pray after hearing the Word of God, they automatically express what meaning the Word has for them, and usually they go on to apply it to their lives. The Word will have enlightened them, questioned their assumptions, rebuked their conduct, or given them guidance and encouragement. All this usually transpires through prayer, which then becomes a response to the challenge of God's Word. We know how enriching shared prayer can be. Different members simply say aloud what the Word has done to them; and as divers responses flow into one another the assembly shares in an ever-enriched pool of understandings and applications.

In some congregations there is the practice of *testimony*. Here individuals attempt to put in communicable words their experience of God's activity in their lives. Often these testimonies are veritable biblical commentaries made in simple terms by ordinary people.

We can see, then, that much scope exists even for the non-literate to receive the biblical message, to interpret and apply it, even if they do not themselves read the written text.

A LIBERATING THEOLOGY FROM THE UNDERSIDE OF HISTORY

What is the point in all this discussion about the Bible and non-literate people? Our concern is for the integrity of the kind of Third World theologies which our Ecumenical Association of African Theologians has been attempting to formulate and promote in the past ten years of its existence. In numerous discussions and exchanges, the gist of which can be found in the written works produced by both EATWOT and EAAT, several basic characteristics of this type of theology have emerged.

I would like to recall three of them. First, it is a committed and liberating theology, as was stressed at the inaugural assembly of the Ecumenical Association for Third World Theologians (EATWOT:

We reject as irrelevant an academic type of theology that is divorced from action. We are prepared for a radical break in epistemology which makes commitment the first act of theology and engages in critical reflection on the reality of the Third World.[10]

Second, this liberation must be achieved ultimately by the oppressed themselves, and not on their behalf, even though others will join them in this commitment. The Asian theologians expressed this felicitously when they said:

To be truly liberating, this theology must arise from the Asian poor with a liberated consciousness. It is articulated and expressed by the oppressed community using the technical skills of biblical scholars, social scientists, psychologists, anthropologists, and others. It can be expressed in many ways, in art forms, drama, literature, folk stories, and native wisdom, as well as in doctrinal–pastoral statements.[11]

Third, the basic source of this liberating theology is the Bible.[12]

If the Bible is the source of liberating theology, those who would engage in doing such a theology must have the Bible realistically available to them, and they must be in a position to reflect on it, not by procuration, but in their own right. Clearly this poses a question for those who cannot read and write, since the Bible offers itself to us today primarily as a written text. Normally only those who are literate will be able to study it directly and base their reflection on this Word of God. Those who are unable to read are in the unenviable position of depending on others.

Unless there is a radical change in methodology, it is not realistic to expect such people to take a creative part in doing theology. Their knowledge of the Scriptures risks being from mere hearsay and to consist only of bits and pieces that are kindly made available to them by those who can read. As we said, the interpretation itself is affected by this dependence. The non-literate would not have full confidence in their own understanding of the Bible, as they would not know whether or not they had all that was required for an informed interpretation. Those who have direct access to the Scriptures would always be tempted to act as judges, with the very real risk of presenting their own interests and viewpoints as the only valid and correct norm of God's Word. The literate would thus have a decided advantage over the non-literate as far as the Bible is concerned.

In the present situation in the Third World, literacy is a key for access to resources of knowledge, power and wealth; and inversely, illiteracy usually bars people from all these. It is natural, therefore, that, all things being equal, the non-literate will tend to be among the less advantaged, among the powerless and those most likely to be oppressed and exploited. If then, they are incapable of taking an active part in reflecting over the Bible, the project of a liberating theology is largely in vain. There is the frightening possibility that theology, dominated by the more advantaged, will not be really for the liberation of those on the underside of history.

CONCLUSION

The gravity of this situation becomes evident in the case of a continent like Africa where illiteracy is so high. And taking the example of Malawi, we see that the predicament of the Catholic population is quite tragic. The conclusion seems to be, then, that a major concern for those interested in developing an effective theology in Africa should be to make sure that literacy is not the only condition for access to Holy Scripture.

This paper attempts to suggest how this could be done: how the Bible could very well become accessible to non-literate people through media adapted to their way of life. It does not pretend to offer elaborate recipes or ready-made prescriptions. All we are saying is that there is need to liberate ourselves from the idea that only those who have the advantage of modern education can take part in developing the kind of liberating theology that Africa needs today.

NOTES

1 'Final Communiqué: Pan-African Conference of Third World Theologians: Dec. 17–23, 1977', in K. Appiah-Kubi and S. Torres (eds.), *African Theology En Route* (Maryknoll, NY, Orbis Books, 1979), pp. 192–3.

2 C. Mesters, 'The Use of the Bible in Christian Communities of the Common People', in N. K. Gottwald (ed.), *The Bible and Liberation* (Maryknoll, NY, Orbis Books, 1983), p. 124.

3 The collective work, ed. N. K. Gottwald, *The Bible and Liberation* (cf. note 2), is a good example of such studies. J. Severino Croatto's penetrating study, 'Biblical Hermeneutics in the Theologies of Liberation', ed. V. Fabella and S. Torres, *Irruption of the Third World* (Maryknoll, NY, Orbis Books, 1983), pp. 140–68, will be familiar to EATWOT members.

4 cf. *1987 Britannica Book of the Year* (Chicago, Encyclopaedia Britan-

nica, 1987), pp. 914–19. Of 55 African countries, 30 have an adult literacy of less than 50 per cent. Except for Lesotho (62 per cent male: 84.5 per cent female), in all other countries the female literacy is below that of the male, sometimes very dramatically so – for example, Chad (35.63 per cent male: 0.5 per cent female).

5   D. B. Barrett (cf. *Schism and Renewal in Africa* (Oxford, Oxford University Press, 1968)) has rightly established, in the case of Africa, a correlation between literacy and availability of the Scriptures in the local language on the one hand and the growth of Church independency on the other. But he surely did not imply that all meaningful contact with the Bible is through direct reading of the Book. The question, then, of liberative or non-liberative use of Scripture is not exactly the same as that of the growth of independency.

6   cf. *1987 Britannica Book of the Year*.

7   I. Linden with J. Linden, *Catholics, Peasants, and Chewa Resistance in Nyasaland* (Berkeley and Los Angeles, University of California Press, 1974), p. 8.

8   'Dogmatic Constitution on Divine Revelation', n. 10; cf. *Vatican Council II*, vol. I, ed. A. Flannery (Northport, NY, Costello Publishing Co., 1984), p. 755.

9   Many new translations of the Bible or portions thereof in African languages have been made or are in progress (cf. J. S. Mbiti, *Bible and Theology in African Christianity* (Nairobi, Oxford University Press, 1986), esp. pp. 22–5). The Catholic Symposium of Episcopal Conferences in Africa and Madagascar (SECAM has set up a biblical apostolate centre in Nairobi with the objective of promoting Bible knowledge among Catholics in Africa.

10   S. Torres and V. Fabella (eds.), *The Emergent Gospel: Theology from the Underside of History* (Maryknoll, NY, Orbis Books, 1978), p. 269.

11   V. Fabella (ed.), *Asia's Struggle for Full Humanity* (Maryknoll, NY, Orbis Books, 1980), pp. 156–7.

12   cf. note 1.

31
A Nicaraguan Example: The Alabaster Bottle – Matthew 26.6–13

A new phenomenon to come out of Latin America in recent years is the establishment of grass-roots Christian communities. One such community that became famous was at Solentiname in Nicaragua. Its popularity was the result of two factors. One was its involvement in the revolutionary struggles, and the other the biblical commentaries that came out of its weekly worship meetings. The community gathered weekly to study the Bible under the leadership of Ernesto Cardenal (the 'I' of this passage). Hermeneutics was undertaken in the face of the torture, death and terror practised by the national guards of Samosa's army.

This piece is reproduced from the fourth volume of the collection *The Gospel in Solentiname* (Maryknoll, NY, Orbis Books, 1982).

It was in Bethany. When they were sitting at the table a girl approached Jesus and poured perfume on his head.

When the disciples saw this, they were angry and they began to say: 'Why this waste? This could have been sold for much money to help the poor.'

WILLIAM: Maybe they were thinking she was bewitching him.

OSCAR: If they'd sold it, it would have gone to only a small number of the poor, and the poor of the world are countless. On the other hand, when she offered it to Jesus, she was giving it, in his person, to all the poor. That made it clear it was Jesus we believe in. And believing in Jesus makes us concerned about other people, and we'll even get to create a society where there'll be no poor. Because if we're Christians there shouldn't be any poor.

I: John, in telling this, says that the one who was criticizing was Judas, and he says that Judas said it because he was in charge of the money and that he was a 'thief'. And he also adds that Judas calculated that it was worth about 300 denarii (which is about 1,000 pesos).

OLIVIA: It would seem that the one who said that said it sincerely, but it was hypocrisy, because he wasn't going to give it to the poor. Just like now, what an abundance of things there are, and the poor don't even get a whiff of anything.

WILLIAM: Everything should really have been given to the poor, not just that perfume, so there was no reason for criticism.

GLORIA: Maybe if she'd poured the perfume on herself nobody would have criticized her.

TERESITA: It's possible that he'd done her some favor, some miracle, and the only way she found of thanking him was to perfume him.

I: It seems that this girl, who John in his version calls Mary, is the same Mary Magdalene out of whom Jesus cast seven devils.

ALEJANDRO: An expensive prostitute, it seems she was, one of the expensive ones.

WILLIAM: Yes, because she was carrying a very precious bottle.

ALEJANDRO: Possibly she saw herself as a slave, an exploited one, and saw in him her liberation.

TERESITA: But why does she have to have been middle-class? She could have been a poor prostitute, a working girl.

WILLIAM: But all that perfume. And the bottle. The alabaster bottle!

I: The alabaster bottle was sealed, and it had to be broken to use the perfume. The perfume could be used only once. And the Gospel says the whole house was filled with the fragrance of nard. It's believed that nard was an ointment that came from India.

TERESITA: Maybe a smuggler paid her with that.

MARIA: Jesus was a poor man, too, and he too deserved to have the perfume poured on him.

I: And worse off than poor, for they were going to kill him two days later. In the passage before this, Jesus said that it was two days to Passover. And in the following passage it's told that Judas went away from there to make the bargain to sell him.

A STUDENT FROM MANAGUA: The Magdalene was used to that perfumed life, and things like that, and so she's being

437

grateful according to her way of life. She's accustomed to a life of perfumes, jewels, carousing. And she pours perfume on him because that's the life she led, she thinks that's logical.

WILLIAM: She's accustomed to squander everything on the man she loves. And she doesn't have that economical mentality of the others. She squanders it right there. And she's not making economical calculations, like Judas.

DONALD: The criticism must have been because that perfume was one of the most costly, but for her it was still cheap to spend it on Jesus, because of what Jesus had done for her earlier. She wasn't paying even a quarter of what she owed him.

JOSE: (*Maria's husband, who works in the San José Bank*): But Jesus hasn't forgotten the poor, because notice that in the following verse he says they will always have the poor among them. He means that if they want to help the poor they can be helping them a lot, later. They'll have the opportunity to give everything to the poor.

> *Jesus heard this and said to them:*
> *'Why do you bother this woman?*
> *This thing that she has done is a good thing.*
> *The poor you will always have among you,*
> *but you will not always have me.'*

BOSCO: That's stupid.

LAUREANO: That's a pretty weak answer because to say you're always going to have the poor is pretty silly.

I: But isn't it true that we've always had them?

LAUREANO: But we're not always *going* to have them.

WILLIAM: This is a phrase much used by reactionaries to say there'll always have to be poor people, because Christ said so. The world can't change, because according to Jesus there'll always have to be rich and poor.

I: He doesn't say there'll always be poor. Let's read it again.

MYRIAM: (*reads*): 'The poor you will always have among you.'

WILLIAM: And the 'always'? How must we interpret that 'always'?

I: Very simply. As long as there are poor, they will always be among us, we shall not be separated from them. Because the Christian community must be with the poor.

WILLIAM: But there's that 'always'. Are there always going to be poor people? That's what disturbs me.

I: He says they are never going to be separated from the poor. That's not the same as saying there'll never stop being poor people. As long as there are poor, they'll always have them at their side, and among them.

TOMAS PEÑA: When there's no more poor they won't.

A STUDENT: I've got it! He says 'among you'. He's referring to *them*, to his disciples, but that doesn't mean there'll never fail to be poor; he's not talking to all of humanity.

LAUREANO: Well, it *was* the disciples that he was saying that to. The disciples always have to be among the poor; they couldn't be among the rich.

TOMAS PEÑA: There's lots of ways of being poor: a poor person can be somebody with an arm missing. A poor person is somebody born stupid, or an orphan child, without parents. These will be in the community. There'll always be people like that in need, but of course if we're Christians they won't be poor, in poverty; if they're among us, that is, we won't let them perish.

NATALIA: Like what's happened in Cuba, where they treat the orphan children with enormous affection, and the insane, the old folks, the crippled, the widows. They're all cared for.

OLIVIA: It could also be that he was telling them instead, it seems to me, that there wouldn't be rich people, that everybody had to become poor. That there must be only poor people. That's what socialism claims. The revolution isn't so we'll all be rich but so we'll all be poor, so there'll be enough for everybody. Not disastrous poor but comfortable poor; tidy, clean, with medicine, with human dignity.

Or is it maybe that since there'll always be progress there'll always be new needs and there'll always be people that are needy? Those would be the poor.

I: That's what the reactionaries say. That even though there may be a lot of progress in humanity there'll always be a difference between rich and poor. That there'll never be a perfect society, a society all equal.

FELIPE: It seems that if things are well-distributed there can't be any rich; then everybody's poor.

I: Jesus is referring to the beggars. It's for the beggars that, according to Judas, they should have sold the perfume. And it seems to

439

me that's not a good prophecy of Jesus, and that it contradicts his announcement of the kingdom of heaven, saying that we'd always have beggars with us. I think what he's saying is that he's going away but that in place of him the poor are left. What that woman was doing with him, they'd have to do later with the poor, because he wasn't going to be there any longer, or rather, we were going to have his presence in the poor. But can it be forever that he'll not be there? The Gospel speaks of a second coming. He was going away and he was coming back.

FELIPE: When there's that society that we dream about, that's when he's coming back, and we'll have him, and there won't be any poor people.

I: Helpless orphans, people who have to go begging, or that sleep under a tree, or die in the streets the way the consumptives die in Managua, that's what's not going to exist when he comes. People for whom you ought to sell a bottle of perfume if you have one. All this now has disappeared in Cuba, and in all the other socialist countries. What supporters of capitalistic inequality say, that there will always be poor, has already stopped being true in socialist countries.

ELVIS: Then there'll be no need to sell any bottles of perfume, and people can use those perfumes, like that alabaster bottle, if they think it's useful to use those perfumes.

MYRIAM: And pouring perfume on anybody will be the same as pouring it on Christ.

I: So you can answer these people who defend inequality: there will always be poor people as long as Jesus isn't here. But when there's only equality and justice, and no needy, no beggars, Jesus will be with us again.

WILLIAM: This passage has also been used to justify big spending for luxury in churches. Because Jesus accepted the pouring of perfume on him. But right here it says that afterwards we'd have to do that with the poor; we couldn't do it to him in church because he wasn't going to be with us in person.

OSCAR: He wasn't going to be with us in person? He was going to be with us in the person of others.

OLIVIA: What that woman did was a lesson for us, and a reminder, so that what's spent in great temples that are good for nothing can be better spent on people, on the poor people he left behind. Now we do have to give to the poor, because the poor are present with us. What she had present was Jesus, his person; now we have him present but in the person of the poor.

FELIPE: Those who now want to spend a lot on church buildings and not on the poor, they're repeating what Judas did in opposing pouring perfume on Jesus. Judas did it because he wanted to get the money, and the people that now want all the spending for the churches, it's for the same reason, because they live off that money. They're thieves.

WILLIAM: What he's trying to tell them is that they're worrying about something silly, and they're not worrying about all the perfume that's been poured on to other stupid things.

I: And that they're going to go on having poor people. And besides, they're not going to do anything for them.

WILLIAM: He's telling them they don't do a damned thing for the poor.

OLIVIA: I also see there, in that woman's attitude, the change in her. It seems to me that for that woman the most valuable thing she's found among her possessions is that alabaster bottle. She's changed her attitude and from that day on she's begun to love, and she's given up the best thing she has. It seems to me that it's also a very good lesson for the bourgeoisie, because poor people don't have anything to give, only love; but for people that do have, Magdalene's lesson is very important: give up what you have, and it's no good to be beating your chest and giving lots of charity to a church, and not give what you have to the poor. She looked at Jesus, she saw him humbler than herself, and more deserving to use that alabaster bottle, that fragrance, and she put the perfume on Jesus. It seems to me that she intended to give herself, all of herself, with that perfume. She looked at him: Jesus looked like a poor man, like a proletarian, because he never was in those big mansions with rich clothes or anything; so she saw him with that simplicity and that humility, and he deserved the best there was.

ALEJANDRO: Besides, he must have needed that cleaning up.

I: That perfume that they poured on people was like a deodorant, because there was no running water then; people weren't always bathing. And Jesus must have been, we might say, just a little smelly.

441

> *What this woman has done,*
> *in pouring this perfumed oil on my body,*
> *is to prepare me for my burial.*

FELIPE: Maybe because they wouldn't pour any on him when they killed him.

I: He is predicting his violent death, without a normal burial. He really wasn't embalmed. When the women arrived with ointments on the third day (and this Mary was with them), he was no longer there. And could it not be that she was doing this on purpose, foreseeing what was soon going to happen to him, and Jesus understood her purpose? Because in the previous passage Jesus had told his friends that it was two days until Passover, and that he was going to be delivered up to the Romans.

> *In truth I tell you,*
> *that wherever this good news*
> *is announced throughout the world,*
> *what this woman did will also be told,*
> *so that you may remember her.*

I: But at the same time he foresees his immediate death, he foresees that his good news about liberation will be announced throughout the whole world. And that whenever his violent death is remembered, with no funeral, like the death of any subversive, they will remember what that woman did, as part of the good news.

OLIVIA: It seems to me that the remembering is for us also to do what she did. So that we do it now, not to him anymore, but to the poor. Or to him in the person of the poor. That's why we must remember her. That woman gave up a luxury. She was used to that kind of life, to those luxuries. As I see it, when she poured that very expensive perfume on Jesus she was giving up all her luxuries and squanderings and that's why Jesus defended her from the criticism. You ought to see how the bourgeois live and what they spend on perfumes and clothes and on the mansions they live in and on their automobiles. And her example and the lesson that Jesus is giving is that you have to give now to the poor.

And people like us who don't have perfumes or luxurious things to give because we're poor?

FELIPE: We can give other valuable things that we have.

LAUREANO: We can offer our lives as Jesus did. Then it'll be also for us, that perfume that the woman poured on Jesus.

32

An Indonesian Example:
The Miraculous Catch –
Luke 5.1–11

Inspired by the Nicaraguan example, the editor of the *International Review of Mission* invited several grass-root communities to send in their comments on selected passages. These were published in the October 1977 issue. These are the reflections of community workers, both professionals and volunteers, who were actively involved in the welfare of those marginalized in Solo, Indonesia. The group included a Muslim. The printed pages may not convey the smiles, anger, surprise and joy that this group experienced but, in spite of this limitation, this example shows how people in different situations appropriate the Word with vigour and freshness.

One of the group reads the first three verses of the text:

> One time Jesus was standing on the shore of Lake Gennesaret while the people pushed their way up to him to listen to the word of God. He saw two boats pulled up on the beach; the fishermen had left them and gone off to wash the nets. Jesus got into one of the boats – it belonged to Simon – and asked him to push off a little from the shore. Jesus sat in the boat and taught the crowd (Luke 5.1–3).

MRS ARIS (*the rural case-worker, listens thoughtfully and says*): In verse 2, Jesus gives us an example of how he conducted his ministry without using any elaborate facilities. He taught from an ordinary boat and not always in the temple. We ought to educate the people to use their simple facilities and not just wait for better ones.

ONE OF THE WOMEN: You're right. We have to educate the people, even though we do it in an open field. Jesus worked outside more often than inside the temple.

BAMBANG (*another rural case-worker*): If Jesus had taught more often in the temple, people wouldn't have believed him. They'd have hated him. But he taught in the midst of the people, outside the temple, and they believed.

He continues with the reading:

When he finished speaking, he said to Simon, 'Push the boat out further to the deep water, and you and your partners let your nets down for a catch.' 'Master,' Simon answered, 'we worked hard all night long and caught nothing. But if you say so, I will let down the nets.' They let the nets down and caught such a large number of fish that the nets were about to break. So they motioned to their partners in the other boat to come and help them. They came and filled both boats so full of fish that they were about to sink (Luke 5.4–7).

A VILLAGE TEACHER: In verse 5 you can see that the disciples obeyed Jesus.

MISS YATI (*the administrator of community development projects*):
Although our job is hard, even risky, we have to obey the Lord's words.

MISS DEBORA (*a labour organizer*): But we shouldn't feel desperate as we face our job. Often, in our most discouraged moments when we're feeling frail and weak, the Lord comes to help us.

MISS ANNA (*a Muslim law student*): You know, it's interesting. Peter didn't catch all those fish for himself; he shared them with his friends, so that others, too, might feel the blessing of the Lord.

ANOTHER STUDENT: One point interested me: In verses 1–3 Jesus taught and preached. In verses 4–7, he did what he taught. Words were followed by deeds.

BAMBANG: Peter and the other disciples helped each other. That means that we have to be able to work together and cooperate with all kinds of groups in society to improve the mutual welfare.

ONE OF THE WOMEN: If we work among the people, we can feel their suffering. Like Peter – he knew the distress of his friends who caught no fish.

MRS ARIS: At night Peter failed to catch fish but after he served Jesus, there was a ray of hope. So often the Holy Spirit comes upon us just at the moment we fail. That's what happened to Peter.

MISS ANNA: Was Peter's catch a matter of fate?

YANIS (*the pastor*): In verses 6 and 7 we see a case of income equality and a spirit in Peter that shows no egotism. But if he hadn't shared with his friends, his ship would have sunk and his friends would have had no fish.

445

BAMBANG: If the other disciples hadn't come to help Peter, they would not have gotten any fish.

MISS DEBORA (*speaking from her experience as a labour organizer*): It seems to happen just the other way round in our society. For instance, foreign employers drain our fish and our properties for their own profit without sharing or making any adequate compensation.

MISS ANNA: It's a case of the strong against the weak.

YANIS: (*reads*):

> When Simon Peter saw what had happened, he fell on his knees before Jesus and said, 'Go away from me, Lord, for I am a sinful man!' He and all the others with him were amazed at the large number of fish they had caught. The same was true of Simon's partners, James and John, the sons of Zebedee. Jesus said to Simon, 'Don't be afraid; from now on you will be catching men.' They pulled the boats on the beach, left everything and followed Jesus (Luke 5.8–11).

MISS DEBORA: Our organization doesn't work long in one spot, but leaves after a certain time, to let people go forward and grow by themselves.

MRS RIBKAH: Perhaps we should say instead that we dare to abandon *our* stake in *them*; we free them from it.

YANIS: There are here, it seems to me, three steps to follow: confession, repentance and then mission.

MISS ANNA: Verse 5 simply stated a matter of fact. That's the way it is, and for us, too: we've already been toiling.

MISS YATI: And it was clear in verse 7 that in that work there was danger.

YANIS: One important thing in verse 7 is that the load of fish was shared equally between the two boats so that both were loaded. We are very much concerned, not for those who have, but rather for the have-nots. We never send funds to, let's say, one of the well-known pre-schools in our city, but, instead, to the children of families of village people for their education.

33

A South African Example: Jesus' Teaching at Nazareth – Luke 4.14–30

This is the other example introduced in the last essay. Here are the reflections of a group from Claremont, Cape Town. It consisted of Blacks, Coloureds and Whites. The names are fictitious. Most of them were involved in some form of social action. Squatters and black unrest were the heremeneutical backdrop for their reflections.

MAG (*after introducing the study*): Maybe we could pretend we are going to make a television film of the incident, first as it happened, then, later, as it might appear in our situation.

REB (*the theological student*) (reads):

Then Jesus went to Nazareth, where he had been brought up, and on the Sabbath day he went as usual to the meeting house. He stood up to read the Scriptures, and was handed the book of the prophet Isaiah. He unrolled the scroll and found the place where it is written:

'The Spirit of the Lord is upon me.
He has anointed me to preach the Good News to the poor,
He has sent me to proclaim liberty to the captives,
And recovery of sight to the blind,
To set free the oppressed,
To announce the year when the Lord will save his people!' (Luke 4.14–21).

Jesus rolled up the scroll, gave it back to the attendant, and sat down. All the people in the meeting house had their eyes fixed on him. He began speaking to them: 'This passage of scripture has come true today, as you heard it being read.'

MAG: Who are the people we need for the film? What are they like?
SALLY (*the ex-nun*): Typical religious congregation ... upholders

447

of the *status quo* ... like the local authority officials we are dealing with.

REB: No, like ANY church congregation, like the people in the church I went to a few weeks ago to talk about squatters, and they got very uptight and some of them went off to another parish where they wouldn't get this sort of thing.

MAG: Were they workers?

WILL (*the community worker*): Yes, they were Nazareth people so they were shepherds and workers, and they knew Jesus from long ago.

LIN (*who works for the Anglican social responsibility board*): And there were visitors, too, probably, because it says Jesus was well known and popular in Galilee.

MAG: Do you think the locals welcomed the visitors?

ANN (*a student*): 'Perhaps they weren't too keen on them, especially if they caused a disturbance.

(*Nobody mentions Jesus as a character in the film. We all take him for granted.*)

MAG: So what happened?

ANN: He went into the synagogue and during the service he was given the scroll and he read from it.

WILL: He chose that bit of prophecy from Isaiah about the deliverer who would set the people free.

MAG: Were they free in Jesus' time?

REB: No, they were under the Romans and they were probably very disappointed in Jesus that he wasn't going to lead a revolution against the Romans, but only give them spiritual liberation.

SALLY: But it wasn't just spiritual ... he did do things like giving sight to the blind.

REB: But he didn't liberate captives.

MAG: Didn't he?

REB: Well, it depends what you mean by captives, because he did set people free from their lusts and selfishness and attitudes like that.

SALLY: Yes, and he gave them hope that things would be better.

WILL: But he was saying that today the prophecy was fulfilled and things were still the same, so they must have been disappointed.

LIN: It depends what your concepts are of how change comes about.

448

He wasn't just promising something invisible and internal that would leave outside things the same.

MAG: Let's look at the different actions promised.

SALLY: He said he would heal the brokenhearted . . . he comforts people and encourages them.

REB: And he gives them insight, helps them to see the things they can't see, or don't want to see.

LIN: He's exposing the truth, exposing people to the truth.

WILL: But people don't always want that.

ANN: They probably reacted in different ways then – some of them enthusiastic and others sceptical.

MAG: The sceptical ones would have been particularly put off by the last bit about the acceptable year of the Lord because the Jubilee Year, every fiftieth year when slaves were to be set free and everything shared out again, never really happened.

REB: Some of the people could have felt threatened because he was saying things were going to change. He attracted people and so could be taking away some of their power.

SALLY: Others would be glad because he was offering them something.

After reading Luke 4.22–30:

> They were all well impressed with him, and marveled at the beautiful words that he spoke. They said, 'Isn't he the son of Joseph?' He said to them: 'I am sure that you will quote the proverb to me, "Doctor, heal yourself." You will also say to me, "Do here in your own home town the same things we were told happened in Capernaum." I tell you this', Jesus added: 'A prophet is never welcomed in his own home town. Listen to me: it is true that there were many widows in Israel during the time of Elijah, when there was no rain for three and a half years and there was a great famine throughout the whole land. Yet Elijah was not sent to a single one of them, but only to a widow of Zarephath, in the territory of Sidon. And there were many lepers in Israel during the time of the prophet Elisha; yet not one of them was made clean, but only Naaman the Syrian.' All the people in the meeting house were filled with anger when they heard this. They rose up, dragged Jesus out of town, and took him to the top of the hill on which their town was built, to throw him over the cliff. But he walked through the middle of the crowd and went on his way.

SALLY: I'm reminded of that little boy from one of our townships here who made good as a singing star and the others acted as if it wasn't anything special. One boy said, 'I knew him when he ran round the streets without any pants on when he was two years old', as if that made any difference to the boy's success now.

WILL: Yes, people don't accept a person for what he is, they always want to classify him.

ANN: When people are familiar we take them for granted. They said Jesus was just Joseph's son, as if that meant they didn't need to listen to him.

MAG: How did Jesus react to their rejection?

WILL: He challenged them. Mentioning Capernaum wasn't very tactful, there was probably rivalry between the villages.

REB: He really confronted them; he used their history to give them examples of other situations of rejection . . . that widow, and Naaman the leper, who was a foreigner.

MAG: Did he upset everybody?

SALLY: No, the 'groupies' were there, the ones who had followed him round, and they were probably on his side.

LIN: And when some wanted to throw him over the hill, others made it difficult and he got away.

MAG: So it wasn't just a quiet Sabbath service?

REB: Far from it; he really caused a disturbance and stirred them all up.

MAG: Perhaps at this point we could turn to the modern situation and look at the parallels like . . .

SALLY: The officials we have to deal with.

REB: And the ordinary church congregations.

WILL: And the people who support the *status quo.*

ANN: And the oppressed who want change and are looking for leadership.

MAG: Who plays the Jesus role in our situations?

REB: The one who tells the truth, especially to the oppressors.

ANN: Anyone who stands up for what is right.

LIN: The people who attack unjust structures.

MAG: You mean people like us here!

REB: Well, yes, though I don't suppose we quite like to put it that way.

SALLY: But that is what we are trying to do.

MAG: So, how do we avoid falling into the trap of self-righteousness?

SALLY: That's where other people come in, why we must be in community, so that we can expose one another to the truth.

REB: We need mutual correction, we can take criticism from people we trust.

LIN: Does that mean we can only expose the truth to people we already trust? Can't we go and confront the officials who are upholding an unjust system?

REB: Yes, but we mustn't be on our own, we need all the time to be checking out with one another.

MAG: What does this say about our churches, where the pattern is: one talks and the rest listen?

WILL: That's all wrong, of course, because we need something different.

REB: Yes, we have to be sharing with one another.

SALLY: We need to be close to people we can trust and be talking with them.

MAG: So, is there a danger of group self-righteousness?

REB AND SALLY: Oh yes, we can easily fall into that. That's why we have to be working with different kinds of people and organizations like the ones who were with us last night [at a meeting about squatters].

LIN: But how did you react to that chap who was giving that great story about volunteers and how he wanted everybody to be coordinated and helping the committee?

REB: We don't want people to work for the [coordinating] committee. We want them to be themselves in their own situation, to get to see the truth and do something about it.

MAG: So, could we look at the meaning in our situation of those actions Jesus quoted?

REB: People are captives to the idea that they must be like somebody else or that they must follow a certain programme; but they need internal liberation and then the other things will follow. It doesn't matter which power rules, people need internal liberation. After we get majority rule, there will still be oppression – if people don't change inside.

LIN: But is that enough? Can you be free inside if the situation is still bad?

REB: People want quite simple things, like a chap I worked with on a building-site who just wanted to save enough money to buy a plot of land to settle on with his family.

ANN: We want deliverance from oppression.

WILL: We want to live freely as we used to before the white man

451

came. When I was a small boy, my grandfather had land, cattle, sheep, goats, plenty of land that they tilled and could reap good harvests and had cows to milk. And life was good. You felt you had what you wanted. But they took the land away from him; something to do with title deeds and white farmers, and that happened to other blacks as well, and the men had to work for the white farmers or come to town to work. So that's how we came here.

MAG: But is that idea of a farm of your own what you want or are you a town man?

WILL: No, I am a town man, I want to live freely in town.

ANN: We want to be accepted as human beings, want the right to be here, live here, have comfortable homes.

WILL: And share in the government of the country.

LIN: Will there still be rich and poor?

WILL: Yes, but not on lines of race.

MAG: Will the country as a whole be changed after, say, ten to twenty years of majority rule?

SALLY: It makes me think of the early church and the way they shared everything and no one was in want.

REB: Political change won't bring that about. There will still be exploitation unless people change inside.

MAG: Can the ideal or principle of sharing apply to a wider society?

LIN: We're in the process of getting concessions towards multi-racial integration, but this could just mean that in twenty years' time the Nationalist Party will still be ruling the country on the basis of Progressive Party policy.

WILL: Blacks can be just as oppressive as whites.

REB: Black slaves in the USA used to sublimate their hopes and sing songs about heaven, and blacks tend to do that here.

ANN: But, lately, at the funerals we have noticed that when we sing the hymns, the words of the first verse are traditional, and then the second verse has different words that the youth have composed, and then, maybe, the third verse is traditional, and so on. And after a while the older people join in with the new words as well as the traditional ones and you can see from their faces that they are sharing the feelings and aspirations of the youth.

LIN: Have these songs been written down? What ideas are being expressed?

ANN: No, it hasn't gone that far.

WILL: It's rather spontaneous.

MAG: So, have we any clearer idea of what good news to the poor means in our situation?

ANN: It means that they will have the chance to share and be accepted as full human beings.

REB: I come back to those early Christians and their experiment. Communal life is possible under any regime – it's a matter of the spirit and just getting on with it.

SALLY: We must live the sharing.

LIN: But we'll go on externally just the same, with war on the border and all the rest of it?

REB: No, things would change. We must clear the communication channels. This sharing life isn't just passive, the togetherness is active and reaches out to other people.

SALLY: You mean it's catchy, infectious?

REB: We must actively persuade people by our example and by our challenging of their values.

MAG: How does this sound to the blacks? Do you think, Will, that black youth would go for what Reb is saying?

WILL: In the black consciousness movement, there is a strong stress on communalism and egalitarianism. We want the kind of society in which there is sharing.

MAG: Does the black consciousness movement rely on education and persuasion or on political action and confrontation too?

WILL: Black community programmes are putting the philosophy into practice, educating people in what communalism means.

MAG: Isn't there a double thrust, educational and political, BCP and BPC (Black People's Convention)? Isn't it a matter of walking on two legs?

WILL: Yes.

LIN: I like that expression, walking on two legs. We need both emphases, on the internal change and on the external confrontation with structures. Otherwise we can end up like some people I know on a rural commune about 200 km from here. They are very happy on their farm, sharing with one another, but they are completely irrelevant to the rest of our situation.

34

A Chinese Example: 'The Silences of the Bible'

K. H. TING

Different people seek different things in the Bible. Here is an attempt to introduce the Bible to new and younger Chinese Christians. This piece, reprinted from Ting's book, *How to Study the Bible* (Hong Kong, Tao Fong Ecumenical Centre, 1981), is a reminder that one has to listen not only to the voices, but also to the silences, in the Bible, in order to discern the word.

Bishop Ting is an internationally known and eminent leader in the Chinese Christian community. A collection of his writings has been published under the title, *No Longer Strangers* (Maryknoll, NY, Orbis Books, 1989).

THE SILENCES OF THE BIBLE

We must listen to what the Bible says to us; we must also pay attention to what the Bible does not say to us. There are some things which the Bible does not say and there are good reasons for this.

In that famous painting entitled 'The Light of the World', Jesus, holding a lamp in one hand, is knocking on the door of a house. There were those who noticed that there was no handle on the door and they raised this point with the artist. The artist said it wasn't that he had forgotten it but that he wanted to use this to tell us that Jesus is standing sorrowfully outside the house knocking on the door. But this door may only be opened from the inside, if the person inside is willing.

In the same way, there are some things which the Bible does not mention, but this is not due to God's forgetting them. In those things which are not mentioned there is also a message which he wants to tell us.

For example, how does the parable of the Prodigal Son end? Does the older brother finally listen to his father's exhortations and return home to make peace with his brother? Or does he continue in his arrogant behavior, remaining outside the house, unwilling to enter? No one knows. This parable ends suddenly just at the point where our interest is greatest. Why? Because we are that elder brother; whether we finally enter the house or remain outside depends on us. The blank space after Luke 15.32 is for each of us to fill in.

In the entire Bible, there is one book which concludes with a question mark. This is the Book of Jonah. God asks Jonah a question but the Bible does not tell us Jonah's reply and the Book of Jonah ends here. And why is this? We must realize, this is not only a question God asked of Jonah. Even more so, he is asking it of us. And he is waiting eagerly for our answer.

The silences in the Bible are important. In its silences, there are also tiny voices speaking in our souls, exhorting us.

Of the sixty-six books in the Bible, there is one – the Book of Esther – which does not once mention God, from beginning to end. What is this particular silence telling us?

Esther is a young woman who accomplished a very wise and courageous thing for the well-being of her people. The book makes clear that God's hand is moving in the affairs of the world, even though God is never mentioned. God himself was glad about what Esther did for her people, and was willing to have this book among those in the Bible.

That the Bible has in it a book which doesn't even mention God, is clearly telling us that the things which God cares for far surpass what we term 'religion'. God does not place importance on mere words. Esther's courageous action, done out of passionate love for her country and people, is not outside God's care and providence.

Therefore, we can say that while whatever is written in the Bible is naturally important, there is also a message in whatever silences the Bible keeps.

Biblical silence has yet another important function. It is like a red light, telling us that we should go no further.

Someone once asked Jesus: 'Lord, will those who are saved be few?' (Luke 13.23.) Jesus answered neither 'many' nor 'few'. he said, 'Strive to enter by the narrow gate.' Peter asked, 'Lord, what about this man?' (John 21.21). Jesus didn't answer this either. He just said, 'What is that to you? Follow me!'

The disciples begged Jesus to tell them about the day when he would come again (Matt. 24.3), but Jesus said to them: 'But of that day and hour no one knows, not even the angels of heaven, nor the son, but the Father only' (v. 36). Later the disciples again asked, 'Will you at this time restore the Kingdom to Israel?' (Acts 1.6.) Still, Jesus said, 'It is not for you to know times or seasons which the Father has fixed by his own authority. But you shall receive power when the Holy Spirit has come upon you; . . . and be my witnesses.' We can see that Christ does not want us to probe deeply into certain questions. When we do ask these questions he answers us with silence, at the same time reminding us to take care of our own responsibilities, to do our present tasks. The Bible tells us, 'the secret things belong to the Lord our God; but the things that are revealed belong to us and to our children for ever, that we may do all the words of this law' (Deut. 29.29). It is obvious that, as human beings, we must recognize that there are some things which we have to be agnostic about.

The conclusion of the Gospel of John says, 'But there are also many other things which Jesus did; were every one of them to be written, I suppose that the world itself could not contain the books that would be written.' Fortunately the Bible was not written to satisfy our curiosity, but to allow those who hunger and thirst for righteousness to know Jesus and to seek to become holy. The Bible offers us sufficient and clear guidance for this goal. We really have no reason to desire more.

What, then, is the truth which the Lord wants us to enter into, and what are the things he does not want us to probe?

Whatever God is willing to reveal to us – the truth which he wants us to enter into – is whatever can help us to become better children of God. Whatever will not aid us in becoming better children of God is, then, not the Biblical truth which God wants us to enter into. In his prayer to the Father, Jesus says: 'Sanctify them in the truth; thy word is truth' (John 17.17).

Sadly, there are times when we are not willing to follow the Spirit humbly, when we are not willing to respect the silences of the Spirit, but, stiff-necked, insist on knowing those things that God does not yet want us to know. Some take human ways of reckoning and presumptuous understanding to be biblical truth and pass them on to others. They even use them to build themselves up to the point of attacking those loyal, humble souls who do not dare to be wildly arrogant. This is extremely dangerous.

Afterword
Cultures, Texts and Margins:
A Hermeneutical Odyssey

R. S. SUGIRTHARAJAH

I would like to begin by sharing with you two texts, both from colonial narratives. The first is from the CMS Missionary Register of 1818. It is about a conversation that went on between a group of Indians who had gathered round under a tree outside Delhi, and a Christian catechist named Anund Messeh. Seeing that these people had gospel portions with them, Anund tells one of the elderly men, 'These books teach the religion of the European Sahibs. It is THEIR book; and they printed it in our language, for our use.' In the ensuing conversation, the elderly man replies, 'That is true; but how can it be the European Book, when we believe that it is God's gift to us? He sent it to us at Hurdwar. God gave it long ago to the Sahibs, and THEY sent it to us.'

The second comes from a children's novel, *The History of Little Henry and his Bearer* by Martha Mary Sherwood, who was engaged in evangelical-educational work in India during the colonial days. Sherwood's work epitomizes the vast quantity of children's literature produced before the 1857 Sepoy Mutiny which was influential in forming colonial attitudes and shaping colonial narratives. *The History of Little Henry and his Bearer* is a moral tale about a scripture-quoting Anglo-Indian, Henry L, aged 7 or 8, and his attempts to convert his Indian bearer, called Boosy. In one scene when Henry and Boosy are travelling to Calcutta, little Henry observes:

> Boosy, this is a good country: that is, it would be a very good country, if the people were Christians. Then they would not be so idle as they now are: and they would agree together and clear the jungles, and build churches to worship God in. It will be pleasant to see people, when they are Christians, all going on a Sunday morning to some fair church built

457

among those hills, and to see them in an evening sitting at the door of their houses reading the *shaster* – I do not mean your *shaster*, but our *shaster*, God's book (1821: 76–7).

I recount these two narratives to reiterate the point that, although the Bible originated largely in west Asia, when it was received in and introduced to the rest of the continent it was seen as an alien text. Thus an Asian Christian reading of the Bible has never been an easy, natural reading. It is not a spontaneous reading as is a Hindu reading of the *Gita* or a Buddhist reading of the *Dhammapada*. It has always been a confected, mapped or manufactured reading worked out amidst different cultures and multiple texts and undertaken inevitably from a situation of marginality. Over the years, this artificial reading has produced a variety of readers – readers with certain pre-understandings. Based on the categories of readers worked out by C. D. Narasimhaiah, the Indian English professor, I identify five types. First, *Archariya*, the discriminating reader, the one who puts into practice what is read; second, the *Panditha*, the academic reader, the one who has considerable knowledge, but not necessarily a committed reader; third, the *Bhakta*, the devoted reader, the reader with a cause and commitment; fourth, the *Rasika*, the aesthetic reader, the reader who reads for satisfaction and whose interest ceases the moment expectations are satisfied; and fifth the *Alpabuddhijana*, the ignorant reader, a reader with an inferior taste (1994: 8,9). Of course these reading positions are not hierarchical, nor are there clear-cut divisions. A reader is likely to identify with a combination of these positions. What is crucial for us is that reading involves taking a conscious position.

What I would like to do here is to narrate briefly the positions we have taken, our hermeneutical journey as Asian readers, the theories we employ to understand our cultures, our texts and our marginality and also how as interpreters our role has evolved over the years – from being nationalistic to being 'postnational'. I would like to make it clear that though I use the plural 'we', I don't pretend to speak for all Asian interpreters. The concerns I am going to share with you are mine – though some Asian biblical scholars may wish to identify with them.

R. S. Sugirtharajah

COLONIAL TOOLS AND HERMENEUTICAL WARS

As readers we first cut our hermeneutical teeth with colonial methods. When I first started as a theological student, the methods which were bequeathed to us by Western teachers were various forms of historical criticism. At that time redaction criticism was seen as a major breakthrough. Later, over the years, other approaches such as social science, post-structuralism, narrative theories and deconstruction, were added to the repertoire. Why do I label these supposedly inoffensive and innocent methods colonial? They are colonial not only in origination, style, content, execution and ideology, but also in the sense that they were used to reshape our minds. Recently, cultural critics have been telling us that the lasting effect of imperialism was not only its political subjugation of people or the economic or ecological devastation it caused, but the ideological and cultural vision it implanted among its subjugated people. The famous minute that T. B. Macaulay wrote in 1835 on how to educate Indians is a testimony to colonialist intentions to control culturally the minds of Indians: 'We must at present do our best to form a class who may be interpreters between us and the millions whom we govern; a class of persons, Indians in blood and colour, but English in taste, in opinions, and in intellect' (Young: 1935, 359). In other words, much more than the territorial and political domination, it was the intellectual and cultural control of the natives which was effective in sustaining colonialism, and also of course in perpetuating its motifs and forms in the post-colonial context. Edward Said in his *Culture and Imperialism* writes:

> . . . the imperial dominion itself, its influence is only now beginning to be studied on the minutiae of daily life . . . the imperial motif woven into the structures of popular culture, fiction, and the rhetoric of history, philosophy, and geography . . . I am discussing an ideological vision implemented and sustained not only by direct domination and physical force but much more effectively over a long time by *persuasive means*, . . . At the most visible level there was the physical transformation of the imperial realm . . . the reshaping of the physical environment, administrative, architectural, and institutional feats such as the building of colonial cities . . . These works show the daily imposition of power in the dynamics of everyday life . . . But the important factor in these micro-physics of imperialism is that . . . a unified discourse . . . develops that is based on a distinction between the westerner and the native so integral and adaptable as to make changes impossible [1993: 132–3].

Colonialism is not simply a system of economic and military control, but a systematic cultural penetration and domination. What is the more damaging is not the historical, political and economic domination, but the psychological, intellectual and cultural colonization. Hence, historical-critical methods were colonial in the sense that they displaced the norms and practices of our indigenous reading methods, but also they were used to justify the superiority of Christian texts and undermine the sacred writings of others, thus creating a division between us and our neighbours. They function as masks for exploitation and abet a voluntary cultural assimilation.

These methods are colonial because of the insistence that a right reading is mediated through the proper use of historical-critical tools alone. For example, look at the opening lines of George Strecker's *The Sermon on the Mount: An Exegetical Commentary:* 'No proper exegesis of the Sermon on the Mount can ignore the results of more than two hundred years of historical critical research into the New Testament.'[1] It rules out at the outset the right of a reader or an interpreter to use any other means to understand the text, and those who do not practise these methods are seen as outside the circle. The implication here is that the Western academy sets the ground rules for interpretation and defines what tools shall be used, and these are paraded as universally applicable in opening up the text. Anyone who does not employ them or does not engage with them is seen as an outcaste. The inference is that any culturally informed reading by a Gandhi, a Tilak, or a Krishnapillai is ruled out. In other words, a culturally diversified approach will never get a look in. The West not only provides the tools but it also controls our textual preferences. What the Indian social scientist, Ashis Nandy, said about colonialism is also equally applicable to biblical interpretation. 'The West has not merely produced modern colonialism, it informs most interpretations of colonialism. It colours even the interpretation of interpretation' (1991: xii). Seree Lorgunpai, the Thai biblical scholar, narrates an example of how the hermeneutical parameters set to work in the Western context make little sense when applied cross-culturally. He says that Westerners find the book of Ecclesiastes strange, but Thai Christians feel at home with it because of its resemblance to Buddhist teaching. However when missionaries started to translate the Bible, Ecclesiastes 'was almost one of the last books to be translated, perhaps because the translators were not aware of the similarity between it and Buddhism or because they just chose to ignore this connection between them' (1994: 155–6. See chapter 24 of this book). Once the rules have been established, those who fail to follow them are seen as outcaste, outside the system and not regarded as doing proper exegesis.

The methods are colonial because they would have us believe that they have universal validity and significance, although they emerged as a contextual response to the specific needs of Western academies. Essentially they are symbols and products of Western culture. What is colonial is the assumption and claim Western scholars make that their work is universal, comprehensive and exhaustive. There is a tacit assumption among Western biblical interpreters that their exegetical works and literary productions on the Bible speak for all and cover the concerns of Asia, Africa and Latin America. If one goes through some of the recent literature on biblical hermeneutics, there is an unwritten assumption that it is dealing with global biblical issues. This applies even when the works are excellent and meticulously researched – such as in the work of Duncan S. Ferguson, Robert Morgan and John Barton, Tom Wright's update of Stephen Neil's *The Interpretation of the New Testament 1861–1961*, and Steven L. Mackenzie's and Stephen R. Haynes' work on different theories of biblical criticism. The questions they address – from demythologization to deconstruction, and from historical methods to literary theories – are in essence Western questions faced, not necessarily by ordinary persons in the West, but by a group of Western academics who are trying to come to terms with the Bible as a piece of literature and its capacity to illuminate their situation. These volumes assume that the responsibility for interpreting the Bible lies in the hands of Western interpreters and that their theories have universal validity. These volumes do not include or address any Asian or for that matter African or Latin American hermeneutical concerns, or mention the interpreters who are concerned with them. Incidentally, the only non-Westerner who gets a look in in these volumes is Gustavo Gutiérrez. He is included not because of his biblical work but because of his prominent role in the Liberation Theology movement. Perhaps the authors of these volumes assume that Asian biblical questions are too theological and Asians as such should not get involved in producing theories because Western exegetical theories will cover Asian concerns.

The institutionalization of these methods in our theological colleges has succeeded in producing successful 'mimics', 'imitators',

461

'translators', 're-writers' and even 'plagiarists' among us. Quite ironically, we began to compare our own interpreters to those in the West to establish our credibility. We hailed Kosuke Koyama as the Karl Barth of Asia or M. M. Thomas as the Niebuhr of India, but in our blind enthusiasm we never bothered to find out who was the C. S. Song of America or the Aloysius Pieris of England. Our hermeneutical arena was littered with exotic symbols and Western hermeneutical figures who had little time for our aesthetic assumptions. Some of them did not even have the remotest understanding of any of the Asian cultures and, worse, they betrayed their Euro-centrism in their exegetical judgements. Though Edward Said's celebrated book, *Orientalism*, does not feature the work of Western biblical scholars, one can see traces of orientalism in their output. Unfortunately the example I am going to highlight comes from the writings of Joachim Jeremias, whose work I admire and value. Some of the exegetical judgements Jeremias comes out with in his near-classic *The Parables of Jesus* betrays a Euro-centric perception of the Orient. For instance, look at the comments he makes on the Parable of the Wicked Servant (Luke 16). When the steward, on hearing of the imminent arrival of his master, alters the account, Jeremias makes an amazing exegetical comment. He justifies the bizarre behaviour of the steward as due to people in the East not knowing anything about book-keeping or audit (1963: 181). At one stroke, he not only claims special European achievements in accountancy, but also denies the possibility that other cultures have different ways of accounting. In other words, he excludes the possibility of the contributions the Chinese, Indians and Egyptians have made towards the development of present-day mathematics – a point very cogently put forward by George Gheverghese Joseph in his recent book, *The Crest of the Peacock: Non-European Roots of Mathematics* (1991). Throughout the book, Jeremias keeps making negative comments about the Eastern people. I am not questioning his integrity, but what Jeremias has done is to unconsciously perpetuate an image of non-Western cultures as lacking vitality, competence and creativity. Incidentally, comments on the same parable which appeared in the *Expository Times* at the height of the colonial era are worth recalling. Commenting on the action of the steward who adjusts the account, Margaret D. Gibson, writing from Cambridge, suggested that this was a custom which prevailed 'whenever Orientals are left to their own methods, uncontrolled by any protectorate of Europeans' (1902–3: 334).

Before anyone gets the impression that all Western reading methods are evil and that we are being crushed under their burden, let me assure you that these methods are alive and kicking in our own theological institutions and put to use with great enthusiasm, even when they are under scrutiny in the West. Our attitude to historical-critical methods is somewhat similar to our use of the English language that we inherited from the imperialists. We do not see the English language as a sign of imperialism but as a vehicle for 'epistemic transformation' (Gayatri Chakravorty Spivak's phrase), namely for transforming the way in which objects of knowledge, especially about humanity, are articulated. Thus interestingly, the very method which is seen as colonial is used by some of us to amplify a variety of subaltern voices – Indian dalits, Japanese burakus, Korean minjung, indigenous people and women. In other words, these tools have been seen to be an effective weapon of de-colonization. For instance, some of the recent exegetical examples of the minority discourse worked out by Ahn Byung Mu, Kuribashi Tero, Hisako Kinukawa and James Massey may appear to be original Korean, Indian or Japanese products, yet in a subtle manner they are based on and a re-work of historical-critical principles. It is worth noting that most of these authors are transplanted or uprooted professionals who return to their caste, community, or tribe in an effort to represent themselves as articulate members of various subaltern groups, after learning their craft and Western theories of oppression at cosmopolitan centres. Since they are denied entry into the local mainstream interpretative arena, they adopt a negative attitude to their local traditions and share an antagonistic relationship to the dominant culture; hence they are attracted to these foreign theories. The dalit hermeneutics is a good example of this. Even a casual reader will notice the tendency to dismiss anything Indian as part of the oppressive brahmanical discourse. Whether caste-based hermeneutics will find its solution in foreign-based theories is something the dalits will have to ask themselves.

FROM COLONIALISM TO ORIENTALISM

Those who have studied the effects of colonialism will tell you that a colonialized person goes through two conflicting processes. In the first, he or she will imitate the colonizer, and in the second he or

she will try to recover indigenous history and retrieve native characteristics. Like the prodigal son, after riotous living among the academic fleshpots of the West and dabbling in fashionable theories,
and our academic purity defiled, we decided to become natives again.
Indian social thinkers egged us on. The National Christian Council
of India's consultation on 'New Patterns of the Social Witness in
India' in 1960 encouraged us to explore our own cultural and philosophical resources. The findings of the consultation state: 'At the
present time very few Christians are making any serious study of
Indian philosophy, history and social thought. Many of us are not
aware of our intellectual heritage ... Since most of us are not
adequately informed, we are not able to contribute our share to the
thinking in these spheres' (*Religion and Society* 1960: 70). Gora,
the eponymous hero in Rabindranath Tagore's novel, echoed our
sentiments. He says at one point:

> If we have the mistaken notion that because the English are strong and
> we can never become strong unless we become exactly like them, then
> that impossibility will never be achieved, for by mere imitation we shall
> eventually be neither one thing nor the other ... come inside India,
> accept all her good and her evil: if there be deformity then try and cure
> it from within but see it with your own eyes, understand it, think over it,
> turn your face towards it, become one with it (1989: 102).

We learnt the same from Fanon; that it would be better for us to
be a native at the uttermost depths of our wretchedness than to be
as our former master. In our enthusiasm to assert our nationalism
we searched for indigenous methods. As an alternative to the importation of inappropriate theories of interpretation, we turned our attention to distinctive national theories for inspiration and for new
directions. We saw this revival of methods of a bygone era as a way
of celebrating and elevating our Asian identity.

In the name of indigenization, we were happy to fill our hermeneutical arena with ancient symbols, stories, and rites, ignoring the crude
realities of our present which was replete with religious rivalries,
caste hierarchies and social inequalities. Blissfully and unconsciously
we were constantly being born and re-born into the past. Among the
many things Western orientalists manufactured for us was a glorious
past in the Sanskritic tradition. At this juncture, the ancient theories
of Sanskrit poetics came to our rescue. To our delight we discovered
that even before the interpretative theories were worked out in the

West, classical writers in Sanskrit literature had come up with extremely sophisticated and well-developed theories of reading. We were proud to claim and celebrate Panini as the world's first grammarian, and ecstatic to know that there was a school of exegetes, the *Mimamsakas*, who were concerned with determining the correct meaning of texts and settling dubious or problematic passages in them. It dawned on us that we could profitably employ various theories of meaning worked out by Sanskritic theoreticians. There was the theory of *rasa*, propounded by the sage Bharata in the fifth century, which holds that poetry is essentially an emotive discourse. There was Ksehemendra's *auchita*, translated as 'propriety', which is a harmonious adaptation of language, figure, imagery etc. Then there was *dhvani*, expounded by Anandavardhana in the ninth century, which stresses the suggestive possibility of a text, its evocative nature and its emotional grip on the reader, hearer, or spectator.

We were ecstatic. But our excitement was short-lived. There was no sustained effort to produce exegetical examples to illustrate how these methods would actually work with biblical texts. A feeble attempt was made in the late '70s to make use of the *dhvani* method as a way of dispensing with Western methods. A special issue of *Biblebhashyam*, the Indian biblical quarterly, featured articles with exegetical examples. Sister Vandana and Anand Amaladass came to be closely associated with this method. However, the enthusiasm for this method waned when serious questions were posed about the whole idea of indigenization. Now, on looking back, we realize that our attempts to search for indigenous methods had inadvertently contributed to a new form of orientalism, but orientalism in reverse worked out this time by the natives themselves. To use Edward Said's phrase, we were participating in our own orientalizing (1985: 325). We were tacitly acquiescing in and reinforcing the images and theories Western orientalists created about us. It was these orientalists who provided us with a new self-perception of ourselves; and it was they who led us to believe in past glories and made us fantasize about their possible return, and in the process caused us to forget present needs and future challenges. Fanon long ago cautioned us that any mindless appropriation of customs and rituals divorced from their historical context in effect not only goes against present realities but also hurts the very people it intends to serve. He warned us that: '. . . the desire to attach oneself to tradition or bring abandoned tradition to life does not only mean going against the current history but also opposing one's own people' (1990: 180). We realized that our efforts to create an India of our dreams, as a reaction to the continual threat of the universalizing nature of Western theories, divorced us from current reality and history, and in a way went against our own people – namely the dalits, the indigenous people and women. We were using the very brahmanical discourse which kept these people outside the mainstream. Paradoxically, the use of an indigenous method ended up being condemned as élitist, oppressive and alienating.

FROM ORIENTALISM TO NATIVISM

While some were busy trying to recover Sanskritic concepts, others who were not part of it or influenced by it, but were suffocating under the double burden of Western and Sanskritic theories, were equally busy trying to animate our own *bhasa* or vernacular tradition. Students of Indian culture draw an important distinction between the *marga*, the highroad, and *desi*, the country road. Sanskrit, which is seen as pan-Indian, ancient, reputable and has hallowed texts, is regarded as the *marga*, while local and vernacular languages of India are seen as the *desi*. The Indian literary critic G. N. Devy calls the search for models in the vernacular tradition 'nativism', which he defines thus:

> It views literature as an activity taking place 'within' a specific language . . . and bound by the rules of discourse native to the language of its origin. It understands writing as a social act, and expects of it an ethical sense of commitment to the society within which it is born. It rules out the colonial standard of literary history . . . and the *marga* claim of the mainstream literature as being the only authentic literature (1992: 119–20).

In other words, nativism is a hermeneutical enterprise which takes place within a specific cultural and language matrix, bound by the rules set by that language.

Nativism draws on both performance traditions and textual traditions. The biblical reflections of Sadhu Sundar Singh, Mungamuri Devadas, Vaman Tilak, Paul Kadamabhavanam, H. A. Krishnapillai, borrow largely form the vernacular mode of story-telling. Hermeneutics, for them, is not only re-reading the ancient texts but also re-telling old stories for a new context. They all articulated their expositions in their own mother-tongues, Punjabi, Telugu, Marathi and Tamil. Most of them were converts from Hindu faith and were familiar with the digressive narrative mode, and influenced by their vernacular narrative thinking. Their re-tellings of the Christian stories are cyclical, episodic and full of asides and parentheses. There are others who draw from the vernacular secular literary tradition. Recently, Dayanandan Francis, applying the devices of Tamil *aham* poetry – the love poems of Tamil literature – has re-narrativized the Song of Songs, with the characterization based on the Sankam tradition of *thalaivan* (lover) and *thalaivi* (beloved) (1992). Lawrence Adigalar, who sees 'biblical ideals inherent in the culture of Tamils', likens the concept of redemption found in the Bible to the one mentioned in the ancient Tamil literature called *Tholkapiam*. He writes: 'A parallel could be drawn between the Genesis story of Satan entering into the garden of Eden to establish dominion over the creature of God and God redeeming the fallen human beings with the story of *Vetchi and Karanthai thinai*' (1993: 72). He reckons that 'the study and use of Tamil literature can only play a vital role for indigenization and of our interpreting methods' (73).

Nativism also draws inspiration from vernacular religious texts, especially from the *bhakti*/devotional writings. Two interpreters come to mind – H. A. Krishnapillai and A. J. Appasamy. As a devotee of Lord Vishnu, Krishnapillai found it difficult to understand the juridical image of expiation used by the pietistic German missionaries to explain the work of Christ. He felt such imagery was a hindrance. Instead, he drew on his own Vaisnavite heritage to arrive at an understanding of the work of Christ. He re-imaged the cross-event as God releasing precious life to make Krishnapillai a devotee. The first poetry Krishnapillai wrote after his conversion has no reference to a juridical transaction. Appasamy advocated the use of *bhakti*/ devotional poets from both Saivite and Vaisnavite traditions to enrich Christian theology. His books, *Christianity as Bhakti Marga* (1928) and *What is Moksa?* (1931) are expositions of the mysticism of John's gospel. The Johannine narratives are illuminated by a wealth of illustrations from *bhakti* poets such as Manikkavacakar, Nammalvar, Tayumanavar, Ramalinga Swami, Tukaram, Kabir, and Guru Nanak. By establishing interconnections between these and Christian texts, and coalescing different spiritual traditions, Appasamy's contention was that these Indian sages belonged to Indian Christians as much as to Hindus, Muslims, and Sikhs. The exegetical insights of

Krishnapillai and Appasamy fall under the rubric of cultural exegesis, which Daniel Christopher–Smith is currently engaged in and trying to promote, but the term 'nativism' may also be helpful in some respects.

Vernacular hermeneutics promoted the awareness of various indigenous traditions. It also compensated for the orientalists' regrettable neglect of literatures in non-Sanskritic traditions. It called into question the hegemonic status of Sanskrit and opened up multiple performance and textual traditions. Significantly, it helped to restore the balance by offering an alternative classical culture in Tamil and paved the way for the shift from vedic vision to *bhakti*. The problem with the vernacular hermeneutics is its isolationism and protectionism. It is culture-bound and hence always in danger of being ghettoized, and understood only by the insiders and irrelevant to the majority. It is accorded a privileged status because it is uncontaminated by external influences. We need to ask again in an emerging complex of global relations whether we can still talk of a pure culture which is not corrupted by the globalization process.

One of the significant contributions of orientalist and nativist approaches is that they give back to people their lost memory – a memory erased by Western discourse. When Chamcha, the postcolonial cosmopolitan Indian, in Salman Rushdie's *The Satanic Verses*, comes out with a list of his favourite movies, predictably all Western masterpieces, another character, Gibreel, exclaims, 'You've been brainwashed. All this art-house crap . . .', and proceeds to give his list of popular Indian cinema. He tells Chamcha, 'Your head is full of junk. You have forgotten everything worth knowing' (1988: 439–40). What was ironical about the whole indigenization process was that while Christians were trying recover elements from the ancient past, or, as Fanon would have put, it 'mummified figments', other Asian religions such as Buddhism and Confucianism were trying to modernize and accommodate themselves to the new urban industrial culture which was sweeping through Asia (Tamney 1993: 65). While we were trying to promote the idea of the distant past as normative, the regional religions of Asia were trying to update and recast their basic tenets to meet the challenges of the mass of industrial development.

Let me pause here for a while and share with you some of the hermeneutical dilemmas we face. There is, of course, the one presented by our tendency to harmonize, which India's ever-recurring religious multiplication makes a constant necessity, but which docs not make it easy always to take an unwavering position. Another question that comes to mind is – why do we need theories?. Like Gita Das, the heroine in Kirin Narayan's novel, I too wonder whether we should analyze 'everything in terms of hidden structures, themes, intentions' and in doing so lose the pleasure of a good read (1994: 85). I would like to ask with the Indian critic Devy, is it a colonial compulsion, to theorize? (1992: 121). Are we wasting our critical talents in the pursuit of such theories? Is biblical criticism really an important activity in its own right? Is it an escapist activity in which critical theorization replaces original production, and critical work replaces our ethical responsibilities? What is the purpose of our reading practice? Is it to produce subtle nuances of emotion and feeling in individuals, or to help communities to face the problems of the contemporary world, as Käsemann proposed: 'I do not know Dom Helder Camara personally, and he – an out-and-out conservative in comparison with myself – will be unacquainted with my work. But were my work no possible help to him in his troubles, I will not want to remain a New Testament scholar. No real service is rendered to the Spirit by one who is unable to assist men under trial' (1973: 236).

What then is the task of a hermeneut? Is it to change the world or understand it? Recently Chaturvedi Badrinath argued for an inversion of Marx's eleventh thesis: 'The philosophers have so far tried to interpret the world, the point however is to change it.' Badrinath turns this round: 'Reformers have so far tried to change India; the point however is to understand India' (1993: 29). Perhaps in the process some service will be rendered such as Käsemann proposed.

SEARCHING FOR A ROLE: FROM NATIONALISM TO POST–NATIONALITY

Little attention has been paid to the social history of the emergence of Asian theological reflection. Unlike modern Christian theology in the West, which emerged amidst various philosophical trends, capitalism, industrial revolution, secularism and interdenominational squabbles, in India it arose as the result of the English-educated middle-class Christians who were attempting to imagine a modern nation. The beginnings of Indian Christian interpretation lie in the encounter between the imported colonial denominational theologies and the newly converted Indian Christians trying to assert their Indian identity in the face of the dominant Western culture. Thus it was in response to colonialism, and the need to construct a homogeneous and unifying Indian culture as against the existing multi-faceted cultural practices, the early Christian converts of India begun to imagine the nation as a unified, pan-Indian entity. The 1857 revolt, which was the beginning of Indian nationalism, was a turning-point also in Indian Christian theological reflection. There were several examples of national stirring (K. Baago's phrase) which took the form of opposition to the colonial theology. When Indian converts of the nineteenth century found themselves faced with a dual existence – their Indian heritage and their Christian faith – and found that the missionaries of that time would not give them the freedom in the exercise of their faith, some of them under the leadership of Lal Behari, a Calcuttan writer and pastor, declared in their journal, the *Bengal Christian Herald*: 'In having become Christians, we have not ceased to be Hindus. We are Hindu Christians, as thoroughly Hindus as Christians. We have embraced Christianity, but we have not discarded our nationality. We are as intensely national as any of our brethren of the native press can be' (Kaj Baago 1968: 3).

This national spirit continued even after independence, when Indian theologians saw their task as helping to build the nation after the end of the colonial era. The theological writings of M. M. Thomas, E. V. Mathew, and Paul Devanandan bear witness to their patriotic consciousness and show these theologians entering upon their task of recovering the biblical message for the building up of the nation after the ravages of colonialism. The Sri Lankan, Celestine Fernando, captures the mood: 'We have been convinced by the pressure of events in our country, over-population, undernourishment, unemployment, grossly inadequate housing, racial conflicts, political corruption . . . to show the relevance of the Bible for nation-building today' (1981: 185).

But today, after nearly forty years of independence and post-colonial rule, the concept of the nation-state has come under severe scrutiny. India may look a valid cultural label on a map, but the question of what it means to an Indian or a Sri Lankan is increasingly difficult to answer in the face of rapid globalization and internationalization. Arjun Appadurai, the social scientist, attributes the emergence of this global culture to five interlinked dimensions of cultural flow which are moving across national boundaries. He calls the five dimensions ethnoscape, mediascape, technoscape, finanscape, and ideoscape. The suffix, '-scape' indicates the varying and unfixed nature of these landscapes and their 'historical, linguistic, and political situatedness' (1990: 7).

1. 'ethnoscape' means the landscape of persons who constitute the shifting world in which we live – tourists, immigrants, refugees, exiles, guest workers, and other moving groups and persons;

2. 'technoscape' means the flow of mechanical and informational technology across 'previously impervious boundaries', through multinational corporations;

3. 'finanscape' means the rapid flow of money through currency markets, national stock exchanges and commodity speculation;

4. 'mediascape' means the distribution of the electronic capabilities to produce and disseminate information through such media as newspapers, magazines, TV, and films;

5. 'ideoscape' means the flow of ideas, terms and images often organized around such key words as freedom, welfare, rights, sovereignty and, these days, democracy (1990: 6–11).

Thus, according to Arjun Appadurai the constant flow of persons, technologies, finance, information and ideology results in deterritorialization, which in his view is 'one of the central forces of the modern world' (1990: 11). Appadurai does not rule out the existence of 'relatively stable communities and networks' nor reject the current tribalism around the world. But his contention is that 'the warp of these stabilities is everywhere shot through with the woof of human motion, as more persons and groups deal with the realities of having to move or the fantasies of wanting to move' (1990: 7). This large-scale movement of people within and between countries has created dislocation, homelessness and disorientation. Homesickness has become the cultural characteristic of our time. One of the stories in Salman Rushdie's recent collection of short stories, *East, West*, raises precisely this issue. The story, 'At the Auction of the Ruby Slippers', is a parable about homelessness, where the exiles, displaced persons, political refugees and orphans perceive that the possession of the magic slippers guarantees not only protection against the witches, but also a safe promise to journey back home. But the question, is where is home?

The exceptional movement of people for a variety of reasons has resulted in the emergence of the diasporic interpreter, who is likewise constantly in search of home. Those of us who are part of the diaspora are equally committed to and disturbed by both cultures – the one we left behind and the one we enter and try to understand. To use Abdul R. JanMohamed's phrase, 'we are specular border intellectuals' endeavouring to stand among and not fall between many stools. JanMohamed defines the 'specular border intellectual' as a person caught between several cultures and groups, and who subjects these cultures 'to analytic scrutiny rather than combining them', and 'utilizes his or her interstitial cultural space as a vantage point from which to define, implicitly or explicitly, other utopian possibilities of group formation' (JanMohamed 1992: 97). We have multiple belongings and multiple loyalties, and, as the demoniac in Mark's Gospel said, we are many. The Iraqi journalist, Kanan Makiya, asks a pertinent question: 'What is the connection between the passport one holds, the views one expresses, the books one writes, and one's innermost emotional and belief system, which is of course what constitutes one's identity?' (1994: 233).

We have come a long way as interpreters, most of us starting by identifying ourselves with nationalism and patriotic causes. I think we need to re-consider our role as interpreters to take into account the multifaceted and enormously complex web of global and local relations, and ask ourselves what is the Indianness or Srilankanness we are craving for. This was what Tagore was trying to address in his novel, *Gora*, which I have already mentioned. Written at a time when nationalism was becoming a potent political force against colonialism in India, we see in Gora, the hero of the novel, a passionate defender of all that is Hindu as a way of overcoming the humiliation of colonialization. But suddenly to his horror Gora discovers that he is not only not a Hindu but not even an Indian, but born to Irish parents. But what Gora learns through the other two characters – Anandamoyi, the surrogate mother who brings him up, and Paresh Babu, the Brahmo leader – is that true Indianness transcends India. By their willingness to redefine traditional Indian purity codes, Anandamoyi and Paresh Babu reaffirm a moral universe which Gora finds it difficult to reject. But to Tagore this shared universe is a universal one, which transcends caste, religion and national boundaries.

At a time when the world is becoming 'a single place' (Roland Robertson's phrase), with the boundaries between cultures blurring, as interpreters we have two options. Let me illustrate these options with two stories. When Alexander the Great invaded India he wanted to meet the philosophers in Taxila, the ancient university town which is now part of modern Pakistan. First he sent his representative. The philosophers did not bother to receive him. The King was in a hurry to see them. So he himself made the journey to meet them. The guards went ahead of him to announce his coming. On arrival, Alexander spoke about his achievements and announced himself as their new patron. There was no response from the philosophers. The King thought that they had not heard him, so he ventured to move closer. As he moved, the sun came behind him and his shadow fell upon one of the philosophers. The conqueror addressed them again: 'I, Alexander the Great, stand before you. All the earth is mine. Speak and tell me what I can do for you. What can I bestow upon you?' The response he got was staggering. The philosopher upon whom the shadow of the conqueror fell replied, 'Nothing much. Just move either a little to the right or to the left so that the rays of sun can fall upon me and their heat can warm my body again.' The response was a stunning indication that there was no point in East and West fraternizing. The gap between the East and the West looked too wide for reconciliation.

The second story comes from one of the short stories in Salman Rushdie's *East, West*, which I have already referred to. The narrator in the story, 'The Courter', is an immigrant in England who comes to a different understanding of bicultural marginality and East–West relations. The comma which Rushdie places between the words East and West, in the title of the book provides us with a clue. At a time when people are concerned with hyphenated identities, Rushdie sees reality from the less polarizing perspective of a comma, where histories of cultural differences can exist side-by side in a state of creative interference and interruption. Either, we could be – in the words of the Vietnamese writer, Le Ly Hayslip, whose life story was immortalized in the Hollywood movie, *Heaven and Earth* – 'the people in the middle', or we could identify ourselves with the philosophers in Taxila and say 'move over' and thereby establish an irreconcilable chasm. To me it is increasingly becoming clear that cultures, nations, and identities can never be defined in simple binary appositions: East–West, and centre–margin. If we try to fix everything into neat categories, we may obscure the more complex perceptions and insights that an ethnocentric approach would permit. In an era of easy polarizations, I for one, like the immigrant narrator in the Salman Rushdie's story, would rather live with the complexities than with easy binary appositions. I would like to end with the words of the narrator: 'But I, too have ropes around my neck, I have them to this day, pulling me this way and that, East and West, the noose tightening, commanding, choose, choose. I buck, I snort, I whinny, I kick ... I refuse to choose' (1994: 211).

NOTE

1   I owe this point to Daniel Patte. See 'Textual Constraints, Ordinary Readings, and Critical Exegesis: An Androcritical Perspective', *Semeia* 62 (1993), p. 62.

REFERENCES

Adigalar, L. T. 1993, 'Concept of Redemption and Vetchi and Karanthi', *Arasardi Journal of Theology* 6 (1), pp. 72–3.
Appadurai, A. 1990, 'Disjuncture and Difference in the Global Economy', *Public Culture* 2 (2), pp. 1–24.
Baago, K. 1968, *Pioneers of Indigenous Christianity* (Madras, The Christian Literature Society).
Badrinath, C. 1993, *Dharma, India and the World Order* (Edinburgh, Saint Andrew Press).
Dayanandan, F. T. 1992, *Vuyar Thani Padal* (Madras, The Christian Literature Society).
Devy, G. N. 1992, *After Amnesia: Tradition and Change in Indian Literary Criticism* (Hyderabad, Orient Longman).
Fanon, F. 1990 (1965), *The Wretched of the Earth* (Harmondsworth, Penguin Books).
Fernando, C. 1981, 'The Use of the Bible in the International Life in Asia', *International Review of Mission* 70 (279), pp. 181–8.
Francis, P. T. 1992, *Vuyar Thani Padal* (Madras, The Christian Literature Society).
Gibson, M. D. 1902/3, 'On the Parable of the Unjust Steward', *The Expository Times* 14, p. 334.
JanMohamed, A. R. 1992, 'Worldliness-without-World, Homelessness-as-Home: Towards a Definition of the Specular Border Intellectual', in Michael Sprinker (ed.), *Edward Said: A Critical Reader* (Oxford, Basil Blackwell), pp. 96–120.
Jeremias, J. 1963, *The Parables of Jesus* (London, SCM Press).
Joseph, G. G. 1991, *The Crest of the Peacock: Non-European Roots of the Mathematics* (Harmondsworth, Penguin Books).
Käsemann, E. 1973, 'The Problem of a New Testament Theology', *New Testament Studies*, 19 (3), pp. 235–5.

Lorgunpai, S. 1994, 'The Book of Ecclesiastes and Thai Buddhism', *Asian Journal of Theology* 8 (1), pp. 155–62.

Makiya, K. 1994, *Cruelty and Silence: War, Tyranny and Cruelty, Uprising and the Arab World* (Harmondsworth, Penguin Books).

Nandy, A. 1991 (1988), *The Intimate Enemy: Loss and Recovery of Self Under Colonialism* (Delhi, Oxford University Press).

Narasimhaiah, C. D. 1994, 'Introduction', *East- West Poetics* (Delhi, Sakhitya Akademi).

Narayan, K. 1994, *Love, Stars, and All That* (New Delhi, Penguin Books).

Religion and Society. 1960, 'Wasrapur Findings IV: Christians and Cultural Foundations of New India', 7 (1), pp. 68–72.

Rushdie, S. 1988, *The Satanic Verses* (Harmondsworth, Viking).

— 1993, *East, West* (London, Jonathan Cape).

Said, E. 1985, *Orientalism* (Harmondsworth, Penguin Books).

— 1993, *Culture and Imperialism* (London, Chatto & Windus).

Sherwood, M. M. 1821, *The History of Little Henry and his Bearer* (Wellington, F. Houlston and Son).

Tagore, R. 1989 (1924), *Gora* (Madras, Macmillan Press).

Tamney, J. B. (1993), 'Religion in Capitalistic East Asia', in William H. Swatos Jr. (ed.), *A Future for Religion? New Paradigms for Social Analysis* (London, Sage Publishers).

Young, G. M. 1935, *Speeches by L Macaulay with his Minute on Indian Education* (London, Oxford University Press).

INDEX OF
SCRIPTURE REFERENCES

Genesis
1.2 157
1.6 157
1.9–10 157
1.20–23 158
2. 190–91
2.9 375
2.18–24 372
3. 51, 52
3.20 159
3.22 375
5.32 209n
6–8. 371
6.1–2 191
6.10 209n
6.11–12 372
6.12–13 372
7.13 209n
8.22 371
9.18–27 195–8, 209n
10. 198–200, 209n
10.1 209n
11.1–9 107, 376
11.3–4 377
12.3 221, 410
15.13 280
15.14 280
15.18–21 280
47.13–26 220

Exodus
22.21 281
22.22–24 109, 115
22.23–27 106
22.26–27 109, 115
23.6–8 111
23.31–33 281
34.6 312

Leviticus
11.1 39
19.17–18 123

20.22 269
25.23 269

Numbers
12. 200–201
14.11 158
27.17 89

Deuteronomy
4.25–26 269
6.21 247
7.6–8 202
7.7–8 223
7.12 281
10.15 202
10.16–18 218
15.3 123
15.17 276
23.18 144
28.63 269
29.29 456

Joshua
23.15–16

Judges
17–18. 220

1 Samuel
8.5 221

2 Samuel
7 111
7.6 384
18.21–32 202

2 Kings
19.9 201

1 Chronicles
1. 199
1.4 209n
2. 1–55 200

Esther
1.1–3 174
1.5–9 174
1.13–14 174
9.10 175
9.15 175
9.16 176
10.1 176
10.3 176

Job
28.19 202

Psalms
9.10 109
12.14 111
15 110
24.1 269
24.1–2 182
24.3–6 110
50.1 10
51.16–17 110
66. 248
68.31 202
72.1–2 111
72.2 109, 115
72.12–14 115
78. 248
95.3 269
96.5 269
97. 269
105. 248
118.23 412

Proverbs
14.31 109
19.17 109
21.3 110
22.22 109
22–23. 111
23.10–11 111
23.26 347

Proverbs – *cont.*
28.15 111
29.14 111
31.8–9 111, 115

Ecclesiastes
2.1–11 342, 344
2.14–17 376
2.18–19 343
2.24 344
2.26 345
3.6 344
3.14 345
4.1–2 108
4.2 345
6.3 345
7.16–17 344
8.8 376
9.1–5 376
9.4–5 345
9.5–9 376
9.7–9 346
12.9 346
12.11 346

Isaiah
1.10 107, 112
1.10–17 108, 110
1.12–15 116
1.17 107, 109, 112
1.21–23 112
1.23 108
1.24–25 112
2.9 108
2.23 108
3.1–9 107
3.12–15 106–116
3.16–41 108
5. 123
5.7 108, 109
5.8 108, 112
5.11–22 108
5.20 108, 112
5.23 112
7.9 111
8.30 108
9.8 106
10.1 111, 112
10.1–4 108
10.2 111, 112
10.3 112
11.2–5 111
11.4 110
11.4–5 115
11.11 202
12.3 162
16.5 111
18.7 202
19.18 221
23. 140

29.13 138
29.19–20 110
32.1–8 110
33.14–16 110
37.9 201
40.6–8 249
41.17–20 248
43.16–21 248
43.20 202
44.3–4 270
45.14 202
49.6 221
52.4–6 248
55.10 116
58.6–7 109
65.9 202
65.25 372

Jeremiah
1.18 106
2.3 202
2.7 269
4.23–26 370
5.28 111
7.5–6 110
7.21–28 110
16.18 269
22.1–5 111
22.13–19 106
22.16 111, 115
23.7–8 271
38.7–13 202
39.15–18 202
46.9 202
47.4 140

Ezekiel
16. 248
16.3–9 248
18.6–9 110
27. 140
28. 140
34.5 89
34.19 109, 115
47.21–23 271

Hosea
2.16–17 248
2.19–20 109, 111
4.1 106, 109, 111
4.4–10 106
6.5 106
6.6 109, 110
11.1 247
13.7–8 106

Joel
3.4–8 140

Amos
3.8 106
3.10 108
4.1 111
5.4–6 109
5.11 111
5.11–12 108
5.12 106, 111
5.14–15 109
5.21–24 110
5.24 110
6.4–7 108
8.4 111
9.7 180

Micah
2. 123
2.2 108
3.1 106
3.1–4 109
3.9–11 108
3.9–12 106
6.1 106
6.1–8 110
6.8 109

Zephaniah
1.1 202
3.10 202

Zechariah
7.1–14 110
7.9–10 110
9.2 140

Wisdom of Solomon
1.17 316

Ecclesiasticus (Sirach)
12.9 346
12.11 346
24.6 316
34.18–22 110
38.24–39.11 346
51.23–30 347

Matthew
5.3 98, 133
5.13–16 331
5.23–24 65
5.46–48 94
5.48 331
6.2–4 129
6.7 94
6.24 129
6.31 128
6.32 94
8.29 161
10. 329
10.5 94

Matthew – *cont.*
10.9–10 126
10.24–25 331
10.42 331
11.5 128
11.19 91, 93
11.25 55
11.28 97, 133
13.12 60
18.6–7 98
21.3 92
22.14 204
24.3 455
25.40–45 109
26.6–13 436–43
28.16–20 327–9, 331

Mark
1.15 102
1.16–20 123
1.18–20 125
1.22 86
1.24 161
1.30 86
1.32 86
1.33 86
1.35–39 141
1.37 86
1.44 86
1.45 86
2.1 141
2.2 86
2.4 88
2.4–6 89
2.5 95
2.11 96
2.13 88, 90
2.13–17 91
2.17 96
2.18 104
2.27 97
3.1 96
3.2–21 89
3.8 87
3.9 88
3.18 95
3.20 88, 141
3.31–35 126
3.32 88, 89
3.34 89
3.35 90
4.1 88, 89
4.11–12 90
4.13 103
4.35–41 103
4.36 88, 89
5.7 161
5.19 96
5.21 88
5.24 88

5.31 88
5.34 96
5.35 96
5.36 95
6.4 122
6.7 332
6.8 128
6.31 141
6.34 89, 103n
6.35–44 128
6.45–46 141
6.51 103n
7.1–13 138
7.4 90
7.6 87
7.15 97, 104
7.17 88
7.18 103
7.24 141
7.24–30 140–8
7.33 88
8.1 88, 103n
8.2 90
8.8 162
8.26 96
8.32 103
8.34 88
9.14 88
9.23 95
9.30–31 141
9.32 103
9.37 97
10.1 88, 90
10.13–15 97
10.17–27 123,
  124–9
10.32 103
10.35–45 129–33
10.42–45 114, 123, 124–9
10.46 88
10.52 96
11.18 89, 90
11.27 89
11.32 89
12.12 89
13. 103
13.10 144
13.18 90
15.8 89
15.15 89
15.38–39 144
23.11–12 136

Luke
1.3 211
1.46–55 182
4.16–21 254n
4.18 128
5.1–11 444–53
5.29 91

6.20 115, 128, 133
6.36 312
9.48 97
9.58 126
9.59–62 126
10.2 332
13.2 95
13.23 455
13.33 122
15. 96
15.1 93
15.7–10 94
15.13 124
15.18 94
16.19–31 60
17.1–2 98
18.25 115
19.41 112
19.42 273
19.47 99
22.44–49 337n
22.66 99, 100
24.27 165

John
1.12 274
1.14 158, 274
1.16 162
1.26 165
1.29 166
2.1 157
2.2 158
2.3 160
2.5 161
2.6 161
2.11 157, 158
2.19 273
3.5 206
3.16 182, 274
3.25 165
4.10 165
5.56 383
6.53 166
7.6 161
7.30 160
7.38 165
8.20 160
8.28 248
9.1 93, 95
12.23 160
12.27 160
13.1 160
13.1–16 114
13.10 163
14.20 384
15.3 163, 164
15.4 384
15.7 384
15.15 183
17.17 456

John – *cont.*
17.20 384
17.23 384
17.26 248
19.25–27 158
19.26 160
20.21–23 337n
21.21 455

Acts
1.1 211
1.6 456
4.8 99
4.32 129
8.26–40 206
9.1–9 308
10.12–48 206–7
11.26 207
13.1 207
22.4–16 308
23.5 99
26.9–19 308

Romans
1.16 143
2.4 311
3.10 311
6.3 383
6.4 313
7. 309
8.15–17 311
8.29 311
9.11 204
10.17 427
11.2 204
11.11 204
11.25 204
11.28 204
11.29 204
12.2 311
13.1–5 211
15.28 205

1 Corinthians
1.9 383
1.27 204
1.28 204
3.16 273
6.19 384
7.14 383
8.3 49–55, 362–4
8.4 188
10.11 411, 416
10.16 383
10.18 203
10.23 188
11.2–16 185–93
12.13 204
13.8 182
14.34–35 75

2 Corinthians
1.1 383
3.12–17 412
5.16 87
7.9–10 311
8.4 383
12.21 311
13.14 383

Galatians
1.11–17 308
1.12 311
1.14 310
3.26–29 274
3.28 204
6.16 204

Ephesians
2.5 383
3. 274
5.22–33 383
6.11–13 43

Philippians
2.1 383
3.6 310
3.10 383

Colossians
1.19 161
2.8 43
2.9 161
3.11–12 204

1 Thessalonians
4.17 384

Hebrews
1.1–3 183
12.10 383

James
1.17 110
2.5 204

1 Peter
2.9 204, 383
5.1 384

1 John
4.12 182, 384
5.6–8 206

Revelation
7.9 87, 207
19.1 87
19.6 87
22.15 144

1 Clement
5.7 205, 210

SELECT INDEX OF
NAMES AND SUBJECTS

Abesan, C. H. 28
Abraham, K. C. 25
Adigalar, L. 467
African Christianity 246–7, 252–4, 421,
    424–6
Ahern, E. M. 360
Ahn Byung-Mu 298
Alexander, D. L. 357
Allen, H. N. 235
'am ha' aretz 100–1
Amalorpavadass, D. S. 24, 28–9
Amore, A. C. 317
Analects 13, 359
Appadurai, A. 470–1
Appasamy, A. J. 467
Ariarajah, W. 72
Asia: Bible in 21–30, 291, 324, 458–63;
    Christianity in 323; dialogue in 295–7
Assmann, H. 38
authority 114–15; of scripture 11–12, 16,
    19, 21–2, 28–9

Barrett, C. K. 164
Barth, K. 314
Beare, F. W. 76
Beker, J. C. 314
Berg, T. 335
Bhagavadgita 13, 17–18, 31, 165, 306, 332
Bhutto, B. 192
Bible 12, 16, 32, 245, 421; authority of
    19–20, 22, 28, 53–4, 299; in Brazil 409,
    411, 413–18; canonization of 75–8,
    300–1; liberation of 79–82; and
    non-literacy 423–34; oppressive use of
    73–5; race in 194–208; rewriting of
    69–73; sacralization and 299–300;
    silences in 454–6; in South Africa
    170–1; translations of 19, 77–8; women
    and 48–57, 75; as Word of God 38,
    67–8, 291, 293; *see also* biblical
    interpretation; New Testament; Old
    Testament

biblical interpretation 301–3, 319–20,
    421–2; Asian 21–30, 291, 294–9,
    323–33; Indian 464–70, 472; Marxist
    59–68; in a multi-faith context 306–7,
    313–17; by non-literates 430–2; and
    politics of truth 290–4; by poor in Brazil
    407–20; Western 293, 460–3
biblical scholarship 23–4, 28–9, 171–2
Black Theology 169, 170–1
Bloch, E. 61
Bodde, D. 368
Boff, L. 79
Borg, M. 311–12
Bruce, F. F. 308
Buck, H. M. 314
Buddha 333, 342–3
Buddhism 13–14, 21, 468; Ecclesiastes
    and 340–1, 342–7; in Korea 233, 234;
    mission commands of 330–3; scriptures
    of 12, 16, 20, 327–9; in Thailand 341–2
Bultmann, R. 98, 141, 143, 166, 203, 314
Burkill, T. A. 143, 144, 145

Cannon, K. G. 294, 301
Carlston, C. E. 316
Chaitanya, K. 18
Chao, T. C. 289, 291–2
Childs, B. 282
Chinese Christianity 289–90, 292–4, 301;
    and ancestor worship 355–61
Christ, C. 301
Christianity: and nationality 470; and unity
    383–4
Christology 78–9
colonial hermeneutics 459–63; opposition
    to 470
community of faith 27, 139, 152, 314; and
    popular interpretation 409–11, 412,
    413–15, 419
Cone, J. 44
Confucianism 12, 13, 356–9, 468; in
    Korea 234

Confucius 13, 15, 357, 358–9
conversion 307–8, 313; of Paul 308–9, 310, 311, 312
creation 180, 379; Chinese myth of 368–74, 377–9
Crenshaw, J. L. 346
Culler, J. 300

De Groot, J. J. M 361
Derrida, J. 299–300
Detweiler, R. 300
Deuteronomic Code 76
Devanandan, P. 382, 470
dhamma 330, 331, 333
dialogical approach 310–13
dialogical imagination 294–9
Dillon, E. J. 340, 344
discipleship 88–9, 123–33
Dufton, F. 146
Dumont, L. 134, 324

Eagleton, T. 171, 172
Eaton, J. 317, 341
Ecumenical Association for African Theologians (EAAT) 421, 432
Ecumenical Association for Third World Theologians (EATWOT) 432
election (of Israelites) 73, 74, 202–4, 223, 269
Esther, Book of 171–2, 173–7, 455

Fanon, F. 464, 465
Fernando, C. 470
filial piety 356–9
Fiorenza, E. S. 53, 141, 177, 301, 302
Fokkelman, J. P. 377
Fortes, M. 360
Foucault, M. 290
Francis, P. T. 467

Gallup, P. 297
Gilgamesh Epic 375
God 123, 215–18, 231–2, 245–6, 249; Bible as revelation of 70–1; the conqueror 279–81; the economist 182; goodness of 127–8; and humanity 374, 376–7; Kingdom of 102, 274; and liberation 217, 219–24, 230, 231, 247, 248, 249–51; as merciful 312; and the oppressed 50, 55, 56, 60, 218, 223–4, 230–1; as Parent 128; presence of 384, 391; in the prophets 106–10; as Yahweh *see* Yahweh
Gora (Tagore) 464, 472
Gossett, T. F. 74
Gottwald, N. 121, 171–2, 279
Gregorios, M. 24, 26–7
Guillaume, A. 44
Guttierez, G. 282, 461

Haenchen, E. 206
Ham, curse of 195–8
Hauerwas, S. 282
head coverings, Paul and 187–9
Hebrews 194–5, 222, 228–32, 242; *see also* Israel
Herskovits, M. 40–1
Hill, E. 40
Hinduism 20, 21; caste and 118; saints of 381–91; scriptures of 12, 16, 20, 29
historical-criticism 319–20, 326
Hollenweger, W. J. 38
households, in the Solomon Islands 180–2
Hsiao Ching 356, 357, 358
Hsieh Yu-Wei 359
Huai Nan Tzu 370–1, 372–3
Hutchison, W. R. 293

I Ching (The Book of Changes) 13
ideology 59–61
India 112–16, 117–18; Christianity in 469–70; church in 114–16; tribe and caste in 118–20, 134
inspiration 29, 53, 70, 77, 78
Islam 13; historical genesis of 395–7; liberation theology in 394, 397, 399, 400–3; private property in 398–9
Israel 134–5, 249, 379; as chosen people *see* election; class consciousness in 224–6; and the exodus 221–4, 248; land of 268, 269, 274–5, 281; origins of 219–20; social organization of 120–2, 124, 221–2; *see also* Hebrews

Jan Mohamed, A. R. 472
Japan 152; ethnic exclusivism in 149–51
Jeremias, J. 60, 61, 92, 462
Jesus Christ 67, 166, 179, 183, 272–3, 274; Bible and 78–9; and gentiles 138–9; and *ochlos* 88–98, 102, 298; Paul and 87, 311–12; and rich and poor 60–1; and the Syrophoenician woman 141–8; tribal values in the teachings of 122–33; and wedding at Cana 160–1, 163, 165–6
jihad 400–1, 402
Judaism 97, 272
justice, in the Qur'an 397–8, 403

kamma 345
Kanzira, R. A. 71–2
Kim Yong Bock 298
Koreans 232–42; in Japan 149–52
Koyama, Kosuke 24–5, 128, 294
Kraemer, H. 291
Krishnapillai, H. A. 467
Kullu, P. 120
Kwok Pui Lan 323

language 20–1, 23, 26, 31
Lao Tzu 13, 15, 374

laos 86–7, 98–100
Lategan, B. C. 335
Latin America 55, 56; Bible reading in 48, 54–5
Le Blanc, C. 374
Lee, A. 296
Lee, S. H. 298
Lewis, N. B. 297
liberation 252–3; exodus and 228–32; hermeneutics of 170–1, 173, 176, 177; Koreans and 240–1
liberation theology 50, 72, 168–9, 171, 282, 307, 337, 422; in Asia 326; Bible and 49, 73, 411, 433–4; in Islam 394–403; of Native Americans 277–9
Lindbeck, G. 282
Linden, I. 425
Lorgunpai, S. 460
Lotus school of Buddhism 13–14

MacRae, G. 311
Mahavagga 327–9
Manikkavacakar 386–8
Marx, K. 58, 59; on religion 61
Mary (mother of Jesus) 158–60
Mencius 358
Mesters, C. 421, 422
minjung 85, 101, 102, 228, 229, 241, 297–9, 302–3; in Korea 234–42 *passim*
mission commands 327–33, 337
missionaries 246, 247, 292–3, 349; in Korea 235–6, 237–9, 240, 241
Moffett, S. A. 238
Moltmann, J. 250
Moon, C. H. S. 298
Moore, G. F. 203
Moses 89, 228–9, 230, 400
Mott, J. R. 291
Mou Tzu 13, 14
Muhammad (the Prophet) 395–6, 399
Mullick, B. 118–19

Nandy, A. 460
nativism 466–9
Nehanda, M. 80–1
New Testament 31, 76, 77, 315; election in 203–4; issue of land in 268, 272–4; secularization in 205–8
Newbigin, L. 43
Nirvana 331, 344
Nolan, A. 79
Nu Kua 368–79

ochlos: in Mark's gospel 86–96; meaning of 98–101
Ogden, G. 341
Ogden, R. A. 380
Old Testament 75–6, 78, 228, 315; issue of land in 268, 269–72; race and sacralization in 195–202

oppression 113–14, 116, 174–5, 284, 398; *see also* God, oppressed and
orientalism 464–6

Palestinians 268, 275
Parkin, R. 134
Parks, S. 295
Paul, Saint 79; conversion of 308–9, 310, 311, 312–13; Jesus and 87, 311–12; and rhetorical hermeneutics 350–5, 362–4; on women 53, 75, 185–93
personhood 358–9
Pfeiffer, R. H. 76–7
Pharisees 97, 103–4
Phillips, G. 334
Po Ch'en Kuang 292
Pongudom, M. 296
poor 110–11, 112–13; and the Bible 409, 411, 414, 415–17, 418; God and 50, 60, 106–8, 108–9, 111–12, 114–15, 128; in Latin America 55, 56
praxis, and interpretation 64–7
purity 138–9

Qur'an 13, 16, 31, 396, 399; and justice 397–8; reinterpreting 400–2

Rad, G. von 203
Radhakrishnan, R. 13, 18
Ramanuja 12, 17
Ratzinger, J. 162–3
revelation 29, 44–5, 78, 249, 250–1
Rice, G. 200
Ricoeur, P. 20
Ringe, S. H. 147
Rissho-kosei kai 14
Rogerson, J. W. 134
Rowley, H. H. 70
Ruether, R. R. 301, 302
Rushdie, S. 468, 471, 473

sacralization 195–202; and election 202–4
Said, E. 5, 7, 459
saints 381–4; in Tamil Saivism 384–91
salvation 246–7, 253
Sambandar 384–5
scripture: authority of *see* authority of scripture; plurality of 11–32, 315–16; *see also* Bible
Seebass, H. 202
selfhood 358, 359
service (*diakonia*) 132, 136–7
Shankara 12, 17
Smith, W. C. 16, 307
Song, C. S. 24, 25–6, 296, 325
Song of Songs 16, 17, 18, 248
Spivak, G. C. 2
spokenness 19–21
Stendahl, K. 309

Strecker, G. 460
suffering 342, 343–6
Suk Nam Dong 298
Sundarar 386, 388, 392

Tao Te 356
Taoism 12, 13, 15, 377–8
tawhid 399–400
Theissen, G. 126, 136
Third World 8, 422; hermeneutics of 4, 7;
  liberation theology in 168–9
T'ien 356–7
Tilak, B. 17, 18
Tamil Saivism 382–3; communion of
  saints in 384–91
Tirukural 316
Tiwari, T. K. 308
Tonghak rebellion 236–7
Torah 31, 76, 272, 311–12
Torres, C. 65–6
tribal values 118–22; in teachings of Jesus
  122–33

uncleanness 139–40, 142–3

Van Beek, G. W. 81
Vempeny, I. 317
vernacular hermeneutics 466–9
visual aids 429

Weber, H-R. 72
West, C. 169, 172, 173
Westermann, C. 196, 197–8
Whybray, R. N. 346
Wiebe, B. 133
Williams, D. 301
Williams, F. E. 164
wisdom tradition 316–17, 346–7
Witherington, B. 146
women 142, 145; equality of 185–93;
  marginalization of, in the Bible 49–51,
  52, 75; perspective on Bible of 55–7; in
  Solomon Islands 184; struggle for
  liberation in Africa 172–3, 175
writtenness 19–21
Wu, Y. T. 292, 293
Wuellner, W. 322

Yahweh 105–16, 121–2, 216–17, 222–4,
  231, 279, 280